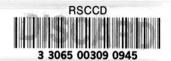

Altering American Consciousness

Santiago Canyon College
Library

Altering American Consciousness

*The History of Alcohol and Drug Use
in the United States, 1800–2000*

Edited by

SARAH W. TRACY AND
CAROLINE JEAN ACKER

University of Massachusetts Press   *Amherst and Boston*

Santiago Canyon College
Library

Copyright © 2004 by University of Massachusetts Press
All rights reserved
Printed in the United States of America

LC 2003013735
ISBN 1-55849-424-3 (cloth); 425-1 (paper)

Designed by Dennis Anderson
Set in Adobe Caslon by Binghamton Valley Composition
Printed and bound by The Maple-Vail Book Manufacturing Group

Library of Congress Cataloging-in-Publication Data

Altering American consciousness : the history of alcohol and drug use in
the United States, 1800–2000 / edited by Sarah W. Tracy and Caroline
Jean Acker.
    p. cm.
Includes bibliographical references.
    ISBN 1-55849-424-3 (cloth : alk. paper)—ISBN 1-55849-425-1 (pbk. :
alk. paper)
    1. Alcoholism—United States—History. 2. Drug abuse—United States—History.
I. Acker, Caroline Jean, 1947– II. Tracy, Sarah W., 1963–

HV5292 .A393 2004
362.29'0973'09034—dc21

                    2003013735

British Library Cataloguing in Publication data are available.

This book is published with the assistance of a generous grant from the
College of Physicians of Philadelphia.

Contents

III. Psychotropics, Psychedelics, and Cigarettes

Acknowledgments

THIS BOOK BEGAN in 1997 with a conference on the history of alcohol and drug use in American society. The meeting was organized by Sarah Tracy and Tom Horrocks and hosted by the Francis C. Wood Institute for the History of Medicine of the College of Physicians of Philadelphia. The conference was supported in part by generous funding from the Barra Foundation, the Groff Family Memorial Trust, and the Benjamin and Mary Siddons Measey Foundation. William H. Helfand graciously loaned a selection of patent medicine posters, prints, and ephemera from his personal collection for display. We gratefully acknowledge the continued interest and generous assistance of both the College of Physicians of Philadelphia and William H. Helfand in producing this volume.

Most of the essays in this collection are revised versions of papers presented at the conference. It bears mentioning that much of the research that went into these essays was conducted within the marvelous historical collections of the College of Physicians. The essays benefited immeasurably from the feedback of conference participants, especially the observations of our commentators: Robin Room, Cheryl Krasnick Warsh, David F. Musto, John C. Burnham, and Charles E. Rosenberg. This volume is a better book because of their insights and advice. David Courtwright also participated in the conference and has lent the editors of this volume significant intellectual and moral encouragement to think about the "big picture" in the history of psychoactive substance use. We have benefited immensely from the suggestions, wisdom, and patience of Clark Dougan, senior editor at the University of Massachusetts Press, and we are grateful for his sustaining vision of this book. In addition, we appreciate the thoughtful comments of the two anonymous readers; they have been helpful in numerous ways. Our greatest debt remains to the contributors of the individual essays; their intellectual excitement and faith in the importance of this volume sustained us through each step of its production.

S. W. T.

C. J. A.

Altering American Consciousness

Introduction

Psychoactive Drugs—An American Way of Life

SARAH W. TRACY AND CAROLINE JEAN ACKER

VIRTUALLY EVERY American alive has at some point consumed at least one, and very likely more than one, consciousness-altering drug. Even those who actively eschew alcohol, tobacco, and coffee are rarely able to avoid drinking from public water supplies. Since the 1980s, even these resources have been laced with a "cocktail of unmetabolized pills and po-tions"[1]—the residues of birth control pills, antidepressants, beta-blockers, steroids, and a host of other psychoactive pharmaceuticals consumed daily by the millions. With many children now taking Ritalin for Attention Deficit Hyperactivity Disorder; professional athletes relying on androstenidione to bulk up; the walking wounded and chronically depressed resorting to selective serotonin reuptake inhibitors such as Prozac; Ginko biloba refreshing flagging powers of memory; and a trip to Starbucks replacing the three-martini lunch, the early twenty-first century appears rife with psychotropic drugs. Yet, psychoactive substances have always been an integral part of American life. As recent scholarship has made plain, psychoactive substances such as nicotine, alcohol, caffeine, and heroin are model commodities, traded freely (or not so freely) for profit. Indeed, in the case of those with strongly addictive properties, demand is built right into the product.[2]

If the use of psychoactive drugs is a constant in American history, the ways drugs and their users are perceived have varied extensively. And these variations in the perception of drug use—from tobacco to cocaine—tell us much about the changing nature of American society. Who would believe, for example, that the corrupting cigarettes ("coffin nails" to their contemporaries) of the 1900s would become the glamorous and heroic habit of Hollywood stars and American soldiers in the 1940s, only to fall on hard times at the end of the twentieth century as an irresponsible, cancer-causing addictive habit?[3] Likewise, the transformation of cocaine's public identity from panacea-like pick-me-up of the late nineteenth century to symbol of Yuppie decadence in the 1980s, to source of urban social decay (especially crack cocaine) in the 1990s provides a sense of the degree to which drugs' identities are transformed over time.[4] History allows us to see that the identity of a psychoactive drug owes as much to its users, their patterns of use, and the political climate in which the drug is taken, as it owes to the drug's documented physiological effects. The essays in this volume explore the ways that Americans have altered their consciousness with and about psychoactive drugs over the past two hundred years. Each work reveals the importance of social, political, economic, and religious contexts in shaping the nature and image of America's drug habits.

It is one of the editors' and authors' working assumptions that America's drug habits cannot be understood, nor effective drug policy made, until we have a clearer picture of the range of drugs used yesterday and today, and the ways in which specific historical circumstances have shaped their use and their regulation. Just as drugs interact with one another, so, too, do their histories. Rather than seeing licit drugs and illicit drugs, recreational drugs and medicinal drugs, "hard" drugs and "soft" drugs, as mutually exclusive categories, we hope that readers will be intrigued by the ways drugs move from one category to another over time. America's current "War on Drugs" has given many a sense that the nation has enjoyed a drug-free past, and that with renewed efforts to stop the use of heroin, cocaine, marijuana, and other illicit substances, there may be a drug-free future. Such thinking is both remarkably naive and historically myopic. It also denies the current and commanding presence of socially acceptable psychoactive drugs such as alcohol, caffeine, sugar, tobacco, antidepressants, estrogen, and testosterone in our daily lives.

Thus, the essays in this volume analyze a diversity of psychoactive substances and their histories. We hope this range will encourage readers to take a broader view of America's consciousness-altering behavior and discover patterns in the ways we favor some drugs and reject others.

Drugs and Alcohol in American History

From the arrival of the first European colonists, drugs have figured prominently in American life. The encounter between European and Native American societies exposed each group to drugs new to them, though familiar to the other group. The British who landed on Virginia's shores in the early seventeenth century found tobacco, which Native Americans smoked to achieve mystical states and to cement social agreements. The English settlers adopted the smoking of tobacco, reinterpreting its use in terms of European humoral medical theory. They also absorbed tobacco as a commodity into the mercantilist economy. Like the coffee bean, the dried tea leaf, and the cocoa bean, dried tobacco shipped well across oceans and satisfied growing European appetites for mild stimulants.[5]

Alcohol has an even earlier history in the exchange between colonials and Native Americans, playing a more central role in America's history than any other psychoactive drug. As early as 1585, members of the first settlement on Roanoke Island achieved some success brewing beer from Indian maize.[6] When the *Arbella* departed England for Boston's shores in 1630, its Puritan voyagers packed in three times as much beer as water, and they stowed some ten thousand gallons of wine.[7] For Europeans and the British, drinking was a way of life essential in societies where most water sources were polluted. They brought this way of life with them to the colonies. Colonial Americans regarded alcohol as the "Good Creature of God." These early settlers drew a strong distinction between drinking and drunkenness, the latter being the work of the Devil. Whether rum distilled from West Indian sugar, home-brewed beer, or imported wines, alcohol was a staple of colonial life. Wine, and opium for that matter, were also among the mainstays of colonial physicians and lay medical practices, and both substances were favored as the heroic bleeding, cupping, and purging gradually fell into disfavor with physicians. Colonials drank socially and they drank a lot—at pubs, harvests, barn and house raisings, weddings, elections, and simply to fortify themselves against the harsh elements of daily life.[8]

The Native American experience with alcohol illustrates what often happens when a new drug in potent form (rum and whiskey, distilled spirits) enters a social group in crisis: in the absence of social experience with the drug, including norms to distinguish acceptable from excessive patterns of use, and in the presence of social turmoil (in this case caused by the colonials' policy of dislocation and annihilation), many drank to excess. Drunkenness contributed to the social displacement and devastating effects of the new infectious diseases resulting from Europeans' incursions into Native Americans' lands and societies.[9]

Although the first temperance reformers may have been American Indians attempting to end the damage colonials introduced to their people through alcohol, the American temperance movement is generally said to have begun with the physician and statesman Benjamin Rush, whose concerns about the health of the young republic led him to write *An Inquiry into the Effects of Ardent Spirits upon the Human Body and Mind* in 1784.[10] Fearful for the new nation's fate, Rush recoiled at the prospect of intoxicated voters shaping its destiny—no small concern at a time when elections often featured heavy drinking, and annual per capita consumption of absolute alcohol figured between four and six gallons (approximately twice the rate in 2000). Rush was the first to articulate the disease concept of intemperance.

Interestingly, he also distinguished between healthful fermented beverages and dangerous distilled alcohol. Evidence suggests that Americans consumed even more alcohol between 1800 and 1830. The efficiency and profitability of turning corn into whiskey, heavy frontier drinking, the spread of urban saloons, and the arrival of beer-drinking Germans and whiskey-swilling Irish all encouraged the nation's bibulous tendencies.[11]

These tendencies elicited a reaction within the Protestant churches, however, which linked salvation with temperance and other reforms such as abolition. The American Society for the Promotion of Temperance (ASPT), founded by evangelical clergymen in 1826, also gained support from farmers, industrialists, and homemakers. Indeed, the temperance campaign, really a series of reform drives, constituted the nineteenth century's longest and largest social-reform movement. Alcohol was seen as imperiling capitalist enterprise, domestic tranquility, and national virtue. By 1836, the ASPT, renamed the American Temperance Society, advocated total abstinence. In the early 1840s, Americans thronged to temperance rallies, "took the pledge" for sobriety, and in record numbers lobbied to end the licensing of saloons. The Washingtonian movement, a grassroots total-abstinence campaign, sponsored parades and speeches, offered recruits financial and moral assistance, and established institutions for inebriates called Washingtonian Homes. Giving way to better organized temperance fellowships such as the Good Templars and the Blue Ribbon societies, the Washingtonian movement faded as quickly as it arrived. The late antebellum era also saw renewed middle-class drives for local and state prohibition. In the 1850s, eleven states passed prohibitory legislation, although most were soon repealed.[12]

Opium and alcohol have been used as medicines since before recorded human history. In the new American republic, a fledgling medical profession administered these drugs in ways consistent with traditional European humoral medicine. Outside of the coastal cities, however, physicians struggled to establish practices in relative geographic isolation and in the face of a democratic citizenry's distrust of a group claiming a monopoly on specialized knowledge. In the Jacksonian era, many Americans not only brewed, fermented, and distilled their own alcohol, they treated their own ills. On farms and in villages and towns, women used herbs and tonics to maintain their families' health and care for them in times of illness. In this system of healing, medicines were expected to restore the body's balance and to relieve symptoms: to revive, to calm, to brace, in short, to make one feel better. Some of these effects we would today call psychoactive.[13]

Far from these scenes of domestic medicine, researchers worked toward a scientific, laboratory-based understanding of how medicines healed. The modern age of pharmaceutical production of medicines opened with the

Swiss pharmacist Friedrich Serteurner's isolation of morphine from opium in 1805. While opium was a complex plant extract with wide variations in potency, morphine was a single compound whose effects could be studied in isolation from other compounds and whose dose could be precisely controlled. Over the course of the nineteenth century, many active compounds were isolated from their plant sources; these included codeine, another extract from opium, and cocaine, taken from the coca plant. Heroin was formed by adding acetic anhydride to morphine to yield a semisynthetic drug which had the same effects as morphine but seemed more powerful because it entered the brain faster than morphine; it was introduced as a cough remedy in 1898. By the early twentieth century, a steady flow of new drugs emerged from pharmaceutical research each year, a process that continues today. While these drugs were introduced as medicines, some had powerful psychoactive effects. The invention of the hypodermic syringe in the 1850s added a new way to deliver drugs to the body that increased the intensity of the felt effects.[14]

The second half of the nineteenth century was a particularly important time for alcohol production, use, and regulation as well. The brewing and distilling industries expanded after the Civil War, and alcohol consumption, especially in the immigrant cities, remained high. But the temperance movement revived as well, linking Demon Rum to concerns about immigration, workplace efficiency, social welfare, and urban political corruption. Frances Willard's Woman's Christian Temperance Union (WCTU) redefined temperance, along with other reforms, as a women's issue involving home protection. At the WCTU's prompting, all states and territories and the District of Columbia included scientific temperance instruction in high school physiology texts by 1902.[15]

This era of social reorganization and professionalization also brought the first widespread attempt to medicalize drunkenness. The American Association for the Cure of Inebriates (AACI), founded in 1870 by physicians and reformers, promoted the disease concept of inebriety, implicating both heredity and chronic debauchery in its etiology. As inebriates' drinking progressed, the AACI contended, inebriates lost control of their actions and required restorative medical and moral treatment. Envisioning a new medical specialty to address the ailment, AACI members built a network of private institutions to treat habitual drunkards. California, Iowa, Massachusetts, New York, and other states followed suit. In this age of industrial capitalism, the goal was to restore inebriates' economic productivity as well as their willpower.[16]

In the final decades of the nineteenth century, the pace of industrialization and urbanization picked up. By the turn of the twentieth century, a number of modernizing trends were in full swing. On the economic and cultural fronts, Americans' identities as consumers rivaled their importance as producers. Following the post–Civil War period in which heavily capitalized industry had created the infrastructure for wide-scale manufacturing and a national market, industry produced a widening array of consumer products for Americans to buy. At the same time, a burgeoning advertising industry adopted new printing technologies and new theories of psychology to create sophisticated, visually arresting pitches for products based on appeals to body image, self-confidence, class identity, and other intangibles.

This was a period of rapid social change in American society, as immigrants flowed in from southern and eastern Europe and, to a lesser extent, from China and Japan, to take jobs in American factories. Beginning around World War I, they were joined by African Americans leaving the South and moving to northern, midwestern and western cities in search of work. These groups swelled the populations of American cities, filling and expanding working-class neighborhoods with people who brought with them their own customs of drug and alcohol use. Those growing up as first- and second-generation Americans (or, in the case of African Americans, urban Americans) amused themselves in dance halls, saloons, and burlesque theaters, where they drank beer or whiskey and sampled powdered drugs: sniffable heroin or cocaine. The advent of the factory-produced cigarette spread the tobacco habit well beyond the adult male cigar smokers who had constituted the majority of tobacco consumers in the past.[17]

Medicines and drugs were bought and sold in an unregulated marketplace and used in a number of distinct patterns. Affluent society women injected morphine subcutaneously to quell their anxieties; taking a drug labeled a medicine and obtained through their physicians was socially acceptable for them in ways that drinking alcohol was not. Businessmen sniffed cocaine to sustain their energies as they strove to meet performance goals. Countless people sipped energizing tonics, including colas containing cocaine, at drug store soda fountains. Countless others sold tonics and patent medicines by mail; many such remedies contained not only cocaine, but alcohol. Young men and women sniffed heroin at dance halls; teenage boys taught each other how to smoke cigarettes and sniff heroin in alley ways and pool halls. Bohemians and artists visited the opium dens of urban Chinatowns. The news and magazine press played up the degradation caused by drug addiction in stories about celebrities and ordinary people who became slaves to the drug habit.[18]

Many white Protestant middle-class Americans recoiled at the social changes they observed in immigrant and African American working class neighborhoods. They took alarm at unfamiliar drug use practices, linking them to unchaperoned mixing of the sexes and outright prostitution. Some cited drug use by Chinese, Irish, or African Americans as evidence of Anglo Saxon racial superiority. Temperance reformers broadened the scope of their concerns, charging that alcohol damaged families when men drank up their paychecks and, returning home drunk, beat their wives and children. The church-based Anti-Saloon League (ASL), meanwhile, founded in 1895 and supported by industrialists such as Henry Ford and Pierre du Pont, spearheaded the prohibition drive.[19]

For the manufacturers and purveyors of medicines—physicians, pharmacists, and pharmaceutical manufacturers—widespread drug use contributed to a crisis of professional legitimacy. Pharmaceutical companies aiming to sell pure, medically effective drugs felt tarred by the false or exaggerated claims made by the hawkers of nostrums. Pharmacists who freely sold morphine or cocaine to any buyer attracted censure. Physicians reported a rising incidence of dependence on morphine and cocaine in their patients and reduced their prescribing of these drugs; nevertheless, many continued to blame the addiction problem on physicians well into the twentieth century. Treatments for addiction enjoyed a brisk market; these included the hospitals managed by inebriety professionals, entrepreneurial clinics, and unlabeled mail-order preparations delivered in plain brown packets (which often contained addictive psychoactive substances).[20]

Progressive reformers sought to bring science, law, and moral authority to bear on social problems, including those associated with drug use. Just as they worked to reform the criminal justice system, Americanize urban immigrants, and close down the red-light districts in American cities, so also they sought to eliminate the causes of drug problems. The 1906 Pure Food and Drug Act, a classic piece of Progressive Era regulation, imposed labeling requirements on medicines containing morphine, heroin, or cocaine. But regulation proved insufficient; increasingly, reformers turned to prohibition as the most effective means of control. From the work of the Woman's Christian Temperance Union and Anti-Saloon League to the efforts of the Anti-Cigarette League to the passage of state and local laws banning the nonmedical use of cocaine, support for prohibitory legislation grew.[21] The Harrison Narcotic Act of 1914 forbade use of opiates, cocaine, and a few other drugs except as authorized by a physician; it was the first federal law to ban nonmedical use of any drug. The American Medical Association supported both Harrison and a 1919 Supreme Court interpretation of the law which prohibited physicians from treating opiate addiction by prescribing opiates to stabilize the patient's dose and prevent withdrawal and subsequent craving. This was a pivotal period in the AMA's quest for professional authority, and the organization aggressively policed its own in an effort to retain control over prescription substances and distance the profession from recreational use.[22]

Under Superintendent Wayne Wheeler, the ASL's innovative bipartisan lobbying approach secured prohibitory state legislation and, by early 1919, ratification of the Eighteenth Amendment, establishing nationwide alcohol Prohibition as the law of the land. A World War I reaction against the German American–owned breweries and fears that alcohol would undermine the nation's military contributed to this success. Within a year's time, Congress had passed the enabling legislation, the Volstead Act, and the country embarked on its "noble experiment."[23]

By the mid-1920s, several factors were in place: for both alcohol and opiate dependence, treatment was disappearing because of the belief that prohibition would end the use and law enforcement would deal with a declining number of perpetrators. The AACI, for example, faded as the prohibition movement grew; by 1920, most of the inebriate institutions had closed, and habitual drunkenness was again viewed as primarily a moral, political, and legal issue. Physicians and the public increasingly accepted a psychological explanation of addiction: those who persisted in using opiates despite legal prohibition and social disapproval were manifesting an underlying psychopathology, a fundamental defect of character.[24]

But many Americans, especially in the cities, rejected Prohibition; speakeasies flourished and bootleg liquor flowed freely in many municipalities. With repeal in 1933, the nation entered what some scholars have called an age of ambivalence about alcohol.[25] The reopened breweries and distilleries advertised heavily to win new customers. As old taboos faded, alcohol consumption spread widely. With the anti-liquor and anti-tobacco movements' decline, the broad contours of modern American drug policy were in place. Alcohol, a drug with long-standing cultural acceptance in many human societies, regained its place as a legally permitted drug, and cigarette smoking, though less deeply entwined in social custom, rapidly assumed a mantle of glamour and sophistication. On the other side of a legal divide, the heroin addict became an increasingly powerful symbol of deviance. In 1937, federal legislation would add marijuana to the list of banned drugs. Federal laws in 1951 and 1956 included mandatory sentences for drug trafficking; they reflected a political consensus that drug users deserved harsh punishment. But even as penalties were stiffened, a growing number of legal and medical professionals questioned the effectiveness of relying on law enforcement to solve the drug problem. In 1958, the American Bar Association and the American Medical Association issued a joint report calling for treating addiction as a medical problem, not a criminal one.[26]

Following disruption of global drug trafficking patterns during World

War II, heroin use gradually increased in the late 1940s and 1950s. Both the market and the use were concentrated in the most disadvantaged sectors of American cities, whose population included growing numbers of African Americans and Hispanics. In the 1960s, this increase in illicit drug use skyrocketed as a new generation, including white middle-class youth, began smoking marijuana, swallowing LSD, and exploring a range of new forms of drug use. Experimentation with illicit drugs reflected the disillusionment of a young generation raised on the expectations nurtured by the rising prosperity of the 1950s and the sweeping moral inspiration offered by the Civil Rights Movement in the early 1960s. By the late 1960s, some civil rights groups shifted to more militant tactics in frustration at the slowness of social change, and the nation's deepening involvement in the war in Vietnam prompted disillusioned youth to experiment with drugs, sex, music, living arrangements, political action, and a wide range of behaviors and attitudes that challenged conventional norms. Over the ensuing decade, drug use as mind expansion gave way to drug use as hedonism. Cocaine took on the aura of glamour, linked to rock and roll celebrity and stock broker excess. The age of first use fell; a group of parents, alarmed as they discovered their twelve-year-olds smoking marijuana, provided political support for a re-energized War on Drugs.[27]

As for alcohol, the late twentieth century witnessed a growing interest in wine connoisseurship. U.S. wine production flourished in California and elsewhere.[28] Although the major breweries dominated the beer market, imported brands and local microbreweries also flourished. America's drinking preferences seemed to be moving away from distilled liquor to fermented beverages. Simultaneously, a strong anti-alcohol sentiment remained within late twentieth-century evangelical Protestantism; in such organizations as Alcoholics Anonymous (AA) and Mothers Against Drunk Drivers (MADD), a grassroots organization founded in 1980 and boasting some six hundred chapters by 2000; and in heightened concern about college binge drinking, alcohol-related domestic abuse, and fetal alcohol syndrome. Beginning in the early 1980s, these efforts, coupled with Americans' health and fitness concerns, spurred a slow decline in per capita alcohol consumption. Taken together, these developments were labeled by some social observers as the neo-temperance movement.[29]

The post-Repeal years also saw renewed debate over the nature of alcoholism. The founders of AA, businessman William Wilson and Robert Smith, a physician, along with the National Committee for Education on Alcoholism, led a crusade to treat alcoholism as a disease. In the 1950s, the biostatistician E. M. Jellinek of the Yale Center of Alcohol Studies promoted a multistage model of alcohol addiction based on his research on AA members.[30] But the disease concept met criticism as well. The American Medical Association in the 1960s and 1970s encouraged physicians to treat alcoholism's "medical aspects" but argued that labeling alcoholism a disease did not relieve individuals of responsibility for their intoxicated behavior. The Supreme Court concurred, declining to exonerate persons for actions committed while drunk. Although the National Institute on Alcohol Abuse and Alcoholism (NIAAA) was established in 1971, lending federal support and funding to alcoholism studies, yet some social scientists, including ones funded by the NIAAA, mustered evidence discrediting the disease model. The 1970s and 1980s witnessed the emergence of a broad-based public health approach oriented toward reducing the mental, physical, and social harm caused by excessive drinking.[31]

As the century ended, the so-called neo-temperance movement appeared to be gaining momentum, linked to the anti-tobacco and anti-drug campaigns. In the mid-1990s, however, the nation still had nearly thirty thousand liquor stores, many supermarkets and convenience outlets sold beer and wine, and more than half of adult Americans regularly drank alcoholic beverages. Alcohol's central role in American culture, if somewhat diminished, seemed firmly entrenched.

For drug addicts, the end of the century spelled dramatic change. President Richard Nixon had reorganized the federal drug policy apparatus, funding community-based drug treatment at the same time that he strengthened drug enforcement in the early 1970s. Federal support for treatment reflected the emergence of new treatment methods such as methadone maintenance and the growing popularity of self-help treatment approaches, including the Twelve Step methods of Alcoholics Anonymous and the therapeutic community techniques of Synanon.[32] Yet under the subsequent Republican administrations of Ronald Reagan and George H. W. Bush, federal funding for law enforcement grew at the expense of support for drug treatment. The head of the Office of National Drug Control Policy under President Bill Clinton, retired general Barry McCaffrey, followed a Nixonesque policy of urging more support for drug treatment while holding a hard line against any reduction in the commitment to drug prohibition, interdiction, and law enforcement. Meanwhile, a private-sector infrastructure developed to meet the demand for drug treatment from those groups least likely to incur criminal sanctions for their drug use and most able to marshal the resources to support recovery and reintegration with family, work, and community. For many, the discovery that HIV, the virus that causes AIDS, was transmitted through shared syringes added a new urgency to concerns about illicit drug use and impelled the rise of a public health response to drug problems. Also called harm reduction, this movement seeks to reduce the risks associated with drug use through such measures as distribution of sterile syringes to reduce the transmission of infectious disease to drug users, their sexual partners, and their infants.[33]

Throughout the late twentieth century, in spite of the political salience of the War on Drugs, many aspects of American culture encouraged the view that drug taking could improve various aspects of life, not just narrowly defined medical problems. From the mid-1950s, a growing range of psychiatric medications offered the promise of mood improvement; during the late 1970s, the anxiety-relieving benzodiazepines, such as Valium, were the most widely prescribed class of medication as patients requested them from their physicians. In the 1980s and '90s, Ritalin held out hope for many young people affected by Attention Deficit Hyperactivity Disorder. And a growing interest in over-the-counter herbal medications from St. John's Wort to Ginko Biloba appears to have captivated a health-conscious public. Different forms of drug chic—from amino acid cocktails to improve brain functioning, to ketamine or ecstasy to fuel the frenzied dancing at raves—continue to come and go, but they are a constant within American society.

The Historical Record

Histories of Alcohol

The historiography of alcohol has been built by a wide variety of players from a wide range of disciplines. Temperance reformers, social historians, political scientists, women's history scholars, sociologists, anthropologists, philosophers, physicians, treatment specialists, literary scholars, and others have spent over a century making sense of alcohol's place in American history.

The earliest alcohol historians were pre- and post-Prohibition temperance agitators. Men and women such as Henry Blair, Ernest Cherrington, Daniel Dorchester, Anna Gordon, and John Krout wrote sweeping "dry" histories that chronicled "Man's Fight against Liquor," a battle that they saw culminating in the drive for Prohibition. These works highlighted the problems caused by drinking and the heroic efforts of temperance leaders to block Demon Rum's destructive path. With Prohibition's repeal in 1933, the social scientists interested in alcohol and alcohol problems tried to distance themselves from the wet and dry camps as they sought a new understanding of the evolving relationship between alcohol and society. Unfortunately, this new understanding paid little heed to history. During the 1940s and '50s, individuals involved with alcohol research groups such as the Yale School of Alcohol Studies—Selden Bacon, E. M. Jellinek, and others—began to probe the "alcoholism" problem, but they took great pains to distinguish their work from the historically minded reformers of years past. For these individuals, promoting a rational discussion of alcohol's present and future place in American life did not include evaluating its past.

The 1960s and '70s, however, were watershed decades for the history of alcohol in the United States. Sociologists, anthropologists, and social historians seemed to "discover" alcohol during this period, producing the first substantial wave of new scholarship on the substance's history. The social ferment of the Civil Rights Era and Vietnam War led to greater scrutinizing of state authority and growing interest in the everyday habits and activities of society's nonelites. Women's history and social history offered new perspectives on traditional historical narratives. Likewise, the remarkable expansion of the medical profession during the 1960s and '70s prompted many scholars outside of medicine to consider topics affecting health and disease in America's past and present. The sociologists Joseph Gusfield, Robin Room, and Harry Gene Levine and the historians William Rorabaugh, Jack Blocker, Ruth Bordin, Jed Dannenbaum, and John Burnham published their initial studies of the alcohol problem during these decades, introducing readers to the Woman's Christian Temperance Union, the measurable effects of Prohibition, and the temperance movement in its many incarnations.

The Alcohol Research Group at Berkeley and its graduates played an influential role in demonstrating how sociologically informed history could illuminate contemporary alcohol issues. Influenced by symbolic interactionism, ethnomethodology, the sociology of knowledge, social movement theory, Marxism, and Michel Foucault, this generation of scholars blended theory and history in new and creative ways. Particularly important here was Harry Gene Levine's article "The Discovery of Addiction," a work referenced by many of the essays in this volume. In this essay, Levine argued that the concept of addiction had a particular historical locus in late eighteenth- and early nineteenth-century America. He revealed the ways in which the rise of the middle class and the industrial capitalist economy placed a premium on self-discipline and facilitated the adoption not only of a temperance ethic, but of a disease concept of addiction that focused on individuals regaining control of their willpower through the assistance of experts and institutions. Levine was hardly alone. Other alcohol historians and sociologists made significant progress integrating alcohol and alcohol regulation into the American cultural narrative, whether analyzing the temperance movement as a vehicle for the expression of gender, class, ethnic, religious, and urban-rural tensions; revealing the ways in which alcohol consumption meshed with the values and habits of the young republic; or focusing on the actual effects of Prohibition.

During the 1980s, '90s, and into the twenty-first century, many of the pioneering academic actors of the previous decades continued to pursue their research in the field, but they were joined by a growing interdisciplinary cadre of anthropologists, sociologists, literary scholars, philosophers, and historians. Continuing the move beyond temperance and Prohibition, scholars of these decades broadened the expanding range of themes and topics within alcohol historiography. They also produced a number of general surveys of the history of alcohol in America. The first in these synthetic overviews was Mark Lender and James Kirby Martin's *Drinking in America*. Andrew Barr followed suit in 1999 with *Drink: A Social History of America*. Later came Griffith Edwards's *Alcohol: The World's Favorite Intoxicant* and Stuart Walton's *Out of It: A Cultural History of Intoxication*. Compilations such as Robin Room and Susanna Barrows's *Drinking: Behavior and Belief in Modern History* provided comparative perspectives on alcohol habits in the United States and European and non-European nations. And many of these works devoted a great deal of time to ethnic differences in drinking practices. Monographs such as Richard Stivers's treatment of Irish drinking, *Hair of the Dog*, focused on the histories of specific ethnicities and their relationship to alcohol in the United States, Denise Herd turned her attentions to African Americans, and Peter Mancall, William Unrau, Nancy Lurie, Steven Kunitz, and Jerrold Levy examined Native Americans' alcohol habits.

The gender and alcohol relationship gained new ground through the works of American studies scholars Catherine Murdock and Lori Rotskoff; historians Barbara Epstein, Jonathan Zimmerman, and Mark Lender, and sociologist Craig Reinarman, among others. These individuals pursued society's changing attitudes toward women who drank and women with drinking problems. By examining such women-led efforts as the campaign for scientific temperance education, the Women's Organization for National Prohibition Reform, or the more recent Mothers Against Drunk Drivers, these scholars also revealed the diversity of roles women played in alternately stemming the liquor traffic and facilitating it. Recently, Janet Golden, a social historian, and Cynthia Daniels, a political scientist, also have explored the links among drinking women, drinking men, and the public discussion of fetal harm. And most recently, Rotskoff has analyzed the evolving relations between men and women through their drinking habits after World War II.

The medical profession's relationship to alcohol and the medicalization of alcohol problems have also drawn recent attention from sociologists and historians. Peter Conrad and Joseph Schneider's second edition of *From Badness to Sickness*, Herbert Fingarette's *Heavy Drinking*, and Lynn Appleton's essay on the problematic case of alcoholism's medicalization offer a variety of critical perspectives on the waxing and waning of the disease concept of alcoholism. The issue of alcohol's place within medicine, meanwhile, has received attention from both medical historian John Warner in *The Therapeutic Perspective* and historian of biology Philip Pauly, who has published two essays on the turn-of-the-century alcohol physiology debates. Treatment professional William White, Jim Baumohl, Robin Room, and Sarah Tracy have examined the creation of medical institutions for the treatment of inebriates throughout the nineteenth and twentieth centuries. Social scientists Ron Roizen and Thomas Babor and medical historian Barbara Rosenkrantz have also analyzed the evolving relationship between the public health community and the definition of alcohol problems throughout the twentieth century.

Perry Duis's comparative study of public drinking in Boston and Chicago between 1880 and 1920 led the way for other studies of drinking establishments. One recent example is Madelon Powers's *Faces along the Bar: Lore and Order in the Workingman's Saloon, 1870–1920*. Colonial historian David Conroy offered a view of the saloon's ancestor in his study of the pub in colonial Massachusetts. Of course, other earlier scholarship, such as labor historian Roy Rosenzweig's *Eight Hours for What We Will*, also addressed the saloon in the context of working-class leisure culture, as did cultural historian Kathy Peiss's *Cheap Amusements*.

Older topics such as Prohibition have continued to be of great interest to historians and sociologists alike, with both groups attempting to extrapolate from the thirteen-year experiment to contemporary drug problems and policy issues. Written in the late 1970s, Norman Clark's work on Prohibition offered readers a counterbalance to Joseph Gusfield's analysis of the movement's symbolic significance for the middle classes. Clark focused on the real problems caused by the saloon and the excessive consumption of alcohol therein, an issue addressed earlier by John Burnham. David Kyvig discussed the opposition to Prohibition in some depth in *Repealing National Prohibition*, while the more recent works of Richard Hamm and K. Austin Kerr have examined the ways different pro-Prohibition reform groups, employing various legal strategies, promoted the cause with varying levels of success. Others, such as Edward Behr, have turned their attentions to Prohibition as a way of illuminating American culture in the 1920s and '30s.

Histories of Drugs Other Than Alcohol

In the nineteenth century, Romantics associated opium and hashish use with exoticism, Orientalism, and stimulation of the imagination. Fitzhugh Ludlow's *The Hashish Eater* exemplified the literature that explored psychoactive drug effects with interest. On a more mundane level, an emerging American middle class sought to relieve the pressures of work and social life in an increasingly complex urban industrial economy through drugs, particularly opiates and cocaine. George Beard described these anxieties and the use of drugs to relieve them in *American Nervousness* in 1881.

By the late nineteenth century, the profusion of new medicines, whether isolated from plants or developed in the laboratory, added to growing awareness of the dependence problems associated with alcohol and opiates like morphine. Although the latter were studied most intensively, Progressive Era observers suspected many substances of being habit forming. Those who developed habits sought relief in a brisk market for treatment methods and medicines. Charles Towns described his own highly popular treatment system in *Habits That Handicap* in 1916.

Others sought to understand addiction as a physiological phenomenon. George Pettey (*The Narcotic Drug Diseases and Allied Ailments,* 1913) and Ernest Bishop (*The Narcotic Drug Problem,* 1920) independently developed theories of opiate addiction influenced by recent findings in immunology. They argued that tolerance, or the need to take larger amounts of the drug to achieve the same effect, developed because the body produced a sort of antibody to counter the drug's toxic effects. They ascribed the severe symptoms that ensued when an addict stopped using the drug to the action of that substance on the body's own tissues. While this theory was discredited by the late 1920s, it focused on two aspects of opiate addiction that have been considered definitive before and since and have influenced thinking about whether other drugs should be considered addictive: the rise of tolerance with steady use and the onset of a clearly recognizable withdrawal syndrome when use is abruptly stopped.

A work that has remained authoritative, *Opium Addiction* by Arthur B. Light and Edward Torrance (1929–30), was based on extensive physiological study of opiate addicts while they were stabilized on morphine, at the height of the withdrawal syndrome, and in the abstinent state. Light and Torrance described the withdrawal syndrome with precision and established that it was not life threatening—and thus did not require careful medical management or palliation.

The Opium Problem by Charles Terry and Mildred Pellens, published in 1928, brought together virtually everything that was scientifically known or believed about opiates up to that time. It consists largely of quoted passages from a broad range of European and American authorities on the physiological, psychological, and, to a lesser extent, social aspects of opiate addiction; it remains an invaluable resource for the historian. Notwithstanding this breadth of perspectives, Terry and Pellens were writing after passage of the Harrison Narcotic Act and its interpretation by the Supreme Court had ushered in the regime of drug prohibition. In this context, the authors' own powerful argument for humane medical treatment of opiate addicts was a lonely protest against policy that favored incarceration over treatment.

From the 1920s onward, the policy of prohibition influenced who used opiates and how, and the heroin addict became a powerful symbol of social deviance in American society. Writers could hardly escape viewing the heroin addict through this lens, but not all came to the same conclusions. In the middle decades of the twentieth century, as policy toward users of illicit drugs became increasingly harsh, psychological and sociological explanations of addiction vied and, in some cases, mingled. Psychologists tended to ground addiction in inherent personality defects, while sociologists were more likely to portray addiction as a behavioral response to a social environment.

In 1925, Lawrence Kolb, a U.S. Public Health Service psychiatrist, explained opiate addiction as arising from a psychopathic personality type, a hypothesis that seemed to justify reformers' hardening view of addicts as social misfits who deserved incarceration. Kolb's theory appeared in such articles as "Types and Characteristics of Drug Addicts" and "Pleasure and Deterioration from Narcotic Addiction." Although these articles helped solidify and popularize the image of a sociopathic addictive personality, Kolb himself went on to advocate medical rather than criminal justice management of addiction. But in the 1930s, sentiment in favor of banning drugs and locking up users was fanned by the publication of "Marijuana: Assassin of Youth" by Harry Anslinger and Courtney Ryley Cooper. Anslinger, head of the Federal Narcotics Bureau, made frequent and effective use of the media to sustain support for his agency.

The roots of a different view of the addict emerged in a sociological strain of research originating at the University of Chicago. Bingham Dai interviewed addicts in jails and clinics and in natural settings. Published as *Opium Addiction in Chicago* in 1937, his dissertation explored addiction as a social phenomenon in which setting and peer norms, as well as anxieties about social identity, influenced how people used heroin. Nevertheless, Dai retained a psychoanalytic framework to explain why certain individuals became addicted to heroin while others did not; in so doing, he sustained a view of addiction as arising from inherent personality traits reflecting an inability to conform to conventional gender and class roles.

Dai's fellow graduate student Alfred Lindesmith achieved lasting prominence as a student of the social aspects of addiction and a champion for medical, rather than criminal justice, management of addicts. He rejected Lawrence Kolb's theory that addiction arose from certain personality types; rather, he argued, heroin addicts' manipulative and sometimes desperate behavior arose from the addiction itself: as the dependent heroin user learned that the pains of withdrawal could be relieved with a single shot of drug, the addict was driven to sustain the addiction and avoid the agony. Lindesmith's research of the 1930s appeared as *Opiate Addiction* in 1947.

Inspired by Lindesmith's rigor in the study of deviant behavior, Howard Becker began studying marijuana smokers among jazz musicians in post–World War II Chicago. Two ideas he developed in *Outsiders: Studies in the Sociology of Deviance* influenced a later generation of ethnographers: first, drug use involved a socially mediated learning process in which neophyte users responded to cues from more experienced users about drug effects and their meanings; second, addiction could be framed as a career, as the addict moved through different stages of addiction and as the addiction interacted with other aspects of a dynamic life course.

Others pursued epidemiological study of heroin addiction or combined sociological investigation with psychodynamic explanations of addiction. During these mid-century decades, as community-based treatment all but disappeared, many heroin addicts spent time as prisoners and patients at the U.S. Public Health Service Narcotic Hospitals in Lexington, Kentucky, and Fort Worth, Texas. The Addiction Research Center at Lexington, and the psychiatric residency program there, exposed researchers and physicians to this captured population and sparked further interest in studying—and treating—addiction outside of institutional walls. Two collections of papers exemplify the studies of these and other leading researchers in the 1950s and early 1960s: *Epidemiology of Opiate Addiction in the U.S.*, edited by John Ball and Carl Chambers, and *Narcotics*, edited by Daniel Wilner and Gene Kassebaum. Isidor Chein and his colleagues studied the prototypical heroin addicts of the 1950s, adolescent males in New York City, to produce a social-psychological explanation of addiction in *The Road to H.*

Marie Nyswander practiced psychiatry in New York after training at Lexington, and by the mid-1950s she had concluded that long-term institutionalization was not the right treatment for every addict. She published her views in *The Drug Addict as a Patient* and later collaborated with Vincent Dole to develop methadone maintenance treatment. Nyswander exemplified a growing number of professionals who, like Lawrence Kolb, came to believe that medical management of addiction was more effective and humane than imprisoning addicts. Kolb argued his case in *Drug Addiction: A Medical Problem*. In 1958, a joint committee of the American Bar Association and the American Medical Association issued a report criticizing the federal government's sole reliance on incarceration as a remedy for heroin addiction. Thus, when large numbers of young people began experimenting with a range of illicit psychoactives in the 1960s, a group of medical and legal professionals had already begun to explore new ways of responding to illicit drug use.

These enormous changes in patterns of drug use also sparked new interest in both the history of drugs and an anthropologically informed understanding of broader meanings of drug use in human culture. Andrew Weil cited a basic human drive to alter conscious through a variety of pharmacological and nonpharmacological means in *The Natural Mind;* the book became a manifesto of youthful middle-class drug exploration. David Musto's *The American Disease*, whose first edition appeared in 1973, remains the most exhaustive historical account of the development of the American policy of drug prohibition. Musto traces in detail the legislative maneuvers that culminated in passage and implementation of the Harrison Narcotic Act and the attitudes and actions of physicians, for whom opiates had become such problematic medicines. In addition, he charts shifts in drug treatment in the early decades of the twentieth century.

Critics of punitive drug policies mined the historical record to bolster their arguments that most drug problems resulted from prohibition; they included psychiatrist Thomas Szasz (*Ceremonial Chemistry*), attorney Arnold Trebach (*The Heroin Solution*), and Edward Brecher, who led a Consumers Union team examining the background of policy and its impact on a range of illegal drugs (*Licit and Illicit Drugs*). The historian David Courtwright challenged these critics' argument that criminalization of opiates and cocaine had created the criminal class of addicts that had predominated through much of the twentieth century. Using tools of quantitative analysis common among social historians of the late 1970s and inspired by the insight that distinguishing use figures for different forms of opiates would reveal the demographic contours of different kinds of users, he produced *Dark Paradise*. This analysis enabled Courtwright to show that young working-class males in deteriorated urban neighborhoods had already established a pattern of heroin use by 1910 and therefore that this pattern of use was not simply a perverse result of policy. H. Wayne Morgan's description of shifting patterns of use and modes of treatment in *Drugs in America* added a another social-historical perspective. The voices of addicts, and some researchers, appear in the oral history collection *Addicts Who Survive;* David Courtwright's introduction to this volume, which he compiled with Don Des Jarlais and Herman Joseph, summarizes what he calls the "classic era of narcotic control."

A new generation of urban ethnographers sought to understand the new patterns of drug use, which involved more kinds of people and younger people, and more kinds of drugs and polydrug use. They typically rejected the essentialism of earlier psychological explanations of addiction which portrayed addicts as passive and retreatist. A 1969 classic of this genre, Edward Preble and John Casey's "Taking Care of Business," portrayed young male heroin addicts as acting with purposeful energy as they did what it took to obtain the heroin necessary to sustain habits requiring four to six injections a day to stave off withdrawal symptoms. Preble and Casey located their subjects, young white, black, and Puerto Rican men in working-class New York neighborhoods, in a heavily policed illicit market in which drug purity had declined and its cost had risen over the decades from the 1920s.

Among the profusion of ethnographic studies of drug use of recent decades (many funded by the National Institute on Drug Abuse, a creation of the Nixon drug policy initiatives), a few examples indicate the range of issues and qualities of the research. In *The Vietnam Drug User Returns*, Lee Robins showed that most heroin-addicted Vietnam veterans, once they returned from the front to their home settings and occupations, did not continue using heroin. These findings helped undermine the idea that, once addicted, heroin users were virtually unreclaimable and encouraged the development of community-based treatment in the 1970s and 1980s. Some ethnographers made use of Howard Becker's career model to relate changes in drug use to identity and social context. Marsha Rosenbaum analyzed how women's deepening involvement with heroin narrowed life options in *Women on Heroin*; Charles Faupel showed how individuals modified levels of heroin use in response to life events in *Shooting Dope*. More recently, Philippe Bourgois's account of crack dealing in East Harlem, *In Search of Respect*, invokes the history of four generations of Puerto Ricans in their home island and New York as a context for understanding the involvement of underemployed youth in the crack market.

Norman Zinberg and Patrick Biernacki produced important studies of heroin users who avoided contact with treatment programs and eluded official data-gathering systems. Zinberg identified enough occasional users of heroin to defy the conventional view of heroin as ineluctably addicting. In *Drug, Set, and Setting*, he discussed the influence of the user's mental attitude and the norms in his or her immediate social environment on levels of use, the experience afforded by the drug, and the ability to contain drug use within chosen limits. Biernacki interviewed people who had been addicted to heroin and ended their use on their own, without recourse to treatment facilities.

While historians were somewhat slower to take up drugs as subject matter, a recent wave of new historical works has enriched our understanding of the multiple roles drugs play in our society. Some historians have focused on individual drugs. Joseph Spillane's *Cocaine* traces this drug's shifting identities from a potential miracle drug to troubling medicine to drug of abuse in the period leading up to passage of the Harrison Act. Cassandra Tate, in *Cigarette Wars*, shows that, though it was never prohibited at the national level, tobacco was nonetheless the target of a long-standing campaign for laws to ban its use. As she brings the story forward to the late twentieth century, she traces the cigarette's dramatic shifts in acceptance and condemnation. In *Creating the American Junkie*, Caroline Acker juxtaposes the lives of morphine and heroin users in the first decades of the twentieth century with the work of researchers who constructed theoretical understandings of addiction from various disciplinary perspectives.

Some historians have focused on particular themes rather than particular drugs. Two works examine not only how women have used drugs but also how women drug users have been portrayed in the media and by policymakers. Stephen Kandall, a physician, surveys the history of women's drug use in America and treatment and policy responses in *Substance and Shadow*. In *Using Women*, Nancy Campbell shows how Cold War concerns about gender roles infused rhetoric—and policy—about drug use. Mara Keire uses gender analysis to a different purpose as she examines the symbolic roles of drug use, dress, and behavior in "Dope Fiends and Degenerates: The Gendering of Addiction in the Early Twentieth Century."

Others have taken a more inclusive approach, building in part on the works of other historians. In *Hep-Cats, Narcs, and Pipe Dreams*, Jill Jonnes casts a broad net as she surveys trends in drug use in America over the last century and a half; she also discusses enforcement efforts in depth and considers drug policy in light of competing policy imperatives such as national security.

From Alfred McCoy's 1972 book *The Politics of Heroin in Southeast Asia* to more recent work by William Walker (*Drug Control Americas* and *Opium and Foreign Policy: The Anglo-American Search for Order in Asia, 1912–1954*) and William McAllister (*Drug Diplomacy in the Twentieth Century*), a number of general points emerge regarding the relation of domestic drug policy to national security concerns and international efforts to control drug trafficking. First, drug revenues are hard to resist, even for states. Second, drug policy almost always takes second place behind national security policy. Third, drug markets (both the supply and demand sides) flourish in areas of political instability and lack of viable economic alternatives for subsistence. For similar reasons, drug trafficking often flows through the same channels as weapons smuggling.

Drug Control Policy, edited by William Walker, contains articles that originally appeared in a special issue of the *Journal of Policy History*. John McWilliams's account of Harry Anslinger's career as commissioner of narcotics (*The Protectors*) emphasizes Anslinger's attention to international concerns as he strengthened domestic enforcement efforts. The intricacies of federal policy toward treatment as well as enforcement during and since the Nixon administration appear in *The Facts about "Drug Abuse,"* produced by the Drug Abuse Council in 1980; *Treating Drug Problems*, a report of the Institute of Medicine; and Michael Massing's *The Fix*. William White's *Slaying the Dragon* recounts the history of many varieties of drug and alcohol treatment over the last two centuries; Lonnie Shavelson provides an intimate view of one city's drug-treatment system in *Hooked*. The discovery of opiate receptors and of the brain's own opiate-like compounds in the 1970s revolutionized understandings of addiction; Solomon Snyder describes his own role in these discoveries and the involvement of politics in addiction research in *Brainstorming*.

One of the most exciting trends of late within the alcohol literature and the history of intoxicants generally has been the consideration of alcohol in relation to other psychoactive substances. In addition to contributing to many of the newer veins of alcohol historiography just outlined, *Altering American Consciousness* makes a significant contribution to this comparative body of literature. Several other collections and monographs have pointed in this direction. The essays in *Consuming Habits* (edited by Jordan Goodman, Paul Lovejoy, and Andrew Sherratt) throw the American experience into comparative perspective, with a particular emphasis on drugs as commodities which are absorbed into the cultural contexts of wherever they are introduced. John Burnham's *Bad Habits* highlights the commercialization of vice in the early twentieth century. David Courtwright's *Forces of Habit* is a sweeping survey of drug use and drug marketing from the early modern period to the present. This movement to consider alcohol as but one of many psychoactive substances whose histories are interrelated comes at an interesting time. Roughly one century after the unifying concept of inebriety was abandoned for the more discrete entities of "alcoholism" and "opiate addiction" and a host of other drug-specific behaviors, many pharmacological researchers are promoting a unitary theory of addiction in which different psychoactive substances are believed to trigger similar neurochemical reactions within the brain.

Of course, the policy side of things may have preceded the pharmacological side by a few decades. The decades-old "substance abuse" moniker encompassed a variety of human-drug relationships before anyone spoke of a "Dopamine Hypothesis." Nevertheless, the interest in considering a variety of psychoactive substances together comes not just from historians, sociologists, and anthropologists, but from psychopharmacologists and clinicians. What's more, these "natural scientists" make plain that culture, social behavior, and learning are key elements in the dopamine equation. To quote a *Time* article devoted to the dopamine hypothesis, "Realistically, no one believes better medications alone will solve the drug problem. In fact, one of the most hopeful messages coming out of current research is that the biochemical abnormalities associated with addiction can be reversed through learning." We believe the essays in this volume will enhance our understanding of the dynamic relationship between culture and chemistry.[34]

The Comparative Approach—Essays in This Volume

The essays in this book originated as papers presented at a conference, Historical Perspectives on Alcohol and Drug Use in American Society, 1800 to 1997, organized by Sarah Tracy and hosted by the College of Physicians of Philadelphia on May 9, 10, and 11, 1997. Designed as a showcase for an emerging wave of new historical scholarship on alcohol and drugs, the conference brought together scholars trained in the history of medicine, women's history, American cultural and social history, literary criticism, sociology, social work, and anthropology. Historians and sociologists whose earlier work had helped inspire these newer investigations were present as commentators. The resulting discussions prompted revisions of the conference papers to emphasize both their connections with one another and their distinct contributions.

The logic of bringing alcohol and drug historians together reflected the understanding that, despite the chasm created by law which separates them into legal and illegal categories, all psychoactive drugs share important commonalities. As mentioned above, this similarity has been recognized for over two decades in the addiction field. But scholars studying the social contexts of drug use, especially historians, had typically remained focused on one side of the divide or the other. On the other hand, humankind's experience with psychoactive drugs has varied tremendously. Drug effects themselves are malleable, shaped by human expectations, constructions, experiences, social contexts, intentions. Different drugs used by different groups of people in different historical times and places have created myriad patterns of use, interpretation, and response. The historian's tools are ideally suited to identify the continuities and reveal the contours of change and difference.

William White, an addiction treatment specialist and author of *Slaying the Dragon: The History of Addiction Treatment and Recovery in America*, maps the linguistic terrain of alcohol and drug-use treatment for the past two hundred years. Drawing on his own clinical and administrative experience, White reveals the complexity and confusion of addiction terminology that physicians, users, patients, policymakers, and others have employed to serve their own distinctive interests. He reminds us that addiction is never a medical or moral problem alone, but a personal, cultural, economic, political, and medical matter. In doing so, he shows what was at stake for each group as they made specific claims about the nature of addiction.

The historical sociologist Ron Roizen analyzes how alcohol problems have been reframed within American society following Repeal of the Eighteenth Amendment. Roizen shows how the alcoholism paradigm of the 1930s and 1940s was promoted as part of scientists', clinicians', and policymakers' efforts to depoliticize alcohol and destigmatize drinking. The idea that alcoholism reflected an inherent susceptibility among a tiny minority gave way in the 1970s as social scientists and epidemiologists formulated a public health approach. This perspective focused on patterns of drinking to define alcoholism and supported the idea that policy adjustments could influence drinking behavior and thus reduce the incidence of problem drinking. Roizen makes a strong case that the transformation of the alcohol problem paradigm resulted not only from pressures within the scientific community, but from larger social and political trends, such as the retrenchment of conservative political and social values in the 1980s and a renewed interest in domestic problems following the end of the Cold War.

In his review of four hundred years of Native American drinking, the historian Peter Mancall challenges whites' persistent stereotyped images and interpretations of Indians' susceptibility to alcoholism. Although yesterday's phylogenetic arguments about the "savage's" predisposition to alcoholism have been replaced by today's genetic explanations, Mancall argues persuasively that we must turn to history, not heredity, for a truer understanding of the complex relationship between Indians and alcohol.

Historian Katherine Chavigny traces the important role that reforming and reformed drunkards played in therapeutic temperance movements from the Washingtonians, through the inebriate homes, to gospel temperance. While some historians stress the continuity across these evangelical and therapeutic fellowships and place the emergence of Alcoholics Anonymous squarely within this tradition, Chavigny points up differences in tone, emphasis, and modes of religiosity in several strains of evangelical temperance in the nineteenth century. These changes notwithstanding, the lay evangelical tradition not only survived, but thrived amid the various articulations of the disease concept of alcoholism and their institutionalization in inebriate homes and asylums.

In her essay, Sarah Tracy addresses Iowa's efforts to create a state-run medical facility for the treatment of alcoholics during the Progressive Era. Tracy's case study of the turn-of-the-century attempt to medicalize habitual drunkenness suggests that the process of promoting and institutionalizing the disease concept of inebriety involved much more than the medical profession's attempting to carve out new turf. It involved ongoing negotiations among temperance and Prohibition forces, state hospital physicians, the state board of control, the state board of health, Iowa's governor, the eugenics movement, the court system, and the inebriates, their families, friends, and employers. Echoing William White's observation that the variety of terms used to label addiction and alcoholism reflects the diverse interests and priorities of their users, Tracy finds that the same diversity of interests that made creating a new medical facility for inebriates possible in Iowa also hindered its success.

Caroline Acker traces the trajectories of two generations of an addicted family and their associates; their experience exemplifies the changing demographics of the addict population at the turn of the century and the circumstances affecting their pathways in and out of treatment. Acker's narrative reveals the transformation of opiate use from its pre–Harrison Act status as palliative medical care for mundane ills such as menstrual pain and seasonal depression, to its post–Harrison identity as stigmatized deviant behavior. In this period, the now-familiar distinction between "medical" and "recreational" (or "thrill-seeking") drug use was first framed. Acker's picture of a family caught in this transition offers insight into the complexity of familial, economic, and cultural circumstances that molded the addict's experience and identity.

In his examination of the same period, the cultural historian Timothy Hickman focuses on those constructing meanings of "addiction" rather than on the direct experience of addicts. Hickman explores the phenomenon's voluntary and involuntary meanings in the context of rapid technological and economic changes taking place in turn-of-the-century America. He sees the concept of addiction as a modern technology itself, one employed by the medical profession to garner new social and cultural authority and reinforce an existing system of class stratification in the United States. By distinguishing the overworked professional who sought relief in drugs from the willful users who could be cast as social misfits, physicians strengthened their claim to expertise in social as well as purely medical problems.

Much as it is for William White and Timothy Hickman, language is very important to the public health and drug historian Susan Speaker. Her analysis of the rhetoric of the anti-alcohol and anti-drug campaigns of the early and mid-twentieth century reveals that the latter adopted the hyperbolic prose and morality tales of the former, with little variation. No surprise, Speaker shows us that a number of the movers and shakers of the anti-liquor and anti-saloon campaigns transferred their energies to the fight against narcotic drugs following Prohibition. Speaker's literary and content analysis of professional, policy, and popular periodical literatures describing the personal and social ills befalling victims of the "narcotics menace" offers students of America's "War on Drugs" tremendous insight into the nature of the contemporary discourse on drug use and abuse. It also calls into question the reality of the public's perception of this troubling social problem.

The sociologist Jim Baumohl provides a detailed study of how federal and state regulatory agencies, medical and pharmaceutical professional organizations, voluntary reform groups, and the media attempted to enforce the Harrison Narcotic Act, address the situation of recently criminalized addicts, and manage the activities of the medical and pharmaceutical professions that had formerly maintained those addicted to opiates. As he charts the tensions between criminal justice and medical management of addiction in California in the 1930s, he foreshadows the challenges posed by the recent passage of Proposition 36 in California, which mandates treatment rather than jail for most nonviolent drug offenders.

Historian Michelle McClellan's examination of physicians' attitudes toward women with drinking problems reveals the extent to which commonly held assumptions about men's and women's gender roles permeated psychiatric thought in the period following World War II. McClellan analyzes the writings of psychiatrists who explained alcoholism as arising from stunted psychosocial development. She argues that the striking differences in how they explained alcoholism in women and men illustrates the heterosexist assumptions that permeated American culture at mid-century: while psychiatrists generally regarded male alcoholics as homosexuals claiming a false heterosexual masculinity through their drinking, they portrayed women who drank as violating their essential femininity by failing to fulfill domestic roles, displaying promiscuity or frigidity, or aspiring to inappropriate occupational roles. These psychiatrists saw women's apparent rejection of appropriate gender roles as more deviant than men's attempts to act out a heterosexual identity they did not truly feel.

The historian Lori Rotskoff offers readers another gendered analysis of men, women, and alcoholism. Focusing on the growth of Alcoholics Anonymous and its auxiliary organizations such as Al-Anon, Rotskoff demonstrates that the therapeutic paradigm employed by AA during the post–World War II decades extolled traditional gender roles. What's more, the wives of the predominantly male AA members were held accountable not only for the management—and often suppression—of the emotional turmoil they experienced because of their husbands' alcoholism, but for their husbands' cure as well. Behind every married and sober alcoholic was a woman who was to support him emotionally and blithely manage affairs on the home front until her husband could resume his role as household head. Rotskoff reveals the paradoxically empowering and confining roles that women were asked to play in reforming their alcoholic husbands, and the ways these roles revealed the nature of the American marriage in the period following World War II.

The final three essays bring us to the contemporary period and broaden the range of discussion to include drugs in their roles as medicines, as market commodities, and as consumer items (and, at times, all three). Nicholas Weiss, both physician and historian, contrasts public perceptions of depression in the 1950s with those of the period since the 1970s by examining medical and popular responses to the introduction of different antidepressants. Debates about the appropriate uses of iproniazid and imipramine in the 1950s were confined to medical circles, while the newer class of serotonin reuptake inhibitors spawned wide-ranging attention in the popular media, including such best-selling books as Peter Kramer's *Listening to Prozac*. Weiss argues that it is not only the technological feat of creating new antidepressants with fewer side effects that allowed for their growing use after 1970, but the economic downturn of the early 1970s, the rise of the "me" generation, the rush of published personal narratives and popular advice books that focused on depression, and the growth of life-enhancing services offered by the medical profession—cosmetic surgery, birth control, obesity treatments—that paved the path for Prozac's widespread acceptance.

Steven Novak's essay on Sidney Cohen's critique of LSD takes us inside the psychedelic drug movement, placing its origins in the experimentation of Cohen and other researchers during the late 1950s. Interestingly, Cohen discovered what other students of alcohol and illegal psychotropic drugs realized in the 1970s, that the user's mindset and the context of use exerted great influence over the user's experience. Novak's treatment of Cohen's experimentation with LSD, his enthusiasm for the drug, and his gradual disillusionment with it, its prescribers, and its promoters likewise reveals the ways in which a psychotropic drug's identity could be molded by its users. Whether it was seen as a CIA truth serum, a Huxleyesque vehicle for transcendence, or a psychedelic cure for alcohol dependence, LSD's identity depended greatly on its user's identity and expectations. The story of LSD's early years also reminds us how much the American public comes to expect of its new drugs and how much it can come to fear them in a short span of years.

Finally, the historian Allan Brandt delves into the great twentieth-century cigarette debate. He nimbly charts how the villainous cigarette at the dawn of the twentieth century came to be an aggressive and popular symbol of autonomy by mid-century, only to fall on hard times following the 1964 and 1988 Surgeon General's reports. Situating cigarette smoking in three sociocultural and temporal frames, Brandt reveals how cultural changes such as Prohibition, World War I, and the rise of Americans' health consciousness, as well as scientific developments such as increased funding for addiction research, and a new epidemiological approach to risk-taking behavior altered the perception of cigarettes and their users. Brandt's essay touches on a number of issues raised by others throughout the volume: the expanding definition of addiction, the substitution of one drug habit for another more acceptable one, the relationship between a drug's identity and the demographics of its users, the tension between individual and social responsibility for drug use and abuse, the role of industry in promoting addictive substances, and the importance of language in describing drug habits.

In bringing addiction back to the forefront, and in drawing on Harry Levine's groundbreaking essay, Brandt brings the discussion of drugs and drug use full circle. From the framing of drug dependence as a disease in the late eighteenth century, in the work of the British physician Thomas Trotter and the American physician Benjamin Rush, to the contemporary notion of addiction as a label for any behavior that seems out of rational control, the specter of dependence on a drug has reflected social fears. As these essays demonstrate, to call addiction or dependence a disease is not to lock it into an unchanging category; social and professional ideas about what constitutes disease also change over time. Nor do we have a national consensus on whether criminal justice or medical experts—or users and ex-users themselves—are the best authorities on the subject. The tobacco situation is still in flux; individual states are experimenting with systems which challenge federal control of drug classification and federal insistence on prohibition of certain drugs; and new psychotropic medications continue to prompt patients', as well as professionals' interpretations of their effects. These ongoing changes reinforce a theme prominent in all these essays: that the meanings of individual drugs and of specific drug-using behaviors change over time in ways that reflect changing cultural concerns, shifting demographics of drug use, evolving medical and scientific understandings of drug use and drug effects, and the experiences of those who use drugs.

Notes

1. Seema Mehta, "The Region Water Reclamation Project to Filter Drugs, Pathogens, Infrastructure: Under Orange County's $600-Million Plan, Extra Levels of Treatment Will Remove Unmetabolized Pills and Potions Flushed Down Toilets," *Los Angeles Times*, 22 January 2002.

2. David Courtwright, *Forces of Habit: Drugs and the Making of the Modern World* (Cambridge: Harvard University Press, 2001); Jordan Goodman, Paul Lovejoy, and Andrew Sheratt, *Consuming Habits: Drugs in History and Anthropology* (London: Routledge, 1995); Rudi Matthee, "Exotic Substances: The Introduction and Global Spread of Tobacco, Coffee, Cocoa, Tea, and Distilled Liquor, Sixteenth to Eighteenth Centuries," in

Roy Porter and Mikulas Teich, eds., *Drugs and Narcotics in History* (Cambridge: Cambridge University Press, 1995), 24–51; Wolfgang Schivelbusch, *Tastes of Paradise: A Social History of Spices, Stimulants, and Intoxicants* (New York: Vintage Books, 1992).

3. Cassandra Tate, *Cigarette Wars: The Triumph of the Little White Slaver* (New York: Oxford University Press, 1999); Allan Brandt, "The Cigarette, Risk, and American Culture," in Judith Walzer Leavitt and Ronald Numbers, eds., *Sickness and Health in America—Third Edition* (Madison: University of Wisconsin Press, 1997), 494–505.

4. Joseph Spillane, *Cocaine: From Medical Marvel to Modern Menace in the United States, 1884–1920* (Baltimore: Johns Hopkins University Press, 2000); Craig Reinarman and Harry G. Levine, "The Crack Attack: America's Latest Drug Scare, 1986–1992," in Joel Best, ed., *Images of Issues: Typifying Contemporary Social Problems*, 2d ed. (New York: Aldine De Gruyter, 1995), 147–90.

5. Courtwright, *Forces of Habit*; Goodman et al., *Consuming Habits*.

6. Andrew Barr, *Drink: A Social History of America* (New York: Carroll and Graf, 1999).

7. Mark Edward Lender and James Kirby Martin, *Drinking in America: A History,* rev. and expanded ed. (New York: Free Press and Collier Macmillan, 1987).

8. David W. Conroy, *In Public Houses: Drink & the Revolution of Authority in Colonial Massachusetts* (Chapel Hill and Williamsburg, Va.: University of North Carolina Press and Institute of Early American History and Culture, 1995); Lender and Martin, *Drinking in America*; William Rorabaugh, *The Alcoholic Republic—An American Tradition* (New York: Oxford University Press, 1979); Daniel Dorchester, *The Liquor Problem in All Ages* (New York: Phillips and Hunt, 1884).

9. Peter Mancall, *Deadly Medicine: Indians and Alcohol in Early America* (Ithaca: Cornell University Press, 1995).

10. Benjamin Rush, *An Inquiry into the Effects of Ardent Spirits upon the Human Body and Mind, with an Account of the Means of Preventing, and the Remedies for Curing Them* (1784; Brookfield, Mass.: E. Merriam, 1814).

11. Madelon Powers, *Faces along the Bar: Lore and Order in the Workingman's Saloon, 1870–1920* (Chicago: University of Chicago Press, 1998); Lender and Martin, *Drinking in America*; Rorabaugh, *The Alcoholic Republic.*

12. William White, *Slaying the Dragon: The History of Addiction Treatment and Recovery in America* (Bloomington, Ill.: Chestnut Health Systems, 1998); Leonard Blumberg and William Pittman, *Beware the First Drink!* (Seattle: Glen Abbey Books, 1991); Jack Blocker, *American Temperance Movements, Cycles of Reform* (Boston: Twayne, 1989).

13. Gerald Grob, ed., *Origins of Medical Attitudes toward Drug Addiction in America: Eight Studies, 1791–1858* (New York: Arno Press, 1981); H. Wayne Morgan, ed., *Yesterday's Addicts: American Society and Drug Abuse, 1865–1920* (Norman: University of Oklahoma Press, 1974).

14. Glenn Sonnedecker, *Emergence of the Concept of Opiate Addiction* (Madison: American Institute for the History of Pharmacy, n.d.).

15. Jonathan Zimmerman, *Distilling Democracy: Alcohol Education in America's Public Schools, 1880–1925* (Lawrence: University of Kansas Press, 1999); Ian Tyrell, *Women's World/Women's Empire: The Woman's Christian Temperance Union in International Perspective, 1800–1930* (Chapel Hill: University of North Carolina Press, 1991); Ruth Bordin, *Woman and Temperance: The Quest for Power and Liberty, 1873–1900* (New Brunswick: Rutgers University Press, 1990); Blocker, *American Temperance Movements.*

16. Sarah W. Tracy, "Contesting Habitual Drunkenness: State Medical Reform for

Iowa's Inebriates, 1902–1920," *Annals of Iowa* (Summer 2002): 1–45; Jim Baumohl and Sarah Tracy, "Building Systems for Inebriates: The Divergent Paths of California and Massachusetts, 1891–1920," *Contemporary Drug Problems,* 21 (Winter 1994): 557–595; Jim Baumohl, "Inebriate Institutions in North America, 1840–1920," in Cheryl Krasnick Warsh, ed., *Drink in Canada: Historical Essays* (Montreal: McGill-Queen's University Press, 1993), 92–114; Sarah W. Tracy, "The Foxborough Experiment: Medicalizing Inebriety at the Massachusetts Hospital for Dipsomaniacs and Inebriates, 1833–1919," Ph.D. diss., University of Pennsylvania, 1992; American Association for the Cure of Inebriates, *Proceedings, 1870–1875* (New York: Arno Press, 1981); Leonard Blumberg, "The American Association for the Study and Cure of Inebriety," *Alcoholism: Clinical and Experimental Research,* 2, no. 3, (July 1978): 235–240.

17. Tate, *Cigarette Wars*; Mara L. Keire, "Dope Fiends and Degenerates: The Gendering of Addiction in the Early Twentieth Century," *Journal of Social History,* 31 (1998): 809–822; Jill Jonnes, *Hep-Cats, Narcs, and Pipe Dreams: A History of America's Romance with Illegal Drugs* (New York: Scribner, 1996; Baltimore: Johns Hopkins University Press, 1999); Denise Herd, "The Paradox of Temperance: Blacks and the Alcohol Question in Nineteenth-Century America," in Susanna Barrows and Robin Room, *Drinking: Behavior and Belief in Modern History* (Berkeley: University of California Press, 1991), 354–375.

18. Caroline Jean Acker, *Creating the American Junkie: Addiction Research in the Classic Era of Narcotic Control* (Baltimore: Johns Hopkins University Press, 2001); David T. Courtwright, *Dark Paradise: Opiate Addiction in America before 1940,* enl. ed., Cambridge: Harvard University Press, 2001 (1982); Jonnes, *Hep-Cats, Narcs, and Pipe Dreams*; Stephen R. Kandall, *Substance and Shadow: Women and Addiction in the United States* (Cambridge: Harvard University Press, 1996); Keire, "Dope Fiends and Degenerates"; H. Wayne Morgan, *Drugs in America: A Social History, 1800–1900* (Syracuse: Syracuse University Press, 1981); Morgan, ed., *Yesterday's Addicts*; David F. Musto, *The American Disease: Origins of Narcotic Control* (1973; 3d ed., New York: Oxford University Press, 1999).

19. Thomas R. Pegram, *Battling Demon Rum—The Struggle for a Dry America, 1800–1933* (Chicago: Ivan R. Dee, 1998); Blocker, *American Temperance Movements*; Bordin, *Woman and Temperance*.

20. Porter and Teich, eds., *Drugs and Narcotics in History*; White, *Slaying the Dragon*.

21. Tate, *Cigarette Wars*.

22. Caroline Jean Acker, "Stigma or Legitimation? A Historical Examination of the Social Potentials of Addiction Disease Models," *Journal of Psychoactive Drugs,* 25 (1993): 193–205; Courtwright, *Dark Paradise*; Musto, *The American Disease*; Porter and Teich, eds., *Drugs and Narcotics in History*.

23. Blocker, *American Temperance Movements*; John J. Rumbarger, *Profits, Power, and Prohibition—Alcohol Reform and the Industrializing of America* (Albany: State University of New York Press, 1989); Lender and Martin, *Drinking in America*.

24. Acker, *Creating the American Junkie*; Tracy, "Contesting Habitual Drunkenness"; Baumohl and Tracy, "Building Systems."

25. Lender and Martin, *Drinking in America*; Robin Room, "Ambivalence as a Sociological Explanation: The Case of Cultural Explanations of Alcohol Problems," *American Sociological Review,* 41 (December 1976): 1047–1065.

26. ABA and AMA Joint Committee on Narcotic Drugs, *Drug Addiction: Crime or Disease* (Bloomington: Indiana University Press, 1961); Acker, *Creating the American Junkie*; Courtwright, *Dark Paradise*; Musto, *The American Disease*.

27. Jonnes, *Hep-Cats, Narcs, and Pipe Dreams*.

28. Barr, *Drink*.

29. Janet Golden, "An Argument That Goes Back to the Womb: The Demedicalization of Fetal Alcohol Syndrome," *Journal of Social History*, 33 (Winter 99): 269–299; David Wagner, *The New Temperance: The American Obsession with Sin and Vice* (Boulder, Colo.: Westview Press, 1997); Gina Kolata, "Temperance: An Old Cycle Repeats Itself: Drinking and Drug Use Fall, A Trend Experts Say May Intensify," *New York Times*, 1 January 1999, 35, 40; Craig Reinarman, "The Social Construction of an Alcohol Problem: The Case of Mothers Against Drunk Drivers and Social Control in the 1980s," *Theory and Society*, 17 (1988): 91–120.

30. Herbert Fingarette, *Heavy Drinking: The Myth of Alcoholism as a Disease*, (Berkeley: University of California Press, 1988); E. M. Jellinek, *The Disease Concept of Alcoholism* (New Haven, Conn.: Hillhouse Press, 1960); Jellinek, "The Phases of Alcohol Addiction," *Quarterly Journal of Studies on Alcohol* 13 (1952): 673–684.

31. Peter Conrad and Joseph Schneider, "Alcoholism: Drunkenness, Inebriety, and the Disease Concept," in Conrad and Schneider, eds., *Deviance and Medicalization: From Badness to Sickness*, expanded ed. (Philadelphia: Temple University Press, 1992), 73–109.

32. Drug Abuse Council, *The Facts about "Drug Abuse"* (New York: Free Press, 1980); Dean R. Gerstein, and Henrick J. Harwood, *Treating Drug Problems*, 2 vols., (Washington, D.C.: National Academy Press, 1990); Michael Massing, *The Fix* (Berkeley: University of California Press, 1998); Solomon H. Snyder, *Brainstorming: The Science and Politics of Opiate Research* (Cambridge: Harvard University Press, 1989).

33. Acker, "Stigma or Legitimation?"; Warwick Anderson, "The New York Needle Trial: The Politics of Public Health in the Age of AIDS," *American Journal of Public Health* 81 (1991): 1506–1517; Nick Heather, Alex Wodak, Ethan A. Nadelmann and Pat O'Hare, eds., *Psychoactive Drugs and Harm Reduction: From Faith to Science* (London: Whurr, 1993); Jonnes, *Hep-Cats, Narcs, and Pipe Dreams*; P. A. O'Hare, R. Newcombe, A. Matthews, E. C. Buring, and E. Drucker, *The Reduction of Drug-Related Harm* (New York: Routledge, 1992).

34. J. Madeleine Nash and Alice Park, "Addicted—Why Do People Get Hooked? Mounting Evidence Points to a Powerful Brain Chemical Called Dopamine," *Time*, 5 May 1997, 68–75.

I

Framing Addiction
and Alcoholism

The Lessons of Language

Historical Perspectives on the Rhetoric of Addiction

William L. White

> *The very naming of something creates new realities, new situations, and often new problems.*
>
> —Thomas D. Watts

THE FIRST SECTION of this essay provides a concise historical account of the evolution of the language used to label the excessive and problematic use of alcohol and other drugs in the United States. The account covers the birth of alcohol rhetoric, the extension of this rhetoric to encompass drugs other than alcohol, and the eventual extension of this language to include problems unrelated to drug use. This initial discussion will proceed with minimal references to the contextual forces that influenced this evolution of language. The second section of the essay, which attempts to analyze such contextual forces in some depth, argues that the confusion and conflict surrounding this evolving language stem from the multiple utilities that these words must successfully fulfill before coming into accepted use in personal, interpersonal, professional, political, and economic discourse.[1]

The Rhetoric of Addiction

The evolution of addiction rhetoric in America emerged out of what Harry Levine has called the "discovery of addiction"—a period in which those who consumed alcohol ceased being a homogenous group of "drinkers" and became separated into normal and abnormal drinkers.[2] The emergence of a new language to characterize and classify these differences marks the birth of American addiction rhetoric. This milestone was, as we shall see, followed by similar distinctions between those using medicines and those addicted to drugs.

The pervasiveness of alcohol and occasional drunkenness in colonial America is well indicated by Benjamin Franklin's treatise *Drinker's*

Dictionary, in which he defined some 235 terms to describe drinking, drinkers, and intoxication. However, there was no term other than *drunkenness* to describe the condition now known as alcoholism. When per capita alcohol consumption began to rise dramatically between the Revolutionary War and 1830, America began to look at excessive drinking in a new way and with a new language.[3] The harbinger of this new view came from an essay by the English physician Thomas Trotter, who referred to chronic drunkenness as a disease, and Dr. Benjamin Rush's 1784 American treatise *An Inquiry into the Effects of Ardent Spirits upon the Human Body and Mind, with an Account of the Means of Preventing and of the Remedies for Curing Them.* Rush's widely circulated pamphlet referenced the "habitual use of ardent spirits" and referred to such use as an "odious disease"—a phrase that marked a bridge between moral and medical conceptions of chronic drunkenness.[4] The Washingtonians, America's first society of recovered alcoholics, referred to themselves in the 1840s as *confirmed drinkers, drunkards, hard cases, inveterate cases, sots, tipplers,* and *inebriates.*[5] Concern about the stigma of such terms, however, led the Washingtonians to call their first residential care facility a home for the "fallen".

The term *alcoholism* is of relatively recent origin. It wasn't until the eighteenth century that the word *alcohol* came to designate the intoxicating ingredient in liquor. The word itself derived from the Arabic word *al-kuhl,* a term first used for an antimony-based eye cosmetic, which later came to mean the essence or spirit of something.[6] The Swedish physician Magnus Huss introduced the term *alcoholism* in 1849 to describe a state of chronic alcohol intoxication that was characterized by severe physical pathology and disruption of social functioning. His new term was intended to replace the German term *methylism,* which Huss judged to be both obscure and technically incorrect.[7] It took nearly a century for Huss's new term, and the accompanying term *alcoholic,* to achieve widespread usage in America.

In the years following Huss's introduction of the term *alcoholism,* other terms emerged for consideration in professional and lay circles to describe the pathological craving for alcohol and the consequences of its excessive use. Dr. Norman Kerr, a prominent nineteenth-century addiction expert, expressed a preference for the term *narcomania* or *intoxication mania.* Kerr chose these terms in the belief that the focal point of the compulsion was the state of intoxication rather than the intoxicating agent.[8] Before the term *alcoholism* became popular, terms such as *intemperance, barrel fever, habitual drunkenness (drunkard), dipsomania (dipsomaniac), inebriety or ebriosity (inebriate), victim of drink,* and *the liquor habit* continued to dominate cultural and professional discourse in the late nineteenth and early twentieth centuries. Harry Levine, whose research traces the historical evolution of the

American language used to label the alcoholic during this period, noted the following additional terms in popular use: *drunk, boozer, alcoholist, rum-sucker, stiff, rummy, souse,* and *wino.*[9] The two terms most frequently used to refer to alcoholism at the end of the nineteenth century were *dipsomania* and *inebriety.*

The term *dipsomania,* taken from the Greek meaning "thirst frenzy," was introduced in 1819 by Christopher Wilhelm Hufeland.[10] Dipsomania came to be associated with a pattern of binge drinking characterized by periods of abstinence followed by what were sometimes called "drink storms." This pattern of explosive drinking was also christened *oinomania* by the Italian physician Salvatori, a term drawn from the word *oinis,* meaning wine.[11] Esquirol in 1838 described dipsomania as a "monomania of drunkenness."[12] Texts such as Wright's 1885 *Inebriism: Pathological and Psychological Study* used the terms *dipsomania* and *oinomania* interchangeably to characterize "an insatiable desire for intoxication."[13] *Dipso* (meaning alcoholic) and *dip shop* (meaning inebriate sanatorium) were common slang terms among the affluent during the early twentieth century.[14]

Inebriety, derived from the Latin root *inebriare*—meaning, to intoxicate—was a generic term for what today would be called *addiction* or *chemical dependency.*[15] Kerr defined *inebriety* in 1894 as a constitutional disease of the nervous system characterized by a morbid craving for intoxication.[16] The term encompassed a wide variety of choices of intoxicants. The type of inebriety was specified in speech or writing, as in *alcohol inebriety,* or *cocaine inebriety.* The term *inebriety* gained prominence through the professionalization of addiction treatment homes and asylums via the American Association for the Study and Cure of Inebriety in 1870 and the founding of the *Quarterly Journal of Inebriety* in 1877.[17]

Alcohol inebriety seems to have encompassed more common forms of chronic drunkenness, while the term *dipsomania* was a more medicalized term for episodic but explosive drinking binges that were thought to be a special form of temporary insanity. The term *inebriety* fell out of favor following the repeal of Prohibition, perhaps in part because the term embraced both good drugs that were to become celebrated and bad drugs that were to become increasingly demonized. The differentiation between alcohol language and "drug" language begins to become solidified in this post-Repeal period. In our continuing story, we will first explore how alcohol language continued to evolve, and then we will return to look at the rhetoric that emerged to depict addiction to drugs other than alcohol.

Psychiatric and Lay Therapy Influences

Huss's term, *alcoholism*, gradually began to replace *inebriety*, first in professional circles and then in popular usage. This new term began to appear in American professional literature during the latter half of the nineteenth century, such as in Hubbard's 1881 treatise *The Opium Habit and Alcoholism* and in articles appearing in such journals as the *Medical Record* and the *Quarterly Journal of Inebriety*.[18] The modern professional shift to the use of the term *alcoholism* seems to have been marked by Karl Abraham's 1908 essay on psychoanalytic perspectives on the disorder.[19] Abraham was one of the first individuals of medical prominence to embrace the terms *alcoholism* and *alcoholic*. The lay therapists Ray Baker and Richard Peabody, and Charles Towns, proprietor of a well-known "drying out" hospital, were the first prominent treatment specialists to begin use of these twin terms in early twentieth-century writings aimed at the general public.[20]

Consensus on the public and professional language to be used in defining problems with alcohol was slow in coming. The terms *alcoholism* and *alcoholic*, while increasingly utilized within the arcane literature of psychoanalysis by 1930, had still gained little popular usage. Charles Towns retreated from his earlier advocacy of the term *alcoholic* and expressed instead his preference for the term *alcoholic excessivist*.[21] A number of authors, including Dr. Robert Fleming of Boston, revived Huss's label *chronic alcoholism* and injected use of the term into the mainstream medical press.[22] Chronic alcoholics who clogged the courts of this period were christened *old rounders*.[23] At this same time, Charles Durfee, another addiction expert, attempted to popularize the terms *problem drinking* and *problem drinker*. Durfee preferred these terms on the grounds that the term *alcoholism* was stigmatizing and because of his belief that alcohol was a problem for many people who were not diagnosable as alcoholic.[24] The founding of Alcoholics Anonymous did much to solidify use of the term *alcoholism* and bring it into widespread popular use, but even in the "Big Book" of AA one finds the terms *problem drinker* and *abnormal drinker*.[25] In 1938, Dr. Robert Seliger uses terms such as *problem drinker, uncontrolled drinker, spree drinker*, and *pathological drinker* interchangeably with the term *alcoholic*.[26] The term *alcoholism* was used frequently enough in the popular and professional press in the late 1930s that Dr. Edward Strecker and Francis Chambers complained that it had become as meaningless as the nineteenth-century terms *nervous breakdown* and *feminine vapors*. They recommended use of the terms *normal drinker* and *abnormal drinker*.[27] In 1942, Dwight Anderson backed Durfee's use of the term *problem drinker* and further suggested that *malady* or *ailment* was preferable to *disease* given that the latter term was usually associated with conditions that had a physical rather than emotional basis. Anderson made a fine distinction in refusing to characterize alcoholism as a *disease* while referring to it as a *sickness*. He further emphasized the importance of the language debate by noting, "If the problem drinker is sick, as is agreed by most authorities, we should avoid terms which are incompatible with this idea."[28]

The Modern Alcoholism Movement

The rise of the "the modern alcoholism movement" in the 1940s under the leadership of the National Committee on Education on Alcoholism (NCEA), firmly embedded the terms *alcoholism* and *alcoholic* in scientific and popular use but did not stop the language debate. The NCEA successfully pushed these terms to the fore in spite of some reluctance from other quarters of the movement. Bruce Johnson, in his oft-cited study of the unfolding of the modern alcoholism movement, notes that many early leaders of this movement had misgivings about the term *alcoholism*. E. M. Jellinek, universally considered the modern godfather of the disease concept of alcoholism, actually preferred the phrases *abnormal drinking, alcohol addiction,* or *compulsive drinking*.[29] Even when he came to reluctantly use the term *alcoholism*, his definition of it evolved significantly over the course of his career.[30] As early as 1941, Jellinek rejected the notion of a singular clinical picture of alcoholism and described fourteen distinct types of abnormal drinkers.[31] He defined as diseases only those types that exhibited "loss of control," but later added to the definitional confusion by dramatically expanding his definition of alcoholism. In 1949, Seldon Bacon warned that the overapplication of the term *alcoholism* was creating a group of "Quasi Alcoholics" whose drinking presented problems for the community but who were hardly appropriate for alcoholism treatment. Included in this category were problem drinkers who were feebleminded, psychotic, or who had severe personality disorders. Bacon referred to these collectively not as alcoholics, but as "chronic social-misfit drinkers."[32] Mark Keller later concurred with Bacon that the term *alcoholism* was destroyed by its popularization during this period. He believed that its embrace by the culture as a whole softened and extended its meaning, thus destroying its utility as a technical and diagnostic term.[33]

The language debate didn't end with the popularization of the term *alcoholism* in the 1940s. Those treating alcoholics continued to struggle to forge a language with clinical utility, but this in itself created problems. In 1955, Dr. Ruth Fox noted the confusion over such terms as *situational drinker, symptomatic drinker, regular* (or *irregular*) *symptomatic excessive drinker, primary addict,* and *secondary addict*.[34] Two years later, the World Health Organization (WHO), agreeing with Strecker, Chambers, Bacon, and Keller that *alcoholism* had lost its clinical specificity, proposed use of the term *alcohol dependence* and further struggled to delineate application of the terms *addiction* and *habituation*. (This action of the WHO marked the rebirth of attempts to generate language that could apply equally to alcohol, opiates, cocaine, and other drugs.) In 1960, Jellinek underscored this linguistic problem by noting the existence of more than 200 definitions of *alcoholism*. After first offering an expansion of his own earlier definition, he tried to recapture the term's specificity by referring to "alcoholisms" and by reducing the historical body of literature on clinical subpopulations of alcoholics into his five "species" of alcoholism, each of which he designated with a Greek letter.[35] Others later followed Jellinek's lead in distinguishing types of alcoholism, using such distinguishing adjectives as "true/reactive," "primary/secondary," "Type I (milieu limited)/Type II (male limited)," "Type A/Type B," and "Apollonian/Dionysian."[36]

Consensus was not to be achieved on use of the term *alcoholism*. At the end of a five-year research project in the 1960s, members of the Cooperative Commission on the Study of Alcoholism were still arguing over whether *person with a drinking problem* was preferable language to the term *alcoholic*. In 1967, they settled on use of the term *problem drinker*.[37] During this same period, the American Psychiatric Association (APA) jumped into the fray recommending the term *alcoholic problems*. It was the APA's position that the terms *alcoholic* and *alcoholism* created the stereotype that all people with problems related to alcohol consumption suffered from a singular affliction. Some medical groups in the 1970s attacked the term *alcoholism* on the grounds that it was a term based on stereotype and biased judgment. There were even proposals that the word be dropped completely and be replaced with the label *Jellinek's Disease*.[38]

When a national institute was established in the early 1970s with the phrase *alcohol abuse* in its title, the semantic battle intensified. Some sought to define *abuse* based on the circumstances of use (nonmedical use), while others tried to define the word based on the consequences of use (harm to the user or society). Mark Keller described *alcohol abuse* as "opprobrious, vindictive, pejorative" and an "inherently nasty" phrase.[39] Other terms that could be found within the field's discourse during the 1970s included *problematic alcohol use, alcohol misuse, deviant drinking*, and *excessive drinking*. The National Council on Alcoholism took a step in 1972 to restore some clarity to this debate by publishing its "Criteria for the Diagnosis of Alcoholism." But major players in the health care arena continued to note the lack of operational definitions governing the alcoholism arena. The World Health Organization in 1974 characterized the situation as follows: "It is clear from a review of the responses to the WHO inquiry that there is no internationally or even nationally accepted definition of 'alcoholism' or of 'problem drinking' but that a variety of definitions and classifications are in use for legal, insurance, treatment, and research purposes."[40]

Impact of Modern Diagnostic Classifications

The continued language debate is most evident in the two modern systems of diagnostic classification—the Diagnostic and Statistical Manual of Mental Disorders (DSM) of the American Psychiatric Association and the International Classification of Diseases (ICD) of the World Health Organization. "Alcoholism" first (1952) appeared in these evolving classifications as a subset of personality disorders and neuroses. This reflected the view that alcoholism was not a primary disorder but a symptom of underlying psychiatric illness. This stance was later (1980) abandoned in favor of two new independent classifications: *alcohol abuse* and *alcohol dependence*. The American Psychiatric Association in its latest (1994) diagnostic classification manual includes generic categories of *substance intoxication, substance dependence*, and *substance-induced disorders*, as well as more drug-specific diagnoses such as *alcohol dependence*.[41] These modern diagnostic systems were, in part, an effort to reflect the growing recognition that alcohol-related problems can exist in the absence of alcohol addiction.

In the late 1980s and early 1990s, the alcohol and drug addiction treatment industry was accused of ethical breaches involving the overdiagnosis of addiction-related disorders, modality misplacement, and clinically inappropriate lengths of stay in treatment. The industry needed some framework to reinstill diagnostic precision and credibility. The Patient Placement Criteria for the Treatment of Substance-Related Disorders of the American Society of Addiction Medicine (ASAM) was to a great extent developed in response to this need. The ASAM criteria replaced the 40–50 sets of criteria being used by insurers and utilization management companies to reduce inappropriate admissions and the propensity for treatment programs to place clients in a more restrictive and expensive modality than clinical characteristics warranted.[42]

During the 1980s, new terms were added to the professional jargon of addiction treatment that sought to capture the untoward effects of alcoholism on family members. Terms such as *co-alcoholism, para-alcoholism, child of an alcoholic*(COA), *adult child of an alcoholic* (ACOA), *dysfunctional family, enabler,* and *codependency* were defined, redefined, overused and misused.[43] This new language came under a flood of criticism following its invasion into the popular culture. The most severe criticisms were that the movement to expand the application of addiction language and concepts was nothing more than a commercially exploitive pseudoscience—a plethora of impressionistic descriptions of new pathologies that had no objective grounding in clinical research.[44] There was also a growing sense that terms like *codependency* and *dysfunctional* had become meaningless because of their indiscriminate and global application.[45]

Creating Language to Embrace Drugs Other Than Alcohol

As if the language surrounding alcohol wasn't complex enough, the development of a professional language that could embrace the problematic use of drugs other than alcohol has been even more difficult in America. The evolution of this language has included nineteenth-century terms named after the user's drug of choice: *narcomania, methomania, vinomania, opiumism, opium drunkenness, morphinism, morphinomania, chloralism, narcotism,* and *pharmacothymia.* The "ism" suffix generally referred to perpetual states of drinking or drug use; the "mania" suffix referred to the rabid craving that could incite periodic episodes of explosive binging. The latter term comes from the Greek word meaning madness.[46] Terms like *morphinist* and *opiophagist* were created to signal the addict's drug choice, and references to *drug drunkards* reflected attempts to apply alcohol language to other drugs.[47]

There have also been attempts to create a generic term that would encompass multiple drug choices: *intoxicomania, narcomania, narcotoxia, drug addiction, drug habituation, drug compulsion, drug abuse, alcohol-and-other-drug-abuse, drug dependence, substance abuse,* and *chemical dependency.* Nearly all of these terms have come under episodic attack.[48] Concern with concurrent and sequential use of multiple drugs dates at least to nineteenth-and early twentieth-century inebriety literature in which we find such phrases as "mixed cases," "multiple inebriety," "combined inebriety," and "alternating inebriety."[49]

Three broadly encompassing terms have vied for modern prominence. The term *substance abuse*—an extension of the 1960s term "drug abuse"—gained some prominence when both clinical data and economic necessity brought about the merger of a growing number of alcoholism treatment and drug abuse treatment programs. A variant of substance abuse was the phrase *alcohol, tobacco and other drug* (ATOD) *use/abuse.* The inclusion of the word *abuse* in these phrases came under considerable attack for its abstractness and for its implied moralism. Jay Renaud went so far as to suggest that use of the term *substance abuse* was an abuse of language that "perpetuates ignorant and moralistic attitudes toward people with chemical dependency." In Renaud's view, references to substance abuse and substance abusers "paint these ill people as perpetrators, not victims."[50]

The term *chemical dependency* emerged within the "Minnesota Model" of alcoholism treatment practiced at Pioneer House, Hazelden, and Wilmar

State Hospital in Minnesota, to conceptualize the pattern of multiple drug use increasingly being seen at these facilities in the late 1950s.[51] This term spread as part of the wider incorporation of the Minnesota Model into a growing number of private and hospital-based treatment programs in the 1970s and 1980s but never achieved universal usage.

As more medical and biological models for conceptualizing alcohol and other drug problems emerged in the 1980s, the term *addiction* vied for professional and popular dominance. *Addiction*, derived from the Latin root *addicere*, meaning to adore or to surrender oneself to a master, has risen in popularity during the last decade. If the term has a certain mustiness about it, it's because it first came into common usage in the professional literature of the mid-1890s—the same period *dope fiend* was coming into common slang usage as a result of its repeated appearance in newspapers and magazines.[52] The term *addict*, or on occasion, *addictee*, emerged around 1910 to replace the earlier term *habitué* used to designate a person suffering from an addiction.[53] Some addiction experts refused to use the term *addict* to apply to those physically dependent upon narcotics because of disease or injury, but instead reserved it for those who developed "the habit" out of their search for pleasure.[54]

The resurgence of the term *addiction* has been accompanied by confusion between its scientific connotations and its popular usage.[55] Its precise scientific usage evolved out of the clinical observations of nineteenth- and early twentieth-century treatment specialists through the more empirically oriented work conducted at the Addiction Research Center in Lexington, Kentucky, in the 1930s and 1940s. Through these influences, *addiction* came to be defined as the presence of three conditions. To say that a drug was physically *addictive* or that one had *an addiction* required demonstration of: (1) increased tissue tolerance to the drug in question, (2) an identifiable and stereotyped withdrawal syndrome when use of the drug was interrupted, and (3) compulsive drug-seeking and drug-using behaviors in spite of adverse consequences. While these elements aptly describe what usually occurs in the regular use of drugs such as heroin, there were other highly destructive patterns of drug use that did not necessarily show either tolerance or stereotyped withdrawal. This prompted respected specialists such as Dr. David Smith, founder of the Haight Ashbury Free Clinic, to suggest in the early 1980s a redefinition of the required elements of addiction to include compulsion, loss of control, and continued use in spite of adverse consequences.[56]

With the popularization of the term *alcoholism*, the words *addiction* and *addict* came to imply drugs other than alcohol, particularly the illicit drugs. But this distinction was not always clear. Some spoke and wrote of *addicts* and encompassed alcoholics within the meaning of this term, while others spoke of *alcoholics and addicts*. Early twentieth-century references to the "drug evil" and to "drug peddlers" reflected the growing use of the term *drug* as a generic term to imply intoxicating and addicting substances. Pharmacy leaders waged an unsuccessful campaign to stop the use of the term *drug* in this manner within professional and popular literature.[57] The umbrella terms *narcotic* and *narcotic addiction* further added to the pollution of language when these terms came, through most of the past century, to embrace cocaine, marihuana and other drugs whose psychopharmacological properties bore no resemblance to opiate drugs.[58] The American Medical Association's *Useful Drugs* even categorized alcohol as a "narcotic" during the first half of the twentieth century.[59] What was included and excluded in the use of these terms became increasingly unclear and remains so.

A century-long thread has led to current efforts to define alcohol as a drug and to find an overarching term that can conceptually embrace alcohol, tobacco, and other psychoactive drugs.

The 1980s saw an extension of addiction concepts to behaviors unrelated to drug use. *Co-alcoholism* and *para-alcoholism* were expanded to *codependence* and then to a broad category of so-called process addictions that included destructive relationships with food, work, people, sex, gambling, shopping, and religion. This was more than a conceptual and linguistic extension. Addiction treatment agencies began marketing products and services to individuals involved in these other activities under the umbrella of addiction treatment. Defining the boundaries of the term *addiction* was an issue for the popular as well as professional worlds when people began referring to themselves as being *addicted* to everything from television to bowling. *Addiction* came to be used in the popular culture to refer to any behavior that was excessive, habitually repetitive, or problematic. People referred to themselves or others as chocaholics, workaholics, and various other "aholics." The skin of the addictions field split open, leaking its language and concepts into what became a passing phenomenon of American pop culture. For a brief period, it looked as though all Americans were addicted to something and saw themselves as potentially in need of "treatment" and "recovery."

Through all of the eras reviewed here, there has been disagreement about how to refer to those who are undergoing treatment for addictive disorders. The terms *inmates, patients, clients, members, residents, guests,* and *students* have been the most common choices during the past century. There has also been an ongoing confusion within the field and the larger culture about what to call those who are no longer actively addicted. (The necessity for such terminology is sparked, in part, by persons in stable recovery who continue to refer to themselves as alcoholics and addicts.) Debate over this designation has for the past 150 years included such labels as *redeemed, on the wagon, sober, drug-free, clean, straight,* or *abstinent.* "Sobriate"—perhaps a takeoff on inebriate—was also used in some quarters. There has likewise been no enduring consensus of what to call institutions that care for people with alcohol and other drug problems. They have gone by such names as *home, asylum, reformatory, institute, sanatorium, sanitarium, hospital, ward, lodge, farm, retreat, agency, center,* and *program.* There hasn't even been agreement on what to call what occurs inside these institutions: *reform, cure, rehabilitation, treatment, counseling, therapy,* or *reeducation.*[60] The trend has been to replace descriptive terms such as "caring for," "dealing with," and "helping," with medicalized terms such as "treatment" that convey the image of a more science-based intervention and attach a greater degree of professional prestige to the intervener.[61]

We have reviewed the struggle to achieve sustained medical and social consensus on (1) how to refer to those whose alcohol and other drug consumption creates problems for themselves or society, (2) how to refer to people who are receiving some kind of intervention to correct these problems, (3) how to refer to this helping process, and (4) how to refer to people who once had, but no longer have, such problems. The review tends to confirm Ira Cusin's observation that *we keep tripping over the same old* (and, I would add, new) *words, loaded with connotative effect, full of sound and fury, signifying nothing.*[62] In the next section, I argue that this failed consensus on the rhetoric of addiction grew out of the multiple utilities such language must simultaneously serve.

Addiction Rhetoric and Its Multiple Utilities

In this section, I offer some personal thoughts on how the words selected to define alcohol and other drug problems reflect personal, social, political, economic, professional, and clinical interests and must simultaneously meet needs in all these zones of activity. I suggest that the tensions that exist within and between these arenas have diminished, and will continue to diminish, the likelihood of American social and professional consensus on the language through which alcohol and other drug problems will be framed.

Personal Utility

The language used to label alcohol and other drug use provides a menu of symbols through which each individual can create, or make sense out of, his or her own relationship with these substances. Language can have a prohibiting, moderating, promoting, or transformative influence in the construction of this person-drug relationship. These labels, whether voluntarily embraced or forced on one by the larger society, may themselves affect the course of alcohol and other drug use and the course of any potential addiction and recovery process.

Let's consider several possible person-drug relationships and the kind of language needed to support each relationship. People who have never used and do not wish to use alcohol and other traditionally defined drugs often embrace a language that demonizes these substances and those who use them. This creates distance between themselves and the problems such substances can cause. Language that evokes repugnance toward these drugs and their use can, in this way, serve as a personal preventative device. Using the defense mechanisms of reaction formation and projection enables one to suppress any latent curiosity or attraction to these substances via an exaggerated animosity toward the substances and those who use them. These same mechanisms may be used by those who formerly experienced problems with alcohol or other drugs, aborted their pattern of use, and subsequently speak with great passion and animus against the drugs and those who use them.

A second group of people are those who use alcohol or other drugs without significant problems associated with such use. These individuals need a language that simultaneously affirms the legitimacy of their own use and helps contain their use within certain defined limits—a language that depicts when the line demarcating abnormal use is crossed. Whereas language serves as a preventative device in our first group, it serves as a rationalizing and moderating influence in our second group. Christie and Bruun noted this potential effect as early as 1969 when they attacked the use of words like *alcoholism* as devices used by "good drinkers" to separate themselves from "bad drinkers" so that the former could drink in guilt-free enjoyment while looking down upon the latter.[63] Language that defines drunkenness as a "vice" can bolster one's resolve to not drink in the same manner that language implying that alcoholism is a "disease" experienced by only a small number of drinkers can provide a rationale for continued drinking for those who don't perceive themselves as part of that vulnerable minority. Both types of language serve to create psychological distance between oneself and the degenerate or diseased other. Similar mechanisms operate within the American illicit drug culture. People who see themselves as responsible users develop intracultural language that stigmatizes certain drug choices or patterns of use, as in the self-righteous castigation of phencyclidine (PCP) as "dummy dust."

A third group includes those individuals experiencing varying degrees of problems related to their alcohol or other drug use. By evoking extreme caricatures via terms like "wino" or "dope fiend," these users can sustain the delusion that their own use, by comparison with such caricatures, is in control and not a problem or, later, a "little" problem but not a "serious" problem. (It is interesting that the psychological needs of both radical abstainers and addicts are similarly met via such linguistic caricatures.) There is also a point at which chronic users may openly embrace such terms as "dope fiend" or "freak" to mock society's efforts to stigmatize them. Embracing such a stigmatized label can mark a significant "career milestone" in one's isolation and alienation from the larger society and one's engagement in a deviant and subterranean culture of addiction.[64]

Some individuals within this third group are in agonizing physical and psychological pain and are desperately searching for a way out of the addiction labyrinth. Such individuals need a language that enhances problem identification and resolution. They need a language that labels and confirms their experience, provides a face-saving means of understanding what happened to them, and points in a hopeful direction for the future. Here language becomes not a preventative or moderating influence, but a catalytic aid to personal transformation. Certain words can serve as keys to unlock frozen, compulsive patterns of drug use. The words that possess such face-saving and transformative power, however, vary from individual to individual and from culture to culture. The label "alcoholism" and the view of alcoholism as a "disease" may serve as a powerful face-saving and sense-making device for one individual while having little meaning for another, who may respond more strongly to the construction of alcoholism as a "tool of genocide." It is not necessary for language to be scientifically "true" to serve this catalytic function, but it must be metaphorically and emotionally true for the addict and his or her family. The language must also be culturally true in that it allows the addict and his or her family to construct a life story and a sobriety-based identity within the cultural context in which they live. A practical implication of this understanding involves the need for addiction treatment agencies to provide within their treatment milieus a broad menu of words, metaphors, and rituals reflecting the diversity of their clientele. The diversity of drug users, the diversity of drug experiences, and the nesting of drug addiction within diverse family and cultural contexts make it highly unlikely that a narrow, highly codified language will emerge to perform this face-saving and sense-making function. In the end, it is personal and cultural viability, not scientific validity, that determines the power of language to incite and solidify the process of addiction recovery.[65]

The traditional therapeutic community perhaps more than any other addiction treatment modality is based on the power of language to shape identity and behavior. When Charles Dederich, the founder of Synanon, was once asked how he had organized hundreds of drug addicts into a self-directed therapeutic community, he responded simply, "It's all done with words."

The extent to which our culture has embraced various terms to describe alcohol- and other drug-related problems has been shaped in part by the degree to which each of these terms could help individuals in the culture banish or make sense out of the role of alcohol and other drugs in their lives. All future language choices will face this same test. The progression of addiction and the stages of recovery involve not only biological processes but a progression of other-applied and self-applied labels.

Social and Political Utility

The language of addiction has meaning for abstainers, users, addicts, and recovering addicts as they interact in their social worlds. In this way, words move beyond personal meaning and take on shared meaning for larger groups. Let's consider what this means for addicts and recovering addicts. Many addicts are enmeshed in drug-using subcultures filled with an elaborate argot that reinforces their drug use and their affiliation with the culture of addiction. This argot not only separates insiders from outsiders, but establishes the elaborate pecking order within the drug culture. Consider for example Lindesmith's story of an early twentieth-century patron of an opium den who, upon finding someone injecting heroin in the bathroom, indignantly reported to the proprietor that there was a "god damned dope fiend in the can" and demanded his expulsion.[66] More recently, language has helped stratify the illicit narcotics subculture from the "righteous dope fiend" to the "gutter hyp" and all points in between.

In a similar manner, the way many people disengage from addiction and the subculture in which it is nested is through a period of equal enmeshment in a language-rich culture of recovery. This recovery culture, whether in the form of Alcoholics Anonymous, Women for Sobriety, or the Nation of Islam, provides a new language through which one's past history is understood and one's identity and lifestyle are reconstructed. This new language has not only personal utility but social utility. It is a way to become fully involved in a new social world. The language of addiction must meet the needs of a large group of recovering addicts within our society. What the growing diversity of sobriety-based support structures have in common is an internally shared and rich language to frame the past and shape the ongoing recovery process.[67]

The social and political utilities that must be achieved in the linguistic construction of the "alcohol problem" or "drug problem" include defining and responding to deviance in a way that promotes social order and the interests of existing social institutions. While there may be pendulum swings between medicalization and criminalization of excessive psychoactive drug consumption and its accompanying sets of language, conceptualizing change within such a dichotomy overlooks the reality that medicalization and criminalization nearly always coexist and that both of these responses are methods of social control. While criminalization may be more personally or socially stigmatizing than medicalization, both processes seek to alter the targeted behavior in ways that enhance social order. Both serve hiding functions through the isolation and pressured sequestration of the addict. Extreme pushes for medicalization and seemingly opposite pushes for criminalization both serve as powerful homeostatic devices that support social order. It is within the legal arena that this definitional process most specifically serves this function by reconciling notions of disease with those of personal freedom, insanity, and criminal responsibility.[68]

The language of addiction also serves a symbolic function in social intercourse. This language might be said to be "coded" in that it is filled with covert, as well as overt, meanings. Each word within the addiction vocabulary can signal a much broader set of values and a broader worldview. Each word has socially symbolic as well as objective meaning. In this way, public surveys showing wide agreement with the proposition that alcoholism is a disease may not reflect knowledge about the biological etiology or course of alcoholism as much as they do the broader notion that alcoholics are in need of help and that public resources should be allocated to provide such assistance. Agreeing that alcoholism (as opposed to drunkenness) is a disease (rather than a vice) says more about ourselves and our social consciousness than it does about the science of alcohol pathology. Pioneers within the "modern alcoholism movement" such as Dwight Anderson and Marty Mann understood, much more than the scientists with whom they worked, that the success of that movement hinged not so much on new scientific discoveries about alcoholism as on changing social perceptions of alcoholism and the alcoholic. Words and images, not scientific evidence, were the tools used to launch this social revolution. What the modern alcoholism movement brilliantly achieved was to make how one spoke about alcoholics a symbol of one's degree of personal compassion and social enlightenment.

The rhetoric chosen to define and discuss drug addiction has often vacillated between defining addicts as diseased patients in need of medical treatment and defining addicts as immoral, criminal deviants who require isolation, punishment, and control. The language moves addicts within or outside our experience through the mechanism of social judgment. Language renders addicts within the boundary of "we" or projects them into the feared and hated world of "they." In more theological terms, language can transform one's contact with an addict from an "I-Thou" relationship to an "I-It" relationship.

Language creates a cultural lens through which outsiders are stigmatized while insiders are excused for exhibiting precisely the same behavior. A person using narcotics prescribed by a doctor is a "patient" using "medicine"; an individual using narcotics without a prescription is a "drug addict" or a "junkie" "strung out" on "dope." The former is said to be "clean"; the latter is said to be "dirty." The doctors and pharmacists who provide the narcotics to the former are "professional healers"; those providing the same narcotics to the latter are "pushers" and "predators."[69]

America has long defined the "drug habit" as evil, but has vacillated on the precise source of this evilness. Linguistic distinctions have helped sustain the logic that bad people (defined as people different from us) use drugs because of their inherent badness, whereas good people (people like us) use drugs because some evil force outside themselves overpowered their goodness. Our labels help distinguish between good and bad drugs and between good people who deserve our sympathy and professional assistance and bad people who should be isolated and punished. Such delineation is often dependent upon much broader political, economic, and social forces. The transition in terms from *intemperance* to *inebriety* to *dipsomania* was, according to Sarah Tracy's investigations, an evolution from the view of drunkenness as vice to that of drunkenness as medical disease. In the nineteenth century these terms were used simultaneously in ways that allowed both vice and disease views to coexist, with social class often determining which judgment and language were to be applied. The wealthy were likely to be viewed as suffering from the disease of dipsomania while their poorer brethren were likely to be viewed as suffering from the vice of willful drunkenness.[70] Motivation as well as social class influences such designations. Those seeking escape from pain are afforded some degree of sympathy in the labels applied to them while those viewed as seeking unearned pleasure through the medium of drug intoxication are subjected to the most pejorative labels.

When one examines the American rhetoric in which alcohol and other drug problems have been constructed, one is immediately struck by the fact that this rhetoric tends to become highly inflammatory during periods of great social conflict. The addiction rhetoric during these times is not so much about drugs as it is about groups of people linked to their use. Struggles between races and social classes and broader concerns about social disorder often get played out metaphorically in prohibitionist campaigns and "drug wars." Racial, class, and intergenerational conflict have exerted a profound influence on American addiction rhetoric. Such conflict birthed the "firewater myths" surrounding early Native American responses to distilled spirits. In the 1870s, it fueled the West Coast anti-opium campaign with its inflammatory images of white children being seduced into Chinese laundries where they were forced to "yield up their virginal bodies to their maniacal yellow captors." Nativism, immigration, racism, and social and class conflict enlarged that campaign and fueled the myth of "Yellow Peril"—the delusion that opium was being used as a political weapon to weaken America as the prelude to Chinese invasion of the United States. We see this pattern of inflammatory rhetoric continuing through the turn of the century anti-cocaine campaign with its images of cocaine-crazed black men attacking white women and rumors of cocaine-inspired black uprisings in the South. It continues with the alcohol prohibition forces tapping anti-Catholic and anti-German sentiment, the anti-marihuana campaign of the 1930s with its repeated references to cannabis-inspired violence among Mexican Americans, the 1950s accusations of communist involvement in American drug trafficking, and the intergenerational and racial underpinnings of the "war on drugs" campaigns of the last half of the twentieth century. We see here how an inflammatory rhetoric is mobilized as a weapon in the struggles between groups of people—conflicts that are first and foremost not about rituals of psychoactive drug consumption or their associated problems. The rhetoric of addiction in these contexts serves the broader function of reflecting, fueling, and sustaining these conflicts.[71]

The language of addiction might be compared to a projective word test revealing prominent or emerging features of the national temperament. Words move into and out of prominence as they reflect or fail to reflect the dominant emotion of the culture. Addiction rhetoric becomes more personalized and medicalized during periods of collective introspection and optimism—optimism about the power of our scientific technology and the potential for human transformation. Addiction rhetoric takes on moral and criminal connotations during periods of lost faith in ourselves and our technology and during periods of increased social disorder. Whether we use language that calls for toleration or language that calls for punishment says as much about our own collective temperament as it does about addicts and addiction. The cycles of addiction rhetoric involve competing, and sometimes alternating, patterns of language that evoke empathy and concern on the one hand and fear and aggression on the other. Science is not the driving force, but more often a self-absorbed bystander in the evolution of this language.

Professional Utility

The rhetoric of addiction reviewed in this essay is also a means of staking out professional territory. It answers by implication what institutions and professional roles have legitimate ownership of the problem.

There could have been no inebriate asylums, no American Association for the Study and Cure of Inebriety, no *Quarterly Journal of Inebriety* without the concept of inebriety. Defining inebriety and declaring this condition a disease shifted ownership for alcohol and other drug problems into a specialized arena. It shifted partial ownership from the jails and psychiatric asylums—institutions that did not want ownership of the problem—and made a marginal peace with a temperance industry that wanted to own the problem but not those people who were products of the problem.

The move was more one toward coexistence within the dominant alcohol problem paradigm than a replacement of that paradigm. Inebriate asylum specialists did not so much declare that inebriety was a disease rather than a vice as much as they said inebriety could be both a disease *and* a vice. In their vocal efforts to screen out hedonists, vicious criminals, and the morally inferior, asylum managers reinforced the view that drunkenness was a function of weak moral character in some people. The delineation of which people suffered from the moral vice of drunkenness and which suffered from the disease of inebriety was based, as earlier noted, primarily upon ethnic and social class distinctions.

In this way, the new inebriety specialists found an escape from the twin challenges of professional emergence: drawing one's arena large enough to procure the needed support and resources to sustain growth while not drawing the boundary so wide as to draw fire from more established and more powerful forces that exist on the field's perimeter. The question is how to emerge and justify one's existence without drawing lethal fire from other stakeholders in the problem to which one has laid claim. Language is an essential medium through which new professions stake their territorial claims. When inebriety was defined and declared a condition that could be a disease *and* a vice, the new inebriety specialists temporarily pacified powerful temperance forces. When they laid claim to dipsomania and defined it as a form of temporary insanity, they built a bridge to the alienists' (nineteenth-century psychiatrists') view of addiction. But perhaps, most important, when they set forth the concept of inebriety as a primary disease requiring specialized treatment, they carved out a niche that formed the foundation of addiction treatment and today's field of addiction medicine.

While the codification of the language of discourse is an essential stage in the emergence of a new profession, the debate over such language can be quickly closed in ways that serve to suppress new research and new ideas.[72] This premature "hardening of the categories"[73] can lead to stagnation and provoke future ideological backlashes. The history of alcoholism treatment from 1940 to 1980 might be depicted as the emergence of a single-pathway model of understanding the etiology, course, treatment, and prognosis of alcoholism, with the years from 1980 to the present marked by professional and public backlash and the emergence of a multiple-pathway model of alcohol problems and alcoholism. The challenge is to construct alcohol and drug problems in a way that enhances professional identity and organizes professional activity, while not constructing that ideology so narrowly as to create stagnation and eventual implosion. This history suggests that professional language can reflect the suppression of science as much as the advancement of science. The images of a professional system defining itself so narrowly as to become professionally extinct or so broadly as to be devoured by neighboring professional arenas are provocative ones.

Language helps create professions and can help place those professions within a pecking order of prestige in relationship to other professions. This is particularly important when a new professional arena embraces issues, problems, or people who have been highly stigmatized. The new language must find ways to not only destigmatize those who have the maligned condition but to destigmatize those who choose to professionally work with that condition. The medicalization of language used to construct alcohol and other drug problems provided an esteem-salvaging legitimacy to those being treated *and* to those doing the treating.[74] Addiction had to be converted into a disease of complex pathology before "drunks" could be converted into "alcoholics" and rendered legitimate patients for the new physician specialty of addiction medicine. The medicalization of addiction was as much about the desired prestige of the caregivers as it was the destigmatization of alcohol- and drug-addicted patients.

In staking out new territory, language is essential to the emergence of new professions. By marking the boundaries of professional territory, language defines the professional perimeters and the outside bodies to whom one must relate. By signaling insider or outsider status, language serves as a litmus test for membership within a professional arena and also for one's membership in various "schools" within that arena. In the case of professions related to alcohol and other drug problems, this professional language must also serve clinical and economic utilities.

Clinical Utility

At a clinical level, language promises precision. It holds out the possibility for the scientific classification of addictive disorders and co-morbidities in ways that allow a careful matching of particular intervention technologies to the characteristics and needs of particular patients. And yet considerable struggle occurs at the boundary of such classifications. When the language of clinical diagnosis is drawn too narrowly, many who could benefit from available helping interventions are deprived of access to such help. When the language of clinical diagnosis is drawn too broadly, there is the risk of people being subjected to unwarranted voluntary or involuntary treatment.

The issue here is not simply that a few people may get unneeded but otherwise benign treatment, but that such misplaced treatment may do great harm. This harm can include the economic costs of unneeded or inappropriate treatment that a patient or family must bear, the harmful effects of having been labeled with a stigmatized condition, and the actual physical or psychological harm resulting from the treatment interventions—what in medicine are referred to as "iatrogenic illnesses" or "iatrogenic effects." It is thus language that defines the boundaries of competence separating fields of professional practice, defines which people will enter a particular arena, and what interventions they will be subjected to within that arena. The more life-threatening the conditions and the more invasive the potential procedures, the more crucial becomes the precision and application of this language.

There has always been in the addictions field a struggle between the desire for clinical precision (particularly in the arena of clinical research), the desire to satisfy the needs of other social institutions such as general and psychiatric hospitals and the courts, and the desire to expand the field's own sphere of professional influence and economic advantage. Recently coined terms such as "checkbook diagnosis" reflect the way in which institutional greed corrupted many of the assessment procedures used by modern addiction treatment programs suffering from low patient census.

Another clinical use of language involves the link between the professional and public arenas, more specifically, communicating to the public in such a way that those suffering with a particular disorder will know how and where to seek appropriate assistance. When professional language is so technical and obscure that it surpasses common understanding, people become vulnerable to charlatans who are successful in attracting those in need simply by virtue of the charlatan's ability to speak clearly, passionately, and hopefully. A similar risk arises when professional language is corrupted by popular usage. When professional language is simplified and fully absorbed into the popular language, perceived distinctions between professional helper, folk healer, and scam artist disappear, and those in need are at great risk of exploitation.

Economic Utility

The language used to construct alcohol and other drug problems is also an economic commodity. It is a designator of who has problem ownership and any associated power and status, and also determines who shall receive the financial resources society has invested in managing the problem. Transforming "drunks" into diseased "alcoholics" created not only a new professional arena but also a new billable diagnosis and a new legitimized medical patient who could serve as a replacement for the diminishing raw materials (patients) that fueled a hospital-based health care industry. Language is also a marketing commodity that determines, through how the problem is framed, the degree of comfort or resistance citizens will have seeking those services. Stigmatizing language ("drunkenness"), as an example, requires coercive tools of engagement, whereas a medicalized, face-saving language ("dipsomania," "alcoholism") holds out the opportunity for voluntary engagement. In a similar manner, language can dictate how much "treatment" can be sold. To pronounce a patient "recovered" after a brief course of inpatient or outpatient counseling communicates that treatment is over. Declaring that this same patient has finished his or her first "stage of treatment" as a "recovering" alcoholic or addict signals the existence of ongoing needs to which the treatment institution may continue to market its products and services.

The economic value of language has important implications for boundary definitions of a professional field. Financial resources (and institutional and personal gain) expand to the extent that the definition of a disorder can be expanded to encompass a larger population. At the same time, such expansion poses the danger of increased conflict with allied professions and the risk of ethical breaches resulting from practicing beyond the limits of one's knowledge and skill. Such financially motivated overextension, by publicly damaging professional credibility, can actually threaten the very future of a professional field. The shift to encompass a broad spectrum of alcohol problems within an alcohol addiction treatment industry, the further extension of that industry to encompass drugs other than alcohol, and the recent extension of the field to encompass "process addictions" stand as clear examples of such expansionism. The explosive growth of the "recovery" industry, the backlashes against industry breaches in ethical practice, and the resulting collapse of much of that industry collectively stand as a morality tale about the risk of a field moving beyond the boundaries of its competence.

Another category of financial stakeholders in the linguistic construction of alcohol and other drug problems includes those public and private institutions responsible for providing the funds that support addiction treatment services. Where private institutions such as insurance companies almost universally benefit (via reduced liability and increased profits) from a very narrow definition of billable diagnoses, federal and state governmental bodies charged with funding addiction treatment have quite mixed interests. Since the status of these agencies is often measured by budget and head count, an expansionist approach to the definition of alcohol and other drug problems often serves to enhance personal and institutional power. At the same time, units (such as medical directors or research departments) within these organizations often advocate very narrow and precise problem definitions. It has been my experience working within such organizations that they dynamically expand the defined scope of their arena until they encounter the boundaries of more powerful organizations within their operating environments.

There are other financial stakeholders in the debate over the language in which alcohol and other drug problems are constructed. Since the repeal of Prohibition, the alcohol beverage industry has actively involved itself in professional dialogues regarding construction of alcohol-related problems. Their financial resources and political power have been used in an effort, more aptly described as haphazard than conspiratorial, to influence this problem construction debate in ways that protected their financial interests. This influence has included efforts to shape the language within which alcohol problems were to be constructed. The first evidence of this influence can be found in the heavy lobbying of alcohol industry representatives in the 1940s to get the Research Council on Problems of Alcohol to avoid using the term *alcoholism*. Alcohol industry representatives preferred terms not named after their product (such as "problem drinking")—terms that shift the locus of the problem from alcohol to the drinker.[75]

While the alcohol beverage industry in the 1930s and 1940s did not like the term *alcoholism*, it was comfortable with the way in which Alcoholics Anonymous, the National Council on Alcoholism, and the major public health institutions defined the totality of the alcohol problem in terms of a small percentage of drinkers whose physiological or psychological sensitivities prevented them from having a normal, healthy relationship with alcohol.[76] For the alcohol beverage industry, either framing alcohol as an addictive poison or focusing on its misuse by the majority has always been much more financially threatening than defining problems in terms of alcoholism. Alcoholism defines the problem as being inside the drinker and allows the industry to divert attention from the much broader and more pervasive problems created by their product—problems that have nothing to do with alcoholism as it has been medically defined. Both the licit alcohol and drug industries have a financial investment in linguistically framing America's alcohol and other drug problems in ways that separate those problems from their own products and promotional activities. Nowhere is this more evident than in the discomfort of the alcohol industry with the "alcohol is a drug" campaign and the prolonged machinations of the tobacco industry to avoid having their product labeled an "addictive drug."

The debate over the language in which alcohol and other drug problems are to be constructed is, at one of its most primitive levels, a fight about money. Nuances of ideological argument mask the fact that the outcome of this debate determines the future of industries, communities, and individual careers.

Prospects for the Future

The struggle to achieve consensus on an accepted language in which to frame alcohol- and other drug-related problems has been and will continue to be plagued by the many uses such language must serve. Language that offers clinical precision related to the diagnosis of addictive disorders severely limits the ability of these constructs to travel across demographic and cultural boundaries to serve as what Room has called a "governing image" for the society as a whole. The personal, social, political, economic, professional, and clinical utilities that the language of addiction must serve will continue to make language a source of more confusion and conflict than consensus. The continued evolution of this language will mark the jockeying for power in the overlapping ownership of alcohol and other drug problems. It will also constitute a reflection of this culture's enduring ambivalence about psychoactive drug use.

Notes

This essay is an expansion of the prologue of *Slaying the Dragon: The History of Addiction Treatment and Recovery in America*. Shortly after I began work on this book in 1994, Ron Roizen challenged me to carefully consider the language through which this story was to be told and suggested that the language was itself an important part of the history. Ron's role in initiating the inquiries that led to this essay is gratefully acknowledged.

The epigraph comes from T. Watts, "The Uneasy Triumph of a Concept: The 'Disease' Conception of Alcoholism," *Journal of Drug Issues* 11 (Fall 1981): 451.

1. This study includes some references to individuals from other countries who exerted a profound influence on the way Americans perceived and labeled addictive disorders. The most significant of these external influences were Dr. Thomas Trotter and Dr. Norman Kerr of England, Dr. Magnus Huss of Sweden, and Dr. Albrecht Erlenmeyer of Germany.

2. H. Levine, "The Discovery of Addiction: Changing Conceptions of Habitual Drunkenness in America," *Journal of Studies on Alcohol* 39, no. 2 (1978): 143–174.

3. Historians variably place per capita alcohol consumption between five and ten gallons at that time, but universally agree on these decades being the highest period in alcohol consumption in American history. J. Rorabaugh, *The Alcoholic Republic* (Oxford: Oxford University Press, 1979).

4. T. Trotter, *Essay, Medical, Philosophical, and Chemical, on Drunkenness and its Effects on the Human Body*, 2d ed. (London: Longman, Hurst, Rees, and Orme, 1804); B. Rush, *Plan for an Asylum for Drunkards to be called the Sober House* (1810), reprinted in G. Corner, ed., *The Autobiography of Benjamin Rush* (Princeton: Princeton University Press, 1948); B. Rush, *An Inquiry into the Effect of Ardent Spirits upon the Human Body and Mind, with an Account of the Means of Preventing and of the Remedies for Curing Them*, 8th rev. ed. (Brookfield, Mass.: E. Merriam, 1814), reprinted in G. Grob, ed., *Nineteenth-Century Medical Attitudes toward Alcoholic Addiction* (New York: Arno Press, 1981).

5. J. Baker, *The Washingtonian Reform: An Address Delivered Before the Hingham Total Abstinence Society June 16, 1844* (Published by the Society, 1844), 1–20; A. Wilkerson, "A History of the Concept of Alcoholism as a Disease," D.S.W. diss., University of Pennsylvania, 1966, 90.

6. S. Lucia, "The Antiquity of Alcohol in Diet and Medicine," in Lucia, ed., *Alcohol and Civilization* (New York: McGraw-Hill, 1963), 171.

7. J. Sournia, *A History of Alcoholism* (Cambridge, Mass: Basil Blackwell, 1990).

8. N. Kerr, *Inebriety or Narcomania: Its Etiology, Pathology, Treatment, and Jurisprudence* (New York: J. Selwin Tait & Sons, 1889).

9. H. Levine, "The Vocabulary of Drunkenness," *Journal of Studies on Alcohol* 42, no. 11 (1981): 1046.

10. J. Marconi, "The Concept of Alcoholism," *Quarterly Journal of Studies on Alcohol* 20, no. 2 (1959): 216–235.

11. Wilkerson, "A History of the Concept of Alcoholism," 65–66.

12. Cited in Marconi, "The Concept of Alcoholism," 225.

13. T. Wright, *Inebriism: Pathological and Psychological Study* (Columbus, Ohio: William G. Hubbard, 1885).

14. B. Johnson, "The Alcoholism Movement in America: A Study in Cultural Innovation," Ph.D. diss., University of Illinois, 1973, 473.

15. W. Bynum, "Chronic Alcoholism in the First Half of the 19th Century," *Bulletin of the History of Medicine* 42 (1968): 161.

16. N. Kerr, *Inebriety or Narcomania: Its Etiology, Pathology, Treatment, and Jurisprudence*, 3d ed. (New York: J. Selwin Tait & Sons, 1894; rpt. New York: Arno Press, 1981), 41.

17. T. D. Crothers, *The Disease of Inebriety from Alcohol, Opium and Other Narcotic Drugs: Its Etiology, Pathology, Treatment and Medico-legal Relations* (New York: E. B. Treat, 1893).

18. C. Douglas, "Historical Notes on the Sanitarium in the Treatment of Alcoholism," *Medical Record* 57 (1900): 410–411.

19. K. Abraham, *Selected Papers on Psychoanalysis* (London: Hogarth Press, 1927).

20. C. Towns, *Habits That Handicap: The Menace of Opium, Alcohol, Tobacco, and the Remedy* (New York: Funk & Wagnalls, 1915, 1920).

21. C. Towns, *Reclaiming the Drinker* (New York: Barnes & Company, 1931), 58, and Towns, *Drug and Alcohol Sickness* (New York: M. M. Barbour, 1932).

22. R. Fleming, "The Treatment of Chronic Alcoholism," *New England Journal of Medicine* 217 (1937): 779–783.

23. V. Anderson, "The Alcoholic as Seen in Court," *Boston Medical and Surgical Journal* 74 (1916): 492–495.

24. C. Durfee, *To Drink or Not to Drink* (Boston: Longmans, Green, 1937); and Durfee, "Re-Education of the Problem Drinker," *Journal of the Connecticut Medical Society* 2 (1938): 486.

25. *Alcoholics Anonymous* (New York City: Alcoholics Anonymous World Services, Inc., 1955), 18.

26. R. Seliger, "The Alcoholic in the Community," *American Journal of Psychiatry* 95 (1938): 701–716.

27. E. Strecker and F. Chambers, *Alcohol: One Man's Meat* (New York: Macmillan, 1938), 21.

28. D. Anderson, "Alcohol and Public Opinion," *Quarterly Journal of Studies on Alcohol* 3, no. 3 (1942): 389.

29. Johnson, "Alcoholism Movement in America," 243, 293.

30. E. M. Jellinek, ed., *Alcohol Addiction and Chronic Alcoholism* (New Haven: Yale University Press, 1942), and Jellinek, *The Disease Concept of Alcoholism* (Highland Park, N.J.: Hillhouse, 1960).

31. K. Bowman and E. Jellinek, "Alcohol Addiction and Its Treatment," *Quarterly Journal of Studies on Alcohol* 2 (September 1941): 98–176; Jellinek, *Alcohol Addiction*, 38–42.

32. S. Bacon, "The Administration of Alcoholism Rehabilitation Programs," *Quarterly Journal of Studies on Alcohol* 10, no. 1 (1949): 8.

33. M. Keller, "On Defining Alcoholism: With Comment on Some Other Relevant Words," in L. Gomberg, H. White, and J. Carpenter, *Alcohol, Science and Society Revisited* (Ann Arbor: University of Michigan Press, 1982), 123.

34. R. Fox and P. Lyon, *Alcoholism: Its Scope, Cause, and Treatment* (New York: Random House, 1955).

35. Jellinek, *The Disease Concept of Alcoholism*, 35–41.

36. T. Babor, "The Classification of Alcoholics: Typology Theories from the 19th Century to the Present," *Alcohol Health & Research World* 20, no. 1 (1996): 6–14. William Rohan later attacked the creation of "alcoholisms" on the grounds that it multiplied rather than discarded a mistaken concept. He called alcoholism a "reified abstract noun" that had contributed to the field's conceptual mess. W. Rohan, "The Concept of Alcoholism: Assumptions and Issue," in E. Pattison and E. Kaufman, *Encyclopedic Handbook of Alcoholism* (New York: Gardern Press, 1982), 31–39.

37. T. Plaut, *Alcohol Problems: A Report to the Nation by the Cooperative Commission on the Study of Alcoholism* (New York: Oxford University Press, 1967).

38. "Jellinek's Disease," *AA Grapevine* 31, no. 4 (September 1974): 42; K. Fitzgerald, "Living with Jellinek's Disease," *Newsweek*, 17 October 1983, 22.

39. Keller, "On Defining Alcoholism," 129–130. The term "abuse" marked the effort to delineate the appropriate and beneficial consumption of alcohol as the "Good Creature of God" from the misuse of God's gift. Early applications of the word "abuse" to excessive alcohol and other drug use include Lender's discovery of one Joseph Birch who was fined and forced to "sit in stocks" for "abusing" himself by drinking: M. Lender, "Drunkenness as an Offense in Early New England: A Study of Puritan Attitudes," *Quarterly Journal of Studies on Alcohol* 34 (1973): 362. An 1830s letter sent by temperance reformer Edward Delevan to the students at Union College implored: "There can be no expediency to the use of a *bad* thing. All use of alcohol as a beverage, in my opinion is evil and evil continually. . . . All use is abuse": quoted in C. Steinsapir, "The Ante-Bellum Total Ab-

stinence Movement at the Local Level: A Case Study of Schenectady, New York," Ph.D. diss., Rutgers University, 1983, 101.

40. J. Moser, "Problems and Programs Related to Alcohol and Drug Dependence in 33 Countries" (Geneva: World Health Organization, 1974), 9.

41. American Psychiatric Association, *Diagnostic and Statistical Manual of Mental Disorders*, 4th ed. (Washington, D.C., 1994), 175–272; see also: M. Schuckit, P. Nathan, J. Helzer, G. Woody, and T. Crowley, "Evolution of the DSM Diagnostic Criteria for Alcoholism," *Alcohol Health and Research World* 15, no. 4 (1991): 278–283.

42. *Patient Placement Criteria for the Treatment of Substance-Related Disorders*, 2d ed. (Chevy Chase, Md.: American Society of Addiction Medicine, Inc., 1996).

43. J. Greenleaf, "Co-Alcoholic . . . Para-Alcoholic . . . Who's Who . . . and What's the Difference?" *Alcoholism: The National Magazine*, May–June 1983, 24–25.

44. E. Gomberg, "On Terms Used and Abused: The Concept of Codependency," in E. Gomberg, ed., *Current Issues in Alcohol/Drug Studies* (New York: Haworth, 1989).

45. E. Scott, "Abusing the Abuse," *Alcoholism Treatment Quarterly* 13, no. 3 (1995): 6.

46. T. D. Crothers, *Morphinism and Narcomanias from Other Drugs* (Philadelphia: W. B. Saunders, 1902).

47. J. Whitaker, "Cocaine in the Treatment of the Opium Habit," *Medical News*, 8 August 1885, 144; J. Greer, I. Albright, and D. Smith, *Tragedies of the Opium Traffic* (Chicago: J. Regan, 1915).

48. D. Wilner and G. Kassebaum, *Narcotics* (New York: McGraw-Hill, 1965), 54.

49. "Remarks on Cocaine and the So-Called Cocaine Habit," *Journal of Nervous and Mental Disease* 13 (1886): 754–759; J. Mattison, "Opium Addicts Among Medical Men," *Medical Record* 23 (1883): 621–623; A. Rogers, "Some Observations during Eighteen Years Experience with Drug and Liquor Habitues," *Wisconsin Medical Journal* 12 (July 1913): 43.

50. J. Renaud, "Substance Abuse Is Language Abuse," *The Counselor* 7, no. 4 (1989): 26–27.

51. One of the earliest references to advocacy of the term chemical dependency is a 1958 presentation by Jane Cain, a nurse at Dia Linn—Hazelden's treatment center for women. D. McElrath, *Hazelden: A Spiritual Odyssey* (Center City, Minn.: Hazelden Foundation, 1987), 112.

52. "Origin and Meaning of the Word Addiction," *Scientific Temperance Journal*, Spring 1936, 9. Mark Lender, in his research on the colonial management of drunkenness, discovered Puritan references to persons "addicted to alcohol": Lender, "Drunkenness as an Offense in Early New England," 357. The term *dope*, which came into usage during this period, was first used to refer to any syrupy preparation and later came to designate products containing opium and cocaine. Persons ordering cocaine-laced soft drinks often simply said, "Gimme a dope." The changing view of drug use was reflected in the term *fiend*, a German derivative referring to a diabolically wicked and hated person: J. Ayto, *Dictionary of Word Origins* (New York: Arcade, 1990), 226. The first known appearance of the term "dope fiend" was in an 1896 article in the *New York Sun*: A. Hess, "Deviance Theory and the History of Opiates," *The International Journal of the Addictions* 6, no. 4 (1971): 593.

53. T. Hickman, "The Double Meaning of Addiction: Habitual Narcotic Use and the Logic of Professionalizing Medical Authority in the United States, 1900–1920," presented at Historical Perspectives on Drug and Alcohol Use in American Society, 1800–1997, College of Physicians of Philadelphia, 9–11 May 1997, 6.

54. S. Hubbard, "Some Fallacies Regarding Narcotic Drug Addiction," *Journal of the American Medical Association* 74 (1920): 1439.

55. S. Vogel, "Psychiatric Treatment of Alcoholism," in S. Bacon, *Understanding Alcoholism* (Philadelphia: The Annals of the American Academy of Political and Social Science, 1958), 99.

56. D. Smith, "Diagnostic, Treatment and Aftercare Approaches to Cocaine Abuse," *Journal of Substance Abuse Treatment* 1 (1984): 5–9.

57. J. Parascandola, "The Drug Habit: The Association of the Word Drug with Abuse in American History," in R. Porter and M. Teich, eds., *Drugs and Narcotics in History* (Melbourne: Cambridge University Press, 1996), 156–167.

58. The word *narcotic* is drawn from the Greek term *narke* meaning numbness.

59. M. Fishbein, *Fads and Quackery in Healing* (New York: Blue Ribbon Books, 1932), 285.

60. Several of these have interesting histories. *Cure,* derived from the Latin *cura,* came to mean "care" or "looking after." *Treat* and *treatment* came to imply "dealing with something by discussion," and *counsel* referred to the act of discussing or consulting. Ayto, *Dictionary,* 133, 150, 527.

61. S. Hiltner, "Who Is Qualified to Treat the Alcoholic? Comment on the Krystal-Moore Discussion," *Quarterly Journal of Studies on Alcohol* 25 (1964): 354.

62. Quoted in: T. Watts, "The Uneasy Triumph of a Concept: The 'Disease' Concept of Alcoholism," *Journal of Drug Issues* 11 (Fall 1981): 452.

63. N. Christie and K. Bruun, "Alcohol Problems: The Conceptual Framework," in M. Keller and T. Coffey, eds., *Proceedings of the 28th International Congress on Alcohol and Alcoholism,* vol. 2 (Highland Park, N.J.: Hillhouse Press, 1969), 69.

64. W. White, *Pathways from the Culture of Addiction to the Culture of Recovery* (Center City, Minn.: Hazelden, 1996).

65. P. Conrad and J. Schneider, *Deviance and Medicalization: From Badness to Sickness* (St. Louis: C. V. Mosby, 1980), 85.

66. A. Lindesmith, *Opiate Addiction* (Bloomington, Ind.: Principia Press, 1947), 187.

67. White, *Pathways,* 51–53, 268–275.

68. T. D. Crothers, in his 1893 treatise, *The Disease of Inebriety,* addresses several chapters to medico-legal questions raised by the conceptualization of inebriety as a disease.

69. W. White, "Themes in Chemical Prohibition," *Drugs in Perspective* (Rockville, Md.: National Drug Abuse Center/National Institute on Drug Abuse, 1979), 179.

70. S. Tracy, "The Foxborough Experiment: Medicalizing Inebriety at the Massachusetts Hospital for Dipsomaniacs and Inebriates," Ph.D. diss., University of Pennsylvania, 1992, 6, 13, 91.

71. This role has been noted by nearly all those who have chronicled American drug use. Samples of the extremes reached in the use of this inflammatory rhetoric can be found in D. Musto, *The American Disease: Origins of Narcotic Controls* (New Haven: Yale University Press, 1973), and J. Helmer, *Drugs and Minority Oppression* (New York: Seabury Press, 1975).

72. Ron Roizen, Personal Communication, 5 December 1996.

73. F. Underhill, quoted in A. Toynbee, *Reconsiderations,* vol. 12 of *A Study of History* (London: Oxford University Press, 1961), 1.

74. The linguistic shift from GRID (Gay-Related Immune Deficiency) to AIDS (Acquired Immune Deficiency Syndrome) in 1982 marked a similar step in destigmati-

zation affecting both persons with HIV/AIDS and their caregivers. See R. Shilts, *And the Band Played On* (New York: St. Martin's Press, 1987), 71.

75. Johnson, "The Alcoholism Movement in America"; A. Wodak, "The Language of Industry: Toward a Definition of Liquorspeak," *Addiction* 90 (1995): 133–134.

76. J. Burnham, *Bad Habits: Drinking, Smoking, Taking Drugs, Gambling, Sexual Misbehavior, and Swearing in American History* (New York: New York University Press, 1993), 81–85.

How Does the Nation's "Alcohol Problem" Change from Era to Era?

Stalking the Social Logic of Problem-Definition Transformations since Repeal

RON ROIZEN

ALCOHOL STOOD considerably higher on the American political and cultural agenda in the nineteenth and early twentieth century than it has over the seventy years since Repeal, in 1933. Why its decline? Over a century of heated conflict about alcohol—and perhaps especially the drawn-out and fractious debate over Repeal—exhausted the nation's patience and interest in the subject.[1] Lingering cultural images of the great controversy and national prohibition's "failure"[2] still operate in effect as historical brakes on alcohol's cultural politics. Moreover, the nation's post-Repeal political plate was full—taken up with the continuing Great Depression, the emergent threat of rising fascism abroad, and, before very long, World War II.[3]

The New Alcoholism Paradigm and Problem Depoliticization

Within what Carolyn Wiener (1981) termed "the alcohol problems social arena" itself, the post-Repeal era soon saw the emergence and successful development of "the modern alcoholism movement"—whose vigorous advocates, led by Mrs. Marty Mann and her National Committee for Education on Alcoholism (NCEA),[4] argued that *alcoholism*, not *alcohol*, was the nation's most important alcohol problem and that alcoholism was *a disease* requiring greatly expanded treatment and research efforts, enterprises quite unlike the political agendas familiar to generations of Americans over the long course of what Selden Bacon (1967) called the Classic American Temperance Movement. The modern alcoholism movement split cultural "ownership" (Gusfield 1996: 249–250) of the alcohol-problem domain between, on the one hand, Alcoholics Anonymous (AA), a voluntary fellowship devoted to the rescue and spiritual renewal of fellow alcoholics,[5] and, on the other, a mainstream scientific enterprise devoted to promoting the importance of research in addressing the nation's alcohol problems.[6] Both interest groups viewed the dry-wet axis of controversy as diversionary and counterproductive—and, especially within the first two or three formative decades following Repeal, struggled hard to distinguish their new agendas from the temperance tradition. In more recent decades, the "war on drugs" and a sustained assault on tobacco have become the focus of heated political exchange in the United States, thus also displacing alcohol from its pre-Repeal station as the nation's original and deeply controversial "drug problem" (Levine 1978).

Figure 1

Figures 1 and 2 offer two pages taken from a draft brochure prepared by the Research Council on Problems of Alcohol ("A Major Public Health Problem Not Being Systematically Attacked—The Misuse of Alcohol," n.d. [1938?]). The canted box on the brochure's title (fig. 1) evidences how eagerly the group sought to distinguish itself from dry and wet interests and as well how much it stressed its own objectivity and disinterestedness vis-à-vis alcohol research. An interior page (fig. 2) provided a visual representation of the "vicious circle" of dry-to-wet-to-dry historical cycling of the nation's alcohol problem.

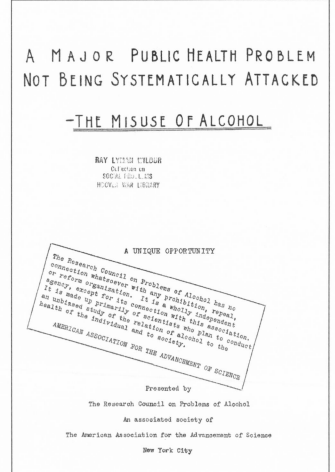

A MAJOR PUBLIC HEALTH PROBLEM NOT BEING SYSTEMATICALLY ATTACKED

-THE MISUSE OF ALCOHOL

RAY LYMAN WILBUR
Collection on
SOCIAL PROBLEMS
HOOVER WAR LIBRARY

A UNIQUE OPPORTUNITY

The Research Council on Problems of Alcohol has no connection whatsoever with any prohibition, repeal, or reform organization. It is a wholly independent agency, except for its connection with this association. It is made up primarily of scientists who plan to conduct an unbiased study of the relation of alcohol to the health of the individual and to society.

AMERICAN ASSOCIATION FOR THE ADVANCEMENT OF SCIENCE

Presented by

The Research Council on Problems of Alcohol

An associated society of

The American Association for the Advancement of Science

New York City

Alcohol's low post-Repeal political profile also had an *intentional* component—and may also be regarded as the product of what Paul Schrecker (1948: 12–18) called historical "work." In the first decade after Repeal, before alcoholism became the consensus theme, a cohort of post-Repeal alcohol activists and enterprises—including, for example, Luther Gulick and his Institute of Public Administration at Columbia University (whence came influential policy studies by Fosdick and Scott [1933] and Harrison and Laine [1936]), Everett Colby's "Council for Moderation" (Roizen 1991a and b), the Research Council on Problems of Alcohol (Roizen 1991a), and an emergent alcohol science center at Yale (Roizen 1993a)—quite deliberately sought ways

Figure 2

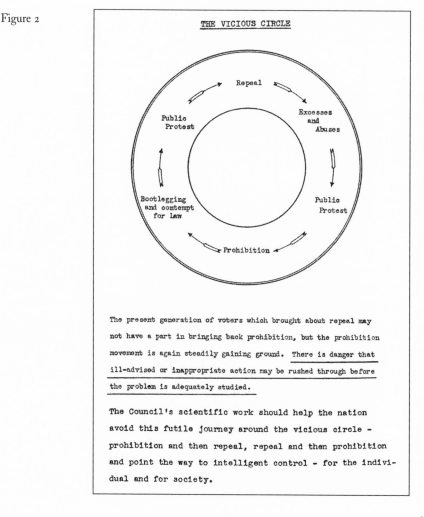

THE VICIOUS CIRCLE

Repeal

Public Protest

Excesses and Abuses

Bootlegging and contempt for Law

Public Protest

Prohibition

The present generation of voters which brought about repeal may not have a part in bringing back prohibition, but the prohibition movement is again steadily gaining ground. There is danger that ill-advised or inappropriate action may be rushed through before the problem is adequately studied.

The Council's scientific work should help the nation avoid this futile journey around the vicious circle - prohibition and then repeal, repeal and then prohibition and point the way to intelligent control - for the individual and for society.

to depoliticize the alcohol problem, thus wresting it from the country's dry-wet tug of war.[7] Each of these enterprises offered its own thematic route to a new neutrality: Gulick suggested his public administration movement's domain assumption that apolitical, purely administrative solutions could be found for formerly political issues (see Gulick 1936; Roberts 1994); Colby suggested that a new normative consensus around moderate drinking would forestall or obviate renewed dry activism in the future; and the nascent scientific organizations at first defined the nation's alcohol problem as either (a) a problem of distorted information (stemming from the long propaganda struggle between wets and drys) (Roizen 1991a: chap. 7) or (b) the failure to adopt an adequately scientific approach to the immense complexity posed by the nation's multifarious alcohol problems (Roizen 1993a).

The American alcohol problem, as these observers saw it, lay less in alcohol, per se, than in the worn-out positions of the dry and wet parties still defining the debate's terms and scrambling for post-Repeal influence. Would-be new players in the post-Repeal arena were particularly mindful of alcohol as a "historical" problem, too—and searched for conceptual and policy tools with which to end the nation's seemingly ineluctable and senseless historical alternation between periods of dry and wet political dominance (Fosdick and Scott 1933; Reports 1938). Their image of pointless historical cycling and wasted political energy doubtless resonated with a larger sense of historical victimization and impotence occasioned by the Great Depression—a social catastrophe widely regarded as the product of an ill-understood boom-and-bust historical mechanism in capitalism not subject to adequate control by actors on the ground.

Institutionally speaking, both AA (with its tradition of nonparticipation in "external" matters and its privatist, spiritual orientation to alcoholism) and contemporary science (whose advocates emphasized its high premiums on disinterestedness, objectivity, and empiricism) nicely fit this spirit of depoliticization. The disease-alcoholism theme, when it came along, inherited this aspiration and managed to provide—almost by accident, as it happened (Roizen 1991a: chap. 8)—a remarkably adept symbolic vehicle and problem focus for its realization. The disease idea also offered destigmatization to the alcoholic and a measure of new symbolic legitimacy for beverage alcohol itself—which, in the new paradigm's lens, harbored little more responsibility for alcoholism or alcohol-related troubles than did sugar for the disease of diabetes. An astute dry critic, Ernest Gordon, got little general attention with his complaint that the new neutralist science looked pretty wet to his tutored eye (Gordon 1946).

Not the least remarkable feature of the modern alcoholism movement was that it in effect represented a trial run for the proposition that modern science could and should take charge of a major American social problem. If Prohibition had been a "noble experiment" in grand-scale, legislatively imposed social uplift, then the modern alcoholism movement represented a bold test of a new, would-be, post-Repeal scientific hegemony. And although it was not science at all, but AA's spiritually oriented approach that provided the new movement's all-important evidence that alcoholics could in fact be helped,[8] the disease concept's message of medicoscientific naturalism defined and premised the new cultural sensibility and spawned the considerable research and treatment enterprises that would emerge over the remainder of the twentieth century.[9]

Origins, Rise, and Faltering of the Alcoholism Paradigm

For all of its high scientific and cultural promise, the actual history of the disease concept's emergence as the new movement's ideological centerpiece reads like a history-of-science shaggy-dog story. In fact, neither the AA nor the new science half of the movement had begun with a disease-concept emphasis. AA—as evidenced for example in its "Big Book" (Alcoholics Anonymous 1939) and a famous article published in the *Saturday Evening Post* by columnist Jack Alexander in 1941—had stressed instead the group's program of spiritual renewal and its members-help-members approach.[10] The new scientific agenda (as noted above) initially focused on misinformation (in the Research Council on Problems of Alcohol) and inadequate appreciation and tools for handling complexity (at Yale). It was the alcoholism focus and the disease theme, however, that provided a crucial bridge, or "boundary object" (Star and Griesemer 1989),[11] between the otherwise quite different institutional halves of the new movement. AA was of course committed to helping the alcoholic from the start. On the science side of the movement, however, the alcoholism focus emerged via a gradual evolution driven by the search for a symbol that would capture the new approach's essence and generate much-needed funding.

The new scientific enterprises—both at the Research Council on Problems of Alcohol (RCPA) and at the Yale center—faced a perplexing structural problem: Their neutralist message about alcohol—attractive as it may have been to a great many middle-of-the-road Americans—was ill suited to inspiring monetary support from traditional research or alcohol patrons (foundations, wealthy individuals, and, perhaps most of all, John D. Rockefeller Jr. and his philanthropic establishment). It happened that only the beverage industry—distilling interests in particular—were impressed enough by the new group's orientation to inquire about offering support. RCPA scientists initially shied away from such offers, fearing derived stigma and charges of biased research. Facing financial collapse, however, RCPA leadership—in a move I've elsewhere described in more detail and dubbed "Bowman's Compromise" (Roizen 1991a: chap. 8)—voted in October 1939 to accept beverage industry funding so long as all future research was devoted solely to the research problem posed by alcoholism.

RCPA Executive Committee Chair Karl M. Bowman pointed out in a memo to the group's membership (see Roizen 1991a: chap. 8) that traditional research focuses on alcohol—research, for example, addressing alcohol's relation to ill health, crime, and poverty—would inevitably generate results that would redound either to the benefit or to the disadvantage of the beverage industry. Especially beneficial outcomes would be problematic where industry funds had been used and would immediately raise suspicions of bias. Research focused on alcoholism, Bowman observed, harbored no such daunting prospect. This odd aspect of alcoholism-focused research, Bowman concluded, implied that the RCPA might ethically accept offers of financial support from major distillers so long as alcoholism provided the main focus of its future research agenda.

In 1942, the public relations specialist Dwight Anderson (1942) further developed this alcoholism theme by suggesting that the idea afforded an excellent symbol with which to clarify the differences between the new scientific approach to alcohol and the dry and wet mindsets. Two years later, in October 1944, E. M. Jellinek and Marty Mann sought to conjoin Anderson's disease concept focus with what the Yale science group regarded as an emergent human resource in AA's potential for rapid national growth. The Yale-based group's idea was to use the disease concept theme as a means for forming a national grassroots organization that would offer information and referral as well as advice to alcoholics and their families, and—not least important—would generate financial support for new scientific research. AA, and particularly the families of AA members, would thus provide a resource for the emergent alcohol science not unlike the relationship between the American Cancer Society (or other single-disease-advocacy organizations) and cancer research.[12]

Mann's NCEA began life as an integral and wholly supported element of the Yale science group—and would remain so for the first five years of its existence. But although Mann proved quite successful in broadcasting the disease concept message to what seemed an enthusiastic American audience, her enterprise was remarkably *un*successful in generating revenues for the parent Yale group, which led finally to NCEA's separation from Yale in 1949. But Mann persevered, and her search led to a denouement of sorts five years later when her disease theme was embraced by a very wealthy and generous patron—IBM-stock heir R. Brinkley Smithers—who welcomed the destigmatizing aspect of the disease conception in its own right and was willing generously to contribute to Mann's public education campaign as well as alcohol science on its behalf. Smithers's support ultimately consolidated a profound change that the disease concept campaign had wrought upon the alcohol science endeavor. Mann's great enterprise had in effect converted the disease-concept theme from a promotional slogan into a field-defining master concept—a transformation that in due course would expose the new movement to the liabilities of overselling the disease concept's scientific credentials and utility.

Virtually from the start, research directed at the disease idea proved unfavorable. Aside from two useful scientific contributions from E. M. Jellinek—a phased symptomatology for alcoholism (Jellinek 1952) and the prevalence estimation formula that bore his name (Jellinek 1951)—alcohol science created more difficulties than support for this central idea. Whether it was Howard W. Haggard's (1944) early empirical rejection of AA's allergy hypothesis, Joan K. Jackson's (1958) disconfirming analyses of the alcoholism syndrome, Leonard Syme's (1957) negative review of the prospects of discerning an alcoholic personality, or—perhaps most disturbing of all—the scientific evidence for the possibility of controlled drinking among alcoholics (see Roizen 1987), the alcohol science that blossomed into existence at least partly because of the success of the disease concept as a public relations enterprise proved hostile to the idea's various empirical test-points.[13] Even the Supreme Court—in *Powell v. Texas* (Fingarette 1970)—could not quite bring itself to ratify the disease concept when it got the opportunity in 1968.

By the mid-1970s the Jellinekian disease concept's scientific liabilities finally caught up with the modern alcoholism movement. A controversial report out of the RAND Corporation, based on outcome data drawn from the U.S. National Institute on Alcohol Abuse and Alcoholism's (NIAAA) demonstration treatment projects around the country, reported that a significant fraction of diagnosed alcoholics were drinking normally at follow-up (see Armor et al. 1976, Roizen 1977 and 1987). Growing unease over the conceptual and scientific liabilities of the traditional alcoholism diagnosis prompted Griffith Edwards and Martin Gross (1976) to fashion the diagnostic criteria for an "alcohol dependence syndrome"—which exercise, despite its own considerable conceptual and empirical difficulties, redefined alcohol addiction as the symbolic property of conventional psychiatry and distanced the diagnosis from the Jellinekian tradition of a discrete, freestanding disease entity with a determinate symptomatology and natural history.

In faraway Finland, a 1969 liberalization of alcohol control policies resulted before long in a sufficiently great increase in popular consumption that Finnish alcohol researchers took the occasion—in combination with a panel of World Health Organization experts—to question whether the alcoholism paradigm's well-known indifference to the alcohol consumption of nonalcoholics, regardless at what level, was truly warranted from a public policy standpoint. The resulting publication (Bruun et al. 1975) brought Sully Ledermann's (1956) provocative "single-distribution" model to greater scientific attention. In the United States, Don Cahalan and Robin Room (Cahalan 1970; Cahalan and Room 1974) began familiarizing a larger scientific audience with the theoretical and policy implications of new survey studies of drinking-related problems. By the mid-1970s, moreover, Room had begun publishing a series of pathbreaking essays articulating a new "problem minimization" perspective on alcohol-problems prevention (e.g., Room 1972 and 1974).[14]

Yet, just how much or how little impact the alcoholism paradigm's accumulating scientific woes may have had on the modern movement is not easy to say. The paradigm's troubles probably had more currency in the worlds of alcohol science and professionally offered treatment, where the disease concept had never held strong sway, than in the world of AA and AA-based lay treatment approaches, where alcohol science was regarded with no little suspicion in any case.

And what happened to Alcoholics Anonymous? It grew and grew (see Room and Greenfield 1993)—and, to a surprising extent, remained a separate and stable estate in the alcoholism social arena. But AA's diffusion also occasioned changes outside its institutional borders. Its famous twelve-step approach and disease language became secularized, routinized, and hypostatized in a derivative tradition of proprietary and state-sponsored treatment enterprises, which included by more recent decades a burgeoning involuntary treatment system—representing an increasing overlap between the substance abuse and the criminal justice establishments. AA's philosophy and institutional structure were also appropriated and adapted to many new territories of perceived excesses in American life—from narcotics addiction to overweight to excessive sexual activity or preoccupation. The result was a widening swath of cultural salience for AA, which in due course introduced more and more Americans to the group's program, special language, and moral coordinates. Widening relevance, however, also attenuated the original philosophy—comingling its thought in the public mind with ideas of codependency, "inner-child," and other personality-theory perspectives drawn from a crowded arena of pop psychology and "alternative medicine."

Rise of a Competitor Public Health Paradigm

Since about 1975, however, the alcohol-problems social arena has once again shown signs of reheating and repoliticization. Perhaps the defining characteristic of this transformation is a reproblematization of alcohol per se. The new trend is by no means a fait accompli, and significant segments of the alcohol-problems domain remain seemingly un- or little affected. For instance, biological and genetic alcoholism research and treatment outcome studies—research agendas still very much set by the modern alcoholism movement—remain high priorities at NIAAA (since its creation in 1970, the most important source of funding for U.S. alcohol research). The nation's alcohol treatment capacity actually expanded dramatically over the decade of the 1980s (see Weisner et al. 1995 and Schmidt and Weisner 1993) even as the nascent repoliticization emerged—though significant signs of trouble and contraction in treatment were evident by the commencement of the 1990s (U.S. House of Representatives 1991).[15]

Yet, clear evidence of the reheating change are visible at a number of levels—in popular culture, in the appearance of a new or redefined array of alcohol-related "moral entrepreneurial" interest groups, and in alcohol science and policy.[16] Though the proportions of drinkers and abstainers in the U.S. adult population (roughly a 2:1 ratio, respectively)—have remained relatively stable over at least the past fifty years (see Room 1991: table 10.1, p. 156), per capita alcohol consumption began a long, slow slide downward in the early 1980s—after a rising trend that increased consumption by about 40 percent from 1962 to 1980. National survey data indicate that interpersonal friction over alcohol went up instead of down in this post-1980 era of downward-drifting consumption (Room et al. 1991)—a finding suggesting that declining consumption may have co-occurred with an even greater relative tightening in drinking norms and associated informal social controls. Signs of a "new temperance" popular sensibility were palpable enough by the mid-1980s to be made the focus of cover stories or feature articles in *Time, Newsweek,* and *Fortune* as well as to draw op-ed or news analysis articles in major newspapers—e.g., in the *Washington Post* (Luks 1983), *Wall Street Journal* (Musto 1984; Heath 1985), *Los Angeles Times* (Keppel 1985), and *New York Times* (Goldberg 1987).[17]

The emergence of a new array of alcohol-related problems and associated moral-entrepreneurial interest groups also signaled the reheating shift[18]—as well as reflected something about the problem focuses, social roots, and value coordinates of the new sensibility. Fetal Alcohol Syndrome (FAS)—the first in the series of new alcohol-related preoccupations—was named in 1973 and came to wider public attention in a May 31, 1977, NBC Evening News broadcast with the introduction of "Melissa," a victim of the condition (Golden 1999). MADD (Mothers Against Drunk Driving), RID (Remove Intoxicated Drivers), SADD (Students Against Drunk Driving) and others (see Marshall and Oleson 1994: 55) launched grassroots campaigns against alcohol-impaired driving in the late 1970s and early 1980s. Though both FAS and MADD activists initially framed their public appeals in terms not uncongenial to the modern alcoholism movement—i.e., stressing the need for more social control of the alcoholic mother-to-be and the alcoholic driver (see Golden 1999, on FAS; Marshall and Oleson 1994, on MADD)—both endeavors' one-problem concentrations and get-tough dispositions were archetypal of the new sensibility.[19] The Center for Science in the Public Interest (CSPI), an offshoot of Ralph Nader's consumer movement, attacked alcohol in the consumerist idiom—promoting increased taxation, reduced alcohol advertising, and monitoring of the beverage industry—and gave rise to Project SMART (Stop Marketing Alcohol on Radio and Television) and CCAA (Citizens Coalition on Alcohol Advertising) (Pittman 1991).

Even the National Council on Alcoholism—Mann's celebrated champion of the modern alcoholism movement in an earlier day—redefined itself in preventionist terms over the 1980s, dropped industry representatives from its board, and in 1990 renamed itself the National Council on Alcoholism and Drug Dependence (NCADD) in tune with alcohol's redefinition as "a drug" and the trend toward conflating alcohol, illicit drugs, and tobacco into a single "substance abuse," "chemical dependence," or "ATOD" (alcohol, tobacco, and other drugs) problem definition. Alcoholics Anonymous may also have widened its salience into a more general asceticism in the American public's eye—thus repositioning the pioneer fellowship with a recast sensibility for the era of the new public health approach. Tightening norms around the American definition of moderate drinking also indirectly marginalized AA's traditional focus on the farthest reaches of the deviant drinking spectrum.

New temperance enterprises found support in a variety of institutional venues—e.g., in philanthropic foundations (e.g., the Robert Wood Johnson Foundation, the Pew Charitable Trusts, the Kaiser Family Foundation, the Rockefeller Family Foundation, and the Buck Fund [which supports the California-based Marin Institute]) (Mosher and Jernigan 1989), in the "parent's movement" (Marcus 1989), in anti-drug advertising, and in a school-based prevention movement. Even an emergent "adult children of alcoholics movement," sparked by Janet Woitiz's (1983) bestseller (Rudy 1991: 717), may be regarded as part of the wider ideological shift to the extent that its perspective tended to revilify the alcoholic—at least as parent.[20] Governmental and quasi-governmental agencies also played important and at times problematic roles in the movement's diffusion (see Mosher and Jernigan's [1989: 252–254] useful roster)—sometimes testing the boundary between the protection of the public's health and political advocacy. Alcohol's increasing salience to the discipline of public health, the growing frequency of alcohol-related articles in the *American Journal of Public Health*, and new alcohol-related deliberations of public health policy groups also bear note (Mosher and Jernigan 1989: 255). Not surprisingly, the emergence of anti-alcohol interest groups prompted the reinvigoration or creation of industry organizations aimed at countering alcohol-control measures and promoting their own approaches to prevention and research. These include the Distilled Spirits Council of the United States (DISCUS), the Beer Institute, the California Wine Institute, the American Vintners Association, Winegrape Growers of America, the Licenced Beverage Information Council, the Alcoholic Beverage Medical Research Foundation, the American Wine Alliance for Research and Education (AWARE), The Century Council, and the International Center for Alcohol Policy (see Marton, n.d.).

The appearance of new problem focuses—notably, those aiming popular attention and opprobrium toward FAS, drunk driving, youthful drinking, and alcohol and violence—redirected the nation's gaze away from the alcoholism movement's focus on the alcoholic. They also reshaped cultural perception of the alcohol-problems domain in subtle but important ways: (1) by redefining "the victim" in the alcohol-problems scenario—moving the victim definition from the misunderstood and wrongly stigmatized alcoholic (i.e., the deviant drinker him- or herself) to the innocent casualty of someone else's drinking (the neonate with FAS, the child run over by a drunken driver, etc.) ; (2) by removing the necessity of an intermediating presence of alcoholism in the causal chain leading to the alcohol problem—meaning that drinking per se, and not necessarily an alcoholic's drinking, might lie behind alcohol-related FAS, crash fatalities, and so on; and (3) by reproblematizing alcohol per se—thus granting new relevance to alcohol control measures as means for addressing such problems via public policy. At the symbolic level, the change was perhaps best reflected in the introduction of federally mandated warning labels in 1989 and the emergence of the problem-redefining slogan that "alcohol is a drug."

New scientific conceptualizations of alcohol problems also appeared on the scene—most coming from alcohol epidemiologists. These came in a number of conceptual forms deriving from different disciplinary or empirical backgrounds and thus afforded a variety of conceptual options rather than a single new paradigmatic monolith. Theory names such as the "disaggregation or alcohol-problems model," the "single-distribution model," the "agent-host-environment model," the "harm reduction model," and the "new public health approach" entered the alcohol policy discourse. Unlike the alcoholism model and focus that preceded them, however, these various designations were unlikely to be widely recognizable to the person on the street—for one reason, because they reflected conceptual developments taking place in a relatively obscure scientific context and had no great campaigning agency (no Marty Mann or NCA) to carry their new message to the public—though new volumes appeared from time to time aimed at a policy-making readership (e.g., Moore and Gerstein 1981, and Edwards et al. 1994). The new conceptualizations focused policy attention once again on drinking per se, and by extension on aggregate or per capita alcohol consumption. The change also expanded the orbit of new alcohol-related policy options—which now stretched beyond the expansion of alcoholism treatment and newly encompassed, for example: increased taxation, warning labels, reduced numbers of outlets, hours of sale, advertising restriction, counter-advertising, and server liability (for a fuller elaboration, see Walsh 1990; Mosher and Jernigan 1989).

Interestingly, the conceptual odyssey that took alcohol science from the "A" of an indifference to alcohol control policy to the "B" of a keen interest therein appears to have traveled across roughly four stages. Consider, for example, the paradigmatic salience of a control measure such as increased taxation: According to the alcoholism paradigm, taxation was a useless and even unjust exercise because its impact would be felt only by nonalcoholic drinkers—the ones who were not causing the alcohol-related problems. The very idea of alcoholism implied someone with a taste for alcohol that was unlikely to be tamed by mere tax increases. Other sorts of alcohol control policies were rendered similarly ineffectual by the alcoholism paradigm.

Next came renewed attention to Ledermann's (1956), single-distribution model—with its intriguing implication that the rigid J-like or lognormal shape of the distribution of consumption in human populations implied that downward shifts in mean consumption should also result in significant declines in the population's proportion of heavy drinkers. At this evolutionary stage—roughly where the argument lay when Bruun et al. (1975) was published—tax measures could be reintroduced into the orbit of legitimate alcohol policy options. Notice, however, that the policy's focus remained, as in the alcoholism model, on the heaviest alcohol consumers.

Next into the theoretical picture came the disaggregationist model, based on new survey studies of the distribution of drinking problems in general populations. Survey studies reported that alcohol-problems indicators did not comport well with the alcoholism paradigm. Instead of finding a few "alcoholics" who accounted for all the problems in the sample and left everybody else more or less problem-free, the survey data showed that lower-level problem scores were commonplace; indeed they were so common that reported problems among less-than-the-heaviest drinkers actually outnumbered those of candidates for the alcoholism label. This finding became known as the "prevention paradox" (Kreitman 1986)—because it suggested that rational prevention policy might actually aim its controlling efforts at the population layer that did not drink the most but nevertheless amassed the greatest aggregate number of alcohol problems. This implication was buttressed along the way by evidence that even the most serious alcohol-related tragedies (e.g., traffic fatalities) more often occurred among nonalcoholic than alcoholic drinkers. Notice that the rationale and focus for alcohol control policies have by now moved away from both the alcoholism model's and even the Ledermann (1956) model's concern with the heavy end of the drinking spectrum and have settled instead on drinkers in a middle range.

The final step in the progression came with the growing salience of dose-response curves—i.e., statistical profiles showing that increasing alcohol intake was associated with increasing levels of risk for one or another sort of alcohol-related problem. Curves with relatively steep slopes at low levels of alcohol intake suggested that drinking, if indulged in at all, should be kept to an absolute minimum. This was roughly where the argument had arrived with the publication of Edwards et al. (1994). The policy span traversed in this evolution is remarkable—taking public health conceptualization from virtual indifference to popular consumption levels to finding them a paramount concern. From the risk-factor vantage point, any alcohol whatsoever poured into the flow of national consumption represented a step upward along one or another risk curve for some drinker somewhere. Only the nettlesome existence of epidemiological evidence of moderate drinking's favorable mortality effects (see Nestle 1996) has kept alcohol's transit from covering the full symbolic distance from benign "social condiment" (as Haggard and Jellinek [1942] described it) to a toxic substance.

Why Transition from *Alcoholism* Back to *Alcohol*?

How should we account for the transition, or would-be transition, from the depoliticizing period of the modern alcoholism movement (1935–1975) to the repoliticized period of the new public health approach (1975–the present)? Interpretive possibilities abound. We might view the emergence of the new public health perspective as a kind of long overdue shucking-off of the early alcohol science's diversionary and self-promotion-based preoccupation with alcoholism—in other words, as a belated expression of alcohol science's intellectual and institutional maturity and independence.[21] Then again, it might be more accurate to characterize the shift as a sign of the new maturity and independence for alcohol *epidemiology*, in particular, and a telling measure of its differentiation from the rest of alcohol science via the development of its own distinctive theoretical perspectives and, perhaps, the emergence of an international scientific community of alcohol epidemiologists as facilitated by the Kettil Bruun Society.[22]

Then again, one might fashion recent changes into a scenario in which the alcoholism paradigm is deeply imperiled and on its way out in alcohol science as a whole—no longer fitted along a variety of dimensions to the nation's more problematized view of alcohol. And yet, it is also possible to read the same changes as suggesting that the alcoholism paradigm simply at some point accomplished its long-term purposes—persuading the public that alcoholism was an illness and building a substantial treatment and research establishment embodying those commitments—and thus obliged alcohol activists to move onward, and outward, into the prevention of a wider orbit of alcohol-rated problems. In this sense, the emergence of the public health paradigm may be regarded as an extension (rather than replacement) of the alcoholism paradigm's action agenda. Finally, it might even be suggested that the public health approach's return to (a) a focus on alcohol per se and (b) the promotion of political and popular responses reminiscent of a dry sensibility suggest the expiration of or a retreat from the post-Repeal dream that modern science would somehow find esoteric and powerful conceptual and policy tools for minimizing the nation's alcohol problems—both in terms of the societal burdens and the wasted and divisive political energy such problems formerly attracted.

The unlikely story of the modern alcoholism movement's origins, with its strongly social-constructionist character and flimsy science base, invites our attention to the relationship between alcohol science and the wider society. The alcoholism movement's story appears to have been framed in externalist social coordinates: notably, in the search for a depoliticized definition of the nation's alcohol problem, in the felt need to establish moderationist drinking norms (which the disease concept indirectly supplied by defining excessive drinking), and in the desire to test modern science's promise in addressing social problems. This social-constructionist account of the emergence and rise to hegemony of the modern alcoholism movement should probably in turn focus our attention on changes in the external social environment that may have occasioned the alcoholism movement's loss of influence and the rise of the new public health approach. The behind-the-scenes significance of the modern alcoholism movement's search for funding also quite naturally invites us to ask if and how the same needs may have remained one of the guiding forces in the emergence of the new public health approach. Room, for instance, characterized the impact of increasing governmental involvement in the alcohol social arena as a problem-widening force:

> As the [alcoholism] movement increasingly became a pressure group for greater governmental effort and funding for alcohol-specific programs, a strong interest developed in underlining alcohol's role in the broadest possible range of problems—particularly those in the forefront of public attention, which concomitantly often carry considerable stigma. To emphasize alcohol's role in a broad range of problems is seen as the primary mechanism for raising alcohol's position on the societal agenda, and also creates a larger negative balance in arguments for the cost-effectiveness of alcohol [programs]. . . . (Room 1978: 195)

At a deeper and more speculative level, research and policy attentions focused on per capita consumption may have had the symbolic subtext of proffering a subtle moral claim on a share of governmental revenues from alcohol sales, which revenues are of course geared to actual consumption. On the other hand—and in light of the alcoholism movement's money-strapped, Depression-era origins—it is also possible to view the new public health approach as in effect a liberation from the money-trail preoccupations of its paradigmatic predecessor. Perhaps time (and a future generation of alcohol historians!) will tell. The alcoholism-to-public-health shift roughly coincided with the commencement of the Reagan years and, as Wagner (1997) has argued, may best be regarded as part of the era's general cultural retrenchment. More recent public interest in the substance abuse problem domain also undoubtedly partly derived from the Soviet Union's collapse and the Cold War's demise—thus allowing for more national attention to be lavished on domestic issues.

The particular set of alcohol-related problem focuses that emerged over the 1970s and early 1980s also harbored important clues to the alcoholism-to-public health shift's social sources. MADD's angry acronym, for example, hints that the alcoholism paradigm may have failed to provide adequate social voice to the victims of alcohol-related harm and for the symbolic expression of their opprobrium or desire for vengeance.[23] Similarly, the emergence of public concern over youthful or underage drinking harbors hints at another kind of cultural failure for the alcoholism paradigm. Though the disease concept engendered an enormous growth in the American formal social control system for alcoholic drinking, it tended to domesticate all drinking by nonalcoholics (Levine 1978; Beauchamp 1980). This feature ill equipped the alcoholism paradigm for the crucially important symbolic task of providing adequate symbolic foundation for our long-standing proscription of youthful drinking. An alcoholism-paradigm-based school pedagogy (which finally became fully articulated and available in McCarthy and

Douglass's *Alcohol and Social Responsibility* [1949]) never fully fit that symbolic desideratum. Indeed, the alcoholism paradigm—with its "alcoholism can strike anyone," democratic ethos—also offered few cultural supports for the maintenance of traditional status-based differentiations in drinking norms. David Pittman (1991) shrewdly observed that the new temperance movement's targeting of drinking by youth, by pregnant women, by women in general, and by ethnic minorities in effect reestablishes a traditional hierarchy of status privilege regarding access to alcohol—i.e., by omission placing the white, middle-class male at the top of the status-access heap.

Ironically, the disappearance of drys from meaningful influence in the alcohol social arena also played a crucial part in the alcoholism-to-public-health transition. At least part of the alcoholism paradigm's rhetorical appeal lay in its capacity to steal the alcohol issue from the clutches of drys and their alcohol-focused temperance paradigm. One cannot read the literature of the early alcoholism movement without being struck over and over again by the persistent references to the fact that the new movement was neither dry nor wet, took no political stand on alcohol, etc.—and, in fact, that the new scientific approach was under siege by the old voices in the alcohol social arena (see, e.g., Haggard 1945). In this way, drys offered a valuable focus and counterpoint for the new alcoholism movement—allowing the new movement to define itself at least as much around what it *was not* as around what it *was*. Social movements benefit greatly by defining disfavored enemies, and the drys in particular fit this bill perfectly for the emergent alcoholism movement. But drys in due course disappeared from meaningful participation in the alcohol social arena—depriving the movement of a valued adversary and, ironically, thus also providing occasion for the reintroduction of a new dry sensibility.

This background change in the alcoholism movement's rhetorical environment had a number of important consequences. For one, it loosed the rhetorical brake that the alcoholism movement had imposed on itself in order that its problem claims not sound too alarmist, too problem-emphasizing, or, in a word, too dry. With drys gone from the scene, however, the alcoholism paradigm could enjoy a new freedom in expanding the borders of problem definition it proffered. David Robinson (1972) insightfully characterized this new expansionism as an alcoholism movement that had "lost control" over its own ideology in the early 1970s. Room (1978) saw quite clearly how the expanding perimeter of the problem domain claimed by the alcoholism movement also thinned the salience of the movement's paradigm, thus also inviting competing "post-addiction" models (as Harry Levine [1978] termed it) of a widening span of alcohol-related problems. Of course, a drying trend in popular sentiment might take a welcoming disposition to this newly reheated alcohol-problems rhetoric. Moreover (and as Room [1978] noted above), the emergence of NIAAA in the early 1970s shifted the payoff matrix strongly in favor of problem amplification—as NIAAA itself required as wide a problem domain as possible to justify its own budget and existence in the context of a great many other social problems competing for Congress's largesse.

Alcohol's shifting moral valence can have far-reaching consequences for problem definition, scientific conceptualization, and public policy. To take just a single example of this sort of connection in moral architecture, consider the link between alcohol's perceived moral valence and alcoholism treatment's perceived appropriateness as public policy. Alcohol, in the early post-Repeal era, was widely touted as a benign commodity, both in the popular (see, e.g., Wickware 1946)[24] and research literatures (see Katcher 1993). The alcoholism paradigm lent support to this moral coloration for alcohol by emphasizing that only the unfortunate few (i.e., the alcoholics) would get into trouble because of their drinking. These few, however, could thereupon lodge credible demands for benevolent handling (i.e., treatment) from society, given that the prevailing cultural definition of alcohol (i.e., as benign) had invited and justified their drinking in the first place. On the other hand, in a society where alcohol's moral valence grows darker—in other words, where "prevention" messages increasingly warn the drinker of a variety of untoward or dangerous consequences of drinking—the moral foundations for the provision of treatment are commensurately undercut. That which society warns one against is that which society also bears less responsibility to treat benevolently when citizens ignore the warning (Roizen 1993b). (It is interesting in this connection to see recent efforts to redefine the societal case for the provision of alcoholism treatment in terms of *minimizing alcoholism's social harm* [i.e., the harm alcoholics cause others] instead of *helping the alcoholic* [see McLellan et al. 1995]).

The old rhetorical themes of the modern alcoholism movement have undoubtedly lost a measure of their resonance in the new sociocultural environment. Heroic allusions to the all-conquering potentials of modern science and scientific method undoubtedly gained a hollower ring as promises of new scientific understanding—perhaps too often packaged in a "just around the corner" timescape—repeatedly proved overly optimistic. Any scientific enterprise—and especially science addressed to a social problem—lacking a core of powerful and esoteric theory will be specially susceptible to exogenous influences. Clearly, the alcohol-problems arena has shifted cultural ground in recent years—to cultural preoccupations with health-and-fitness, consumerism, the anti-drug and anti-tobacco enthusiasms, social order, and even, perhaps (as Pittman [1992] noted), the partial retrenchment of traditional status relationships. What was once a great call for the genius of modern science to shed a problem-fixing enlightenment and esoteric technological fix on America's alcohol problem has more recently seen alcohol shift to a lifestyle issue.

The new public health paradigm emerged from a number of credible scientific critiques of the alcoholism paradigm. There is a lively tradition of epidemiological thought and research behind the new paradigmatic contender—ranging from Ledermann's (1956) daring single-distributionist generalization, to Ole-Jorgen Skog's (1985) hypotheses about how the herd-like implications of Ledermann's model might be understood at the level of group and individual drinking behavior, to Cahalan and Room's (1974) survey-based effort to reinterpret problems that were once subsumed under the alcoholism label into a series of more discrete phenomena. The presence of this record of research enterprise gives the new public health paradigm a scientific "past" that the alcoholism paradigm in effect lacked in the 1930s and 1940s (putting aside a nascent psychiatric tradition of speculation on alcoholism). But even good scientific credentials do not, of course, obviate a connection between the scientific and the popular realms in the alcohol-problems domain. Perhaps a Darwinian image of that relation is best— namely, a view of alcohol science that sees it as providing society with an array of paradigmatic choices (and their associated symbolic subtexts) from which to select the emphases that best suit current concerns and trends. Such a perspective may help us understand how alcohol scientists can quite accurately see themselves as following out the dictates of a perfectly scientific, internally driven research course while an externalist perspective on that same science offers ample suggestion of social construction.

Forward into the Past?

The Sixty-Four-Dollar Historical Question in all this is of course: Should we regard the current drift away from the depoliticizing alcoholism paradigm and toward the new, repoliticizing public health approach as historical progress or retrogression? In other words, does the new paradigmatic direction truly offer a better understanding and truer grasp of something called our "alcohol problems"—at last cutting through the alcoholism paradigm's limits—or are we kidding ourselves, and is the new public health approach instead simply providing an apt scientific vehicle for a new dry-direction swing of the same old American historical pendulum, the one that that Fosdick and Scott (1933) and the early RCPA (Reports, 1938) warned us about? Does the public health approach really embody better science, or does it instead reflect a different value orientation to alcohol—one, say, more in tune with the times?

Remarkably, the alcohol-problems domain has by and large retained its cultural integrity over the years since Repeal: the alcoholism movement's designation of alcoholism as a disease did not result in alcoholism (much less alcohol problems) becoming melded into the nation's mainstream or general health and mental health institutional systems; similarly, a more recent designation of alcohol as a drug has not (yet, at least) resulted in alcohol becoming fully subsumed within a new "substance abuse" problem definition. Alcohol problems have for the most part remained a recognizably separate department of life and society over the full post-Repeal era. Jack Blocker (1989) has suggested that the post-Repeal era reflects another (the fifth, to be more precise) revolution in an ongoing saga in which temperance cycles move from benevolent to coercive dispositions before they restart.

We might also profitably characterize the story of alcohol's post-Repeal American experience as an exercise in historical forgetting in the nation's alcohol-problems social arena. That first generation of post-Repeal analysts I spoke of at the beginning of this essay set their sights on understanding and, ultimately, reducing the amplitude of the historical arc of the nation's dry-wet-dry pendulum swings. Two successive generations of alcohol imagery—the modern alcoholism movement and the new public health approach—have in effect displaced and downgraded that *historical* problem with their own particular problem focuses. To the extent that new-public-health advocates increasingly concentrate their analytical attentions once again on alcohol per se, their conceptual viewfinder returns the nation's attention to the very topic and problem-source claim that both post-Repeal depoliticizers and the alcoholism movement sought to displace and retire. If the new public health trend continues—with its risk-factor sensibility setting the empirical, analytical, and policy-related agenda—we as a nation will have less and less reason to expect a wider historical sensibility to emerge from the cultural elites to whom we entrust our best-informed thought on the matter. Not knowing whether what we're seeing of late in alcohol science, in alcohol-related interest groups, and in popular sentiment is progress or retrogression is partly a by-product of losing touch with the important place of the historical dynamic in our studies of this very American terrain. As the focus returns to alcohol per se, our scientific elite and interest groups tacitly invite us to a vision in which history and society represent little more than the battleground for a war between preventionist and industry perspectives on alcohol use. If that sounds familiar, well. . . .

References

Alcoholics Anonymous: The Story of How More Than One Hundred Men Have Recovered from Alcoholism. New York: World, 1939.

Anderson, Dwight. 1942. "Alcohol and Public Opinion." *Quarterly Journal of Studies on Alcohol* 3: 376–392.

Appleton, Lynn M. Personal communication (email), 17 April 1997.

Appleton, Lynn M. 1995. "Rethinking Medicalization: Alcoholism and Anomalies." Pp. 59–80 in Joel Best, ed., *Images of Issues: Typifying Contemporary Social Problems,* 2d ed. New York: Aldine de Gruyter.

Armor, D. J., J. M. Polich, and H. B. Braiker. 1976. *Alcoholism and Treatment.* Santa Monica: Rand Corporation.

Bacon, Selden D. 1967. "The Classic Temperance Movement of the U.S.A.: Impact Today on Attitudes, Action and Research." *British Journal of Addiction* 62: 5–18.

Beauchamp, Dan E. 1980. *Beyond Alcoholism: Alcohol and Public Health Policy.* Philadelphia: Temple University Press.

Bishop, Charlie, Jr., and Bill Pittman. 1994. *To Be Continued . . . The Alcoholics Anonymous World Bibliography 1935–1994.* Wheeling: The Bishop of Books.

Blocker, Jack S., Jr. 1989. *Cycles of Reform: American Temperance Movements.* Boston: Twayne.

Bruun, Kettil, et al. 1975. *Alcohol Control Policies in Public Health Perspective.* Helsinki: The Finnish Foundation for Alcohol Studies, 25.

Burnham, John C. 1968. "New Perspectives on the Prohibition 'Experiment' of the 1920s." *Journal of Social History* 2: 51–68.

Cahalan, Don. 1970. *Problem Drinkers: A National Survey.* San Francisco: Jossey-Bass.

Cahalan, Don, and Robin Room. 1974. *Problem Drinking among American Men.* New Brunswick, N.J.: Rutgers Center of Alcohols Studies, Monograph No. 7.

Clark, Norman C. 1976. *Deliver Us from Evil: An Interpretation of Prohibition.* New York: W. W. Norton.

Conrad, P., and J. W. Schneider. 1980. *Deviance and Medicalization: From Badness to Sickness.* St. Louis: Mosby.

Edwards, Griffith, et al. 1994. *Alcohol Policy and the Public Good.* Oxford: Oxford University Press.

Edwards, Griffith, and Martin Gross. 1976. "Alcohol Dependence: Provisional Description of a Clinical Syndrome." *British Medical Journal* 1: 1058–1061.

Fingarette, Herbert. 1988. *Heavy Drinking: The Myth of Alcoholism as a Disease.* Berkeley: University of California Press.

———. 1970. "The Perils of Powell: In Search of a Factual Foundation for the 'Disease Concept of Alcoholism'." *Harvard Law Review* 83: 793–812.

Fosdick, Raymond B., and Albert L. Scott. 1933. *Toward Liquor Control.* New York: Harper & Brothers.

Golberg, Howard G. 1987. "[Wine Talk column:] An Industry Symposium Grapples with the 'New' Temperance Movement." *New York Times,* 6 May, C16.

Golden, Janet. 1999. "'An Argument That Goes Back to the Womb': The Demedicalization of Fetal Alcohol Syndrome. 1973–1992." *Journal of Social History* 33, no. 2: 269–298

Gordon, Ernest. 1946. *Alcohol Reaction at Yale.* Francistown, N.H.: Alcohol Information Press.

Graham, John D. 1993. "Injuries from Traffic Crashes: Meeting the Challenge." *Annual Review of Public Health* 14: 515–543.

Gulick, Luther. "Foreword." Pp. vii–xx in Harrison and Laine, *After Repeal.*

Gusfield, Joseph R. 1996. *Contested Meanings: The Construction of Alcohol Problems.* Madison: University of Wisconsin Press.

———. 1967. "Moral Passage: The Symbolic Process in Public Designations of Deviance." *Social Problems* 15: 175–183.

H.W.H. [Haggard, Howard W.]. 1945. "The 'Wets' and 'Drys' Join against Science." *Quarterly Journal of Studies on Alcohol* 6: 131–134.

Haggard, Howard W. 1944. "Critique of the Concept of the Allergic Nature of Alcohol Addiction." *Quarterly Journal of Studies on Alcohol* 5: 233–241.

Haggard, Howard W., and E. M. Jellinek. 1942. *Alcohol Explored.* Garden City, N.Y.: Doubleday, Doran..

Harrison, Leonard V., and Elisabeth Laine. 1936. *After Repeal: A Study of Liquor Control Administration.* New York: Harper & Brothers.

Heath, Dwight B. 1985. "In a Dither about Drinking." *Wall Street Journal,* 25 February, 28.

"How Can I Help an Alcoholic?" Reprint: *Guideposts Magazine,* Carmel, N.Y., 1954. This item is available at the Library of The New York Academy of Medicine (and was kindly sent to me by Patricia E. Gallagher there).

Jackson, Joan K. 1958. "Types of Drinking Patterns of Male Alcoholics." *Quarterly Journal of Studies on Alcohol* 19: 269–302.

Jellinek, E. M. 1952. "Phases of Alcohol Addiction." *Quarterly Journal of Studies on Alcohol* 13: 673–684.

[Jellinek, E. M.] 1951. "Expert Committee on Mental Health, World Health Organization. Report of the first session of the Alcoholism Subcommittee. Annex 2: Jellinek estimation formula." (WHO Tech. Rep. Ser., No. 42) Geneva.

Johnson, Bruce Holley, 1973. "The Alcoholism Movement in America: A Study in Cultural Innovation." Ph.D. diss., University of Illinois at Urbana—Champaign.

Jones, Bartlett C. 1961. "The Debate over National Prohibition, 1920–1933." Ph.D. diss., Emory University.

Katcher, Brain, 1993. "The Post-Repeal Eclipse in Knowledge about the Harmful Effects of Alcohol." *Addiction* 88: 729–744.

[Keller, Mark], 1991. "Interview with Mark Keller." Pp. 57–66 in Griffith Edwards, ed., *Addictions: Personal Influences and Scientific Movements.* New Brunswick, N.J.: Transaction.

Keller, Mark. 1979. "Mark Keller's History of the Alcohol Problems Field." *The Drinking and Drug Practices Surveyor* 14: 22–28.

———. 1975. "Multidisciplinary Perspectives on Alcoholism and the Need for Integration: An Historical and Prospective Note." *Journal of Studies on Alcohol* 36: 133–147.

———. 1972. "On the Loss-of-Control Phenomenon in Alcoholism." *British Journal of Addiction* 67: 153–166.

Keppel, Bruce. 1985. "More Criticism, Less Consumption: Alcohol under Attack by 'New Temperance.'" *Los Angeles Times,* 8 September, sec. V, pp. 1, 5.

Kreitman, Norman. 1986. "Alcohol Consumption and the Preventive Paradox." *British Journal of Addiction* 81: 353–363.

Kurtz, Ernest. 2002. "Alcoholics Anonymous and the Disease Concept of Alcoholism." *Alcoholism Treatment Quarterly* 20, no. 3/4: 5–40. Co-published simultaneously in Thomas F. McGovern and William L. White, eds., *Alcohol Problems in the United States: Twenty Years of Treatment Perspective*. Binghamton, N.Y.: Haworth Press.

———. 1979. *Not-God: A History of Alcoholics Anonymous*. Center City, Minn.: Hazelden Educational Services.

Kyvig, David E. 1979. *Repealing National Prohibition*. Chicago: University of Chicago Press.

Ledermann, S. 1956. *Alcool, Alcoolisme, Alcoolisation*. Vol. 1. Paris: Presses Universitaires de France.

Levine, Harry Gene. 1978. "The Discovery of Addiction: Changing Conceptions of Habitual Drunkenness in America." *Journal of Studies on Alcohol* 39: 143–174.

Luks, Allan. 1983. "'Neo-Prohibition': Pouring Taxes and Stigmas on Drunks." *Washington Post*, 4 September, C1–2.

Mann, Marty. 1950. *Primer on Alcoholism*. New York: Rinehart.

Marcus, Carol. 1989. "The Parent's Movement: An American Grassroots Phenomenon." Pp. 133–138 in Stanley Einstein, ed., *Drug and Alcohol Use: Issues and Factors*. New York: Plenum.

Marshall, Mac, and Alice Oleson. 1996. "MADDer Than Hell." *Qualitative Health Research* 6: 6–22.

Marshall, Mac, and Alice Oleson. 1994. "In the Pink: MADD and Public Health Policy in the 1990s." *Journal of Public Health Policy* 15: 54–68.

Marton, Rebecca Murphy. "The Role of Government and the Non-Profit Sector in the New Temperance Movement." World Wide Web address or URL: <http://sunset .backbone.olemiss.edu/~phjuerg/newtemp.html>

McCarthy, Raymond, and Edgar M. Douglass. 1949. *Alcohol and Social Responsibility: A New Educational Approach*. New York: Thomas Y. Crowell Co. and Yale Plan Clinic.

McLellan, A. Thomas, et al. 1995. "Is Treatment for Substance Dependence 'Worth It?': Public Health Expectations, Policy-Based Comparisons." In *Training about Alcohol and Substance Abuse for All Primary Care Physicians*. New York: Josiah Macy Jr. Foundation.

Merz, Charles. 1930. *The Dry Decade*. New York: Doubleday, Doran.

Milam, J. R., and K. Ketcham. 1983. *Under the Influence: A Guide to the Myths and Realities of Alcoholism*. New York: Bantam Books.

Miller, William R., and Ernest Kurtz. 1994. "Models of Alcoholism Used in Treatment: Contrasting AA and Other Perspectives with Which It Is Often Confused." *Journal of Studies on Alcohol* 55: 159–166.

Moore, M., and D. Gerstein. 1981. *Alcohol and Public Policy: Beyond the Shadow of Prohibition*. Washington, D.C.: National Academy Press.

Mosher, James F., and David H. Jernigan. 1989. "New Directions in Alcohol Policy." *Annual Review of Public Health* 10: 245–279.

Musto, David F. 1984. "New Temperance vs. Neo-Prohibition." *Wall Street Journal*, 25 June, n.p.a.

Nestle, Marion. 1996. "Alcohol Guidelines for Chronic Disease Prevention: From Prohibition to Moderation." *Social History of Alcohol Review* 32–33: 45–59.

Pauly, Philip J. 1994. "Is Liquor Intoxicating? Scientists, Prohibition, and the Normalization of Drinking." *American Journal of Public Health* 84: 305–313.

Pittman, David J. 1991. "The New Temperance Movement." Pp. 775–790 in David J.

Pittman and Helene Raskin White, eds., *Society, Culture, and Drinking Patterns Reexamined.* New Brunswick, N.J.: Rutgers Center of Alcohol Studies.

Plaut, Thomas F. A. 1967. *Alcohol Problems: A Report to the Nation by the Cooperative Commission on the Study of Alcoholism.* New York: Oxford University Press.

"Reports: The Research Council on Problems of Alcohol." 1938. *Science* 88 (7 October): 329–332.

Roberts, Alasdair. 1994. "Demonstrating Neutrality: The Rockefeller Philanthropies and the Evolution of Public Administration, 1927–1936." *Public Administration Review* 54: 221–228.

Robinson, David. 1972. "The Alcohologist's Addiction: Some Implications of Having Lost Control over the Disease Concept of Alcoholism." *Quarterly Journal of Studies on Alcohol* 33: 1028–1042.

Roizen, Ron. 1994. "Norman Jolliffe, the Rockefeller Foundation, and the Origins of the Modern Alcoholism Movement." *Journal of Studies on Alcohol* 55: 391–400. Also see Roizen 1991a, chap. 4.

———. 1993a. "Paradigm Sidetracked: Explaining Early Resistance to the Alcoholism Paradigm at Yale's Laboratory of Applied Physiology, 1940–1944." Paper presented at the Alcohol and Temperance History Group's International Congress on the Social History of Alcohol, Huron College, London, Ontario, Canada, 13–15 May.

———. 1993b. "Merging Alcohol and Illicit Drugs: A Brief Commentary on the Search for Symbolic Middle Ground between Licit and Illicit Psychoactive Substances." Paper presented at the International Conference on Alcohol and Drug Treatment Systems Research, Addiction Research Foundation, Toronto, Canada, 18–22 October.

———. 1991a. "The American Discovery of Alcoholism, 1933–1939." Ph.D. diss., Sociology, University of California, Berkeley.

———. 1991b. "Redefining Alcohol in Post-Repeal America: Lessons from the Short Life of Everett Colby's Council for Moderation, 1934–1936." *Contemporary Drug Problems* 18: 237–272. Also see Roizen 1991a, chap. 3.

———. 1987. "The Great Controlled-Drinking Controversy." Pp. 245–279 in Marc Galanter, ed., *Recent Developments in Alcoholism*, vol. 5. New York: Plenum.

———. 1977. "Comment on the 'Rand Report.'" *Journal of Studies on Alcohol* 38: 170–178.

Room, Robin. 1991. "Cultural Changes in Drinking and Trends in Alcohol Problem Indicators: Recent U.S. Experience." Pp. 149–162 in Walter B. Clark and Michael E. Hilton, eds., *Alcohol in America: Drinking Practices and Problems.* Albany: State University of New York Press.

———. 1978. "Governing Images of Alcohol and Drug Problems: The Structure, Sources and Sequels of Conceptualizations of Intractable Problems." Ph.D. diss., Sociology, University of California, Berkeley.

———. 1974. "Minimizing Alcohol Problems." *Alcohol Health and Research World*, n.v.a. (Fall): 12–17.

———. 1972. "Notes on Alcohol Policies in the Light of General-Population Studies." *Drinking and Drug Practices Surveyor* 6: 10–12, 15.

Room, Robin, and Thomas Greenfield. 1993. "Alcoholics Anonymous, Other 12-step Movements and Psychotherapy in the US population, 1990." *Addiction* 88: 555–562.

Room, Robin, Tom Greenfield, and Connie Weisner. 1991. "People Who Might Have Liked You to Drink Less: Changing Responses to Drinking by U.S. Family Members and Friends." *Contemporary Drug Problems* 20: 499–519.

Rubin, Jay L. 1979. "The Wet War." Pp. 235–258 in Jack S. Blocker, Jr., ed., *Alcohol, Reform and Society: The Liquor Issue in Social Context*. Westport, Conn: Greenwood Press.

Rudy, David R. 1991. "The Adult Children of Alcoholics Movement: A Social Constructionist Perspective." Pp. 716–732 in David J. Pittman and Helene Raskin White, eds., *Society, Culture, and Drinking Patterns Reexamined*. New Brunswick, N.J.: Rutgers Center of Alcohol Studies.

Schmidt, L., and C. Weisner. 1993. "Developments in Alcoholism Treatment: A Ten Year Review." Pp. 369–396 in Marc Galanter, ed., *Recent Developments in Alcoholism*, vol. II. New York: Plenum.

Schrecker, Paul. 1948. *Work and History: An Essay on the Structure of Civilization*. Princeton: Princeton University Press.

Skog, O.-J. 1985. "The Collectivity of Drinking Cultures: A Theory of the Distribution of Alcohol Consumption." *British Journal of Addiction* 80: 83–99.

Star, Susan Leigh, and James R. Griesemer. 1989. "Institutional Ecology, 'Translations' and Boundary Objects: Amateurs and Professionals in Berkeley's Museum of Vertebrate Zoology, 1907–1939." *Social Studies of Science* 19: 387–420.

Syme, Leonard. 1957. "Personality Characteristics and the Alcoholic: A Critique of Current Studies." *Quarterly Journal of Studies on Alcohol* 18: 288–302.

"Temperance Union Is Seeking a New Image." *New York Times*, 26 August 1984, 34.

U.S. House of Representatives. 1991. "The Drug War in America: Crisis in Alcoholism Treatment." Subcommittee on Health and Long Term Care of the Select Committee on Aging. 102nd Congress, First Session.

Wagner, David. 1997. *The New Temperance: The American Obsession with Sin and Vice*. Boulder, Colo.: Westview Press.

Walsh, Diana Chapman. 1990. "The Shifting Boundaries of Alcohol Policy." *Health Affairs*, n.v.a. (Summer): 47–62.

Weisner, Constance, Thomas Greenfield, and Robin Room. 1995. "Trends in the Treatment of Alcohol Problems in the US General Population, 1979–1990." *American Journal of Public Health* 85: 55–60.

Wickware, Francis Sill. 1946. "Liquor." *Life*, 27 May, pp. 68+.

Wiener, Carolyn L. 1981. *The Politics of Alcoholism: Building an Arena around a Social Problem*. New Brunswick, N.J.: Transaction.

Woitiz, Janet. 1983. *Adult Children of Alcoholics*. Hollywood, Fla.: Health Communications.

Notes

The research and preparation of this essay have been supported by National Institute on Alcohol Abuse and Alcoholism Grant No. AA09623. I thank Kaye Fillmore for helpful comments on an earlier draft.

1. For the great Repeal debate, see especially Kyvig 1979, Jones 1960, and Merz 1930.

2. Compare Burnham's (1968) trenchant analysis of the notion of national prohibition as a "failed experiment."

3. Recall, however, that World War I actually energized the dry campaign for the Eighteenth Amendment. (See Jay L. Rubin's [1979] superb study of the differences between the First and Second World Wars re alcohol in America.)

4. Later better known as the National Council on Alcoholism (NCA), and, since 1990, named the National Council on Alcoholism and Drug Dependence (NCADD).

5. AA has generated an immense historical literature, much of it by grateful members (see Bishop and Pittman 1995). The definitive history remains Ernest Kurtz's *Not-God* (1979).

6. The literature on the history of post-Repeal alcohol science is very thin—comprising two dissertations (Room 1978 and Roizen 1991a), Carolyn Wiener's monograph (1981), and a variety of reminiscences by the long-time *Journal of Studies on Alcohol* editor, Mark Keller (e.g., 1975, 1979, and 1991). Bruce Holley Johnson's (1973) dissertation remains the starting place for historical examination of the combined AA-and-science movement.

7. The search for a neutralist idiom for the post-Repeal handling of alcohol-related problems and alcohol's symbolic relegitimation began even before Repeal itself, with the "dilutionist" and "carbon monoxide" metaphor offered to Congress by Yale physiologist Yandell Henderson (see Pauly's [1994] wonderful account).

8. See Keller's (1972) commentary on this curious "capitulation" of alcoholism's treatment to AA (also Room 1978: 138–139).

9. Lynn M. Appleton (1995) has recently offered a welcome and on-target critical review of the tendency among American sociologists (as in Conrad and Schneider's *Deviance and Medicalization* [1980]) to regard the modern alcoholism movement's disease campaign as a paradigmatic case of medicalization; "folk medicalization," argues Appleton, offers a better characterization of the actual social history. My sense is that the disease-alcoholism case requires that the issue of "medicalization" be distinguished from that of "scientific ownership" and the growth of research. For the depoliticizing aspects of disease designations, see Gusfield 1967—made conveniently available in Gusfield's (1996) more recent book.

10. Interestingly, Miller and Kurtz (1994) have recently pointed out that the most familiar and standard form of the disease concept (as available, for instance, in Ketchum and Morris [1985]) was neither borrowed from nor central to AA thought. Kurtz (1979: 212ff.) noted that AA co-founder William Wilson harbored serious reservations about the disease idea and has recently published an article (Kurtz 2002) developing and strenthening the point that AA is not so closely linked to the disease concept as many have thought. Jack Alexander's AA article appeared in the *Saturday Evening Post*'s 1 March 1941 issue.

11. I thank Caroline Acker for pointing out this very useful paper.

12. Incidentally, this is one of the reasons Mann's (1950) book on alcoholism addressed its narrative primarily to the families of alcoholics. A "Q&A" format article, titled "How can I help an alcoholic?" (1954)—and undoubtedly authored by Mann herself—describes the NCA in just these terms. The response to a question about the differences between AA and NCA reads in part: "The National Committee on Alcoholism, on the other hand, is a voluntary health agency, like the TB Association, the American Cancer Society, the American Heart Association. Its Board members are professional and lay citizens, mostly non-alcoholic."

13. Fingarette (1988) brought this nether side of science's relationship to the disease concept to a wider public audience.

14. If I may add a personal observation at this point: In retrospect, these various happenings certainly both undercut the reigning alcoholism paradigm and laid important foundations for the emergent competitor paradigm, the "new public health approach" (NPHA). Nevertheless, if you had asked me in 1975—or, for that matter, in 1980 or even

in 1985—whether they represented serious challenges to either public perceptions or interest-group conceptualization of alcohol problems, I would have most assuredly said "no." The public health perspective was—as far as I knew, at least—a little-known challenger deriving from a little-known research specialty (survey research, redubbed "alcohol epidemiology" in part to improve its appearance in a field dominated by a medical or quasi-medical sensibility) whose main purpose was to waffle on the important question it was ostensibly sent forth to answer: how many alcoholics were there? I recently asked my good friend and colleague Robin Room whether he had the feeling when Bruun et al. (1975) was being published that a shift in alcohol's popular paradigm was under way; he said "yes." This means I (who did not travel much or discourse with the alcohol research elite) and Robin (who did) might be separated by as much as fifteen years (1975–1990) in our estimate of when the NPHA began to exert a meaningful influence on policy and popular thought and practice.

15. I thank Lynn Appleton (personal communication) for pointing out this reference and providing a useful synopsis of proprietary alcoholism treatment's troubled condition by the early 1990s.

16. Alcohol and temperance historians have themselves been going through a revisionist transformation in recent years—sparked by John C. Burnham's (1968) seminal paper and carried forward in the work of Clark (1976) and Blocker (1989).

17. The *Time* article appears in the 20 May 1985 issue; the *Newsweek* article in the 31 December 1984 issue; and the *Fortune* article in the 18 March 1985 issue (S. P. Sherman, "America's New Abstinence," n.p.a.). See Room 1991: 149 et seq., for more coverage of shifts in popular culture. Sociologist David Wagner's (1997) insightful monograph, *The New Temperance: The American Obsession with Sin and Vice*, locates changing sentiment toward alcohol within a broader new asceticism comprehending illicit drugs, sexuality, smoking, and fitness.

18. Walsh (1990: 59–60) notes the remarkable frequency of such changing interest-group ownership of the alcohol problem in our U.S. historical experience.

19. Marshall and Oleson (1994) examined the internal evolution of MADD from an alcoholism to a NPHA focus. Musto (1984) early on placed the new anti-drunk-driving initiative at the heart of the new temperance shift. His *Wall Street Journal* discussion began: "For the second time in this century, a serious, effective and popular temperance movement is gathering force in this country. However, it is not a campaign for prohibition but for realistic efforts to curb the harmful effects of alcohol, especially the damage wrought by drunk drivers" (n.p.a.). Interestingly, the new grassroots movement was not sparked by increases in the nation's traffic crash fatality rate. In fact, this rate (per 100 million vehicle miles driven) has fallen steadily and substantially over the entire post–World War II era, and enjoyed a particularly sharp decline in the 1970s (see Graham 1993: 515–516), i.e., in the decade just before MADD et al. came on the scene. According to Graham's five-year averages (as offered in his table 1), the U.S. traffic fatality rate (per 100 million miles of travel) fell by 20.62% from 1965–69 (during which period, the rate was 5.47) to 1970–74 (4.34) and by another 21.57% from 1970–74 to 1975–1979 (3.40). The rate of decline slowed in the 1980s: from 11.47% from 1975–79 to 1980–84 (3.01) and 11.87% from 1980–84 to 1985–89 (2.47).

20. Rudy (1991: 717) cites a *Newsweek* cover story (18 January 1988) on the adult children of alcoholics movement; the associated illustration offered "a shattered family portrait with a spilled booze bottle and the caption 'Growing Up with Alcoholic Parents Can Leave Scars for Life.'"

Notable for their absence from the list of active players are the Woman's Christian Temperance Union (WCTU) and the Anti-Saloon League, though occasional newspaper reports note an approving disposition toward the new temperance by group representatives (e.g., "Temperance Union," 1984).

21. Such a view might draw a relatively straight developmental line from Haggard and Jellinek's (1942) articulation of an "alcohol-problems" paradigm, through the reassertion of that scientific perspective in the Cooperative Commission report published the mid-1960s (Plaut 1967), to the recent ascendancy of the new public health approach. It is interesting in this connection, however, that the original formulation of an "alcohol problems" perspective at Yale was intended to take attention away from a preoccupation with alcohol per se—which preoccupation was viewed as a dry fixation. The plural form, "alcohol problems," was deliberately intended as marking a sharp divide from the dry focus on "the alcohol problem," a singular form and focus on alcohol (see Roizen 1993a). Indeed, a striking historical puzzle and clue may be said to reside in the fact that current advocates of the new disaggregationist, public health approach wish to restore alcohol per se to causal significance in "alcohol-related problems" whereas the early formulators of the "alcohol-problems perspective" at Yale had quite the opposite goal in mind— namely, distancing alcohol problems from alcohol per se!

22. The Kettil Bruun Society for Social and Epidemiological Research on Alcohol— named for the Finnish sociologist Kettil Bruun (1924–1985), who pioneered many areas of alcohol social research—serves several purposes in the international alcohol epidemiological community, including sponsoring an annual meeting.

23. For an analysis of MADD's emotional topography, see Marshall and Oleson (1996).

24. Wickware (1946: 68), in *Life*, for example wrote: "Of the estimated 50,000,000 drinkers in the U.S., all but a fraction use alcohol moderately and more or less regularly because it makes them feel better and more appreciative of themselves and their fellows. It also gives them better appetites, since it is an excellent condiment. Taken for purposes of social relaxation or as a gustatory adjunct, alcohol never has damaged anyone. Even when taken in fairly large amounts over a long period of time, the purely physical effects of alcohol by itself are almost negligible."

II

Alcohol and Narcotics in the American Context

"I Was Addicted to Drinking Rum"

Four Centuries of Alcohol Consumption in Indian Country

PETER C. MANCALL

"I WAS ADDICTED to drinking rum and would sometimes get quite intoxicated." So wrote the Pequot memoirist William Apess in his account of his own life, published in 1829. Apess was no casual observer of Native American society. During the antebellum period he wrote five books, thereby becoming the most prominent American Indian author of his age. It is thus significant that Apess told his readers that he was abused by relatives (notably his grandparents) when they were intoxicated, and that he saw all around him the signs of despair caused by the liquor trade. In his opinion, the responsibility for the domestic violence committed by inebriated men and women lay not with the drinkers themselves but with the non-Indians who had supplied them with alcohol. "My sufferings were through the white man's measure," he wrote in 1833, "for they most certainly brought spirituous liquors first among my people. For surely no such sufferings were heard of, or known among our people, until the burning curse and demon of despair came among us: Surely it came through the hands of the whites."[1]

Apess's views on abusive drinking provide an ideal opening for understanding the troubled relationship between Indians and alcohol in America. His writings seem to confirm the opinion of scores of other Native Americans in North America during the eighteenth and nineteenth centuries: alcohol was for many Indians a "deadly *beson*"—as the Delaware Prophet Neolin put it in 1737—a deadly medicine that wreaked havoc on Indian communities.[2] Like Apess, many native commentators blamed European colonists for alcohol's costs. "[H]ere is One thing You Yourselves are to Blame very much in," the Catawba headman Hagler told North Carolina officials in 1754, "That is You Rot Your grain in Tubs, out of which you take and make Strong Spirits You sell it to our young men and give it them, many times," leading them to lives of criminality and early death.[3] This logic persisted, in modified form, well into the twentieth century. As John Trudell, chairman of the American Indian Movement, wrote in 1975, alcohol had been used by Europeans to weaken the native peoples of North America and undermine any collective solidarity they needed to prevent the conquest of the continent. "This is how our land has been taken from us," he declared, "because every time an inhuman act has been committed against our people, we have been disoriented with the madness of alcohol."[4]

"Sufferings" unleashed by the "white man," "deadly medicine" provided by colonists who "rotted their grain" to produce a substance that led to criminality and mortality, "the madness of alcohol"—such accounts suggest that liquor has always been a menace everywhere it has appeared in Indian country. Yet was this always the case? As twentieth-century anthropologists and historians pointed out, many Native Americans did not drink to the point of intoxication every time alcohol was available. Many Indians have found benefits in drinking, even if they have realized at the same time that excessive drinking has often led to a variety of social pathologies and individual ailments.[5] Further, long-term studies of some indigenous communities have revealed that the allure of alcohol has been stronger for certain members of communities—notably young men—than for others; over time, many Native Americans who acknowledged abusive drinking early in their lives eventually decided to abstain from alcohol.[6] Specific groups, including Navajo communities, Omahas, and the Nebraska Winnebago, also developed effective means for controlling abusive drinking; such indigenous anti-alcohol movements have at times included use of sweat lodges or the adoption of the so-called Peyote Road in which admitted alcohol abusers ingest a mild hallucinogen and establish links with traditional cultural values, including a recognition of the destructive consequences of alcohol use.[7]

What emerges, then, are two distinct strands in the existing literature. On the one hand are numerous accounts, especially evident in the surviving documentary evidence, of the social pathologies that alcohol seemingly has caused in native communities since the early seventeenth century. If alcohol had never been introduced into these societies, so this logic suggests, Indians would have been better able to respond to the threats posed by colonization. Such historical accounts are supported by numerous recent studies analyzing the deleterious impact that abusive drinking has had on native communities.[8] On the other hand are accounts of twentieth-century scholars, notably anthropologists, whose observations of particular communities suggest that it is a great overstatement to presume that alcohol has inevitably been a destructive force.[9] In addition to these two distinct academic interpretations there exists a veneer of popular culture in which all Indians are assumed to be potential alcoholics waiting to plunge into inebriated despair: Indians' fates, seemingly determined by genetic predispositions, are beyond their control in this ongoing tragedy. Such notions have contributed to the creation of reservation, state, and federal laws regulating the sale of alcohol to Native Americans.[10]

To make sense of these interpretations we need to set out, at least briefly, the larger historical context. From contact until the present day, there has been no single Native American response to liquor. Consumption patterns have differed over time and by region and even within specific communities; gender and age have played a role in drinking patterns.[11] Patterns of alcohol-related illness, disease (including fetal alcohol syndrome), and trauma are not uniform within the Native American population today, and were not in past centuries either.[12]

But for all the historic differences that exist, Americans—Indian and non-Indian—have shared a history that has shaped both Indian drinking patterns and commentary on Indian drinking. Most of the native peoples of North America, with the notable exception of Native Americans in the American Southwest and modern-day Mexico, possessed no alcoholic beverages before the sixteenth century.[13] Native Americans who lacked long traditions of producing and consuming fermented beverages thus encountered alcohol at the same time that they had to cope with the other dislocating forces associated with European colonization: the appearance in North America of people wanting to take control of Natives' lands; of European livestock trampling Indians' fields; of Catholic and Protestant missionaries determined to control Natives' souls; and, most significant of all, of Eurasian microbes that devastated Native American peoples who possessed no acquired immunities to them. It is impossible to overstate the significance of these developments, which led, by 1800 or so, to population loss estimated at 90 percent for the Western Hemisphere and the radical shrinking of lands still in the control of Indians. Although that demographic catastrophe is no longer taking place—Indian populations stabilized around 1900 and have demonstrated substantial growth since[14]—modern American Indian history (and the history of alcohol consumption by Native Americans) is inexplicable if we forget the long-term context.

"Intemperance Is Now Doing Its Work Rapidly."

In colonial America, as the surviving documentary record has made abundantly clear, many Native Americans craved alcohol. Some eastern woodlands Indians, for whom the only purpose of consuming alcohol was to become intoxicated, did all they could to get drunk. As the Choctaw headman Captain Houma informed a British official in July 1778, rum was "like a Woman—when a man wanted her—and saw her—He must have

93

her."[15] Many Indians condemned the seemingly insatiable thirst of members of their communities yet recognized an inability to remain sober.

Indian drinking in early America led to all sorts of maladies, ranging from the physiological effects of drinking binges (including, according to the documentary record, miscarriages)[16] to domestic violence, poverty, and death. One missionary in New France in 1693 claimed that "[a]ll the pregnant women addicted to drink either abort or seek abortions, or cause the death of their infants by throwing them into the fire, or the waters, or by bashing them against the ground; or [infants also die] because their [mother's] milk dries up or is spoiled by the repeated use of eau-de-vie and they can provide no substitute for it."[17] Throughout the eastern woodlands, such complaints, which first surfaced in the late seventeenth century, were all too common. When liquor was present, some Native Americans had to have it, regardless of the consequences. Those complaints persisted through the eighteenth century, surfacing in treaty discussions through the revolutionary period and into the nineteenth century.[18]

During the nineteenth century, ethnographers and physicians who traveled around the United States studying Indians made similar reports. The historian John Halkett wrote in 1825 about the "fit of insanity" produced when Native Americans drank, a "frenzy" that sent the inebriated into violent rampages.[19] Many Onondagas, the physician Jonathan Kneeland reported in 1865, drank themselves into stupors and died from exposure, drowning, or in fights; "many have been the victims of diseases from their habits of surfeiting and drunkenness, alternating with hunger and want, who would else have recovered."[20] Indians in Washington Territory fared no better. "Intemperance is now doing its work rapidly," a physician reported to the American Medical Association in 1857. "Alcohol, with syphilis, will soon complete the work of the destroyer, and the Red man, in this territory too, will be extinct."[21] Iroquois Indians, one physician reported at mid-century, fell ever deeper into poverty when fur traders offered alcohol for pelts, and depletion of the animals forced the Indians off their lands.[22] Into the twentieth century, Indians unable to control their thirst for alcohol continued to indulge in pathological behavior. Inability to remain temperate landed some in the Asylum for Insane Indians at Canton, South Dakota; alcohol abuse led others to violence and murders.[23]

By the late nineteenth century some Native Americans were so bent on becoming inebriated that they drank, as an emissary of the Indian Rights Association reported in 1884, "alcoholic drugs, like cologne, painkiller, essence of lemon, etc. .... for their intoxicating effect with disastrous results."[24] Greater availability of alcohol in the twentieth century has not prevented

Indians from consuming noxious potions such as "Montana Gin," a combination of cleaning fluids and other poisons. "I wasn't a social drinker, that's for sure," a forty-year old Cree woman from northern Manitoba recently told an interviewer. "I drank heavy. I drank every day. I drank without eating. I drank Lysol, Listerine, rubbing alcohol, after-shave. You name it, I drank them all. I seen people drinking them. . . . You mix Lysol with water, lukewarm water. You mix it in a big bottle. That tall part, whatchyoucallit, the foam, that has to settle down first, then you drink it. [Rubbing alcohol] and after-shave you just put cold water. Listerine is 22 percent alcohol, you drink it straight."[25] Clinical observations from the mid-to-late twentieth century suggest that alcohol-related pathologies are more prevalent in Native American communities than for the mainstream population, though one long-term study of three Navajo populations reveals that such figures need to be set into their proper context.[26]

These brief observations have an underlying theme: the Indians involved and those who observed them shared the belief that the consumption of alcohol destroyed individual lives. Many recognized as well that alcohol abusers often acted in concert with others, thereby destabilizing families and even entire communities. But if the participants recognized the destructive consequences of their behavior, why did they continue to drink? Were many, as Apess claimed for himself, addicted to alcohol?

"The Chronic Habit of Intoxication"

Americans did not fear addiction to alcohol until Anthony Benezet and Benjamin Rush defined the problem in late eighteenth-century Philadelphia.[27] But though colonial Americans lacked a notion of addiction to alcohol, they nonetheless recognized that some men and women in their own society could not repress their thirst for intoxicating beverages. During the colonial period, when average consumption of distilled beverages was approximately seven shots per day, abusive drinking was typically linked to moral failings: drunkenness, scorned in the Bible, was a sign of degeneration and savagery. Those who could not control their desires were denied entry into public houses, thereby not only losing the opportunity for tippling but also forfeiting the personal and political relationships that so often formed in such buildings.[28]

After Rush had identified the potential dangers of addiction to alcohol, nineteenth-century physicians proposed multiple causes for alcohol abuse, all of which pointed toward addiction. Some physicians contended that pregnant mothers who drank or mothers who drank while they were nursing their babies passed on a desire to drink to their offspring, and that desire developed into addictive behavior over time.[29] One physician insisted in 1833 that "the habitual use of spirituous liquors in a vast proportion of the cases in which it is now drunk, is the result of the medical use [of alcohol], by which men are taught that it is not only right to drink rum, but useful and necessary."[30] Others asserted that vices picked up in childhood transformed otherwise normal people into addictive drinkers.[31] One physician in the late 1880s told an audience at the American Social Science Association that addictions to drinking could be caused by heredity, injuries to the brain, or perhaps unexplainable social cycles in which "inebriety moves in waves or currents, or, like an epidemic, prevailing for a time with great activity, then dying away; both endemic and epidemic at times."[32]

Yet while some argued for the heritability of addiction to alcohol, others contended that no such trait could be inherited and that the causes of such drinking lay elsewhere.[33] One physician in 1866 offered up perhaps the most intriguing cause of addictive drinking: "I firmly believe that the chronic habit of intoxication," claimed Forbes Winslow, "has often owed its origin to the powerful influence which certain anacreontic drinking songs [have] exercised over the minds of weak persons who unfortunately are too prone, if associating with what is termed 'good company' and 'jolly fellows,' to indulge in vinuous excesses."[34]

Such medical opinions shaped popular conceptions of alcohol use, especially during times of widespread fears of moral turpitude associated with alcohol use. Such opinions also shaped interpretations of Indian drinking.

"An Inherent Appetite for Alcohol"

It is a matter of some importance that non-Indians speculated about the causes of alcohol abuse among Native Americans long before Rush appeared on the scene. Colonists believed that they understood why Indians consumed alcohol as they did. Indians could not control their drinking because they were uncivilized; lacking the trappings of European society, they never mastered what James Boswell had termed "the art of getting drunk."[35] The prevailing logic of that age dictated that Indians were unable to control their thirst. As the British governor of West Florida wrote in 1774, "It is often bad enough with white people when they are [drunk]. . . . [W]hat can be expected from Indians who are void of sense and reason, born in savage ignorance and brought up in the same way, but the most barbarous and inhuman murders and cruelties?"[36] Having failed to convert to English ways, Indians in the late colonial period retained what one governor of Virginia termed "the passion for strong drink."[37] In these accounts, Indians' seeming addiction to alcohol was but one notable symptom of their real affliction: they had not yet cast off what European observers routinely termed their "savage" ways.

Colonists frequently lamented that Native Americans needed to become civilized; without civilization, Indians would remain dangerous presences, always lurking (in the minds of colonists) in dark forests on the edges of colonial settlements. Periodic stories of Indian raids on outlying villages, whether these involved actual widespread destruction of a community (as in Deerfield, Massachusetts, in 1704) or the more common taking of hostages, circulated repeatedly in early America in a genre of literature known as "captivity narratives." These narratives, which were the most popular form of reading material in the colonies, more widely read than any other books besides the Bible, informed colonists' sensibilities about Indians. Native Americans, whether they were Creek or Choctaw, Iroquois or Abenaki, were always a threat, in large measure because they were, as the French put it, *sauvage*. Colonists feared Indians because Indians acted without reason, and when they did so colonial writers of captivity narratives or newspaper articles were on the spot to recount the horrors to a captive public.[38]

It was in this context that the notion of Indian addiction to alcohol emerged. That stereotype was based on the seeming irrationality of Indian actions. If alcohol had sedated Native Americans and made them calm, the stereotype might not have developed. But alcohol, so many observers claimed, led Indians to lessen their customary inhibitions and to act out in destructive ways. Lurid accounts of alcohol-induced orgies spiced the literature circulating about Native Americans, and some of those accounts appeared in the work of natural historians who saw it as their duty to report the eccentricities of the Indians they witnessed.[39] Drunken Indian men and women ran naked through the streets of Quebec in the late seventeenth century, one missionary reported, and "in full view and to the great horror of all, they engaged openly, like wild beasts, in shameful and unspeakable acts with one another."[40] In most surviving accounts, alcohol was a problem because inebriated Indians acted with reckless abandon.

In this world, the notion of addiction thus became a central concern. Colonists, that is, believed that Indians did things under the influence of alcohol because they could control neither the urge to become intoxicated nor their inebriated desires. Significantly, many Indian commentators agreed. One group of Mohawks told the superintendent of Indian Affairs in the mid-eighteenth century that the liquor trade kept "them all poor, makes them Idle and Wicked, and if they have any Money or Goods they lay it all out on Rum, it destroys Virtue and the progress of Religion amongst us."[41] A Tuscarora chief offered a similar depiction of Indians spending all their resources on alcohol, apparently unable to resist its lure. He noted that his people had recently moved northward from Carolina "where they lived but wretchedly being Surrounded by white People, and up to their Lips in Rum, so that they cou'd not turn their heads anyway but it ran into their mouths. [T]his made them stupid, so that they neglected Hunting, Planting, &c."[42]

These complaints, and many others, testify to the common belief that Indians craved alcohol and their pursuit of it would be their ruin. The Native American spokesmen used not the language of addiction per se, but a language of despair. Their argument was based on their belief that Indians were so enamored of alcohol that they needed help to end their abuse of it. From such a perspective it made sense to appeal to colonial authorities and to seek their assistance in ending what was, throughout British America, an illegal business.

Nineteenth-century observers often shared the cultural assumptions of earlier witnesses, but they tended to accept that Indian drunkenness had physiological as well as cultural causes. Indians suffered because of "[t]heir propensity to intoxication," as one observer termed it in 1824.[43] An anonymous correspondent for the *Boston Medical and Surgical Journal* wrote in the mid-1840s that when Indians could get liquor "the thread of life is made shorter still, and the red man, perhaps the best specimen of physical development on the globe, struggles with death like a giant contending for his rights, ..." But Indians succumbed, the report continued, because the drinker "falls in the vigor of his age, a sacrifice, often, to an appetite he neither understands nor attempts to control."[44] Another observer noted in 1840 that Indians had a "*morbid thirst* for strong drink" and that Europeans took advantage of them as a result.[45] Or, as an observer of the San Carlos Agency in Arizona reported in the early 1880s, Indians "like the people of all races, [seem] to have [an] inherent appetite for alcohol."[46] When Charles Meserve toured Indian communities and Indian schools in the Southwest at the end of the nineteenth century, he reported to the Indian Rights Association that whiskey was "one of the worst enemies that the Indian meets, and it has more to do with preventing him from advancing along the road to civilization than anything else."[47] Observers tended to believe that Indians were "addicted to drunkenness" as one reported in 1908, or had acquired a habit "at an early age" which "seems more completely to control the individual than it does with any other people."[48] In 1883 one observer, who claimed he was one-eighth Wyandot, offered up his assessment in doggerel: "Our tribe it never run saloons," he began,

Called whisky shops and gambling rooms.
Fire-water maddens nerve and brain,
And causes bitter woe and pain. . . .
You gave us fire-water bad,
And set our warriors raving mad.[49]

The historical record provides ample documentation of behavior that led observers to argue that many Native Americans were addicted to alcohol. But not all Indians were abusive drinkers; many in the past remained sober, and abstainers and former drinkers each battled the alcohol trade, recognizing that the only way to stop the horror was to prevent liquor from entering their community, or at least limiting the opportunity for its consumption.[50] But the stereotype drawn in the colonial period has nonetheless survived: Indians cannot hold their liquor because they are somehow predisposed toward becoming addicted to alcohol.

Contemporary evidence at times supports the notion that Indian alcohol abuse has stemmed from innate tendencies and that some Native Americans have developed a physical dependence on alcohol.[51] Testimony from drinkers suggests that some individuals at least have a seemingly insatiable desire for alcohol. "Yeah, I do have a drinking problem," reported one forty-three-year-old Yupik in Alaska. "I like the taste of booze and when I start, I can't stop. If I want to stop drinking, I can stop *for two weeks*. But to go *completely dry*, to *never, ever* drink again—I won't say that. I *can't say, I won't say*, that I will stop for ever and ever because I know I won't. I can't stop forever. I enjoy it too much."[52] If one person's testimony is insufficient, then we can resort to surveys, including a 1980s survey of Navajo Indians in which two-thirds of the women and over one-half of the men contended that they had a "physical weakness" for alcohol that non-Indians lacked; older members of the community held that belief in even higher numbers than younger men and women.[53] As psychiatrists have recently reported, in some Indian communities three-fourths of the men and over one-third of the women have been diagnosed at some point as abusive drinkers, a pattern suggesting widespread social pathology.[54]

Rejecting the cultural chauvinism of early modern Europeans, we twenty-first-century observers no longer speak of the causes for alcohol abuse in terms of civilization and savagery. Instead, those who believe that Indians are more prone to alcohol abuse employ more scientific language: Native Americans' problems with alcohol stem from a genetic predisposition to abuse alcohol. There is only one difficulty with this construct: most recent inquiries into the genetics of alcoholism and American Indians' particular susceptibility to alcohol abuse reveal that Indians have no peculiar inherited traits leading them to become alcoholics. Some individuals, perhaps some

Indians, seem to possess an inherited predisposition toward alcohol abuse. But there is no convincing evidence suggesting that Indians as a group are more inclined to possess these traits than the general American population.[55]

LOOKING AT THE historical record now, we cringe at the arrogant assumptions of some earlier observers. We reject any notion that Indians could not control their drinking because they were *sauvages*. We reject the assumptions of earlier observers who believed that Indians needed to progress along a certain predetermined route to civilization. But like those earlier commentators, observers today, Indian and non-Indian, seek to discover why many Native Americans drank alcohol when the effects were often disastrous. That is, we seek explanations for baffling episodes of self-destructive behavior and its causes.

What can we learn from a historical approach to the concept of Indian drinking? The historical record and clinical studies reveal an enduring and widespread belief that American Indians were somehow often addicted to alcohol. That belief, which has been shared over the centuries by Indians as well as non-Indians, has not changed, despite the fact that there is abundant evidence that points to widespread variation in drinking patterns in Native American communities.[56] Instead, what has changed in those centuries is the vocabulary used to describe apparently addictive behavior.

There seems little doubt that alcohol caused problems in many Native American communities because members of those communities suffered as a result of the expansion of European and Euro-American culture and society. Times of widespread social change have seemingly always led some individuals to seek ways of coping that have included ingestion of mood-altering substances when such substances were available. It should be remembered that Europeans, who possessed alcohol for centuries and had developed rules for its consumption, at times suffered from periods of widespread alcohol-related problems. For example, the "gin craze" in mid-eighteenth-century England, the social phenomenon that led the social reformer and artist William Hogarth to create those enduring images of "Beer Street" and "Gin Lane," occurred in part because of wider availability of more potent alcohol during the early phases of the industrial revolution; when the English and other Europeans drank more alcohol then, they were apparently seeking in liquor an escape from the disorienting social changes of their everyday lives.[57] In the Western Hemisphere, even many Native Americans who possessed fermented beverages before the arrival of Europeans and had long-established rules for proper consumption suffered greater rates of alcohol abuse during the colonial period when traditional rules limiting consumption broke down and Europeans sold more potent alcohol to

Indians.[58] Given the fact that colonization of Indian country in territory that became the United States led to constant pressures on Native Americans, it is perhaps not at all surprising that some Indians who never had alcohol earlier chose to drink, even to abuse alcohol, in an effort to escape the physical, spiritual, and mental turmoil that were part of the colonization process. Their societies were, after all, under siege, and alcohol seemed to promise a means of temporary escape. History, not biology, holds the key to understanding Native American drinking patterns, just as history, not biology, holds the key to understanding alcohol consumption in other American populations. Rather than relying on genetic explanations for alcohol abuse among American Indians, which is perhaps just another manifestation of the age-old European notion that non-Western peoples are somehow deficient when compared to Westerners, it makes more sense to place alcohol use among Native Americans into its proper historical context.

William Apess thought he was addicted to drink, but he realized that his situation was complex. His autobiographical writings from the early nineteenth century seem to confirm the idea that the psychiatrist and anthropologist Arthur Kleinman has suggested: illness has cultural and historical, as well as physiological, causes.[59] The historical record, which contains stories of seemingly inescapable descents into alcohol abuse as well as accounts of recovery from destructive behavior, reaffirms the complexity of drinking experiences in Indian country.[60] The accounts we inherit from the past remind us that human behavior springs from the context and contingency of events and not, as some would prefer, from innate, racially determined predispositions. To understand alcohol use in Indian country, present-day observers would do well to recognize that tragedies associated with such use have no single cause. Alcohol problems among Native Americans, like those experienced by other Americans, need to be understood in their complexity, and understood as well as the product of specific historic circumstances.

Notes

1. Barry O'Connell, ed., *On Our Own Ground: The Complete Writings of William Apess, A Pequot* (Amherst: University of Massachusetts Press, 1992), 31–32, 121.

2. "Narrative of a journey, made in the year 1737, by Conrad Weiser . . . ," trans. H. H. Muhlenberg, in *Historical Society of Pennsylvania Collections* I: 117; Peter C. Mancall, *Deadly Medicine: Indians and Alcohol in Early America* (Ithaca: Cornell University Press, 1995), esp. 85–100, 110–129.

3. William L. Saunders, ed., *Colonial Records of North Carolina*, 10 vols. (Raleigh, 1885–1890), 5:143.

4. John Trudell, "Before We Were 'Indians,'" *Akwesane Notes* 7 (1975): 38–39.

5. Nancy O. Lurie, "The World's Oldest Ongoing Protest Demonstration: North

American Indian Drinking Patterns," *Pacific Historical Review* 40 (1971): 311–332; R. C. Dailey, "The Role of Alcohol among North American Indian Tribes as Reported in the *Jesuit Relations*," *Anthropologica* 10 (1968): 45–59; Wesley R. Hurt and Richard M. Brown, "Social Drinking Patterns of the Yankton Sioux," *Human Organization* 24 (1965): 222–230; Jack O. Waddell, "For Individual Power and Social Credit: The Use of Alcohol among Tucson Papagos," *Human Organization* 34 (1975): 9–15; Susan M. Stevens, "Alcohol and World View: A Study of Passamaquoddy Alcohol Use," *Journal of Studies on Alcohol*, supp. 9 (1981): 122–142; Christian F. Feest, "Notes on Native American Alcohol Use," in Pieter Hovens, ed., *North American Indian Studies: European Contributions* (Gottingen: Edition Herodot, 1981), 201–222; Jack O. Waddell, "Malhiot's Journal: An Ethnohistoric Assessment of Chippewa Alcohol Behavior in the Early Nineteenth Century," *Ethnohistory* 32 (1985): 246–268; Mancall, *Deadly Medicine*, 63–84.

6. See Stephen J. Kunitz and Jerrold E. Levy, *Drinking Careers: A Twenty-Five Year Study of Three Navajo Populations* (New Haven: Yale University Press, 1995), passim.

7. Roberta L. Hall, "Alcohol Treatment in American Indian Populations: An Indigenous Treatment Modality Compared with Traditional Approaches," in Thomas F. Babor, ed., *Alcohol and Culture: Comparative Perspectives from Europe and America*, Annals of the New York Academy of Sciences 472 (1986): 168–178; Thomas W. Hill, "Peyotism and the Control of Heavy Drinking: The Nebraska Winnebago in the Early 1900s," *Human Organization* 49 (1990): 255–265; Benson Tong, "Allotment, Alcohol, and the Omahas," *Great Plains Quarterly* 17 (1997): 27–29; Kunitz and Levy, *Drinking Careers*, 27–28, 110–117. For an account of one Native American who abused alcohol until he adopted the peyote road, see Paul Radin, *The Autobiography of a Winnebago Indian* (1920; rpt. New York: Dover, 1963).

8. See, among other sources, Ronald J. Lamarine, "Alcohol Abuse among Native Americans," *Journal of Community Health* 13 (1988): 143–155; Patricia Silk-Walker et al., *Alcoholism, Alcohol Abuse, and Health in American Indians and Alaska Natives*, American Indian and Alaska Native Mental Health Research, monograph no. 1 (1988), 65–67; Margaret M. Cortese et al., "High Incidence of Invasive Pneumococcal Disease in the White Mountain Apache Population," *Archives of Internal Medicine* 152 (1992): 2277–2282; L. P. Peterson et al., "Pregnancy Complications in Sioux Children," *Obstetrics and Gynecology* 64 (1984): 519–523; Albert DiNicola, "Might Excessive Maternal Alcohol Ingestion during Pregnancy Be a Risk Factor Associated with an Increased Likelihood of SIDS?" (letter), *Clinical Pediatrics* 24 (1985): 659; John C. Godel et al., "Smoking and Caffeine and Alcohol Intake during Pregnancy in a Northern Population: Effect on Fetal Growth," *Canadian Medical Association Journal* 147 (1992): 186–187; Ronet Bachman, "The Social Causes of American Indian Homicide as Revealed by the Life Experiences of Thirty Offenders," *American Indian Quarterly* 15 (1991): 471, 484–487; Richard Goodman et al., "Alcohol and Fatal Injuries in Oklahoma," *Journal of Studies on Alcohol* 52 (1991): 156–161; J. David Kinzie, "Psychiatric Epidemiology of an Indian Village: A 19-Year Replication Study," *Journal of Nervous and Mental Disease* 180 (1992): 33–39; Philip A. May, "Suicide and Self-Destruction among American Indian Youths," *American Indian Culture and Research Journal* 1 (1987): 62; Margaret M. Gallaher et al., "Pedestrian and Hypothermia Deaths among Native Americans in New Mexico," *JAMA* 267 (1992): 1345–1348; Lawrence R. Berger and Judith Kitzes, "Injuries to Children in a Native American Community," *Pediatrics* 84 (1989): 152–156; Carol Lujan et al., "Profile of Abused and Neglected American Indian Children in the Southwest," *Child Abuse and Neglect* 13 (1989): 449–461; Robert Blum et al., "American Indian–Alaska Native Youth Health," *JAMA* 267 (1992): 1642–1643; David

Swanson et al., "Alcohol Abuse in a Population of Indian Children," *Diseases of the Nervous System* 32 (1971): 835–842; and Duane Sherwin and Beverly Mead, "Delirium Tremens in a Nine-Year-Old Child," *American Journal of Psychiatry* 132 (1975): 1210–1212. For an overview of nineteenth-century patterns see William E. Unrau, *White Man's Wicked Water: The Alcohol Trade and Prohibition in Indian Country, 1802–1892* (Lawrence: University Press of Kansas, 1996).

9. For one important work taking this approach see Mary Douglas, ed., *Constructive Drinking: Perspectives on Drink from Anthropology* (Cambridge: Cambridge University Press, 1987); for the uses of alcohol in Indian communities in early America see Mancall, *Deadly Medicine*, 63–84.

10. An excellent review of the legal issues can be found in Robert J. Miller and Maril Hazlett, "The 'Drunken Indian': Myth Distilled into Reality through Federal Indian Alcohol Policy," *Arizona State Law Journal* 28 (1996): 223–298.

11. For discussions of gender, with particular reference to the drinking practices of Native American women, see Joy Leland, "Women and Alcohol in an Indian Settlement," *Medical Anthropology* 2, no. 4 (Fall 1998): 85–119, and Kunitz and Levy, *Drinking Careers*, 117–127; for a more general discussion of clinical studies relating to women's drinking, see especially Frances K. Del Boca, "Sex, Gender, and Alcoholic Typologies," in Thomas F. Babor et al., eds., *Types of Alcoholics: Evidence from Clinical, Experimental, and Genetic Research*, Annals of the New York Academy of Sciences 708 (1994): 34–48.

12. See Dwight B. Heath, "Alcohol Use among North American Indians: A Cross-Cultural Survey of Patterns and Problems," *Research Advances in Alcohol and Drug Problems* 7 (1983): 343–396; Philip A. May, "The Epidemiology of Alcohol Abuse among American Indians: The Mythical and Real Properties," *American Indian Culture and Research Journal* 18, no. 2 (1994): 121–143; Stephen J. Kunitz and Jerrold E. Levy, "Changes in Alcohol Use among Navajos and Other Indians of the American Southwest," in Roy Porter and Mikuláš Teich, eds., *Drugs and Narcotics in History* (Cambridge: Cambridge University Press, 1995), 133–155. For differing rates of FAS see Myra Shostak and Lester B. Brown, "American Indians' Knowledge about Fetal Alcohol Syndrome: An Exploratory Study," *American Indian Culture and Research Journal* 19, no. 1 (1995): 45–46.

13. For pre-contact drinking see Jack O. Waddell, "The Use of Intoxicating Beverages among Native Peoples of the Aboriginal Greater Southwest," in Jack O. Waddell and Michael W. Everett, eds., *Drinking Behavior among Southwestern Indians: An Anthropological Perspective* (Tucson: University of Arizona Press, 1980), 1–32.

14. See Russell Thornton, *American Indian Holocaust and Survival: A Population History since 1492* (Norman: University of Oklahoma Press, 1987).

15. Report of the Proceedings of the Honble. Charles Stuart . . . on his late Tour thro the Choctaw Nation . . . , July 1, 1778, Colonial Office [CO] 5/78, Records of the British Colonial Office, Class 5 (microfilm), reel 7.

16. Henry Flower, *Observation on the Gout and Rheumatism . . . with a Short Account of Some Medicines, and Ways of Curing Diseases, used by the Native Indians* (London, 1766), 10.

17. "Mémoire touchant l'yvrognerie des sauvages en Canada," 1693, Archives des Colonies C 11, 12–2, f. 380–387, Archives Nationale, Paris.

18. See Peter C. Mancall, "Men, Women, and Alcohol in Indian Villages in the Great Lakes Region in the Early Republic," *Journal of the Early Republic* 15 (1995): 425–448.

19. John Halkett, *Historical Notes Respecting the Indians of North America, with Remarks on the Attempts Made to Convert and Civilize Them* (London, 1825), 165.

20. Jonathan Kneeland, "On Some Causes tending to Promote the Extinction of the Aborigines of America," *Transactions of the American Medical Association* 15 (1865): 255.

21. Geo. Suckley, "Report on the Fauna and Medical Topography of Washington Territory," *Transactions of the American Medical Association* 10 (1857): 214–215.

22. Thomas Stratton, "Contribution to an Account of the Diseases of the North American Indians," *Edinburgh Medical and Surgical Journal* 71 (1849): 281–282.

23. H. R. Hummer, "Insanity among the Indians," *Proceedings of the American Medico-Psychological Association*, 68th annual meeting (1912): 454–455, 459; Thomas Williamson, "Diseases of the Dakota Indians," *Minnesota Medicine* 23 (1940): 725.

24. S. C. Armstrong, *Report of a Trip made in behalf of The Indian Rights Association to some Indian Reservations of the Southwest* (Philadelphia, 1884), 19. Fears about the addictive potential of such substances were not confined to reports about Native Americans; see The American Association for the Study and Cure of Inebriety, *The Disease of Inebriety from Alcohol, Opium, and Other Narcotic Drugs, Its Etiology, Pathology, Treatment and Medico-Legal Relations* (New York: E. B. Treat, 1893; rpt. New York, 1981), 383–385.

25. Brian Maracle, ed., *Crazywater: Native Voices on Addiction and Recovery* (Harmondsworth, England: Penguin, 1994), 75.

26. T. Kue Young, *The Health of Native Americans: Toward a Biocultural Epidemiology* (New York: Oxford University Press, 1994), 200–204; Levy and Kunitz, *Drinking Careers*, 168–191.

27. Harry G. Levine, "The Discovery of Addiction: Changing Conceptions of Habitual Drunkenness in America," *Journal of Studies on Alcohol* 39 (1978): 143–174; Roger E. Meyer, "The Disease Called Addiction: Emerging Evidence in a 200-year Debate," *Lancet* 347 (1996): 162–166.

28. See William Rorabaugh, *The Alcoholic Republic: An American Tradition* (New York: Oxford University Press, 1979); Richard P. Gildrie, "Taverns and Popular Culture in Essex County, Massachusetts, 1678–1686," *Essex Institute Historical Collections* 124 (1988): 158–185; Peter Thompson, "'The Friendly Glass': Drink and Gentility in Colonial Philadelphia," *Pennsylvania Magazine of History and Biography* 113 (1989): 549–573; Paton Yoder, "Tavern Regulation in Virginia: Rationale and Reality," *Virginia Magazine of History and Biography* 87 (1979): 259–278; David Conroy, "Puritans in Taverns: Law and Popular Culture in Colonial Massachusetts, 1630–1720," in Susanna Barrows and Robin Room, eds., *Drinking: Behavior and Belief in Modern History* (Berkeley: University of California Press, 1991), 29–60; Conroy, *In Public Houses: Drink and the Revolution of Authority in Colonial Massachusetts* (Chapel Hill: University of North Carolina Press, 1995).

29. See anon., "The Nursing Mother," *The Medical Brief . . .* 21 (June 1893): 786; William Sweetser, *A Dissertation on Intemperance* (Boston, 1829), 56–57; Dr. Thomeuf, "Alcoholism in Women," *Wood's Medical and Surgical Monographs* 7 (New York, 1890): 352.

30. David M. Reese, *A Plain and Practical Treatise on the Epidemic Cholera . . .* (New York, 1833), 88–89.

31. See, e.g., Franklin D. Clum, *Inebriety: Its Causes, Its Results, Its Remedy*, 3d ed. (Philadelphia, 1892), 61.

32. T. D. Crothers, *The Disease of Inebriety and Its Social Science Relations* (n.d., n.p.), 4–6.

33. Leslie E. Keeley, *The Non-Heredity of Inebriety* (Chicago, 1896).

34. Forbes Winslow, *On Uncontrollable Drunkenness Considered as a Form of Mental Disorder* (London, 1866), 21–22.

35. James Boswell, *Life of Johnson* (1791), ed. R. W. Chapman (Oxford: Oxford University Press, 1980), 1022.

36. Peter Chester to the Earl of Dartmouth, 4 June, 1774, in K. G. Davies, ed., *Documents of the American Revolution, 1770–1783*, 21 vols. (Shannon, Ireland: Irish University Press, 1972–1981), 8: 128.

37. William Nelson to the Earl of Hillsborough, 5 February, 1771, in Davies, ed., *Documents of the American Revolution*, 3: 37.

38. Captivity narratives came, essentially, in two genres: those produced by former captives who were "redeemed" (rescued) and could thus write about their captivity from the safety of colonial society; and those produced by friends and family members of captives who either could not be rescued or who refused to leave families and communities into which they had been adopted. The literature on these narratives and what they meant is extensive; for a start see Alden T. Vaughan and Edward W. Clark, eds., *Puritans among the Indians: Accounts of Captivity and Redemption, 1676–1724* (Cambridge: Harvard University Press, 1981); James Axtell, "The White Indians of Colonial America," *William and Mary Quarterly*, 3d ser., 32 (1975): 55–88; June Namias, *White Captives: Gender and Ethnicity on the American Frontier* (Chapel Hill: University of North Carolina Press, 1993); and John Demos, *The Unredeemed Captive: A Family Story from Early America* (New York: Alfred Knopf, 1994).

39. See, eg., Nicholas Denys, *The Description and Natural History of the Coasts of North America* (1672), trans. William F. Ganong (Toronto, 1908), 448–450; Bernard Romans, *A Concise Natural History of East and West Florida* (1775; rpt. New Orleans: Pelican Pub. Co., 1961), 55; William Bartram, *Travels through North and South Carolina, Georgia, East and West Florida, the Cherokee Country, the Extensive Territories of the Muscogulges, or Creek Confederacy, and the Country of the Choctaws* (1791; rpt. New York: Penguin, 1988), 214–215.

40. "Mémoire touchant l'yvrognerie des sauvages," f. 388.

41. E. B. O'Callaghan, ed., *Documentary History of the State of New York*, 4 vols. (Albany, 1849–1851), 2: 592.

42. "Journal of Indian Affairs," in James Sullivan et al., eds., *The Papers of Sir William Johnson*, 14 vols. (Albany: University of the State of New York, 1921–1965), 12: 273–275.

43. Samuel Morewood, *An Essay on the Inventions and Customs . . .* (London, 1824), 190–191.

44. [Anon.], "Indian Medicines," *Boston Medical and Surgical Journal* 30 (1844): 183–184.

45. Ralph B. Grindrod, *Bacchus: An Essay on the Nature, Causes, Effects, and Cure, of Intemperance* (New York, 1840), appendix.

46. Frederick Lloyd, *Special Report on Indians at San Carlos Agency* (n.p., [1883?]), 6.

47. Charles F. Meserve, *A Tour of Observation among Indians and Indian Schools in Arizona, New Mexico, Oklahoma, and Kansas* (Philadelphia, 1894), 7–8. Henry R. Schoolcraft, in his massive study of American Indians in the early nineteenth century, also wondered why Indians drank and if any solutions could be found that would enable them to learn "the principles of temperance" that presumably existed in civilized societies; see Schoolcraft, *Information respecting the History, Condition, and Prospects of the Indian tribes of the United States*, 4 vols. (Philadelphia, 1851–1854), esp. 1: 547, 557. Schoolcraft, it should be noted, was inclined to blame non-Indians for Indians' failings in this respect, but the tone of his inquiries suggested that he endorsed existing notions that Indian drinking represented an impediment to Native Americans' cultural progress.

48. Aleš Hrdlička, *Physiological and Medical Observations among the Indians of the Southwestern United States and Northern Mexico* ... (Washington: Govt. Print. Off., 1908), 35–36; A. D. Lake, "The Civilized Indian, His Physical Characteristics and Some of His Diseases," *New York Medical Journal* 75 (1902): 407.

49. J. I. Lighthall, *The Indian Household Medicine Guide*, 2d ed. (Peoria, Ill., 1883), 34.

50. See Mancall, *Deadly Medicine*, 110–129.

51. For example, Levy and Kunitz report that some alcohol abusers among the Navajo suffer withdrawal symptoms when they do not drink; see *Drinking Careers*, 103–105.

52. Maracle, ed., *Crazywater*, 85.

53. Philip A. May and Matthew B. Smith, "Some Navajo Opinions about Alcohol Abuse and Prohibition: A Survey and Recommendations for Policy," *Journal of Studies on Alcohol* 49 (1988): 324–334.

54. See Kinzie, "Psychiatric Epidemiology of an Indian Village." It should be pointed out that Indian drinking patterns could be self-reinforcing: once young Native Americans observed the ways that others drank, they learned that normal imbibing typically led to intoxication. In other words, their "drunken comportment" was the result of social forces, not biological imperatives. Such an argument, first proposed to explain that Indians learned destructive drinking practices from non-Indians, has recently been employed to describe patterns of drinking within Navajo society. For the model see Craig MacAndrew and Robert B. Edgerton, *Drunken Comportment: A Social Explanation* (Chicago: Aldine, 1969); for the Navajo see Levy and Kunitz, *Drinking Careers*, esp. 231. See Mancall, *Deadly Medicine*, 252–253, for a critique of this aspect of *Drunken Comportment* and how it relates to the initial introduction of alcohol into Native American societies.

55. See David Goldman et al., "DRD$_2$ Dopamine Receptor Genotype, Linkage Disequilibrium, and Alcoholism in American Indians and Other Populations," *Alcoholism: Clinical and Experimental Research* 17 (1993): 199–204; Lynn Bennion and Ting-Kai Li, "Alcohol Metabolism in American Indians and Whites: Lack of Racial Differences in Metabolic Rate and Liver Alcohol Dehydrogenase," *New England Journal of Medicine* 294 (1976): 9–13; Bernard Segal and Lawrence Duffy, "Ethanol Elimination among Different Racial Groups," *Alcohol* 9 (1992): 213–217; Arthur W. K. Chan, "Racial Differences in Alcohol Sensitivity," *Alcohol and Alcoholism* 21 (1986): 93–104; Lillian E. Dyck, "Absence of the Atypical Mitochondrial Aldehyde Dehydrogenase (ALDH$_2$) Isozyme in Sasketchewan Cree Indians," *Human Heredity* 43 (1993): 116–120; and Shi-Han Chen et al., "Gene Frequencies of Alcohol Dehydrogenase$_2$ and Aldehyde Dehydrogenase$_2$ in Northwest Coast Amerindians," *Human Genetics* 89 (1992): 351–352. For summaries of this literature see May, "Epidemiology of Alcohol Abuse," 124; Mancall, *Deadly Medicine*, 6–7.

56. As Kunitz and Levy have noted, "The heterogeneity of Navajo drinking styles should help put to rest the idea that the high rate of alcohol abuse among certain Indian populations is biologically based." See *Drinking Careers*, 230.

57. George Vaillant, *The Natural History of Alcoholism* (Cambridge, Mass.: Harvard University Press, 1983), 99–100.

58. This phenomenon is clearest in Mexico; see William B. Taylor, *Drinking, Homicide, and Rebellion in Colonial Mexican Villages* (Stanford: Stanford University Press, 1979), 28–72.

59. Arthur Kleinman, *Patients and Healers in the Context of Cultures* (Berkeley: University of California Press, 1980). See also Stephen J. Kunitz, *Disease and Social Diversity:*

The European Impact on the Health of Non-Europeans (New York: Oxford University Press, 1994).

60. For one notable eighteenth-century description of an Indian alcohol abuser over-coming his "addiction" to drink see [Jean] Bossu, *Travels through that part of North America formerly called Louisiana*, trans. John Reinhold Forster, 2 vols. (London, 1771), I: 117–123; for twentieth-century accounts see Maracle, ed., *Crazywater*, 149–214.

Reforming Drunkards in Nineteenth-Century America

Religion, Medicine, Therapy

KATHERINE A. CHAVIGNY

HISTORIANS OF ADDICTION argue that at the end of the eighteenth century a new medical interpretation of habitual drunkenness began to challenge prevailing moral and religious views. Here and there, American drunkards reported an inability to stop drinking despite their desire to do so. Observers began to speculate that these habitual drunkards, rather than simply being vicious or sinful, suffered from an alcohol-induced disease that resulted in a progressive loss of control over drinking. This disease concept of addiction went on to inform the ideology of nineteenth-century temperance reform and prompted new medical therapies for the inebriate. The only treatment for the drunkard, who was now perceived as a victim of the disease, was total abstinence from all intoxicating beverages. Moderation was no remedy: A single drink could rouse the imperious appetite. Temperance advocates recommended total abstinence for all Americans. Alcohol was too addicting to be trifled with.[1]

Drunkards reporting on their experiences helped birth the disease concept of addiction. Yet evidence for the further dissemination of that concept in nineteenth-century America has been drawn almost entirely from the literature produced by temperance reformers and doctors. The tacit assumption is that professionals and reformers more or less directly translated those popular experiences into ideology and prescriptions. Lately the reported experiences of drunkards have received some scholarly attention, but as a vernacular literary genre, rather than for the popular ideas about addiction and treatment within them.[2] In fact, the narratives of reformed drunkards were at least as widely heard as speeches as read as texts. Moreover, these narrators had a few ideas about the malady from which they suffered, ideas that they translated into action. These men (women were supporters, but rarely confessed to alcohol addiction) agreed with temperance reformers about the universally addicting properties of alcohol. As might be expected, however, they declared that the addicted could be made sober again, and offered themselves as examples. But they rarely claimed to be suffering from a disease, and they routinely rejected medical assistance on the grounds that such treatment relied on enforced rather than voluntary abstinence. They reformed, they said, with the help of the pledge, sympathetic fellowship, and the grace of God.

The views of reformed drunkards appear to constitute a minor variation of the disease concept of alcohol addiction already studied by addiction historians. Yet this variation was widely promulgated throughout nineteenth-century America, largely by reformed drunkards willing to make public their experiences in speeches and in autobiographical writing. The tradition of collective confession and experience-telling (as it was commonly called) arose in the antebellum period, partly to redress the neglect of drunkards by established temperance reformers. The revival of 1857–1858 transformed experience-telling into a religious therapeutics for drunkards that was broadly embraced by evangelical Protestants. After the Civil War, this therapeutics, which consisted of public confession, fellowship, and temperance work, overshadowed physicians' attempts to found a medical treatment for alcohol and other addictions (a disease they called inebriety). Reformed drunkards established institutions, clubs, and associations to help men become sober but also to promote total abstinence temperance. The inebriety doctors developed a national professional association, a journal, and what they believed to be a systematic knowledge about habitual drunkenness. The reformed drunkards and their supporters, in contrast, operated within regional and local evangelical and temperance networks that nonetheless spread across the nation. Their decentralization has effectively hidden this popular therapeutic tradition from historians' view. Understanding it provides key insights into the historical roots of Alcoholics Anonymous and subsequent confessional treatments of addiction and addictive behavior, in particular their peculiar mix of disease concept and spirituality.

Reforming Drunkards in Antebellum America: The Washingtonians

The revolutionary-era physician Benjamin Rush argued as early as 1790 that drinking alcohol could induce a disease manifesting itself as a progressive loss of control, the treatment for which was total abstinence. It was evangelical temperance reformers of the 1820s, however, who popularized the idea in an all-out assault on national drinking habits. Sin and disease intermingled in their thinking about addiction, and though these reformers believed that only total abstinence could help the drunkard, they had little hope that he could sustain it. Lyman Beecher, a Presbyterian minister and reformer, launched the total abstinence phase of the national temperance movement in the mid-1820s with his *Six Sermons on Intemperance*. He argued that it was possible for drinkers to reform only in the early stages of their habit. Intemperance was "a sin so deceitful," he warned, gaining such "physical and moral influence . . . upon its victims," that to advise moderation was disastrous: "if we cannot stop men in the beginning, we cannot separate between that and the end." The "end," he went on, was extinction of religious affections and finer sensibilities.[3] Confirmed drunkards, though victims of sin and disease, could not easily be reformed because of their ruined morality; it was better to focus on moderate drinkers, who could be saved. For practical purposes, evangelical reformers treated drunkards not as victims but as warnings, leaving the state to deal with them under laws addressing drunkenness, disorderly conduct, and other offenses against public order.[4] Although several physicians in the 1830s suggested drunkards might benefit from therapeutic incarceration in institutions especially designed for the purpose, nothing concrete came of such proposals until the 1860s.[5]

Evangelical temperance reformers such as Beecher had larger goals in mind than reforming the drunkard. They demanded personal and social purification to save the nation from cosmic catastrophe. Moderate drinkers had to be made aware of their sin and the awful consequences, which were medical, familial, and national, as well as spiritual.[6] Impelled by religious fervor, evangelical temperance advocates were the radicals of the temperance movement. They excoriated moderate drinkers and liquor sellers for their sinfulness and campaigned for laws to end the sale of liquor. By the end of the 1830s, however, their strident rhetoric and insistence on prohibition had alienated many who supported temperance.[7]

In 1840 a group of artisans in Baltimore developed a new kind of temperance society intended to appeal to hard-drinking men like themselves. Adopting a total abstinence pledge, the Washingtonians, as they called themselves, related their own experiences with drunkenness and sobriety rather than relying on lecturers or preachers sanctioned by established temperance societies. They avoided chastising the moderate drinker, preferring to boast of their former drinking prowess while using humorous and pathetic anecdotes to persuade drinkers of the benefits of total abstinence. Most notably, however, they drew on their own experiences to illustrate how sympathy could save the drunkard from his appetite. Coercion, they insisted, never had such an effect, and for that reason they refused to endorse the use of legislation to stamp out drinking.

Washingtonians soon found that their personal stories about drunkenness and reformation fascinated a broad range of audiences. Reformed men quickly fanned out across the United States, giving experience speeches, promoting the total abstinence pledge, and explaining the principles of Washingtonian societies.[8] The movement's appeal depended partly on the familiarity of its cultural and social forms and partly on the novel construction the Washingtonians placed upon them. The Washingtonians' insistence on extemporaneous testimony and personal commitment from participants recalled the social religion of the Methodists, who used similar sorts of gatherings to orchestrate a sense of shared mission among the laity. Washingtonian gatherings, where reformed men related their experiences while drunkards and other audience members trooped up to sign the pledge, were compared to revivals. But the Washingtonians shared republican suspicions of the divisive influence of denominational religion. They were committed nonsectarians, banishing religious discussion from their proceedings so as to maintain focus on personal abstinence. They refused to set up national organizations or establish membership qualifications, arguing that such devices led to a concentration of power and distance from the citizenry that naturally led to corruption. Meetings and pledge signing were completely public. By making the recently reformed, rather than ministers or other notables, speakers at weekly meetings, and by passing the pledge often, the Washingtonians created a participatory atmosphere that emphasized egalitarian fellowship rather than hierarchy.[9] Republican and Christian in orientation, the Washingtonians appealed to both men and women, to skilled laborers and newer members of the middle class, to northerners as well as southerners.

To extract ideas about the etiology of drunkenness from Washingtonian oratory is to misrepresent their rhetoric, which offered arguments embedded in anecdotes drawn from personal experience. It was a pragmatic discourse, intended to motivate listeners to sign the total abstinence pledge. In the course of their speeches, however, many (though not all) Washingtonians admitted to a progressive inability to control their drinking habits. Charles Woodman, a former baker whose habit had landed him in jail on many occasions, referred to the "chain of servitude" forged by drinking alcohol that had bound him before his reform.[10] Some confessed that the chain was so strong that even after experiencing the terrifying hallucinations of *delirium tremens*, they returned to drinking.[11] Others admitted, sometimes in a boasting fashion, of the extremities to which the alcohol appetite had driven them. Only rarely did Washingtonians attribute this loss of control to a disease-like process, however, and only then to buttress their contention that drunkards were not naturally vicious, as they were conventionally represented in most popular and religious literature. William Mitchell, president of the original Baltimore Washington Society, explained the relationship between drinking and the drunkard's nature: "Drinking is a social vice. Men of generous habits and feelings, are the men who fall prey to intemperance."[12] Alcohol insinuated itself into men's lives via their better impulses, not their sinful ones.

Drink dragged men down into intemperance, but intemperance did not destroy their moral nature, the Washingtonians asserted. Reformed men frequently referred to how much they had suffered as drunkards. The point of such anecdotes was not merely to elicit pity, but to demonstrate that the drunkard still possessed the moral sensibilities required for suffering. These sensibilities apprised them of their degradation and made them wish for reform. Social rejection, however, robbed them of hope and deepened their misery. John H. W. Hawkins, a Baltimore hatter who became a well-known experience speaker, testified that during his struggles to stop drinking, "Not a being [came] to take me by the hand, and lead or help me along and say YOU CAN. I was friendless, without help, or light, an outcast."[13] Drunkards were indeed victims of the addicting properties of alcohol and of their own generous natures, but the most dangerous victimization arose out social ostracism. The dismissive attitudes of the respectable convinced drunkards they were incapable of reform. The Washingtonians "endeavored to gain their confidence . . . and to awaken the moral power of disenthralled manhood within them."[14] Experience speaker Jesse Vickers illustrated how such efforts worked. Vickers accompanied a delegation of Washingtonians to visit a drunkard living in squalor outside of Cincinnati.

> I asked him if he would not like to become a respectable man once more. "Yes I would," said he. "Well now, said I, you can live to be a respectable man yet." "Well if you will show me how, I will try," was his reply. Now, said I, in the first place, you must get your own will to do it, and then you must sign the total abstinence pledge—well he did.

Vickers had his colleagues prepare some soup and fill a tub with water. "While they were washing him we'd occasionally give him some soup; and it appeared to me as that every spoonful you could see a joint of his back bone slip into its place—well we dressed him up, and on the fourth night he gave his experience."[15] They approached him not as a degraded drunkard, but as a man who could find the will to stop drinking if properly assisted. They offered the pledge as a gesture of their faith in him. Decent food, a bath, and clothes bolstered the drunkard's self-image. Finally, relating his experiences as a reformed man completed the process of creating a sober subject. Reforming drunkards demonstrated their newly found moral power by testifying on behalf of total abstinence temperance.

Telling one's story before a sympathetic audience probably had a therapeutic effect on men trying to sustain sobriety. This therapeutic effect should be conceived in broad terms, however. It derived from a vision of social reform based in universal voluntary total abstinence, rather than in a therapeutic that alleviated a condition from which particular individuals suffered.[16] The Washingtonians never intended their movement for drunkards primarily. They believed the reformed man's experience narrative constituted the most powerful inducement to sign the total abstinence pledge, and for that reason they gave former drunkards leadership roles. Their task was to create totally abstinent communities that sympathized with and assisted the drunkard rather than ostracizing him. Praising the Washingtonians, the rising politician Abraham Lincoln reminded the Springfield Washingtonian Society, "When [the drunkard] casts his eyes around him he should be able to see all that he respects, all that he admires, all that he loves, kindly and anxiously beckoning him onward and none beckoning him back to his former miserable 'wallowing in the mire.'"[17] By putting the reformed man's experience at the center of their movement, Washingtonians provided a rationale for signing the temperance pledge rooted in sympathy and practical philanthropy, rather than purely in anxiety about sin or disease.

By 1845, the Washingtonian temperance movement was in rapid decline, attacked by evangelical temperance reformers for (among other things) refusing to label drunkenness a sin, besmirched by widely publicized incidents of reformed men returning to drink, and internally fragmented by the issue of prohibition. Temperance fraternal societies rose up to take their place. Though they devoted most of their energies to recruiting the already respectable, the Rechabites, the Good Samaritans, the Sons of Temperance, and the Good Templars kept alive the idea that the drunkard was not necessarily a sinner, and could be reformed if given sympathy and assistance. Indeed they argued that their form of organization, with its closed meetings, secret rituals, membership qualifications, and fines for backsliding, was better able to help men become totally abstinent and stay that way. Nonetheless, as the temperance movement threw its energies into passing "preventative" prohibition laws in the 1850s, "remedial" efforts to help the drunkard reform through voluntary means languished.[18]

Reforming Drunkards in the Gilded Age: Gospel Temperance

Reforming individuals continued to resonate with evangelical Christians, who believed that social change must begin with a change in an individual's convictions and behavior. By the mid-1850s, the nation was reeling from sectional strife over slavery, controversial prohibition laws, and an economic depression. During the winter of 1857–1858, anxious Christians turned to more purely religious solutions to the problem of sin; religious revival gripped urban areas across the country. The secular press, aided by telegraph communication and searching for news during a slow season, extensively covered the revival. Once again, the reformation of drunkards gained national attention.[19]

A ubiquitous feature of the revival was the prayer meeting, a devotional gathering led by the laity rather than by a minister. It consisted primarily of prayer and testimony by members of the audience. The simple structure of the meetings—placards were printed with the "rules" and placed in plain view—allowed for their proliferation. In Boston, for example, meetings were held not only at noon (a time that accommodated businessmen and laborers) but also throughout the day, for special constituencies such as women, and in secular venues to attract those persons, such as drunkards, prostitutes, and urban pleasure-seekers, who might not enter a church. Both religious and secular commentators interpreted the conversion of drunkards as a sign that the revival was reaching notorious sinners. While secular papers focused on more sensational conversions, such as that of Orville "Awful" Gardiner, a hard-drinking professional boxer, religious writers recorded the testimony of more ordinary reformed drunkards.[20] During a Boston prayer meeting, a man gave this account of his conversion not four months earlier. After mustering the courage to enter a prayer meeting for the first time, he reported, "I stood up and told them I was a poor miserable sinner, and asked them to pray for me; and I prayed for myself. I had been drinking, but I knew what I was about. I signed the pledge that night, and I thank God I have kept it ever since. I never have had any desire to drink since; God has taken the appetite away. I went home and prayed to God to have mercy on my soul, and in a few days I found peace."[21] Given the frequency of meetings at the height of the revival and the preference for prayers of thanks such as his, this man probably gave his testimony dozens of times. Notable as well was the use of the pledge, a device of the temperance movement, and the man's claim that conversion took his appetite for alcohol away. These features came to characterize "gospel" temperance, a post–Civil War temperance movement that used prayer meetings and pledging as means of rousing support. This movement revived efforts to help drunkards reform voluntarily through confession and missionary work and endowed such reformations with explicitly religious and evangelical meanings: drinking and drunkenness were sins; repentance and God's grace could save the drunkard; giving public testimony could stir others to sign the pledge and experience conversion.[22]

The 1857–1858 revival inspired a generation of lay evangelical activists, for whom prayer meetings, the temperance pledge, and missionary work to reform the sinner were the method, and personal conversion was the means and goal. Their organizations, which included a revitalized Young Men's Christian Association and the early Woman's Christian Temperance Union, gained fresh impetus from the urban revivals of Dwight Moody and Ira Sankey in the mid-1870s (Moody himself was converted during the revival of 1857–1858 in Chicago). Moody continued the practice of spotlighting archetypal reformed sinners such as drunkards, and included some reformed drunkards in his entourage, entrusting them with responsibilities such as organizing prayer meetings for drinking men in neighborhood locales. Men willing to make public testimony about the renunciation of the sin of drinking through the grace of God became exemplars of divine power for many evangelical Protestants in the late nineteenth century. For some believers support went beyond a sympathetic ear to contributing energy and resources to reforming drunkards.[23]

Men reformed through gospel temperance drew on local and regional evangelical networks to create institutions to help drunkards. Reformed men in Massachusetts and Maine formed "ribbon" clubs (members wore blue or red ribbons on their lapels) for men who wished to stop drinking. Assisted by the Woman's Christian Temperance Union and welcomed at evangelical churches, ribbon reformers traveled through the Midwest giving their experiences, holding temperance revivals, and forming ribbon clubs. In Illinois, their activism produced dozens of clubs, a series of annual state conventions, and at least one journal.[24] In Boston, Chicago, Philadelphia, and New York, evangelicals Christians, inspired by the urban revivals, joined with reformed men to open inebriate homes, where drunkards could repair to practice total abstinence and find an experience of God's grace. A separate arm of the gospel temperance movement arose in urban slums. Jerry McAuley, a former "river thief" who was evidently inspired by the visit of the redeemed drunkard "Awful" Gardiner to Sing Sing prison where McAuley was incarcerated, later converted to evangelical Protestantism and total abstinence. In 1871, McAuley founded the Water Street Mission, an institution that offered food and shelter to homeless drunkards in Manhattan. McAuley led them to redemption and sobriety at nightly public prayer meetings. Supported by leading holiness Methodists and evangelical Presbyterians, McAuley and his successor, reformed drunkard Samuel H. Hadley, made the Water Street Mission into the model for the gospel rescue mission movement. By the end of the century, hundreds of gospel rescue missions had sprung up in cities across the country. Many of them were staffed by former drunkards who served a clientele they knew from personal experience.[25]

Like the Washingtonians, the reformed men of the gospel temperance movement insisted that the drunkard deserved sympathy, not censure, and the institutions they created were predicated on the principle that reformation could not be coerced. Yet they warned the drunkard not to rely on his own will to reform. Their stories emphasized helplessness instead. One early gospel temperance autobiographer confessed to having had his arms lopped off after he fell asleep, drunk, across a railroad track.[26] Another told of suffering from delirium tremens for four sleepless days and nights, without food or shelter, until voluntarily incarcerating himself to keep from drinking again.[27] Gospel temperance men excelled in telling tales of what twelve-step groups in the twentieth century would call "hitting bottom." In the nineteenth century, however, the failure of willpower arose from man's sinful nature, which had precipitated the addiction in the first place. A chronicler of the ribbon movement explained, "If you have suffered the evils of intemperance, you are in a position to fully realize man's weakness . . . never does he fully realize [this] till sin has severely punished him."[28] The drunkard's struggle against drinking epitomized the sinner's struggle against sin.

But with the awareness of helplessness came hope and then relief. Gospel temperance advocates promised that signing the pledge and seeking God's grace could produce the most miraculous effects. Holiness doctrines popular in evangelical circles in the post–Civil War period held that God's grace could restore sinners to a state of sinlessness. For drunkards, conversion could eradicate the appetite for alcohol. As Jerry McAuley put it, "Blessed Jesus . . . saved me from desiring to do those things which I had been doing."[29] This was the message that ribbon workers and rescue mission leaders carried across the country at prayer meetings, temperance revivals, and gospel lectures.

Medical Treatment of Addiction in Late Nineteenth-Century America

When physicians advocating the medical treatment of alcohol and other addictions—which they called inebriety—formed the American Association for the Cure of Inebriety (the AACI) in 1870, they had two goals: to convince a skeptical medical profession of their disease concept, and to convince the public of the efficacy of asylum treatment of inebriates. By the mid-1870s it had become clear that their main competitors in the field of treating alcohol addicts were the gospel temperance advocates. Gospel temperance had a phalanx of proselytizers in the reformed drunkards and a host of evangelical supporters. They had a religious therapeutics organized around pledging and conversion, public confession, and missionary work. Moreover, gospel temperance activists, recognizing that some drunkards needed more support in their struggle for total abstinence, had founded at least five treatment institutions, called inebriate homes, that used those therapeutic techniques. These private institutions, which were located in urban centers, hosted ribbon reform groups and temperance fraternities, and were supported by local evangelical organizations and voluntary societies. Drunkards reformed through gospel temperance sometimes ended up in inebriate homes, while drunkards reformed in inebriate homes often became lecturers on gospel temperance circuits.[30]

The growing divergence between medical and religious concepts of alcohol addiction in late nineteenth-century America becomes clearest in comparisons between the ideas of the inebriety doctors and those expressed by the superintendents and inmates or graduates of the inebriate homes (often the superintendents and staff were graduates). Though all inebriate home personnel supported prohibition (as did most gospel temperance reformed men) they insisted that coercion would always fail to reform the drunkard. D. Banks McKenzie, superintendent of the Appleton Home in Boston and a reformed drunkard, explained: "The longer an inebriate is kept forcibly from his beloved cup, the more anxious he will be for a debauch on his restoration to liberty."[31] Officials at the Boston and Philadelphia homes expressed similar sentiments: "Threats stimulate resentment that could lead to renewed excesses," and "constraint might make [the drunkard] a hypocrite—it could never promote his reformation."[32] The officials of the inebriate homes did not fully dispense with the disease concept of inebriety in their discourse or practice. McKenzie believed that drunkards suffered from a "physical thralldom." Yet, in a fashion typical of gospel temperance beliefs, he argued that "the only safety for men who have once yielded to their appetite for drink," was "a change of heart, involving a complete change of life" sustained by "Divine Grace."[33] David Harrisson, a graduate of the Boston Washingtonian Home and staunch defender of the disease concept, thought that the Home's treatment allowed the inmate to feel "the soothing and sustaining power of grace shine in upon his troubled soul."[34]

Inebriety physicians defended a relentlessly somatic and increasingly hereditarian disease concept of addiction. They argued that alcohol poisoned the body and weakened the constitution. According to Thomas Davison Crothers, editor of the AACI's *Quarterly Journal of Inebriety* and a leading spokesperson of the inebriety movement, "impairment of the moral perceptions is one of the first symptoms of the disease," and those moral perceptions were the last to recover in a successful cure.[35] An effective therapeutics focused on restraint of the patient until healing had occurred and the moral capacity had been restored enough so that he could resist temptation. Rural isolation was more important, Crothers believed, than locks and bars. Nonetheless, model commitment laws drafted by the AACI in 1872 recommended that directors of asylums be given the legal power to retain even their voluntary patients for at least six months.[36]

Inebriety physicians doubted that reformed drunkards could be effective in helping other drunkards to reform. One inebriate asylum physician declared that such men were "especially disqualified" to serve as staff in inebriate institutions because of the abnormal constitutions that had predisposed them to inebriety in the first place.[37] In language suggesting the involuntary responses of those afflicted with the disease of inebriety, Thomas Crothers derided the "wave-like temperance agitations" that encouraged drunkards to take the pledge.[38] He explained that inebriates "may honestly make many exertions to recover, but unless the organism sustains the mind in its endeavors, failure will be the rule and not the exception."[39] These physicians recommended exposure to religion and culture as part of asylum treatment. In keeping with their scientific worldview, however, they rejected a key evangelical belief, that a miraculous gift of grace from God could reform a drunkard. Instead inebriety physicians drew upon liberal Christian traditions, in which piety, morality, and health were cultivated over time, rather than achieved through a spiritual rebirth and missionary zeal to save others.[40]

By the 1880s, inebriety physicians, in step with the progressive scientific theories of the day, had endorsed a more pessimistic hereditarian disease concept of addiction. This move also bolstered their arguments in favor of state-financed inebriate asylums. Those persons who had inherited a constitutional weakness for alcohol had little chance of becoming sober without long-term quarantine from temptation. Given that such persons usually exhibited a host of degenerative symptoms, which included pauperism, vagabondage, and criminality, along with their inebriety, the AACI argued that society would be well served by an archipelago of inebriate asylums tended by professional inebriety doctors. Legislatures, however, found their arguments unconvincing.[41] In contrast, inebriate home officials strongly objected to hereditarian interpretations of inebriety that made drinking the expression of an inborn flaw. Superintendents of the homes believed that such views discouraged drunkards from trying to reform and provided them with a ready excuse for backsliding.[42]

THE DISEASE CONCEPT of addiction in which habitual, excessive drinking is believed to arise from somatic causes and becomes progressively worse over time would come to play a central role in twentieth-century therapeutic approaches to addiction. The image of the addict promulgated by twelve-step programs—that is, of a person suffering from a disease whose therapy consists of submission to a higher power and a life-long struggle to do right, owes as much to gospel temperance doctrine as it does to the antebellum Washingtonians. It was evangelical reformed men who enshrined the admission of helplessness and dependence upon God for salvation from the alcoholic appetite. The highly structured Alcoholics Anonymous meetings, which are dominated by confessional testimony, are far more similar to late nineteenth-century experience and gospel rescue meetings than the freewheeling Washingtonian gatherings of the antebellum period. Moreover, Alcoholics Anonymous adopted a fundamentally religious concept of addiction, in which sin leads to habituation and misery, which bears little relation to medical disease concepts of addiction prevalent in the nineteenth or the early twentieth centuries.

It is nonetheless a significant leap, socially and culturally, from gospel temperance to Alcoholics Anonymous. Gospel temperance meetings were largely public; AA maintains privacy through its policy of anonymity. Gospel temperance therapeutics spilled over into temperance reform and evangelical proselytizing; AA admits into its therapeutic circle only those suffering from the disease of alcoholism. The process by which this transformation was achieved I explore more fully elsewhere. Like their forebears in the nineteenth century, however, the reforming drunkards of Alcoholics Anonymous have promulgated a powerful ideology about and therapy for their own addiction, overshadowing the doctors and altering American consciousness.

Notes

The author would like to thank Jim Baumohl, Ernest Kurtz, Harry Gene Levine, Ron Roizen, Robin Room, Sarah, Tracy, and two anonymous reviewers for their comments and suggestions on earlier versions of this paper.

1. The originator of this influential thesis is Harry Gene Levine, "The Discovery of Addiction: Changing Conceptions of Habitual Drunkenness in America," *Journal of Studies on Alcohol* 39 (1978): 143–174.

2. John W. Crowley, *Drunkard's Progress: Narratives of Addiction, Despair and Recovery* (Baltimore: Johns Hopkins University Press, 1999). Crowley follows standard interpretations of the roots of Alcoholics Anonymous in overlooking the rich confessional tradition arising from religiously reformed drunkards of the late nineteenth century. For a similar view, see Leonard U. Blumberg with William L. Pittman, *Beware the First Drink! The Washington Temperance Movement and Alcoholics Anonymous* (Seattle: Glen Abbey Books, 1991).

3. Benjamin Rush, *An Inquiry into the Effects of Ardent Spirits on the Body and Mind, with an Account of the Means of Preventing and of the Remedies for Curing Them*, 8th ed. (Brookfield, Mass.: E. Merriam 1814); Lyman Beecher, *Six Sermons on the Nature, Occasion, Signs, Evils and Remedy of Intemperance* (Boston: T. R. Marvin, 1828), 25, 47, 39, 35–36.

4. Robert Abzug, *Cosmos Crumbling: American Reform and the Religious Imagination* (New York: Oxford University Press, 1994), chap. 3, passim; as Abzug points out, Beecher pursues all of these arguments in his *Six Sermons*.

5. Samuel B. Woodward, *Essays on Asylums for Inebriates* (n.p., 1838). These essays first appeared in 1835 as a series in the Boston *Mercantile Journal*. Other proposals for inebriate asylums include those of Benjamin Rush, *Medical Inquiries and Observations upon the diseases of the Mind* (Philadelphia: Kimber & Richardson, 1812), 354–355; and [Eli Todd et al.], *Report of a Committee of the Connecticut Medical Society Respecting an Asylum for Inebriates* . . . (New Haven, 1830). Dr. J. Edward Turner founded the first inebriate asylum in 1864. See Thomas Davison Crothers, "Sketch of the Late Dr. J. Edward Turner: Founder of Inebriate Asylums," *Journal of Inebriety* 11 (1889): 1–25; Charles H. Shepard, "The First Inebriate Asylum and its Founder," *Journal of Inebriety* 39 (1898): 1–34.

6. Abzug, *Cosmos Crumbling*, chap. 3 and passim.

7. Ian Tyrrell, *Sobering Up: From Temperance to Prohibition in Antebellum America, 1800–1860* (Westport, Conn.: Greenwood Press, 1979), 110–113, 148–151; John Allen Krout, *The Origins of Prohibition* (New York: Alfred A. Knopf, 1925); Emil Christopher Vigilante, "The Temperance Reform in New York State," Ph.D. diss., New York University, 1964; cf. Robert Hampel, *Temperance and Prohibition in Massachusetts 1813–1852* (Ann Arbor: UMI Research Press, 1982), 57–58; 91–94.

8. [John Zug], *The Foundation, Progress and Principles of the Washington Temperance Society of Baltimore, and the Influence it has had on the Temperance Movement in the United States* (Baltimore: John D. Toy, 1842). Historians who discuss the Washingtonians include Hampel, *Temperance and Prohibition*, chaps. 7 and 8; Bruce Laurie, *Artisans into Workers: Labor in Nineteenth-Century America* (Urbana: University of Illinois Press, 1989), 74–75, 92–94; Tyrrell, *Sobering Up*, chaps. 7 and 8; Jed Dannenbaum, *Drink and Disorder: Temperance in Cincinnati from the Washingtonian Revival to the WCTU* (Urbana: University of Illinois Press, 1984), chap. 2; Sean Wilentz, *Chants Democratic: New York City and the Rise of the American Working Class, 1788–1850* (New York: Oxford University Press, 1984), 310–314; Teresa Anne Murphy, *Ten Hours' Labor: Religion, Reform, and Gender in Early New England* (Ithaca: Cornell University Press, 1992), chap. 5; and Jonathan Zimmerman, "Dethroning King Alcohol: The Washingtonians in Baltimore, 1840–1854," *Maryland Historical Magazine* 87, no.4 (1992): 374–398; see also Abzug, *Cosmos Crumbling*, 102–104.

9. "Extraordinary Temperance movement," *Journal of the American Temperance Union* (hereafter *JATU*) 5 (April 1841): 52, 53; [Zug], *Washington Temperance Society of Baltimore*, 40–41; [Aaron B. Grosh and G. Bigelow], *Washingtonian Pocket Companion, containing a choice collection of temperance hymns, songs, &c* . . . (Utica: R. W. Roberts Printer, 1842), 6.

10. Charles T. Woodman, *Narrative of Charles T. Woodman, A Reformed Inebriate*, (Boston: Theodore Abbot, 1843), 25.

11. John B. Lecraw, *A Sketch of the Life, Travels, and Sufferings of a Reformed Man* . . . *Written by Himself* (Pawtucket: B. W. Pearce, 1844), 25; A. V. Green, *The Life and Experience of A.V. Green, the Celebrated Ohio Temperance Sledge Hammer* . . . (Wooster: Printed for the author, 1848), 43.

12. [Zug], *Washington Temperance Society of Baltimore*, 40, 11; *JATU* 5 (1841): 51.

13. Maryland State Temperance Society, *11th Annual Report of the Temperance Society for the Year 1841*, (1842), 15.

14. "National Temperance Convention," *JATU* 5 (1841): 131, reporting on a July meeting in Saratoga Springs at which reformed drunkards spoke.

15. *11th Annual Report of the Maryland State Temperance Society* . . . *1841*, 17.

16. On the various senses of the therapeutic, see Philip Rieff, *The Triumph of the Therapeutic: Uses of Faith after Freud*, rpt. ed., (Chicago: University of Chicago Press,

1987), and Martha C. Nussbaum, *The Therapy of Desire: Theory and Practice in Hellenistic Ethics* (Princeton: Princeton University Press, 1994).

17. Abraham Lincoln, *An address, Delivered before the Springfield Washingtonian Temperance Society . . . February, 1842* (Springfield: Illinois State Register Press, 1908), 9.

18. For an interesting account of the internal dynamics of this shift among women reformers, see e.g., Lori Ginzberg, *Women and the Work of Benevolence: Morality, Politics and Class in the Nineteenth-century United States* (New Haven: Yale University Press, 1990), chap. 4.

19. Kathryn Teresa Long, *The Revival of 1857–58: Interpreting an American Religious Awakening* (New York: Oxford University Press, 1998); cf. Timothy L. Smith, *Revivalism and Reform* (New York: Harper, 1957).

20. On Gardiner, see New York *Tribune*, 5, 8, and 13 March 1858.

21. *Old South Chapel Prayer Meeting: Its Origin and History . . .* (Boston: J. E. Tilton, 1859), 192; see also Talbot W. Chambers, *The Noon Prayer Meeting at the North Dutch Church, Fulton Street, New York . . .* (New York: Reformed Protestant Dutch Church, 1858), 45–52.

22. For contemporary works describing gospel temperance, see W. H. Daniels, *The Temperance Reform and its Great Reformers. An Illustrated History . . .* (New York: Nelson & Phillips, 1878); T. H. Arthur, *Strong Drink: The Curse and the Cure* Philadelphia, 1877) 569–629; A. M. Morse, *Lost and Rescued*, 7th ed. (Chicago: Jennings & Pye, 1901), chaps. 5, 8, and 10; J. E. Stebbins, *Fifty Years History of the Temperance Cause* (Hartford, Conn.: J. P. Fitch, 1976); and Charles Morris, *Broken Fetters: The Light of Ages on Intoxication* (New York: N. D. Thompson, 1888), chaps. 13, 14, and 15. See also Helen Campbell et al., *Darkness and Daylight; or Lights and Shadows of New York Life: A Woman's Story of Gospel, Temperance, Mission and Rescue Work* (Hartford, Conn.: A. D. Worthington 1892), esp. 54–88.

23. Long, *The Revival of 1857–58*, chap. 7. On Moody, see James F. Findlay, *Dwight L. Moody, American Evangelist, 1837–1988* (Chicago: University of Chicago, 1969), esp. chap. 6; and William McLoughlin, *Modern Revivalism: Charles Grandison Finney to Billy Graham* (New York: Ronald Press, 1959), 217–248. On reformed drunkards in Moody's revivals, see Daniels, *The Temperance Reform*, 527–532, and William H. Daniels, ed., Moody: *His Words, Work, and Workers . . . with Thrilling Experiences of Converted Inebriates* (New York: Nelson & Phillips, 1879), esp. 511–512.

24. See Massachusetts Total Abstinence Society, *Annual Reports*, [Report of the Treasurer], 31 December 1874; George T. Ferris, "The life and work of Francis Murphy and Dr. Henry Reynolds," in Thurlow Weed Brown, *Minnie Hermon: Or the Cure of Rum. A tale for the Times* (Chicago: J. W. Goodspeed, 1876), passim. On support offered by the early Woman's Christian Temperance movement for reforming drunkards, see Annie Wittenmeyer, *History of the Woman's Temperance Crusade* (Philadelphia: Published at the Office of the Christian Woman, 1878), 89–98. See also James M. Hiatt, *The Ribbon Workers* (Chicago: J. W. Goodspeed, 1878); *Fourth Annual Report of the Illinois State Temperance Reform Club to the Fourth Annual Convention held at Bloomington, Illinois* (Chicago: R. W. Crampton, 1879); the journal is the *Chicago Ribbon Review*.

25. R. M. Offord, ed., *Jerry McAuley, his Life and Work, with an Introduction by the Rev. S. Irenaus Prime and Personal Sketches by A. S. Hatch* (New York: Ward & Drummond, 1885); Jerry McAuley, *Transformed; or The History of a River Thief* (New York, 1876); and Samuel H. Hadley, *Down in Water Street: A Story of Sixteen Years of Life and Work in Water Street Mission, A Sequel to the Life of Jerry McAuley*, memorial ed. (New

York: Fleming H. Revell, 1906), esp. 67–82. On McAuley and his impact on evangelical welfare initiatives, see Norris A. Magnuson, *Salvation in the Slums: Evangelical Social Work, 1865–1920*, (Metuchen, N.J.: The Scarecrow Press, 1977), 2–13, 137–140; and Aaron Abell, *The Urban Impact on American Protestantism, 1865–1900*, (Hamden, Conn.: Archon, 1962), 122–123.

26. Thomas Doner, *Eleven Years a Drunkard or the Evils of Intemperance Showing What Whiskey Did For me* (Sycamore, Ill.: Arnold Brothers, 1874). The cover of the cheaply produced edition shows Doner writing his narrative with a pen held in his mouth. See also Festus G. Rand, who reported in his *Autobiography of Festus G. Rand. A Tale of Intemperance* (Romeo, Mich.: J. Russell, 1866) that he had lost his lower legs and his hands to frostbite incurred after falling asleep drunk outside on a cold night.

27. Mrs. S. May Wyburn, *"But, Until Seventy Times Seven": Jeremiah, Samuel, John* (New York: Loizeau Brothers, 1936), 63–68.

28. Hiatt, *Ribbon Workers*, 16.

29. Offord, *Jerry McAuley*, 114.

30. These institutions are the Washingtonian Home in Boston, founded as the Home for the Fallen at the height of the revival of 1857–1858, the Chicago Washingtonian Home, the Appleton Home also in Boston, the Philadelphia Franklin Reformatory, and the New York Christian Home for Intemperate Men. For the origins of these institutions, see Katherine Chavigny, "American Confessions: Reformed Drunkards and the Origins of Therapeutic Culture," Ph.D. diss., University of Chicago, 1999. On men reformed through gospel temperance who had been treated in the Chicago Washingtonian home, see, e.g., W. T. Cox, *Out of the Depths; A Personal Narrative of My Fall Under the Power of Strong Drink and My Complete Reformation* (Sycamore, Ill.: Baker & Arnold, 1876), and D. N. Tucker, *A Struggle for Life and Victory Through the Lamb* (Sycamore, Ill.: Baker & Arnold, 1879).

31. [D. Banks McKenzie], *The Appleton Temporary Home: A Record of Work*, rev. and enlarged ed. (Boston: Published for the Home, 1876), 130–31.

32. See *8th Annual Report, Boston Washingtonian Home, 1865* (1866), 12–13 (first quotation), and *21st Annual Report, Philadelphia Franklin Reformatory 1893* (1894), 52 (second quotation).

33. [McKenzie], *Appleton Temporary Home*, 72–77, quotation 76.

34. David Harrisson, *Voices from the Washingtonian Home, Being a History of the Foundation, Rise, and Progress of the Washingtonian Home . . .* (Boston: Redding & Co., 1860), 185.

35. The American Association for the Study and Cure of Inebriety, *The Disease of Inebriety* (1893), 122. By 1885, Albert Day, the longtime superintendent of the Boston Washingtonian Home, had come to agree with the AACI's interpretation of inebriety. *28th Annual Report, Boston Washingtonian Home, 1885* (1886), 9, 14.

36. [T. D. Crothers], "Curability of Inebriety," *Quarterly Journal of Inebriety* 6 (1884): 14–27; quotations from 23–24; see also D. G. Dodge, "Restraint as a Remedy in the Treatment of Inebriety," *Proceedings of the First Meeting of the American Association for the Cure of Inebriety* (1872): 51–57; "Report of the Committee on Legislation," *Proceedings of the Third Meeting of the American Association for the Cure of Inebriety* (1873): 62–77; Crothers, "Sketch of the Late Dr. J. Edward Turner."

37. *Proceedings of a Complimentary Dinner Given to Dr. Joseph Parrish* (Hartford, Conn., 1890), 12.

38. E.g., "Agitation Period of the History of Inebriety," *Journal of Inebriety* 6 (1884): 187–195.

39. "Reform Movements," *Journal of Inebriety* 1 (1878): 243.

40. Cf. Jim Baumohl and Robin Room, "Inebriety, Doctors, and the State. Alcoholism Treatment Institutions before 1940," *Recent Developments in Alcoholism* 5 (1987): 135–174; Jim Baumohl, "Dashaways and Doctors: The Treatment of Habitual Drunkards in San Francisco from the Gold Rush to Prohibition," Ph.D. diss., University of California, Berkeley, 1986, esp. chap. 3; Jim Baumohl, "On Asylums, Homes, and Moral Treatment: The Case of the San Francisco Home for the Care of the Inebriate, 1859–1870," *Contemporary Drug Problems* (1986): 395–445; and Leonard U. Blumberg; "The Institutional Phase of the Washingtonian Total Abstinence Movement: A Research Note," *Journal of Studies on Alcohol* 39 (1978): 1591–1606. These works overlook the confessional and evangelical components of inebriate home treatment. Jim Baumohl briefly discusses religious treatment facilities in his later article "Inebriate Institutions in North America, 1840–1920," in Cheryl Krasnick Warsh, ed., *Drink in Canada: Historical Essays*, (Montreal: McGill-Queen's University Press, 1993).

41. Baumohl and Room, "Inebriety, Doctors, and the State." See also Edward M. Brown, "'What Shall We Do with the Inebriate?' Asylum Treatment and the Disease Concept of Alcoholism in the Late Nineteenth Century," *Journal of the History of the Behavioral Sciences* 21 (January 1983): 48–59, esp. 55–57.

42. See, e.g., Daniel Wilkins of the Chicago Washingtonian Home, who wrote that "out of every 36, 35 have acquired the habit [of] drinking themselves; their parents were total abstainers" (*25th Annual Report, Chicago Washingtonian Home*, 1888 [1889], 24). An official of the Philadelphia Reformatory asked why, when roughly half the progeny of drunken men were females, were so many fewer women afflicted with habitual drunkenness? (*3rd Annual Report, Philadelphia Franklin Reformatory, 1874* [1875], 45).

Building a Boozatorium

State Medical Reform for Iowa's Inebriates, 1902–1920

SARAH W. TRACY

FROM HIS ROOM in the State Hospital for Inebriates at Knoxville, Ed Harris, a businessman and patient, penned his request for "parole" to Iowa Governor William Harding. It was January 1917, and Harris, who had spent several weeks in the state "jaghouse," claimed to have "finished taking the treatment."[1] As evidence for his rapid recovery, the dry goods merchant from Salix, Iowa, offered his current position as the hospital's barber—a job that occupied him three days a week. No sick man could manage such a schedule, Harris claimed. Then he begged the governor to remember their meeting years back, under happier circumstances, when Harris had traveled to the Sioux City executive offices to discuss business. Might the governor not attend to his case personally? Harris asked, for he desperately wanted to return to his store in Salix. In his absence the business "had gone to blazes." Harris also confided, "My little boy of 12 years is taking this [Harris's absence from home] very hard and I will never take another drink for his sake alone."[2] Further reassuring the state's executive officer, Harris added that there was considerable distance between him and the "common drunkard" in residence at Knoxville.[3] Harding's reply came just over a month later. By that time the governor received another handwritten note, this one from Harris's son, closing with the query: "Know [*sic*] will you try and help get [my dad] out so he can take care of me?"[4]

Harris's letter and that of his son struck a responsive chord in Harding. Within a week, the state's executive officer had consulted with the hospital superintendent on Harris's behalf and learned that the superintendent and the Board of Control were the only parties responsible for "paroling" patients. Deferring to Superintendent M. C. Mackin's authority, the governor informed Harris that his case had been judged a favorable one, but that "there is an element of time which is very necessary to complete recovery." Harding hoped that Harris would "feel disposed to accept and act upon the advice of those who have your case under observation and when you are really ready for release on parole or discharge, there should be no difficulty about it."[5]

Harris was not satisfied with the governor's reply, though, and he quickly revamped his campaign for freedom. Having resided at the hospital for a month, the businessman pronounced himself "cured" in a subsequent letter, adding "I have thoroughly made up my mind to quit drinking and smoking not only for a few months, but the rest of my life, and I don't like to stay here when I am perfectly well and see my shop and living go to the dogs."[6] Once more, Harding was prompted to act, inquiring a second time into the possibility of Harris's early release. And this time M. C. Mackin acquiesced, reasoning in a letter dated March 6, "were [Harris] to lose his business by reason of his detention here, it probably would be a factor in discouraging him and causing him to again take up his former habits of inebriety. I really think it would be much better for the boy to remain for a period of four or five months but owing to his worried condition it might really be of no value to keep him longer than the first of April. This is the date on which he seems to be anxious to be released and I think I would be justified in giving him a trial at home."[7]

On April 11, Governor Harding received a final note from Salix. Ed Harris expressed his and his son's thanks for Harding's personal interest in the businessman's case. "I am on the water wagon for good," he assured the governor. "The good people here as a rule have given me the glad hand and while at first I thought the measure [commitment to Knoxville] was rather drastic, I am now pleased that I am rid of the Habit."[8]

So ends this—as far as we know—happy tale of one of Iowa's inebriates, but what are we to make of it? The story of the Salix, Iowa, businessman raises a variety of questions: How did medical and lay authorities understand the condition of inebriety, as a bad habit or as a disease? How did the conflicting priorities of the patient, his family, and inebriate hospital physicians affect the course of treatment? What distinguished treatment in the inebriate hospital from treatment in jail? Why was Iowa committing habitual drunkards to state hospitals in the first place?

This essay examines the evolution of Iowa's eighteen-year, state-sponsored medical program for inebriates, an early attempt to medicalize habitual drunkenness. It presents an analysis of the changing relations among the state's executive office, the inebriate hospitals, and other interested parties—families, physicians, the temperance lobby, legislators, the Iowa State Medical Society, and the Board of Control for State Institutions.[9] The medicalization of habitual drunkenness proved a difficult task, not only because of the strong moral valence surrounding drinking problems—a force that made it impossible for many to view the inebriate as an innocent victim of a disease—but also because of the competing interests of those affected by the alcoholic and his or her actions: judges, physicians, hospital superintendents, temperance reformers, eugenicists, legislators, and friends and family members. The attempt to medicalize habitual drunkenness in Iowa was *not* a top-down enterprise imposed upon the state by physicians. It was a politically and socially negotiated process. Indeed, a central irony of inebriate reform in turn-of-the-century Iowa is that the same congeries of interests that made medical treatment for the inebriate a pressing public issue also impeded its successful implementation. Though it took place at a time when the medical profession was expanding both its social and cultural authority within Iowa and across the United States, the effort to medicalize habitual drunkenness in the Hawkeye State revealed both the limits of this authority and the difficulty inherent in defining a protean, chronic condition with connections to a host of social problems and political causes.[10]

For some, it may come as no surprise that Iowa—a state with a rich temperance and prohibition heritage—would have attempted such an innovative therapeutic course. The Iowa historian Dorothy Schwieder has remarked that temperance concerns "proved the most emotional, politically significant and tenacious of all issues in nineteenth- and twentieth-century Iowa."[11] As I show, however, there was no single impetus for inebriate reform; there were many. The temperance and prohibition movements of the late nineteenth and early twentieth centuries clearly nurtured related concerns about the plight of the habitual drunkard.[12] Legal reformers and medical practitioners also promoted the effort to medicalize habitual drunkenness and provide for its cure. The initial, and unheeded, calls for medical treatment in Iowa came in the 1850s from judges, tired of seeing the same alcoholic recidivists in their courts year after year. By the end of the nineteenth century, Iowa's reform-oriented State Board of Health and a growing medical profession with a meliorist bent supported medical treatment. Likewise, an increasingly centralized state administrative apparatus—with a newly created Board of Control of State Institutions—nurtured the cause through its efforts to efficiently manage Iowa's impoverished, diseased, and disabled citizens. State administrators and physicians alike defined inebriate reform in pragmatic terms, focusing on the good it might effect in the daily lives of individual drinkers, their families, their friends, and the state's economy. Indeed, the campaign to build a state system of care for inebriates was emblematic of a variety of changes taking place in turn-of-the-century Iowa.

By 1902, when the first state hospital opened its inebriate ward, Iowa was well on its way to building a network of specialized social welfare and medical institutions for the treatment of the state's defective, delinquent, and dependent classes. As early as 1888, Iowa had established a department for the criminally insane at the state prison in Anamosa. The revised Code of 1897 provided for two new state hospitals for the insane—Clarinda and Cherokee, which opened in 1888 and 1902 respectively. In 1903, Iowa financed the construction of the University of Iowa Hospital in Iowa City. Oakdale, the state's tuberculosis sanitarium, opened its doors in 1908. The Perkins Act, passed in 1913, underwrote the treatment of children at University of Iowa Hospital, before the state bankrolled a separate institution for children in 1917. In 1919, the Iowa General Assembly passed a law to establish the state's first psychopathic hospital, linked to the University of Iowa Hospital.[13] In short, the state of Iowa expended more funds on medical care for its citizens between 1898 and 1919 than ever before.

If the establishment of inebriate hospitals was of a piece with the state's expansionist healthcare policy, it also had significant symbolic value. By placing their state on the cutting edge of institutional expansion and reform across the country, Iowans could rank themselves with states such as Massachusetts and New York in enlisting "men of science" to conserve their human and economic resources. To offer medical care to the inebriate said, in effect, "Everything's up-to-date in Iowa City," not to mention Des Moines. It was an act of enlightened compassion, scientific expertise, and rational administration that signified the heartland's participation in the modern world. The reform of inebriates, dipsomaniacs, and alcoholics was a classic Progressive reform with origins in the Gilded Age.[14]

The Inebriate Reform Movement

As early as 1870, a group of physicians, clergy members, social workers, and reformers of all stripes joined hands to recast habitual drunkenness as a disease and create new institutions—private and public—for the medical management of inebriety. Gathering in New York City to form a new professional organization—the American Association for the Cure of Inebriates (AACI)—these reformers declared to the world:

1. Intemperance is a disease.
2. It is curable in the same sense that other diseases are.
3. Its primary cause is a constitutional susceptibility to the alcoholic impression.
4. This constitutional tendency may be inherited or acquired.
5. Alcohol has its true place in the arts and sciences. It is a valuable remedy, and like other remedies, may be abused.
6. All methods hitherto employed having proved insufficient for the cure of inebriates, the establishment of asylums for such a purpose, is the great demand of the age.

7. Every large city should have its local or temporary home for inebriates, and every state, one or more asylums for the treatment and
care of such persons.
8. The law should recognize intemperance as a disease, and provide
means for its management, other than fines, stationhouses and
jails.[15]

The AACI founded its own journal, the *Quarterly Journal of Inebriety*, edited
by Thomas Crothers, a physician and the superintendent of the Walnut Hill
Lodge in Hartford, Connecticut. Over the next forty-eight years, Crothers
became the leading spokesperson for the medicalization cause, as he put
forth the association's principles in the *Quarterly Journal*, the *Alienist and
Neurologist*, the *Medico-Legal Journal*, the *Journal of Social Science*, and other
popular, social reform, and medical venues.

Promoting a medical understanding of habitual drunkenness in Gilded
Age and Progressive Era America consumed the efforts of hundreds if not
thousands of social reformers, and captured the attention of individuals as
diverse as Nathan S. Davis, the first president of the American Medical
Association; the Boston settlement house reformer Robert Archey Woods;
Frances Willard, the founder of the Woman's Christian Temperance Union;
and the neurologist George Miller Beard, who coined the term "neurasthenia."[16] In the late nineteenth and early twentieth centuries, superintendents
of insane hospitals and prison wardens alike attributed a significant number
of their patients and inmates to intemperance. General hospitals, if private,
often refused to treat the habitual drunkard, or if public and required to treat
all classes of patients, found the alcoholic "a source of ever-recurring trouble."[17] By 1910, several decades after the founding of the AACI and the
establishment of facilities for inebriates up and down the east coast and
throughout the Midwest, Homer Folks, the secretary of the New York State
Charities Aid Association, asserted, "No one fact, other than the hard fact
of poverty itself, confronts social workers, in whatever field they may be
engaged, so constantly as alcoholism." As Folks further reported, even the
"conscientious almshouse superintendent finds his best plans miscarried, and
the discipline and regime of his institution broken up, by the in-and-out
alcoholic rounder."[18] From prostitution to penury, the problems associated
with inebriety were manifold. To turn-of-the-century reformers, inebriety
appeared to nurture a growing population of defectives, delinquents, dependents, and the depraved.

It is hardly surprising, then, that social workers, physicians, and jurists all
became preoccupied with "the alcoholic menace" during the fifty years between 1870 and 1920. These were the years in which the Woman's Christian
Temperance Union, the Prohibition Party, and the Anti-Saloon League

waged a far more visible, and arguably successful, war against drink. Whether concerned with feeblemindedness, domestic violence, lawlessness, or lost wages, reformers expended tremendous efforts to medicalize habitual drunkenness, efforts that must be seen against the backdrop of great urban growth, the rise of industrial capitalism, the arrival of millions of culturally diverse newcomers, the construction of the modern bureaucratic state, *and* the professionalization of medicine and the social sciences in the United States. Within all these contexts, chronic drunkenness came to be seen as an unprecedented threat. Yet, at least initially, it also appeared to offer physicians, especially psychiatrists and neurologists, an unprecedented opportunity to acquire cultural and social authority and to advance their specialties while serving both private and public good.

The construction of specific institutions for drunkards was a key element of the campaign to medicalize habitual drunkenness.[19] Reformers established more than one hundred private and public institutions for inebriates and dipsomaniacs between 1870 and 1920. (Most were closed during the years immediately following the passage of national Prohibition.) At least a dozen states and the District of Columbia attempted to establish public inebriate hospitals, but only California, Iowa, Massachusetts, Minnesota, and New York were successful in creating their own institutions. By far, the longest lived state hospital systems for inebriates belonged to Massachusetts (1892–1920) and Iowa (1902–1920). Indeed, in the same issue of *The Survey* where Homer Folks bemoaned the situation of the alcoholic rounder and the rounder's management within the social welfare and criminal justice systems, Folks's assistant Bailey Burritt pointed to both Iowa's State Hospital for Inebriates at Knoxville and the State Hospital for Inebriates at Foxborough, Massachusetts, as blazing the path for other states.[20]

Origins of Iowa's Inebriate Reform Campaign

At the April 1902 quarterly meeting of the Iowa Board of Control, a new and controversial issue arose. A debate took place over the nature of the inebriates treated within the state hospitals for the insane and the Home for Old Soldiers. Josiah F. Kennedy, secretary of the State Board of Health, initiated the exchange with his paper "Inebriety and Its Management."[21] With the legislature considering several bills to provide state care for inebriates, the Board of Control had decided to study the matter. They had commissioned Kennedy, whose anti-tobacco sentiments were widely known in the state, to conduct the investigation. Kennedy regarded tobacco as what today is called a "gateway drug," one leading to alcohol consumption and, ultimately, to inebriety and crime. Moreover, he regarded the state's swelling inebriate population as a blot on the crest of the State Board of Health, noting:

> here is a large class of acquired and preventable diseases patent not only to the physician and sanitarian, but to the layman as well, and as yet the State Board of Health has not discovered any effectual, if possible, way of prevention; nor has the legislature, the press, or the forum been more successful. Moral suasion, legal suasion, education, the teaching in our public schools of the evil effects of alcohol, the daily exhibition by its unfortunate victims of its dangerous results have all been tried and are still on trial, and yet, as the ranks of the inebriates are thinned by death, there seems to be an on-coming army to take their places.[22]

Kennedy related in detail the story of inebriate hospitals across the country, quoting extensively from the annual reports of the State Hospital for Inebriates in Massachusetts. He concluded with several recommendations from alienists and reformers across the globe in support of the inebriate hospital idea. For Kennedy, however, the construction of institutions for inebriates was just a beginning. Far-ranging in his reform vision, the Board of Health secretary declared that the battle against habitual drunkenness required not only prevention through temperance instruction at school and home, but prohibitions against drinking within "the great corporations"; the termination of state employees who use intoxicants—cigarettes, tobacco, and alcohol; rigorous laws against the sale of alcohol and tobacco to minors; and the elimination of confirmed inebriates' "right to beget a tainted offspring."[23]

Nothing if not comprehensive, Kennedy's plan bore the stamp of Iowa's vigorous temperance movement and presaged the state's eugenics concerns by about a decade.[24] It represented the sort of Progressive Era activism that had characterized Iowa's medical profession. And it was of a piece with the centralizing administrative reforms taking place in Iowa's state government. As historians Amy Vogel and Lee Anderson have shown, the temperance lobby, medical profession, and eugenics movement in Iowa were far from isolated communities.[25] And during the early years of the twentieth century, all three were poised to take advantage of the agenda of the new centralized administrative agency in the state, the Board of Control. Indeed, the success of Iowa's experiment in state-sponsored medical treatment for inebriates depended largely upon the ties among these groups.

If it was unusual for the topic of medical care for inebriates to receive such prominent attention from the Board of Control in 1902, it was hardly surprising, given the ongoing alcohol concerns of Iowa's physicians. As early as 1871, Josiah F. Kennedy had presented several resolutions before the Iowa State Medical Society to recognize the existence and agenda of the American Association for the Cure of Inebriates, founded in the previous year. Ken-

nedy lobbied to appoint an ongoing committee on inebriety that would report on the topic "as upon any other medical subject."[26] In 1880, a
temperance-minded contingent within the state medical society presented
the Iowa General Assembly with a petition to ban the sale of intoxicating
liquors at state, district, and county fairs.[27] And two presidents of the society
devoted significant portions of their inaugural speeches to the topic. In 1885,
H. C. Huntsman of Oskaloosa encouraged "the medical profession to support this fearless young State in its gigantic struggle with a social disease
that honeycombs society."[28] In 1892, George F. Jenkins of Keokuk, noting
that inebriety "more seriously and disastrously affected the moral and civil
affairs of the State and Nation than any other disease that comes under the
notice of the physician," urged the state to consider a law that would recognize inebriety as a disease and provide medical treatment for "the alcohol
habit," in a special facility.[29]

Concerns about the alcohol problem in Iowa, and the medical treatment
of inebriates in particular, reflected an increasing commitment on the part
of the state medical society to serve the public's health and consolidate their
own social authority.[30] Indeed, in 1906, just a year before the State Hospital
for Inebriates at Knoxville opened its doors, Sioux City's William Jepson,
the president of the society, observed: "A constantly recurring necessity seems
to exist of impressing upon our legislative bodies, including those charged
with the moulding of public thought and directing legislative action, that
we are vitally concerned in all that pertains to the health and welfare of the
public. . . . From this organization must ever flow in the future that thought
which will be the guiding light to our law-makers in making matters per-
taining to the betterment of the physical and mental welfare of our citizens."[31] In short, stewardship of the individual patient *and* the body politic
were priorities for Iowa's leading physicians.

The medical society's litany of interests in the alcohol problem was not
unusual in Iowa. Another prominent organization, the State Board of
Health, was preoccupied throughout the 1880s with similar concerns. The
founding of specific facilities for inebriates at two of the state's insane hospitals in 1902 coincided with unprecedented growth in the Board of Health's
administrative authority. After its establishment in 1880, the Board of Health
had served as little more than a state advisory agency, maintaining the power
to recommend, but not enforce, sanitation and anti-nuisance measures it
deemed in the public's interest. In 1902, smallpox struck Iowa's capital, Des
Moines. The disease disrupted city life and led other major midwestern cities
to reconsider their economic ties to Iowa's capital, where officials were slow
to put costly quarantines into effect. A legislative "panic" ensued, and the
board was given the authority not only to recommend, but to enforce its

policies.[32] Strengthening the Board of Health was very much a political expedient to secure Iowa's business status within the Midwest. In one stroke, the state relieved its trade partners' fears of contagion and took a significant step toward securing the health of the state's citizens through rational administration.

Politics, however, was nothing new for the Board of Health. The temperance lobby, and the Woman's Christian Temperance Union in particular, had courted the agency throughout its first two decades. Fighting to maintain its mantle of scientific objectivity and political neutrality, the Board consistently stopped short of adopting a strong pro-temperance position. Instead, its members used their organization "to inject medical science into the temperance debate," winning the favor of an important political constituency—the WCTU—while addressing a legitimate public health concern.[33]

Nor was the Board of Health the only state organization to don the mantle of science, or at the very least, scientific or rational management. Iowa's Board of Control of State Institutions was established in 1898 to improve the efficiency and management of Iowa's charitable and correctional institutions through central governance. Prior to the Board's formation, the individual institutions functioned autonomously: they were, in essence, small fiefdoms, competing with one another annually for the state's largesse. Poor relief and its attendant institutions were managed with near autocratic authority by county judges from 1851 to 1860, when county boards of supervisors assumed these responsibilities. It is not surprising, then, that the very first pleas for a state inebriate asylum, voiced in 1863, arose from the judicial sector, long responsible for the welfare of the state's dependent paupers and insane.[34] Even after control of the county charities and corrections institutions had been ceded to the new boards of supervisors, inspections of the institutions remained the province of the county judges and their prosecuting attorneys, a system that obtained until 1868.[35] Between 1870 and 1898, there were repeated calls for a central state agency to manage Iowa's welfare and correctional institutions, all unsuccessful.

By 1897, though, Iowa's emerging constellation of state institutions for the deaf, dumb, insane, orphaned, and criminal classes was shrouded in controversy. Local corruption and general mismanagement had led to "a feeling of hostility between institutions and a feeling of opposition toward them on the part of [the] public and Legislature, induced by sentiment that institutions were the vehicles of special interests, and not unselfishly representative of a beneficent purpose of government."[36] To combat this skepticism and ill will, the General Assembly appointed the Healy Investigating

Committee, which delved into the administration of the state's asylums, homes, and prisons, and ultimately recommended that a new, rationally and centrally organized governing board be created for their supervision. The Board of Control was appointed as a direct result of the Healy Committee's report, and charged with three basic responsibilities: general, including financial, control of the state charitable, penal, and reformatory institutions; financial control of the state's institutions of higher education; and administrative control of the county and private institutions for the insane.[37]

Efficient management also meant that the General Assembly encouraged the Board of Control to make sure that the state's institutions were kept abreast of the latest developments in the care of their respective populations. Thus, it was the Board's task to undertake investigations regarding the management of "soldiers' homes, charitable, reformatory and penal institutions in this and other countries" and to encourage "scientific investigation of the treatment of epilepsy by the medical staff of insane hospitals and the institution for the feeble-minded . . . to publish from time to time bulletins and reports of the scientific and clinical work in such institutions."[38] It was in this capacity that the Board asked J. F. Kennedy, secretary of the State Board of Health of Iowa, to present the overview contained in his paper "Inebriety and Its Management" at its quarterly meeting in March 1902.[39]

Finally, turn-of-the-century developments within Iowa's temperance movement—specifically, the weakening of the state's prohibition policy—created a more hospitable climate for novel alcohol control measures, including medical care for inebriates. In 1889, Iowans elected a Democratic governor, Horace Boies. Boies's election spelled an end to thirty-two years of Republican rule in the state and signaled Iowans' dissatisfaction with prohibition, a staple of the Republican platform. Republicans eventually gave up their strong support for prohibition, ceding control over such issues to the legislature, and they won the governorship back in 1893. One year later the legislature voted in the Mulct Law, which did not repeal prohibition, but gave individual communities the option of modifying it within their borders upon a favorable local vote and the payment of a certain fee. Now cities were able to exercise a certain level of control over their own wet or dry status.[40] With the state's policy on prohibition easing, legislators initiated what Dorothy Schwieder termed "an almost bewildering array" of new liquor legislation to keep the traffic and the problems associated with drinking in check. In 1909 alone, there were at least nineteen bills on liquor reform introduced at the General Assembly.[41] Six years later, in 1915, however, statewide prohibition won the day again. By the time national Prohibition was enacted, "almost every known method of regulating the liquor traffic [had] been given a trial in Iowa."[42] In short, the establishment of the state inebriate hospital should be seen as but one of many new checks placed on the alcohol trade by Iowans during the Progressive Era.

From "Nuthouse" to "Jaghouse": An Iowa Chronology

State legislators, however, were not eager to expend the necessary funds to establish a separate institution for the treatment of inebriates, so they first imposed a less expensive solution on an unwilling Board of Control. In February 1902, House representative Mahlon Head of Greene County introduced a bill before the General Assembly to establish a special ward for inebriates at one of Iowa's state hospitals for the insane. The bill, approved by the House the next month, and by the Senate and its Committee on Public Health in April, was significant for its originality and for its placement of inebriety squarely within the medical domain. Yet there was little support for the measure among the state hospitals' executive officers. The superintendents of Mount Pleasant and Clarinda State Hospitals, Charles Applegate and Max Witte, and the chairman of the Board of Control, Judge John Cownie, countered that the treatment of inebriates at a *separate* institution, as Kennedy's report had proposed, offered Iowans the best solution. But the economy-minded legislature disagreed. A few weeks after the Board of Control's March meeting, the bill cleared the Senate. The new inebriate law went into effect on the Fourth of July.[43]

On July 21, the *Cherokee Democrat* noted that the state had received its first inebriate, one S. N. Bidne, a blacksmith from Norma. Bidne was "in the habit of getting drunk, and when in this condition, sometimes dangerous."[44] Most recently, while intoxicated, he had attempted to shoot a woman. As the first person to be tried under Iowa's new inebriate law, Bidne had to tough it out in the Forest City jail until the Board of Control decided which hospital would receive the state's habitual drunkards. Unlike the insane, who rarely, if ever, were held in jail as they awaited room at Iowa's insane asylums, inebriates were sentenced to the state hospitals under the same conditions that governed the commitment of individuals to the state's industrial schools[45] The state's policy reflected both the moral and the medical dimensions of inebriety: in order to receive medical treatment, the prospective inebriate was first detained in jail, then tried before a judge; then "sentenced" to the state hospital for a period of time designated by the district court judge rather than determined by hospital physicians; and the governor, not the hospital superintendent, held the power to "parole" patients. Medical authority was far from complete.[46]

Within twenty-four hours of Bidne's trial, the Board of Control reached its decision, the *Des Moines Register and Leader* reported: "Inebriates to go to Mount Pleasant—the Board is Hostile. . . . The board does not approve of the new law and believes it was a mistake to make the inebriate depart- ment a part of one of the state hospitals. . . . It is expected there will be an ample number of patients, and that it will not be long until the new de- partment is overtaxed."[47] So began Iowa's eighteen-year experiment in the medical management of the state's inebriates.

By September 1902, just two months after Mount Pleasant had established its inebriate ward, referred to in official documents as "the inebriate hospital," sixty-nine habitual drunkards were receiving treatment, and the rate of ad- mission for inebriates was outpacing that for the insane. In October, the Board of Control designated Cherokee State Hospital, the newest (and emp- tiest) of the state hospitals, the institution to care for inebriates from the northwestern part of the state. As in virtually all other state hospitals in the country, and certainly those in Massachusetts, the mixing of inebriates and insane patients proved difficult. Opening up Cherokee to habitual drunkards might have relieved congestion, but it did not ease the tensions between the two patient populations. Upon making his monthly inspection of the Mount Pleasant State Hospital, for example, Board of Control Chairman John Cownie reported that the insane held the inebriates in utter contempt. Chat- ting with a patient whom he mistakenly thought an inebriate, Cownie had "spoke sympathizingly with him and consoled with him over his unfortunate habit." The patient, confined by reason of insanity, shouted in indignation, "Mr. Cownie, I want you to know I'm no drunken sot; I'm here for my health."[48] Matters had not improved by the end of the year, when a well- respected general manager of a Des Moines insurance company was sen- tenced to the Mount Pleasant facility for his drinking and complained bit- terly about the treatment he received. In short, the inebriates, once sober, were insulted by their confinement with individuals who had lost their minds; the insane were offended by being housed with those they regarded as immoral and vicious in habit; and the superintendents were piqued by the resulting discord and the ease with which the inebriates, once sober, escaped from the hospital grounds. Nor did it help that Cherokee's superintendent, Max Voldeng, proclaimed after a mere six months of treating inebriates at his hospital: "Caring for inebriates properly at a state hospital for the insane is as impossible as its attempt is injudicious. Besides the uselessness of keep- ing the inebriates, their presence is injurious to the insane patients and to the discipline of the institution. Usually, they are dirty and lazy. . . . They won't work. All they do is sit around and spit tobacco juice all over every- thing, making their rooms dens of filth."[49]

Responding to the complaints of both the superintendents and the patients, and to the critique and recommendations offered by the Board of Control, the state legislature in 1904 set aside over $100,000 to revamp the abandoned State Home for the Blind in Knoxville as the new State Hospital for Inebriates. The General Assembly also put the Board of Control in charge of the state's inebriate facilities, removing the authority from the governor's hands.[50] Creating the new Knoxville State Hospital took two years. Local opposition to the facility fell away as the promise of jobs became a reality for Knoxville's citizens. In January 1906, the *Knoxville Express* reported with great fanfare:

> From the survey a two hours' visit to the new institution affords, we are impressed with the fact that the state has undertaken in seriousness to afford men addicted with the drink habit an opportunity to reform. ... A special study of each patient's case will be made by the medical directors, and an earnest attempt made to combat and eradicate the disease of alcoholism. It is hoped that when patients are dismissed from the hospital that they will have been built up into the best physical condition they are capable of. As Superintendent Willhite says, the work of the hospital must necessarily be, in a large measure experimental, and if it proves to be successful in any large degree it will be the greatest thing in the world.[51]

Finally, the inebriates had a home of their own. Over the next fourteen years, five different superintendents served terms at the State Hospital for Inebriates at Knoxville. In 1913, the hospital developed a two-tiered system which separated "hopeful" inebriates from the so-called incorrigible inebriates, who, although deemed unlikely to reform, were thought to benefit from prolonged confinement within a structured farm setting.[52] Parole became largely a discretionary procedure controlled by the superintendent and Board of Control, and a pay system for patient labor was established that compensated the working inebriate, funneled money back to the hospital for his support, and sent what was left to the patient's dependents, if he had any.[53] The inebriate hospital at Knoxville never served women, who comprised between 4 and 10 percent of the inebriates treated in the state between 1902 and 1920. Female inebriates continued to take the cure at Mount Pleasant State Hospital for the Insane, where a ward remained open specifically for their care.[54] In 1919, with the passage of the Volstead Act, Knoxville closed its doors to the state's alcoholics, and the state sold the facility to the federal government as a hospital for returning veterans of World War I.[55] The dwindling numbers of inebriate men were sent to the Independence State Hospital, and the women continued to be treated at Mount Pleasant.[56]

Recurring Desires, Conflicting Priorities:
Treatment at Knoxville

Treating Iowa's inebriates was a difficult, unenviable task. As with the condition itself, treatment often pitted the physical and psychological needs of the drinker against the emotional and economic needs of his or her family. The correspondence of Ed Harris and his son with the governor makes this plain. Initially, treatment also opposed the needs and desires of inebriates to those of the insane; this much is clear from the report of Chairman Cownie. What's more, shortly after Iowa initiated its inebriate reform program in 1902, doctors at the state hospitals realized that their own therapeutic intentions were being thwarted by the needs and priorities of the court system, especially the county judges who committed patients. Addressing these and other challenges posed a frustrating problem for all involved and one that was constantly renegotiated, much like the disease concept of inebriety itself. How then did each of these parties make sense of the problem of inebriety and its treatment?

The Cultural Framing of Inebriety

At least rhetorically, Iowa's state hospital physicians conceived of inebriety as a disease of modern civilization, somewhat akin to George Miller Beard's concept of neurasthenia. Classifying the condition as "one of the most serious menaces accompanying the twentieth-century civilization," whose "direful effects seem to have been fully realized in all civilized countries," Charles Applegate, superintendent of the Mount Pleasant State Hospital, voiced an opinion shared by most of the directors of Iowa state institutions.[57] Dealing with this "defective class" was "becoming more difficult as our modern social life becomes more complex. . . . Not in the whole field of medicine is there a disease so far-reaching in its ruinous effects upon the habitue himself, home, family, and society at large," added W. S. Osborn, who became the second superintendent at Knoxville in 1906.[58] The comments of Applegate and Osborn highlight the perceived seriousness of the problem they confronted. They are also interesting for the connections the physicians drew between Iowa and "modern civilization."[59] Applegate made this tie more explicitly when he observed, "The statistical records of the police courts of Paris, London, New York, and Chicago, show a rapid increase in juvenile criminality, and charge this increase to alcohol. Our small towns, too, have caught the disease."[60] The problems of the metropolis had become the problems of the heartland; and it followed that Iowa should engage in reform efforts on par with nations such as Great Britain and France and states such as Massachusetts and New York, places keeping "abreast of the times by enacting restrictive laws to enable us to protect, treat, and if possible, cure this unfortunate class of citizens."[61]

Yet even if inebriety was a disease of modern civilization demanding a modern, scientific response, it was by no means clear to Board of Control members that the state had a moral or financial obligation to provide the most up-to-date care to inebriates. Even after three state hospitals had established inebriate wards, Judge L. G. Kinne, a member of the Board of Control, noted that inebriates, whether diseased through defective heredity or vicious habit, did *not* deserve the state's largess, though they should receive it anyway because "the state can do no better service to society at large than to restore to health and to the ranks of the productive laborers these men and women who, without such aid become mental and physical wrecks and who tend to sap the morals and health of the people, thereby greatly adding to the vast army which is a constant public burden."[62] Kinne, who had spent many an hour considering the plight of the "defective, delinquent, and criminal" classes, articulated two related arguments in favor of state care for inebriates: inebriety was a fount of other physical, mental, and social diseases, and inebriety turned productive citizens into beings obsessed with the consumption of alcohol.

Relying on Benedict Morel's theory of degeneration, Kinne and his comrades in reform believed that one generation's inebriety could be hereditarily transmitted to the next as a defective nervous constitution, which subsequently could appear in the form of inebriety, epilepsy, insanity, nervousness, moral depravity, or criminal behavior.[63] If those possessing such debilitating and destructive constitutions chose to reproduce with individuals similarly affected, their children in turn would suffer from an even greater array of disabling conditions, until finally, the hereditary line would terminate. Thus, in the minds of Board of Control members, if no effort were made to confine and treat the inebriate ranks of Iowa, they had the potential to spawn a race of physical and moral degenerates that would tax the state and national coffers as never before. Eugenical arguments such as this were a staple of discussions of the state's duties.[64] Inebriate reform was promoted as enlightened and scientific statecraft.

Similarly, in a mostly agricultural state that prided itself not only on its productive farms but on its metal mining firms and a host of Mississippi River industries, inebriety posed a particularly disturbing threat. The unchecked consumption of alcohol violated the productive ethic that Iowans held dear and foreshadowed the public's rising concern with addiction, a concern that became a staple of twentieth-century consumer society.[65] Some reformers believed that the desire for alcoholic stimulation originated on the one hand in the mentally taxing work of the professional and merchant classes and on the other hand in the debilitating work conditions and standard of living that burdened the unskilled laborer—in other words, in the demands of production (whether in the office or on the farm). However, most focused on the act of consuming alcohol itself as the force which turned men, and to a lesser extent women, into unrestrained consumers. Thus, Knoxville's first superintendent, W. S. Osborn, recommended gardening and farm work as restorative pursuits for inebriates, not only because the physical activity might strengthen weakened physiques, but because these pursuits substituted "healthy activity for unhealthy activity, sober thought to produce instead of drunken craving to consume."[66] In a state as agriculture-oriented as Iowa, gardening and farm work also could be seen as vocational training. Treatment was meant to restore inebriates to productive citizenship.

At the same time that reformers in Iowa perceived inebriety as a disease of consumption run amok in modern civilization, threatening to compromise future generations, they also reluctantly regarded it as an "American" disease. This is not to say that they were ignorant of the toll habitual drunkenness took in other nations. Far from it. Inebriety was a disease that connected Iowa to the metropole, whether Boston or Paris. Yet, the statistics collected by the superintendents of insane hospitals treating inebriates between 1902 and 1906 demonstrated conclusively that second- and third-generation Americans dominated patient censuses—not Germans, not the Irish, not Scots, not Britons, not Slavs, not even Scandinavians.[67] Of course, relatively speaking, Iowa did not have the burgeoning immigrant populations of the northeastern or western United States or of midwestern cities such as Chicago. Nevertheless, the perception was that foreigners drank more than Americans, especially Iowans who had lived under prohibition for so long. Reformers expected to find foreigners or first-generation Americans presenting at the inebriate hospitals in disproportionately high numbers. When Charles Applegate reported his findings to the contrary—137 of 155 admissions to the inebriate hospital at Mount Pleasant in 1902–1903 were second- or third-generation Americans—the directors of Iowa's penal, medical, and social welfare institutions were shocked. In the words of Board of Control Chairman John Cownie: "It is really surprising that the nations of Europe where a great majority of the people indulge in intoxicating liquors should furnish so few confirmed inebriates for treatment . . . while the American, where [sic] food is better and more abundant than in Europe, and where there is less temptation for the use of intoxicating liquors on account of poverty, should lead all others with one hundred and thirty-seven."[68] All was not well in the land of milk and honey. Cownie asked, "What could account for the fact that although more Europeans than Americans drank, the Americans were more likely to become inebriates?" Answering his own question, he claimed it was the American character—"the persistency with which the American goes after everything he undertakes." In other words, the strength of the American drive was a weakness when it came to inebriety. The commandant of the old soldiers' home suggested that it was simply Americans' "pernicious habit of treating," something not shared by foreigners, who generally paid only for themselves.[69] Superintendent M. T. Gass of the soldiers' orphans home thought that Americans recognized their drinking problems more easily and sought out treatment more frequently.[70] This was a sanguine interpretation, but one with which the matron at the same institution disagreed. Instead, Mary Hilles, who claimed familiarity with "with mothers of all classes," believed simply that "the foreign mother is a better homekeeper than the mother of the same class among the Americans."[71] Foreign mothers prepared more wholesome meals than their American counterparts, claimed Hilles. Thus, foreign families were better nourished and less in need of artificial stimulants such as alcohol to help them through the day. No explanatory consensus was ever achieved with regard to the abundance of American patients, but the fact was undeniable: inebriety in Iowa was an American disease. It was also a disease that revealed the state's caretakers' prejudices for and against the foreign presence in Iowa. Ultimately, its new nativist image may also have helped garner support for medical reform efforts.

Varieties of Inebriety: Medical versus Lay Understandings

Iowans held many different views of inebriety between 1902 and 1920. "Periodical inebriate," "environmental or associational inebriate," "vicious and incorrigible inebriate," "incurable inebriate," "hopeful and respectable inebriate," "weak and self indulgent inebriate," "nervous, impulsive, and easily led inebriate," "chronic, selfish, ignorant, lazy and criminal inebriate," "gentleman, tippler inebriate," "honest, hereditary victim inebriate," "dipsomaniac," "simple inebriate," "common drunkard," and "alcoholic"—Iowa's physicians used each of these terms in patient records and journal articles when describing the habitual drunkards they confronted at the state's inebriate hospitals.[72] With so little terminological consistency among the doctors treating inebriates, it should not come as a surprise that medical and lay understandings of inebriety frequently conflicted.

In actuality, however, there was a good deal of overlap among a number of these terms. Generally, physicians distinguished between various types of inebriety according to their presumed etiology, the duration of the inebriate's behavior and symptoms, the supposed proximity of the symptoms to insanity, the degree of morality or immorality displayed, and the strength of the individual's desire to reform. Those who had become inebriates by dint of heredity were deemed at once the least to blame for their condition, and the most difficult to cure. Frequently, dipsomaniacs, whose desperate craving for drink struck at odd intervals, were understood to have inherited a debilitated nervous constitution. Often termed "true inebriates" or "honest hereditary victim inebriates," these individuals suffered from "a well recognized abnormal mental condition," and were deemed incapable of experiencing a "normal intoxication."[73] By contrast, physicians saw those who became inebriates solely through the habit of drinking as at least partially responsible for their disease. Simple inebriates' condition originated in repeated habitual indulgence—the habit of drinking nurtured through the pleasures of "normal" intoxication, the urgings of drinking associates, the pain associated with some physical debility, or the emotional trauma of losing a loved one or job. In these cases, the "willpower" of the inebriate was compromised over time. Gradually the voluntary habit of drinking to excess became the disease of inebriety. For the "innocent" inebriate, then, a defective nervous constitution, hereditarily transmitted, provoked the habit of chronic intoxication. For the "guilty" inebriate, the habit of intoxication brought about the disease of inebriety. The distinction here was not unlike that made between the "worthy" and "unworthy" poor.

The duration of one's habitual drunkenness, the presence of a criminal record, the number of times an individual had attempted to "take the cure," and the degree to which a patient appeared to desire reform all figured prominently in his or her diagnosis as "incurable," "hopeful," or "incorrigible." Similarly, physicians anticipated a higher rate of cure in those with the financial resources to support their stays and to facilitate their gradual return to employment. In other words, class mattered.[74]

Doctors declared those with several years of inebriety under their belts unlikely candidates for cure, while they deemed individuals in the earlier stages of their disease both desirable and promising patients. Such an opinion bore remarkable similarity to physicians' stance on insane patients and those with another chronic disease, tuberculosis. Yet, most of the patients committed to Iowa's inebriate hospitals had been inebriates for fifteen to twenty years, and many of these individuals had sought out "specific" cures prior to admission. Specific cures, also known as patent or secret remedies—Leslie E. Keeley's bi-chloride of gold is the most famous—were common at the turn of the century. They were administered at private "institutes" for inebriety and nervous disease, or obtained by mail order.[75] A patient's repeated attempts to "take the cure" cut both ways: such efforts testified to the individual's genuine desire for reform, but they also indicated the difficulty of successfully helping that person. More often than not, a long duration of inebriety matched with a history of taking "specific" cures resulted in an "incurable" diagnosis.

What troubled the superintendents of Mount Pleasant, Cherokee, Independence, and eventually Knoxville most, though, were not the incurable patients per se, but the stream of so-called incorrigible inebriates who were committed to the hospital from the county courts. Such patients were recognizable to physicians not only by their symptoms and chronicity, but by their moral taint. Frustrated after his first year as the director of the Knoxville State Hospital, Superintendent W. S. Osborn declared, "The indiscriminate commitment of persons because they are given to drink brings degenerates, criminals and men of low moral standing in which there is little or no hope of benefit. The last named class of patients do not want to be benefited, but prefer the life they have been leading."[76] Two years later, Osborn's successor, H. S. Miner, reported that the problem persisted, for county courts regarded the hospital as "a dumping place for all the good-for-nothing bums and petty criminals in the community. Everyone who was a menace to society, whether an inebriate or not, if he indulged in intoxicants at all, ought to go to Knoxville."[77] The results of such commitments were devastating to hospital order and efficacy. Escapes and elopements were rampant among this class of patients, who diverted the hospital staff's energies and diluted the institution's "cure" rates.[78]

The problem of the "incorrigible" inebriate revealed much about the difficulties of medicalizing habitual drunkenness. First, the managerial priorities of each institution—court and hospital—were instrumental in defining who was an "inebriate" requiring medical treatment. At least initially, the courts wished to get rid of their worst recidivist cases and regarded these individuals as appropriate candidates for medical care (after all, nothing else had worked!), while the hospital wished to treat "hopeful" cases early in their drinking careers. Ultimately, the inebriate hospital struck a bargain with the courts and state legislators, agreeing to take the incorrigible cases, if they might be detained in a new branch of the facility, the inebriate "reformatory."[79] Physicians saw the separation of these two patient classes as essential to maintaining a hopeful and uplifting atmosphere for those who might benefit from hospital confinement.

The case of the "incorrigible" inebriate, indeed the term itself, further reminds us that inebriety was perceived as a hybrid medico-moral condition, one that doctors believed involved the power of the will and the power of heredity, and one that likewise addressed issues of criminal justice and medical treatment.[80] If hospital physicians saw teaching the courts how to select appropriate candidates for medical care as an important step toward effective hospital treatment; they regarded educating the public as another. The families and friends of inebriates routinely committed their loved ones to the hospital while harboring two false assumptions: first, that treatment required but a few weeks—much like the Keeley cure—and second, that their committed relatives would be returned to them upon request.[81] Moreover, it was not clear that the Iowa public regarded inebriety as a disease in the first place, despite the state's imprimatur. Between 1902 and 1906, the superintendents of Iowa's state hospitals for the insane could pride themselves on their up-to-date understanding of the disease of inebriety, but bringing the public in line was a more difficult matter. As Mount Pleasant's Charles Applegate lamented in 1903: "There seems to be but little charity, and less sympathy, shown the poor unfortunate inebriate by the general public, and it may all be due to the fact they do not consider inebriety a disease, but the results of the victim's own sin and folly."[82] Newspaper coverage of the inebriate hospitals' work suggested a similar reluctance on the public's part to regard inebriety as just another disease. For example, initially Knoxville's residents so vigorously protested the state's decision to place the inebriate hospital in their town that one Iowa paper concluded that "the drunkard [was] considered by all classes as on a lower level than lunatics or convicts."[83] It is hard to tell if public opinion had changed much by 1906, when the inebriate hospital at Knoxville opened, and when the *Knoxville Journal* editorialized that it "was impressed with the fact that the state has undertaken in seriousness to afford men addicted with the drink habit an opportunity to reform. Those incarcerated in the institution will not be permitted to rest on flowery beds of ease, nor will they be subjected to unnecessary harsh discipline. They will be furnished good comfortable rooms, good diet, proper medical treatment and those who are physically able will be required to work."[84] Language such as this only fed the ambiguous identities of inebriety and its institutions. Was addiction a habit or a disease? Was inebriate reform medical or penal? Were inebriates incarcerated or admitted? Addressing the Thirty-Fourth General Assembly in his biennial message on January 9, 1911, Governor B. F. Carroll offered his own answer: "Some of the persons sent there need medical attention, perhaps when first committed most all of them do, so that it would be necessary to maintain a hospital, but a larger percent of the inmates, after the first few days or weeks, at most, are abundantly able to work and need to be thoroughly disciplined. . . . In other words, the institution should partake *both* of the nature of a hospital and a reformatory."[85]

Medico-Moral Therapy in Iowa: Tonics and the "Wheelbarrow Cure"

The superintendents of the state institutions for inebriates and the members of the Board of Control shared Governor Carroll's concerns. Daily they confronted the challenges of curing a morally loaded, chronic disease that took men and women away from their families and often compromised their financial security. Meanwhile, the taxpayers and legislators, conflicted in their attitudes toward the inebriates, wanted assurance that their dollars were being put to effective use. Devising a treatment regimen that attended to the medical and psychological needs of patients and their families' financial needs, as well as the political demands of legislators and citizens-at-large, was no easy task. Searching for models of successful state programs for reforming inebriates, the Board of Control turned to other states. Of these states, Massachusetts appeared to offer the most guidance.

In truth, the treatment protocol established at the Iowa institutions was remarkably similar to that offered inebriates in the Bay State.[86] Elements of this regimen were quite standard, though matters were a bit more complex than Mount Pleasant's Charles Applegate claimed when he averred that the object was to "simply confront the disease and treat it."[87] Most patients arrived in an intoxicated state. Before putting these individuals to bed, the admitting physician and his assistants made preliminary mental and physical exams. Blood and urine samples were sent to the pathologist. Once the patient had sobered up, usually after 24 to 72 hours, a second exam was performed; this included the patient's own narrated history and an attempt to verify previous diagnoses. At this point, the admitting physician often learned that the patient's alcohol habit had begun as an effort to relieve the pain of some underlying injury, disease, craving, or personal tragedy. Medicines, tonics, and physical therapies followed, according to the case. Strychnine, the active ingredient in nux vomica, was used frequently as a digestive aid and nervous tonic, especially in cases of difficult withdrawal. The same held true for tincture of cinchona and tincture of gentian, which were both used as digestives. Physicians also employed chloral, sulphonal, and bromides, all powerful nervous system depressants, in conjunction with strychnine, especially when sleep proved difficult. Hydrotherapy, electrotherapy, and massage supplemented these tonics.[88]

Once the immediate effects of alcohol and its withdrawal had passed, physicians started inebriates on a light diet of toast, oatmeal, and milk accompanied by large quantities of coffee and tea—"stimulation without intoxication," they proclaimed. When the patients' health improved, the diet became more varied. Patients continued to receive their daily doses of strychnine, just as they did at many private sanitaria. If, after a few weeks, patients progressed to this stage, they started a program of physical culture, exercise, and employment, usually within and around the hospital grounds. Physicians also considered entertainments, lectures, and general socializing essential elements of therapy. Through these means, and the gradual awarding of liberties around the grounds for good behavior, physicians hoped to reform their patients and return them to productive citizenship.[89]

Though the medico-moral elements of therapy were evident in the Iowa superintendents' prohibitions against card playing and the hospital lectures "along moral lines," the therapeutic issue that best highlighted the moralistic frame of inebriety was employment. Light occupation—vocational therapy—routinely played a part in the treatment of the insane, but the inebriates' situation was more complicated. Simply put, if the state was willing to care for its inebriated ranks, legislators believed that the taxpayers of Iowa should receive something in return. The Board of Control agreed, reasoning that inebriety might be a disease, but it was a largely self-inflicted disease, an illness whose victims' moral failings frequently were responsible not only for their condition, but also for their loved ones' financial worries and the state's bloated roster of dependents, defectives, and degenerates.

The contrast between the "innocent" insane and "guilty" inebriates is clear when we consider the rehabilitative labor expected of each group. The insane might engage in gardening, farming, domestic labor, and some lighter oc-cupational pursuits, but the Board of Control actually considered coal mining a potential form of "vocational therapy" for inebriates. Although many of the men who were admitted to Knoxville were so-called unskilled labor, more than their shortage of skill led the Board to suggest coal mining. According to Board member John Cownie, coal mining was ideal for several reasons. First, mining required little skill; second, a mine might supply fuel econom-ically to all state institutions; third, the prospect of mining coal at the state hospital for inebriates was so loathesome an image that it might deter many from alcoholic excess; fourth, it was easy to keep watch on the inebriates if they were underground; fifth, after laboring in the mine, inebriates would be too tired to escape; and sixth, mining might be done all year round, as opposed to farm work, which was seasonal. Coal mining was thinly veiled punishment for inebriates. The real appeal of mining lay in its punitive ability to deter drinkers from alcoholic excess and to provide for the state's economic interests. If leg irons and locks were not a part of the inebriate hospital, a mine shaft might serve instead.

The state never constructed its coal mine at the inebriate hospital. Instead it supplied a fleet of wheelbarrows. Most patients who stayed at Knoxville for more than a few weeks ended up taking "the Wheelbarrow cure." The hospital loaned its inebriate patients to local farmers at harvest time, and it employed patients to grade the land around the institution and manage the hospital farm. With Knoxville employing more than fifty men to landscape the grounds, John Cownie eagerly reported to the *Knoxville Express*: "Our wheelbarrow cure for dipsomaniacs is working wonderfully well . . . [it] is the best thing we have found yet . . . I tell you when the men get through with that cure they will hesitate a long time before they touch whisky [sic] again and have to go back to the wheelbarrow."[90] Through their employment, inebriates earned a wage that was split between the hospital and the patients' families, if they had them, or the hospital and the patients, if they had no relatives. The wheelbarrow cure was meant to appease a treatment-shy public and return dollars back to the state's coffers; it also was intended to train patients to provide for themselves and their dependents. In 1911, the state built a brick works at Knoxville to keep the men at work year round.

Ed Harris in Context: The Patients and Their Stories

If the Board of Control, the state legislature, the superintendents, and the newspapers helped mold the medical and penal identity of the inebriate hospital, so did patients, their families, and friends. Indeed, the last three parties put the inebriate asylum to uses that were frequently at odds with the therapeutic goals of reformers. Iowans might concede that the state needed a medical facility for its inebriates, but they wished to serve their own social, and often personal, ends.

Take, for example, the case of women seeking divorces from their habitually drunk husbands. In 1903, shortly after the passage of the new inebriate law, the *Cherokee Democrat* reported that "wives are taking advantage of the new dipsomaniac law to get divorces." Habitual drunkenness had been considered grounds for divorce in Iowa for some time, but it was a difficult condition to prove. With the opening of the inebriate asylum, wives had a new way to certify that their husbands drank to excess regularly: they could have their men committed to the inebriate hospital. Within weeks of the opening of the Mount Pleasant Hospital for Inebriates, at least five women committed their husbands as inebriates and promptly filed divorce petitions.[91]

Matters had not changed much by the time Knoxville opened its doors in 1906: the *Des Moines Register* regaled readers with the story of Harvey Connor, a sometimes abusive inebriate who had "turned his wife and children out of doors and converted his house into a sort of wholesale liquor establishment." When Mrs. Connor could take no more, she threatened divorce. But in a peculiar twist of fate, Mr. Connor actually avoided the divorce proceeding by agreeing to be committed to the state inebriate hospital. In his case, the act of taking the cure indicated to civil authorities an earnest desire to put his life back in order and return to the ranks of responsible husbands. Connor received a term of "three years, or until cured."[92] In these cases, whether the condition was considered a disease or not mattered less than the legal recognition that the condition was "real," and therefore grounds for civil action.

Some inebriates were remarkably adept at enlisting not only their families, but also their friends and concerned townspeople in the commitment and parole processes. Consider the case of Karl Pedersen, a horse buyer from Decorah, a small river town in northeastern Iowa and home of Luther College. Though this Norwegian immigrant's "pecuniary status" was listed as "poor," upon his admission to the Independence State Hospital for Inebriates in September 1903, Pedersen proved rich in friends. According to his admitting history, Pedersen had bought horses successfully for seventeen of his thirty-five years, but in the previous two years he had lost a considerable sum in the horse trading business. Subsequently, Pedersen had turned to drink. A willing and cooperative patient, he was well liked by the hospital staff, one of whom noted on 30 October: ". . . gets along very nicely. Is quiet and well behave [sic], and [works] in the dining room where he is a very good helper. Is not very profane."[93] Such comments reveal the priorities of both staff and institution: successful institutional management required compliant behavior; successful treatment meant the patient's adoption of good manners and work habits.

That same fall day, the citizens of Decorah also cast their vote in Pedersen's favor, petitioning W. P. Crumbacker, the Independence superintendent, to recommend the horse trader's parole to the state's governor, Albert Cummins.[94] Signed by Decorah's mayor (who was a physician), by the city's district court clerk, sheriff, marshal, hotel manager, and several bankers and businessmen, the petition was also endorsed by W. D. Lawrence, M.D., medical director of the Lawrence Sanitorium for the cure of inebriety and the drug and tobacco habits in Minneapolis, Minnesota, where one of Pedersen's best friends had been a patient. Though Pedersen's original "term" at the inebriate hospital was listed as eighteen months, he was paroled just seven weeks after the arrival of the petition, upon his taking a pledge to avoid both drink and drinking establishments. Like his fellow parolees, Pedersen was asked to make monthly reports to the governor, approved by the clerk of the district court, certifying his abstinence. One year later, a report from the Decorah sheriff indicated that Pedersen was again drinking, but significantly less than before his confinement.[95]

Pedersen was not alone in having his community rally behind him. Jan Vickers, a twenty-six-year-old printer from Jones County, near the State Penitentiary at Anamosa, was committed to the inebriate ward of the Independence State Hospital for the Insane in January 1903 by his mother. Concerned about the "bad company" her son kept when drinking, and alcohol's pernicious influence on Vickers's behavior and ability to earn his living, Mrs. Vickers thought his case warranted medical treatment. Though its exact date is not recorded, a petition was filed with the hospital superintendent on Vickers's behalf, requesting his parole. Signed by the clerk of the district court who had processed Vickers's original commitment papers, as well as several attorneys, merchants, a newspaper editor, a physician, the mayor of Anamosa, and others, the petition proclaimed that personal acquaintance with the printer had convinced residents that "if paroled . . . [he] will keep the obligations of his parole and abstain from the use of all intoxicating liquors."[96] Vickers, however, took matters into his own hands, escaping on April Fools Day, after two and a half months of confinement at Independence. The Anamosa sheriff, W. A. Hogan, returned Vickers to Independence a month later, and his parole was granted in early June. Six months later, the same sheriff reported that Vickers was serving a jail sentence of fifteen days for violating the terms of his parole by drinking. "We want him returned [to the state hospital] as soon as he is discharged," added Hogan.[97]

The discourse shaping patients' commitment, treatment, and release was hardly confined to petitions. The committing parties—family, friends, or officers of the court—played an essential part in supplying the patient's history. When Dennis Rowley, a forty-one-year-old Cedar Rapids railroad worker of Irish ancestry, entered the Inebriate Hospital at Cherokee in December 1902, the law firm that had helped Rowley's wife initiate commitment proceedings previously (only to be dissuaded by a number of Rowley's friends, including the Catholic priest of Cedar Rapids) reported that Rowley was a good worker in spite of his hard drinking; that he had been abusive toward family and friends because of his drunkenness; and that his family struggled to support themselves since his earnings were spent on alcohol: "We hope that you will be able to reclaim Mr. Rowley and if you are able to correct his habits he will be able by industry and application, both of which he possesses in a high degree, to make restitution for his former misconduct and mistreatment of his family. He keenly appreciates the abuses and mistreatment they have received at his hands, and if he can but be cured of the drink habit, he will become a faithful citizen. We hope you will succeed in righting him and in sending him home in complete possession of himself."[98] The language of the lawyers highlights several issues. First, the inebriate's character was an important element in the treatment process. The law firm emphasized Rowley's potential for productive citizenship, should the hospital succeed in curing him of the liquor habit. Again, the institution's missions were both clinical and social. The disease of inebriety was a "habit" which required the "righting" of the individual, as well as his being "cured." Finally, it is interesting, but not surprising, that a law firm rather than a physician supplied the useful patient history. It was, after all, usually aberrant social behavior—violence, domestic abuse, squandered wages—that made habitual drunkenness so disturbing, not the clinical manifestations of alcohol consumption. The hospital treated both. And the inebriate's personal and clinical histories offered hospital physicians clues as to how well that treatment might take. These narratives also identified difficulties at work, troublesome associates, or poor family relationships. Each of these environmental factors and others could portend failure, no matter how much progress was made inside the hospital walls.

Cases such as Pedersen's, Vickers's and Rowley's reveal the socially negotiated nature of treatment, and ultimately, the way in which the public and physicians viewed inebriety. The cooperation between medical and lay agents—the townspeople, lawyers, the hospital superintendent, and the governor—make the political nature of treatment for the inebriate clear. Medicalization, in this case, was neither complete, nor a top-down, physician-orchestrated affair. Inebriety was both clinical entity and social disease. Even the term "parole," typically applied in penal contexts, confirmed inebriety's hybrid moral-medical disease persona. In violating his or her physical constitution through drink, the inebriate had also transgressed Iowa's civil polity. All manner of citizens had a say in the path the inebriate followed before, during, and after treatment.

Conclusion: Iowa and the Progressive Cause of Medicalization

The Progressive Era has received more attention from historians of Iowa than almost any other period in the state's history.[99] A passing glance at John Briggs's tome *Social Legislation in Iowa* gives a sense of the remarkable diversity of social reforms—from domestic relations to defective delinquency, from prostitution to public health—that swept across the Hawkeye State in the early twentieth century. What makes the state's experiment with medical care for habitual drunkards so integral to Iowa's history is its resonance with the full spectrum of social reform concerns. Indeed, as much as any reform passed in turn-of-the-century Iowa, the creation of inebriate hospitals embodied a diversity of elements that characterized Progressivism in America: the search for order; the rise of "issue-focused coalitions"; the secular institutionalization of Protestant moral values; the growth of an increasingly regulatory state with a well-articulated, efficiently organized, social reform mission; the maturation of the professions; and the expansion of scientific and medical authority.

I have argued that we should understand Iowa's efforts to provide medical care for inebriates as part of the larger changes taking place within the state at the dawn of the twentieth century: the reform of Iowa's government and the centralization and expansion of state authority for health and social welfare institutions; the professionalization of Iowa's physicians, and their attendant commitment to both clinical medicine and public health; and the cyclical tides of temperance and prohibition reform. In essence, Iowa was able to put in place an unusual medical and social reform measure thanks to its ties to these larger developments. The eugenics movement, active in Iowa from the 1890s through the 1920s, also nurtured a public socio-medico-economic discourse that placed priority on curtailing drunkenness.[100] For Iowa's turn-of-the-century medico-moral entrepreneurs, to reform the inebriate was to stem the tide of liquor-induced hereditary degeneration and its attendant disease, poverty, and crime.[101] Inebriate hospital advocates repeatedly offered this rationale for their work. In short, the Progressive Era was an opportune moment to propose an alternative to the failed "treatment" solutions of the mental asylum and jailhouse. The inebriate hospital idea drew ideological and institutional support from a variety of important political, economic, social, and medical sources that typified Iowa's participation in the Progressive Movement between 1900 and 1920.

It is also important to see the Iowa story within the larger disciplinary context of American psychiatry's growth and its expansion into the realm of everyday life. As the historians of medicine Elizabeth Lunbeck and Jack Pressman have argued, turn-of-the-century American psychiatrists embraced a new and expansive vision of their specialty, one in which mental illness and aberrant behavior were caught early. In an effort to transform their specialty into an active, treatment-oriented branch of medicine, psychiatrists, neurologists, and neuro-psychiatrists distanced themselves from their custodial forbears, the alienists and asylum keepers. Neuroses and bad habits were to be nipped in the bud, before they blossomed into full psychotic flower. Just as preventive medicine and hygiene became the watchwords of the new public health, so too, prophylactic psychiatry, mental hygiene, and the psychopathic hospital became staples of psychiatric medicine in the early twentieth century. In their psychopathic hospitals, and increasingly in their private offices, physicians practiced the psychiatry of adjustment, helping their patients reform their attitudes and behaviors in cases of broken marriages, delinquency, petty crime, prostitution, depression, and habitual drunkenness. As Lunbeck notes, psychiatrists wished to treat the psychopathology of everyday life.[102] And for many, whether in twentieth-century Boston or Progressive Era Iowa, heavy drinking was part and parcel of their routine existence.

Yet, Iowa's experiment in inebriate reform speaks more specifically to the difficulty inherent in expanding medical authority to treat social problems.

This is the process of medicalization—a process too often characterized as the medical profession's heavy-handed, near unilateral efforts to bring certain physical conditions or behaviors into its domain. Perhaps the archetypal example of medicalization is the case of madness. Medieval Europeans understood madness in theological terms, as punishment for sinful behavior; early moderns regarded the mad as socially noxious, dependent, and sometimes dangerous. Not until the Enlightenment, however, when Britain began to require medical certification to confine the mad to asylums, did physicians become the keepers of the mad. The late eighteenth century and early-nineteenth-century moral therapy employed at asylums in Europe, Great Britain, and the United States was heralded by the medical profession and the public as an unprecedented humanitarian and therapeutic advance. In America, efforts to build asylums for the insane were led by the "father of American psychiatry," Benjamin Rush, who took charge of the Pennsylvania Hospital in 1783. The social reformer and school teacher Dorothea Dix picked up where Rush left off in the early nineteenth century, campaigning vigorously and successfully throughout the country for the construction of new asylums. Thus, by the mid-nineteenth century, madness had become mental illness, falling squarely within the physician's domain.

In calling for new inebriate asylums, reformers from Benjamin Rush on routinely invoked the story of madness's medicalization, arguing that the same level of humanity that was shown the insane should be given the inebriate. Chronic inebriety and its neurological lesions were not only thought to precipitate mental illness, but some types, "dipsomania" for example, were regarded as forms of insanity. As W. S. Osborn, superintendent of Knoxville, remarked in 1907,

> The application of present day methods in treating inebriates is not unlike the unscientific measures resorted to in the treatment of that kindred disease, insanity, during the middle ages. In the light of such experience, in view of the great number of crimes committed, the nameless havoc wrought together with the fact that inebriety is the most fruitful and prolific source of all diseases which afflict mankind, can we say that inebriates receive just and proper consideration from their fellow men? Must not the state recognize its responsibility, and recognizing such, owe it to the safety and welfare of its people . . . to isolate and treat these unfortunates? . . . [Inebriates] are diseased individuals . . .[103]

The comparison between inebriates and the insane is a useful one in large measure because it begs the question of how the process of medicalization works. The powerful position of psychiatry today may be attributed in part to the expansive disciplinary actions of Progressive psychiatrists wishing to extend their medical domain, but some territories proved more difficult to claim than others, and some proved less attractive in the course of time. In Iowa, it is clear that physicians were hardly alone in advocating for the disease concept of inebriety and the medical treatment of the condition. The first cries for an inebriate asylum came not from doctors but from judges in the county court system. Indeed, some hospital superintendents actively opposed offering medical care to habitual drunkards when the issue was first raised. The legislature, however, voted the state's new medical policy into place, and the superintendents were left no alternative but to accept it.

Thus, the story of Iowa's inebriate hospital experiment makes clear that offering medical care for inebriety was hardly a top-down process. Though the policy was initiated "from above," by the state legislature, and carried out by hospital physicians, court systems, and even the governor, the commitment and treatment processes involved inebriates' families, friends, and fellow citizens. The involvement of these latter parties, as we have seen, suggests limitations to both state and professional authority in the medicalization process. Although each of these agents participated in the inebriate hospital experiment, they frequently did so on their own terms, and it is difficult to say whether their participation in initiating treatment or demanding its end signaled an endorsement of the disease concept of inebriety. Ironically, the medicalization process may have received support from parties uninterested in the medical perspective per se, but interested in its particular social utility. Recall the example of frustrated women seeking divorce from their chronically drunk husbands. The women used commitment to the hospital as a means of validating their complaints against their spouses and facilitating divorce. Court systems, similarly frustrated by their worst drunkard recidivists, deemed these individuals "worthy" of medical treatment—this in spite of the protests of hospital superintendents, who found such cases both "incorrigible" and "incurable." In short, both individual and institutional priorities influenced participation in the medical enterprise, and such involvement did not necessarily denote a change of perspective on the nature of inebriety from vice to disease.

Thus, though the political, professional, and institutional circumstances in Iowa were propitious for the creation of a new medical approach to caring for the habitual drunkard, the implementation of the medical model—medicalization—proved less successful because the various nonmedical parties involved continued to pursue their own goals, and these objectives often clashed with treatment regimens, undermined the authority of hospital physicians, and frequently sabotaged patients' chances of successful reformation. Had the hospital's success rate been more promising, matters might have been different. But the superintendents' resistance to using the term "cured"—a reasonable reluctance on their part, given the intractability of the condition they treated and the difficulty they had in keeping their patients for the desired therapeutic course—loudly broadcast the problematic nature of their medical mission. Moreover, two other factors worked against the wholesale adoption of the medical perspective: first, the fact that the medical facilities for drunkards addressed a small percentage of the alcoholic population; that is, many more drunkards were sent to jail for their petty crime of public drunkenness than were confined at the inebriate hospitals. Thus, medical care could hardly supplant the traditional criminal justice solutions to this vexing problem. Second, Prohibition and World War I cut short the medical efforts of physicians, drying up much of the political concern for the treatment of drunks. Many legislators doubted the necessity of medical care for the inebriate when the manufacture and sale of alcoholic beverages was banned. And wartime prohibition and the tendency for down-and-out drunks to either enlist in the armed services or obtain employment in a desperate labor market diminished the patient censuses at inebriate hospitals across the land. In the end, Iowa's efforts to medicalize habitual drunkenness were unsuccessful for as wide a range of reasons as they were initiated.

Notes

Reprinted in slightly different form from "Contesting Habitual Drunkenness: State Medical Reform for Iowa's Inebriates, 1902–1920," *Annals of Iowa* 61 (Summer 2002): 241–285. Copyright 2002 State Historical Society of Iowa. Used with permission of the publisher.

My thanks to the State Historical Society of Iowa for awarding me a publications grant that made completing this work possible. The staff at the SHSI has provided outstanding support and made doing research in Des Moines a pleasure. I am also grateful to *Annals of Iowa* Marv Bergman, who has provided insightful suggestions since he first heard this material presented at the Iowa History Forum in April 2000. I thank the anonymous readers of this essay for their helpful comments and encouragement.

1. Ed Harris to Governor William L. Harding, 5 January 1917, "State Institutions: Inebriate Hospital, Knoxville," in Governor Harding Papers; General Correspondence of the State's Institutions, box 29, folder 1-3732, State Historical Society of Iowa, Des Moines, (SHSI-DM). Unless otherwise noted, all archival materials are held at the SHSI-DM. The patient case files and records are kept at each of the state hospitals where they were originally recorded.

2. Ibid.

3. Little did Harris know that the superintendents of the hospitals treating inebriates (Mount Pleasant for women; Knoxville for men) thought the "common drunkard" had a better prognosis than the "the true inebriate." See George Donohoe, "The Inebriate," *Bulletin of the Iowa Board of Control* 16 (March 1914). Of course, Harris might have been making a distinction based on economic class rather than pathological status, though the two have never been unrelated in discussions of inebriety or alcoholism. Nevertheless his use of the term "common drunkard" was in stark contrast to the views of the superin-

tendents of the inebriate hospitals, highlighting two important issues: the difference between lay and medical understandings of inebriety, and the changing terms used to describe those with hopeful versus pessimistic prognoses.

4. Robert Harris to Governor William L. Harding, 13 February 1917, Governor Harding Papers.

5. William L. Harding to Ed Harris, 17 February 1917, Governor Harding Papers. As we shall see, the length of time required for successful treatment was a hotly contested issue. Harris's "favorable" patient status quite likely had to do with the fact that he was better off financially than most inebriates and had a job waiting for him upon his return—indeed a position that was beckoning him during his stay at Knoxville.

6. Ed Harris to Governor William L. Harding, 28 February 1917, Governor Harding Papers. By 1917, the inebriate hospital at Knoxville was not eager to use the term "cure" in relation to inebriety. They preferred to refer to patients as improved sufficiently for parole, and offered as a comparative case the insane patient who was discharged as cured from the state hospital, but who might easily return there at a later date suffering again from mental illness. In addition, the term "cure" smacked of the patent medicine trade that sold "specifics" or "cures" for inebriety—a business that virtually every superintendent of an Iowa institution found loathesome professionally and therapeutically.

7. M. C. Mackin to Governor William L. Harding, 6 March 1917.

8. Ed Harris to Governor William L. Harding, 11 April 1917.

9. The uneven nature of the archival correspondence and patient records from Iowa's turn-of-the-century inebriate experiment makes it hard to judge the representativeness of Harris's case, even if we can determine how frequently businessmen were admitted to the state inebriate hospital for their alcohol problems. The minutes of the Iowa State Medical Society's annual meetings, the quarterly reports of the Board of Control, the annual reports of the inebriate hospitals, and the daily reportage of local newspapers tell an interesting tale of Iowa's Progressive Era struggle to define the nature of habitual drunkenness and to devise an acceptable socio-medical solution to this vexing problem.

10. Here I borrow the terms "social" and "cultural" authority from Paul Starr, who uses them in his *Social Transformation of American Medicine* (New York: Basic Books, 1982). He writes, "Social authority involves the control of action through the giving of commands, while cultural authority entails the construction of reality through definitions of fact and value." Physicians may possess both types of authority, for they may direct other medical personnel—say, physician assistants or nurses—as well as patients, to follow their orders. When patients go to a physician, however, to learn what's "wrong" with them, they are relying on the doctor's "authority to interpret signs and symptoms, to diagnose health or illness, to name disease, and to offer prognoses.... By shaping the patient's understanding of their own experience, physicians create the conditions under which their advice seems appropriate" (Starr, *Social Transformation*, 13–14).

11. Dorothy Schwieder, *Iowa: The Middle Land* (Ames: Iowa State University Press, 1996), 212. For a discussion of the nineteenth-century temperance debates, see also Richard Jensen, "Iowa, Wet or Dry? Prohibition and the Fall of the GOP," in Marvin Bergman, ed., *Iowa History Reader* (Ames: State Historical Society of Iowa and Iowa State University Press, 1996), 263–288.

12. Throughout the nineteenth century and into the twentieth, temperance reformers and those concerned with reforming individual inebriates were frequently one and the same group. The physician and social activist Benjamin Rush, a founder of the American temperance movement in the late eighteenth century, also advanced a disease concept of

alcoholism and urged the creation of special "sober houses" for the treatment of drunkards. The immensely popular, if short-lived, Washingtonian temperance movement of the 1840s made the reclamation of the individual drunkard and the support of his or her family its chief cause. This was also true of the fraternal temperance orders—the Sons of Temperance, the Good Templars, and the various Ribbon movements—of the later nineteenth century. And while the Woman's Christian Temperance Union (WCTU) is perhaps best remembered for its late nineteenth- and early twentieth-century parades of women in white and campaigns against the liquor traffic, the organization maintained close ties with the Blue and Red Ribbon Reform Clubs for individual drinkers and advanced their own White Ribbon movement. With mission-like zeal, the WCTU also sought out drunkards in their homes, in hospitals, in jail, at saloons, and in the workplace to preach the "gospel temperance" and reclaim lost souls. They also published illustrated pamphlets about the ravages wrought on the drunkard's body through his or her consumption of alcohol. In short, the reform of individual drunkards was a vital part of the American temperance movement. For broader views of the temperance movement see, Jack Blocker, *American Temperance Movements: Cycles of Reform* (Boston: Twayne, 1989); Joseph Gusfield, *Symbolic Crusade: Status Politics and the American Temperance Movement* (Urbana: University of Illinois Press, 1963); and Mark Edward Lender and James Kirby Martin, *Drinking in America: A History,* 2d ed. (New York: Free Press, 1987). For the efforts of the WCTU, see Ruth Bordin, *Women and Temperance: The Quest for Power and Liberty, 1873–1900* (New Brunswick: Rutgers University Press, 1981); Catherine Gilbert Murdock, *Domesticating Drink: Women, Men, and Alcohol in America, 1870–1940* (Baltimore: Johns Hopkins University Press, 1998); Philip Pauly, "The Struggle for Igorance about Alcohol: American Physiologists, Wilbur Olin Atwater, and the Woman's Christian Temperance Union," *Bulletin of the History of Medicine* 64 (1990): 366–392; and Jonathan Zimmerman, *Distilling Democracy: Alcohol Education in America's Public Schools, 1880–1925* (Lawrence: University of Kansas Press, 1999).

13. For more on the history of the Iowa State Psychopathic Hospital, see Paul E. Huston, "The Iowa State Psychopathic Hospital (part one)," *The Palimpsest* 54, no. 6 (November/December 1973): 11–27, and Huston, "The Iowa State Psychopathic Hospital (part two)," *The Palimpsest* 55, no. 1 (January/February 1974): 18–30. For an earlier discussion of the value of such an institution to Iowa, see Max N. Voldeng, M.D., "The Present Status of Mental Hygiene and Mental Control," *Journal of the Iowa State Medical Society* 3, no. 6 (December 1913): 378–385. Voldeng, who was one of the first superintendents to treat inebriates at Cherokee State Hospital for the Insane, noted (381): "All observation hospitals, all institutions with psychopathic departments are replete with instances where early and proper control resulted in speedy recovery of various mental diseases. The prompt response to immediate supervision and treatment of alcoholic cases is apparent to everyone."

14. California, Massachusetts, Minnesota, and New York are other states that attempted to develop extensive treatment services for the chronically intoxicated. See Sarah Tracy, "The Foxborough Experiment: Medicalizing Inebriety at the Massachusetts Hospital for Dipsomaniacs and Inebriates, 1833–1919," Ph.D. diss., University of Pennsylvania, 1992, and Jim Baumohl and Sarah Tracy, "Building Systems to Manage Inebriates: The Divergent Paths of California and Massachusetts, 1891–1920," *Contemporary Drug Problems* 21 (Winter 1994): 557–97.

While I date the origins of the inebriate reform movement to the founding of the American Association for the Cure of Inebriates, it is worth noting that there were earlier calls for asylums for inebriates. During the late eighteenth century, Benjamin Rush issued a plea for homes for drunkards in *An Inquiry into the Effects of Ardent Spirits upon the Human Body and Mind, with an Account of the Means of Preventing and of the Remedies for Curing Them,* 8th revised ed. (Brookfield, Mass.: E. Merriam, 1814; this text was first published in 1784). Samuel Woodward, the superintendent of the Massachusetts Asylum for the Insane at Worcester, further urged the construction of hospitals for inebriates in *Essays on Asylums for Inebriates,* collection of essays originally appearing in 1833 in the *Boston Daily Mercantile Journal* and in 1838 in pamphlet form. It is republished in Gerald Grob, *Nineteenth-Century Medical Attitudes toward Alcoholic Addiction* (New York: Arno Press, 1981).

This characterization of the inebriate reform movement as a classic Progressive reform effort derives in large part from treatments of the Progressive Era and the development of the state apparatus and the professions in Robert Wiebe, *The Search for Order, 1877–1920* (New York: Hill and Wang, 1967); Louis Galambos, "The Emerging Organizational Synthesis in Modern American History," *Business History Review* 44 (1970): 279–290; Daniel T. Rodgers, "In Search of Progressivism," *Reviews in American History* 10 (1982): 113–132; Thomas Haskell, *The Emergence of Professional Social Science: The American Social Science Association and the Nineteenth-Century Crisis of Authority* (Urbana: University of Illinois Press, 1977); Starr, *The Social Transformation of American Medicine;* Andrew Abbott, *The System of Professions: An Essay on the Division of Expert Labor* (Chicago: University of Chicago Press, 1988); and Camilla Stivers, *Bureau Men, Settlement Women: Constructing Public Administration in the Progressive Era* (Lawrence: University Press of Kansas, 2000).

15. Joseph Parrish, "Minutes of the First Meeting of the American Association for the Cure of Inebriates," American Association for the Cure of Inebriates, *Proceedings, 1870–1875* (New York: Arno Press, 1981), 8.

16. Nathan Smith Davis was founder of the Medical Temperance Society, which met annually at the American Medical Association meetings. He was also editor of the *American Medical Temperance Quarterly* and helped found the Chicago Washingtonian Home for the Reformation of Inebriates in 1863. Although the Home was based largely on Christian temperance principles, Davis believed that inebriety was a disease. See Nathan Davis, "Inebriate Asylums: The Principles that Should Govern Us in the Treatment of Inebriates," *Quarterly Journal of Inebriety* 2 (1877): 80–88; and Mark Lender, "Nathan Smith Davis," *Dictionary of American Temperance Biography: From Temperance Reform to Alcohol Research, the 1600s to the 1980s* (Westport, Conn.: Greenwood Press, 1984). At its founding in 1784, the Woman's Christian Temperance Union pledged its support for homes for inebriate women, and it established at least five homes in New York City, Philadelphia, New Hampshire, and Chicago. Frances Willard voiced her support for both the disease concept of alcoholism and the creation of industrial homes for male inebriates as well. See Willard, "Homes for Inebriates" and "Habitual Drunkards," in Anna Gordon, *The Beautiful Life of Frances Willard* (Chicago: Woman's Temperance Publishing Association, 1898), 173–175; and Murdock, *Domesticating Drink.* Woods, an outspoken settlement house reformer in Massachusetts, was instrumental in securing public and legislative support for the Massachusetts Hospital for Dipsomaniacs and Inebriates (later the State Hospital for Inebriates at Foxborough, and finally the Norfolk State Hospital [for Inebriates]). See Robert A. Woods, "Massachusetts State Hospital for Inebriates and Dipsomaniacs," *Pennsylvania Medical Journal* 12 (November 1908): 144–148; Woods, *The Prevention of Inebriety: Community Action* (Washington: Government

Printing Office, 1912) and Woods, *Drunkenness: How the Local Community Can Be Brought to Do Its Part* (Boston: Massachusetts Commission on Probation, 1916). Beard, whose ideas about nervous disease "illustrate[d] the utility of scientific metaphor in helping rationalize a rapidly changing and stress-filled world" is best known for his *American Nervousness* (New York, 1881) and his discovery of neurasthenia. However, prior to this work, he wrote extensively on inebriety and the hereditary nervous weakness that frequently contributed to it. See George M. Beard, *Stimulants and Narcotics: Medically, Philosophically, and Morally Considered* (New York: Putnam, 1871); Beard, "Causes of the Recent Increase of Inebriety in America," *Quarterly Journal of Inebriety* 1 (1876): 25–48; and Charles E. Rosenberg, "George M. Beard and American Nervousness," in his *No Other Gods: On Science and American Social Thought* (Baltimore: Johns Hopkins University Press, 1976), 98–108. The interest of these prominent figures suggests the visibility and salience of the inebriate reform cause.

17. Homer Folks, "Social Aspects of Alcoholism," *The Survey* 25 (1910): 14.

18. Ibid.

19. For excellent overviews of the inebriate hospital movement, see William L. White, *Slaying the Dragon: The History of Addiction Treatment and Recovery in America* (Bloomington, Ill.: Chestnut Health Systems/Lighthouse Institute, 1998), esp. 21–63; and Jim Baumohl, "Inebriate Institutions in North America, 1840–1920," in Cheryl Krasnick Warsh, ed., *Drink in Canada: Historical Essays* (Montreal: McGill-Queen's University Press, 1993), 92–114.

20. Bailey Burritt, "The Habitual Drunkard," *The Survey* 25 (1910): 25–41.

21. Josiah F. Kennedy, M.D., "Inebriety and Its Management," *Bulletin of Iowa Institutions* 4, no. 2 (April 1902): 184–95.

22. Ibid., 185.

23. Ibid., 186. Kennedy's recommendations to corporations that they enforce a temperate workplace and "homeplace" for their workers presaged Henry Ford's creation of the Sociological Department by a few years. The Ford Sociological Department inspected workers' homes to see if their homelife qualified them for the famous $5 Day. Drinking was grounds for exemption from this level of pay.

24. Iowans' concerns about alcoholism and degeneracy were plain to see in the state's first eugenics law, enacted in 1911. Said to be among the country's strictest eugenics legislation, the law encouraged the sterilization of "habitual criminals, degenerates and other persons," which included "criminals, rapists, idiots, feeble-minded, imbeciles, lunatics, drunkards, drug fiends, epileptics, syphilitics, moral and sexual perverts, and diseased and degenerate persons" held within state institutions—in other words, any person who was believed to run the risk of producing "children with a tendency to disease, deformity, crime, insanity, feeble-mindedness, idiocy, imbecility, epilepsy, or alcoholism" (*Supplement to the Code of Iowa [1913]*, sec. 2600). Likewise, in a less extreme vein, the WCTU, according to historian Hamilton Cravens, saw eugenics as a means of "socialization into the proper habits of health, diet, and sobriety for the young." (Cravens, *Before Head Start: The Iowa Station and America's Children* [Chapel Hill: University of North Carolina Press, 1993], 36–7).

25. See Amy Vogel, "Regulating Degeneracy: Eugenic Sterilization in Iowa, 1911–17," *Annals of Iowa* 54 (Winter 1995): 119–43; and Lee Anderson, "'Headlights upon Sanitary Medicine': Public Health and Medical Reform in Late Nineteenth-Century Iowa," *Journal of the History of Medicine and Allied Sciences* 46 (1991): 178–200. See also Lee Anderson, "A Case of Thwarted Professionalization: Pharmacy and Temperance in Late

Nineteenth-Century Iowa," *Annals of Iowa* 50 (Winter 1991): 751–771; and Philip L. Frana, "Smallpox: Local Epidemics and the Iowa State Board of Health, 1880–1900," *Annals of Iowa* 54 (Spring 1995): 87–118. For more on alcoholism and eugenics, see Leila Zenderland, *Measuring Minds: Henry Herbert Goddard and the Origins of American Intelligence Testing* (New York: Cambridge University Press, 1998), esp. 186–221, and Ian Dowbiggin, *Keeping America Sane: Psychiatry and Eugenics in the United States and Canada, 1880–1940* (Ithaca: Cornell University Press, 1997), esp. 85–88.

26. "Minutes of the 1871 Annual Meeting," in Historical Committee of the Iowa State Medical Society, ed., *One Hundred Years of Iowa Medicine: Commemorating the Centenary of the Iowa State Medical Society, 1850–1950* (Iowa City: Athena Press, 1950), 37.

27. "Minutes of the 1880 Annual Meeting," in ibid., 43.

28. "Minutes of the 1885 Annual Meeting," in ibid., 46.

29. "Minutes of the 1892 Annual Meeting," in ibid., 51. See also A. W. McClure's presidential address in "Minutes of the 1887 Annual Meeting," in ibid., 48. McClure, an advocate of "mental therapy," was for many years the president of the board of trustees of the Mount Pleasant State Asylum for the Insane (later the Mount Pleasant State Hospital) and had firsthand knowledge of alcohol's role in mental illness.

30. See for example "Minutes of the 1878, 1879, 1881, 1884, 1886, 1890, 1893, 1903, and 1906," in ibid., 41–43, 45, 47, 49, 51, 61, and 65.

31. "Minutes of the 1906 Annual Meeting," in ibid., 65.

32. For more on the Board of Health's acquisition of state administrative power, see Harold Martin Bowman, *The Administration of Iowa: A Study in Centralization* (New York: AMS Press, 1903), 129–58, esp. 139–41; and Frana, "Smallpox: Local Epidemics and the Iowa State Board of Health, 1880–1900."

33. Anderson, "Headlights upon Sanitary Medicine," 196.

34. Hubert Wubben in his *Civil War Iowa and the Copperhead Movement*, (Ames: Iowa State University Press, 1980), notes, "Dubuque's Judge Hamilton thought the state needed a center to deal with problem drinkers, a state Inebriate Asylum" (186).

35. In 1868, the brief-lived circuit judges (who replaced the county judges) and district attorneys were charged with these responsibilities. See Bowman, *The Administration of Iowa*, 96–98. Between 1870 and 1898, these remained the only administrative agencies for charitable and correctional institutions. One exception to this supervisory trend was the 1872 establishment of a gubernatorially appointed visiting committee to monitor the treatment of patients at the state's institutions for the insane. See ibid., 106–107.

36. Ibid., 110.

37. Ibid., 115.

38. Ibid., 21.

39. Kennedy, a prominent general practitioner and public health activist, who had turned down an appeal from the reorganized state medical school to become its first professor of medical theory and practice in 1870, devoted his energies instead to the State Board of Health, where his role and influence were legendary. See also Anderson, "Headlights upon Sanitary Medicine," 193, and L. F. Andrews, "Iowa State Health Board's Grand Old Man," *Des Moines Register and Leader*, Sunday morning edition, 23 February 1908, 2.

40. Dan Elbert Clark, "The History of Liquor Legislation in Iowa," *Iowa Journal of History and Politics* 6 (1908): 55–87, 339–374, 503–608; Jensen, "Iowa, Wet or Dry?" 263–288.

41. Schwieder, *Iowa: The Middle Land*, 216–217.

42. Dan E. Clark, "Recent Liquor Legislation in Iowa," *Iowa Journal of History and Politics* 15 (1917): 42–43.

43. *Journal of the House of the 29th General Assembly of the State of Iowa* (Des Moines), 1902, xxxviii; *Acts of the 29th General Assembly of the State of Iowa* (Des Moines), 1902, 58–59; *Journal of the Senate of the 29th General Assembly of the State of Iowa* (Des Moines), 1902, 883, 1187. The Senate committee's vision of inebriety as a mental health problem rather than a penal problem is significant. The Massachusetts legislature had followed a similar course, establishing a state hospital for inebriates and dipsomaniacs in 1893 that fell within the jurisdiction of the State Board of Lunacy and Charity. When that institution was reorganized as the Norfolk State Hospital for Inebriates in 1911, the Commonwealth had already split its Board of Lunacy and Charity into a Board of Insanity and a Board of Charities, locating it outside the state's mental health system, even though its protocols for admission, treatment, and release were modeled on those of the insane. In the Massachusetts case, the switch signaled the state's view of the inebriate as a drain on the Bay State's economy first, and as a person with mental disease second.

44. "Dipsomaniac Law put into Effect," *Cherokee Democrat*, 22 July 1902, 2.

45. Charles Applegate, the superintendent of the Mount Pleasant State Hospital voiced his objections to the new inebriate law's penal aspects in his biennial report to the Board of Control: "I believe that the inebriate should be committed by the commissioners of insanity the same as in the case of an insane person, and not allowed to remain in jail awaiting trial when in need of treatment, and when the greatest amount of good could be accomplished. If inebriety is a disease and the inebriate is to be treated in a hospital, his commitment should not convey the penal aspect of a criminal until he has been found guilty of a criminal offense." *Twenty-second Biennial Report of Iowa State Hospital, Mount Pleasant, to the Board of Control of State Institutions—for Biennial Period ending June 30, 1903* (Des Moines: The State of Iowa), 65.

46. At the request of the state hospital superintendents, the General Assembly revised the inebriate commitment laws in 1904 and again in 1907, giving hospital physicians more governing power over their inebriate patients, taking the power to parole patients away from the governor and placing it in the hands of the hospital superintendents, and making it possible for inebriates to voluntarily commit themselves to the hospital without a court trial. By 1907, the courts and inebriate hospitals (by then Knoxville for men and Mount Pleasant for women) further restricted admission to people "not of bad character or repute aside from the habit for which the commitment was made," and individuals who stood a reasonable chance of being cured. See John Briggs, *The History of Social Legislation in Iowa* (Iowa City: State Historical Society of Iowa, 1915), 185–195.

47. "Inebriates Go to Mt. Pleasant," *Des Moines Register and Leader*, 22 July 1902.

48. "Dislike Dipsomaniacs—Insane Patients Incensed at Being Confined with Bestial Drunks," *Cherokee Democrat*, 21 October 1902, 2.

49. "Are a Big Nuisance: Such is Dr. Voldeng's Opinion of the Inebriates," *Cherokee Democrat*, 19 November 1903, 1.

50. The governor, however, still could issue a patient's parole upon the recommendation of the Board or the hospital superintendent.

51. "New Hospital Open—Superintendent Willhite now Ready to Extend Hearty Welcome to the 'Dipsies,'" *Knoxville Journal*, 26 January 1906, 2.

52. Briggs, *History of Social Legislation in Iowa*, 185–95.

53. Ibid., 194–95.

54. Board of Control of State Institutions, *Laws of Iowa Relating to the Care of Ine-*

briates in State Hospitals (Anamosa: The Penitentiary Press, 1910). Cited in this pamphlet is a note that on 18 January 1906, the Board of Control designated the Mount Pleasant State Hospital as the one to which female inebriates would be sent.

55. Coincidentally, this is what happened to the Massachusetts Hospital for Dipso-maniacs and Inebriates, although Knoxville, unlike MHDI, remains a VA Hospital to this day. Westborough State Hospital in Massachusetts remained the state institution that treated women, just as Mount Pleasant continued to receive female inebriates. Iowa, however, designated Independence State Hospital as the facility for the treatment of the dwindling number of inebriate men, while Massachusetts sent inebriates to state hospitals throughout the state. See Tracy, "The Foxborough Experiment"; "Laws of the 39th General Assembly of the State of Iowa, Chapter 187, Board of Control, S.F. 790," *Acts and Joint Resolutions Passed at the Regular Session of the Thirty-Ninth General Assembly of the State of Iowa* (Des Moines: The State of Iowa,) 194; and *Twelfth Biennial Report of the Board of Control of State Institutions for the Period Ending June 30, 1920.* (Des Moines: The State of Iowa,) 11–12.

56. Whereas Knoxville had customarily had patients censuses ranging in the 200–300 range, Independence treated less than one hundred persons per year immediately follow-ing Knoxville's closing. See *Twelfth Biennial Report of the Board of Control of State Insti-tutions*; and *Thirteenth Biennial Report of the Board of Control of State Institutions for the Period Ending June 30, 1922* (Des Moines: The State of Iowa).

57. Charles Applegate, "Inebriety, and the Care and Treatment of Inebriates in the Mt. Pleasant State Hospital, Mt. Pleasant, Iowa," *Bulletin of Iowa Institutions* 5 (1903): 155.

58. W. S. Osborn, "State Care and Treatment of Inebriates," *Bulletin of the Iowa Board of Control* 9 (1907) 3.

59. Of course, Applegate's remarks are also colored by his own desire to win the support of others in this cause and obtain a separate facility for their inebriate charges.

60. Applegate, "Inebriety, and the Care and Treatment of Inebriates," 165.

61. Ibid., 155.

62. L. G. Kinne, "Alcoholism," *Bulletin of Iowa Institutions*, 6 (1904) 184.

63. On Benedict Morel and his theory of degeneration, see Charles Rosenberg, "The Bitter Fruit: Heredity, Disease, and Social Thought," in Rosenberg, *No Other Gods*, 25–53. See also Leila Zenderland, *Measuring Minds: Henry Herbert Goddard and the Origins of American Intelligence Testing* (Cambridge: Cambridge University Press, 1998), esp. 145–50. According to Rosenberg, "Morel, a pious French psychiatrist, also assumed that de-generation meant, literally, a deterioration from the state of physical perfection granted man before the fall. Drugs, alcohol, environments inimical to human health and devel-opment—such as mines and urban slums—progressively impaired the ability of men to pass on to their children even that tenuous state of health which they had themselves inherited" (*No Other Gods*, 43). Morel believed in the inheritance of a neuropathic con-stitution which tended to deteriorate from one generation to the next (alcoholism in one generation might lead to feeblemindedness in the next), each generation more compro-mised than its predecessor, until ultimately the last generation was rendered sterile, and thus truly the last. In light of Rosenberg's comments on degeneration, the Iowa Board of Control's recommendation of coal mining as a "therapy" for inebriates was ironic. After all, mining was a dangerous and debilitating occupation. The recommendation also high-lights the balance of punishment and treatment deemed appropriate for those with a moral-medical disease.

64. For eugenical discussions of inebriety, see Applegate, "Inebriety, and the Care and Treatment of Inebriates"; Osborn, "State Care and Treatment of Inebriates"; Kinne, "Alcoholism"; and M.C. Mackin, "The Effects of Alcohol on the Nervous System," *Bulletin of the Iowa Board of Control* 18 (1916). 122–127. For a classic and contemporaneous eugenical treatment of alcoholism in families, see Arthur H. Estabrook and Charles B. Davenport, *The Nam Family: A Study in Cacogenics* (Cold Spring Harbor, N.Y. Eugenics Record Office, 1912). The extremism of the eugenics movement is seen in the words of Estabrook and Davenport's concluding remarks: "Nam Hollow [ancestral home of the Nam Family] is a social pest spot whose virus cannot be confined to its own limits. No State can afford to neglect such a breeding center of feeble-mindedness, alcoholism, sex-immorality, and infanticide as we have here. A rotten apple can infect the whole bowl of fruit. Unless we abandon the ideal of social progress throughout the State we must attempt an improvement here" (84). See also fn. 24.

65. For more on the history of addiction, see Harry Gene Levine, "The Discovery of Addiction: Changing Conceptions of Habitual Drunkenness in American History," *Journal of Studies on Alcohol* 39 (1978): 143–74. For an excellent discussion of workingmen's and workingwomen's consumption habits and middle- and upper-class concerns about their drinking habits see Roy Rosenzweig's local study of Worcester: "The Rise of the Saloon," in Chandra Mukerji and Michael Schudson, eds., *Rethinking Popular Culture: Contemporary Perspectives in Cultural Studies* (Berkeley: University of California Press, 1991), 121–156. Perry Duis, *The Saloon: Public Drinking in Chicago and Boston, 1880–1920* (Urbana: University of Illinois Press, 1983), offers an invaluable comparative perspective. On the rise of consumer society in America, see Daniel Horowitz, *The Morality of Spending: Attitudes toward the Consumer Society in America* (Baltimore: Johns Hopkins University Press, 1985), and Lawrence B. Glickman, ed., *Consumer Society in American History: A Reader* (Ithaca: Cornell University Press, 1999).

66. Osborn, "State Care and Treatment of Inebriates," 9.

67. I have chosen to focus on the male patients in this essay, because they were the chief concern of the physicians, reformers, and judicial officials who wrote about inebriety and shaped the state's policy toward inebriates. Such a focus is not undeserved: between 90 and 95 percent of the patients treated in Iowa's inebriate wards and hospital were male. The Board of Control's biennial reports contain a wealth of demographic data that suggest that prior to their institutionalization between 26 and 36 percent of male patients were occupied in "domestic and personal" services (ranging from bar tending to hotel clerking and egg candling; the largest job category was "laborer"); 25 to 29 percent were in "manufacturing, mechanical, and building" trades (ranging from painters to bakers to watchmakers to miners); and 15 to 17 percent were in agricultural and rural trades (ranging from farmers to nurserymen and horsemen; farmers were consistently the second largest single occupation listed, after laborers). Geographically, by far the largest group of inebriates hailed from Polk County, seat of the state's capital, Des Moines; the ten most populous counties contributed approximately 40 percent of the patients. Half of the men were married, while another third were single; the widowed and divorced made up a fifth of the male patients. Over 80 percent of the inebriates had received their common school certificates; another 15 percent had obtained their high school diplomas or college degrees. "Constant users" were most common, with "occasional" and "periodic" drinkers together making up half of the male patients. Their average age at the time of their admission was about 40 years, with the largest ten-year cohort between the age of 40 and 49. The average age at which most men began getting intoxicated was about 25 years, with ap-

proximately half beginning between the ages of 15 and 24. On average, 90 percent of the men smoked and/or chewed tobacco.

68. John Cownie in "Minutes of the Quarterly Meeting of Executive Officers of the Board of Control," *Bulletin of Iowa Institutions*, 5 (1903): 246.

69. Ibid., 246–247. "Treating" was the term used to describe the practice of paying for another's drink. In the United States during the first half of the nineteenth century, political candidates and political bosses would often hire the saloons and groceries who sold liquor to provide it free for voters several weeks before an election. Following the Civil War, however, treating was done on a more individual level, with saloon keepers buying a round of drinks for their patrons, thus starting a custom that the drinkers themselves kept up. Treating was a sign of masculine solidarity, or camaraderie with the other patrons. It brought saloon keepers a small fortune. See Lender and Martin, *Drinking in America*, 10, 54–56, 60, 104, and Madelon Powers, *Faces along the Bar: Love and Order in the Working-Man's Saloon, 1870–1920* (Chicago: University of Chicago Press, 1998), 93–118.

70. M. T. Gass in "Minutes of the Quarterly Meeting," 248.

71. Mary Hilles in "Minutes of the Quarterly Meeting," 247.

72. These terms are taken from patient records, annual reports of Iowa's inebriate hospitals, and published accounts of the treatment of Iowa's inebriates between 1902 and 1920.

73. Donohoe, "The Inebriate," 104.

74. Of course, socioeconomic status continues to matter in treatment outcomes. There is a wealth of literature that indicates a patient's financial resources affect his or her ability to gain access to treatment programs and are a good indicator of a patient's chances for a successful treatment outcome. Those with more resources are believed to have more of an incentive to complete treatment, for they usually have a higher level of social functioning and a more comfortable lifestyle to rejoin upon achieving sobriety. See F. Baeklund, L. Lundwall, and B. Kissin, "Methods for the Treatment of Chronic Alcoholism: A Critical Approach," in R. J. Gibbons et al., *Research Advances in Alcohol and Drug Problems*, vol. 2 (New York: Wiley, 1975); and P. Nathan and R. Niaura, "Behavioral Assessment and Treatment of Alcoholism," in J. Mendelson and N. Mello, eds., *The Diagnosis and Treatment of Alcoholism* (New York: McGraw-Hill, 1985), 391–455.

75. Linking these cures to medical quackery, regular physicians, or those with conventional medical training, disdained them, and Iowa's hospital superintendents were no exception. One could argue, however, that in spite of their tainted image within the regular medical profession, the Keeley Cure and the Keeley Institute did more to promote the disease concept of alcoholism than any other medical remedy or organization. For more on Leslie E. Keeley, see White, *Slaying the Dragon*, esp. 51–71; Cheryl Krasnick Warsh, "Adventures in Maritime Quackery: The Leslie E. Keeley Gold Cure Institute of Frederickton, N.B.," *Acadiensis* 17 (Spring 1988): 109–30; Leslie Keeley, *The Non-Heredity of Inebriety* (Chicago: S. C. Griggs, 1896); Keeley, "Inebriety and Insanity," *Arena* 8, no. 3 (1893): 328–337; Keeley, "Does Bi-Chloride of Gold Cure Inebriety?" *Arena* 7, no. 4, (1893): 450–460; and Keeley, "Drunkenness, A Curable Disease," *American Journal of Politics*, (July 1892): 27–43.

76. *State Hospital for Inebriates, Knoxville, Iowa– First Biennial Report* (1906), 6.

77. H. S Miner, "For What Was Our Inebriate Hospital Established and What Should Be Its Aim?" *Bulletin of the Iowa Board of Control* 10 (1908): 152.

78. The institutional chaos created by inebriates was not a new phenomenon. See

Nancy Tomes, *A Generous Confidence: Thomas Story Kirkbride and the Art of Asylum-Keeping, 1840–1883* (Cambridge: Cambridge University Press, 1984), 252–253; Tracy, "The Foxborough Experiment," 59–65; and Baumohl and Tracy, "Building Systems."

79. Interestingly, a similar scenario unfolded in Massachusetts. There separate facilities for incorrigible, chronic, and hopeful cases were also established. See Tracy, "The Foxborough Experiment," and Baumohl and Tracy, "Building Systems."

80. For a philosophical examination of the definition of inebriety as a disease of the will in the United States and Great Britain, see Mariana Valverde, *Diseases of the Will: Alcohol and the Dilemmas of Freedom* (Cambridge: Cambridge University Press, 1998).

81. The courts were often agents of misinformation in this regard. As the Knoxville superintendent, George Donohoe, remarked in 1914 ("The Inebriate," 108), "It is discouraging day after day to see cases come into the institution drunk or half drunk, in the peculiarly fatuous mental condition produced by persistent intoxication, and have them tell you that they have come for the 'cure' and want to now how many days it will take. Upon questioning them when they are sober, you learn that the person himself has been led to believe, if not actually promised, that if he pleads guilty when charged with being an inebriate, he will be sent to Knoxville for a few days or a few weeks to be cured of a disease from which he is suffering. The drinker who is easily led while drinking, pleads guilty and is committed under the inebriate laws for a term until cured, not to exceed three years. Is it any wonder that he rebels and is discontented when he finds conditions not at all as pictured to his family?"

82. Applegate, "Inebriety, and the Care and Treatment of Inebriates," 164.

83. "Lo the Poor Drunkard," *Knoxville Express*, 7 December 1904, 2.

84. "New Hospital Open–Superintendent Willhite now Ready to Extend Hearty Welcome to the 'Dipsies'," *Knoxville Journal*, 26 January 1906, 2.

85. "Biennial Message of B. F. Carroll, Governor of Iowa, to the Thirty-Fourth General Assembly,"*Legislative Documents Submitted to the Thirty-Fourth General Assembly of the State of Iowa* (Des Moines: Emory H. English, State Printer and Edward D. Chassell, State Binder, 1911), 29.

86. For more on Massachusetts' efforts to treat inebriates through state institutions, see Tracy, "The Foxborough Experiment," and Baumohl and Tracy, "Building Systems."

87. Applegate, "Inebriety, and the Care and Treatment of Inebriates," 162.

88. For more on the treatment regimens for patients, see O. C. Willhite, "The Care and Treatment of the Inebriate at the Cherokee State Hospital," *Bulletin of Iowa Institutions 5* (1903); Applegate, "Inebriety, and the Care and Treatment of Inebriates"; Kinne, "Alcoholism"; Osborn, "State Care and Treatment of Inebriates"; and H. S. Miner, "Cause, Prevention, and Cure of Inebriety," *Bulletin of the Iowa Board of Control* 11 (1909): 152–159.

89. In addition to the citations in the previous note, see also Irwin Neff, "The Modern Treatment of Inebriety,"*Proceedings of the American Medico-Psychological Association* (1914): 463–471. Neff was the superintendent of the State Hospital for Inebriates in Massachusetts between 1908 and 1919. Interestingly, that hospital relied less on cathartics, emetics, and sedatives than its Iowan counterpart. The reasons for this discrepancy are unclear.

90. "The Wheelbarrow Cure—A New Way of Making Teetotalers of the Dipsos," *Knoxville Express*, 8 August 1906, 2.

91. "Terrors of Dipsomaniac Ward Now Increased by Probability of Wife's Divorce," *Cherokee Democrat*, 6 February 1903, 2–3.

92. "Quits Drink to Stop Divorce: Harvey Conner Agrees to Go to Inebriate Asylum for Cure in Order to Keep His Wife," *Des Moines Register and Leader*, 5 February 1906, 3.

93. Karl Pedersen, 30 October 1903 notes, Patient no. 93, Case Files of the Independence State Hospital for Inebriates, Independence Mental Health Institute, Independence, Iowa. Recall that the Independence State Hospital for Inebriates was really an inebriate ward at Independence State Hospital for the Insane.

94. At this time, only the governor could issue an official letter of parole.

95. Karl Pederson, 15 September 1904 "Mental Condition notes," Patient no. 93, Case Files of the Independence State Hospital for Inebriates.

96. Petition from the Undersigned Citizens and Residents of Anamosa and Jones County, (no date), Jan Vickers, Patient no. 4, Case Files of the Independence State Hospital for Inebriates.

97. Sheriff W. A. Hogan to W. P. Crumbacker, Superintendent, 17 January 1905, Jan Vickers, Patient no. 4, Case Files of the Independence State Hospital for Inebriates.

98. Cooper, Clemens, and Lamb, Lawyers, to Superintendent to M. N. Voldeng, 13 December 1902, Dennis Rowley, Patient no. 14, Case Files of the Independence State Hospital for Inebriates. Though Rowley was initially committed to Cherokee State Hospital, he was transferred to Independence to relieve the overcrowding at Cherokee, once the new Independence facility opened in 1903.

99. For a sampling of the literature on turn-of-the-century and Progressive Iowa, see Thomas J. Morain, *Prairie Grass Roots: An Iowa Small Town in the Early Twentieth Century* (Ames: Iowa State University Press, 1988); Morain, "To Whom Much Is Given: The Social Identity of an Iowa Small Town in the Early Twentieth Century," John L. Larson, "Iowa's Struggle for State Railroad Control," and Jensen, "Iowa, Wet or Dry?" all in Bergman, ed., *Iowa History Reader*; Frana, "Smallpox: Local Epidemics and the Iowa State Board of Health" Vogel, "Regulating Degeneracy" Keach Johnson, "The Roots of Modernization: Educational Reform in Iowa at the Turn of the Century," *Annals of Iowa* 50, no. 8 (Spring 1991); 892–918; Joyce McKay, "Reforming Prisoners and Prisons: Iowa's State Prisons—The First Hundred Years," *Annals of Iowa* 60, no. 2 (2001): 139–173; Anderson, "A Case of Thwarted Professionalization"; and H. Roger Grant, "Railroaders and Reformers: The Chicago and North Western Encounters Grangers and Progressives," *Annals of Iowa* 50, no. 7 (Winter 1991): 772–786.

100. See Vogel, "Regulating Degeneracy."

101. The term "medico-moral entrepreneur" recalls Howard Becker's term "moral entrepreneur," a concept he developed long ago in *Outsiders: Studies in the Sociology of Deviance* (New York: Free Press, 1963). Becker was concerned with social reformers who sought to redefine what was morally, socially, and legally acceptable within their societies; they sought to define deviance. Increasingly in the twentieth century, moral entrepreneurs employed the expertise of psychiatrists to support their claims. In the case of inebriate reform, the moral entrepreneurs not only employed psychiatrists, many of them *were* psychiatrists making disciplinary claims that brought the already socially deviant behavior of habitual drunkenness within the medical domain.

102. See Elizabeth Lunbeck, *The Psychiatric Persuasion: Knowledge, Gender, and Power in Modern America* (Princeton: Princeton University Press, 1994), esp. 3–7, 46–77, and 244–253; and Jack D. Pressman, *Last Resort: Psychosurgery and the Limits of Medicine* (New York: Cambridge University Press, 1998), esp. 18–46.

103. Osborn, "State Care and Treatment of Inebriates," 4.

Portrait of an Addicted Family

Dynamics of Opiate Addiction in the
Early Twentieth Century

CAROLINE JEAN ACKER

IN JANUARY 1927, two men met on the narcotics ward of Philadelphia General Hospital, where both were seeking a cure for opiate addiction. William Schmidt, a salesman from a small town in eastern Pennsylvania, had arrived at the hospital with his wife, Kate, who had been admitted
to the women's narcotics ward; both were addicted to morphine. Frederick
Beckman, addicted to heroin, was a gangster and drug dealer from Brooklyn.
After going through the standard regimen of hyoscine treatment to manage
the withdrawal syndrome, all three were released.[1]

In May of the same year, Bill and Kate Schmidt returned to Philadelphia
General for a second attempt to cure their addiction; this time they were
accompanied by Kate's parents, Adelaide and Richard Zauberin, who were
also addicted to morphine. Kate reported that, as local sources of morphine
had become harder to maintain, the Schmidts had begun buying heroin
through the mail from Bill's new acquaintance, who had returned to New
York. In about March, Beckman wrote the Schmidts to announce that he
had gotten into trouble with the New York authorities and, since he had
done so trying to supply them, it was up to the Schmidts to help him out.
Soon thereafter, he appeared at the house the Schmidts shared with Kate's
parents and stayed with them for three weeks. The unwelcome houseguest
kept the family up late at night with longwinded stories and persuaded them
to share their drug supplies with him; at one point, he terrorized them by
brandishing a gun. After threatening to expose the family's addiction to their
friends and neighbors, he disappeared.

This encounter between a respectable small-town family and a Brooklyn
gangster occurred as the structures of national drug prohibition were being
erected.[2] Thirteen years earlier, the Harrison Narcotic Act had prohibited
nonmedical use of opiates and cocaine. In 1919, the Supreme Court had ruled
that maintaining addicts on supplies of opiates to prevent withdrawal (ad-

diction maintenance) constituted a violation of the Harrison Act. The American Medical Association (AMA), representing physicians concerned about their profession's reputation for causing addiction through indiscriminate prescribing of opiates, supported this view. Community-based options for addiction treatment were disappearing rapidly. Private practice physicians were becoming increasingly reluctant to take on addicts as patients both because they saw addicts as troublesome and because they lacked therapeutic resources to provide effective help. In enforcing the Harrison Act, the Treasury Department, with the cooperation of the AMA, prosecuted and imprisoned physicians whose prescribing records suggested excessive prescription of opiates, and fear of arrest added to physicians' motivation to shun addicted patients.[3] By 1927, the men's and women's narcotics wards at Philadelphia General Hospital constituted one of the few remaining recourses for addicts seeking a cure and lacking the funds to pay for private sanitarium care.

As prohibition of opiate use was enacted and enforced, and as the medical profession by and large withdrew from the business of treating addicts, the context for the use of opiates was transformed. The market for them shifted from unregulated sale to a combination of highly regulated sale for medical purposes and a growing illicit market for any purchase not authorized by a physician. This shift intensified a demographic shift in the types of people likely to become addicted to opiates.[4] And, as the context for the use of opiates changed, so did the meanings of opiates for those who used them. New patterns of drug-using behavior, new strategies for managing addiction, and new identities to incorporate addiction all emerged in the period between about 1900 and 1930.

In the late nineteenth century, the distinction between "medicine" and "drug" was fluid. Drug use included a set of vaguely bounded, overlapping patterns including some that we might characterize as quasi-medical. The ability of psychoactive drugs to make one feel better was consistent with popular and professional conceptions of the function of medicine through much of the nineteenth century: the relief of troubling symptoms. Alcohol retained its status as a medicine in therapeutics textbooks into the 1920s. People took pills and drank tonics and pick-me-ups to improve physical and mental well-being in ways that physicians sought increasingly to control in the twentieth century. Conversely, the middle-class woman taking morphine supplied by her physician—the modal late-nineteenth-century addict described by David Courtwright[5]—was taking officially sanctioned medicine in an attempt to manage psychic discomforts.

After 1914, as the Harrison Act was implemented, a binary set of categories emerged to distinguish legal from illegal, and medically approved from medically condemned, patterns of use. The Progressive Era anti-vice campaigns helped create this polarity as they cast drug use in a moral framework. In this formulation, "vicious" or "pleasure-seeking" use was seen as undermining the bourgeois values of thrift, self-denial, and future orientation, and rejecting conventional middle-class norms regarding class, gender and sexuality. Meanwhile, reform-minded physicians sought increased authority to control the uses of medicine. The Harrison Act's creation of prescription requirements for the sale of opiates and cocaine added to this authority; additional legislative and regulatory supports for physician control of the dispensing of medicines would follow. Medical use was sharply demarcated from use for pleasure, in conjunction with amusement, or in the context of socialization. Today, this classification appears as the distinction between "medical" and "recreational" drug use.

However, this binary opposition belies the realities as addicts knew them in ways that are illuminated by examining the experience of the cohort of opiate addicts who lived through the period of transition from freely sold opiates to tight legal restrictions on their use. As law and medical practice altered the market for opiates, and as medically managed maintenance was outlawed and treatment options all but vanished, addicts developed their own strategies for maintaining their addiction. These strategies became aspects of a new form of addict identity as the behaviors to maintain addiction were criminalized.

The Schmidts, the Zauberins, and Frederick Beckman were patients at Philadelphia General Hospital at a time when the physicians managing the narcotics wards were engaged in a thoroughgoing study of the effects of opiates on addicts under the guidance of the Philadelphia Committee for Clinical Study of Opium Addiction. Funded by the Rockefeller-financed Bureau of Social Hygiene, this research took advantage of the availability of addicted patients to examine various clinical aspects of addiction. Subjects were recruited from among the ward patients; in some cases, hospital fees were waived in consideration of patients' participation in the study. Most of the work, including that which was published, consisted of physiological examination of subjects while on morphine, at the height of the withdrawal syndrome, and again in the abstinent state which followed withdrawal.[6] This research established that the withdrawal syndrome, in otherwise healthy patients, was not dangerous or fatal; these findings, which suggested that medicating or palliating the withdrawal syndrome was not necessary, further eroded physicians' sense of obligation to deal with patients they increasingly saw as troublesome.

A less successful aspect of the research, from the point of view of its sponsors, consisted of psychiatric and psychological interviews intended to uncover the causes of addiction and suggest more effective means of treatment. Transcripts of these interviews and of medical and drug-use histories taken by the internists working on the ward allow the historian to reconstruct the experiences of the cohort of opiate users who had become addicted in the preceding few decades. The accounts of a middle-class family from a small town and a Brooklyn gangster illustrate the transition in the demographics of addiction that occurred during this period. In doing so, they highlight the plight of addicts who struggled with addiction in a period when the kinds of available treatment and the numbers of treatment institutions were shrinking, and they illustrate the patterns of managing addiction and kinds of addict identities that emerged in that historical context.

Adelaide and Richard Zauberin, Kate's parents, began using opiates in ways typical of white middle-class individuals in the late nineteenth century. Richard Zauberin was born in 1864 in a Pennsylvania village; as a boy he loved to hunt and fish. In his teenage years, his family moved to a small town outside of Hazelton, Pennsylvania.[7] Richard's family had come from Switzerland; his father, a Swiss German, owned a prosperous dry goods store. A street in the town bore the family's name; in Kate's words, the grandfather "owned the street."

Adelaide was born in 1873 in New Jersey to a carpenter and his wife. In her childhood, her family also moved to this town, and when Adelaide was about nine, she met Richard, who was then about eighteen. When she was sixteen (in 1889) and began menstruating, Adelaide, on her mother's advice, began taking morphine once a month for the severe cramps she experienced. For years, she continued taking morphine every month, but only during her menstrual periods. In 1891, when Adelaide was eighteen and Richard was twenty-seven, they married.

When he was about twenty, Richard had begun drinking with his male friends, and he soon fell into a pattern of drinking sprees. Throughout his adult life, he moved in and out of a series of jobs. For a time, he worked in the family store; then he cleaned machinery at a silk mill; then made bobbins for another silk mill; then worked as weighing master for a coal storage company. He worked for a time as an examiner of railroad cars to determine if repairs were required, and so on, losing jobs because of his drinking (and later, because of morphine addiction), but securing new jobs and holding them for some time because when sober he was apparently a skillful and conscientious worker. Moreover, Richard held a kind of sinecure as town assessor—obtained no doubt through family influence—which seemed to involve little work but produced some modest annual income.

Richard was sent away several times for cures, sometimes at the insistence of his father. At a sanitarium in northern Pennsylvania, he was introduced to morphine as part of the cure for his drinking. In his daughter's words, "They simply loaded him up with it there." For some years, he took the morphine only after these sprees.

At some point in his adult life—difficult to pin down from the narrative accounts—Richard contracted a painful leg condition which he called neuritis and which was treated periodically with morphine. The pain and partial withering of one leg forced him to give up roller skating and ice skating, two of his favorite pastimes even in adulthood.

Adelaide had not known Richard drank when she married him; she learned of his sprees during the first year of their marriage. She said, "It broke my heart the first time and he promised never to do it again, of course. No, he did not keep [the promise]." At this point in the interview, Kate, in the ward bed next to her mother's, added, "When I was a child I was so ashamed I would go to school by the back streets." At the same time, she was deeply fond of her father; in her words, "my father and I were inseparable."

Richard's sprees caused Adelaide considerable and ongoing worry. His checkered job history and his practice of borrowing money from friends to buy liquor kept the family from achieving economic security or living up to the status of his parents' family. After a series of miscarriages, Adelaide had a baby girl, Kate, in 1897. When Kate was still an infant, Richard's mother lost her sight and became a permanent invalid. Richard and Adelaide gave up their own home and moved in with his parents, where Adelaide cared for her mother-in-law for the next nine years until the older woman died in 1909. Three years later, Richard's father, a kindly and intelligent old man whom Kate had loved, also died. The family may have inherited the parents' home; in any case, they became homeowners again at some point.

According to Kate, her mother and father had shifted from episodic to chronic use of morphine a few years before their admission to the hospital. About two years before, Adelaide recounted, her own father had become paralyzed. She said, "He was sick and to take care of him I had a few quarter grain morphine pills and I would once in a while take one of them to boost me up and that was the beginning." Over the course of the eight weeks her father stayed with them, Adelaide gradually took larger and more frequent doses of morphine.

Meanwhile, Richard had been receiving courses of morphine for his neuritis for some years. A physician gave him injections of morphine for the pain and, occasionally, strychnine, to counter the weakness caused by the courses of morphine. The physician occasionally gave him large amounts of morphine—apparently frequently enough to cause addiction, because Richard said that at one point the physician had put him through a reduction regimen to end his use. Richard corroborated Adelaide's account that she had begun taking morphine on a regular basis at about this time in response to her father's invalidism.

The elder Zauberins exemplify the typical patterns of late nineteenth-century opiate use.[8] Each took morphine on an episodic basis for many years for medical reasons, and in an unregulated market they could easily obtain the drug from a pharmacy or a physician. Each slipped from episodic to chronic use at a time of pain or crisis. Adelaide's adult life had been punctuated with disappointment: the discovery of her husband's drinking, a succession of miscarriages, the loss of the family's own household as they moved in with in-laws. These misfortunes were doubtless augmented by the restricted feminine caretaking role she assumed through much of her adult life, caring for a blind and demanding mother-in-law and then for her own father in his final illness. In this last crisis, during which morphine was available through the supplies a physician was providing for her father, Adelaide resorted to its solace with increasing frequency and became addicted.

Morphine was commonly prescribed as a "cure" for alcoholic sprees in the late nineteenth century, and Richard's introduction to opiates was thus typical as well. He ascribed his own shift to addiction to the painful leg neuritis which had laid him up. For a man whose favorite forms of play were roller and ice skating in a region where special train cars brought skaters to a nearby rink, this ailment must have constituted a serious loss. His addiction to morphine came after years of binge drinking that consistently disrupted his work life.

In contrast to the Zauberins, Frederick Beckman typified the new type of opiate addict that emerged in the context of urban amusement venues. He, too, had middle-class origins (in this respect, he was unlike the more typically working-class men who began sniffing heroin in pool rooms and dance halls in the early 1900s); born in 1886, he was a generation younger than Richard Zauberin. Frederick grew up in Brooklyn, the son of parents descended from a Catholic German family; his father was an undertaker. He attended public school, graduated from high school at fifteen in 1901, and took a job as an office boy in a publishing company. At about the same age, he reported, he had first visited a "sporting house." Occurring at about the time he finished high school and began working, this rite of passage was common among young men at a time when red-light districts were still tolerated in American cities and when a male sporting scene flourished in New York City.[9] Frederick changed jobs three times during the next three years, working as a clerk, then at Wanamaker's (occupation not specified), then as a horse driver for the Macy Company. These menial jobs hardly seem the path toward a middle-class future, and it is likely that Frederick was developing social bonds with other teenage boys, middle- or working-class, in similar situations: single, living with their parents, working at a job, and having time and money to spend in Brooklyn's restaurants, bars, sporting houses, pool halls, and theaters. But in 1904, an emergency brought Frederick to work in the family business. On June 15, an excursion boat, the *General Slocum*, caught fire in the East River,[10] and resulting deaths among passengers overburdened the Beckman family's funeral parlor. Frederick joined his father's staff and then attended embalming school. However, the death of his mother three years later, when Frederick was twenty-two, altered the pattern of his life again. He began drinking heavily; as he put it, he "was drunk steadily for several years." He quit working with his father and moved through a series of odd jobs, including a stint as a singing waiter.

Frederick's involvement with opiates dates from this period. He described first being offered opiates in his social circle: he once said a fellow waiter offered him some smoking opium; at another point, he said "a girl" had given him some heroin at the beach (probably Coney Island). He portrayed his drug use in purely social terms, part of what he and his friends did for amusement and relaxation. Yet the circumstances also echo the pattern of Richard Zauberin: he began using opiates during a time when he had been drinking heavily following the death of his mother. Thus, although he encountered opiates in a social and recreational setting rather than at a sanitarium for alcoholics, he, like many others, found that they relieved the symptoms of hangover. Moreover, unlike Richard, he quickly substituted chronic opiate use for the pattern of heavy, chronic drinking. In doing so, he joined an indeterminate but significant number of individuals who found opiate addiction less disruptive of their work and domestic lives than alcoholism or a pattern of binge drinking.

Frederick did not provide a clear narrative of his gang involvement, but by the time he arrived at Philadelphia General, he had served several jail and prison terms, he had sold drugs to New York theater people, and he claimed to have shot a man in a gang dispute. A seasoned criminal, he was also charming and sociable. Between his several admissions to the narcotics ward, he maintained a friendly correspondence with hospital staff and some former patients. Although his third admission ended with premature discharge from the hospital because he had caused a disturbance on the ward, he wrote later to apologize, and he resumed a chatty correspondence with the ward staff to help kill time as he served a sentence at the federal penitentiary at Atlanta in the summer and fall of 1927. The combination of tantalizing detail and absence of clear accounts of his criminal activity suggests a man who, with long practice, had become adept at managing both his affect and what he said about himself to suit the environment he found himself in.

Kate and her husband Bill, eleven years younger than Frederick, belonged to the age cohort who were adolescents as the Harrison Act was implemented. Both were born into families that had settled in eastern Pennsylvania in the early nineteenth century and achieved local prominence. As a child Kate played mostly with boys; she never particularly liked girls as friends. She liked to wade in the creek despite maternal prohibition; as the roots of the hazel trees that gave nearby Hazelton its name colored the creek water black, Adelaide could tell from Kate's stained legs when she had been disobeyed. Kate enjoyed fishing with her father. An avid reader, she wore out three copies of *The Swiss Family Robinson*.

When Kate was fifteen, in 1912, she had her first menstrual period, accompanied by painful cramps. Adelaide, like her mother before her, gave her daughter a dose of morphine for the pain. The same year, Kate also began dating a young man named John. Kate finished high school and wanted to go to college but her paternal grandfather, who might have paid the cost, had died when she was twelve. "My father could have afforded it," Kate said, "but I was too young to insist and they thought one year in business college was better than four years in college somewhere. . . . Everything would have been different if I had had that chance." After nine months of business college, "I then worked in an office and I hated it. I made a good job of it, but I wanted to teach English somewhere." She worked in various offices— the phone company, a steel company. Then at the Lehigh Valley Railroad she did requisition work. She worked at the kinds of clerical and secretarial jobs reserved largely for women, and encountered the less formal aspects of office gender relations as well: one boss expected her to lie to his wife when he took a female companion along on a business trip, and she quit a job because her employer "got affectionate." She continued to see John through his college years, first at Lafayette and then at Columbia. Their relationship was on and off, as she would occasionally spend time with other young men and he also developed a relationship with a woman in New York. Following a spat in which Kate refused to break off a date with another man, John ended their relationship.

At this point, an acquaintance of John's, Bill Schmidt, began wooing Kate assiduously. In August 1925, Kate and Bill were married. "Why did I marry him?" Kate asked rhetorically in response to the psychiatrist's question. "He was the sort that needed taking care of so badly." She later said, "I ran away and ran away from him and finally I married him," though she denied that she had done so on the rebound from John. Following their marriage, Kate gave up her job, despite hating to do it, because her husband insisted she was working too hard. With the onset of bad economic conditions, what Richard called "this business depression," Bill lost his job at a coal mine; thereafter he spent some time selling vacuum cleaners and another stint selling brushes.

Apparently because of economic hardship, the young couple lived with Kate's parents. Thus, despite some education and a brief working history, Kate's life assumed some of the contours her mother's had: she and her husband lived with her parents rather than maintaining an independent home. Disappointed at missing out on a college education and the profession it might have made possible, Kate experienced further loss when she acceded to her husband's demand that she give up her job. Although Kate's close relationship with her loving parents was clearly more affectionate than Adelaide's relationship with her parents-in-law, the family's slide into addiction, as we shall see, pushed Kate increasingly into the role of caretaker for her parents.

Bill had been born the same year as Kate, 1897, in the town where both lived. As only one brief interview with him occurs in the records, and the others' accounts of him are not entirely consistent, one can only piece together fragments of his life. It appears, though, that he had wanted to become a physician. He entered the Navy during World War I and spent four years working at a hospital, and he began using opiates in this setting which afforded easy supply. Afterward, according to Kate, he lacked the money to finish his education: "The only thing he wanted to do was to study medicine. Everything else has been a disappointment to him and to us."

Although the entire family blamed their opiate addiction on Bill Schmidt, the parents' account of increasing morphine use at times of crisis makes this point unclear. Bill did, however, introduce his wife to a new route of administration, hypodermic injection, and this shift seems to have caused her addiction. Kate had always taken the morphine by mouth for her menstrual cramps. Once, seeing the pain she was in, Bill suggested he give her an injection. Kate described her response to this experience: "One dose hypodermically and you are an addict. You can take it by mouth, but the effect is entirely different. . . . It's more powerful and more pleasant hypodermically." (This was subcutaneous rather than intravenous injection. Although the latter practice was becoming increasingly prevalent during the 1920s, subcutaneous injection remained common, and high purity levels of morphine and heroin in this period meant a powerful addiction could be sustained in this way. Kate also told of accidentally hitting a vein once and finding the experience terrifying.)

The shift to injection changed the drug experience for Kate; she quickly began escalating her use: "Yes, it is pleasant. Oh, nothing worries you very much. It's the worrying sort of people that take drugs. I have always worried, over nothing, in particular." She began using more, moving up to a cube a day. "Any one will do that," she said; "I took it for the sense of relief it gave me." Adelaide had taken her morphine by mouth and while Richard's physician had administered injections of morphine for the neuritis, Richard had never injected himself. It is clear, though, that shortly after Bill and Kate's marriage, all four were addicted, and they faced the challenges of managing their addiction in a small town.

Juggling fear of exposure with the need to sustain daily supplies for a family of four created a serious challenge for which Kate seems to have assumed the primary responsibility. Both the Schmidt and Zauberin families had enjoyed decades of local social and political prominence in a small-town setting where everyone knew everyone. Kate begged for assurances that the information she provided would not be communicated outside the hospital, and she expressed alarm that one of the nurses who worked on the narcotics ward came from her hometown; they had many acquaintances in common. She later blamed this nurse for telling Bill's family he was addicted.

Kate had always been able to get morphine from a doctor for her menstrual cramps, but when she began asking him for more, he cut her off, and she began buying morphine, and occasionally heroin, from an addict acquaintance. She also continued some attempts to wheedle drug supplies from physicians; she recounted the following exchange: "He said he would not give me a thing but I said I knew he would and so what was the use of pretending to be so hard boiled." Another time, Kate expressed reluctance to seek help from a physician (perhaps the same one) because "he is just the kind that's out for a good time" who repeatedly propositioned her. Her father had lost his most recent job two months earlier because he was taking drugs. Asked how she obtained money to keep buying them, Kate replied, "Any man will loan me money if I ask him." As a rule they never asked for it back, but, she said, "It is humiliating." Sometimes she was able to persuade a physician to provide the family with drugs for a short period while they were waiting for readmission to Philadelphia General.

The connection with Frederick Beckman created a new opportunity, and Kate traveled to New York alone to establish a connection with him (she said Bill had been afraid to go). Frederick seems to have introduced her to other suppliers there. She then ordered supplies from New York in the mail, but also at times traveled to Scranton to buy drugs.

When Frederick found it expedient to leave New York, a household in rural Pennsylvania must have seemed an ideal place to lie low. One day in the late winter of 1927, he appeared on the family's doorstep claiming that he was fleeing the authorities who had caught him selling drugs. In Kate's words, Frederick said that because he had been buying drugs for them, "it was up to us to take care of him and so he came to our house." He stayed three weeks, making life miserable for the family. He lived off of them and did nothing to help around the house. Kate said, "We had no home life, no privacy at all . . . [H]e would come up and sit in our bed room until way late at night." She later heard (from a friend of his, whom she also met through Philadelphia General) that Frederick actually had run out of town with some money he owed someone—although he had claimed he had no money with him. Moreover, Adelaide had looked in a bag of his and found a stash of heroin, although Frederick had claimed he had no drugs and was expecting them to supply him with what he used. After Frederick left, Kate tried to break off connections with all suppliers as a means of ensuring they might stay off drugs by lacking access to them. But Frederick wrote threatening letters insisting they continue to buy drugs from him and telling them he had once shot a man; Kate reported, "He told us all kinds of stories and I learned all sorts of terms."

This visit seems to have marked a crisis for the family. As Frederick waved his gun, plundered their drug supplies, and threatened them with exposure, they encountered at first hand the violence and coercion that accompanied the illicit trade in opiates. Meanwhile, they were becoming increasingly isolated, and breaking off connections with dealers apparently had not worked. In a letter begging for readmission for herself and her parents, Kate wrote to E. G. Torrance, the resident in charge of narcotics admissions at Philadelphia General, on March 7, 1928: "We have been out of drugs for twenty four hours and I must write to you while I can. . . . It is cold here. The fires are both out. We have not eaten for two days. Our home will be sold for taxes." Dr. Torrance wrote back that he could receive them, and Kate and her parents reentered the hospital on March 30.

Kate appears to have had a compelling personality which she deployed in increasingly desperate ways. From a girl who preferred male friends to female, she grew into a young woman who attempted to provoke her long-time boyfriend John into deeper commitment by dating other men. When she lost at this game, she married Bill, whom she described as "the sort that needed taking care of so badly." Like many intelligent, educated women of her time, and like her mother before her, she channeled her energies and skills within the constraints of gender expectations ("educated" may seem exaggerated, but she graduated from high school at a time when many did not, her high school studies included geometry and Latin, and but for her parents' unwillingness to pay for it, she would likely have attended college). Within these constraints, she used her charm and gender (parrying passes from bosses and physicians; borrowing money from men) as she assumed management of procuring the family drug supplies. The unusually personal and complimentary tone in letters written to her by a physician and a psychologist (both males) at Philadelphia General add to the impression that she was adept at engaging men's personal sympathies through a combination of charisma and pitiable pleading.

In returning repeatedly to the hospital, both the family and Frederick Beckman acted out a common pattern: a cycle of attempts at cure followed by relapse to the use of drugs. Kate and Bill returned home after their first admission to the household where Kate's parents were still using morphine. Kate resumed responsibility for supplying them, and quickly began using again. She said later, "I not only had to live in the environment of other people taking the drug after I left here, but I had to find it for them to take. I knew that it would be difficult but I thought I could leave it alone." However, her quick resumption of use forced her to conclude, "If it is there you will take it, that's all." Bill ascribed his own relapse to the recurrence of a painful ear condition. During his second visit, Richard said he had thought he could fool with it without losing control; experience had proved him wrong as well.

When Kate and her parents came to Philadelphia General in December 1928 (her fourth visit; their third), both Kate and her father reported that they had all started using drugs again even before they had gotten out of Philadelphia after their previous visit in March. Kate knew where to buy it because "one of the girls in the ward told me." She took it because she was disappointed her husband had not met her when she came out of the hospital. Kate had urged Bill's mother to help him in some way. Bill's mother had responded, in Kate's account, by virtually kidnapping her son and refusing to let him return to his wife. Kate had come to realize that Bill had left her. She had heard that he was working for his father, a railroad dispatcher, at an "easy job" as a call boy who assembled train crews. According to her source, Bill had been off drugs for eight months. Kate, on the other hand, had an abscess of three weeks' duration on her left shoulder as a new complication of repeated injections.

Frederick Beckman also described the conditions in which he resumed drug use after his various cures (which included withdrawal while in jail). The psychologist who interviewed him reported, "He feels all right when off drug but gets a kind of depression occasionally—it is as though something is 'kind of lacking' perhaps for a week or so . . . he could even get over his depression without drugs." However, this depression did create vulnerability, as Frederick recounted returning to drug use in 1919 after a cure at Riverside Hospital in New York followed by eight months of abstinence: "I was working steady and was getting along fine and then I met a fellow when I was coming home from work. He was an addict and he asked me to have some again. I was depressed and it was hailing and snowing and I lost hold of myself and let him give me a little shot and that's the fatal one, the first one. A few days after that the desire got me." On a bleak fall day while he was at Philadelphia General, Beckman again suggested a link between depressed mood, gloomy weather, and resumed opiate use: "Many a fellow with broken habit will go back on a cold wet day like this."

These accounts of resuming drug use echo those of dozens of other interviewed patients. Many reported that they felt normal only when they were taking opiates, and feelings of depression or other malaise during abstinence created continuing vulnerability. The moment of relapse was often described in one of three ways. It was recognized that addicts returning directly to scenes of former use often relapsed, but chance encounters with associates from the social group where they had used drugs were also hazardous. Caught off guard as the unexpected meeting triggered craving, former users accepted casual invitations to share some drugs; they quickly resumed chronic use. Second, crises could cause relapse. Third, seasoned addicts sometimes used treatment episodes to bring high levels of tolerance back to more manageable levels. They sometimes indicated they had supplies of opiates waiting at home, ready for the first dose following discharge from the hospital. While such behavior might not constitute "relapse" in the contemporary sense, it added to clinicians' observations that treatment failures were common.

Kate went through several of the experiences typical of relapsers. Following her first admission, she returned to her household where she resumed her role as drug procurer for the family. Her father indicated that when she left the hospital for the third time, the discovery that her husband had not come to meet her drove her to resume use before she and her parents had even left Philadelphia. She indicated that she had learned where in Philadelphia to acquire drugs from another patient on the ward. It is impossible to untangle the relative influences of her marital disappointment and another possibility: that Kate made a point of learning, while in the hospital, how to procure drugs immediately upon release. The desperate tone of her letter begging for readmission, and her occasional need to obtain drugs from a physician with a promise that she and her parents would seek treatment, make it possible that she would have seen another hospital visit as a temporary respite from the struggle to keep the family supplied with drugs.

Nevertheless, on the fourth visit (the last which appears in the records), Kate indicated that this time, when she and her parents left the hospital, they would move to a new location and stay with a sympathetic aunt, and she would look for a job of some kind. She hoped, with some reason, that this change of scene would improve her chances of remaining abstinent. As the record stops here, we cannot know what happened to her and her parents; but when Richard was asked "Are you going to stay off?" he replied with fatalism: "I was good the last time, I would not have touched it if the rest had not but this time if they are going on I will go too. If they go, the hell, I go along. If they stay away I will stay away."

IN THE YEARS following 1928, the situation did not improve for addicts like Kate and her family. Lacking effective treatments for them and prohibited by law from providing drugs to maintain their addiction and prevent withdrawal, many physicians accepted the emerging psychiatric consensus that addicts' drug-seeking stratagems evidenced an underlying psychopathic personality.[11] This view was consistent with the view promulgated by the Treasury Department's Division of Narcotics in its enforcement of the Harrison Act: addicts were criminals and, as such, should be incarcerated.

The physiological research conducted at Philadelphia General Hospital with subjects like the Schmidts, the Zauberins, and Frederick Beckman provided strong evidence that the withdrawal syndrome was not dangerous or life-threatening. These findings undermined the argument for short-term palliation of withdrawal, which, by bringing patients to an abstinent state, was considered a "cure," albeit one that often failed. The growing recognition that many addicts went through detoxification only to fall back to drug use strengthened the view that only long-term institutionalization could break the grip of stubborn drug habits. In this way, too, medical views paralleled those in criminal justice. In 1929, Congress passed the Porter Act, which called for the creation of two prison hospitals for addicts, to be run by the Public Health Service. The first opened at Lexington, Kentucky, in 1935 and the second, at Fort Worth, Texas, in 1938. Federal prisoners who were addicted to opiates served their sentences there; addicted federal probationers were incarcerated there until the physicians determined they were "cured"; and a small number of voluntary patients came to seek relief from their addictions.[12] For those unable to avoid arrest and without the means to pay for sanitarium care, jail or prison terms became a standard part of addict life.

The elder Zauberins, like many elderly addicts in the 1920s who had begun using opiates decades earlier in ways that violated no medical or social norms, lived to a time when patients had to receive compassionate exemptions from the Harrison Act in order that their physicians might provide opiates on a maintenance basis without violating Harrison. Both Adelaide and Richard met criteria by which the Public Health Service granted such exemptions, but they may have been unaware of this possibility, and in any case, the process was cumbersome, involving travel and examination by authorized physicians. As their own physicians cut them off, they were forced to rely on Kate to keep themselves supplied.

The ways that the family became connected to the illicit market and the ways that Beckman used opiates to help manage depression and stop a destructive pattern of drinking reflect more similarities of experience than the differences in their lives might suggest. The patient records for Philadelphia General's narcotics wards indicate that many individuals who became addicted to opiates both before and after implementation of Harrison did not fall as neatly into categories of respectable and gangster as did the Zauberins, the Schmidts, and Frederick Beckman.

Bill and Frederick illustrate two common patterns that continued into the post-Harrison period. Bill, like many health professionals or aspiring health professionals, became addicted as a result of occupational exposure (while working in the Navy in some medical capacity). Frederick most closely typifies the criminally involved heroin addict that came to dominate medical and criminal discourse regarding addiction. He may well have already been involved in gang and criminal activity at the time he began his opiate use. He went on to become a career criminal, serving repeated sentences—finally in a federal penitentiary. He combined drug and nondrug criminal activity in a way that has confounded scholars' attempts to sort out the relationship between illicit drug use and other crime. Nevertheless, his recourse to drugs also related to other life issues: the heavy drinking for several years following his mother's death followed by the shift to opiates, which appear to have functioned as a more satisfactory substitute for the alcohol; the capacity of depression or even gray skies to contribute to relapses.

The family's respectable status and residence in a small town did not shield them from either the shame and burden of addiction or the risks of arrest or violence endemic to urban drug markets. Thus, Kate and her parents began opiate use in ways that typified nineteenth-century patterns, but by the mid-1920s, their experience paralleled that of many who began opiate use neither in a medical setting nor in direct connection with a criminal gang, but in settings where opiates were used socially. The majority of patients seeking help in the narcotics ward at Philadelphia General Hospital were working-class individuals who were introduced to opiates by friends and associates. After 1914, these people would have begun use in an illicit market, where they confronted forces that encouraged the assumption of an addict identity. Reduced treatment options meant there were fewer paths out of addiction (though many undoubtedly achieved lasting abstinence on their own).[13] Physicians remained a potential source for opiates, but as they incorporated fear of causing addiction and fear of being caught over-prescribing opiates into their behavior toward patients, addicts became more likely to lie to doctors. The main source for the opiates necessary to sustain addiction remained the illicit market, and maintaining one's addiction meant acquiring the skills to move in a criminal underworld sustained in part by the threat of violence. Deepening social stigma surrounding addiction encouraged passing, or behaving in ways that hid addiction from family and associates.[14] Many addicts developed a dual identity as they navigated markets and social circles where drugs were available while they struggled to maintain families and jobs. As relapses frustrated attempts to sustain abstinence, many addicts confronted narrowing options, and addiction became the central fact of their lives.[15]

Across the spectrum of legitimacy of social roles—and the spectrum of motives for beginning drug use—many positions are possible, and these are represented among the patients who appeared to be treated and studied at Philadelphia General: people living in the working-class neighborhoods where urban vice was centered, where young adults weighed opportunities in legitimate venues and visible, lucrative illegitimate ones, and where many would seek to combine opiate use with sustaining their family relationships and pursuing legitimate occupations. For such individuals, forced and sustained contact with the illicit market must have been a powerful force eroding legitimate social roles and reinforcing connections with the increasingly deviant social world in which opiates were bought and sold.

Notes

1. Records of the Philadelphia Committee for Clinical Study of Opium Addiction, Library of the College of Physicians of Philadelphia. Patient names have been changed. The cases discussed in this essay are numbers 26–35 (vol. 18) and 26–52, 26–29, 26–70, and 26–28 (all in vol. 13).

2. David F. Musto, *The American Disease: Origins of Narcotic Control* (New Haven: Yale University Press, 1973).

3. Caroline Jean Acker, "From All-Purpose Anodyne to Marker of Deviance: Physicians' Attitudes toward Opiates in the U.S., 1890–1940," in Roy Porter and Mikulas Teich, eds., *Drugs and Narcotics in History* (Cambridge: Cambridge University Press, 1995), 114–132.

4. David T. Courtwright, *Dark Paradise: Opiate Addiction in America before 1940* (Cambridge: Harvard University Press, 1982).

5. Ibid.

6. Arthur B. Light et al., *Opium Addiction* (Chicago: American Medical Association, 1929–1930).

7. Information on the town and region is drawn from Robert F. Archer, "The Route

of the Black Diamond," *A History of the Lehigh Valley Railroad* (Berkeley, Calif.: Howell-North Books, 1977); Thomas D. Eckhart, *The History of Carbon County*, vol. 1 (Published by author and the Carbon History Project, 1992); Wilbur A. Myers and Edward Hanlon, *Historical Album of Wilkes-Barre and Wyoming Valley in Luzerne County, Pennsylvania 1729–1976* (Wilkes-Barre, Pa.: Luzerne County Bicentennial Commission, 1976); Daniel Rupp, *History of Northampton, Lehigh, Monroe, Carbon and Schuylkill Counties* (Lancaster, Pa.: G. Hills, 1845).

8. Courtwright, *Dark Paradise.*

9. Timothy J. Gilfoyle, *City of Eros: New York City, Prostitution, and the Commercialization of Sex, 1790–1920* (New York: W. W. Norton, 1992).

10. Irvin S. Cobb, *Exit Laughing* (Indianapolis: Bobbs-Merrill, 1941), 141.

11. Caroline Jean Acker, *Creating the American Junkie: Addiction Research in the Classic Era of Narcotic Control* (Baltimore: Johns Hopkins University Press, 2001), chaps. 4 and 5.

12. Ibid., chap. 6.

13. Patrick Biernacki, *Pathways from Heroin Addiction: Recovery without Treatment* (Philadelphia: Temple University Press, 1986).

14. Erving Goffman, *Stigma: Notes on the Management of Spoiled Identity* (New York: Touchstone, 1963).

15. On narrowing options, see Marsha Rosenbaum, *Women on Heroin* (New Brunswick: Rutgers University Press, 1981).

The Double Meaning of Addiction

*Habitual Narcotic Use and the Logic of Professionalizing
Medical Authority in the United States, 1900–1920*

Timothy Hickman

> *Owing to the present advance of medicine, new words are being rapidly
> coined, therefore, if you desire to keep abreast of the times, keep your
> dictionaries and encyclopedias at your elbow: patronize them freely,
> and, when your reading or musing entices your curiosity on any subject,
> or in any direction, turn to them and be informed. They are both
> convenient and useful in looking up facts and meanings when you have
> but a few moments to devote to an inquiry, and will save you from
> many mistakes and uncertainties.*
> —D. W. Cathell, M.D., and W. T. Cathell, M.D.,
> *The Book on the Physician Himself and Things That
> Concern His Reputation and Success* (1913)

THOUGH NOTED AT least as early the 1830s, habitual narcotic
use did not become a subject of large-scale public attention in the United
States until after the Civil War. Changes in medical technology and practice,
such as the isolation of morphine from opium in 1805 and the growing use
of the hypodermic syringe after the middle of the century, encouraged the
widespread administration of narcotics by American physicians.[1] Beginning
in the 1870s, an increasingly animated discussion of what many writers characterized as a spiraling national "drug problem" became evident in both the
medical and popular presses.

The drug problem entered American consciousness during a period that
historians have identified as a time of cultural crisis.[2] They have shown that
fin-de-siècle cultural life was characterized by a struggle to redefine the terms
of human agency in ways that made sense during a period typified by its
rapid technological and economic changes. People have faced challenges to
the definition of the self in every historical epoch, but the effort seems to
have been particularly acute at the turn of the twentieth century. As the

literary critic June Howard observes, "to immerse oneself in the documents of the period is gradually to come to recognize the depth of [these people's] sense of confusion and danger and to respect the historical specificity of their reported discomfort."[3]

The historian T. J. Jackson Lears concurs with Howard's point, explaining that the cornerstone of nineteenth-century bourgeois identity "was the autonomous individual, whose only moral master was himself."[4] Yet accounting for responsibility and obligation, terms essential to the coherent assertion of self-mastery, was no simple task for the (mostly white and mostly male) beneficiaries of the rapidly corporatizing end-of-the-century economy. Corporate, managerial capitalism was a means of financial organization that served to relieve individual businessmen of the burden of personal risk and responsibility.[5] When compared with the swiftly passing entrepreneurial economy, the new system often seemed to behave of its own will, independent of human cause and certainly beyond the "mastery" of any individual actor or agent. Because it seemed that "individual will and action were hemmed in by the emerging iron cage of a bureaucratic market economy,"[6] Lears argues that "bourgeois culture entered . . . a 'weightless' period, marked by hazy moral distinctions and vague spiritual commitments." He concludes that the result of such "weightlessness" was that "personal identity itself came to seem problematic" in the waning years of the nineteenth century.[7]

If economic transformation wasn't challenging enough, relentless mechanization and technological expansion further complicated the assertion of human agency in a world of machines, electricity, and the rudiments of mass communication. Between the end of the Civil War and the beginning of the new century, railroad lines grew from 35, 000 to nearly 200,000 total miles.[8] In 1880 Thomas Edison made electric lighting practical, and in 1882 New Yorkers gaped as the new bulbs illuminated Wall Street.[9] Communication technology also boomed. Both the multiplex telegraph and the telephone debuted at Philadelphia's 1876 Centennial Exhibition.[10] Steam-powered printing presses contributed to the proliferation of periodical publications, and the circulation of big city newspapers increased dramatically.[11] These are but a few examples, yet they help to anchor the historian Thomas Haskell's claim that the close of the nineteenth century represented the culmination of what was "undoubtedly the most profound and rapid alteration in the material conditions of life that human society has ever experienced."[12]

These combined forces of technological and economic change threatened middle-class identity by increasing the public's perception of regional and individual "interdependence" according to Haskell, who argues that "as society became increasingly interdependent, we may speculate that the effect, as experienced by sensitive persons within the society, must have been a tendency for efficient causation to recede from the observer."[13] Haskell thus describes the turn-of-the-century cultural crisis as a widely sensed decline in the causal power of human intention, rooted in the perception of the formerly *in*dependent subject's entanglement within a newly *inter*dependent society. Like Lears, Haskell finds that "the individual, the irreducible atomic constituent of society" was "devalued" within the context of a transformed society that was typified by its perception of increased interdependence.[14]

Many self-proclaimed experts in a variety of fields suggested "professionalism" as a solution to the challenges posed by turn-of-the-century interdependence. Haskell defines "professionals" as "persons who claim to possess esoteric knowledge which serves as the basis for advice or services rendered to the public for remuneration."[15] He further defines "professionalization" as "a measure not of quality, but of community," explaining that "a social thinker's work is professional depending on the degree to which it is oriented toward, and integrated with, the work of other inquirers in an ongoing community of inquiry."[16] Haskell argues that boosters of professional expertise believed that they offered the specialized skills and knowledge required to lead the lay public's search for causality along the complex paths of an interdependent modernity.[17] The professional, a member of a self-defined and regulated community of experts, thus sought to restore and redefine a sense of human causal agency for a society whose concept of the self was grounded on deeply imperiled notions of individual autonomy and self-mastery.

The concept of modern professionalization helps us to make sense of the way that turn-of-the-century experts "solved" their drug problem because many doctors and national lawmakers believed that the professional control of the access to narcotics (through prescription) could subdue the threat of addiction.[18] The drug addict, whose condition was often described as an affliction that attacked its victim's power of will, served as a particularly strong example of the way that modern technology threatened older formulations of individual human agency. Many addiction experts found in narcotics a product of modern (medical) technology that, rather than fulfilling optimistic predictions of a world made better by science, turned its human subjects into the slaves of their own discoveries.[19] Narcotic addiction thus embodied the otherwise abstract threat that stalked the autonomous individual in a newly interdependent, modern society. It signified the annulment of the bourgeois subject's autonomy, willpower, and self-mastery. The unregulated use of narcotic drugs thus served many experts and reformers as an example of modernity's worst-case scenario, and they invoked the authority of the professional expert to confront the menace.

This essay investigates several connections between the addiction concept of habitual narcotic use and the modern logic of medical professionalization. By engaging multiple voices of the medical mainstream, whose work was published in the nation's leading medical journals, I argue that the addiction concept of habitual narcotic use was embedded in the early twentieth-century paradigm of professionalizing medical authority—an important element of which suggested that state and professional authority could join together in order to meet the challenges of an interdependent modernity. Anti-narcotic legislation, which was grounded in the turn-of-the-century concepts of the addict and of addiction, both reflected and enhanced this broader medico-cultural logic.

From Morphinomaniac to Narcotic Addict

To contend that the concept of addiction was embedded in a turn-of-the-twentieth-century movement toward professional organization is to suggest a modification to what is perhaps the most influential study of the concept of addiction. In a path-breaking 1978 essay, Harry Gene Levine argued that the concept of addiction was the product of a change in medical thinking about alcohol at the end of the eighteenth and the beginning of the nineteenth centuries. He claims that "this new paradigm or model defined addiction as a central problem in drug use and diagnosed it as a disease, or disease-like."[20] The chief symptom of this "disease" was the loss of control over drinking, and thus the habitual drinker was relieved of the moral responsibility that seventeenth-century theorists and theologians had assigned the drunkard.

Levine further argues that this new paradigm was consistent with what he terms "the ideology of the Temperance Movement"[21] and was first worked out by physicians "whose orientation led them to look for behavior or symptoms beyond the control of the will and whose interests lay precisely in the distinction between Desire and Will."[22] He thus finds a cultural and social basis for this new explanation of habitual drunkenness and demonstrates the way that allegedly "value-free" medico-scientific descriptions of human behavior are often sociocultural productions of their historical moment.

Contrary to Levine's assertion, however, the "disease concept" of drug and alcohol use and the concept of "addiction" are not the same thing. He cautions his audience that "the modern reader translates the behavioral description of the habitual drunkard into modern terms—into the alcoholic,"[23] but he makes the same move himself when he quickly translates the older disease concept into the modern notion of addiction, which is something that did not appear until years later. He argues that the seventeenth- and eighteenth-century view, which held that "habitual drunkards simply loved to drink and get drunk, and that they could stop at any time" did not simply die out, but that it "continued to exist alongside the addiction—that is, the temperance—model."[24]

Yet the words "addict" and "addiction" were only rarely used to denote drug users or their condition before the turn of the twentieth century. Most nineteenth-century authorities preferred more colorful words like habitué, morphinist, morphinomaniac, opium eater, and opium slave. Though Levine finds the word occasionally employed in the sermons of eighteenth-century Puritan theologians as well as in ante bellum medical texts, the word is never used as a noun in his examples. It is not used to identify a condition called "addiction," nor is the word "addict" invoked as a name for a person who suffers from that condition.[25]

This is not a quibble. Levine convincingly shows that the disease concept signaled a shift in the medical paradigm of the late 1700s. In much the same way, the general adoption of the addiction concept, signaled in part by the growing use of the term itself, was a part of a shift to the paradigm of organized, professional, scientific medicine in the first years of the twentieth century. An important part of the addiction concept was the supposed scientific knowledge of the condition that the use of the term seems to imply. To employ the word "addict" was to turn away from the older, more dramatic phrases that became far less common in medical discourse after about 1900.[26] Its use offered doctors a way to identify themselves as a part of a professional/scientific/legal community and, as we will see, the term's popularity coincided with the increasing power and prestige of organized medicine marked by the rise to dominance of the American Medical Association in the first years of the twentieth century.

Second, Levine's association of the disease concept with that of addiction misses the addiction concept's chief distinction. "Addiction" did not "exist alongside" an older, voluntary notion of habitual drug use because the term contained *both* concepts within itself. This is, quite literally, its definitive feature. We can better understand these two contradictory concepts and the way that the term "addiction" contains them both by examining the earliest English uses of the word.

Originally, addiction signified the assignment of a status or condition by a court of law. The *Oxford English Dictionary* lists the word "addict" as derived from the Latin *addict-us*, meaning "assigned by decree, made over, bound, or devoted." The word first appeared in English around 1529 as a legal adjective, describing the state of someone who was "formally made over or bound (*to* another); attached by restraint or obligation; obliged, bound, devoted, consecrated." This usage soon was made obsolete by a related verb (*to* addict, or to have been *addicted*) whose most recent manifestation is the one that we still use today. Its first meaning was "to deliver over formally by sentence of a judge (*to* anyone). Hence, . . . to make over, give up, surrender." This definition was paired with a second, reflexive meaning that emphasized a greater degree of volition than the strict juridical sense of the legal term: "To bind, attach, or devote *oneself* as a servant, disciple, or adherent (*to* any person or cause)" and also "to devote, give up, or apply habitually to a practice."[27] Both these contradictory senses of the word, first, the notion of addiction as an assigned or *juridical* condition and second, of addiction as a self-willed or *volitional* condition are at play in the noun "drug addict," a designation which became the dominant name for a habitual drug user (someone who suffered from an "addiction") sometime around 1910.

The discrepancy between the voluntary and compulsive—which, following etymological precedent, I will call the volitional and juridical definitions of the words "addict" and "addiction"—is of central importance in any discussion of habitual drug use.[28] In the first years of the twentieth century, this double meaning of addiction was put into play within the context of the turn-of-the-century cultural crisis. The resolution of addiction's contradictory double meaning, which was signaled in part by the general acceptance of the term "addiction," was merely an affirmation of the concept's status as paradox: the addiction concept contained *both* meanings of the word within itself. Most important, the addiction concept provided a formula for the assessment of moral culpability for the addict's condition that held dire consequences for those who were left without an excuse for their drug taking.

Many turn-of-the-century medical authorities believed that the necessity of living with modern social, technological, and economic pressures caused middle- and upper-class Americans—who were still, at least physically, creatures of "nature"—to become particularly susceptible to the seduction of narcotics.[29] This move greatly reduced the volitional sense of the word "addict" by minimizing the role of individual choice for middle-class drug users and thus spared them the moral responsibility for their condition. These people were *juridical* addicts because they were addicted *by* the conditions of a changing world.

The *volitional* meaning of the word was generally reserved for those whose class, and often racial, position was deemed inferior to white, middle-class America. It also served to illustrate the depths which beckoned the "more respectable" members of society should the "drug hazard" go unchecked. Nonwhite and demimonde "others" were supposedly free of the commercial and cultural strains of modern life and were, with few exceptions, denied an excuse for taking drugs. They were thus assigned a greater degree of moral responsibility for their habit than were "juridical" addicts.

The Harrison Narcotic Act of 1914 affirmed the addiction concept's double meaning in that it provided a solution to the problems posed by both groups of addicts. By 1920, volitional addicts came to be defined as *criminals* and were thus proper subjects of the penal system.[30] The juridical addicts, on the other hand, were defined as innocent *patients*, something that was shown in part by their willingness to place themselves under the authority of professional medicine. The Harrison Act thus carved up the addict population and divided the spoils between medical and penal authorities, who in turn reinforced each other in their pursuit of the act's goals. We can observe this operation at work if we look more closely at what the doctors had to say for themselves.

The Responsibilities of the Professional Physician

The American Medical Association was the paradigmatic voice of professionalizing medicine at the turn of the twentieth century. The century's first twenty years saw the AMA, founded in 1847, rise from its disorganized and somewhat marginal nineteenth-century position to the place of dominance over the medical profession that it enjoys today. Between 1900 and 1910, total AMA membership skyrocketed from 8,401 to 70,146. By 1920 total membership, partially due to a 1913 reform of its constitution, stood at 83,338.[31]

In June 1900 the Association gathered in Atlantic City, New Jersey, for its fifty-first annual meeting. A future president of the organization, Dr. John A. Witherspoon of Nashville, Tennessee, delivered the "Oration on Medicine" to that year's assembly and he called it "A Protest against Some of the Evils in the Profession of Medicine." He used his opportunity to explore a host of challenges that confronted AMA physicians at the beginning of the Association's remarkable expansion. Witherspoon found "the indiscriminate use of narcotics" looming large among these problems, prompting him to one his more excessive flights of sentiment:

> Ah, brothers! we, the representatives of the grandest and noblest profession in the world, with the God-given mission of making growth more perfect, life more certain and death more remote, must shoulder the responsibility, follow in the footsteps of the Great First Physician, and warn and save our people from the clutches of this hydra-headed monster which stalks abroad throughout the civilized world, wrecking lives and happy homes, filling our jails and lunatic asylums, and taking from these unfortunates the precious promises of eternal life.[32]

Witherspoon thus connected the control of narcotic addiction with professional responsibility and set very high stakes for the linkage. He asserted that the physicians of the AMA held proprietary responsibility for perfecting the growth of their people, a notion which helped to anchor his claim that the AMA conventioneers were "the representatives of the grandest and noblest profession in the world." Yet Witherspoon feared the obstacles that could impede professional medicine's "God-given mission" to perfect human growth. He noted that "there are but a few men here of wide experience who do not daily come in contact with practitioners whose panacea for everything is opium in some of its forms."[33]

Witherspoon, who worried that "the morphin habit is growing at an alarming rate,"[34] blamed his audience for spreading the condition: "We can not shift the responsibility, but must acknowledge that we are culpable in too often giving this seductive siren until the will-power is gone, and a moral and physical wreck is sent down to shame and degradation."[35] Patients were thus seduced into taking their first steps on a downward path by those entrusted with their care—their family physicians. Witherspoon's solution, however, was not simply to ban this potent form of modern medical technology. He followed popular medical opinion when he found the narcotic to be "a wonderful remedy, capable of great good when judiciously used," but he felt himself "bound to say that when used as it is by some doctors, it is productive of terrible results."[36]

Witherspoon thus made an important distinction when he accused his colleagues of spreading narcotic addiction. He blamed *some*, not all, doctors and thus set a standard based on the mastery of modern medical technology by which to measure the professional quality of a physician's care. It was thus the duty and measure of the *true* professional to arrest the public's slide into addiction.[37] Part of that task required the doctor to take exclusive possession of his knowledge—a key marker of a professionalized occupation. Witherspoon felt that physicians often compounded their mistakes by sharing their pharmacological wisdom with their patients. He argued that by dispensing "the unnecessary and hurtful information too often given the laity of [the drug's] seductive influence on human beings"[38] the physician contributed to the habit's spread.

Witherspoon's oration thus highlighted several crucial themes in the rhetoric of medical professionalization that we find at work in the construction of the addict and of addiction at the turn of the century. First, while acknowledging the drug's therapeutic value, he warned that its potential for medical misuse was great and that physicians were to blame for the growing prevalence of addiction. Second, he suggested that professionalization might mean a purging of those physicians who failed to live up to approved prescribing practices. Finally, he staked a claim for professional ownership of the esoteric knowledge of narcotic prescription. These themes together demanded that professionally responsible physicians come to grips with and master this new form of technology in order to meet the demands implied by the term *professional*.

Criminals and Patients

Witherspoon's concerns continued to play themselves out in the first twenty years of the new century. Doctors repeatedly blamed themselves and also modern conditions for fastening narcotic addiction upon their middle- and upper-class patients.[39] Physicians often paired the description of what they envisioned as a victimized middle-class addict with a drug user who became addicted or continued her drug use through channels outside of the medical profession and was thus assigned the burden of responsibility for her own condition. These addicts, unlike their "respectable" counterparts, were not given the sanctuary of a condition *assigned* by their doctors or by the challenge of meeting the demands of changing social conditions. They were instead blamed for becoming addicts through their own *volition*.

In a 1914 study conducted in a Manhattan city prison, Dr. Perry Lichtenstein claimed that "the number of victims who directly trace their addiction to physicians' prescriptions is very small; I have found but twenty such people out of 1,000."[40] Because so many of the addicts in his sample of prisoners learned to use drugs from sources other than medical, Lichtenstein concluded that the information regarding these drugs had spread independently of medical agency. He thus suggested that these addicts were responsible for their own addiction, implying that volitional drug use be added to the list of criminal activities that had already landed his subjects behind bars. Lichtenstein argued that the M.D. needed to protect his knowledge, to hoard it as his private property, and to keep it from the public. He concluded that "the information given by physicians to patients, that they had been receiving morphine, cocaine, etc., is to be deplored. Patients should be kept in ignorance as to medication."[41]

The significance of Lichtenstein's study lies in its comparison to a contrasting account given by Dr. Alexander Lambert only one year before, in 1913. The powerful and influential Lambert, an M.D. and professor of medicine at Cornell, who was Theodore Roosevelt's personal physician and later became president of the AMA, described in the *Journal of the American Medical Association* "the striking fact that nearly 80 percent of those addicted to the use of morphine have acquired their habit through legitimate prescribing by their physicians or by self-medication."[42] At the time, Lambert was engaged in promoting Charles B. Towns's addiction cure. We therefore must note that the addicts in his sample had come to him for cure. Lambert referred only to those who acknowledged the physician's authority and trusted in his power to dispense a cure—people who approached the physician in the role of *patient*. It is to these people only that Lambert's assertion of (80 percent) medical responsibility applied. They had contracted the habit through the ministrations of a doctor and were therefore free from personal responsibility for their habit. But, as the 1914 study made clear, the drug users who accepted their role as patients were not the people in jail, where only 20 out of 1,000 could trace their habit to the family doctor.

The juxtaposition of these two studies, which are representative of the poles of the early twentieth-century medical debate about addiction, illustrates the way that the 1914 Harrison Act would reflect and enhance these doctors' findings by dividing the control of the addict population between medical and penal authorities. Addicts who came to their condition at the hands of a doctor—in other words, patients—were considered to be proper subjects of medical rather than penal attention, while those who failed to acknowledge the authority of the physician—those who came to their condition at their own doing—would be regarded as criminals. This assignment of differing positions within the addict population follows what I have described as a contrast between the juridical and volitional elements that constitute the concept of addiction. It shows the way that drug use by people who were unable to receive professional medical attention or uninterested in doing so could be classified as criminal, while a proper patient was simultaneously defined by her willingness to submit to the authority of her doctor. We see here a construction of narcotic addiction whose implied remedy required both classes of addicts to surrender to powerful social institutions. Professional medicine was positioned to accept those who were willing to assume the role of "patient"—those of the "better class"—while the correctional system lay in wait for the recalcitrant "criminals" of the other class.

Criminals, Patients, and the Medico-Legal Authority of Professional Medicine

In April 1920, five years after the passage of the Harrison Act, the AMA held its seventy-first annual meeting in New Orleans. Here the assembled physicians received the Report of the Committee on the Narcotic Drug Situation in the United States, which presented the AMA's version of the history of the country's "narcotic drug situation" as well as its recommendations for a future course of action. This document, which summarized much of what had been written about narcotics between 1870 and 1920, contains the AMA's medico-legal solution to the double meaning of addiction and is the period's most sophisticated statement of the relationship between narcotic addiction and professional medicine in their turn-of-the-century cultural context.

For the AMA, addiction was a peculiarly modern malaise. The committee's first goal was "to point out . . . that drug addiction in the sense in which we ordinarily use the word at the present time is a modern problem."[43] The members were unambiguous in their placement of narcotic addiction within the context of the mid-to-late nineteenth-century technological and scientific discoveries that typified the coming of what they self-consciously identified as "modernity." This passage, which was concerned with "the sense in which we ordinarily use the word at the present time," also made clear that the addiction concept was an idea that was particularly attuned to its modern context. It was a different way of conceptualizing habitual drug use from the ideas which had gone before.

This difference is clear in the committee's description of the narcotic addicts themselves. If addiction itself was a product of modern technology, then so were the addicts. The committee members distinguished between drug users past and present when they claimed that "the facts stated indicate that we are not dealing with the opium smokers or eaters of another age and civilization but with a problem which in one phase dates back to the middle of the nineteenth century with the introduction into use of the hypodermic needle" (1325). Here we see the syringe figured as a modern instrument of technological subjection, but we also see that the committee believed that "addiction," as a medico-scientific term, meant something quite different from older formulations of habitual drug use.[44] The doctors made it clear that a "drug addict" was a creature quite different from an "opium eater" and that their difference lay in an intensification of effect caused by the development of modern medical technology.

Modern problems required modern solutions, and thus the committee suggested that the combined forces of professional and legal authority were best suited to stamp out the modern "pestilence" of narcotic addiction. Fearing that the medical profession might be "compelled to follow in the wake of the great work already begun of stamping out drug addiction," the committee urged the physicians of the AMA to "take the lead to which their position entitles them" and to "get control of the situation through law and the care of those already victims" (1324). The AMA's committee suggested a medico-legal strategy that emphasized the leadership of the medical profession in the mobilization of both "law" and "care" in the eradication of drug addiction and thus met what I earlier suggested was an important element of the paradigm of early twentieth-century professional medicine. The committee felt that professionalism, paired with and backed by legal authority, could protect Americans from the dangerous side effects of modern medical technology.

The determination of who was subject to "law" and who was considered a proper candidate for medical "care," however, was closely linked to what I have identified as the paradoxical double meaning embedded within the concept of addiction. We have seen that the assessment of medical responsibility was one way to determine the addict's culpability for his condition, but one's socioeconomic position also made a great deal of difference. This is particularly clear in the special committee's division of the addict population into distinct groups.[45]

The committee took up a familiar theme when it suggested that "the habitual users of narcotic drugs may be divided into two classes." The doctors immediately excluded the first group, composed of patients under the direct supervision of a physician, from its consideration, leaving only "those who are addicts—those who use narcotic drugs for the comfort they afford and continue their use solely by reason of an acquired habit." This second class of drug users, whom the committee described as "those who are suffering from a functional disturbance with no physical basis expressed in a pathologic change" (1326), were the only group to which it applied the word "addict."

The committee suggested four subgroups within this second class, and it is here that the social significance of the AMA's medico-legal solution to the double meaning of addiction becomes clear. In this second group—the "addicts"—the committee placed "correctional cases, mental defectives, social misfits and otherwise normal persons" (1326). The AMA's different approaches to the problem of addiction within these four subgroups show quite clearly the way that the modern concept of addiction operated as a formula to divide the addict population based on social class.

Though the committee identified four subgroups within the population of addicts, it sought to confine the first three of these groups in one institution. They claimed that "under a proper system of classification, in the institution for the after-care of the addict, it will be necessary to segregate the correctional, the mental defective, and the social misfit groups" (1327). The fourth group, "otherwise normal persons," was not to be institutionalized, and I will return to it later. In the meantime, we need to be clear on the nature of this "institution" and on the care and identity of its inmates.

The AMA committee argued that "the correctional cases should be committed to institutions with no age limit—from the cradle to senility, if necessary."[46] Further, they seemed to rule out the possibility of permanent cure for this group when they suggested that, upon improvement, "they could be put on probation under the care of a technically trained person acting as probation officer." The doctors suggested a similar treatment for the "defectives," arguing that "institutional care must be provided where they can be comfortable and often self-supporting, but where they shall not be permitted to reproduce their kind" (1326). For both of these groups, then, the committee suggested permanent confinement or, at the least, a lifetime of close professional supervision.

Though the committee made no overtly racial or class-based judgments in its brief discussion of the first two subgroups, it had less reticence in making class-based judgments for the "misfits," the third group to be institutionalized. Though it stated that "misfits are found in all social strata" (1326), the committee reserved its apprehensions for those misfits of the "drifting industrial population," whom it felt had become visible within the last generation. While noting that "the facilities may have to be increased," the committee affirmed that "we already have state provision for the care of correctional cases and mental defectives." But the doctors worried that "the problem of the misfit and of the drug user who appears normal except for the drug weakness has yet to be solved" (1327). They warned that "the misfit can no longer be ignored. He is too numerous; he has learned the lesson of organization; and he has learned through association means of cheap satisfaction that deaden for a time his elemental cravings, even though they return him to society more of a menace and a care than before" (1326). The "means of cheap satisfaction" that he had "learned through association" were narcotic, and this method of discovery situated him firmly within what Perry Lichtenstein had described in 1914 as the volitional class of addict.[47]

The committee argued that the social misfit was, like all addicts, a product of modern intellectual, economic, and technological change. It felt that social misfits were produced by a cultural environment that precluded the resigned acceptance of "unhappiness and disease" as the work of "the hand of Providence." This intellectual predisposition was aggravated by an economy that differed from older models whose "unremitting toil and consequent deadened nerves prevented such problems as arise with the change from a 'pain economy' to a 'pleasure economy,' so that it may be said that a society which has enough of a surplus for leisure will also have more misfits." Heightened nervous sensitivity, combined with what the committee described as an individualistic, rational culture, was thus to blame for the phenomenon of the social misfit, whose problem was, according to the doctors, "getting into the right place to enjoy the surplus and the leisure" generated by the new "pleasure economy" (1326).

It was still more problematic, according to the committee, that such a drifting misfit had a penchant for "listening to any agitator who assures him that this dissatisfaction and restlessness are the fault of some one besides himself" (1326). The committee concluded that, for the modern worker, "the minute subdivision of labor of the modern factory system" meant that "if he has 'nerves,' some day he will get a nightmare vision of himself as a piece of social waste, a victim of conditions far more far-reaching than his individual life. When he becomes organized and vocal, society awakens to the fact that he is an I.W.W., a Bolshevik, or what not" (1327). In other words, what the doctors saw as the workers' growing leisure provided these people with the opportunity to reflect on their condition, and thus a particularly sensitive individual who realized himself to be caught up in what Thomas Haskell characterized as a complex, interdependent society—"a victim of conditions far more far-reaching than his individual life"—was likely to organize in order to challenge that society's legitimacy.

The committee's proposals show the way that medical professionals could use the concept of narcotic addiction as a means to address social conditions that far exceeded their (narrowly defined) field of medical expertise. Though the committee described the misfit as *partially* blameless for his condition, which is what spared him from the certainty of lifelong institutionalization with the "mental defectives" and "corrective cases," the misfit still required the close guidance and supervision of professional experts who were well acquainted with the source of his problems. The doctors therefore suggested "vocational guidance" as the solution to the social misfit's problems. They emphasized the professional's role as a pilot through the labyrinth of modernity when they explained that "this whole movement is based on the belief that happiness is a by-product of normal, useful activity, and that the child can be directed along the way, whether he be brilliant, mediocre or stupid. Its social philosophy teaches that the goal of society is to provide so flexible a social system that there shall be no misfits among the normal members of a population as a result of lack of guidance and training." The committee thus emphasized professional "guidance and training" as a way to channel and refocus human drives whose expression was frustrated by modern economic conditions and then appropriated by the destructive forces of radical politics, narcotic addiction, or both. By suggesting that guidance was to be continued beyond the addicted misfit's "recovery," the committee posited continued professional supervision throughout the addict's life. It argued that, in order "to counteract [restlessness] with the cured addicts, it will be imperative to devise a wise probation system. Many an otherwise hopeless misfit can be permanently saved by the supervision of a wise and experienced probation officer, acting with authority" (1327).

The suggestion of assertive professional guidance for the misfit class was combined with recommendations for the permanent institutionalization of "mental defectives" and "correctional cases" (i.e., uncooperative misfits) in work camps. The committee hoped that this aggressive medico-legal intervention would solve the problem of these three groups, which together approximated the "volitional" side of the concept of addiction. But the problem of what to do with the last group remained. The doctors therefore turned their attention to the challenge of the "otherwise normal" addict.

The committee made the class position of this final group of addicts clear, especially in comparison to the misfits of the drifting industrial population, when it placed among them "the literary genius who has to finish his manuscript for the publisher; the social worker whose district must be covered at whatever cost to herself; the physician or nurse with an epidemic sweeping the city, and who must not stop—any of these may realize too late that he has become a slave to the drug." Clearly, this group was composed of a different set of individuals from those in the misfit class. Though the misfits weren't "wholly to blame" for their condition, the otherwise normal addict was much less so. The committee explained the incidence of this type of addict, writing that "we may have such a person working under too great strain. Then the 'last straw' is laid on the burden, and in the altogether human search for relief . . . the drug is perhaps taken occasionally, and the habit finally formed." Thus, the addict otherwise normal was subject to an "altogether human search for relief" from the pressure of maintaining his position atop the socioeconomic pyramid (1327). This was quite different from the misfit's inability to accept his unhappy lot in life. The otherwise normal addict, whom the committee depicted as a physician or nurse, a literary genius or a social worker, was a victim of the demands of society upon an individual whose only fault was trying too hard to serve that society. Because modern society's demands were so great, these people were relatively free from responsibility for their condition. They therefore represented more closely the *juridical* aspect of the concept of addiction.

Aggressive vocational guidance backed by penal authority was clearly an inappropriate form of professional intervention for the "otherwise normal" addict. The committee suggested instead "Psychanalysis" as the most productive way to help these people and it described this treatment as a form of "mental therapy," whose goal was "the reclamation of [the unconscious] part of the ego." They believed that it offered "the greatest hope for the salvation of the otherwise normal person whose will is not strong enough to shake off the drug habit" (1328).

The professional expert could, in fact, turn the addict's powerful desire to his own and to society's good. The committee declared that the otherwise normal addict's "strong desire is a measure of his energy. Let him be taught to direct that energy into wholesome channels which will give him as great pleasure and which will recreate his soul." The report concluded: "Such is the task of the men and women in charge of the institution for the educated men and women who are drug addicts: They are to be both trained and sympathetic, wholesome and strong-willed; friends and guides into a new life in which the base desire for self-gratification is, not suppressed, but directed into new channels which will make for the happiness of the individual and the race" (1328). The professional's role was not the same in this case as it was when engaging the misfit class. It was transformed from that of a "probation officer, acting with authority," to a "sympathetic, wholesome and strong-willed friend." Besides demonstrating the committee's suggestion for differing degrees of social control for the different classes, this report offers a blueprint of the way that the addiction concept could serve to extend the social power of organized medicine. The committee envisioned a modern professional whose social task was to focus the desire of the "better class" into more "productive" channels while at the same time identifying the "mental defectives" and "corrective cases" for incarceration in prisons and work camps. The committee thus affirmed the paradoxical double meaning of addiction by assigning the juridical addicts—those of the "better class"— to the supervision of professional medicine while sentencing the volitional addicts (i.e., criminals) to the supervision of the correctional authorities.

THE MEDICO-LEGAL approach, signified in part by the widespread adoption of the terms "addict" and "addiction," had different effects for different members of the addict population. We have seen the way one class of addicts—the "volitional"—came to be seen as criminal while the other "juridical" class came to be regarded as a group of patients. Both groups, however, were forced to submit to the authority of powerful social institutions, medical or penal, because they took narcotic drugs. On January 1, 1920, the enforcement of anti-narcotic laws was turned over to the newly created Narcotic Division of the Prohibition Unit of the Internal Revenue Bureau. Armed with a set of Supreme Court decisions that augmented the prohibition element of the Harrison Act, the federal government was well equipped to launch its enforcement of this newly minted medico-legal logic. It was authorized to begin the "War on Drugs" whose battles remain undiminished until the present.

Notes

In addition to the editors and anonymous readers of this volume, I wish to thank Alice Fahs, Jonathan Judaken, Brook Thomas, and Jon Wiener for their insights.
    1. For a thorough description of the patterns of opiate prescription and use in the

early and mid-nineteenth century, including a detailed discussion of Civil War battlefield application, see David T. Courtwright, *Dark Paradise: Opiate Addiction in America before 1940* (Cambridge: Harvard University Press: 1982), 35–61.

2. This is a persistent theme in the historiography of the Gilded Age and Progressive Era. Besides the works cited and discussed at greater length in the text, one might begin with "classics" such as Robert H. Wiebe's *The Search for Order, 1877–1920* (New York: Hill and Wang, 1967) and Henry F. May's *The End of American Innocence: A Study of the First Years of Our Own Time, 1912–1917* (New York: Alfred A. Knopf, 1959). Also fundamental are Alan Trachtenberg, *The Incorporation of America: Culture and Society in the Gilded Age* (New York: Hill and Wang, 1982), and Nancy Cott, *The Grounding of American Feminism* (New Haven: Yale University Press, 1987). Theoretical takes on modernity abound, but a good start is to be found in Marshall Berman's *All That Is Solid Melts into Air: The Experience of Modernity* (New York: Penguin, 1988) and Matei Calinescu's *Five Faces of Modernity: Modernism, Avant-Garde, Decadence, Kitsch, Postmodernism* (Durham: Duke University Press, 1987). Most recently, scholars have applied and sometimes challenged the crisis model according to specific experiences marked by race, class, and gender difference. Exemplary here are Gail Bederman, *Manliness and Civilization: A Cultural History of Gender and Race in the United States, 1880–1917* (Chicago: University of Chicago Press, 1995), Grace Elizabeth Hale, *Making Whiteness: Southern Segregation, 1890–1940* (New York: Random House, 1999), and sections of R. G. Lee, *Orientals: Asian Americans in Popular Culture* (Philadelphia: Temple University Press, 1999).

3. June Howard, *Form and History in American Literary Naturalism* (Chapel Hill: University of North Carolina Press, 1985), xi.

4. T. J. Jackson Lears, *No Place of Grace: Anti-Modernism and the Transformation of American Culture, 1880–1920* (New York: Pantheon, 1981), 12–13. Lears is far from alone in suggesting that autonomy and self-mastery were crucial components of nineteenth-century bourgeois identity, Gordon S. Wood, writing about the Revolutionary and Early National Periods, locates a similar definition of the self in what he describes as "the classical republican tradition," which held that "man was by nature a political being, a citizen who achieved his greatest moral fulfillment by participating in a self-governing republic." To fulfill one's humanity was, by definition, to follow the virtuous path, but "to be completely virtuous citizens, men—never women, because it was assumed they were never independent—had to be free from dependence and from the petty interests of the marketplace. Any loss of independence and virtue was corruption." The "virtuous citizen" was thus both autonomous and his own master. See Gordon S. Wood, *The Radicalism of the American Revolution* (New York: Vintage, 1991), 104.

In a somewhat different vein, C. B. Macpherson writes in his classic study of the foundations of liberal thought that "the central difficulty" of "original seventeenth-century individualism . . . lay in its possessive quality . . . [which] is found in its conception of the individual as essentially the proprietor of his own person or capacities, owing nothing to society for them." Macpherson further argues that in liberalism "the human essence is freedom from dependence on the wills of others, and freedom is a function of possession." The notion of liberal independence, then, like republican autonomy, rested in the more fundamental assertion of self-possession. To surrender or to lose one's "possession" was to relinquish independence and to corrupt the essence of the whole. The maintenance of autonomy from forces outside of the self was thus the key to both public and private virtue. See C. B. Macpherson *The Political Theory of Possessive Individualism: Hobbes to Locke* (Oxford: Oxford University Press, 1961), 3.

5. See Alfred D. Chandler Jr., *The Visible Hand: The Managerial Revolution in American Business* (Cambridge: Belknap/Harvard University Press, 1977), 1–14.

6. Lears, *No Place of Grace*, 32. The core of Lears's argument lies in his claim that fin-de-siècle elite cultural critique had lost its formerly solid grounding in communitarian social institutions, especially the Protestant church. Turn-of-the-century cultural elites therefore turned to various ideologies of the individual in what Lears argues were their multiple resistances to "modernity." Lears concludes that this "therapeutic" approach to individual selfhood was (and is) precisely the logic of the modernity supposedly under attack and thus, paradoxically, served to strengthen an emergent world of corporate capitalism and its consumer ethos.

7. Ibid.

8. Mark Wahlgren Summers, *The Gilded Age, or, The Hazard of New Functions* (Upper Saddle River, N.J.: Prentice-Hall, 1997), 78.

9. Ibid., 2–3.

10. Trachtenberg, *The Incorporation of America*, 41.

11. Ibid., 122–123.

12. Thomas Haskell, *The Emergence of Professional Social Science: The American Social Science Association and the Nineteenth-Century Crisis of Authority* (Urbana: University of Illinois Press, 1977), 1.

13. Ibid., 39–40.

14. Ibid., 40

15. Ibid., 27. There is a vast literature on the history of the professions and professionalization in the United States. I have chosen to focus on Haskell's work because of the way that he links professionalization with a broader cultural crisis, rooted in the perception of an increasingly "interdependent" society. Haskell's notion of interdependence and its threat to the coherent assertion of causality helps to explain much of what was said about narcotic addiction. Those wishing to read more fully in the history of professionalization might begin with the excellent anthology of essays edited by Haskell, titled *The Authority of Experts: Studies in History and Theory* (Bloomington: Indiana University Press, 1984). Also helpful is Alexandra Oleson and John Voss, eds., *The Organization of Knowledge in Modern America, 1860–1920* (Baltimore: Johns Hopkins University Press, 1979). More recent work can be found in Dorothy Ross, ed., *Modernist Impulses in the Human Sciences, 1870–1930* (Baltimore: Johns Hopkins University Press, 1994). Those specifically interested in medical professionalization might begin with Paul Starr's *The Social Transformation of American Medicine: The Rise of a Sovereign Profession and the Making of a Vast Industry* (New York: Basic Books, 1982). Judith Walzer Leavitt and Ronald L. Numbers, eds., *Sickness and Health in America: Readings in the History of Medicine and Public Health* (Madison, University of Wisconsin Press, 1978), is also quite helpful as is Joel D. Howell's *Technology in the Hospital: Transforming Patient Care in the Early Twentieth Century* (Baltimore: Johns Hopkins University Press, 1995). In addition to its suggestive and useful insights, Martin S. Pernick's *A Calculus of Suffering: Pain, Professionalism, and Anesthesia in Nineteenth-Century America* (New York: Columbia University Press, 1985) offers a thorough bibliography of both primary and secondary sources in the study of the history of medical professionalization.

16. Haskell, *Emergence of Professional Social Science*, 18.

17. Throughout this essay, I use the word *modernity* in reference to the objective conditions of turn-of-the-century life, especially the period's movement toward a corporate economy and its rapid technological change. A *modernizing* culture is thus one

where these changes are occurring. The notion of the *modern* will signify the elements of turn-of-the-century culture that contemporaries considered to be radically new or different from those that had gone before.

18. Calls for professionalization are abundant in the medical journals published in the first years of the twentieth century. As the medical historian David F. Musto has observed, "medicine and pharmacy were in active stages of professional organization when they became involved with the issue of narcotic control." Musto examines the way that the interests of organized medicine influenced the final shape and the progress of anti-addiction legislation. I hope to add an exploration of the way that the rhetoric of medical professionalization and the concepts of the addict and of addiction affected one another to Musto's insight. See David F. Musto, *The American Disease: Origins of Narcotic Control* 3d ed. (New York: Oxford Press, 1999), 13. For the specific strategies for control employed by the medical profession see Caroline Jean Acker's "From All-Purpose Anodyne to Marker of Deviance: Physicians' Attitudes toward Opiates in the U.S., 1890–1940," in Roy Porter and Mikulas Teich eds. *Drugs and Narcotics in History* (Cambridge: Cambridge University Press, 1995).

19. My sense of medical technology is drawn from Howell's *Technology in the Hospital*. On page 8 he defines technology as being comprised of three layers. Technology can be physical (an artifact or machine), it can be an activity (a treatment or practice), or it can be a specific knowledge. Though they are not a perfect fit, I believe that the refined products of opium and coca had elements of all three of these aspects of technology and can thus be seen as a part of the modernizing medical technology of the late nineteenth and early twentieth centuries.

20. Harry Gene Levine, "The Discovery of Addiction: Changing Conceptions of Habitual Drunkenness in America," *Journal of Studies on Alcohol* 39, no. 1 (January 1978): 143. Levine's notion of a paradigm shift is drawn from Thomas Kuhn, *The Structure of Scientific Revolutions*, 2d ed. (Chicago: University of Chicago, 1970). Kuhn's work is also fundamental to my own.

21. Levine, "Discovery of Addiction," 144.

22. Ibid., 151.

23. Ibid., 148.

24. Ibid., 158.

25. Levine first quotes Reverend S. Danforth who in 1709 wrote that "God sends many sore judgments on a people that addict themselves to intemperance in drinking" (147). He contrasts this with Benjamin Rush's 1814 contention that "the persons who have been addicted to [strong liquors] should abstain from them suddenly and entirely" (152). In the first example the word is used as a reflexive verb, in the second it is passive but still a verb. While demonstrating a shift in the assertion of moral responsibility for habitual drunkenness, the term does not refer to a distinct physiological condition that these earlier writers would have recognized as "addiction."

26. This change in terminology is clear in an examination of Charles E. Terry and Mildred Pellens, *The Opium Problem* (1928; Montclair, N.J.: Patterson Smith, 1970). The older terms for habitual drug use continue to appear after the turn of the century, but their use diminishes as they are rapidly replaced by the words "addiction" and "addict."

27. *The Oxford English Dictionary*, Compact ed. (1971), s.v. "addict."

28. Most historians refer to this discrepancy as a conflict between the disease and vice concepts of habitual drug use. Rather than arguing over which notion is dominant at which time, I hope that my turn to something like the literal meaning of the word

"addiction" itself demonstrates how both notions could operate simultaneously, in one concept. It is also important to note that the division of the sick into guilty and innocent camps was not inaugurated at the turn of century. The addiction concept helped to formalize this older medical approach to "social" diseases. For further exploration of this tendency, see Alan Brandt, *No Magic Bullet: A Social History of Venereal Disease in the United States since 1880*, expanded ed. (New York: Oxford University Press, 1987). Caroline Jean Acker explores this process as it operated in medical attitudes regarding the opiates and addiction in "Stigma or Legitimation: A Historical Examination of the Social Potentials of Addiction Disease Models," *Journal of Psychoactive Drugs* 25, no. 3 (July–September 1993): 193–205.

29. Such arguments can be found in many places. Among the most interesting and influential are George Miller Beard's *Stimulants and Narcotics; Medically, Philosophically, and Morally Considered* (New York: G. P. Putnam & Sons, 1871), 24; Leslie E. Keeley, *Opium: Its Use, Abuse and Cure; or, From Bondage to Freedom* (Chicago: Banner of Gold, 1897), 39–41; T. D. Crothers, *Morphinism and Narcomania from Other Drugs: Their Etiology, Treatment and Medicolegal Relations* (Philadelphia: W. B. Saunders, 1902), 33; and L. L. Stanley, "Morphinism," *Journal of the American Institute of Criminal Law and Criminology* 6 (1915–1916): 586.

30. This interpretation of the Harrison Act required several years of legal haggling. Especially important were the Supreme Court's 1919 decisions in *Webb et al. v. United States* and *United States v. Doremus*. See Musto, *American Disease*, 131–132.

31. James G. Burrow, *AMA: Voice of American Medicine* (Baltimore: Johns Hopkins University Press, 1963), 49–50. Still more significant, according to Burrow, was the growth in the number of AMA fellows. This number, which referred to those who paid full fees and subscribed to the *Journal of the American Medical Association*, rose by 500 percent during these years. While the number of subscribers to the *JAMA* rose from 4,633 in 1900, to 30,032 in 1920, its influence was probably much greater because, according to Burrow, it was available to about 80 percent of the profession.

32. J. A. Witherspoon, M.D., "A Protest against Some of the Evils in the Profession of Medicine," Oration on Medicine before the fifty-first Annual Meeting of the American Medical Association, Atlantic City, N.J., 5–8, June 1900, published in *JAMA*, 34; no. 25 (23 June, 1900): 1591. David Musto cites this passage in order to demonstrate the growing medical consciousness of the narcotic habit in *American Disease*, 303.

33. Witherspoon, "A Protest," 1591.

34. Ibid. Witherspoon believed that morphine was not the only product of modern medical technology requiring professional attention. On page 1592 he argued that "the same can be said of cocain [sic], which is rapidly becoming a national evil, because of its indiscriminate use in minor surgical operations."

35. Ibid., 1591.

36. Ibid.

37. This was a common and important move. See J. B. Mattison, "Morphinism in Women," *Atlantic Medical Weekly* 5 (20 June 1896), 392. Archibald Church and Frederick Petersen, *Nervous and Mental Diseases*, 8th ed. (1914), quoted in Terry and Pellens, *The Opium Problem* 113; and F. X. Dercum, "Relative Frequency of Drug Addiction among Middle and Upper Classes; Treatment and Final Results," *Pennsylvania Medical Journal* (February 1917), quoted in Terry and Pellens, 117.

38. Witherspoon, "A Protest," 1592.

39. David Courtwright has argued that national anti-addiction legislation became

possible only when the perception of a change in the addict population—from white, middle-class women to a demimonde fringe—became widespread. It is clear, however, that even though medical researchers often noted demographic changes, the argument that the majority of the blame be placed upon the physician who had inflicted the condition upon an innocent patient remained a vital part of the discourse. While Courtwright makes a compelling argument regarding the criminalization of narcotic use, I hope to point out the way that the noncriminal addict was likewise placed under the authority of a powerful social institution. See *Dark Paradise*, 1–8.

40. P. M. Lichtenstein, "Narcotic Addiction," *New York Medical Journal*, 14 November 1914, quoted in Terry and Pellens, *Opium Problem*, 112. He went on to explain the presence of these twenty among the others, invoking a gender distinction that was very important to the definition of addiction. He mobilized notions of an inherent women's weakness, based on reproductive biology, when he explained that "most of these victims were women who had been suffering from tubal disease," thus designating one group of addicts who, because of the weakness signified and imparted by their gender, were somewhat less to blame for their addiction, while still maintaining the existence of another group whose active agency in their drug use rendered them proper objects of penal attention.

41. Ibid.

42. Alexander Lambert, "The Treatment of Narcotic Addiction," *JAMA* 60 (21 June 1913), quoted in Terry and Pellens, *Opium Problem*, 110.

43. Committee on the Narcotic Drug Situation in the United States, "Report," *Proceedings of the New Orleans Session, Minutes of the seventy-first Annual Session of the American Medical Association*, New Orleans, 26–30 April, 1920, *JAMA* 74, no. 19 (8, May 1920): 1324. Page numbers hereafter are given in the text.

44. For more on the syringe as a threatening piece of modern medical technology, see Harry Hubble Kane, *The Hypodermic Injection of Morphia. Its History, Advantages and Dangers* (New York: Chas. L. Bermingham, 1880), 13, 19. The authoritative source on the history of the syringe remains Norman Howard-Jones, "A Critical Study of the Origins and Early Development of Hypodermic Medication," *Journal of the History of Medicine and Allied Sciences* 2, no. 2 (Spring 1947): 201–249.

45. This is among the most common and important moves in the discourse of addiction. The U.S. Treasury Department, in what could be viewed as a companion piece to the AMA's report, makes a similar division in *Traffic in Narcotic Drugs*, Report of Special Committee of Investigation Appointed March 25, 1918, by the Secretary of the Treasury, June, 1919. (Washington: Government Printing Office, 1919). See especially page 23. For a popular version of the same division as it was applied to racial difference, see William Rosser Cobbe, *Doctor Judas, A Portrayal of the Opium Habit* (Chicago: S. C. Griggs, 1895).

46. The committee's suggestions for the treatment of the first two groups, the "defectives" and the "correctional cases," mirror Charles B. Towns's nearly fanatical suggestion of work camps for what he termed hopeless cases. See Charles B. Towns, *Habits That Handicap: The Menace of Opium, Alcohol, and Tobacco, and the Remedy* (New York: The Century Co., 1916), 211–212.

47. Besides demonstrating these addicts' class position, this passage made clear that, for the most part, they were not iatrogenic addicts.

Demons for the Twentieth Century

The Rhetoric of Drug Reform, 1920–1940

SUSAN L. SPEAKER

CRITICS OF THE war on drugs have long noted that rational public discussions about drugs of abuse are difficult in America, partly because anti-drug rhetoric has demonized drugs and drug users and exaggerated the extent of abuse. "Drug" stories in newspapers and magazines, movie and television dramas, and talk shows frequently portray "drugs" as instantly addictive, impossible to resist, and sure to bring violence, insanity, or economic and social ruin. The drug-crazed criminal and drug-dealing gang member have become familiar American villains. Addiction and abuse are often described as "scourges," "plagues," or "epidemics" that will engulf the entire nation. Any apparent increase in drug use, especially by young people, elicits worried predictions that it will continue indefinitely. Politicians also use this language, and continue to characterize drug control efforts as a "war" on drugs, often insisting that it can and must be won at any cost. Such dramatic, uncompromising rhetoric seems to hit the mark: respondents to polls frequently name "drugs" as one of the top four problems currently facing America.[1]

Drug abuse *is* a significant and difficult public health problem. Some drugs carry risks and dangers best avoided, and there are indeed some people—many more than we would like—whose lives are damaged or destroyed through drug abuse. At the same time, however, there has been an immense amount of scientific, psychological, and sociological research done in the past thirty years which has greatly enhanced our understanding of psychoactive drugs, their effects, hazards, and use patterns. It is clear, for example, that drug use is a highly individual phenomenon, the outcome of which is very dependent upon personality, set and setting, and other factors. The experience of the past thirty years also suggests that at least some people can use drugs moderately without becoming abusers, that even heavy abuse may not be a lifelong pattern, and that many "outbreaks" of drug abuse are self-limiting and fairly short-lived.[2] Popular discourse seems hardly affected by this information, however, and continues to use terms, images, and assumptions reminiscent of those used by alcohol prohibitionists a century ago. And this, as this essay will show, is no coincidence. Although Americans have since become accustomed to talking about "alcohol" and "drugs" as somewhat separate problems, and many view nineteenth-century prohibitionists as stuffy, puritanical, and even ridiculous, the rhetorical lineage of recent "just-say-no" campaigns extends directly back to the long campaign against "Demon Rum."

From the 1830s to the early twentieth century, the temperance and prohibition movements routinely characterized alcohol as a great social "evil," capable of causing any and all possible social or personal disasters, tempting people from all social classes to moral turpitude and certain ruin. After about 1900, however, the popular bugaboo "Demon Rum" was joined increasingly by "the narcotic evil," that is, problems of addiction, crime, and vice associated with other psychoactive drugs such as cocaine, opiates, and marijuana. Although these other drug problems were quite different in magnitude and character from the alcohol problem, anti-narcotic reformers such as Richmond Hobson used prohibitionists' well-established rhetorical form to alert Americans to the "drug menace." The extension of anti-alcohol rhetoric to anti-drug crusades began in earnest during the 1920s, with the activities of groups such as Hobson's International Narcotic Education Association, and was complete by the late 1930s, when Harry J. Anslinger, head of the Federal Bureau of Narcotics, became the most frequently quoted "authority" on drug problems. Even as Americans were making an uneasy peace with alcohol during the early 1930s, their stance toward other drugs was crystallizing into intolerance. Long after Prohibition ended and public concern about alcohol subsided, the rhetoric used in that crusade continued to be applied to other drugs and drug problems. And although popular articles about drug abuse no longer use the terms "demon" or "evil," they still employ many of the assumptions embodied in Prohibition and early anti-narcotic rhetoric: for example, that the drugs in question are powerful, seductive, and rapidly addictive; that everyone is at risk for addiction; that drugs *by themselves* are sufficient to cause any imaginable deviant behavior and are directly responsible for most crime and violence; that the problem is very large, even if we cannot see it; and that the problem is closely associated with feared outgroups (e.g., criminals and foreigners) and possible conspiracies.

This extension of rhetoric and assumptions is interesting for several reasons. First, while the magnitude and nature of alcohol abuse in the nineteenth century may have in part justified crusaders' strong rhetoric, the social problems associated with opiates, marijuana, and cocaine were comparatively minor, and their abuse patterns were often quite different. Even granting certain similarities between alcohol abuse and other drug habits, the anti-narcotic rhetoric seems greatly disproportionate to the threat. (And alcohol then, as now, caused much more damage than other drugs.) Second, Americans stopped demonizing alcohol after Prohibition, and chose to deal with its risks largely through regulation, education, and harm-reduction strategies. They have resisted redeeming many other psychoactive drugs in the same way, however. This has had significant consequences for public discussion of drug problems, framing such problems in uncompromising terms that preclude open and realistic debate.

This essay is based on my initial research for a larger work in progress that will trace anti-alcohol and anti-drug rhetoric from 1830 to the present, examining their common elements, and social and cultural contexts, as well as the enduring usefulness of such rhetoric in American politics and culture. Here I examine the "crossover" decades 1920–1940, when the anti-alcohol movement was declining and the anti-narcotic campaigns were growing, and show how prohibitionists' basic rhetorical elements were incorporated into anti-drug literature. I then use a content analysis of anti-drug themes in fifty-four popular periodical articles published between 1920 and 1940, along with *New York Times* articles to show how early narcotic reformers' themes, images, and "facts" diffused to broader popular discussion of drug problems.[3] I suggest that as Prohibition rhetoric was extended into anti-narcotic campaigns, and Prohibition itself was winding down, "drugs" took on the mantle of "evil" that alcohol had worn for many generations.

Prohibition Rhetoric

A series of campaigns against alcohol, diverse in both constituency and strategy, were carried on from the early 1800s to the early twentieth century. They were prompted to some extent by increased alcohol use and subsequent damage to individuals, families, and communities, but also by the demands of an industrial society, and the complex social tensions produced by industrialization, immigration, and demographic change. Their aims and emphases varied and often overlapped: some of the campaigns focused on sobriety as a necessary condition of success in an industrial economy (e.g., the Washingtonians, Sons of Temperance, and other fraternal groups); some, such as the American Temperance Society, were more concerned with controlling the drinking practices of workers and immigrants in the growing cities; others, like the Woman's Christian Temperance Union (WCTU), worried more about domestic violence and poverty resulting from drunkenness. The Anti-Saloon League (ASL), whose efforts finally achieved Prohibition, focused exclusively on closing saloons and getting alcohol outlawed throughout the nation, in the interest of wiping out crime, poverty, and vice. Many anti-alcohol crusades were connected to other reforms, and influenced by the evangelical revivals of the nineteenth century.[4] Despite the differences between the various groups, their rhetoric—in speeches, illustrative stories, and pamphlets and newsletters—displays many consistent elements. They emphasized the power and seductiveness of alcohol, the insidious ways it could enslave and then destroy, and the inevitability of addiction. They used scientific as well as moral appeals. And the strongly evangelical Protestant base of nineteenth-century reform led temperance reformers to talk about their work as struggles between good and evil, in which there could be no compromise.

Temperance reform was initially based on Benjamin Rush's 1784 theory that distilled alcohol ("ardent spirits") was addictive for some people. Within several decades beer, wine, and hard cider were deemed potentially addicting as well. Reformers urged complete abstinence for everyone, so as to keep susceptible citizens safe from temptation and destructive addiction. Although many temperance advocates knew that only some people developed serious problems with alcohol, their literature (especially the popular illustrative stories) rarely mentioned this. There alcohol was described as a tool of the devil—tempting at first, irresistible after initial acquaintance, leading away from God and, ultimately, to moral decline and material ruin. The *Temperance Tales* published in the 1850s pulled no punches on these themes: one narrator, describing a drunkard, asked:

> What had blasted those hopes, what had cast a shadow over those prospects? What was bowing that manly form, tearing his heart and burning his brain? What had rendered him an alien and an outcast? Was it not the demon, personified in the bottle he held in his trembling hand? Was he not charmed by a serpent whose sting was death, and consuming his very vitals?[5]

In some stories, young women were warned not to encourage young men to take even a single drink, for what a man might avoid on his own might still tempt him if the good regard of a young lady were at stake:

> Never put a glass into the hand of a young man. You know not how terrible shall be the issue of that one thoughtless act. He has, ere he met you, perhaps felt his danger. He has been compelled to confess to his heart the growing power of a habit which he traces back to some such scene as this in which he stands by your side. On the brink of the abyss he has started back and sought to untwine the chords that were dragging him down. He is struggling like a wrestler with his appetite. He is yet weak before its giant power. If he yield a hair, if he allow it the least vantage, it will re-assert its dominion, he is its slave for life.

... You are his temptress! With pleasant smiles and kind words, you reach him the ruby draught. How can he resist? You have armed his old enemy against him.[6]

Alcohol could also masquerade as beneficial medicine, only to trap the unsuspecting users of "medicinal spirits," as one writer noted:

Here is an influence of a nature so secret and subtle as almost to escape suspicion, yet ever at work, in the past and now, baffling our efforts, ruining our hopes, thrusting back the reformed, ensnaring the unwary, and infecting whole classes and regions with false notions and a fatal practice.[7]

To temperance reformers and many other Americans during the 1800s, temperance or abstinence seemed crucial to maintaining a good society, because patterns of alcohol consumption were changing, often for the worse. As industrialization proceeded and cities grew larger and their populations more mobile, drinking increasingly took place not with family or known neighbors, but away from home with strangers. With the growth of the liquor industry and the saloons, and the development of a "cult of domesticity," social drinking also became a predominantly male activity. As immigrants from Germany and Ireland, and rootless young American men from the rural areas swarmed into the cities looking for work after 1830, drunkenness became associated with vice and loose living, with the seduction of innocents, with "Romanism," and with rioting and political corruption.[8] Nativism and racism were often woven into the anti-alcohol literature as well. After 1870 temperance reformers increasingly directed their attacks not just at alcohol itself but at the "liquor interests,"—saloons and their proprietors, and the distillers and brewers who supplied (and sometimes owned) them. In *The Saloon under the Searchlight* the minister and long-time temperance worker George Stuart neatly summed up who the enemies of temperance were, inviting readers to ascertain the righteousness of the prohibition cause by looking at who was for the saloon and who was against it.[9] Those for it, he said, included those in the liquor trades, of course, a dangerous class of godless, vicious, manipulating men ("the majority of these are foreigners"); these were joined by professional gamblers, anarchists, robbers, counterfeiters, and burglars, as well as "scarlet women," un-Americanized foreigners ("becoming more dangerous and ... *without exception* in favor of the saloon"), and drunken bums ("lost to all good, vicious from head to foot, and having no desire to reform").[10]

As Norman Clark has noted, public drinking in saloons, especially after the Civil War, also posed a clear threat to family life: workingmen spent too much time and money at such places, often exhausting the family budget.

Tempted by cheap drinks and "special deals," young men, often fathers, drank excessively, squandered the family income, abused or abandoned their wives and children, damaged their health, and became unfit for work. Post-war temperance groups, such as the Woman's Christian Temperance Union (founded in 1873) focused heavily on saving families from the ravages of alcohol. Collections of temperance stories and the WCTU's *Union Signal* featured many accounts of drunkards' wives. These routinely highlighted alcohol-induced violence and insanity, as well as general criminal behavior. For example, in "Married to a Drunkard," a prematurely aged woman tells how her husband, in the throes of an alcohol psychosis, killed their two daughters with a carving knife, then cut his own throat. Worse yet, her remaining child, a boy, having apparently inherited his father's tendencies, ended up a drunk as well, and was dead at eighteen. The woman warns her audience not to "blast your life as I blasted mine" by marrying a drunk:

> You will marry him and reform him, so you say. Ah! A woman sadly overrates her strength when she undertakes to do this. You are no match for the giant demon, drink, when he possesses a man's body and soul. What is your puny strength beside this gigantic force? He will crush you too![11]

The "demon alcohol" described in this literature is very powerful: even one drink, authors implied, could begin transforming a decent, law-abiding person into a gaunt, wild-eyed, homicidal maniac, or a ragged, stuporous derelict. It could take credit for most, if not all, of society's problems:

> One drink is what gives the policeman his job, pays the salary of the police judge, puts silk on the saloonkeeper's wife, fills the drunkard's wife's closet with skeletons and rags, and is the primary ingredient in a mixture that paints a cartoon of misery and woe on the drunkard's face that is not duplicated anywhere else this side of hell.

> As we look in the madhouse, monster Drink cries: "One-third of these are mine!" As we survey the inmates of our prisons, he cries, "Two-thirds of these are mine!" As we look at the paupers sustained by public charity, he cries, "These are all mine!" And when we gaze in horror at the one hundred thousand corpses with which his dungeon is annually gorged, he shouts exultingly: "Mine! Mine! All these are mine!" When we tremblingly ask: "What have you done with their souls?" he sneeringly answers, "You'll know at the Judgement!"[12]

After about 1870 prohibitionists also began incorporating new medical and scientific knowledge into their rhetoric, drawing on the work of physiologist Benjamin Ward Richardson and others. These researchers insisted that alcohol was not a medicine or a tonic or a food, but simply a poison.

They detailed its ability to cause direct physical changes to cell membranes and to virtually every organ in the body, including the brain. Temperance writer T. S. Arthur noted, "No substance in nature, as far as yet known, has when it reaches the brain, such power to induce mental and moral changes of a disastrous character as alcohol. Its transforming power is marvelous, and often appalling. It seems to open a way of entrance into the soul for all classes of foolish, insane or malignant spirits, who, so long as it remains in contact with the brain, are able to hold possession."[13] These findings strengthened the "dry" argument that alcohol had no medicinal or other beneficial effects, and formed the basis of the WCTU's Scientific Temperance Instruction campaign, which sought to have the dangers of alcohol and other drugs explicitly included in the hygiene texts used in primary and secondary schools, and to have temperance instruction made mandatory in public school curricula.[14] Physiological arguments also added dramatic weight to prohibitionists' literature and public speeches. A favorite "demonstration" used by Anti-Saloon League lecturers, for example, was to break an egg into a glass of pure alcohol, and tell audiences that the resulting curdle was similar to the effects of alcohol on the stomach's lining.[15]

One of the Anti-Saloon League's star lecturers was Richmond P. Hobson, who made extensive and imaginative use of the "scientific" rhetoric, and later transferred these "facts" to his anti-narcotic campaigns. Hobson was a Spanish-American War hero, and Democratic congressman from Alabama in 1906–1915, and joined the prohibition campaign around 1909. In 1913, he introduced a measure into Congress that would become known as the Hobson Amendment. With some modification, this later became the Eighteenth Amendment prohibiting the manufacture, transport, or sale of intoxicating liquors. He was enlisted as a lecturer by the Anti-Saloon League in 1910, and was heard or read by thousands of people during the next ten years. On the lecture circuits Hobson, like William Jennings Bryan, was a popular speaker, and the highest paid as well, often getting $525 per week plus expenses.[16] His standard speech, titled "Alcohol the Great Destroyer," appeared in several versions in the *Congressional Record* and also (greatly expanded) in his book *Alcohol and the Human Race* (1919). Many of the essential points were condensed for a series of public education pamphlets. Hobson told his audiences that "alcohol is a poison . . . produced by the process of fermentation, and is the toxin, or liquid excretion or waste product of the yeast or ferment germ. According to the universal law of biology that the toxin of one form of life is a poison to all forms of life of a higher order, alcohol, the toxin of the low yeast germ, is a protoplasmic poison to all life." He warned that it induced disease by paralyzing the white blood cells: "They behave like drunken men. In pursuit they cannot catch the disease germ. In conflict they cannot hold the disease germs for devouring."[17] In *Alcohol and the Human Race*, Hobson would provide more gruesome detail, explaining that alcohol has a special affinity for nervous system tissue, dehydrating its aqueous portion, dissolving its lipid portion, and coagulating its protein. And since the sheathing of nerve tracts was largely lipid, alcohol would eat through these in no time, eroding morality and other "higher" functions first, then attacking the intellect, the physical coordination, and so on, and bringing on degeneracy. Retrograde evolution, said Hobson, was a cardinal danger for any creature, especially human, which regularly consumed alcohol:

> If a peaceable red man is subjected to the regular use of alcohol, he will speedily be put back to the plane of the savage. . . . If a negro takes up regular use . . . , in a short time he will degenerate to the level of a cannibal. . . . No matter how high the stage of evolution, the result is the same. A white man . . . will be degenerated to the point where he will strike with a dagger or fire a shot to kill with little or no provocation. . . . he will be cruel to his own flesh and blood. It is conservatively estimated that 95 percent of all the acts and crimes of violence committed in civilized communities are the direct result of men being put down by alcohol toward a plane of savagery. . . . In every living thing there is the evolutionary impulse to rise and progress. . . . man is not changing much in his physical nature, but is evolving chiefly in his nervous system, building up those delicate centers of the brain upon whose activities rests the moral sense. Nature is trying to produce men of high character, a race of true, noble men. Alcoholic beverages even in moderation reverse the processes of nature and set back the purposes of creation.

By using the degeneracy argument, Hobson and other writers could blend older moral rhetoric about alcohol's actions with a modern "scientific" explanation loosely derived from Darwin's theories.[18] Hobson's preoccupation with race suicide was unusually strong, but it was a concern shared by other Americans, especially after 1910 when America's emergence as a world power and the prospect of war heightened worries about our collective strength and fitness. The threat of "degeneracy" added new urgency to anti-alcohol campaigns, anti-vice crusades, and efforts to restrict immigration. Hobson, along with many other writers, referred to alcohol as a "disease," a "parasite," and a "social cancer." He also framed many of his proposals for action in immunological terms, calling for "innoculation" of the public with the "serum" of truth through education. This was especially urgent, crusaders believed, because this "disease" affected the "germ plasm" or reproductive cells just as it ravaged the nervous system tissues. While alcohol degenerated the individual, it also cursed his or her offspring with insanity, hysteria, epilepsy, idiocy, and various deformities, along with inherited moral deficits. No family could escape this fate if either parent drank even a little. Further, within several generations, the "taint" would render descendants sterile, thus ending the family line altogether. And the character of the nation suffered as the number of degenerates grew; so too would freedom and civilization suffer if the "great destroyer" were not stopped. Indeed, Hobson said, "all the pages of history cry out to America, 'Conquer the great destroyer or perish.'"[19] Hobson frequently drew criticism for exaggerating or distorting medical and scientific information (e.g., claiming that "alcohol is killing off as many Americans every year as all the wars of the world have killed in battle in 2,300 years"), but this did not affect his popularity with most audiences.[20]

The war with Germany intensified the racial elements in anti-alcohol rhetoric. Hobson's wartime speeches noted that German hostility and degeneracy were caused by the drinking habits of German mothers. The ASL traced the war's origins to the rise of a people who "drink like swine" and whose "sodden habits have driven them constantly toward brutality and cruelty."[21] The prohibitionists were thus able to equate abstinence with patriotism, and this probably contributed to the successful enactment of Prohibition as a wartime measure in 1917, and its eventual ratification as the Eighteenth Amendment in 1919.

The nineteenth- and early twentieth-century temperance campaign rhetoric depicted alcohol not just as a personal temptation to be avoided for the sake of one's character and soul, but also as the primary cause of poverty, violent crime, vice, degeneracy, and civil unrest. It was a pervasive and urgent problem, reformers said, and might also have sinister connections to those who would overthrow our nation. After several decades of relentless agitating, lobbying, and propagandizing, the Woman's Christian Temperance Union and the Anti-Saloon League not only achieved their goal of nationwide Prohibition, but had familiarized Americans with a well-defined rhetorical style for talking about mood-altering substances.[22]

Anti-narcotic Rhetoric

Although anti-alcohol education campaigns continued after Prohibition was enacted, some reformers, including Hobson, were drawn to the cause of narcotic control during the 1920s.[23] The Harrison Narcotic Act of 1914 had made the first step toward controlling domestic consumption, but the details of enforcement (especially the medical maintenance question) were still being worked out.[24] Meanwhile, Americans after World War I were caught up in fears of anarchy, communism, and foreigners generally, and often associated narcotics addiction and traffic with these "elements." Addiction among the "lower orders" of society had increased, even as iatrogenic addiction had declined, and opiate use, especially, had acquired sinister connotations.[25] Reformers such as Hobson, Sara Graham-Mulhall (who had served as a deputy commissioner on the New York State Narcotic Board from 1919 to 1921), and Hearst newspaper journalist Winifred Black insisted that education and vigilance were crucial to wiping out this evil, soul-destroying bondage, not just for Americans but for the entire civilized world. Accordingly, in 1920, Hobson helped get a twenty-five-page textbook for teachers written and distributed, so that schoolchildren could be warned about the dangers of narcotic addiction.[26] Following this he helped establish several anti-narcotic organizations: the International Narcotic Education Association (INEA) in 1923, the World Conference on Narcotic Education (WCNE) in 1926, and the World Narcotic Defense Organization in 1927.[27] These groups worked hard to raise public awareness, using many of the tactics that had worked so well for the ASL and WCTU: getting prominent citizens (e.g., physicians, attorneys, judges, and legislators) involved (usually via letter-writing campaigns), holding international conferences, and pressuring politicians to tighten controls on narcotics. They sent out (by Hobson's account) millions of pamphlets and article reprints, contributed articles to magazines and newspapers, and contacted teachers and school superintendents.[28] Hobson and other reformers such as Graham-Mulhall regularly gave speeches to women's clubs and other groups in New York City. Using the new medium of radio (just introduced in 1920), Hobson was able to reach a wide audience with his fervent pleas for action against "the narcotic evil," and the anti-narcotic campaign also had the support of W. R. Hearst and his journalists.[29] Beginning in 1927, anti-narcotic reformers drew the press, politicians, and civic organizations into a nationwide effort called Narcotic Education Week, held in the last week of February. The INEA's report on the first Narcotic Education Week noted that over 21,000 "constructive programs" were done by various organizations, including religious and educational associations. About half the country's radio stations carried some narcotic education messages, and seventy-six of these produced a "well-prepared drama" on the dangers of drug use. Mayors and governors issued statements of support, and both local papers and national chains cooperated with the effort.[30]

That same year, *Narcotic Education*, the bulletin of the INEA and WCNE, began publication. It featured updates on the activities of the organizations, informative articles on the drug-using populations and the "addiction problem," and texts of addresses given by Hobson and other notables at various meetings and on the radio. This bulletin furnishes many examples of the anti-drug rhetoric used by these groups, and shows how closely many of these writers followed the pattern of anti-alcohol literature, emphasizing the power of the drugs, the ubiquity and growth of the problem, and the connections between drugs and vice, crime, individual ruin, and threats to American society.[31]

The "degeneration" argument was applied to narcotics use just as it had been to alcohol, with a few adjustments. Hobson continued to worry that the American race would suffer serious decline if narcotic use spread, and to warn that we would not be able to stand up to our enemies. But because narcotics (unlike alcohol) are not produced domestically, the elements of conspiracy in his rhetoric are not the American liquor interests but shadowy foreign "enemies" rarely specified. In the first issue of *Narcotic Education* he asserted that America was being deluged with dangerous drugs because those drugs were profitable to the countries who trafficked in them; naturally, such countries would target wealthy nations such as our own. They would also, however, have the "motive to weaken a financial, commercial, or industrial rival or an imagined enemy in war." In an earlier *New York Times* article, Hobson had noted, "The United States is assailed by opium from Asia as a base, by cocaine with South America as a base, and by heroin and synthetic drugs with Europe as a base. This deadly drug warfare that is striking from three sides . . . is more destructive and biologically more dangerous to our future than would be united warfare against us from these three continents."[32]

In the wake of the war, amid growing nativism and calls for immigration restriction, this rhetoric found a ready audience. Other contributors also argued that the world would not be safe for civilization until the traffic had been stopped. This theme was also very common in the popular periodical literature: over half the articles I examined for the 1920s made direct reference to foreigners and possible conspiracies by foreign countries or foreign drug smugglers. The *New York Times* regularly ran articles on the drug traffic and short pieces on arrests, raids, and convictions, always highlighting the illegal activities of the Italians, the Greeks, the Chinese, and the Mexicans.[33]

The reformers characterized "narcotics" as poisons and addiction as a disease, just as temperance advocates had done with alcohol. Hobson transferred his "facts" about alcohol's ability to dissolve the sheathing on nerve tracts directly to heroin, with a similar warning about the subsequent degeneration of higher, more evolved faculties. Likewise, he asserted that narcotics had a special affinity for the reproductive tissues and could blight the children as well as the parents. Narcotic addiction, like alcohol addiction, was seen as a habit innocents acquired when they were lured into it by "bad company" or the drug sellers. But there was an added twist with narcotics, according to many writers: the drug itself induced in the users a "mania" to bring everyone else into addiction. The addict, said Hobson, "thinks, dreams, plots to bring all whom he contacts into addiction. All addiction tends to spread. . . . Drug addiction is more communicable and less curable than leprosy." U.S. Attorney Frank Catinella told a group of pharmacy students that "the drug . . . kills body, soul, and spirit. It not only destroys the person who acquired the habit, but that person becomes in turn the medium by which he transfers the habit to someone else." This vampire-like characterization of addiction turned up in many popular articles, some written by judges, physicians, and prison superintendents, and was used as a justification for isolating addicts in prisons and hospitals.

Although Hobson's anti-alcohol tracts had warned of the dangers of even one drink, he moderated this opinion to play up the addictive properties and deadly potentials of heroin and morphine: "Five ounces of alcohol is considered a fatal dose. Five ounces of morphine taken at one time will kill 1500 men. It requires months and often years of repeated regular drinking with many drinks a day to produce a drunkard. One dose a day for six days will make a youth a drug addict. An ounce of heroin could make two thousand addicts within a week."[34] Dope peddlers, he said, take advantage of this rapid addiction potential, introducing their victims—especially high school children—to heroin at seemingly harmless "snow parties" where they are urged to sniff it. "But once is once too often. The poison is so swift that the poor youth will seek the next party for relief, and the next." Within a week the victim would be suffering a bondage worse than death and from which there was no escape. The dangers of drugs, like the dangers of alcohol described by temperance writers, could be insidious indeed. Even worse, Hobson warned, was the possibility that European chemists would continue to discover more potent synthetic addicting drugs, and flood our country with them, much as the "foreign" distillery and brewery owners had done with alcohol.[35]

Because the habit could spread so rapidly, and because medical use alone could not account for the volume of opiates imported each year, anti-narcotic crusaders assumed that a million or more Americans were addicts and that this number was increasing all the time, especially among young people.[36] Public health and law enforcement officials' estimates were much lower (100,000–200,000), and they sometimes criticized the inflated figures, but to no avail. Hobson and his fellow reformers insisted that the "narcotic peril" was even more dangerous than "Demon Rum."

Anti-narcotics crusaders also blamed drugs for violence, crime, and insanity, just as prohibitionists had blamed alcohol. Although Hobson had earlier claimed that 95 percent of violent crime could be traced to the degenerative effects of alcohol, his anti-narcotic essays noted that the "great majority of daylight robberies, daring holdups, cruel murders, etc., are being committed by youthful heroin and cocaine addicts." Sidney Brewster, Warden of City Prisons in New York City noted in a *Narcotic Education* article that "with the use of drugs, every drug addict may be termed not only a derelict, as far as society is concerned, but a potential criminal as well." Earlier, Brewster had noted, "The man who uses heroin is a potential murderer, the same as the cocaine user. He loses all consciousness and moral responsibility." Another *Narcotic Education* writer warned of "prostration of the will and demoralization; Criminal excursions . . . culminating in banditry, burglary, and murder committed under the brutalizing stimulus of the drugs or impelled by the craving to get them."[37]

Several years after Harry J. Anslinger became chief of the newly created Federal Bureau of Narcotics (FBN) in 1930, he initiated a propaganda campaign to help rouse public support for uniform state narcotic laws, including the prohibition of marijuana (which had not been included in the Harrison Act.) His strategy was similar to Hobson's: frequent public addresses on the dangers of the "killer weed" and its connections to crime and violence; enlisting the help of civic and religious organizations (including Hobson's and the WCTU); and offering the FBN's expert advice to journalists wishing to write about marijuana and the drug problem. As previous anti-narcotic writers had done with heroin, Anslinger told audiences that this new drug was "the worst evil of all," that "fifty percent of the violent crimes committed in districts occupied by Mexicans, Spaniards, Latin-Americans, Greeks, or Negroes may be traced to this evil," that marijuana induced violent, atrocious crimes, including murder and rape, and caused permanent insanity in users. Its use, he said, was increasing at a frightening rate, especially among young people. This campaign was successful, in that eighteen more states had adopted the uniform narcotic law by 1936, but it also led to a demand for a federal marijuana control law, which Anslinger had not wanted.[38]

The Rhetorical Legacy

How much effect did these anti-narcotic crusaders have on the wider public discourse? While it is difficult to make direct causal connections, I believe that Hobson, his fellow reformers, and Anslinger had a considerable influence on the way Americans talked about drugs. Hobson was already well known as a congressman and Prohibition lecturer, and attracted quite a bit of attention during the 1920s, as did other socially prominent crusaders. For example, Hobson was featured in at least two large-circulation national magazines during the 1920s—the *Saturday Evening Post*, and *Lit-*

erary Digest; Sara Graham-Mulhall was written up in *Current Opinion* and in *Pictorial Review*, which awarded her $5,000 for her book *Opium: The Demon Flower*. More important, however, they were very active in New York, using their social and political contacts to recruit other influential people to the cause. Not only did they produce and distribute large amounts of campaign literature, but in the *New York Times*, at least, their activities were routinely reported, if only in short paragraphs noting "Captain Hobson warns of narcotic peril" or "Federation of women's clubs to fight marijuana evil." Hobson had two large feature articles in the Sunday *New York Times* during the 1920s, and daily articles covered his World Conference on Narcotic Education meeting in Philadelphia, held on July 5–9, 1926. The activities of the World Narcotic Defense Association and the International Narcotic Education Association were also often noted in the *Times*. Likewise, during the 1930s, Anslinger, in his official position as FBN commissioner, could reach a wide audience via the newspapers and civic groups eager to help with the "narcotic problem." And although I did not examine the Hearst papers for this study, it is likely that, with their consistent support of the anti-narcotic cause and their large circulation figures (in 1935 the twenty-eight Hearst papers had a combined circulation of 5.5 million daily and 7 million on Sunday), they played a large role in defining the rhetorical style for talking about drugs.[39]

Certainly, some of the anti-narcotic rhetoric was already in place by the time Hobson and others got involved. Narcotic addiction was being described as "evil" and a "menace" well before 1920. And earlier writers had sometimes characterized the problem in "epidemic" terms, that is, virulent (with everyone equally susceptible) and rapidly growing. But before 1920, the bulk of periodical articles concerning drugs focused on the international opium traffic, particularly its effects on China, and not on America's domestic drug problem. The campaigns of the 1920s and 1930s, through constant repetition, helped establish an anxious and inflated anti-drug rhetoric in American popular periodicals, making "evil," "epidemic," and similar descriptions almost obligatory. Roughly two-thirds of the fifty-four periodical articles I examined, and virtually all of the *Times* articles more than three paragraphs in length called the problem an "evil," a "menace," an "infection," or used similar terms. Between 70 and 73 percent of magazine articles which mentioned size described the problem as large or very large (that is, asserting that the number of addicts was between one and five million), and half stated that it was growing rapidly.

The crusaders' emphasis on nefarious dope peddlers was echoed strongly in the periodical articles. Fifty-three percent of the 1920s items and 60 percent of the 1930s items described users as victims of pushers. Connections of addicts with violence and criminal behavior were equally strong. Sixty-five percent of articles in the 1920s and 86 percent in the 1930s highlighted violent behavior, and almost all noted the connection between drug use and crime, as did many of the *New York Times* articles.

The sharp increase in articles mentioning crime and violence during the 1930s is partly due to the rash of articles that followed the passage of the 1937 Marijuana Tax Act. Following Harry Anslinger's lead (in his article "Marihuana—Assassin of Youth"),[40] accounts of marijuana intoxication almost jumped off the page at readers: young men and women leapt off buildings, or indulged in sexual abandon, or attacked strangers, or robbed stores, or murdered their entire families with axes under the influence of this vile drug. This emphasis on marijuana horror stories seems to have originated with Anslinger's need to raise Americans' awareness about the drug at a time when most Americans outside the South and Southwest knew very little about it and public opinion regarding its control was largely apathetic. (This apathy may be apparent in the fact that very few magazines ran articles on marijuana before 1937, even though sympathetic newspapers had been editorializing about the "menace" since 1932.) Crime, during the desperate Depression years, was a reliable "hook" Anslinger could use to focus attention on marijuana.

The increased emphasis on crime and violence during the 1930s may also be due to the waning of protest against addict stereotypes. About one-fourth of the 1920s magazine articles were sympathetic to addicts' situation rather than fearful. Robert Schless, who worked with addicts at the Philadelphia Department of Public Welfare, noted that most addicts looked and behaved nothing like their popular stereotypes. On the contrary, users were most often generally responsible, well behaved, and not too different from average citizens. He also informed readers that opiates cause little of the physical damage or mania often found with other drugs, and attributed much of the "addict trouble" to restrictions imposed by the Harrison Act.[41] Samuel Hopkins Adams wrote a series of articles for *Collier's* in 1924 in which he argued that addiction was a disease, not a vice, and that laws made it worse by persecuting physicians who try to help addicts, and allowing peddlers and quack cure clinics to get rich.[42] Other writers also argued that addicts were just everyday folks who happened to have an unfortunate physical condition, or perhaps just a weak, not pathological, personality. Only two sympathetic articles appeared in the 1930s, and neither concerned marijuana users. In the *Times*, moreover, there seem to be no sympathetic articles at all in these decades.

By the late 1930s, when marijuana became a hot issue, Americans had apparently accepted a sensationalistic rhetoric as the "normal" language for describing drug problems. This is not surprising, all things considered. The rhetoric of a drug "evil" was familiar to most Americans from generations of anti-alcohol campaigns, and it also gave expression to their postwar fears of foreigners, crime, and social disorder, and perhaps fed a public appetite for sensational stories. The anti-narcotic activists were often socially well placed, which gave them credibility as well as publicity, and they used Prohibition-style saturation strategies to keep their cause in the spotlight. Together with law enforcement officials such as Anslinger they were able to dominate public discussion of narcotic use and addiction. Unlike prohibitionists, these crusaders faced little opposition: there was no large population of addicts agitating for their right to use drugs; even before the Harrison Act, addiction was regarded as unfortunate and embarrassing. And the physicians and others who advocated a medical approach could offer no real workable alternatives to enforcement, short of maintenance, which most considered intolerable. Perhaps, too, many Americans found it easy to accept the stereotypes because the narcotic problem *was* relatively small, and was increasingly outside their direct experience as various controls reduced the number of medical and middle-class addicts.

Anti-drug campaigns, like anti-alcohol campaigns, have gone through several cycles since then, but the rhetoric forged during the initial efforts has remained with us. During the 1940s and 1950s, Harry Anslinger (who remained chief of the Federal Bureau of Narcotics until his retirement in 1962) continued to insist that marijuana caused insanity, and warned that drugs, especially heroin, were part of a communist conspiracy to undermine national security by fostering addiction in Americans, particularly in military personnel.[43] In the 1960s and 1970s, despite a softening of cultural attitudes and official redefinition of addiction as a disease, drugs of abuse were demonized by some writers and legislators. For example, during the 1964 Senate hearings on the Drug Abuse Control Amendments, Senator Thomas Dodd told the committee that illegal use of amphetamines and barbiturates had "flooded the country" and "reached epidemic proportions . . . increasing at a fantastic rate among juveniles and young adults," and added that the drugs had "a direct causal relationship to increased crimes of violence." During House hearings the following year, Rep. Florence Dwyer deplored the "devastating effects of the easy availability of . . . dangerous drugs—crimes of violence and depravity, widespread delinquency among the young, . . . the graduation to the hard narcotics, the ruined lives of countless individuals, the misery and heartbreak and dislocation of innocent and helpless families." A physician testifying at the 1969 House Select Committee on Crime hearing on amphetamine abuse concluded, "historians may someday compare our problems with drugs to the ravages of the Black Death during the Middle

Ages when a third of the population was struck down." Senator Edward Kennedy opened the 1979 hearings on tranquilizer abuse by noting that "no one is immune from this problem; it affects doctors and priests, teachers and laborers, business executives and housewives." He believed that the hearings would reveal only the "tip of the iceberg—that thousands of Americans are hooked and do not know it."[44] Popular accounts in magazines such as *Reader's Digest* told how even one dose of a drug could bring on disaster, from nervous breakdowns to addiction to suicide. In 1970, President Richard M. Nixon declared that drugs were "public enemy number one" and initiated the "war on drugs."

Since Ronald Reagan's second term, much public discourse about drugs has used the "just say no" and "zero tolerance" approach. The Partnership for a Drug-Free America's television campaigns showed viewers that "drugs" were to one's brain what a hot frying pan was to an egg. Another early PDFA effort showed the supposed EEG of a marijuana smoker to be as flat as that of a coma patient. Media coverage has focused heavily on the victims of the crack cocaine "epidemic," running hundreds of stories about ruined lives, crimes and violence, and crack babies.[45] In 1985 the journalist Peggy Mann published *Marijuana Alert*, featuring many horror stories about good, sweet teenagers transformed into lazy, moody, rebellious, promiscuous monsters by (as Nancy Reagan said in her foreword) "a drug that is taking Americans captive." And so it goes.

In this essay I have attempted a brief demonstration of the consistency and longevity of American public discourse concerning mood-altering drugs. Such a survey raises more questions than can be answered in this space, and I hope to address them in future work. First, to what extent is this characteristic rhetoric a reflection of genuine drug problems (and how do we define "drug problem"?); and to what extent is it an expression of various social tensions—class struggles, demographic changes, racial and ethnic conflicts, labor struggles, etc.—or an expression of particular social values and ideologies (especially those surrounding deviance in the nine-teenth century, and the various views of the social and world order derived from Darwin, Spencer, et al.)? Second, what accounts for the persistent use of these themes and images over time? Do they have a special resonance for Americans, and if so, where does it come from, and why is it functional? Third, to what extent has this popular rhetoric not only reflected but shaped public perceptions and drug policy itself during this century? The answers probably won't change policy, but they may tell us much about what mean-ings alcohol and other psychoactive drugs have carried for Americans during the past two hundred years, and why we talk about them as we do.

Notes

1. See, for example, Craig Reinarman and Harry G. Levine, "The Crack Attack: Politics and Media in the Crack Scare," pp. 18–51 in Reinarman and Levine, eds., *Crack in America: Demon Drugs and Social Justice* (Berkeley: University of California Press, 1997); Thomas Szasz, *Ceremonial Chemistry*, rev. ed. (Holmes Beach, Fla.: Learning Publications, 1985); Steven Wisotsky, *Beyond the War on Drugs* (Buffalo, N.Y.: Prometheus Books, 1990), 174–84; Craig Horowitz, "The No-Win War and Its Discontents," *New York* 5 (February 1996); Joseph McNamara's commentary in "The War on Drugs Is Lost," *National Review*, 12 February 1996; and *The Drug Policy Letter*, published quarterly by the Drug Policy Foundation, Washington, D.C.

2. Reinarman and Levine, "Crack in Context," pp. 1–17 in *Crack in America* includes a good summary of this research, especially work done by Norman Zinberg and Howard Becker.

3. For this study I have used articles indexed in *Readers Guide* and the *New York Times Index* under the headings "drugs," "drug habit," "drug traffic," "narcotics," and names of individual drugs (opium, cocaine, marijuana, morphine, heroin, etc.) The magazine articles were "coded" with a checklist which noted how the drugs, their users, and their sellers were portrayed, what (if any) explanations for the drug problem were given, the size of the problem (if mentioned), and associations made between drugs and deviant behaviors or drugs and various "outgroups." The range of possible positions in these areas was determined from a preliminary random survey of anti-drug literature (including the magazine articles) between 1920 and 1950. A comprehensive content analysis of *New York Times* articles was not possible, but I have examined and used many of them here.

4. See Jack S. Blocker, *American Temperance Movements: Cycles of Reform* (Boston: Twayne, 1989); Paul Boyer, *Urban Masses and Moral Order in America, 1820–1920* (Cambridge: Harvard University Press, 1978); and Norman Clark, *Deliver Us from Evil: An Interpretation of American Prohibition* (New York: W. W. Norton, 1976).

5. S. F. Cary, "The Story of the Bottle," in Cary, ed., *The National Temperance Offering* (New York: R. Vandien, 1850), 25.

6. A. L. Stone, "Appeal to the Ladies of America," in Cary, ed. *National Temperance Offering*, 216–217; also see T. S. Arthur, "The Circean Cup," in the same volume.

7. H. D. Kitchel, "Brandiopathy; or, 'Just a Little for Medicine,'" in Cary, ed., *National Temperance Offering*, 45.

8. Paul Boyer has described a sense of "urban threat" that developed in the early nineteenth century as older neighborhoods changed hands, immigration increased, and urban life seemed to become more hurried and impersonal. Because of these changes, he suggests, traditional family and community regulation of drinking behavior and social problems such as poverty, crime, and insanity diminished, and they seemed increasingly threatening. See *Urban Masses and Moral Order*, 3–21 and 23–24. William Rorabaugh also explored the anxieties of antebellum Americans and how these affected drinking behavior in *The Alcoholic Republic: An American Tradition* (New York: Oxford University Press, 1979), 125–181. Drunkenness and rioting were not confined to urban settings, however. Irish canal and railroad workers were notorious for this, as were cowboys, fur trappers, and other frontier types. See Rorabaugh, 140–46. Paul E. Johnson's *A Shopkeeper's Millennium: Society and Revivals in Rochester, New York, 1815–1837* (New York: Hill & Wang,

1978) provides a fine analysis of the social tensions and changes in a fast-growing new city, and how residents used revival and reform to address them.

9. Stuart (1857–1926) had a long and varied career as an evangelist minister and well-regarded temperance lecturer in the South, campaigned for the Prohibition Party, and often addressed Anti-Saloon League gatherings. *Saloon under the Searchlight* went through five editions, the last in 1908.

10. George R. Stuart, *The Saloon under the Searchlight* (New York: Fleming H. Revell, 1908), 8–16.

11. From "Touching Incidents and Remarkable Answers to Prayer," in Elton R. Shaw, ed., *The Curse of Drink, or, Stories of Hell's Commerce: A Mighty Array of True and Interesting Stories and Incidents, Striking Articles, Touching Home Scenes, and Tales of Tender Pathos, all Thrilling with Graphic Details and Eloquent Language of the Fearful Consequences of the CURSE OF DRINK* (n.p.; copyright 1909 by editor.) This collection was published somewhat after the WCTU's peak period, but, since temperance stories were very formulaic, "Married to a Drunkard" is not too different from earlier stories of drunkards' wives. I use it here only because it is more compactly written and thus easier to quote.

12. Ibid., pp. 496, 501.

13. T. S. Arthur, *Grappling with the Monster* (Philadelphia: Hubbard Bros., 1877), 63.

14. See Philip J. Pauly, "The Struggle for Ignorance about Alcohol: American Physiologists, William Olin Atwater, and the Woman's Christian Temperance Union," *Bulletin of the History of Medicine* 64 (1990): 366–92; Jonathan Zimmerman, "The Queen of the Lobby: Mary Hunt, Scientific Temperance, and the Dilemma of Scientific Education in America, 1879–1906," *History of Education Quarterly* 32 (1992): 1–30; and Zimmerman, "The Dilemma of Miss Jolly: Scientific Temperance and Teacher Professionalism, 1882–1904," *History of Education Quarterly* 34 (1994): 413–432.

15. Andrew Sinclair, *The Era of Excess: A Social History of the Prohibition Movement* (New York: Harper, 1962), 39. Note the close similarity to the Partnership for a Drug-free America's television ads nearly 100 years later, which showed an egg ("This is your brain") broken into a hot frying pan ("This is your brain on drugs.") ("Any questions?").

16. According to Walter Pittman, the League paid Hobson $171,250 between 1914 and 1922; Hobson was also able to push the sale of his own books on the circuit, selling 200–300 copies per month. See Pittman, "Richmond Pearson Hobson, Crusader," Ph.D. diss., University of Georgia, 1969, 127–140.

17. *Congressional Record*, 61st Cong., 3rd sess., 1911, XLIV, pt. 2, p. 1868.

18. Temperance writers and some physicians had written about the effects of hereditary alcoholism in individuals and families since at least the 1870s, but the "race suicide" and eugenics arguments for prohibiting alcohol appear later. See John Higham, *Strangers in the Land* (New York: Atheneum, 1966), 131–157, on the origins and growth of eugenics thought, and Charles Rosenberg, "The Bitter Fruit: Heredity, Disease, and Social Thought," pp. 25–53 in Rosenberg, *No Other Gods: On Science and American Social Thought* (Baltimore: Johns Hopkins University Press, 1976), for nineteenth-century hereditarian thought more generally.

19. *Congressional Record*, 61st Cong., 1911, 3rd sess., XLIV, pt. 2, pp. 1870–1871.

20. According to Pittman, Hobson drew ridicule from the wet press, who liked to publish his inaccuracies with corrections, and was also reminded by other temperance workers not to exaggerate so much. See "Richmond Pearson Hobson," 141–143.

21. Quoted by Sinclair, *Era of Excess*, 117.

22. The organizations produced millions of newspapers, newsletters, pamphlets, and posters which they distributed to churches, corporations, labor unions, fraternal organizations, and women's clubs, and also placed "dry" slogans on billboards and in newspapers. See ibid., 106–116; Ruth Bordin, *Woman and Temperance* (Philadelphia: Temple University Press, 1981), 72–94; Blocker, *American Temperance Movements*, 80–119; and K. Austin Kerr, *Organized for Prohibition: A New History of the Anti-Saloon League* (New Haven: Yale University Press, 1985).

23. Pittman notes that these people needed a new focus for their moral fervor. Prohibition enforcement was often a fiasco, and Prohibition itself was becoming more controversial, so reformers "welcomed the narcotics struggle as one where the issues, evil and good, were clear cut and an almost unanimous public opinion favored the reformers. Gangsters and drug addicts have never had a good public image nor were they effective lobbyists" ("Richmond Pearson Hobson," 162).

24. For details on the maintenance question see David Musto, *The American Disease: Origins of Narcotic Control*, rev. ed. (New York: Oxford University Press, 1987), 121–182, and Jim Baumohl's essay in this volume.

25. See Musto, *American Disease*, 132–134, and David Courtwright, *Dark Paradise: Opiate Addiction in America before 1940* (Cambridge: Harvard University Press, 1982).

26. Pittman, "Richmond Pearson Hobson," 167. Apparently reformers had little success getting this widely adopted.

27. Other citizens' organizations included the White Cross and the Inter-State Narcotic Association.

28. Hobson did much of the fundraising for these organizations himself, primarily through giving speeches to civic and church groups around the country, but they also received generous support from larger donors, such as Josiah K. Lilly of Lilly Pharmaceuticals. Hobson was also able to persuade the National Educational Association to join the fight against narcotics. Financial supporters were often a source of political support as well, as when Hobson was agitating for the passage of uniform state narcotics laws. See Pittman, "Richmond Pearson Hobson," 170–180. Hobson also claimed that in 1926–1927 the organization had been able to get out 2,500,000 documents on a small budget by using "the services of the public printer and the Congressional frank, and the machinery of education and of great organizations" (*Narcotic Education*, July 1927, 6).

29. The INEA specifically mentions its debt to Hearst in its reports on Narcotic Education Week for 1927 and 1928: "The cooperation of the press was gratifying. Mr. William Randolph Hearst led in putting the force of his whole national system behind the movement" (*Narcotic Education*, April 1928, 65–66). In the foreword to Winifred Black's *Dope: The Story of the Living Dead* (New York: Star, 1928), Fremont Older remarked that Hearst "never forgets Narcotic Week, nor forgets to remind his editors when it is approaching. . . . He keeps this subject alive whenever the occasion arises, forces it under the noses of his readers and continues to demand that the Government kill this dreadful traffic. And finally, when it is killed, he will have done more than any man in the United States to accomplish its death."

30. The General Federation of Women's Clubs, the Parent Teacher Associations, and the WCTU were among these. See *Narcotic Education*, July 1927, 13–14.

31. Although *Narcotic Education* did not begin publication until 1927, much of Hobson's material (and that of other contributors such as Sara Graham-Mulhall) had been reworked from articles and speeches given in the early 1920s. As he had with anti-alcohol campaigns, Hobson tended to stick with the same spiel.

32. *New York Times*, 9 November 1924, IV, 4.

33. The *New York Times Index* listed an average of 100 items on the drug traffic per year between 1921 and 1931; for the period 1920–1940 inclusive, the average is 80 items per year.

34. *New York Times*, 9 November 1924, IV, 4.

35. "Saving Youth from Heroin and Crime," *Literary Digest*, 24 May 1924, 32–33; "Heroin Heroes," *Saturday Evening Post*, 20 September 1924, 42; "One Million Americans Victims of Drug Habit," *New York Times*, 9 November 1924, IV, 4; "The Struggle of Mankind against Its Deadliest Foe," *Narcotic Education*, April 1928, 52–54.

36. This figure was originally offered in 1919 by A. G. DuMez in a government report based, as it turned out, on grossly distorted survey data and fictitious draft statistics. The errors were soon acknowledged, but so quietly that many politicians and reformers, perhaps unaware, continued using the earlier figure. See Courtwright, *Dark Paradise*, 9–34.

37. Sidney W. Brewster, "Actual Trend of Drug Addiction and Its Relationship to Crime–I," *Narcotic Education*, July 1927, 11–13; Brewster quoted by Hobson, "One Million Americans Victims of Drug Habit," *New York Times*, 9 November 1924, IV, 4; Stephen Anderton, "Public Enlightenment and Uniform State Laws to End Narcotic Darkness and Chaos," *Narcotic Education*, July 1927, 22–25.

38. The federal legislation put further enforcement duties on the FBN at a time when its budget and personnel resources were already strained. Thus Anslinger hoped to keep the enforcement responsibilities with the states. See Richard Bonnie and Charles Whitebread, *The Marihuana Conviction: A History of Marihuana Prohibition in the United States* (Charlottesville: University Press of Virginia, 1974), 92–117, and John McWilliams, *The Protectors: Harry J. Anslinger and the Federal Bureau of Narcotics, 1930–1962* (Newark: University of Delaware Press, 1990), 51–80.

39. Hobson was the subject in "Heroin Heroes," *Saturday Evening Post*, 20 September 1924, and "Saving Youth from Heroin and Crime," *Literary Digest*, 24 May 1924. Graham-Mulhall authored "The Increasing Drug Menace and Its Serpentine Trail," *Current Opinion*, May 1922, and was featured in the *Pictorial Review* issue of January 1927. The figures concerning the Hearst papers are from Alfred Lee, *The Daily Newspaper in America: The Evolution of a Social Instrument* (New York: Macmillan, 1937), 220; Lee also noted that Hearst papers tended to carry quantities of the same features: "Local autonomy amounts to freedom to collect necessary local news and to fight the crusades with which Hearst sensationalizes his sheets . . ."; see also "Hearst," *Fortune*, October 1935, 43–55.

40. Harry J. Anslinger and Courtney Ryley Cooper, "Marihuana: Assassin of Youth," *American Magazine*, July 1937, 18–19, 151–153.

41. Robert A. Schless, "The Drug Addict," *American Mercury* 4 (February 1925): 196–199, and "Pitting Drugs against Alcohol," *Current Opinion* 78 (April 1925): 449–450.

42. Samuel Hopkins Adams, "The Cruel Tragedy of Dope," *Collier's*, 23 February 1924, 7–8; "How People Become Drug Addicts," *Collier's*, 1 March 1924; and "How to Stop the Dope Peddler," *Collier's*, 8 March 1924.

43. See Harry J. Anslinger, "Marihuana . . . the Assassin of the Human Mind," *Law Enforcement* 1 (October 1951): 7–10; "Criminal and Psychiatric Aspects Associated with Marihuana," *Union Signal*, 5 February 1944, 77–78; "Drug Addiction," *JAMA* 144 (1950): 333; Anslinger and William Thompkins, *The Traffic in Narcotics* (New York: Funk & Wagnalls, 1953); Anslinger and Will Oursler, *The Murderers: The Story of the Narcotics Gangs* (New York: Farrar, Straus, & Cudahy, 1961).

44. U.S., Congress, Senate, Committee on Labor and Public Welfare, Subcommittee

on Health, *Control of Psychotoxic Drugs: Hearing before the Committee on Labor and Public Welfare, Subcommittee on Health on S 2628*, 88th Cong., 2nd sess., 1964, pp. 46–47; U.S. Congress, House, Committee on Interstate and Foreign Commerce, *Drug Abuse Control Amendments of 1965; Hearings before the Committee on Interstate and Foreign Commerce on H.R. 2*, 89th Cong., 1st sess., 1965, p. 223; U.S. Congress, House, Select Committee on Crime, *Crime in America—Why 8 Billion Amphetamines? Hearings before the Select Committee on Crime pursuant to H. Res. 17*, 91st Cong., 1st sess., 1969, pp. 20, 23; U.S. Congress, Senate, Committee on Labor and Human Resources, Subcommittee on Health and Scientific Research, *Use and Misuse of Benzodiazepines: Hearings before the Committee on Labor and Human Resources, Subcommittee on Health and Scientific Research*, 96th Cong., 1st sess., 1979, pp. 1–2.

45. See Reinarman and Levine, "The Crack Attack," on media coverage of the crack "epidemic" during the 1980s.

Maintaining Orthodoxy

The Depression-Era Struggle over Morphine
Maintenance in California

Jim Baumohl

Behold now a ghost—the vagrant spectre of a dead mistake: Narcotic
Clinics. Innocent in origin but vicious in effect, the mistake died young.
But the evil spirit it awoke now and again roams the land, even to
this day finding advocates to renew its mischief.

—Harry J. Anslinger, ca. 1941

A clinic may not be a panacea, but even its most bitter enemies can
offer nothing better.

—Dr. George Parrish, 1935[1]

Introduction

At the close of the nineteenth century, American legislators
began to make into law their aversion to freely available opiates. Strict control
accorded with temperance objectives, seemed likely to prevent a great deal
of addiction and accidental poisoning, and appealed to the aspirations of
doctors and druggists for greater income and respectability: licensed dispensing might help regulate ruinous competition; restricted prescribing
might give doctors some moral distance from the blighting addict trade and
close the infamous all-night drug stores of the country's vice districts. As
the *Pacific Pharmacist* opined, the sooner each druggist declined "to make
money by trading upon the ignorance, the weaknesses or the vices of his
customers, the sooner will pharmacy be looked up to as an art or a profession." Alas, there were some practitioners "who must be whipped into line
by the sharp lash of the law."[2]

In 1903 the American Pharmaceutical Association (APhA) adopted a
model state law which based the availability of opiates on prescriptions written by licensed medical practitioners (including dentists and veterinarians)

and filled by certified pharmacists. It banned prescriptions for habitual users except "for the treatment of such habit." The APhA did not explicitly forbid the indefinite furnishing of maintenance doses to keep addicts out of withdrawal ("to satisfy their craving," in the language of the time). However, in 1909, the California State Board of Pharmacy specified the lawful, "good faith" use of opiates in treating addiction to be gradual withdrawal over several weeks. The California standard subsequently shaped enforcement of the epochal Harrison Narcotic Act, a federal statute effective March 1, 1915.[3]

Written as a revenue measure which enabled physicians and pharmacists to register as licensed handlers and dispensers of certain drugs, the Harrison Act avoided the appearance of regulating the practice of medicine, a responsibility guarded by the states. However, the Treasury Department, which administered Harrison, issued regulations in early 1915 which declared prescriptions valid only when written for "normal" doses. Addicts, including patients with advanced tuberculosis or severe, chronic pain, now would be dependent on registered physicians who were prohibited from prescribing the high doses necessary to exceed the tolerance levels of habitual users. As David Musto argued, from the implementation of Harrison, Treasury officials used it as the basis for an assault on maintenance. This reflected a growing consensus among physicians that "ambulatory treatment"—either as gradual reduction or maintenance—was always inferior to the asylum model of lengthy custody and enforced abstinence that had dominated the treatment of alcoholism since the 1880s.[4]

Still, the first years of Harrison Act enforcement were marked by conflict between Treasury's Narcotic Division and thousands of physicians who were principled, or unwitting—or occasionally unscrupulous—violators of Harrison's alleged anti-maintenance warrant. Indeed, during the first years of the Harrison era, when doctors chose to fight rather than conform, local and district courts tended to hold that physicians acting in good faith could treat addiction as they saw fit, or that Harrison, as a mere revenue measure, could not infringe on a state's right to regulate medicine. At first, maintenance proved difficult to eliminate. But on the same day in March 1919, the Treasury Department got two critically important, if razor-thin (5–4), rulings from the Supreme Court. *U.S. v. Doremus (249 U.S. 86)* affirmed the constitutionality of Harrison's requirement of valid prescriptions. *Webb et al. v. U.S. (249 U.S. 96)* put maintenance beyond the pale. Writing for the majority in *Webb*, Justice William R. Day cast aside the subtleties of good faith and clinical necessity. Doubtless irritated with Dr. Webb, who prescribed huge quantities of morphine that likely were resold, Day wrote bluntly: "[T]o call such an order . . . a physician's prescription would be so plain a perversion of meaning that no discussion of the subject is required." *Webb* drove an effective (if fragile) wedge between addicts and legal sources of supply, and the decision's potential scope immediately alarmed local officials, for a real end to maintenance seemed to promise widespread suffering, crime, inundation of jails, and an overwhelming demand for hospital care. Treasury came under considerable pressure to help locals cope with the situation.[5]

Within two weeks of *Webb*, Treasury formally defined exceptions to antimaintenance policy: essentially, the elderly or incurably ill could be maintained if doctors affirmed that the drug was "necessary to sustain life." Such exceptions were already tolerated, and some states had rules and procedures for these cases. Since 1909, California's Board of Pharmacy had required physicians to register "medical" addicts. A Pennsylvania law of 1917 also required registration. This limited form of morphine maintenance became a little-known facet of therapeutic orthodoxy throughout the Harrison era, and although not without major ambiguities and attendant problems for doctors and patients, the practice was not insignificant: Between November 1918 and the end of September 1932, more than 17,000 addicts were registered in Pennsylvania, the registry adding about 1,000 persons per year even at the end of this period, almost two-thirds of whom suffered with cancer.[6]

At the end of July 1919, Treasury supported local initiatives to organize outpatient dispensaries—narcotic clinics—in response to *Webb*. Whether clinics were ardently encouraged or merely permitted depended on the views and organizing zeal of any given regional Collector of Internal Revenue, but whatever its quality, this support was expedient. As the Commissioner of Internal Revenue saw it, in the wake of *Webb*, "a system of relief" was required "whereby these unfortunate persons may be prevented from becoming menaces to the community and be ultimately salvaged." In the absence of available hospital treatment, clinics might examine addicts and give them "the minimum dose required to prevent their physical and nervous collapse." But the clinics were intended only as therapeutic staging areas. As the Surgeon General advised the Commissioner: "They serve to relieve the present crisis and later will serve as feeders to the institutions where real cure can be carried out."[7]

As local and state officials were desperate for revenue in the midst of postwar recession and inflation, Treasury looked to the United States Public Health Service (PHS) to provide institutional care. The PHS had earlier resisted this idea; however, after *Webb*, and impressed by the fiscal and administrative architecture of the venereal disease clinics established during the war, the Surgeon General found merit in a similar federal, state, and local partnership to manage addicts. The PHS would assume a coordinating role and, of vital importance, take responsibility for addicts without legal residence anywhere. The France Bill, introduced in Congress in mid-August

1919, reflected this plan. France intended to create a federal matching grant program allowing states to establish Treasury-approved treatment systems drawing on PHS and military hospitals. Opposed as a harbinger of state medicine by substantial conservative elements in the American Medical Association (AMA), and spurned by a budget-slashing Senate, France failed on October 10th.[8]

Despite the defeat of the France Bill, more than forty local clinics operated in the United States for some period between 1919 and 1923. They had in common the low-cost sale of morphine (and sometimes heroin and cocaine), but they were otherwise a mixed lot. Whatever their individual approaches and merits, however, all soon operated without the blessing of Treasury, which backtracked on clinics once it was clear that the France Bill was dead. Fortified by an April 1920 AMA resolution condemning ambulatory treatment, the Narcotic Division effectively discredited the clinics, closing most without resistance. As the rest of the story is usually told, after February 10, 1923, when the last, stubborn clinic closed in Shreveport, Louisiana, the United States entered a four-decade period when no lawful opiate maintenance was available anywhere. From the closure of Shreveport to the establishment of methadone maintenance in New York City in 1965, American drug policy was, in the words of David Courtwright and his colleagues, "simple, consistent, and rigid." Addicts were demonized, hounded, subjected to draconian criminal penalties, and never treated except in the confines of hospital or jail. For the most part, only the patients of private sanitaria were spared immediate withdrawal. Abstinence was the only legitimate goal of treatment.[9] Allowing for the oft-forgotten maintenance of the elderly or incurably ill and a "gray market" of private maintenance for the well-to-do, this story seems accurate.

But notably absent is more than passing attention to how therapeutic orthodoxy was maintained, particularly in the face of continuing divergence and dissent. It was not reproduced effortlessly. In September 1930, when Harry J. Anslinger (1892–1975) began his thirty-two-year reign as chief of the new Federal Bureau of Narcotics (FBN), he assumed command of a corps of agents recently infamous for feeding on street addicts while neglecting large dealers, and for "black-jacking" doctors and druggists "into line." Anslinger promised a new dispensation, especially for "the professional classes" hounded by "field men" looking "to build up a good record" at their expense.[10] He could hardly have done otherwise. Rash enforcement, in part, caused Treasury important legal and political setbacks during the mid-1920s. In 1926 Congress rejected all six amendments to Harrison proposed by the Department to "clear up certain points which have been raised in certain courts to the disadvantage of the government." One of these, which would have outlawed ambulatory treatment, intended to nullify a unanimous 1925 Supreme Court ruling (*Linder v. U.S., 268 U.S. 5*) that severely threatened *Webb*. *Linder*, involving a well-known Spokane (Washington) doctor who in 1922 prescribed small amounts of cocaine and morphine to an addict "stool pigeon," resuscitated the defense of professional good faith and reminded federal enforcers that Harrison could not trespass on a state's right to regulate medical practice. While the Court reaffirmed Harrison's constitutionality in 1928, like Congress, it did nothing to blunt *Linder*'s specific threat. That would require vigilant political work by the FBN.[11]

One site of heresy was California, where maintenance advocates were concerned with a variety of related problems: the criminalization of addicts who were otherwise respectable citizens; the property crime (particularly car theft and burglary) attributed to addicts raising money for morphine (then the opiate of choice on the Coast); the dreary parade of addicts in and out of city and county lockups to no seeming end; the failure of a few months of state hospital care to do more than detoxify, treat abscesses, and promote weight gain; the prohibitive cost of massive, long-term confinement; and the corruption of local, state, and federal police by drug money. After weighing such matters, the Berkeley criminologist and former police chief August Vollmer (1876–1955) concluded in 1936 that "the first step in any plan to alleviate this dreadful affliction should be the establishment of federal control and dispensation—at cost—of habit-forming drugs." Vollmer's was a minority voice, but he was eminent and by no means alone.[12]

Maintaining Orthodoxy

> I can't save enough to take a cure because it takes just a day's wages to keep down the craving. What I used to get in a drug store for twenty[-]five cents [five grains] costs just exactly five dollars now to peddlers. If I have it I can work with the rest of the huskies. But if I just get up in the morning and go to work without it I would not be able to walk in about six or eight hours. I therefore would lose my job. . . . If I had a place where I could go and buy my ration . . . then I know I could taper off in a few weeks till I'd be nearly or all through with it.
>
> —G. A. Horner, Sacramento, August 9, 1919

> I have seen myself in the dark cold of the night, board the blinds . . . of a fast express train, in the mountains of northern California, and ride long and hard . . . to get a shot of morphine. I have kicked habits, cold turkey, in the box car, jungles, and in many a cold and dreary jail

house cell. . . . [W]hen a victim goes through all this misery, and continues to wade in said misery, it must thereby have an awful holt [sic] upon [him]. . . . [G]ive these who can prove incurable, a permit to use said medicine.

—Anthony Votta, Rikers Island, New York, May 18, 1939[13]

The Jost Bill

By January 1931, when William P. Jost, an obscure Alameda County Republican, introduced a maintenance bill in the California Assembly, the State Board of Pharmacy and its political allies had spent twenty years trying to create an effective alternative to incarceration on the one hand or maintenance on the other. A 1911 state commitment law sponsored by San Francisco's sheriff (who was also a powerful state senator) resulted in the wholesale transfer of addicts from county jails to state hospitals, but this merely enraged the asylum keepers, who by 1916 had regained substantial control of the commitment process. Successful bills to create a state hospital for addicts and alcoholics were pocketed by governors in 1913 and 1917 on grounds of economy.[14] Thus, following *Webb* and the demise of the France Bill, and with the active collaboration of regional Treasury officials, the City of Los Angeles established a narcotic dispensary in February 1920.

This clinic treated 564 people during its short life. Over three-quarters of its registrants had been addicted for longer than five years, almost exclusively to morphine, and most were between twenty and forty years old. Over 90 percent were white and native born. Almost all were unskilled and semi-skilled workers, and in no position to pay one dollar per grain for morphine, the going price on the street. The clinic sold only morphine, for 10 cents per grain, and attempted to "balance" an addict on six to eight grains per day. Doses were reduced and withdrawal recommended consistent with the addict's health. Above all, the clinic attempted to support employment, as it was "infinitely better to have [addicts] at work using a moderate amount of morphine than turned loose on the streets desperate." Almost 20 percent of the registrants applied for hospitalization, which the clinic doctors considered "necessary for the last stage of treatment." The city health department paid for the private care of a few of these, and a few more were treated at the county hospital, but for most, the clinic was "simply tiding [them] over an emergency."[15]

Savagely disparaged by William Randolph Hearst's *Los Angeles Examiner*, and quickly disowned by the Treasury Department, the clinic was closed by federal order in August 1920. Even so, the experiment persuaded some of the wisdom of the clinic model and even organized maintenance per se. The

Los Angeles Times vigorously defended the "Hearst-assailed" clinic. The Board of Pharmacy, originally opposed to the Los Angeles clinic and a much smaller one in San Diego, ultimately supported them. Frank Hutton, the attorney in charge of Board prosecutions, wrote to the Commissioner of Internal Revenue: "It is incomprehensible that a fair and impartial investigation of the Clinic idea would stamp it a failure." In Hutton's view, clinics accomplished "more good . . . in one day than all the prosecutions in one month." Neither Dr. L. M. Powers, the Los Angeles Health Commissioner, nor John P. Carter, Treasury's Collector of Internal Revenue for Southern California, could understand opposition to the clinics; Carter was flummoxed by his agency's change of course. The committee of physicians and laymen advising the Los Angeles clinic was appalled by the "hidden . . . and lying influence" marshaled against it.[16]

Carter's bafflement testified to his distance from policymaking. From its first enforcement of Harrison, Treasury's strategy was to subordinate treatment methods to drug control, and clinics, no less than private physicians, seemed likely sources of supply to the black market. Treasury also worried that clinics could undermine *Webb* by raising the question of why government was permitted to engage in a medical activity forbidden to private doctors. As regional supervisor Harry Smith explained to the press when closing the California clinics: "[A]mbulatory treatment is not legal, whether [by] a municipality or an individual."[17]

In October 1923, some members of the defunct clinic's advisory committee, Powers and Carter among them, formed the nucleus of the Los Angeles–based Bureau of Drug Addiction. This was an ambitious organization with an unmistakably critical cast. Its Medical Division intended to establish "a properly equipped hospital unit" to treat addicts "within the limits of existing law," but its other divisions, one chaired by Vollmer, another by former Treasury Secretary William Gibbs McAdoo, aimed to produce reports with "particular emphasis" on cases where the Medical Division's work was hamstrung by existing law.[18] The Bureau of Drug Addiction was also short-lived, but with the encouragement of the Board of Pharmacy, the mission of its Medical Division was assumed in late 1924 or early 1925 by the Narcotic Committee of the Los Angeles County Medical Association (LACMA).[19] For a number of years, one or more of the Committee's doctors seem to have discreetly provided examinations and morphine prescriptions out of their own offices. By 1931, however, the Committee was openly maintaining several dozen sick or elderly addicts at a clinic in the psychopathic ward of Los Angeles County General Hospital, and the clinic's director was paid 60 dollars per month by the city health department.[20]

Writing in 1937, Dr. Henry Smith Williams (1863–1943) observed that in the early '30s the LACMA clinic "was an institution of rapidly-growing fame. . . . The work was known to the White Cross Societies, and projects were pending to petition legislatures to sanction the similar treatment of ambulatory addicts whose sole malady was drug addiction disease." Williams was referring most immediately to the Seattle-based White Cross Association on Drug Addictions, a group which advocated expanded treatment options for addicts, including maintenance. He also had in mind William Jost's White Cross–inspired Assembly Bill 1433. This would have allowed city and county health officers to prescribe up to four grains of morphine per day to "addicts of long standing . . . classed as incurables."[21]

The LACMA Narcotic Committee's clinic was one referent for the Jost Bill; the California State Narcotic Hospital at Spadra was the other. Spadra was the work of Republican State Senator Sanborn Young, of Santa Clara County, who in 1927 authored and steered a successful bill to create it after hospital bills failed in the legislature in 1921 and 1925. Located about thirty miles southeast of Los Angeles, Spadra opened in August 1928, superintended by Thomas F. Joyce, formerly the resident physician at New York City's Riverside Hospital and an experienced manager of addicts. Spadra was a modest attempt to provide institutional treatment (of eight months to two years duration) outside of county jails and existing state hospitals.[22]

Predictably, Spadra failed to escape the powerful gravity of California's decades-old struggle among state hospitals, jails, and commitment courts. From the Gold Rush on, state hospital superintendents, superior court judges, and county jailers had wrestled over the definition of appropriate candidates for hospital care. Hospital administrators always wanted promising therapeutic material; jailers always wanted to be rid of unruly drunkards and, by the 1880s, addicts and the drug trade that followed them inside the lockups. For their part, committing magistrates responded to earnest pleas for lenience or medical treatment from the sometimes visibly ill people before them (or from their families), or acted on their own or a sheriff's inclination to remove troublesome and frequent offenders to more convenient and perhaps salutary custody. To accommodate all interests, Young envisioned Spadra as both a hospital for "hopeful" cases and a separate work farm for incorrigibles. But a parsimonious Republican governor regarded Spadra as "a test tube experiment which we can later enlarge and expand." Thus, one facility was asked to serve both functions. Moreover, the equally thrifty legislature located Spadra on land already owned by the state, an unfortunate site with no natural barriers to elopement. The result was large numbers of escapes—almost one per day through 1929—to which Joyce responded in time-honored fashion: He built higher walls, employed more guards, and installed a searchlight "that could detect escaping inmates at night over a distance of three-quarters of a mile." He also tried to educate superior court judges about suitable candidates for treatment: "We would welcome the man who has no criminal record or who has not lived on his wits or been the recipient of the proceeds of prostitution, or worse." Escapes finally were cut to about one per month, but the judges were hard to educate, so Joyce sought greater discretion for the superintendent, a tried and true way to dispose of undesirable patients. He got approval in principle in January 1931, a week before the Jost Bill was introduced in the Assembly. Joyce's enlarged discretion would allow him to refuse addicts who had failed in treatment at other state hospitals and those with criminal histories. This would substantially hamper the sheriffs, probation officers, and judges who would use Spadra as an alternative to the county jail or state prison.[23]

Such an exclusive approach to rehabilitation was controversial given its timing. An "intensive narcotics drive" in San Francisco had produced 424 drug arrests (with 350 convictions) between June 1930 and February 1931, along with hundreds of "vagrant addict" arrests.[24] It was a terrible time for San Francisco's addicts, not only because of the heightened threat of arrest, but because supply was disrupted by the disorganization of a major dealing network. Anthony Votta, a long-time addict, recalled it later (from a New York jail cell) as "the biggest panic in the history of Frisco."

> Cube morphine was in the market at that time, and what little of it was in circulation, the price went up from $1.50 for about a three grain cube to $5.00 per cube. . . . Men and women of all walks, and stations in life, roamed the city in search for this drug—night and day—and would pay any price. . . . Not being able to get the drug, we stormed the drug stores, and bought all the cough syrup that contained narcotics and drank the same. Some left the city, while others . . . actually kicked their habits upon their feet. . . .[25]

With legions of addicts already going "cold turkey" in jail, San Francisco's police court judges dismissed 95 percent of the "vag-addicts" who came before them. The San Francisco White Cross launched a drive to raise funds and promote medical alternatives to incarceration (including maintenance). And the Jost Bill proposed to put Spadra to wider use by allowing superior court judges to send to Spadra any addict convicted of possessing less than one ounce (roughly 437 grains) of morphine. Moreover, this option applied even to peddlers so long as they were addicts themselves and had been "entrapped . . . by another addict acting as a stool pigeon for enforcement officers." The last provision was a slap at state and federal police methods, of course.[26]

Jost's attempt to commandeer Spadra for the jailers was extremely offensive to Young and Joyce (who called it "nothing short of a calamity"); but it was the Jost Bill's catholic provision for maintenance that set off alarms at the brand-new Federal Bureau of Narcotics. The bill was "a vicious piece of legislation," the seasoned agent Harry Smith advised Anslinger, "such as will tend to destroy much of the work . . . during the past twelve years" (i.e., since *Webb*).[27] Relying on dubious evidence about the evils of the 1920 Los Angeles clinic supplied by Smith and Anslinger, Hearst's *San Francisco Examiner* excoriated the bill. Winifred Black Bonfils, writing in her prominent "Annie Laurie" column, warned her Hearst syndicate readers that the Los Angeles clinic "flooded [the state] with addicts, who rushed in here from all over the country." The Jost Bill would "invite every poor, wretched addict to California, and ask him to bring his friends and relations along." Smith recruited Earl Warren (1891–1974) to make similar dire predictions. Warren, later governor of California and then Chief Justice of the U.S. Supreme Court, was in 1931 the Alameda County district attorney.[28]

The political bum's rush was effective. Unlike the 1920 Los Angeles clinic, the Jost Bill found no defenders in the press and every authority condemned it in hair-raising terms. After a March 17th hearing, the Assembly Committee on Medical and Dental Laws unanimously tabled it. Jost pledged to cooperate with Young and Joyce to work out the apportionment of addicts among the jails, Spadra, and other state hospitals. But Spadra's problems in this respect were only beginning.[29]

The End of the LACMA Clinic

On April 24, 1934, in what the *Examiner* called "a series of spectacular sorties," FBN agents arrested five physicians, four druggists, and a male nurse in different sections of greater Los Angeles. They had allegedly prescribed or conspired to furnish morphine to addicts in violation of the Harrison Act. Harry Smith, who coordinated the arrests, announced that they were the result of a continuing investigation of diversion from legitimate channels.[30] A LACMA clinic doctor, Frank T. Cary, was among those arrested. The following day, the clinic's director and chair of LACMA's Narcotic Committee, Dr. Edward Huntington Williams (1868–1944), turned himself in. The arrests of Cary and Williams occurred only ten days after the city health officer had persuaded the city council to resume modest stipends for the two clinic doctors, who had been volunteers since 1932.[31]

The city health officer, Dr. George Parrish (1872–1941), was a feisty veteran of acrimonious public battles with religious fundamentalists and health faddists, and he was not cowed. However, after the arrests, he was hard-pressed to maintain the clinic, and came under terrific pressure from the FBN and the Los Angeles police to acquiesce in seven onerous conditions for its continuation. These included provisions for the reexamination of all clinic patients, as well as their finger-printing, photographing, and registration with state and local narcotics police. Most important, a six-grain maximum daily allowance would be imposed.[32]

On May 11th, Parrish met with federal and local representatives to discuss these terms. Harry Smith and the Los Angeles police chief insisted that such conditions were required by the Harrison Act. Parrish firmly disagreed and prevailed upon Dr. Edward H. Anthony (b. 1878), physician to federal prisoners in various area jails, to take over the clinic with health department financial support and political cover. With reluctance, which grew as federal agents and Los Angeles police began to harass him, Anthony served as the sole clinic doctor for seven weeks—until he and a cooperating druggist were arrested by the FBN for violating the conditions laid out by Smith, particularly that concerning the permissible daily ration. In spite of the mayor's remonstrations with Anslinger, that was the end of the clinic. But it was not the end of the arrests: on August 1st, a federal grand jury indicted Williams and his office partner, Dr. Edson Hun Steele (1895–1953), on numerous counts of issuing "so-called prescriptions" in violation of Harrison, and one count of conspiring to violate the law.[33]

Williams believed (correctly) that he was the FBN's principal target, but until Anthony was arrested, he was angry but not overly concerned. "The whole thing is one of the rankest and clumsiest frame-ups that I have ever seen," he wrote to Vollmer early in June. "And make no mistake—I intend to have the last laugh in this case." Williams's early confidence was based on a naive conviction that he would be supported by his medical peers and by the Roosevelt administration, but as the arrests of Los Angeles physicians continued throughout the spring and summer of 1934, Williams began to take his position quite seriously. "The reign of terror now in progress to suppress medical men is without precedent," he wrote to Vollmer. A recently arrested physician, he reported, "gave morphine to a man who has cancer of the rectum as well as tuberculosis. The officers used him—this perfectly legitimate case, a dying man—as a stool pigeon." The purpose of his own arrest was clear to him: "The whole object of the attack seems to be to use me . . . so that the medical fraternity may be frightened into closing the Clinic and refusing to prescribe morphine." Williams recognized "the moving spirit[s] in this conspiracy" to be Sanborn Young ("a paranoid fanatic who has run wild"), and Harry Smith ("his actions indicate the grandiose ideas of paresis"). Williams's supporters had appealed directly to the secretary of the Treasury, he told Vollmer, because "his Narcotic Department, headed by Anslinger, is not to be trusted."[34]

Williams was right to be suspicious of the FBN, for Harrison Act enforcers had been marking him since 1920, when he was a member of the Los

Angeles clinic's advisory committee. His faith in his fellow physicians was misplaced, however. While Williams had the private support of prominent members of the AMA and the California State Medical Association, neither of these organizations, nor even LACMA, was willing to come to his defense publicly. In part, this was because over the years the LACMA clinic became an organizational loose cannon. The Narcotic Committee was a presidentially appointed group with ill-defined responsibilities. Although it had twenty-four members in 1934, no more than a handful participated. As no regular reports were made on the clinic, few of the Committee's own members knew much about it. When the FBN moved in the spring of 1934, LACMA's president was unaware of the clinic; in fact, he claimed that the Narcotic Committee "was never authorized by the County Medical Association to create a clinic or to enter into group treatment for addicts"—an activity of which he disapproved. Such controversy among LACMA's councilors about the clinic's history and legitimacy and, doubtless, real fear of the FBN produced caution, if not foot-dragging. Resolutions calling for a full hearing by the membership, and for public support for the arrested doctors, were voted down by LACMA's leadership.[35]

While LACMA did not offer public support to Williams or any of the arrested doctors, a special committee, comprised largely of past presidents of the organization, did try to intercede with the FBN. However, this committee's internal division about ambulatory treatment was exploited by FBN agents who systematically misrepresented clinic procedures and Williams's professional history. In meetings that agents characterized as confidential, the doctors were told, for instance, that in May 1921 Williams was charged with "prescribing large quantities of narcotic drugs for 32 addicts, under the guise of so-called ambulatory treatment." The agents claimed that a federal grand jury warned Williams that if he failed to stop, "the case would be reopened." The doctors were informed further that in early 1928 Williams had been "reported for sending drugs through the mails to an addict physician," but that no action was taken because "the addict died." And apparently most damaging, in the eyes of at least one LACMA representative, Williams and Steele had prescribed for a dead man.[36]

When finally made aware of these claims in early 1935, Williams called the first "an unmitigated, purposeful lie." No documentary evidence ever was produced to support the FBN's contention. In the matter of the addict physician sent drugs through the mail, Williams had an impressive and ironic rejoinder: The Pasadena doctor in question had at one time been former Treasury Secretary Andrew Mellon's family physician; he was brought to Williams "with the knowledge of the Secretary himself" because the old man was dying of cancer. With respect to prescriptions for the dead, Williams could not resist pointing out that prescribing for a dead man was perfectly legal. It was illegal, he continued, for a living person to use any such prescription—but no one had suggested this had happened. He then detailed how the clinic doctors worked out with state narcotic officers, whom he named, a procedure for using a trusted addict—a man with advanced tuberculosis who was also a state informer—to fill prescriptions for clinic patients too sick to attend. He then delivered their morphine. The "dead man" was a patient who had died between the writing of the prescription and the morphine delivery. According to Williams, the courier "reported the situation and no more prescriptions were written."[37]

The interesting question is why the FBN worked so hard and played so rough to prosecute doctors connected with a clinic that made no claim to maintain "mere" addicts. Williams did not support indiscriminate maintenance. Like most other maintenance advocates of this era, he regarded all forms of ambulatory treatment as second best to hospitalization and abstinence. Further, like Spadra Superintendent Joyce, Williams distinguished "deserving and decent addicts" from those who were "dishonest and degenerate," the former deserving "great sympathy," the latter "permanent penitentiary residences." The LACMA clinic's patients were desperately sick by every account. Ample evidence was presented in court that some patients referred by physicians for clinic enrollment were refused after examination and laboratory work because Williams or one of his associates thought that hospital treatment was indicated. Why, then, were physicians at the LACMA clinic treated differently from doctors in, say, Pennsylvania, who maintained a similar population of addicts?[38]

There were several reasons. First, there was considerable symbolic value in bringing Edward Huntington Williams to heel. He was an associate editor of the tenth edition of the *Encyclopedia Britannica;* with his brother, Henry Smith Williams, he was also a prolific and well-known popular science writer. Second, he had been an outspoken opponent of the Harrison Act since its passage, arguing that the law should be repealed in favor of the medical management of addiction by the PHS. In a newspaper editorial that Anslinger brought to Assistant Treasury Secretary Gaston's attention, Williams was portrayed as a medical eminence and quoted as follows: "The peddler is the great problem of the drug situation. The Harrison Narcotic law, by preventing doctors from prescribing morphine [to addicts], created the peddler. . . . There would be no peddlers now if that law were repealed. But that would throw the officers out of work." The editorialist concluded that "the Doctor's proposals have been attracting widespread attention. It is well to withhold judgment on the recent charges against him."[39]

But most inflammatory to Anslinger, Williams was not a lone dope doctor: He was associated with the White Cross, which was touting the LACMA clinic as a model for a revived maintenance movement. In fact, this connection was incidental; Williams was more an intellectual fellow traveler than a comrade in arms. Even so, explaining to Gaston why the FBN was proceeding against Williams, Anslinger emphasized that Williams was "connected with the International [San Francisco] White Cross," an organization "making a drive to repeal the Federal narcotic laws and to set up in their place a system . . . under which licensed addicts are supplied with narcotics." Anslinger saw Williams, like the White Cross, as a brazen political enemy, and he intended to play Nemesis: "The moral effect of his conviction upon other practitioners," Anslinger wrote in a memo to himself, "will most certainly result in greater circumspection in the prescribing and dispensing of narcotic drugs along the West Coast." This was the motive Williams had asserted all along.[40]

In their criminal trial, Williams and Cary hung their defense on *Linder*. The United States District Attorney asserted that clinic patients paid Williams five dollars for a physical examination and then were referred to Cary "with an 'O.K.' for a morphine prescription," for which they paid an additional five dollars. However, the only evidence of such crass practice came from an addict of long standing brought from Chicago to work as an informer. The FBN paid him by the day and also gave him a "reward" following the arrest of Williams and Cary. The doctors' attorneys claimed that the FBN was maintaining the man on morphine so that he would testify (ironic proof that well-supplied addicts could function normally), and insisted that he be kept in custody without drugs so that the jury could see him in withdrawal. The judge refused, but Williams's lawyer tried to keep the issue before the jury: When a pellet of morphine rolled off a scale during the testimony of a government chemist, he remarked that it "had better be given" to the informer. The judge held him in contempt.

After an acrimonious six-week trial in which all seventeen medical experts supported the doctors, the judge instructed the jury that such professional testimony and the *Linder* standard of good faith were "advisory only." Told to rely on its "experience in human affairs," which is to say, on a common sense notably jaundiced on drug matters, the jury convicted Frank Cary on five counts of violating the Harrison Act. He was sentenced to twelve months in a federal road camp and five years probation. Convicted on one count, Williams spent a year on federal probation and was forbidden to hold a narcotics license for two years. Their appeals were thwarted on technical grounds owing to a filing error by their attorneys. Both doctors were acquitted of conspiracy. After three years, in July 1937, the FBN dropped charges against Williams and Steele. At about the same time, the FBN agent-in-charge who helped make the Williams-Steele case, was arrested for selling a large quantity of morphine to gangsters. He pleaded guilty and went to prison.[41]

The trial of Edward Anthony and pharmacist William Dickinson resulted in a deadlocked jury, and the case was taken up for decision by Federal District Judge Leon R. Yankwich. Finding that Anthony acted in good faith by the *Linder* standard, Yankwich noted acerbically that "neither [Los Angeles Police] Chief Davis nor the federal authorities can give an ultimatum to a physician as to the manner of treatment by him . . . the violation of which would constitute a violation of the law." Anthony, Yankwich asserted, lived up to his Hippocratic oath—and was then punished for doing so. In acquitting Anthony and Dickinson, Yankwich had the following message for the FBN: "It is not the law that a medical officer can give absolution for criminal offenses, any more than it is the law that the enforcement officers, by placing their own interpretation on the law, can create an offense which does not exist."[42]

SEVEN OF THE LACMA clinic's last seventy-two patients died shortly after the clinic closed—of pulmonary tuberculosis, diabetes, heart disease, advanced syphilis, all complicated by years of addiction and the therapeutic necessity of large doses of morphine. An eighth patient, a forty-year-old, tubercular woman, went to work as an informer for the Los Angeles police and not long after was beaten to death on the job. Between May 29 and July 10, 1934, of seven clinic patients committed to Spadra, six were quickly released by Superintendent Joyce because they were too sick to benefit from treatment. On February 26, 1937, a former clinic patient ended as follows an open letter to the major Los Angeles newspapers and the city's public officials: "Today I am without narcotics and am having [pulmonary] hemorrhages. Physicians will not prescribe narcotics for me as they fear arrest. . . . I have been refused treatment at the Spadra State Hospital. I have been refused admittance to the Los Angeles General Hospital because I am addicted. . . . I am not financially able to go to a private institution. Unless I receive narcotics I will die. Yours in distress."[43]

A Debacle for the San Francisco White Cross

"I am commencing to work on the [San Francisco] White Cross," Sanborn Young wrote to Anslinger in March 1934, a month before the first LACMA clinic doctors were arrested. Young knew that the San Francisco group, recently incorporated as the International White Cross as the result of conflict with the Seattle parent organization, was planning an independent fund-raising and membership drive in southern California. The organization walked right into the "reign of terror" and found Young and Anslinger ready to exploit its estrangement from the founding chapter. By August, when Williams and Steele were indicted, the San Francisco or International White Cross was an outlaw among charities.[44]

The American White Cross Association on Drug Addictions was founded in Seattle in December 1920 by an Episcopal rector and four friends. Throughout its history, the organization drew heavily on Protestant clerics for leadership and relied for sustenance on membership fees, the sale of White Cross postal seals, and small grants from the Seattle Community Fund. Despite attempts to establish other branches, only in San Francisco did the association take root outside of Seattle.[45]

The San Francisco chapter was founded in 1927. Like the Seattle group, it did educational work, publishing and distributing literature and providing speakers on addiction, particularly in the schools; and it took an interest in treatment, arguing publicly for leaving the management of addiction to physicians. Its secretary worked with addicts who brought problems to the Market Street office and, doubtless, she put in a good word for them with local judges. In 1934, the director was Reverend James S. West, formerly pastor of San Francisco's First Baptist Church.[46]

Like its parent organization, the San Francisco White Cross raised money by soliciting memberships and selling postal seals. In 1932 it mounted its first membership and fund-raising drive in southern California, systematically canvassing the residents of Los Angeles, Long Beach, and San Diego.

Charitable organizations customarily sought approval by local philanthropic elites in advance of such campaigns. In San Francisco, this meant review by the Indorsement Council, a private body closely connected to the Chamber of Commerce; in Los Angeles, it was the Social Service Commission, a municipal body. The endorsement groups guarded against fraud; they also bounded political acceptability. Failure to seek their approval had no enforceable consequences, but could result in crippling publicity. Perhaps out of ignorance, perhaps in defiance, in 1932 the White Cross did not go through the endorsement committees of the cities in which it solicited. The complaints about the membership drive were many and loud. Members of the Los Angeles Social Service Commission were themselves solicited by telephone, a practice its president considered "inherently crooked." When the White Cross returned for another campaign in the Southland in the spring of 1934 and applied for endorsement, Commission members were primed to be critical. So was Sanborn Young, put on the FBN payroll by Anslinger at one dollar per year to serve as an official spokesman. And Young had mobilized his cadres: the Los Angeles police, the state Division of Narcotic Enforcement, the Los Angeles county jail physician, the Los Angeles district attorney, among others. Young also got help from Everett G. Hoffman (1876–1953) and Earle Albert Rowell, Seattle White Cross stalwarts who confirmed reports of corruption in the 1932 campaign. Rowell told the Social Service Commission that of $7,500 collected from Los Angeles residents, the organization had seen but $900. The solicitors spent the rest on themselves. West, who was not in charge at that time, conceded that this was true, but claimed that the organization had since "devised a system by which solicitors could not appropriate collections." His assertion was greeted skeptically. Given the previous ineptitude of the San Francisco White Cross, and the improbable help of Hoffman and Rowell, Young and Anslinger easily executed their strategy to cripple the organization's ability to raise money. The Social Service Commission pounded the White Cross on technical matters and withheld its endorsement.[47]

Young also wanted to attack the group's ideas in a highly visible public forum. Therefore, instead of allowing the Commission to confine the matter strictly to professional and technical considerations, Young and his allies tore into West with the extraordinary hostility they usually reserved for communists. After calling the organization's "teaching" nothing more than "the desire of the dope addict," Young continued: "It is a crying shame that our public schools are open to [the] vile educational propaganda that this organization . . . is espousing. Their theories are more dangerous to our school children than any pestilence." West was on his feet before Young finished. After defending himself as a father of three and a man of God, he invoked the First Amendment: "I have just as much right as Mr. Young to speak anywhere for a cause which I believe is just and right; any American citizen has that privilege." Before West could turn to matters of substance, however, Young regained the floor and launched a bitter attack on narcotic clinics.[48]

It was a rout. At one point or another in the several hearings held before large audiences from mid-June to mid-July, all three commissioners expressed their disagreement with White Cross doctrine, whether on modifying the Harrison Act to specifically permit clinics or on the question of whether addiction created "criminal desire," as one commissioner put it. Although the Commission's decision was couched in technical terms, its repudiation of White Cross philosophy was clear. Even the *Los Angeles Times*, which had supported clinics in 1920 and was not given to fanning the flames of drug war, nonetheless augmented its approval of the Commission's technical objections with an editorial condemnation of White Cross policy.[49]

The hearings before the Social Service Commission seem to have started the San Francisco White Cross on a steep decline, probably because it could no longer effectively raise money by its accustomed means in either Los Angeles or San Francisco. Although the White Cross was not campaigning in San Francisco, and had no request pending, the Indorsement Council withdrew its support just as the Los Angeles Commission began hearings.[50] The gratuitous quality of this action strongly suggests a political motive, and one suspects the intervention of Sanborn Young. In the event, when William Walker, a key Commission witness hostile to the White Cross, embraced clinics a few years later, he looked for support to Seattle, not San Francisco.

The Defection of William Walker

By late 1938, William G. Walker (1885–1956), Chief of California's Division of Narcotic Enforcement, was convinced that Spadra was a failure and that federal morphine dispensaries made more sense. At a December 6th budget hearing held by Governor-elect Culbert Olson, Walker said this publicly for the first time. He pronounced Spadra "a useless expense," and proposed that "addicts be registered, fingerprinted, examined and then permitted Government rations . . . according to need, with doses gradually decreasing to a minimum." His statement made news all over the country. "I told him the truth," Walker wrote subsequently to a Washington state senator and White Cross advocate. "[W]e have a problem of incurable people on our hands that cannot be cured by ordinary methods. . . . There certainly is a better plan than arresting the addicts time and time again, only to have them contact peddlers immediately on their release. If anyone could see the suffering of these poor devils while withdrawal symptoms are present, they would understand why we should have a change."[51]

This extraordinary admission came from a teetotaler with solid credentials in police work: in addition to running California's Prohibition Administration from 1929 to 1932, Walker had been a highly regarded chief of police in Fresno for five years, taking that position when his predecessor and thirteen other officers were arrested for Prohibition violations. He was on cordial terms with Anslinger, and Anslinger had praised his appointment to Division Chief to Sanborn Young.[52]

It is not clear exactly when Walker became an apostate. He was appointed Chief in July 1933, after the Division had been mired in controversy, declining morale, and an economizing legislative attempt to do away with it and leave all drug law enforcement to local police and the FBN. (Only massive Hearst protests and Anslinger's intervention prevented this.) Through the mid-1930s, certainly, Walker hewed to the conventional line. In November 1933, as part of the Hearst papers' campaign to defend state and federal enforcement budgets, Walker cooperated with a reporter in the fabrication of a morphine and white-slave-trade story that was a sensational item—until the *San Francisco News* revealed it to be bogus. Throughout 1934, he helped Young and Anslinger discredit the San Francisco White Cross. As late as

1935, he faithfully intoned the "murder weed" characterization of marijuana that was becoming part of the orthodox canon. In 1937, however, Walker split with Young. They had serious differences over the potential menace of marijuana, the wisdom of the federal Marijuana Tax Act of 1937, and the danger of Asian morphine to the Pacific Coast. But they came into sharpest conflict about the utility of Spadra. By 1937, Spadra had been in political trouble for several years, and Walker sided with its critics.[53]

In March 1931, seeking to head off Jost, Young had promised: "Give us two years more in the handling through hospitalization of the narcotic addict and . . . California will solve the problem of whether or not the addict as such can be permanently cured." He was optimistic. In early 1931, Spadra not only held its capacity of 95, but was referring patients to nearby state hospitals. Superintendent Joyce may not have been getting exactly the sort of patients he wanted, but he had gained significant control over admissions and business was booming. By November 1933, however, Spadra's census was 55 and slipping. Joyce's assistant told a visiting Hearst reporter: "The only explanation I can find is that the narcotic enforcement bureaus have been so reduced in personnel and funds that they cannot . . . bring in the dope victims for treatment." As this was in the midst of the aforementioned funding drive, it was an obliging assessment, and superficially plausible: The Division's budget had been cut dramatically. But according to Walker, this impaired only the pursuit of substantial peddlers, a job the Division shared with the FBN. It did not affect the apprehension of addicts eligible for Spadra, most of whom were arrested by local narcotic squads and came from county jails. The state's Director of Institutions got it right when he blamed Spadra's declining census on economies "adopted by many counties." Obliged to pay 25 dollars per month for each addict committed to Spadra, as well as to absorb the cost of transportation and accompaniment, most counties stopped making commitments or made them rarely. Once the Depression matured, the teeming county jails had to serve. By the end of 1934, Spadra's census was down to 45; by October 1937, it was 17. Like his good friend Herbert Hoover, Young had not reckoned with the consequences of protracted hard times.[54]

Spadra's falling census jeopardized its survival. Indeed, only Anslinger's direct intervention and the vocal support of Spadra's traditional constituencies (particularly women's groups and the Hearst papers), persuaded Governor James Rolph against scrapping the hospital late in 1932. But although Rolph had been won over, his administration was paralyzed by the Depression and financial scandal. As it happened, Rolph became mortally ill early in 1934 and died on June 2nd, but it was apparent much earlier that he would not be a gubernatorial candidate again. By January 1934, with only 50 patients at Spadra, Young knew that he needed a plan to keep the hospital alive under a new governor.[55]

One proposal, floated by Young at the beginning of the year, was to have state and federal narcotics officers "pick up addicts that meet the requirements of the officials in charge of Spadra." Walker did not object to this rather desperate plan, but reminded Anslinger that as the state had very few enforcement officers, the burden of its achievement would be largely on the FBN. He then reiterated Spadra's desire to avoid "the habitual criminal or 'alley hype' type, or incurables." There is no record of Anslinger's response, but regardless of his support for Young, it is inconceivable that he would have allowed his own relatively small force of agents to be sent out to rustle up worthy young patients for Spadra.[56]

Harry Smith forwarded to Anslinger a next-best proposal: Spadra could be used as a probationary alternative to prison for selected federal drug offenders. This was to be one function of the federal narcotic hospital at Lexington, Kentucky, authorized by Congress in 1929, but not due to open until 1935. Smith made a creative pitch to get Spadra a piece of this market and Anslinger sent the idea to the Director of the Federal Bureau of Prisons, who pursued the matter with Joyce. No agreement was reached, however, probably because no statutory mechanism allowed the commitment of federal criminal offenders to a state hospital.[57]

As these ideas were being discussed, Spadra's chief parole officer returned bad news. Spadra's "cure rate," that is, the percentage of addicts abstinent two years after release, was just under 18 percent for 1928–1931, and this did not include in the denominator "the escaped or the unsuitable cases that were discharged or returned to court." Young found this a "great disappointment," but he was forthright about the carefully collected data: "It is convincing evidence," he wrote to Anslinger, "that the hospital alone is not a success, that the farm in connection with it for incurables is an absolute necessity. . . . At present we have more than five hundred addicts on our streets that have been given the cure at a cost of almost $1000 each and are still stealing and begging and a source of great expense to us." Lexington, he thought, had better profit from Spadra's experience, or it "will make no better record."[58]

A "farm" or "colony" for the incarceration of addicts for three, five, or perhaps even ten years, as Young and Joyce favored, was not the only logical response to such a concession. However, it was consistent with the orthodox views that only permanent abstinence counted as therapeutic success, and that incarceration had a powerful preventive effect because addicts were relentless proselytizers. The colony plan also fit Young's reluctant conclusion that the only addicts Spadra could get were "just the kind which we can not help." Thus, the promotion of addict colonization, envisioned in Spadra's original design, became fundamental to Young's strategy for keeping Spadra open. The hospital would now be sold as a way to reduce crime and the spread of addiction by way of specific deterrence. Regardless of what it was called, Spadra would now be marketed as a prison.[59]

Maintenance advocates took a different lesson from their pessimism, emphasizing the management rather than cure of addiction. Still, while maintenance was sharply at odds with the Treasury Department's obsession with supply reduction and the FBN's consequent persecution of physicians, it was not inconsistent with tough law enforcement. George Parrish, for instance, favored a "clinic-hospital and legal plan." This combined maintenance clinics (to reduce illicit traffic) with involuntary institutional treatment of six months to two years (for addicts motivated to be "cured" or addicts caught peddling) followed by welfare and vocational support, as needed. These efforts were to be combined with a federal law that imposed on nonaddicted smugglers or peddlers "a minimum penalty of such uniform severity . . . that no one would or could try it twice." This was roughly the position of the White Cross, and it seems to be the view at which Walker arrived. Although Walker supported maintenance, he also asked Olson for more enforcement money; and although he regarded Spadra as a failure, he was happy to have addicts sent to the new federal hospitals at Lexington (opened in 1935) and Fort Worth (1938), albeit because they were federally supported.[60]

For his candor, Walker endured a month-long blitz of well-orchestrated vilification. The Hearst papers dusted off their earlier warnings about clinics as migration magnets, recalled the specter of the disgraced Jost Bill and, disregarding the stricter commitment requirements achieved by Young and Joyce, claimed that Spadra was curing addicts "of the worst type," thus putting its low cure rate in a novel light. Young publicly characterized Walker as an inefficient administrator who put politics above integrity and called his ideas about clinics "ridiculous." Anslinger provided unsubstantiated information which, with suitable embellishment by San Francisco judge Twain Michelsen, was used to characterize Walker as a cynical, failed federal job-seeker looking to curry favor with the new governor. Michelsen, whose vitriol sometimes raised even Young's eyebrows, accused Walker of catering to the "perverted tastes" of criminals. The California Federation of Women's Clubs and its various chapters weighed in with petitions denouncing Walker, as did the still-redoubtable Woman's Christian Temperance Union. In all, it was a loud and long public hiding. "Maybe that will teach Mr. Walker not to stick his neck out so far," Assistant Secretary Gaston wrote to Anslinger approvingly.[61]

By February 1939 it was apparent that Olson, although he favored state control of wholesale and retail liquor distribution, was going neither to support morphine clinics nor to retain Walker. Young, planning an anti-narcotic exhibit for the San Francisco World Fair, nonetheless wanted to press the assault. Anslinger advised against it now that Walker had lost. "One of the most effective weapons against these agitators is not to dignify their arguments by taking them too seriously," Anslinger wrote. "Walker is a skunk and we have all learned from childhood never to engage in a battle with that animal. They usually go into seclusion by themselves."[62]

William Walker returned to Fresno and sold real estate. However, as Young feared, Walker's defection had doomed Spadra. Olson never made appointments to the hospital's advisory board, and he pocketed a successful colonization bill because his new Director of Institutions, Los Angeles psychiatrist Aaron Rosanoff, was determined to relieve the state of Spadra's cost. Failing to get Anslinger's help in negotiating the systematic commitment of California's addicts to the federal hospitals, Rosanoff closed Spadra over the noisy protest of its political friends. The institution's few remaining patients were distributed to other state hospitals on June 28, 1941.[63]

A Letter from Friend Earl

In April 1940, a veteran Oakland police officer, Frederick Barbeau, told a Fresno gathering of the Women Peace Officers Association that narcotic clinics, or a wholesale supply plan, would stop "the illegal sale of . . . narcotics and would take care of the old addicts and reduce addiction 90 per cent. The old addicts are the ones who start the new ones," Barbeau explained, "and by stopping the illegal traffic and registering all the users we could make great progress in controlling this age old curse." There was no "cure" for addiction, he averred.[64]

Among his auditors was a California State Federation of Women's Clubs worker who was sufficiently scandalized to write immediately to Twain Michelsen. Michelsen replied that Barbeau was spreading "the propaganda of the notorious White Cross." Michelsen was actually less concerned with the White Cross than with August Vollmer, whose views Barbeau seemed to be promoting. Michelsen wrote to Anslinger about Barbeau's address and included a sheet on which he typed selected offensive passages from Vollmer's *The Police in Modern Society* (1936). He recommended "constructive protest" of the officer's remarks. Anslinger already knew about the speech as the FBN district supervisor in San Francisco had sent him a clipping from the *Fresno Bee* that summarized it. The supervisor intended "to have a little talk" with Barbeau "to convince him of the impracticability of such a procedure."[65]

Anslinger's San Francisco man never contacted Barbeau, and the matter might have ended there except that in September 1940, at the convention of the International Association of Chiefs of Police, Harry Smith took matters into his own hands, approaching the police chief whom he took to be Barbeau's boss. As it happened, Barbeau's association with Vollmer, formerly the Berkeley chief, caused Smith to accost the wrong man. Barbeau was an Oakland officer, and the Berkeley chief had no idea whom Smith was talking about. (He subsequently sent Anslinger a list of Berkeley officers so that he might identify the man.) Smith contacted his old friend Earl Warren for help. Warren, by then California Attorney General, had been the district attorney in Alameda County (where Oakland and Berkeley are located), and had helped Smith derail the Jost Bill in 1931. Warren did, indeed, know Barbeau, and assured Smith that he would "do whatever I can to bring about a change in his views." On October 1, Warren wrote Barbeau a letter worth quoting at length:

> I have just received a letter, a copy of which is enclosed, from Harry D. Smith. . . . As you will observe . . . , his Bureau is somewhat disturbed because of your recent address at Fresno. Of course, it is no concern of mine except that all of us are interested in sound and effective narcotic control. Evidently your views on the subject have been cited in other parts of the country, which is the reason for his writing to me.
>
> I know you have given a lot of thought to the subject and I presume that if you are correctly quoted it is your considered opinion that clinics of this character would bring about more effective control. I have never thought that it [sic] would do so but I realize that whenever we are in the field of speculation, reasonable persons will differ. After reading Mr. Smith's letter I wondered if perhaps reconcilement of your views and those of the Federal Bureau might not be effected by a conference between one of its representatives and yourself. I would be glad to endeavor to arrange such a meeting if agreeable to you.
>
> I am sure that you will understand that I do not consider this a matter of official business as conflicting views on law enforcement methods are peculiarly personal. However, where mutual friends in the law enforcement business disagree on policies of vital importance, I presume it is not out of order as a friend to suggest something that may bring them together. It is in this spirit that I am writing to you and with full realization that conflicting views have been honestly and sincerely arrived at.
>
> I am sorry that I do not get an opportunity to see the boys in the Oakland department more often but this job takes me away from the Bay district so much that I have very little opportunity to do more than sleep there.[66]

Barbeau was suitably impressed, but also savvy. Rather than treating the letter as a personal matter, he did not reply until he had discussed it with his boss. On October 8th, he wrote "Dear Friend Earl" that he would be "only too glad to meet any member of the Federal Bureau to talk things over." He continued: "As for the article in the Fresno Bee, . . . they did not particularly mis-quote me but they did not fully quote me[,] which made a lot of difference as to meaning. I hope you dont [sic] feel that I have changed my mind to any degree as to law enforcement work, far be it from such." Warren sent Barbeau's reply to Smith, suggesting that "sometime when either you or some ranking officer of the Bureau is in this part of the country you arrange to sit down with Fred and discuss the entire subject." Then, in conclusion, he interposed himself, noting that such "an informal discussion" would "help bring me up to date on narcotic enforcement and give me an opportunity to see old friends again."[67]

Warren simultaneously put Barbeau on notice, handed him an out (mis-quotation), and refused to let him face the FBN without himself as intermediary. He achieved the FBN's goal of silencing Barbeau without allowing one of his "boys" to be bullied. It was neat work. Smith wrote Anslinger that he was immensely "gratified" by "such prompt and cooperative action," characterizing Warren's letter as "a master-piece of diplomacy . . . [that] without doubt will attain the desired ends." "However," he closed, "if there should be any repetition, and you will let me know, I have still other ways of attending to the matter."[68]

Lindesmith's Mythology

There is a last episode to consider. At the 1940 police chiefs' convention where Harry Smith inquired about Fred Barbeau, a former New York City police official gave Anslinger a copy of the July-August issue of the *Journal of Criminal Law and Criminology*. This contained "Dope Fiend Mythology" by the social psychologist Alfred Lindesmith (1905–1991). The article was a passionate dissent from American drug policy and the practice of demonizing addicts. Its last paragraph read:

> The "dope fiend" mythology serves . . . as a rationalization of the status quo. It is a body of superstition, half-truths, and misinformation which bolsters up an indefensible repressive law, the victims of which are in no position to protest. The treatment of addicts in the United States today is on no higher plane than the persecution of witches in other ages, and like the latter it is to be hoped that it will soon become merely another dark chapter of history.[69]

Anslinger was not pleased. "It is unfortunate that an article containing such misinformation and half-truths should be carried in a magazine devoted to the education of law enforcement officers," he wrote to Assistant Secretary Gaston upon his return from the convention. He went on to lump Lindesmith with Vollmer (whom Lindesmith cited) and others with "similar views as to the ambulatory treatment of drug addicts." In keeping with his earlier advice to Young about the World Fair exhibit, Anslinger continued: "I do not wish to place the Bureau on the level of having to answer Lindesmith, and would like your suggestions as to counteracting this vicious propaganda." Gaston responded that "Lindesmith's piece is an apology for addiction written from the standpoint of an addict. We ought to look for a college professor, ex[-]district attorney or other lawyer or law professor to answer him."[70]

Anslinger decided on Twain Michelsen, who hammered out a bellicose, several-thousand-word assault on Lindesmith, the White Cross, and particularly the World Narcotics Research Foundation (WNRF), a Los Angeles–based, pro-maintenance organization to which Lindesmith, the Williams brothers, William Walker, and numerous other veterans of dissent had lent their names at the end of 1938. "Lindesmith's Mythology" outlined a conspiracy against the noble but beleaguered FBN, and took up twenty-six pages in the same journal which had devoted ten pages to Lindesmith. Its last sentence captures its tone: "Neither narcotic monopolies nor narcotic clinics, with their 'low cost legitimate drugs,' as advocated by Dr. Lindesmith, will be permitted to gain a foothold in America as long as we have the protection of such dynamic agencies as . . . the Federal Bureau of Narcotics, nor will any narcotic racket of the pseudo-scientist be permitted to flourish in our midst."[71]

This was published only months after an FBN agent, insisting that Lindesmith belonged to a "criminal organization" (the WNRF), had threatened him with the loss of his teaching position at Indiana University. As Lindesmith recalled the encounter in 1965: "He intimated that I might jeopardize my position . . . by expressing my views and expressed the opinion that I was unfit to teach. I sought to defend my position and indicated that I thought British methods of handling the drug problem [by physician prescribing] were more sensible and effective than our own. He replied that I was living in the United States, not in England, that he didn't like the 'damned Limeys' anyway, and that loyal citizens ought not criticize existing laws or policies of the government." Later, a second agent, sent in part to apologize for the threats of the first, explained to the incredulous professor that the FBN, in addition to enforcing the criminal law, "also had the duty of 'disseminating right information and preventing the dissemination of wrong information.'"[72]

Conclusion

> *To stay experimentation in things social and economic is a grave re-*
> *sponsibility.... It is one of the happy incidents of the federal system*
> *that a single courageous State may, if its citizens choose, serve as a*
> *laboratory; and try novel social and economic experiments without risk*
> *to the rest of the country. This Court has the power to prevent an*
> *experiment.... But in the exercise of this high power, we must be ever*
> *on our guard, lest we erect our prejudices into legal principles.*
>
> —Louis D. Brandeis, March 21, 1932[73]

Irene Danford was a San Francisco area club woman. In the mid-1920s she went through several surgeries and in the course of managing "unbearable pain" became addicted to morphine. In 1928 she spent eight months in Patton State Hospital in southern California; in 1929 she was four months at Agnews State Hospital near San Jose. In both cases, she was discharged as "cured." But in February 1930 Mrs. Danford was arrested for forging prescriptions and sent to Spadra. She was released in December, cured once more. In May 1931 she was again arrested for forging prescriptions. The federal judge, who usually dispensed five-year sentences to repeat Harrison offenders, let Mrs. Danford off with a three-year term in an institution to be chosen by the state attorney general. He would recommend parole after a year, he said, "if she had overcome the dope habit."[74]

The judge's lenience reflected a diligent effort to match punishment to offender, to yoke the law to social custom. Mrs. Danford was in most ways absolutely respectable. She was an educated woman of high social standing, "an involuntary slave of the dope habit," according to her attorney, "having acquired it through sickness." Pleading guilty, Mrs. Danford insisted that she "adored her children," and "had never harmed any one" in her life. "It is difficult to associate with law breakers," she confessed to the judge. "I do not know how to get narcotics from peddlers so I adopted the only method I knew to get them." Here, indeed, was an innocent; and here, as well, was a three-time loser who confounded those who would help her.[75]

Before Harrison, Mrs. Danford might have been discreetly maintained by her physician, had that been her choice. The California State Board of Pharmacy was forbearing and flexible in such matters, especially for reputable addicts. But by the 1920s Harrison Act enforcement put a great burden on doctors to justify maintenance, especially in cases like Mrs. Danford's, for she did not require morphine to sustain her life but merely to manage pain and withdrawal. Only a liberal interpretation of medical necessity would have put her doctor on the safe side of Harrison, a law that Treasury had never interpreted liberally.

Mrs. Danford was the kind of "victim" championed by the White Cross, which struggled to introduce the public to representations of "normal" addicts: ordinary, working people who were not "dope fiends." Maintenance advocates, after all, could not make the predatory "dope fiend," the sinister poster child of repressive policy, represent the possibility of benign (or less than catastrophic) opiate dependence any more than pension advocates could use an old soak of a tramp to advertise the Social Security Act. Conflict about morphine maintenance in the 1930s was also and inevitably about the public representation of addicts. There was no recourse to authoritative science: the durability of addiction was mysterious; its secretive nature and the primitive epidemiology of the era made it impossible to know much about how many addicts there were and what they were like on the whole. However, as Lindesmith recognized, empirical evidence was beside the point for the FBN, for the demonization of addicts was critical to the maintenance of orthodoxy. The White Cross's evidence was better only in the sense that it effectively disputed FBN assertions about the addict's inherent depravity. The White Cross's normalization of addiction is best understood as a plausible but essentially rhetorical counterpoint to orthodox claims.[76]

On the other hand, there was little conflict about curability: By the mid-1930s, both supporters of maintenance and its orthodox critics believed most addicts to be incurable. Public Health Service doctors would be more optimistic until the end of the 1940s, however, and the PHS's Dr. Lawrence Kolb probably was more optimistic than most. Unlike Young, Anslinger, and even Thomas Joyce, all of whom tended to characterize addicts in blunt demographic and social terms, Kolb was subtle and clinically attuned. He sent Anslinger a particularly revealing comment on Anthony Votta, the Rikers Island epistler from whom we heard at earlier points in this narrative. Votta was a South Philadelphia Italian, a man of forty-one (in 1939), addicted from the age of eighteen, a career "hype" and shoplifter, arrested ninety times by his own count. Votta was convinced of the injustice and folly of his twenty-month sentence for possession of heroin. "I know," he wrote, "that I would live a much happier and longer life if I could get it according to law."[77] In Anslinger's view, Votta was a typical "dope fiend." But here are Kolb's observations:

> [I]t is quite obvious that he is an incurable case . . . because he knows that he cannot be cured, and obviously does not intend to cooperate in efforts made to help him. I am quite in agreement with him that punishment is useless in his case, and doubtless irrational. . . . Nevertheless,

> every addict is not like Mr. Votta, and it would require an extensive machinery honestly to separate hopeless cases like his from other cases for whom repression in the way of strict regulation, along with scientific treatment, might do good.[78]

As Kolb appreciated, under the regime proposed by Votta, a determination of incurability would confer a valuable privilege (maintenance), and thus there would be considerable incentive for addicts to be so diagnosed, including those who might succeed in "scientific treatment." While conceding that the Harrison Act "has not improved [Mr. Votta] at all," Kolb shared Anslinger's opinion that "in practical application" maintenance schemes ran the great risk of providing narcotics "to persons who, unlike Mr. Votta, might be cured." To separate "honestly" the curable from the hopeless, it would be essential to rely on evidence that could not be manipulated by the individual whose qualifying condition was to be verified. But clearly, no test of an addict's incurability could meet such a standard, for as Kolb observed, incurability was "a state of mind," specifically, the addict's own assumption of incurability, expressed in confessional terms and by a lack of cooperation in treatment.[79]

In the absence of a reliable validation mechanism, "an extensive machinery" would be required to enforce some workable surrogate. The FBN and a few states already had gone part way down this road by codifying exemptions from anti-maintenance policy, but these terms of exception turned out to be ambiguous and often arbitrary. It simply was not clear what complex combinations of disease and age made withdrawal from morphine life-threatening or cruel. Nor was there any established norm of endurance to apply to sufferers of intractable pain, even if it were possible to validate pain. How to measure cruelty? Nothing, it seemed, would substitute for medical judgment, and yet it was just such discretion that Harrison enforcers so mistrusted. After *Webb*, as morphine maintenance became hedged with limitations and made perilous by an imperious police power, doctors feared to err on the side of relieving simple suffering. The result was that some addicts died, coughing up blood in buckets like so many unattended paupers in a Victorian pesthouse.

In the age of methadone, one is struck by the severity of Kolb's standard; and indeed, by 1955 Kolb supported widely expanded maintenance. In the 1930s, however, orthodox reasoning about addiction was dominated by the antinomy firmly established by the nineteenth-century temperance movement: The confirmed, habitual user could be either abstinent or abjectly enslaved. Intermittent abstinence was a species of failure, not a kind of success. Nor was there readily intelligible language in which to represent the drug dependence of people who suffered no necessary, gross incapacity. This put maintenance supporters at a distinct disadvantage. No matter how care-fully the Williams brothers, for instance, explained that morphine was not intrinsically harmful, and that addiction could be managed without horrible consequences, they seemed to be temporizing with (if not encouraging) an obvious evil. The Williams brothers clearly recognized that the maintenance of law-abiding addicts would promote many practices associated today with "harm reduction" (disinfecting and dressing abscesses, discouraging needle sharing, and promoting an addict's nutrition and overall health), but along with ambulatory treatment, these practices were tainted as tending to cater to vice by making it a sustainable project. Therapeutic orthodoxy had become rooted in deterrence by punishment, whether by human law or as the "nat-ural" result of transgression. Dissidents argued that a history of addiction, combined with documented failures to remain abstinent after treatment and a defeated or defiant attitude about cure, should be adequate indication that maintenance was a more useful course than institutionalization. They were untroubled by the moral hazard posed by Kolb and would have made phy-sicians responsible for managing registered addicts, the practice in England after 1926. Institutions would have been for those who wished to enter them.

If American federalism were thoroughly Brandeisian, federal authorities might have viewed the approach of the White Cross, or the activities of the Los Angeles clinics of 1920 and 1934, as useful, even welcome experiments in social policy. But American federalism is selectively Brandeisian. The famous metaphor of the state as the laboratory of democracy is neglected or invoked throughout the political spectrum as strategy on a particular issue dictates. The decentralization of authority is a double-edged sword, and like that weapon, it is a means, not an end.

From the beginning, Harrison Act enforcers in the Treasury Department rejected an experimental approach to treatment policy. The presiding strategy was to keep the development of treatment completely subordinate to iron-fisted supply-control measures, the consequences for addicts notwithstand-ing. State legislatures and citizens' groups were to support and carry out this federal policy, not to criticize or innovate. Experimentation was an evil por-tent of backsliding into an era of lax regulation, not an opportunity to address the problems of regulation itself. Harry Anslinger inherited this staunchly prohibitionist organizational culture, with its anti-maintenance prejudice "erected into legal principle" in the form of *Webb*. Under Anslinger, the culture of the FBN was shaped by long-time Treasury men like Harry Smith. They were honest, loyal—and narrow. A few, like Smith, came from families bruised by addiction, and their work was intensely personal. They knew "wrong information" if not the First Amendment.[80]

Anslinger shifted the FBN's attention toward peddlers and away from street addicts, but despite his post-appointment rhetoric, he enforced no perceptible new dispensation for physicians who in good faith relieved the suffering of addicts. He had no inclination to reexamine evidence from the clinic era, accepting uncritically the official tale of universal ineffectiveness and corruption. Perhaps most important, Anslinger, like his predecessor, ignored *Linder*, engaging in a bold, unstated policy of "agency nonacquiescence" with the judicial branch. This permitted the FBN's "lusty applications" of its police power to be driven by administrative regulations and its preferred judicial precedent of *Webb*. Anslinger knew that an acquittal achieved by a physician at a dear price was as good as a conviction when it came to frightening others. By such means, the FBN, in effect, regulated an area of medical practice that doctors were not anxious to reclaim.[81]

This is not to say that Anslinger discouraged the medical treatment of addicts. Treatment was important to the FBN because it helped make tough law enforcement politically palatable and kept the agency in tune with important constituencies like the Woman's Christian Temperance Union and the array of influential women's clubs throughout the country. Cure, though, was less important to Anslinger than the surety of therapeutic custody as a specific deterrent. It was the "free and perambulating addict" whom Anslinger wanted to corral—whether in hospital or jail made little difference to him. Indeed, the more like a jail, the better he liked the hospital. A narcotic clinic, on the other hand, was more anathema than a writ of *habeas corpus*.[82]

For decades, this view of treatment was rarely challenged, but in 1958, after three years of study, an expert interdisciplinary panel issued *Narcotic Drugs: Interim Report of the Joint Committee of the American Bar Association and the American Medical Association on Narcotic Drugs*. The report raised the usual objections to orthodoxy, and went so far as to recommend the creation of experimental outpatient clinics that might supply addicts under strict controls. Anslinger promptly organized his own advisory committee which, in *Comments on Narcotic Drugs* (also 1958), countered that clinics were demonstrated failures, sources of addiction, and threats to national defense (they would abet World Communism's destruction of democracy's capacity to resist). *Comments* even allowed Twain Michelsen to reprise his role in the Lindesmith affair, which he did with relish, summarizing his earlier attack on villains past and updating it to light anew into Lindesmith, the now-traitorous Lawrence Kolb, Rufus King (of the American Bar Association), and the "free-spending," irresponsibly liberal Russell Sage Foundation. The *Interim Report*, Michelsen complained, was "a libel upon the intelligence of the people of America." Surely it remained true that "only under the impact of heavy prison sentences can we hope to rout the scum of the criminal world."[83]

For all its belligerence, the FBN did not radically alter the treatment of opiate addicts in California during the Depression. Anti-maintenance sentiment had been entrenched in medical circles for at least a decade before the Jost Bill, and despite men like Vollmer, Walker, and Barbeau, law enforcement officials probably were no more sympathetic even when substantially more frustrated. The ideological battle for organized opiate maintenance was lost in the few years following *Webb*, not in the 1930s. More materially, absent the stimulation of federal funds proposed in the failed France Bill of 1919, public drug treatment innovations were not politically feasible in California during the Depression. Not even the small, politically well-connected State Narcotic Hospital at Spadra could survive the state's financial collapse. Despite the New Deal, bond issues, and the adoption in 1935 of a controversial state personal income tax and a revised scheme of corporate taxation, California's governments remained cash-starved. With 700,000 unemployed by mid-1932, the state legislature stiffened residence requirements for public assistance, and the cities made themselves as unattractive as possible to the impecunious. Indeed, as the "migration magnet" rhetoric aimed at the Jost Bill suggests, the Depression greatly aggravated county governments' long-standing terror of vagrant undesirables and the fiscal burden of providing for newly arrived poor folk. In the infamous, short-lived "bum blockade" of February 1936, Los Angeles Police Chief Davis deployed 150 officers to seal the state's borders![84]

Still, by dogging physicians and stifling public debate about maintenance, the FBN ensured that there would be no working models, no matter how modest, upon which dissent might build. As the LACMA clinic case shows, Anslinger fully understood the importance of vigilance. When crossed in such ways, the FBN and its allies did not merely defend their position by appeal to science and reason in public forums, nor did they stop at the political strong-arming that so infuriated conservative opponents of the New Deal when undertaken in more controversial areas of social policy. Rather, the FBN harassed, intimidated, and occasionally jailed detractors like so many feckless "dope fiends" or scheming "reds." Nonconforming organizations were not just contrary, they were "illegal." Functioning with little political restraint given the profound bipartisan consensus on drug policy and crime, the FBN carefully marked and strictly defended the boundaries of therapeutic orthodoxy. And beyond these lay dragons—or at any rate, federal narcotics agents.

Abbreviations Used in the Notes
(Manuscript Collections and Names of Archives)

AP   Harry J. Anslinger Papers, Pattee Labor Library, Pennsylvania State
          University, State College, Pa.
CSA   California State Archives, Sacramento, Calif.
DEA   Department of Justice, Record Group 170, Records of the Bureau of
          Narcotics, Drug Enforcement Administration, Pentagon City, Va. (Most
          of these records are now available at the National Archives Record
          Center, College Park, Md., but they are cited here as cataloged at the
          DEA.)
FDR   Franklin Delano Roosevelt Library, Hyde Park, N.Y.
LACMA   Archives of the Los Angeles County Medical Association, Los Angeles,
          Calif.
LP   Alfred R. Lindesmith Papers, held by Dr. John Galliher, Department of
          Sociology, University of Missouri–Columbia.
PHS   Public Health Service, Record Group 90, National Archives,
          Washington, D.C.
RP   James Rolph Papers, California Historical Society, San Francisco, Calif.
VP   August Vollmer Papers, Bancroft Library, University of California,
          Berkeley, Calif.

Notes

This paper was published previously in *Contemporary Drug Problems* 27 (2000): 17–75. It is reprinted here by permission of Federal Legal Publications, Inc.

For the time being, my many important debts must be acknowledged cryptically. The following people gave me editorial help and research assistance of one sort or another: Caroline Acker, Raymond Albert, Greg Bradsher, Chuck Burke, Diane Castle, David Courtwright, John Galliher, Kim Hopper, Pat Keats, Harry Levine, David Lewis, Shirley Lewis, Julia Littell, John McWilliams, Jennifer Nelson, David Pfeiffer, Judy Regueiro, Craig Reinarman, Richard Rogers, Fred Romanski, Sandy Schram, Ursula Sherman, Marianne Smith, Bill White, and Dea Zugby. Bryn Mawr College and the Lindesmith Center of the Open Society Institute generously defrayed the expenses.

1. [Harry J. Anslinger], "The Fallacy of Narcotic Clinics," AP, Box 8, File 4; George Parrish, in "Institutions for Morphin[e] and Other Addiction-Forming Drugs," an open forum in *California and Western Medicine* 43 (1935): 368–370 (quoted remark, 369).

2. "Editorial Notes," *Pacific Pharmacist* 1 (1907),: 65–67 (cited passage, 66–67). The editorial was in praise of the State Board of Pharmacy's Los Angeles crackdown on unlicensed purveyors and druggists "selling habit-forming drugs to 'fiends'." On the confluence of temperance and professional influence, see Joseph F. Spillane, "Making a Modern Drug: The Manufacture, Sale, and Control of Cocaine in the United States, 1880–1920," in Paul Gootenberg, ed., *Cocaine: Global Histories* (New York: Routledge, 1999), 27–34 especially.

3. On the APhA model act: David F. Musto, *The American Disease: Origins of Narcotic Control* (New York: Oxford University Press, 1987), 17–18, 22. On California: *Statutes of*

California, Thirty-Eighth Session (1909), Chapter 279, Section 8; *Statutes of California, Forty-Third Session (1919)*, Chapter 612, Section 8 1/2. The California "good faith" standard influenced Harrison enforcement from the outset; for its incorporation into Treasury regulations, see Charles E. Terry and Mildred Pellens, *The Opium Problem* (New York: Bureau of Social Hygiene, 1928), 758.

4. Musto, note 3, 121–126; quoted passage, 125–126. A fair-minded discussion of the complexities of "ambulatory treatment" is Edward Huntington Williams, *Opiate Addiction: Its Handling and Treatment* (New York: Macmillan, 1922), 17–93. The asylum model in the treatment of alcoholism: Jim Baumohl, "Inebriate Institutions in North America, 1840–1920," in Cheryl Krasnick Warsh, ed., *Drink in Canada* (Montreal: McGill-Queens University Press, 1993), 92–114 (text); 218–231 (notes); public inebriate asylums just before and after Harrison: Jim Baumohl and Sarah W. Tracy, "Building Systems to Manage Inebriates: The Divergent Paths of California and Massachusetts, 1891–1920, *Contemporary Drug Problems* 21 (1994): 557–597.

5. Ambulatory treatment in private practice: see the March 16, 1915 remarks of Dr. J. W. McConnell in "Philadelphia West Branch," *Pennsylvania Medical Journal* 18 (1914–15): 762. Ambulatory treatment in New York during this period: Musto, note 3, 104–120. In addition to the case texts, see Musto, 131–132; Rufus G. King, "The Narcotics Bureau and the Harrison Act: Jailing the Healers and the Sick," *Yale Law Journal* 62 (1952–53): 736–749; Terry and Pellens, note 3, 745–806.

6. Treasury's adoption of exceptions: Terry and Pellens, note 3, 756–757. California: California State Board of Pharmacy (hereafter CSBP), *Minutes, Volume 1* (October 22, 1909), 83b, CSA. Pennsylvania: *Laws of Pennsylvania, Session of 1917*, No. 282, Section 8; *Session of 1921*, No. 98, Section 8. Pennsylvania data: Harold V. Smith to H. J. Nugent, October 5, 1932, Treasury Department File (hereafter TDF) 0120–9, Folder 2, DEA.

7. Daniel C. Roper (Commissioner of Internal Revenue), "Memorandum for the Secretary," July 15, 1919; Rupert Blue (Surgeon General) to Roper, July 28, 1919, PHS, Box 204.

8. Blue to Roper, note 7. The France Bill and the role of the PHS: Musto, note 3, 144–145, 332–333 (his note 64). The control of venereal disease during World War I: Allan M. Brandt, *No Magic Bullet: A Social History of Venereal Disease in the United States since 1880* (New York: Oxford University Press, 1987), 52–121.

9. David Courtwright, Herman Joseph, and Don Des Jarlais, *Addicts Who Survived: An Oral History of Narcotic Use in America, 1923–1965* (Knoxville: University of Tennessee Press, 1989); quoted passage, p. 1; Musto, note 3, 151–182; Dan Waldorf, Martin Orlick, and Craig Reinarman, *Morphine Maintenance: The Shreveport Clinic, 1919–1923* (Washington, D.C.: Drug Abuse Council, 1974).

10. See Musto, note 3, 346–347 (his note 9), for an FBN field supervisor's admission in 1932 that "enforcement in the 1920s was perhaps as bad as physicians and druggists claimed." This note includes the supervisor's candid language about "black-jacking" and "field men" promoting their careers at the expense of "the professional classes." See also Henry Smith Williams, *Drug Addicts Are Human Beings* (Washington, D.C.: Shaw Publishing, 1938). Narcotic agents were not so renegade a lot as Volstead Act enforcers, but for the occasionally critical reminiscences of federal agents who worked from the 1920s through the 1930s, see Maurice Helbrant, *Narcotic Agent* (New York: Vanguard Press, 1941), and William Spillard, *Needle in a Haystack* (New York: McGraw-Hill, 1945).

11. Purpose of the amendments (in the words of Assistant Treasury Secretary Andrews): "Strengthening the Harrison Narcotic Act," *Journal of the American Medical As-*

sociation 86 (1926), 1473–1474. With the failure of its proposed amendments, which the AMA forcefully opposed in the editorial cited above, Treasury supported a model state law to accomplish many of the same ends, including the abolition of ambulatory treatment and maintenance. The resulting Uniform Narcotic Drug Act was written by a committee of the National Conference of Commissioners on Uniform State Laws between 1927 and 1932. While the Conference demurred on specific methods of treatment, in the spirit of *Webb* it did not consider a prescription for maintenance to be "in the course of [a physician's] professional practice." Section 8(a) of the Uniform Act specifically forbade the dispensing or prescription of more than 1/2 grain of morphine to the same patient within 48 hours. [National Conference of Commissioners on Uniform State Laws, *Uniform Narcotic Drug Act* (Chicago: Author, 1932).] By October 1938, 40 states had passed the Uniform Act, but California was not among them. On the progress of the Act: Harry Anslinger (hereafter HJA), "Address Before the *New York Herald Tribune* Forum, October 25, 1938," AP, Box 1, File 7.

12. August Vollmer, *The Police in Modern Society* (Berkeley: University of California Press, 1936), 117.

13. G. A. Horner to James Rolph (Mayor of San Francisco), August 9, 1919, RP, Box 49, Folder 591; Anthony Votta to Federal Bureau of Investigation, May 18, 1939 (quoted passages, pp. 8, 10), AP, Box 3, File 1.

14. See Baumohl and Tracy, note 4.

15. Los Angeles clinic: Terry and Pellens, note 3, 872–876. The patient data: "Report of the Narcotic Committee, 1920," *The Bulletin* [of the Los Angeles County Medical Association], 51:8 (April 21, 1921): 6–8. The clinic charged 10 cents per grain because required to make a profit. Originally, this $2,000 or so per month was earmarked for institutional treatment of patients, but with recession, inflation, and rapid population growth, the city council appropriated most of it for the general fund.

16. "City's Drug Clinic an Astounding Failure," *Los Angeles Examiner*, April 22, 1920, sec. 2, pp. 1, 3; Lee Shippey, "Truth About City Drug Clinic," *Los Angeles Times*, May 2, 1920 (sec. 2, pp. 1, 5). The clinic committee's disparagement of "lying influence" (by which it meant the *Examiner*'s): "Report of the Narcotic Committee," note 15, 8. Hutton's letter (Frank S. Hutton to Commissioner of Internal Revenue, May 13, 1921, TDF 0120–1, Folder 2, DEA) refers to the Board's opposition to "some of the initial methods" of the clinic. In April, this resulted in the replacement of its first medical director and the formulation of 18 rules of procedure by the Board and the clinic committee ["Rules for the Narcotic Clinic of Los Angeles," TDF 73221, DEA; CSBP, note 7, *Minutes, Volume 5* (April 26, 1920): 116a–b.] Powers and Carter: Terry and Pellens, note 3, 875–876.

17. Lee Ettelson, "U.S. Banishes Dope Clinics," *Los Angeles Examiner*, August 13, 1920, sec. 1, pp. 1, 4.

18. H. L. Kirby to Hugh S. Cumming, October 26, 1923, PHS, Box 206. The Bureau's director, Kirby came from the Committee on Drug Addictions in New York, of which Dr. Charles Terry (1878–1945) was executive. Terry was the father of organized morphine maintenance, having established the first such clinic in Jacksonville, Florida, in 1912.

19. The membership of this committee overlapped substantially with the Bureau's Medical Division. And just as the Bureau arose in part from the dissatisfaction of some Board of Pharmacy members with Treasury's revised clinic policy, the LACMA committee was organized by the Board's Los Angeles attorney to "examine certain addicts who claimed for one reason or another that they required narcotics." If the committee found good cause, it would provide treatment "in accordance with the law." The Pharmacy

Board's dissatisfaction with Treasury's clinic policy: Hutton to Commissioner, note 16, and Board of Councillors, *Minutes*, March 28, 1921, LACMA. On the establishment of the LACMA's review and treatment function, about which its councillors became confused in later years: CSBP, *Minutes*, note 6, *Volume 8* (January 10, 1925): 148.

20. Board of Councillors, *Minutes*, August 13, 1934, LACMA. The clinic's director at this time was Dr. Joseph J. O'Brien (1881–1958).

21. H. S. Williams, note 10, 37. Jost would have underdosed most addicts, but its critics never mentioned that it provided too little rather than too much. See AB 1433 (1931), Original Bill File, CSA.

22. Spadra's enabling legislation: *Statutes of California, Forty-Seventh Session (1927)*, Chapter 89; Statutes of California, Forty-Eighth Session (1929), Chapter 406. Joyce in New York: Thomas F. Joyce, "Denarcotizing the Addict," *Monthly Bulletin of the Department of Health* (New York City), June 1921, 132–136.

23. Baumohl and Tracy, note 4 (the struggle over commitments); Sanborn Young, "A Relentless War," *State Government*, ca. 1933, AP Box 6, File 1 (Governor Clement Young's incremental approach); "Report of Medical Superintendent of State Narcotic Hospital," in *Appendix to the Journals of the Senate and Assembly of the Forty-Ninth Session of the Legislature of the State of California* (Sacramento: State Printer, 1931), *Volume 1*, 176 (changes in security); State Narcotic Committee, "The Trend of Drug Addiction in California," in *Appendix to the Journals of the Senate and Assembly*, as above, *Volume 5*, 29 (Joyce on desirable patients); William H. Jordan, "Larger State Dope Hospital Plan Adopted," *San Francisco Examiner*, January 16, 1931, AP, Box 6, File 5; "Assembly Passes Bills to Strengthen State Narcotic Act," *San Francisco Examiner*, April 9, 1931, 20; "Spadra Measure Signed by Rolph," *San Francisco Examiner*, April 25, 1931, 11 (superintendent's discretion).

24. "Police Will Push Campaign on Dope," *San Francisco Examiner*, February 27, 1931, 2. Although detailed San Francisco arrest data are elusive for the 1930s, there were 106 "vag-addict" arrests there between June 9 and October 10, 1930, and 658 during calendar year 1935 [State Narcotic Committee, note 23, 34; State of California, Senate Interim Narcotic Committee, *Report on Drug Addiction in California* (Sacramento: State Printer, 1936), 67]. Along with his maintenance bill, Jost introduced unsuccessful legislation in 1931 to repeal the state's "vag-addict" law, passed in 1929 and sponsored by Young. The vagrancy law had been used to prosecute addicts since 1875, but Young broadened its scope. See Jim Baumohl, "The 'Dope Fiend's Paradise' Revisited: Notes from Research in Progress on Drug Law Enforcement in San Francisco, 1875–1915," *The Surveyor* 24 (June 1992): 3–12.

25. Votta to FBI, note 13, 7–8. Other evidence supports Votta's account of the rapid escalation of morphine's street price: see "2 Admit Guilt as Dope Chiefs," *San Francisco Examiner*, April 3, 1931, 6. Federal agents in California seized over four times the weight of drugs in the last five months of 1930 than during the whole year preceding July 1, 1930. Most seizures occurred in San Francisco, where the FBN was going after "the larger dealers" rather than "chasing vagrant addicts." (Smith to HJA, December 29, 1930, AP, Box 3, File 10.)

26. Dismissal of cases: Senate Narcotic Committee, note 24, 35; AB 1433, note 21, Sections 3 and 4.

27. Smith to HJA, March 7, 1931, TDF 0120–1 Folder 2, DEA; Joyce's opinion: William H. Jordan, "Narcotic Foes Unite Against Jost's Bills," *San Francisco Examiner*, February 20, 1931, 4.

28. Herbert L. Phillips, "'Dope Clinic' Bill Killed," *San Francisco Examiner*, March 18, 1931, 4; Annie Laurie, "Legislators, Do We Want 'Dope Clinics' to Return," *San Francisco Examiner*, March 12, 1931, 13. Federal agents had long promoted the magnet theory: see J. S. Considine to Federal Prohibition Commissioner, August 4, 1920, TDF 73221, DEA, and C. D. Writesman to L. G. Nutt, May 1, 1924, TDF 0120–9, Folder 1, DEA.

29. William H. Jordan, "State to Gain New Power Over Addicts," *San Francisco Examiner*, March 19, 1931, 4.

30. The "drive" against "physicians dispensing . . . freely to addicts" was planned on Anslinger's December 1933 visit to Los Angeles ("California," ca. December 1934, AP, Box 8, File 8). Its seeds were sown a month earlier, however, when the Hearst papers began a related campaign to help Anslinger and William Walker, Director of California's Narcotics Enforcement Division, defend their budgets against Depression cost-cutting. See "Unscrupulous Doctors Complicate Task of Handicapped Dope Squads," *Los Angeles Examiner*, November 5, 1933; Walter Naughton, "Dope Selling Doctors Increase as U.S. Cuts Enforcement Fund," *San Francisco Examiner*, November 6, 1933, AP, Box 6, File 1.

31. "5 Doctors Seized on Dope Charges; City Clinic Probed," *Los Angeles Examiner*, April 25, 1934, sec. 2, p. 1; "Sixth Doctor Surrenders; Denies U.S. Dope Charges," *Los Angeles Examiner*, April 26, 1934, sec. 1, p. 5. The pharmacists were quickly released with warnings. LACMA volunteers: "Council Votes Dope Funds," *Los Angeles Examiner*, April 14, 1934, sec. 1., p. 7.

32. On Parrish: membership file, LACMA. Conditions: "Police Seek Supervision of Dope Addicts," *Los Angeles Examiner*, May 1, 1934, sec. 1, p. 5. These conditions were based on the FBN's interpretation of Treasury Decision 2809 of March 20, 1919, which spelled out exceptions to anti-maintenance policy. This decision also warned: "Physicians will be held accountable if through carelessness or lack of sufficient personal attention the patient secures more narcotic drugs than are necessary for medical treatment, and devotes part of his supply to satisfy addiction." Since maintenance and medical treatment often were inseparable, this regulation was a license for harassment.

33. The May 11th meeting and Anthony's subsequent experience: *United States v. Anthony et al. (15 F. Supp. 553)*, and "Two Dope Suspects Face Trial Oct. 16," *Los Angeles Examiner*, October 2, 1936, sec. 2, p. 16; Williams and Steele: clipping from the *Los Angeles Times*, August 2, 1934, E.H. Williams membership file, LACMA; "Cal–1698," Department of Justice, Mail and Files, File No. 12–12, Sub. 55, National Archives, Washington, D.C.

34. Williams to Vollmer, June 6, August 10, and August 23, 1934, VP, Box 33. For a partisan but penetrating view of "The Los Angeles Reign of Terror," see Henry Smith Williams, *Drugs Against Men* (NY: Robert M. McBride & Company, 1935), 167–181.

35. Marking Williams: Considine to Federal Prohibition Commissioner, note 28; the LACMA discussion can be followed in Board of Councillors, *Minutes*, May 7, 1934; July 2, 1934; August 13, 1934; January 7, 1935; February 4, 1935; December 2, 1935; January 6, 1936; February 3, 1936, LACMA. At the beginning of the Williams-Cary trial, discussed below, Dr. Clifford Wright, of the Narcotic Committee, did make a widely publicized speech in support of the doctors to the Los Angeles County Federation of Women's Clubs (Jean Loughborough, "Better Narcotic Control Urged at Club Meeting," *Los Angeles Examiner*, October 12, 1934, sec. 2, p. 3).

36. For the FBN's allegations, see HJA, "Memorandum for Mr. Gaston," June 28, 1934, AP, Box 3, File 6.

37. Williams did not become aware of the charges in Anslinger's memo until after his trial with Cary. They were revealed during a subsequent misconduct proceeding against the federal prosecutor. For quotations from the transcript, further discussion of the FBN's claims, and a detailed refutation, see Williams to Harry H. Wilson, March 26, 1935, VP, Box 33.

38. Williams, *Opiate Addiction*, note 4, 20–21; *U.S. v. Anthony et al.*, note 33. Even the FBN conceded the grave illnesses of most patients, but disputed the appropriateness of maintenance and the size of the morphine doses.

39. Editorial, *Hollywood Citizen-News*, May 21, 1934, VP, Box 33. Biographical information: E. H. Williams, membership file, LACMA; "E. H. Williams, Noted Alienist, Succumbs at 75," *Los Angeles Times*, June 25, 1944, sec. 2, p. 7. Williams is best known to drug historians as a contributor to the myth of the "cocainized Southern negro" (Musto, note 3, 282–284, his notes 15, 20).

40. HJA, "Memorandum for Mr. Gaston," note 36; "California," note 30. An article that appeared in the *Washington Herald* (a Hearst paper) in December 1934 had Anslinger assailing the International White Cross's "notorious" clinic proposal and naming Williams as the organization's founder ("Medical Group Fighting 'Dope' Curb, Is Charge," *Washington Herald*, December 7, 1934, AP, Box 5, File 15). But neither of the Williams brothers were "joiners" or optimists about "organized reform" (H. S. Williams to Alfred R. Lindesmith, November 9 and November 10, 1939, LP; E. H. Williams to Vollmer, September 30, 1934, VP, Box 33).

41. Cary's sentence: "Dope Case!" *Los Angeles Examiner*, January 10, 1935, sec. 2, p. 8; his trial: "Trial of 2 Doctors Charged with Dope Conspiracy Starts," *Los Angeles Examiner*, October 10, 1934, sec. 2, p. 1; "Legal Right to Prescribe Narcotics, Doctors' Defense," *Los Angeles Examiner*, October 11, 1934, sec. 1, p. 16; "Lawyer in Federal Dope Trial Cited for Contempt," *Los Angeles Examiner*, October 13, 1934, sec. 1, p. 3; H. S. Williams, note 10, 187–193. Denial of appeal: *Cary et al. v. United States (86 F.2d 461)*. On the outcome for E. H. Williams, see his letter to Vollmer, May 28, 1939, VP, Box 33. Dropped charges: Department of Justice, note 33. The agent-in-charge (Chris Hanson): Alfred Lindesmith, *The Addict and the Law* (Bloomington: Indiana University Press, 1965), 15–16.

42. *U.S. v. Anthony et al.*, note 33.

43. H. S. Williams, note 10, 66–67 (summary of committed cases); 68–70 (deceased patients); 109–110 (former patient's letter). On informer Madge Surber, promoted to "secret dope sleuth" by the *Examiner* upon her demise: "Dope Sleuth Slugged, Dies," *Los Angeles Examiner*, October 1, 1934, sec. 1, p. 3. Most of the data Williams presented were gathered by Everett G. Hoffman, of the Seattle White Cross, during the summer of 1937. By examining Los Angeles court records, Hoffman found that of sixty-five patients tracked over three years of clinic attendance, none had been in court during that time. Prior to clinic enrollment, this group had 311 arrests over an unspecified period of time. In the three years after the clinic's closure, forty-one of the former patients accounted for sixty-three arrests (Hoffman to Lindesmith, January 24, 1938, LP).

44. Young to HJA, March 24, 1934, AP, Box 3, File 6.

45. There is no secondary literature on the White Cross. My understanding of its history comes from promotional material and Alfred Lindesmith's correspondence with Everett G. Hoffman.

46. "Anti-Narcotic League's Fund Campaign Hit," *Los Angeles Examiner*, July 3, 1934, sec. 1, p. 8.

47. "Inherently crooked": "White Cross Wins Delay," *Los Angeles Times*, June 13, 1934, sec. 2, p. 3; "Anti-Narcotic League Bitterly Denounced at Social Service Hearing," *Los Angeles Examiner*, July 4, 1934, sec. 1, pp. 3, 6; "Drive Fund Losses Told," *Los Angeles Times*, July 3, 1934, sec. 2, pp. 1–2; "White Cross Plea Denied," *Los Angeles Times*, July 11, 1934, sec. 2, pp. 1, 5.

48. "Anti-Narcotic League Bitterly Denounced," note 47; "White Cross Inquiry Ends," *Los Angeles Times*, July 4, 1934, sec. 2, pp. 1–2. Although Young did not call West a communist—not publicly, at least—his vilifying rhetoric borrowed from the contemporaneous anti-communist crusade in California of which he was a leader, supported in part by anti-narcotic regulars like the WCTU. See, for example, "Red Menace Rouses City," *Los Angeles Times*, May 17, 1934, sec. 2, p. 8.

49. "The White Cross Decision," editorial, *Los Angeles Times*, July 12, 1934, sec. 2, p. 4. "Criminal desire": "Anti-Narcotic League Bitterly Denounced," note 47; "White Cross in New Row," *Los Angeles Times*, June 20, 1934, sec. 2, pp. 1–2.

50. "Anti-Dope Body Loses Support," *Los Angeles Times*, June 11, 1934, sec. 1, p. 3.

51. "Dope Addicts: Olson Studies New Aid Plan," *San Francisco News*, December 10, 1938, TDF 0120–1, Folder 2, DEA; Walker to Washington State Senator Paul Thomas, December 29, 1938, LP.

52. HJA to Young, July 6, 1933; HJA to Walker, July 6, 1933; Walker to HJA, October 30, 1933, AP, Box 3, File 7; Bernard Taper, "A 'Prohi' Remembers Volstead Era," *San Francisco Chronicle*, August 4, 1952, p. 17; "William G. Walker," *San Francisco Chronicle*, February 24, 1956, p. 25.

53. The Division's turmoil and near abolition: "Narcotics Charge Examples Given," unidentified clipping, ca. November 14, 1932, AP, Box 6, File 4; "Senator Young Dope Charges Hit by Rolph," *San Francisco Examiner*, November 17, 1932, 3; William H. Jordan, "Government Acts to Prevent California Wrecking Laws Against Dope," *San Francisco Examiner*, February 16, 1933, AP, Box 6, File 7; "Levey Opposes Abolition of Dope Bureau," *San Francisco Examiner*, February 18, 1933, AP, Box 6, File 3. Walker's "coloring": "Faking the News," editorial, *San Francisco News*, November 11, 1933; "Walker Admits Dope Charges Propaganda," *San Francisco News*, November 11, 1933, AP, Box 6, File 1. The colored story: [Wooster Taylor], "Dope Ring Linked to Traffic in Girls," *San Francisco Examiner*, November 3, 1933, AP, as above. Walker on marijuana ("horrible in its effects") in late 1933: Wooster Taylor, "Dope Officials Helpless to Curb Marihuana Use," *San Francisco Examiner*, November 7, 1933, AP, Box 6, File 1. He expressed similar views ("serious menace") in a February 18, 1935 radio address, quoted at length in Michelsen to Olson, December 17, 1938, TDF 0120–1, Folder 2, DEA. Differences: Young to HJA, December 23, 1938, TDF 0120–1, Folder 2, DEA.

54. "Two years more": William H. Jordan, "California Hailed as Dope Fight Leader," *San Francisco Examiner*, March 2, 1931, 8. Division budget cuts and effects: "Dope Bureau Urges Support," *Los Angeles Examiner*, October 5, 1934, sec. 1, p. 11. County obligations: Spadra's enabling legislation (note 22). Implications: Paul E. Madden (Chief, Division of Narcotic Enforcement) to Randal F. Dickey (California Assemblyman), March 13, 1941, TDF 0120–8, DEA. Director of Institutions (Dr. J. M. Toner): "State's Dope Patient List Shows Decline," *San Francisco Examiner*, November 20, 1933, AP, Box 6, File 1. Joyce's assistant (Dr. Robert Wyers): Marjorie Driscoll, "Two Congressmen Visit Spadra; Rap Dope Budget Cut," *Los Angeles Examiner*, November 13, 1933, AP, as above. Spadra's census in October 1937: Hoffman to Lindesmith, January 8, 1938, LP.

55. Winning Rolph: R. E. Hall (Acting District Supervisor) to HJA, August 26, 1932;

HJA to Rolph, September 12, 1932; Toner to HJA, September 23, 1932, TDF 0120–8, DEA. Constituencies: "Save State Narcotic Hospital at Spadra," editorial, *Los Angeles Examiner*, February 20, 1933, AP, Box 6, File 3; Bonfils to HJA, February 20, 1933, AP, Box 3, File 7; Joyce to HJA, February 24, 1934; Laura Seeley-Thomson (Federation of Women's Clubs) to HJA, February 24, 1934, TDF 0120–8, DEA. Rolph's health: Young to HJA, March 24, 1934, AP, Box 3, File 6. Rolph's administration: H. Brett Melendy and Benjamin F. Gilbert, *The Governors of California* (Georgetown, Calif: Talisman Press, 1965), 363–380.

56. Walker to HJA, January 23, 1934, TDF 0120–8, DEA.

57. Smith to HJA, January 31, 1934; HJA to Sanford Bates (Director of the Federal Bureau of Prisons), February 2, 1934; Bates to HJA, February 6, 1934; HJA to Walker, Young, and Smith, February 7, 1934, TDF 0120–8, DEA.

58. John Knox to Young, January 26, 1934; Young to HJA, February 8 and March 23, 1934, TDF 0120–8, DEA.

59. Young to HJA, October 1, 1934, TDF 0120–8, DEA; Thomas F. Joyce, "What Shall We Do with California's Incurable Narcotic Addicts?" in Senate Interim Narcotic Committee, note 24, 49–51. After 1932, Young pursued a secondary strategy of adding to Spadra a facility for women, who as of 1931 went to Norwalk State Hospital because sex segregation at Spadra proved difficult. (At first, Young favored sending female addicts to the women's prison due to open in Tehachapi in 1932, but that put him in conflict with the Hearst papers and women's groups.) By the end of 1934, with public drunkenness arrests and state hospital admissions for alcoholism rising with the Depression, Repeal, and population growth, Joyce wanted to admit alcoholics to Spadra. See Otheman Stevens, "Need of Dope Hospital to Cure Women Stressed," *San Francisco Examiner*, April 2, 1931, 19; "Hospital Care Needed for Women Victims of Dope," editorial, *San Francisco Examiner*, April 3, 1931, 36; Otheman Stevens, "Women Dope Victims Face Prison Brand," *San Francisco Examiner*, April 4, 1931, 15; "Same Care Should Be Given Dope Victims of Both Sexes," editorial, *San Francisco Examiner*, April 28, 1931, 34; William H. Jordan, "Rescue Addicts!" *Los Angeles Examiner*, December 21, 1934, sec. 2, p. 1.

60. Parrish, note 1.

61. Examples of press criticism: "Narcotics Free Clinic Plan Rapped," *San Francisco Chronicle*, December 9, 1938; "Experts Denounce Walker Dope Plan," *San Francisco Examiner*, December 15, 1938; "Walker Ouster Study Revealed," *San Francisco Examiner*, December 16, 1938; "Neglect Laid to Walker," *San Francisco Call-Bulletin*, December 20, 1938; "Walker's Dope Plan Assailed by Anslinger," *San Francisco Examiner*, December 20, 1938; "Walker's Plan Denounced by Senator Young," undated, unidentified clipping, TDF 0120–1, Folder 2, DEA. In "Federal Narcotics Bureau Refuses Job to Walker," a *San Francisco Examiner* piece of December 14 (TDF 0120–1, as above), the reporter claimed that "leaders in the fight to curb drug addiction" pointed out that "Walker's policies . . . undoubtedly were well known to Commissioner Anslinger long before the State official made his declaration at the budget hearing. . . . The rejection of Walker's plea for a federal post, it was indicated, was based on careful study of his administrative methods and ideas over a period of years." This was sheer fabrication, phrased so that the words were not put in Anslinger's mouth. In a December 7 telegram to Michelsen, Anslinger did say that Walker had "applied for position this bureau but could not find it possible to place him." Note that he did not say that the inquiry was recent or that Walker was objectionable. Moreover, in letters to Michelsen and Young, Anslinger implied that he was completely unaware of Walker's views on clinics. (HJA to Michelsen,

December 7 and 28, 1938; HJA to Young, December 28, 1938, TDF 0120–1, as above.) Gaston's handwritten, undated note to Anslinger is in the same file.

Michelsen's remark about Walker catering to "perverted tastes" was in a San Francisco political newsletter that he sent to Anslinger, who liked the phrase and repeated it back in his answering letter (HJA to Michelsen, February 9, 1939, TDF 0120–1, Folder 3, DEA). Petitions from chapters of the California Federation of Women's Clubs are also in this file. Anslinger forwarded one of these to Governor Olson, probably as an excuse to register his displeasure with Walker by including his response to the women's club president. In this Anslinger remarked that "we have found the clinic-system far more dangerous than narcotic peddlers in causing a tremendous increase in drug addiction." (HJA to Mrs. I. H. Teilman, February 7, 1939, TDF 0120–1, Folder 3, DEA.) There was no evidence for such a conclusion.

62. HJA to Young, February 13, 1939, TDF 0120–1, Folder 3, DEA. Olson's views of alcohol control: "Olson Asks State Take Over Liquor," *Los Angeles Examiner*, January 18, 1935, sec. 1, p. 8.

63. Walker's career after 1939: Taper, note 52. Doom: Young to HJA, December 23, 1938, TDF 0120–1, Folder 2, DEA. It seems that only the intervention of Elizabeth Bass, a doyenne of the Democratic Party and a Roosevelt appointee to the FBN (she was Anslinger's top political operative), persuaded Olson to keep Spadra open during the early part of his administration (Elizabeth Bass to Franklin Delano Roosevelt, June 18, 1939, FDR, OF, Box 919, Eliz. Bass). Rosanoff's views: Michelsen, "An Open Letter to Dr. Aaron J. Rosanoff," TDF 0120–8, DEA; Madden to Dickey, note 54. Anslinger told Rosanoff in February 1940 that California could not use federal courts to commit addicts to Lexington, Fort Worth, or Alderson (West Virginia, for women) without federal legislation to permit it. "Furthermore," Anslinger wrote, such a law would encourage the states "to shirk their duty." (HJA to Rosanoff, ca. February 1940, cited in Madden to Dickey.)

64. "Police Aide Urges Free Narcotics for Dope Addicts," *Fresno Bee*, April 17, 1940, TDF 0120–1, Folder 3, DEA.

65. Michelsen to Mrs. Maddux, April 22, 1940; Michelsen to HJA, May 13, 1940; Joseph Manning to HJA, April 30, 1940, all TDF 0120–1, Folder 3, DEA.

66. J. A. Greening (Berkeley Chief of Police) to HJA, October 7, 1940; Warren to Smith, October 1, 1940; Warren to Barbeau, October 1, 1940, all TDF 0120–1, Folder 3, DEA.

67. Barbeau to Warren, October 8, 1940; Warren to Smith, October 14, 1940, both TDF 0120–1, Folder 3, DEA.

68. No meeting had occurred by mid-December, and Smith, having called a significant chip, was by then frustrated with Anslinger's failure to thank Warren personally for the intervention. Smith to HJA, October 5, 1940; Smith to Warren, December 19, 1940, both TDF 0120–1, Folder 3, DEA.

69. Alfred Lindesmith, "Dope Fiend Mythology," *Journal of Criminal Law and Criminology* 31 (1940), 199–208 (cited passage, 208).

70. HJA to Gaston, September 17, 1940; Gaston to HJA, ca. September 17, 1940, both TDF 0120–1, Folder 3, DEA.

71. Twain Michelsen, "Lindesmith's Mythology," *Journal of Criminal Law and Criminology* 31 (1940): 375–400 (cited passage, 400). Although the Williams brothers' names appeared on WNRF literature, Henry denied to Lindesmith that they were in any way

involved and wrote that Edward had explicitly requested that his name be removed (H. S. Williams to Lindesmith, note 40).

72. Lindesmith claimed that the FBN was behind Michelsen's attack, and there can be no doubt of it. On his harassment by the FBN, see Lindesmith, note 41, 254–257.

73. *New State Ice Co. v. Liebmann (265 U.S. 262)*.

74. "Former Club Woman Faces Dope Trial," *San Francisco Examiner*, May 6, 1931, 19; "Former Club Leader Given Dope Sentence," *San Francisco Examiner*, May 10, 1931, sec. 1, p. 16.

75. "Former Club Leader," note 74.

76. Historian David Courtwright, in *Dark Paradise: Opiate Addiction in America before 1940* (Cambridge: Harvard University Press, 1982), argued that as conservative medical practices reduced iatrogenic addiction, the locus of opiate addiction moved from middle-class to lower-class and sporting circles in the decades before Harrison. Historical epidemiology is something of an empirical rabbit hole, but his point seems accurate. Even so, there were many addicts not caught up in a wider pursuit of vice, and this was the point hammered on by the White Cross.

77. Votta to FBI, note 13.

78. Kolb to HJA, June 29, 1939, AP, Box 3, File 1.

79. Kolb to HJA, note 78. For an explication of this dilemma in disability determination, see Deborah A. Stone, *The Disabled State* (Philadelphia: Temple University Press, 1984).

80. For the biographical origins of Smith's "natural hatred for narcotic drugs in any form and for any person who trafficked in them," see Smith to HJA, September 5, 1940, AP, Box 2, File 21.

81. The FBN's disregard for *Linder* went well beyond typical "agency nonacquiescence." Usually, this is a formally declared or informal practice whereby a federal agency chooses not to change its regulations on the basis of an adverse *circuit* court decision. The most common form is called "intercircuit nonacquiescence," and it occurs when an agency chooses not to honor the ruling of a circuit other than the one that will review whatever case is at hand. "Intracircuit nonacquiescence" is more rare and confrontational, in that the agency refuses to abide by the decision of a circuit court even within that court's jurisdiction. The Internal Revenue Service (a Treasury Department agency) began to practice such tactics at about the time of *Linder*. See Samuel Estreicher and Richard L. Revesz, "Nonacquiescence by Federal Administrative Agencies," *Yale Law Journal* 98 (1989), 679–772. "Lusty applications": King, note 5, 748. Dr. David Lewis (personal communication) notes that Anslinger's FBN regarded *Linder* as *obiter dictum* and thus beside the point of legal precedent and substantive policy. Even so, the Supreme Court does not seem to have regarded the decision's provisions for good faith practice as mere legal aside. The White Cross's Everett Hoffman claimed that Justice McReynolds (*Linder's* author) told him in 1926 that "the recent Linder decision would protect the doctors henceforth." Hoffman was skeptical: "I told him that he did not know the Narcotic Bureau," he recalled (Hoffman to Lindesmith, January 8, 1938, LP). In any event, the failed Smoot Amendments to Harrison in 1926, and the subsequent development of a uniform state narcotic law (see note 11), clearly indicate that Treasury officials took *Linder's* practical threat to *Webb* quite seriously. The decision was thus ignored at every opportunity.

82. Anslinger's views on treatment: "The Narcotic Problem," speech to the Attorney

General's Conference on Crime, December 13, 1934 (AP, Box 1, File 7). Anslinger thought highly of German eugenic colonization, and of an Alaskan version proposed by a Washington state hospital doctor opposed to the program of the Seattle White Cross. Harry Smith was similarly enthusiastic, but Kolb called the idea "absurd." H. L. Sharman, Anslinger's Canadian counterpart, offered a more polite dissent: Addiction was in decline, he wrote from Ottawa, even without extreme policies like "narcotic bar-rooms" (maintenance clinics) or "permanent leper islands." See HJA to Dr. J. W. Doughty, October 14, 1936; HJA to His Excellency the Governor of Washington, January 10, 1941; Smith to HJA, January 30, 1941; Kolb to HJA, February 5, 1941; Sharman to HJA, February 3, 1941, all TDF 0120–8, DEA. For the proposal, see J. W. Doughty, "State Farm Colony," in *Third Annual Report of the Department of Finance, Budget and Business* (Olympia: State Printer, 1940), 160–161.

83. Joint Committee of the American Bar Association and the American Medical Association on Narcotic Drugs, *Drug Addiction: Crime or Disease?* (Bloomington: Indiana University Press, 1961; this volume includes both the interim and final reports of the Joint Committee); Advisory Committee to the Federal Bureau of Narcotics, *Comments on Narcotic Drugs[,] Interim Report of the Joint Committee of the American Bar Association and the American Medical Association on Narcotic Drugs* (Washington, D.C.: U.S. Treasury Department, Bureau of Narcotics, 1958). Michelsen's comments: 72–104; quoted passages: 86, 95.

84. Depression-era tax mechanisms: Marvel M. Stockwell, *Studies in California State Taxation, 1910–1935* (Berkeley: University of California Press, 1939); federal, state, and local financial relationships: Winston W. Crouch, *State Aid to Local Government in California* (Berkeley: University of California Press, 1939); hostile treatment of impoverished migrants: Walter J. Stein, *California and the Dust Bowl Migration* (Westport, Conn.: Greenwood Press, 1973); Carey McWilliams, *Southern California: An Island on the Land* (1946; Santa Barbara: Peregrine Smith, 1973); Gregory R. Woirol, *In the Floating Army: F. C. Mills on Itinerant Life in California, 1914* (Urbana: University of Illinois Press, 1992).

"Lady Tipplers"

Gendering the Modern Alcoholism Paradigm, 1933–1960

Michelle McClellan

During the mid-1940s, a thirty-two-year-old "career woman" in a northeastern American city was hospitalized and treated by a psychiatrist for alcoholism. Recounting her case in a professional journal, the psychiatrist attributed her problem drinking to underlying psychological weaknesses that stemmed from her difficult relationship with her parents, especially her mother, and to romantic disappointments. The woman first started to drink soon after she began work in an office, where she had an affair with a co-worker, a "thoroughly unsuitable married man," according to the psychiatrist. She reported that she would have intercourse with him only when she had been drinking. She became pregnant, and "[her lover] deserted her when, under sordid circumstances, she had an abortion the horrors of which realized all the fears of woman's suffering which the [patient's] mother had described. It was following the abortion that the patient's excessive drinking began."[1] Interestingly, the psychiatrist emphasized the woman's height—she was six feet tall—and the patient herself believed that her "troubles" originated when she was forced to take men's parts in school plays because of her height. Combining as it does alcoholism, adultery, abandonment, and a rejection of motherhood, this woman's story could be read as a cautionary tale of what could happen to any woman who strayed outside the boundaries governing "proper" sexual and social behavior.

During the middle decades of the twentieth century, medical professionals and the general public alike sought to explain an apparent increase in the number of women with drinking problems. Reflecting the long-standing cultural associations of drinking with gendered public spaces and issues of sexuality, many commentators interpreted women's drinking during these years as a sign of the breakdown of conventional gender roles. While this essay focuses primarily on the writings of psychiatrists, their central themes—the ways in which women's drinking interacted with motherhood and sexuality—were echoed in the popular media and by female alcoholics themselves.

The discourse surrounding alcoholism both contributed to and reflected a preoccupation with gender in the wider society. As a number of historians have shown, the middle decades of the twentieth century were characterized by anxiety regarding traditional gender ideology in the midst of widespread social, economic, and political changes. The economic dislocation of the Great Depression, the family separation and mobility of the World War II years, and the political and cultural pressures of the Cold War all seemed to pose an unprecedented threat to the family.[2] Even as scientific and medical experts attempted to formulate a modern, nonmoralistic model of alcoholism as a disease, they remained enmeshed in a social and cultural context that included complex, long-standing links between gender and liquor. Alcoholism seemed to be a problem of gendered boundaries that were too often crossed: the boundary between a "manly" social drinker and an "effeminate" male alcoholic, and the boundary that was intended to preserve alcohol consumption, particularly in public spaces, as a specifically masculine prerogative. Psychiatrists used their cultural authority to attempt to monitor and enforce those boundaries through a medicalized language of deviance, a language applied to alcoholics of both sexes but one in which alcoholic women seemed especially problematic.

Although "effeminate" male and "masculine" female alcoholics might seem to threaten conventional gender roles equally, the woman alcoholic was viewed as more deviant and disturbing than the male because of a persistent association between drinking and masculinity. New drinking customs evolved during and after Prohibition, and women increasingly partook of alcohol in a variety of settings.[3] Yet not all Americans welcomed these new habits; many interpreted women's liquor consumption as a troubling indication of changing gender role conventions. Discomfort with women's drinking—especially heavy drinking or imbibing in traditionally male public spaces—shaped views of female alcoholics in a variety of ways. For one thing, the distinction between the "normal" social drinker and the pathological drinker, a central element of the modern definition of alcoholism, was more difficult to draw in the case of women, for whom anything more than an occasional cocktail might be considered suspect. A drinking woman did not have to be regarded as a technical "alcoholic" to be considered "masculine" and therefore deviant. This is not to say that psychiatrists thought that any woman who drank would automatically become an alcoholic; but psychiatrists and the lay public alike often viewed social drinking and alcoholism among women as two symptoms of the same social problem: women's increasing "masculinity" and its threat to conventional gender roles. Further, psychiatrists often assumed that any woman who violated traditional gender boundaries in order to drink must be especially ill; as a result, they considered women alcoholics to be more pathological than their male counterparts. Moreover, this view of drinking as a gender transgression—and alcoholism as a problem of gender identity—served to obscure differences among women who drank. While racial, ethnic, and class differences among women shaped drinking patterns and access to treatment for alcoholism, at the level of medical discourse such differences were subsumed into a single gendered category: the woman alcoholic. Finally, the perception that problem drinking among women, itself read as sign of social disintegration, was on the increase lent a particular urgency to discussions of the issue.

The Modern Alcoholism Paradigm

For the American medical and scientific communities, the repeal of Prohibition in 1933 brought an opportunity to reassert authority over the issue of alcohol use and abuse. As one physician explained, "The prohibitionists have done much damage by insisting that alcoholism is a political problem, thus preventing men from recognizing that alcoholism is a disease to be treated."[4] In the decades following Repeal, several groups of research scientists, including the Research Council on Problems of Alcohol and the Yale Center for Alcohol Studies, along with clinicians and educational and self-help groups, such as the National Committee for Education on Alcoholism and Alcoholics Anonymous, formed what scholars have called the "modern alcoholism movement." These individuals and groups, some loosely affiliated and other working independently, formulated and promoted the ideas that scholars have since labeled the "modern alcoholism paradigm." According to this paradigm, the cause of alcohol-related problems, particularly problem drinking, was located in the individual, not the substance. Thus, a central element of this model was the distinction between a normal person who drank socially or recreationally, and the person who became alcoholic (for reasons that, according to many scientists, were not yet understood). At the same time, alcoholism was considered a disease, not a vice or simple bad habit resulting from a lack of willpower.

Yet even as this disease model of alcoholism gained prominence, research scientists and practicing physicians offered few coherent definitions of alcoholism or explanations of its causes. Many researchers relied on vague or circular operational definitions of alcoholism and its criteria as a diagnostic category, noting only that the subjects they studied were being treated for "alcoholism" (and were therefore "alcoholics"). E. M. Jellinek, a physiologist at the Yale Center who is generally considered the father of the disease model, offered a more precise explanation, defining alcoholism as a chronic, progressive disease with distinct stages. Some social scientists and clinicians cataloged the drinking habits of their subjects or patients, fitting them into various categories devised by Jellinek. Rather than focusing on the amount of alcohol an individual consumed, the Jellinek model emphasized drinking patterns (for example, drinking in the morning) and the extent to which drinking interfered with the person's ability to function either occupationally or socially. Yet Jellinek did not use any data on women alcoholics when he formulated his model, and his interpretation was clearly gendered, assuming the alcoholic to be man, as evidenced by his focus on occupational adjustment and the "ability to be a good provider."[5]

Compared to physiologists and social scientists, many of whom emphasized how much was still unknown about alcoholism, many psychiatrists offered what seemed to be a comprehensive interpretation of its causes, consequences, and treatment. As a result, psychiatry played a key role in shaping the medical and popular understanding of alcoholism. As the historian Elizabeth Lunbeck has shown, psychiatrists gained cultural authority during the first decades of the twentieth century by expanding their jurisdiction to include aspects of everyday life, including gender roles; psychoanalytic language and concepts increasingly permeated popular culture as well.[6] Alcoholism, which seemed a much more everyday malady than, for example, schizophrenia, provided another opportunity for psychiatrists to extend their authority and offer their expertise to the lay public. In addition, the concern, frequently expressed in the popular press, that both recreational and abusive drinking were increasing among women provided a context in which expert analysis of this "social problem" seemed especially appropriate and welcome. Even as social drinking among women became more common, then, psychiatrists stepped in to mediate the gendered line between acceptable drinking and alcoholism.

A number of elite psychiatrists and psychoanalysts thus addressed the problem of alcoholism during the middle decades of the twentieth century, writing in prestigious medical journals such as the *Journal of the American Medical Association* and specialized publications like the *Quarterly Journal of Studies on Alcohol,* as well as in popular magazines and books. Since many of these psychiatrists were affiliated with the major institutions for alcoholism treatment, their views undoubtedly shaped the care that many patients received, even though it is difficult to know the extent to which the average physician knew and applied these writings. Further, the themes these doctors emphasized were echoed by social workers, in the popular media, and even by female alcoholics themselves. (It is always possible, of course, that psychiatrists were in fact echoing their patients.) There were important differences in the precise ways in which psychiatrists and their patients articulated these themes. Despite such variations, however (which will be discussed more fully below), the consistent return to these themes by all these voices demonstrates how strongly issues of gender and sexuality resonated in mid-twentieth-century American society.

To a great extent, psychiatrists shared the perspective of the modern alcoholism paradigm that alcoholism should be considered a disease (rather than a sin or lack of willpower) and that there was a fundamental difference between the normal, moderate drinker and the alcoholic. Within that framework, however, they offered their own definition. Adopting psychoanalytic language regardless of whether they had received formal training as analysts, psychiatrists interpreted alcoholism primarily as a behavioral symptom of underlying emotional problems related to gender identity. Drawing on theories of personality development and psychopathology which emphasized parent-child relationships, sexuality, and gender roles, these doctors sought to explain the psychological conflicts that led an alcoholic to drink. These psychiatrists were not the first to connect alcoholism with issues of gender, as medical professionals and social commentators had done so since at least the last decades of the nineteenth century. Mid-twentieth-century mental health experts were thus able to build on resonant cultural images even as they reformulated interpretations especially suited to their time.

"Mom in a Bottle": Alcoholism and the Crisis of Masculinity

Following the modern alcoholism paradigm, which underscored the importance of the distinction between normal or social drinking and alcoholic drinking, psychiatrists attempted to interpret the significance of both recreational and pathological drinking. Concluding that alcohol consumption had highly gendered associations, they maintained that issues of masculinity served to distinguish the male alcoholic from the normal male drinker.

After Prohibition was repealed, social drinking was generally viewed as an acceptable, normal behavior for men. As the language and imagery surrounding it shows, social drinking was gendered as a masculine activity: one had a beer with his buddies in the manly atmosphere of the bar or saloon; learning to "hold one's liquor like a man" was an important coming-of-age ritual; drinking capacity was linked to sexual prowess.[7] As one physician explained, "One of the most powerful attractions in drinking is the *demonstration of masculinity*. To drink someone under the table, to carry one's liquor well, has always been held in high estimation."[8] Drinking thus appealed to men because of its masculine connotations. These very connotations, however, ensnared those men who, according to psychiatrists, turned to alcohol in an attempt to compensate for an inadequate psychosexual development. Because they tried to use alcohol to cope with psychological and emotional problems, these men were unable to maintain normal drinking patterns and became alcoholic.

Drawing on psychoanalytic theory, then, many psychiatrists interpreted alcoholism in men as the result of a failure to achieve psychological and sexual maturity. One doctor, in fact, maintained that alcoholism was a "special masculine neurosis" because the "excessive use of alcohol makes it possible to realize, in a fantastic subjective way, the primitive solution of the oedipus complex." He explained further, "In the elation of alcohol we may find the attempt to realize the deepest unconscious desires to kill the father and be united with the mother. The symbolic satisfaction involves simultaneously and automatically the impending punishment—death by the physiological consequences of alcohol, i.e., the condition of unconsciousness and coma."[9] Drawing on similar themes, most psychiatrists located the origins of alcoholism in men in a particular constellation of early family relationships. The typical male alcoholic, according to psychiatrists, had an overprotective, indulgent mother and a remote father. As a result, the boy was dependent on the mother, passive, and unable to form a masculine self-image. Instead, he identified with his mother and developed a "feminine" constitution. After describing the "typical mother attachment" of alcoholic male patients, one psychiatrist explained that "out of this situation there developed a feminine identification, a dynamic factor of determined force in leading to a feminine approach to life in these unfortunate individuals."[10] Similarly, Edward A. Strecker, a well-known psychiatrist who was involved in alcoholism treatment, argued that "Momism"—the phenomenon in which American mothers allegedly ruined the next generation through their smothering behavior toward their children—was the "basic, underlying cause" in about 80 percent of the alcoholic cases he studied. He proclaimed, "Alcohol is a mom that can be poured into a glass."[11]

According to psychiatrists, these men turned to alcohol, often during adolescence, in the hopes that its associations with masculinity would compensate for their own feelings of confusion and inferiority. Robert P. Knight, M.D., a psychoanalyst at the Menninger Clinic in Kansas, explained how such a young man would feel caught between his "passive, childish, feminine wishes" and the "masculine strivings inculcated by the father and by the cultural ideology absorbed from schooling and from conflicts with other boys." The doctor continued, "Excessive drinking supplies a compromise solution to both aspects of this conflict. It affords implicit gratification of passive oral wishes, and, at the same time, through the distorted standards of masculinity of late adolescence, provides the illusion of being masculine through his trying to be a hard-drinking he-man who can 'hell around' with the boys."[12] Another psychiatrist described the motivation of a forty-five-year-old man who had been drinking heavily for twenty years: "He felt that alcohol relieved his tension and made him feel more masculine and less aware of the effeminate component in himself."[13] Excessive drinking as a strategy to feel more masculine ultimately and inevitably failed; psychiatrists explained that alcoholic men were unable to realize that the masculinity they sought in this way was "superficial," "spurious," and "distorted" and could not resolve their conflicts, only leaving them, in the words of one psychiatrist, "as frustrated as ever."[14]

Psychiatrists argued that homosexuality was closely related to alcoholism in men; they maintained that both conditions were the result of psychosexual immaturity that was itself caused by exaggerated dependency on the mother. As one doctor wrote, "With such strong feminine identification, the development of a passive homosexual male is understandable."[15] While the medical literature on alcoholism contained relatively few examples of homosexual behavior—one study of alcoholics treated at a state-operated outpatient clinic, for instance, reported only two "active" homosexuals out of sixty-three patients[16]—psychiatrists nevertheless discussed the issue extensively, citing frequent examples of "latent" homosexuality, "sexual maladjustment," and marital failure among male alcoholics.[17] Doctors reported that many alcoholic men had difficulty sustaining relationships with women and seemed to prefer the company of other men. The homosocial world of the saloon, in which alcohol lowered inhibitions, provided, according to psychiatrists, the ideal environment for alcoholic men to express their unconscious desires in a socially acceptable manner. Knight described one patient: "He showed the typical behavior of alcoholics toward men friends in drinking and getting tenderly affectionate with them, swearing eternal friendship, becoming lovingly demonstrative toward them, thus acting out strong and thinly disguised homosexual attraction. When he was sober, on the other hand, he feared he would be regarded as a 'sissy' or a 'fairy.'"[18] Another doctor, while acknowledging that the "stage of direct genital homosexual acts is omitted, due to the remaining resistance," nevertheless insisted that bar fights and even "paying another man's debts in the bar" represented a "direct manifestation" of homosexual drives.[19]

Psychiatrists defined alcoholic men as effeminate, dependent, passive, and often homosexual—in short, the opposite of what, in their view, a mature man should be. This "crisis of masculinity" had tremendous resonance during the middle decades of the twentieth century, as "Momism" and the "homosexual menace" seemed to threaten American military preparedness and democracy.[20] These issues of gender were used to differentiate the normal man, who could engage in routine social drinking with his friends, from the alcoholic, whose failure to achieve a masculine identification and heterosexual adjustment led to pathological drinking.

"The Increasing Masculinity of Women": Alcoholism among Women as a Sign of the Times

Psychiatrists' interpretation of alcoholism in women featured a similar focus on the gender identity and sexual behavior of the alcoholic. While alcoholic men seemed effeminate, displayed homosexual leanings, and were often unable to hold jobs, according to doctors, women with drinking problems displayed masculine traits such as aggressiveness, were often promiscuous or frigid, and failed to care for their children adequately. Just as the alcoholic man's immaturity and feminine constitution were at the root of his problems according to psychiatrists, so the common denominator behind the alcoholic woman's pathologies was her failure to adjust to the feminine gender role. One doctor reported, for example, that the alcoholic women he studied all demonstrated "a rather clear-cut desire to assume the masculine role."[21]

While quantitative proof is difficult, if not impossible, to find, available evidence indicates that women's recreational drinking became increasingly common during the three decades following the repeal of Prohibition. Further, the *perception* of a rise in women's drinking was widespread, reflected in medical and social science literature and the popular media alike. One group of sociologists reported, for example, that while there had been little systematic or longitudinal study of changes in women's drinking patterns, "the consensus is that social drinking [among women] is definitely increasing." The authors continued, "the transformation of the traditional tea party into the cocktail party; the presence of women in public bars, cocktail lounges, taverns, and other drinking places; the phenomenon of drinking parties made up exclusively of women, all attest to a widespread change in mores." Advertising and films contributed to this trend, according to these researchers. Further, the authors noted, the recent increase in women's drinking—and thus the break with convention—was most noticeable among women of the middle class; only "in the highest and in the lowest social levels" had women's drinking been acceptable in the past. In addition, while these social scientists noted that women seemed to be drinking more in a variety of settings, including women-only groups, women's participation in mixed-gender drinking, especially in public settings, often attracted the most attention as it resonated strongly with long-standing cultural associations between drinking and sexuality. Among college women, for example, other researchers found a high correlation between alcohol consumption and dating, reflecting, they believed, the fact that women could more easily obtain alcohol while on dates.[22]

Social scientists in such studies usually conveyed or at least affected a tone of detached neutrality. Articles in the popular media, on the other hand, frequently adopted a much more shrill, alarmist tone. "Lady Lushes on the Loose!" trumpeted one 1944 headline. "Alibis Galore Given for Feminine Feet on Bar Rails," the article continued, with illustrations showing a blonde and a brunette engaged in a "catfight" over the blonde's escort with the caption, "Our women drunks are not above slugging it out."[23] These articles often expressed men's indignation and bitterness that women were invading the male world of the saloon. One writer, for example, criticized women who drank in public for ordering elaborate fruity drinks and monopolizing the bartender's time, while another admonished women who dared drink in a bar to sit near the door and leave after thirty minutes.[24] Lamenting the decline of the double standard, many writers criticized the changing character of the corner saloon, now festooned with pink decorations and cluttered with lipstick-stained glasses, and of the typical female customer, who no longer slunk in through the "Ladies' Entrance" but rather sat at a table in the front room. "Women Nowadays Called 'Hard' Drinkers," declared a 1947 headline in the *New York Herald Tribune*, while a similar article worried over "A Growing Liability: The Woman 'Bar Fly.'"[25]

Observers perceived women's drinking as threatening because they interpreted it as a reflection of women's increasing masculinity. In fact, many commentators, including psychiatrists and journalists alike, attributed increased rates of social drinking among women to the fact that more women were acting like men by working and socializing in public. Doctors offered a number of possible reasons for this increase in women's drinking, including feminism, the "emancipation of women," and the growing number of women who worked in factories and offices.[26] The comments of one psychoanalyst demonstrated that any behavior perceived to be masculine in women could be linked to alcohol use: "With the increasing masculinity of women, apparent in the choice of professions, in clothes, and in women's attitude toward life, we find an increased inclination toward alcohol and drunkenness."[27] By linking women's alcohol consumption with their changing employment patterns, attire, and public demeanor, these psychiatrists both reflected cultural anxiety regarding perceived threats to conventional gender roles and reinforced the assumption that women's alcohol use was symptomatic of these unwelcome social changes.

Newspaper and magazine articles featured similar themes: women who drank invaded male space, both the saloon and, often, the workplace. For (male) bartenders and patrons, the worst aspect of women's saloon drinking was simply that such women tried to behave like men.[28] Not a few women, according to another article, "have taken to drink in their effort to keep up with their men."[29] Such fears were especially prominent during World War II. As one newspaper opined, "In this war, the fact that so many women have worked at men's jobs has played its part in stimulating drinking. Sociologists observe that when women enter a male environment, they tend to adopt the ways of men."[30] Some alcoholic women themselves echoed this connection between drinking and entering a man's world. "Marty" Mann, the founder of the National Committee for Education on Alcoholism, recalled that she too had attributed some of her heaviest drinking to her career involvement; she had "used the excuse that many men do—that I had to drink in my business, that I did my best work over cocktails, that it was a business in which it was essential to entertain." Mann explained that she eventually learned, after her recovery, that "it may be essential to serve others drinks but that does not mean you have to drink with them, and it certainly doesn't mean that you have to get drunk."[31] By arguing that she could both continue in her career and be surrounded by liquor as a woman, and as a recovering female alcoholic at that, Mann asserted her claim to the doctrines of the modern alcoholism paradigm.

The perception that women's social drinking was increasing shaded easily into a concern that alcoholism was becoming more common among women as well. All observers agreed that alcoholism was less frequent among women than among men. Estimates of the sex ratio among alcoholics varied widely but tended to cluster around 6:1 (six male alcoholics to every female). While some scientists, including Jellinek, maintained that the sex ratio was consistent over time and any apparent increase resulted from the willingness of more women to seek treatment, the dominant view—and that which reflected and reinforced cultural concerns about changing gender roles—held that alcoholism among women was increasing.[32] It may be impossible for historians to determine the actual incidence of alcoholism among women during these years, but the important point here is the widespread perception that it was increasing. Newspaper articles reported that drunk driving, arrests for public intoxication, and hospitalization for alcoholism were all increasing among women. One headline proclaimed, for example, "National Report on Lady Booze Hounds a Cause of Concern."[33]

In any case, even contemporary psychiatrists asserted that statistics alone failed to convey the real scope of the problem of alcoholism among women. As the psychiatrist Benjamin Karpman, M.D., expressed it, "what alcoholic women seem to lack in quantity, they certainly do make up in quality." He and other psychiatrists contended that alcoholic women's participation in an activity that contradicted traditional gender roles was itself evidence of severe pathology. Even as they maintained that alcoholism was less common among women than among men because of regulatory gender norms, many doctors concluded that those women who did become alcoholic were therefore, by definition, sicker than their male counterparts. Karpman stated the prevailing view directly: "alcoholic women," he asserted, "are more abnormal than alcoholic men." He explained that even in this "sophisticated age, women are still subject to more repressions than men, and in attempting to solve their conflicts, they must seek outlets that are still within the limits of conventional social acceptance of their sex." But alcoholic women violated these boundaries when the "pressure becomes so great as to be beyond control"; their alcoholism, then, "naturally must be more vehemently expressed, being in proportion to the tension behind it."[34] Psychiatrists argued that the masculine connotations of social drinking appealed to both the ordinary male drinker and the male alcoholic. While the "effeminate" male alcoholic was unable to maintain normal drinking patterns because of his gender role deficiencies, he at least attempted, through his drinking, to reclaim what was natural for him—namely, masculinity. On the other hand, the same association of social drinking with masculinity could dissolve the distinction between a female recreational drinker and a female alcoholic and render even women's moderate drinking potentially threatening.

Articles in the popular media echoed—in many cases quoted—the experts who maintained that alcoholic women were sicker and more difficult to treat than their male counterparts. Further, newspaper and magazine articles went beyond the psychological and health costs of alcoholism to any individual woman to focus on the social costs of women's excessive drinking. The authors of such articles clearly viewed women's drinking, whether "alcoholic" or not, as a index of the breakdown of gender roles and a sign of social disintegration. The belief that women's drinking was increasing lent even more urgency to their discussion. Reflecting ambivalence regarding women's changing roles and the extent to which observers viewed women's drinking as a symbol of those changes, one columnist opined, "The lady lusher, the girlish guzzler and the woman-wowzer are among 1947's Problem People. . . . The Bistro Berthas, Cocktail Lounge Lorettas and Barfly Beatrices are becoming something more than sickening to people who respect womanhood and think that women's place, while it may no longer be strictly in the home, is certainly not in the corner dive, with or without pink and white furnishings, soft music and a couple of groggy canaries."[35] Similarly, another argued that women's new freedom to drink came at too high a price: "Shattered homes, blasted lives, and an increasing drain on society are the result of the 'emancipation' that permits a women to sip a social cocktail and does not criticize her for doing so."[36]

Finally, the emphasis on drinking as a masculine activity and therefore a gender transgression for women served to obscure important differences among women. Clearly, gender issues shaped the construction of alcoholism among men as well; but perhaps assuming that a certain amount of alcohol-related health and social problems among men was natural, researchers usually balanced gender with other variables in their analysis of men. Not so with women. A few female social workers who studied women alcoholics during the 1940s and 1950s did discuss class and ethnic differences among their subjects, but they were exceptions; their writings only highlight the lack of such attention in the vast majority of the literature.[37] This silence is especially striking given the numerous studies by social scientists and psychiatrists of ethnic and class differences among male alcoholics. If women were mentioned in these studies at all, they were included as simply another category (for example, "Irish," "Negroes," "Women"). Defining women as an already "other" classification, researchers did not attempt to break down that category by class, race, or ethnicity.[38] Thus, while class and cultural differences clearly shaped the patterns of women's drinking, the consequences they faced for their drinking, and their opportunities for treatment for problem drinking, few physicians or scientists attempted to explore those variables because they interpreted women's drinking primarily as a *gender* transgression. Women's increased public, social drinking during the middle decades of the twentieth century served, in fact, to blur boundaries that the behavior had once established between "good" and "bad" women, making the gender transgression all the more salient. One commentator lamented the possible risk a man now faced of meeting a female family member in a drinking establishment, noting with regret that at least before Prohibition, "a man would never meet his wife, his sweetheart, his daughter, his sister or his grandma there." Revealingly, one New York newspaper claimed that several drunken women who got into a fight in a run-down bar were in fact identical to their "better-dressed sisters under the skin" at a swanky uptown nightclub.[39]

Tomboys and Temper Tantrums: Alcoholism as a Failure of Femininity

Just as they located the cause of male alcoholism in gender identification problems determined by early family dynamics, psychiatrists interpreted alcoholism in women as the result of a failure to adjust to the feminine role, which they traced to the alcoholic woman's childhood experiences.

Learning the appropriate gender role in childhood—and fulfilling that role in adulthood—constituted fundamental elements of the mid-twentieth-century understanding of psychological development and of assessments of mental health. Further, this focus on a psychological—rather than a strictly biological—basis for gender roles, while apparently less constricting, strengthened the cultural authority of psychiatrists, who labeled behavior that contradicted traditional gender roles as "deviant," "pathological," or "neurotic." By emphasizing the importance of learning the proper gender role, mental health experts revealed at the same time that the socialization process could go awry, suggesting that gender roles were neither automatic nor perhaps as stable as people had once assumed. In this context, the re-inforcing of gender boundaries became more important than ever, and any-one who displayed unconventional behavior could be subject to psychiatric scrutiny—if not actually on the analyst's couch, then through the many pop-ular books and articles published by prominent psychiatrists. The dominant psychiatric definition of alcoholism as a psychological and behavioral prob-lem resulting from emotional conflicts associated with gender identity thus reflected and served as a focus for cultural anxiety about changes in the gendered patterns of behavior of mid-twentieth-century men and women.[40]

According to experts, many alcoholic women had displayed masculine and therefore deviant behavior as children—some had acted like tomboys, for example, while others exhibited unfeminine temper tantrums—which had not been sufficiently discouraged by the parents, whether as a result of divorce or the death of a parent or simple parental "ignorance."[41] While such childhood problems laid the psychological groundwork, psychiatrists main-tained that stressful experiences or emotional difficulties later in life were usually necessary to precipitate the development of alcoholism, especially in women. Perhaps reflecting an assumption that women would not turn to such an unnatural activity as drinking without some external pressure or stimulus, doctors reported that many alcoholic women had begun drinking in response to a particular situation or problem. Although a number of psy-chiatrists concluded that alcoholism in women was therefore more "idio-syncratic" than the condition in men, the most frequent "triggers" alcoholic women reported for their excessive drinking in fact formed a consistent, highly gendered picture: they were almost always related to sexual and re-productive matters (for instance, painful menstruation, menopause, miscar-riage and abortion, marital problems, or difficulty coping with the respon-sibilities of motherhood).[42] Doctors believed that alcoholic women's responses to these situations—their drinking—demonstrated their inability or unwillingness to accept and fulfill the feminine gender role. Yet psychi-atrists did not interpret the connection between stressful life events associated with the adult female role and alcoholic drinking as a straightforward cause-and-effect relationship. Rather, they asserted that underlying psychosexual adjustment problems led both to alcoholic women's drinking and to their failure to fulfill conventional responsibilities of motherhood and domesticity. For their part, alcoholic women similarly focused on marital conflicts, the challenges of motherhood, and reproductive and sexual difficulties as critical elements of their drinking problems. To a significant extent, alcoholic women spoke the same cultural language as their doctors, yet their explanations for their own drinking contained a critical difference. Unlike psychiatrists, who focused on various underlying psychological causes for both domestic "failure" and alcoholism, alcoholic women explained simply that they drank *because* of these family and household problems, even though the drinking, in turn, only worsened them.

According to psychiatrists, alcoholic women had significant difficulties coping with the biological and social aspects of reproduction; the ways in which psychiatrists framed these issues reflect the mid-twentieth-century focus on psychological elements of gender roles. Although the custom was probably less frequent than it had been in the late nineteenth century, when alcohol-based patent medicines aimed at "female complaints" were common, some women turned to alcohol for relief from the pain and discomfort associated with menstruation and menopause. As late as 1949, for example, one author noted, "Many popular remedies used by women to relieve painful menstruation usually contain a high concentration of alcohol." He then warned that some doctors considered it "ill advised" to use "alcoholic beverages or alcohol-containing preparations during periods of pre-menstrual tension."[43] Either women continued to use alcohol for these symptoms despite such warnings, or psychiatrists simply continued to interpret problem drinking in these terms; doctors cited numerous cases of "menstrual dipsomania" and described cases like Mrs. L.K., a fifty-four-year-old woman who began drinking when "menopausal symptoms became manifest." In one oft-cited 1937 study of alcoholic women, forty out of fifty patients suffered from dysmennhorea, reporting pelvic discomfort and "premenstrual depression of spirits" and expressing annoyance with this "periodic physiological dysfunction." Unwilling simply to accept these women's complaints, the psychiatrist had them examined by a gynecologist, who found "no pelvic pathology to which the pain could be attributed." The psychiatrist explained, "Careful psychological investigation revealed deeper motives behind the symptoms and emotional attitudes toward menstruation."[44] Reflecting the pervasiveness of these issues, a female psychologist echoed this theme more than two decades later, suggesting while menstrual pain and premenstrual tension, postpartum depression, and menopause might be linked to alcoholism in women, the main factor was probably "the woman's emotional adjustment to and acceptance of these feminine physiological functions."[45]

Thus, while nineteenth-century physicians had understood women's use of alcohol in these circumstances as a straightforward—if misguided—response to pain which was naturalized as part of the female experience, mid-twentieth-century psychiatrists dismissed alcoholic women's complaints of physical discomfort, maintaining instead that women's *emotional* conflicts regarding these processes—and, by extension, the feminine gender role—led to alcoholic drinking.[46] It is worth noting that this type of quasi-medical drinking represented the most familiar and accepted drinking style for otherwise respectable women, and it did not necessarily trigger the same kinds of concerns as did women's recreational drinking in public spaces. Women's drinking in the home could certainly cause problems, according to *Life* magazine, "but at least it does not constitute a public menace" as did the female invasion of the saloon.[47] Still, even private imbibing at home could threaten children and complicate women's sexual and marital adjustment, according to psychiatrists and social workers.

"For Goodness Sakes, Mom, Don't Die a Drunkard"

As a fundamental element of the feminine gender role, the theme of motherhood played a major role in the construction of female alcoholism. In both its biological and social dimensions, indeed, motherhood has historically been a central issue in the discourse surrounding the relationship between women and alcohol. During the nineteenth century, temperance campaigners rallied to the slogan of "Home Protection" as they targeted the saloon and men's liquor consumption as a threat to the family, which they represented. As a result of this kind of gendered association of women with temperance and men with liquor, women's use of alcohol has historically been rendered almost invisible, except in cases where the women involved were already considered deviant, such as prostitutes or certain immigrant groups. When alcohol consumption by women has been defined as a more general problem, reproductive concerns have often been at the core of the discussion, with attention focused on the ways in which women's alcohol consumption threatened to harm children. While the ways in which this potential danger was defined changed over time—by the middle decades of the twentieth century, social and psychological models supplanted the biological explanations common at the turn of the century—the focus on motherhood remained a central element in the construction of alcoholism in women.

Around the turn of the twentieth century, physicians and reformers argued that women's alcohol consumption—which most commentators believed to be primarily in the form of patent medicines—threatened to poison the race.[48] Progressive Era reforms, such as the Pure Food and Drug Act of 1906, alleviated much of this anxiety, and Prohibition held the promise that alcohol-related problems would disappear. The failure of Prohibition brought a new set of issues to the fore, and the eugenic discourse of the turn-of-the-century period did not reappear as part of the post-Prohibition (and post-immigration restriction) attention to alcoholism. In fact, in a striking reversal of many of the ideas of the earlier period, scientists and physicians denied many previous conclusions about the biological consequences and genetic bases of alcoholism.[49] The question and answer column of *Hygeia,* a magazine published by the American Medical Association and aimed at a popular audience, asserted that "the injurious effects of alcohol on the male and female germ cells or on the product of conception have been, to say the least, greatly exaggerated."[50] The *Journal of the American Medical Association* even denied that drinking during pregnancy posed any danger, reassuring a physician who inquired about a patient who had drunk a significant amount of beer before she knew she was pregnant, "The patient need have no worries about the effect of her beer debauch on her unborn baby."[51]

But although they dismissed earlier warnings about the biological and genetic consequences of women's alcohol use, mid-twentieth-century psychiatrists shared their predecessors' concern with alcoholic women's capacities as mothers. They simply replaced warnings about alcohol as a racial poison with concern over the psychological "deficiencies" that made alcoholic women unable or unwilling to fulfill the conventional responsibilities of motherhood and domesticity. Thus, just as these doctors regarded gynecological problems as matters less physical than emotional, so too they emphasized the psychological and environmental—rather than the biological and genetic—aspects of motherhood. As portrayed in the medical literature, alcoholic women demonstrated a constellation of difficulties associated with the domestic role: studies were filled with references to their marital failures, abortions, and indifferent, neglectful, and hostile mothering.[52]

In mid-twentieth-century America, the normal woman was expected to desire children as the fullest expression of her sexual maturity and feminine identity. According to psychiatrists, a substantial number of alcoholic women did not seem to want children, which only underscored their pathology and deviance. One psychiatrist reported the case of a thirty-eight-year-old married woman who began drinking after her marriage: "[she] had an abortion as she 'did not want to be bothered with children'. . . . She was a poor manager and housekeeper and engaged in none of the domestic arts. . . . Sexually she was frigid."⁵³ When they did have children, psychiatrists maintained, alcoholic women frequently were indifferent or hostile to them. One doctor described an alcoholic woman who began drinking heavily after her first child was born: "She showed little interest in the child, and was bored and irritated by the other young mothers who were naturally her companions. . . . Drinking commenced."⁵⁴ Another woman, who was treated at the Washingtonian Hospital in Boston during the early 1950s, reported that she "associated the onset of heavy drinking with performing the role of housewife and mother."⁵⁵

For these women, it seemed, frustration and boredom with domestic roles contributed to the development of alcoholism. Excessive drinking, in turn, often interfered with a woman's capacity to care for children and fulfill other responsibilities, and contributed to further problems. Most reports of women alcoholics' experiences were filtered through a social worker or psychiatrist, and it is difficult to know how some social workers and psychiatrists defined "good" and "bad" mothering. Regardless of the bias that may have colored these reports, though, it is easy to imagine how a mother's alcoholism could cause emotional distress and even physical danger for her children.

For the most part, psychiatrists maintained that a woman's inability or unwillingness to be a mother was an indication of deviance and should be a source of guilt. Occasionally, however, psychiatrists' attitudes toward the difficulties these alcoholic women experienced were more complex. The connection the doctors drew between the frustrations women faced in their domestic role and the development of alcoholism contained an implicit acknowledgment of the limitations of that role and of the greater social value attached to the adult male role. Still, psychiatrists did not support or encourage women to abandon their conventional role or even seek to change it systemically. For example, Karpman noted that one of the alcoholic women he treated suffered from feelings of guilt, but he explained that she had "definite social reasons for her self-accusatory attitude. She knew that she was an incompetent and unsatisfactory mother, and she had upon her conscience the fact of a most distressing abortion." While he was careful not to align himself completely with these "definite social reasons," providing instead a professional distance on the social conditions by describing them "objectively," he nevertheless offered no solution for the woman except that she learn to conform to them and resolve her feelings through psychotherapy.⁵⁶

In one unusual study during the early 1950s, women social workers at the Washingtonian Hospital in Boston encouraged alcoholic women who felt unable to cope with domestic responsibilities to "shift roles" by developing interests and getting a job outside the home and yielding the care of their children to others (it is unclear whether there was any element of coercion in the removal of the children). These women were able to return to or find jobs in fields such as clerical or sales work; a few held managerial and professional positions. Some children were placed in foster care, while others lived with a relative. The researcher reported that a significant proportion of the subjects found a job much easier to handle than raising children and managing a household, and the staff supported the women who made these changes.[57] These therapists were rare in their recognition of the stresses involved in domestic roles and their validation of women who made other choices. Yet even this study illustrates the constraining nature of mid-century gender roles. Although they addressed family and work issues, these social workers did not advocate any social or systemic responses to the difficulties these women faced. Further, this program did not allow for the possibility of dual roles; women could change from housewife to worker, but the program provided no guidance or support for combining those roles.

In fact, alcoholic women themselves seemed to share these assumptions about the importance of motherhood to their identity, which should not be surprising given the central position of motherhood in conventional ideas about female identity, on the one hand, and the emotional significance of family for women, especially women with relatively few choices outside the home, on the other. One alcoholic woman who had had three miscarriages, for example, explained that the "experiences made her feel rather inferior and an incomplete woman."[58] Another woman recalled that she agreed with the advice she received from the psychiatrist she consulted about her excessive drinking: "I did finally go to a psychiatrist and he told me, 'Your only problem is that you don't have children,' and that if I had a baby my drinking would stop. Which, of course, is what I thought too."[59]

While many psychiatrists discussed the effect of women's alcoholism on their children in a relatively detached, abstract manner, viewing (or at least describing) their patients' difficulties as simply more clinical evidence, alcoholic women's own voices, recorded in the case files of several groups of social workers and in Alcoholics Anonymous narratives, relay the anguish they frequently felt over the effects their drinking had on their children. Some alcoholic women, particularly after they had achieved sobriety, recounted stories about their children as a way to show the severity of their alcoholism and perhaps also the magnitude of their recovery. The poignancy and power of these stories came from the shared cultural understanding of the extent to which their actions—impulsive, selfish—deviated from the way in which a mother was supposed to behave. One woman, for example, drank the brandy that a doctor had prescribed for her son. Another, denied access to the family car and money by her husband, robbed her son's piggy bank.

A third went to a "gin mill" instead of to her son's wedding. She explained (after achieving sobriety), "That's the kind of a mother I was."[60]

The physical danger an alcoholic mother could pose to her children appeared often in fictionalized form, as for example in the 1947 film *The Smash-Up*, in which the main character accidentally sets the house on fire, nearly killing herself and her young daughter. In many cases, alcoholic mothers lost custody of their children. Following a divorce, the ex-husband of one alcoholic woman was awarded custody of their child because the mother exposed the child to her excessive drinking.[61] The son of another alcoholic woman was cared for by strangers since the mother was "either drunk, in jail, or in a mental hospital."[62] In yet another case, the children of an alcoholic woman had been placed in foster care; according to a court order, she could have them back only if there were another responsible person in the house, so the wife of another AA member stayed with her for several weeks.[63] The class status and ethnic background of the woman and her family had a significant effect on these issues, as families with more resources—of money, time, and relatives who could provide extra support and childcare—were less likely to come to the attention of social workers. Yet a mother's drinking could disrupt any family, regardless of their circumstances. One woman reported that she felt guilty that she was not able to counsel her children when she was drunk, and many mothers painfully recalled that their behavior when intoxicated had frightened their children. "Nelly," for example, fell out of bed when she was drunk, which made her daughter cry in fear; Nelly herself felt she was unfit to raise her daughter. In addition, a mother's drinking could affect her children's lives outside the family: as a result of their mother's drinking, many children were socially isolated or even ostracized (one researcher noted that alcoholic fathers probably would not even have noticed that their behavior affected their children in this way).[64]

While the necessity of caring for children often interfered with treatment opportunities, many alcoholic women felt that their children provided an incentive for recovery. As "Mrs. L." improved, for instance, she was "pleased that her children regarded her as 'all right' again."[65] Recovery did not always proceed smoothly, however, and the process could be especially difficult and upsetting when children were involved, with guilt and anxiety leading to still more drinking. The son of one alcoholic woman, "Olivia," wrote to her while he was away at school, "for goodness sakes, Mom, don't die a drunkard." Upon receiving this letter, Olivia resolved not to drink again, but she "went only to the next weekend" before taking another drink. In another case, a woman's ex-husband accused her of being an unfit mother; in response, she avoided seeing him or the child and drank more "to forget it." Even getting drunk did not guarantee oblivion, however; some alcoholic women reported alcoholic hallucinations in which they heard their children's voices or voices accusing them of going out drinking and leaving the children at home.[66]

Clearly, motherhood remained a central element in the discourse on women's alcohol consumption. In marked contrast to the scientists and physicians who spearheaded the "race poison" panic of the turn of the century and cast women's drinking as a social problem, however, mid-twentieth-century psychiatrists regarded any maternal deficiencies that alcoholic women displayed as individual, psychological issues. Rather than expressing concern for the fate of the children in these situations, they focused on the ways in which the mother's attitude seemed to indicate her rejection of her proper role and hence her pathology. This shaping of alcoholism as an individual and psychological, not social, problem reflected the orientation and the cultural authority of psychiatry. Following from this interpretation, the solutions were also individual rather than systemic. Even as they identified women's dissatisfaction with domestic roles and the pressures of childrearing as contributing factors in the development of alcoholism, psychiatrists and other medical writers maintained that the answer was not social change but individual adaptation to be achieved through psychotherapy.

"A Futile and Mad Career of Promiscuity and Drunkenness"

In addition to motherhood, sexuality was the other central theme in the literature on alcoholic women, both because of the emphases of psychoanalytic views of personality development and because, for women, drinking and "deviant" sexuality had long been associated. Because of long-standing stereotypes about women's sexual behavior, many experts probably expected to find evidence of promiscuity among some alcoholic women—those whose race, class, or upbringing made them, according to psychiatrists, more likely to engage in deviant sexual behavior, such as prostitutes and other women who were examined in prison settings, African American women, and the occasional actress.[67] By the middle decades of the twentieth century, moreover, added to these assumptions was a new view of the sexuality of the ideal middle-class wife and mother, whose respectability no longer shielded her sexuality from the scrutiny of experts. Historians have described the mid-twentieth-century gender system as neo-Victorian: ideally, as during the nineteenth century, men were to work outside the home while women maintained the domestic sphere. But there was an important difference from the earlier formulation in that the idealized wife and mother was now regarded as a sexualized being, and marriage was supposed to bring sexual fulfillment for both partners. Yet while this new paradigm of "sexual liberalism" brought more freedom for some kinds of sexual expression, it also made possible the increasing regulation and medicalization of the sexuality of all women. While nineteenth-century associations of alcohol and female sexuality had often focused on the image of the prostitute, mid-twentieth-century discourse held that alcoholism in any woman could be linked with a host of sexual problems, often defined in medical terms, including frigidity, promiscuity, and homosexuality.[68]

While women's drinking produced considerable anxiety in some circles, as already demonstrated, moderate recreational drinking as a component of mixed-gender socializing nevertheless became increasingly common among some social groups by the middle decades of the twentieth century. Yet in a culture in which female sexuality could be expressed, but was properly contained only within marriage, the combination of alcohol—with its promise of lowered inhibitions and loss of control—with female sexuality seemed potentially threatening. Even within marriage, drinking habits could cause conflict. Some alcoholic women reported that they had begun drinking at their husband's urging. One, for example, recalled that her husband "taught her to drink and then shamed her as a prude until she drank with him."[69] Even in these relationships, however, the husbands had strict standards that they expected their wives to uphold, criticizing them if they became intoxicated at a party and or if they drank at home alone. One wife began drinking with her husband, and they "frequently got drunk together." But when he found out that she "continued drinking when he was not at home," he "resented" it.[70] Husbands' attitudes toward their wives' problem drinking, of course, varied widely. While one husband did not understand or accept his wife's alcoholism and urged her to drink with him when she was trying to stay "on the wagon," another blamed himself for her condition because she learned to drink only after marrying him.[71] Excessive drinking could be both cause and effect of marital problems: some women reported that they had begun drinking as a result of a husband's infidelity or a divorce, while in other cases couples separated or divorced because of a husband's or wife's drinking. In general, alcoholics had high rates of marital disruption, and rates of separation and divorce were especially high for women alcoholics.[72]

Women's drinking that was not "contained" within marriage could seem even more threatening, and could also be dangerous for women. A number of alcoholic women recounted situations in which they had been subjected to unwanted sexual advances from strangers when they were drunk. While late nineteenth-century discourse used terms like "seduction" to warn of the dangers liquor and sexuality held for women, mid-twentieth-century doctors were more likely to consider such incidents further evidence of these women's pathology. One psychiatrist, for example, blamed an alcoholic woman who had been raped, claiming that a normal woman would have resisted more

and suggesting that she may have received some gratification from the experience since she was "most unattractive physically." He did not blame her
primarily for being drunk, but he maintained that her alcoholism was a
symptom of her underlying psychological and sexual problems, which caused
her to "want" the rape.[73]

While psychiatrists considered homosexuality a central component of
male alcoholism, they afforded the issue much less attention in their discussions of alcoholism in women. Researchers reported few, if any, lesbians
or bisexuals among the alcoholic women they studied.[74] One notable exception was the case of Frances, a twenty-six-year-old alcoholic who was treated
by the psychiatrist Dr. Benjamin Karpman. Frances attributed her alcoholism to fear, explaining that the "'greatest fear of all was that of my homosexuality being found out.'" The psychiatrist described her situation this way:
"Realizing her homosexual tendencies and fearing them, she embarked on
a futile and mad career of promiscuity and drunkenness. When she wasn't
seeking an escape from homosexuality in the embraces of some man, she
was seeking it in alcohol and often she sought it simultaneously in both."[75]
His discussion of her case shows how easily alcoholic and sexual excess could
be linked in the image of the alcoholic woman.

Indeed, psychiatrists' findings about homosexuality and alcoholism
among women had less to do with the behavior or identity of the women
they studied than it did with the assumptions they held about sexuality and
with the gendered and sexual associations of social drinking patterns. Psychoanalysts asserted, for example, that the homosocial nature of men's drinking patterns provided cover for the expression of latent homosexuality among
alcoholic men. Researchers came to contradictory conclusions, however, as
to whether female alcoholics preferred the company of other women or of
men while drinking.[76] While some women drank with female friends, both
at home and in public, and could, therefore, theoretically have been labeled
"latent homosexuals"—and historians have, indeed, documented the existence of a lesbian bar culture during this period[77]—the much more familiar
stereotype about alcoholic women was that they were heterosexually promiscuous. Focused as it was on women's participation with men in what had
previously been male public space, including both the bar and the office, the
anxiety about the perceived increases in women's drinking and alcoholism
further contributed to the preoccupation with women's problematic heterosexual—rather than homosexual—activities. In addition, the censure of alcoholic women's alleged heterosexual promiscuity, often described as of a
piece with their public liquor consumption, conjured the familiar image of
the drunken prostitute and served to enforce the boundaries governing
"proper" sexual and social behavior for women in a way that discussion of

drinking and lesbianism, which was less familiar and could perhaps be more easily dismissed as irrelevant to the majority of women, might not. Interestingly, even the hallucinations alcoholics experienced reflected these assumptions: while alcoholic men frequently heard voices accusing them of being homosexual, alcoholic women were much more likely to be called "prostitute" in their hallucinations.[78]

In fact, the familiar stereotype that alcoholic women were heterosexually promiscuous dominated discussion of alcoholic women's sexuality in various ways. As noted above, any women who were already regarded as deviant because of race or class status were considered especially likely to be promiscuous. Although African American women received very little attention in the alcoholism literature generally, the way they were portrayed reflected assumptions about their sexuality. In one study of fifty alcoholic women, only eight were "colored," but they were disproportionately represented in the group that had "conscious knowledge of sexual relations before puberty." Another study that reinforced and perhaps reflected both racial and gender stereotypes reported that more alcoholic women than alcoholic men were infected with syphilis, and of the women, more black than white women were infected.[79]

Still, it was not just the "deviant" or "public" woman (or the woman who drank in public) whose sexuality was open to scrutiny. As historians have shown, by the middle decades of the twentieth century, even middle-class housewives were expected to be sexual beings, and psychiatrists had extended their authority over formerly private behavior such as the emotional dimensions of marital sexuality. Many psychiatrists labeled the alcoholic women they treated "frigid" (how the therapist came to this conclusion was often unclear). While frigidity might seem more respectable than promiscuity—after all, a housewife who drank all day at home and then failed to respond to her husband's advances was certainly a different image from a bar-hopping working-class woman with multiple sexual partners—to psychiatrists, frigidity and promiscuity were simply different manifestations of sexual deviance. In fact, promiscuity was often interpreted by psychiatrists as an attempt to flee from a homosexual identity (as in the case of Frances) or, more commonly, as an effort to compensate for frigidity. With the addition of alcohol, one woman, even an apparently respectable one, might demonstrate both frigidity and promiscuity. One physician relayed the case of a "young woman, of good family background and fair educational training, married to a bank official, and the mother of three children, who indulged, while under the influence of liquor, in indiscriminate sexualities with strange men; under the same conditions she was rejecting and frigid in her relations with her husband."[80]

THE PREOCCUPATION with gender issues that so influenced American medical and popular thought during the middle decades of the twentieth century thus also shaped the construction of alcoholism. The continued association of alcohol consumption with masculinity provided a language to analyze excessive drinking by both sexes. Psychiatrists defined alcoholism, among both men and women, as an attempt to compensate for psychosexual immaturity. Doctors and social scientists believed that alcoholics, as exemplars of failed gender socialization and consequent identity problems, provided evidence of serious underlying troubles in American society. Yet, while a "feminine" man and a "masculine" woman might seem in these terms to be equally threatening, the specific gendered meanings attached to liquor consumption rendered female alcoholics more problematic than their male counterparts. Alcoholic men might seem effeminate, but at least they were seeking (through their drinking) to recover their masculinity. Alcoholic women's drinking, by contrast, demonstrated a flight from femininity. They could thus be judged failed—rather than self-medicating—women. Psychiatric and popular depictions of alcoholics thus served as cautionary tales regarding the importance of maintaining proper gender boundaries.

The modern alcoholism paradigm was predicated fundamentally on a distinction between moderate drinking, which was normalized, and habitual or excessive drinking, which was medicalized. As such, it claimed universal applicability, framed in terms of science and expressed in ostensibly gender-neutral language. But the line between excess and moderation was not, after all, a simple matter of quantity (or frequency). Women's recreational drinking, in particular, had become more common during the middle decades of the twentieth century—a development that was by no means universally welcomed in American society. The continuing ambivalence regarding excessive, or transgressive, drinking by women functioned to blur the boundary (in both medical and lay discourses) between "alcoholic" women and "drinking" women. As a result, alcoholic women were excluded, both rhetorically and practically, from the disease model of alcoholism, and social *and* pathological drinking by women were interpreted as symptoms of the same social problem—the allegedly increasing "masculinity" of American women. Drinking women who "acted like men" served as a troubling demonstration of the instability of mid-century gender roles that, many Americans claimed, threatened the family and society.

Notes

1. D. Noble, "Psychodynamics of Alcoholism in a Woman," *Psychiatry* 12 (1949): 416.

2. See, for example, Elaine Tyler May, *Homeward Bound: American Families in the Cold War Era* (New York: Basic Books, 1988); John D'Emilio and Estelle B. Freedman, *Intimate Matters: A History of Sexuality in America* (New York: Harper and Row, 1988); Susan M. Hartmann, *The Home Front and Beyond: American Women in the 1940s* (Boston: Twayne, 1982); William H. Chafe, *The American Woman: Her Changing Social, Economic, and Political Roles, 1920–1970* (London: Oxford University Press, 1972); and Maxine L. Margolis, *Mothers and Such: Views of American Women and Why They Changed* (Berkeley: University of California Press, 1984).

3. Catherine Gilbert Murdock, *Domesticating Drink: Women, Men, and Alcohol in America, 1870-1940* (Baltimore: Johns Hopkins University Press, 1998), uses domestic evidence like cookbooks and table-setting guides in creative ways, arguing convincingly that respectable American women did drink in the home during the late nineteenth and early twentieth centuries. But she perhaps overstates the extent to which women's *public* drinking was accepted during Prohibition and the post-Prohibition period. See especially 164–65.

4. L. Sillman, "Chronic Alcoholism," *Journal of Nervous and Mental Disease* 107 (1948): 147.

5. For a classic statement of the "disease model" of alcoholism, see E. M. Jellinek, "Phases of Alcohol Addiction," *Quarterly Journal of Studies on Alcohol* 13 (1952): 673–684. For the philosophy of Alcoholics Anonymous see *Alcoholics Anonymous: The Story of How More Than One Hundred Men Have Recovered from Alcoholism* (New York: World, 1939) and subsequent editions. On the "modern alcoholism movement," see Ronald Roizen, "The American Discovery of Alcoholism, 1933–1939," Ph.D. diss., University of California at Berkeley, 1991, and Bruce Holley Johnson, "The Alcoholism Movement in America: A Study in Cultural Innovation," Ph.D. diss., University of Illinois, 1973. For historical discussion of alcohol consumption patterns, theoretical models of alcoholism, and treatment, see Mark Edward Lender and James Kirby Martin, *Drinking in America: A History* (New York: Free Press, 1987); W. J. Rorabaugh, *The Alcoholic Republic: An American Tradition* (New York: Oxford University Press, 1979); Genevieve M. Ames, "American Beliefs about Alcoholism: Historical Perspectives on the Medical-Moral Controversy," in Linda A. Bennett and Genevieve M. Ames, eds., *The American Experience with Alcohol: Contrasting Cultural Perspectives* (New York: Plenum Press, 1985), 23–39; Mark Edward Lender, "Jellinek's Typology of Alcoholism: Some Historical Antecedents," *Journal of Studies on Alcohol* 40 (1979): 361-373; Harry Gene Levine, "The Discovery of Addiction: Changing Conceptions of Habitual Drunkenness in America," *Journal of Studies on Alcohol* 39 (1978): 143–174; A. E. Wilkerson Jr., "A History of the Concept of Alcoholism as a Disease," D.S.W. diss., University of Pennsylvania, 1966; Edith S. Lisansky Gomberg, "Historical and Political Perspectives: Women and Drug Use," *Journal of Social Issues* 38 (1982): 9–23; and Kaye Middleton Fillmore, "The Epidemiology of Alcohol Use and Abuse among Women: A History of Science Approach," *Bulletin of the Society of Psychologists in Addictive Behaviors* 3, no. 3 (1984): 130–136.

6. For a fascinating discussion of the ways in which psychiatrists remade their discipline and influenced early twentieth-century American culture, see Elizabeth Lunbeck, *The Psychiatric Persuasion: Knowledge, Gender, and Power in Modern America* (Princeton: Princeton University Press, 1994). On psychoanalysis, see Nathan G. Hale Jr., *The Rise*

and Crisis of Psychoanalysis in the United States: Freud and the Americans, 1917–1985 (New York: Oxford University Press, 1995).

7. R. S. Banay, "Cultural Influences in Alcoholism," *Journal of Nervous and Mental Disease* 102 (1945): 265–275; A. Meyerson, "Alcohol: A Study of Social Ambivalence," *Quarterly Journal of Studies on Alcohol* 1 (1940–1941): 13–20; J. P. Shalloo, "Some Cultural Factors in the Etiology of Alcoholism," *Quarterly Journal of Studies on Alcohol* 2 (1941–1942): 464–478. A classic psychoanalytic essay on the relationship between alcoholism and gender and sexuality was published in 1908, appearing in English in 1926: Karl Abraham, "The Psychological Relations between Sexuality and Alcoholism," *International Journal of Psycho-Analysis* 8 (1926): 2–10. A number of American psychiatrists drew on this essay.

8. Banay, "Cultural Influences in Alcoholism," 269.

9. S. Weijl, "Theoretical and Practical Aspects of Psychoanalytic Therapy of Problem Drinkers," *Quarterly Journal of Studies on Alcohol* 5 (1944–1945): 206–208.

10. J. H. Wall, "A Study of Alcoholism in Men," *American Journal of Psychiatry* 92 (1936): 1391.

11. Edward A. Strecker, *Their Mothers' Sons: The Psychiatrist Examines an American Problem* (Philadelphia: Lippincott, 1951), especially the chapter "Mom in a Bottle." Strecker was of course not alone in blaming American mothers for a psychological and social problem; other "experts" blamed mothers for a host of problems, including juvenile delinquency, homosexuality, autism, and schizophrenia. See, for example, Molly Ladd-Taylor and Lauri Umansky, eds., *"Bad" Mothers: The Politics of Blame in Twentieth-Century America* (New York: New York University Press, 1998). For an example of the ways in which psychological theories could dovetail with cultural stereotypes, see the discussion of Irish-American drinking patterns in Richard Stivers, *A Hair of the Dog: Irish Drinking and American Stereotype* (University Park: Pennsylvania State University Press, 1976).

12. R. P. Knight, "The Psychoanalytic Treatment in a Sanatorium of Chronic Addiction to Alcohol," *Journal of the American Medical Association* 111 (15 October 1938): 1444.

13. M. M. Miller, "Treatment of Chronic Alcoholism by Hypnotic Aversion," *Journal of the American Medical Association* 171 (14 November 1959): 167.

14. R. P. Knight, "The Psychodynamics of Chronic Alcoholism," *Journal of Nervous and Mental Diseases* 86 (November 1937): 544; Harold W. Lovell, *Hope and Help for the Alcoholic* (Garden City, N.Y.: Doubleday, 1951), 76; Knight, "The Psychoanalytic Treatment in a Sanatorium of Chronic Addiction to Alcohol," 1444.

15. J. Levine, "The Sexual Adjustment of Alcoholics," *Quarterly Journal of Studies on Alcohol* 16 (1955): 680.

16. Ibid., 679.

17. Banay, "Cultural Influences in Alcoholism," 273.

18. Knight, "The Psychodynamics of Chronic Alcoholism," 545.

19. Weijl, "Theoretical and Practical Aspects of Psychoanalytic Therapy of Problem Drinkers," 202.

20. See John D'Emilio, "The Homosexual Menace: The Politics of Sexuality in Cold War America," in Kathy Peiss and Christina Simmons, eds., *Passion and Power: Sexuality in History* (Philadelphia: Temple University Press, 1989), 226–240.

21. Sillman, "Chronic Alcoholism," 140.

22. C. A. Hecht, R. J. Grine, and S. E. Rothrock, "The Drinking and Dating Habits of 336 College Women in a Coeducational Institution," *Quarterly Journal of Studies on Alcohol* 9 (1948–1949): 252. Prior quotations are from J. W. Riley Jr., C. F. Marden, and

M. Lifshitz, "The Motivational Pattern of Drinking," *Quarterly Journal of Studies on Alcohol* 9 (1948–1949): 353–362.

23. "Lady Lushes on the Loose!" *New York Daily Mirror Sunday Magazine*, 20 December 1944, Oversize Package no. 1, Mann Collection, Syracuse University Archives (hereafter SUA).

24. See, for example, Noel F. Busch, "Lady Tipplers," *Life*, 14 April 1947, 85; "Mrs. Drunkard," *Newsweek*, 8 March 1948, 22–23; "Dressing for the Cocktail Lounge," *Christian Century*, 20 January 1937, 75–77.

25. "Women Nowadays Called 'Hard' Drinkers," *New York Herald-Tribune*, 5 January 1947; "A Growing Liability: The Woman 'Bar Fly,'" *New York Daily Mirror*, 5 January 1948, Oversize Package no. 1, Mann Collection, SUA.

26. F. J. Curran, "Personality Studies in Alcoholic Women," *Journal of Nervous and Mental Disease* 86 (1937): 647; Sillman, "Chronic Alcoholism," 136; D. B. Rotman, "Alcoholism: A Social Disease," *Journal of the American Medical Association* 127 (1945): 566; N. D. C. Lewis, "Personality Factors in Alcoholic Addiction," *Quarterly Journal of Studies on Alcohol* 1 (1940–1941): 33; C. H. Durfee, "Some Practical Observations on the Treatment of Problem Drinkers," *Quarterly Journal of Studies on Alcohol* 7 (1946–1947): 237.

27. Weijl, "Theoretical and Practical Aspects of Psychoanalytic Therapy of Problem Drinkers," 203.

28. "A Growing Liability: The Woman 'Bar Fly.'"

29. "Women Are Drinking Too Much," *Facts*, n.d., Oversize Package no. 1, Mann Collection, SUA.

30. "Why Some Women Should Not Drink," *Cosmopolitan*, n.d., Oversize Package no. 2, Mann Collection, SUA.

31. Marty Mann, "Mrs. Mann Tells of Cheap Bar Life," *Washington, D.C. Times-Herald*, 23 May 1945, Oversize Package no. 1, Mann Collection, SUA.

32. See, for example, Jellinek, "Recent Trends in Alcoholism and in Alcohol Consumption," *Quarterly Journal of Studies on Alcohol* 8 (1947): 1–43; N. Jolliffe, "The Alcoholic Admissions to Bellevue Hospital," *Science*, 27 March 1936, 306–309; F. Lemere, P. O'Hallaren, and M. A. Maxwell, "Sex Ratio of Alcoholic Patients Treated over a 20-Year Period," *Quarterly Journal of Studies on Alcohol* 17 (1956): 437–442; J. V. Lowrie and F. G. Ebaugh, "A Post-Repeal Study of 300 Chronic Alcoholics," *American Journal of Medical Science* 203 (1942): 120–124; and B. Malzberg, "First Admissions with Alcoholic Psychoses in New York State," *Quarterly Journal of Studies on Alcohol* 10 (1949): 461–470.

33. "National Report on Lady Booze Hounds a Cause of Concern," *Mitchell, S.D. Republic*, February 26 [?], Oversize Package no. 1, Mann Collection, SUA. See, for example, "Women Are Drinking Too Much," *Facts;* "Women Who Drink," *Sunday Mirror*, both n.d., Oversize Package no. 3, Mann Collection, SUA.

34. Benjamin Karpman, *The Alcoholic Woman: Case Studies in the Psychodynamics of Alcoholism* (Washington, D.C.: Linacre Press, 1948), vii.

35. H. I. Phillips, "The Sun Dial," *New York Sun*, 27 January 1947, Oversize Package no. 1, Mann Collection, SUA.

36. "Women Who Drink."

37. Twila Florence Fort, "A Preliminary Study of Social Factors in the Alcoholism of Women," M.A. thesis, Texas Christian University, 1949; Dorothy Jean Deex, "A Study of the Housewife Role among Alcoholic Women In-Patients at the Washingtonian Hospital," M.S. thesis, Boston University School of Social Work, 1954. See also Edith S.

Lisansky, "Alcoholism in Women: Social and Psychological Concomitants." *Quarterly Journal of Studies on Alcohol* 18 (1957): 588–623.

38. See, for example, Meyerson, "Alcohol: A Study of Social Ambivalence," 13–20; Shalloo, "Some Cultural Factors in the Etiology of Alcoholism," 464–478.

39. Phillips, "The Sun Dial"; "Lady Lushes on the Loose!"

40. See Lunbeck, *Psychiatric Persuasion*, 69, on the "psychiatry of adjustment" that was applicable to everyone. For an example of a popular polemic on gender written by a psychiatrist, see Ferdinand Lundberg and Marynia F. Farnham, M.D., *Modern Woman: The Lost Sex* (New York: Harper & Brothers, 1947), in which the authors maintain that the "increasing masculinization of women" causes great conflict for women.

41. One study calls the mothers of the alcoholic women in her study "ungiving" and the fathers "ineffectual": B. Rosenbaum, "Married Women Alcoholics at the Washingtonian Hospital," *Quarterly Journal of Studies on Alcohol* 19 (1958): 85–86; Deex, "Study of the Housewife Role," 18, cites a "lack of preparation" for the role of homemaker. See also Karpman, *Alcoholic Woman* ("Case of Elizabeth"); Fort, "Preliminary Study," 169; Curran, "Personality Studies in Alcoholic Women," 649, 656–664; R. J. Van Amberg, "A Study of 50 Women Patients Hospitalized for Alcohol Addiction," *Diseases of the Nervous System* 3–4 (1943): 250; J. H. Wall, "A Study of Alcoholism in Women," *American Journal of Psychiatry* 93 (January 1937): 944; and H. Wortis and L. R. Sillman, eds., "Case Histories of Compulsive Drinkers," *Quarterly Journal of Studies on Alcohol* 6 (1945–1946): 320–321; on the pattern of masculinity, see Sillman, "Chronic Alcoholism," 140–141. Interestingly, medical discourse on infertile women echoed this theme, emphasizing the unconventional childhood behavior of women who sought treatment for infertility; in both cases, the women had somehow "failed" and were outside the mainstream of what a woman's role should be. See Elaine Tyler May, *Barren in the Promised Land: Childless Americans and the Pursuit of Happiness* (New York: Basic Books, 1995), 174.

42. Lisansky, "Alcoholism in Women," 614; see also Wall, "A Study of Alcoholism in Women." Men's reasons for drinking often included vague moods, such as boredom, irritability, or shyness.

43. Joseph Hirsh, *The Problem Drinker* (New York: Duell, Sloan, and Pearce, 1949), 50.

44. Wall, "A Study of Alcoholism in Women," 944.

45. Lisansky, "Alcoholism in Women," 591.

46. C. Landis and J. F. Cushman, eds., "Case Studies of Compulsive Drinkers," *Quarterly Journal of Studies on Alcohol* 6 (1945–1946): 167; Lewis, "Personality Factors in Alcoholic Addiction," 41; Van Amberg, "A Study of 50 Women Patients Hospitalized for Alcohol Addiction," 249; Durfee, "Some Practical Observations," 237–238; Fort, "Preliminary Study," 121, 152; Rosenbaum, "Married Women Alcoholics at the Washingtonian Hospital," 88.

47. Busch, "Lady Tipplers," 85.

48. See, for example, R. Demme, "The Influence of Alcohol upon the Organism of the Child," in Wood's *Medical and Surgical Monographs*, 12 (1891): 225; T. D. Crothers, "Degeneration Common to Alcoholism and Inebriety," *Illinois Medical Journal* 24 (1913): 229–234; F. Lentz, "Alcoholic Heredity," *Quarterly Journal of Inebriety* 10 (1888): 101–106; E. S. Talbot, "Alcohol in Its Relation to Degeneracy," *Journal of the American Medical Association* 48 (1907): 399–401; W. M. Eccles, "The Relation of Alcohol to Physical Deterioration and National Efficiency," *Journal of Inebriety* 30 (1908): 69; A. Gordon, "Pa-

rental Alcoholism as a Factor in the Mental Deficiency of Children," *Journal of Inebriety* 35 (1913): 65; A. H. Arlitt and W. G. Well, "The Effect of Alcohol on Reproductive Tissues," *Journal of Experimental Medicine* 26 (1917): 769–771; H. Hoppe, "Procreation during Intoxication," *Journal of Inebriety* 32 (1910): 105–110; C. R. Stockard, "The Influence of Alcoholism on the Offspring," *Proceedings of the Society for Experimental Biology and Medicine* (1911–12): 71–72; L. M. Maus, "Alcohol and Racial Degeneracy," *Medical Record* 85 (1914): 104; and W. C. Sullivan, "A Note on the Influence of Maternal Inebriety on the Offspring," *Quarterly Journal of Inebriety* 21 (1898): 331–332.

49. Some of the most prominent researchers on alcohol questions, including E. M. Jellinek, dismissed the idea that alcohol damaged germ cells or produced deformities in children. See Moira Plant, *Women, Drinking, and Pregnancy* (London: Tavistock, 1985), 14–15. While Prohibition played a key role in reshaping the research agenda—and con-clusions—regarding the effects of alcohol on reproduction, Philip J. Pauly argues con-vincingly that it was not the only factor. He analyzes a series of experiments performed by biologists during the 1910s and 1920s that generated a "total negativity," rendering the question a non-issue. See his "How Did the Effects of Alcohol on Reproduction Become Scientifically Uninteresting?" *Journal of the History of Biology* 29 (1996): 1–28.

50. "Questions and Answers," *Hygeia* 14 (March 1936): 285. See also T. Swann Har-ding, "Alcohol, Health, Longevity, and Offspring," *American Journal of Pharmacy* 111 (1939): 351–358, and Paul Popenoe, "Heredity and Environment as Related to Alcohol-ism," *Eugenical News* (1946–47): 35–38.

51. "Queries and Minor Notes: Effect of Single Large Alcohol Intake on Fetus," *Journal of the American Medical Association* 120 (1942): 88; "Queries and Minor Notes: Effect of Alcoholism at Time of Conception," *Journal of the American Medical Association* 132 (1946): 419; "Queries and Minor Notes: Smoking and Drinking during Pregnancy," *Journal of the American Medical Association* 154 (1954): 186; "Queries and Minor Notes: Alcoholism and Heredity," *Journal of the American Medical Association* 136 (1948): 849; "Notes and Queries: Alcohol and Pregnancy," *Practitioner* 160 (1948): 73. See also Hirsh, *The Problem Drinker*, 50–51: he maintains that alcohol consumed by the mother is not harmful to the fetus or to the nursing infant. The fact that the attention this issue did receive tended to be in the question and answer sections of medical journals suggests that many practicing physicians—and presumably their patients as well—continued to wonder about whether alcohol did damage offspring, although the predominant medical view was that it did not.

52. H. H. Hart, "Personality Factors in Alcoholism," *Archives of Neurology and Psy-chiatry* 24 (1930): 130; Rosenbaum, "Married Women Alcoholics at the Washingtonian Hospital," 86; I. Wolf, "Alcoholism and Marriage," *Quarterly Journal of Studies on Alcohol* 19 (1958): 511–513; Wortis and Sillman, "Case Histories of Compulsive Drinkers," 310. On hostility toward children: Deex, "Study of the Housewife Role," 55.

53. Wall, "A Study of Alcoholism in Women," 948.

54. Ibid., 947.

55. Deex, "Study of the Housewife Role," 67.

56. Karpman, *Alcoholic Woman*, 231. See Lunbeck, *Psychiatric Persuasion*, 72–74, for a discussion of psychiatrists' "faintly feminist" but inconsistent perspective on issues of gender and sexuality.

57. Deex, "Study of the Housewife Role."

58. Fort, "Preliminary Study," "Victoria," 176.

59. Brett Harvey, *The Fifties: A Women's Oral History* (New York: HarperCollins, 1993), 125–126.

60. *Alcoholics Anonymous: The Story of How Many Thousands of Men and Women Have Recovered from Alcoholism* (New York: Alcoholics Anonymous World Services, Inc., 1955 [New and Revised Edition] hereafter cited as *Alcoholics Anonymous*), 378; Fort, "Preliminary Study," 119; *Alcoholics Anonymous*, 518.

61. *Alcoholics Anonymous*, 409.

62. On alcoholic women being unable to care for their children, see Karpman, *Alcoholic Woman*, 70, 227, and Rosenbaum, "Married Women Alcoholics at the Washingtonian Hospital," 87. (Example is Vera, in Karpman, 227.)

63. *Dr. Bob and the Good Oldtimers* (New York: Alcoholics Anonymous World Services, Inc., 1980), 242–243.

64. Fort, "Preliminary Study," "Nelly," 59, 63; for counseling children, 125.

65. Deex, "Study of the Housewife Role," "Mrs. L.," 86.

66. Fort, "Preliminary Study," "Olivia," 155; "unfit," 210; Curran "Personality Studies in Alcoholic Women," on hallucinations, 654–655.

67. See, for example, Van Amberg, "A Study of 50 Women Patients," 250.

68. See May, *Homeward Bound*, on the sexualized wife and mother and sexual containment; D'Emilio and Freedman, *Intimate Matters*, 241, on "sexual liberalism"; and Lunbeck, *Psychiatric Persuasion*, 308.

69. Fort, "Preliminary Study," 224, also 82, 130.

70. Ibid., 269; Landis and Cushman, "Case Studies," 166–167.

71. Fort, "Preliminary Study," 226, 175.

72. Rosenbaum, "Married Women Alcoholics at the Washingtonian Hospital," 86; Wolf, "Alcoholism and Marriage," 511–513; Fort, "Preliminary Study," 19, 25 (on marriage being an independent and dependent variable in alcoholism, for examples, see 193, 197, 242, 280); Deex, "Study of the Housewife Role," 76, 80; Karpman, *Alcoholic Woman*, 125–126.

73. Karpman, *Alcoholic Woman*, 227.

74. Curran, "Personality Studies in Alcoholic Women," 665, Levine, "The Sexual Adjustment of Alcoholics," 677.

75. Karpman, *Alcoholic Woman*, 128, 137, 141.

76. Hart, "Personality Factors in Alcoholism," 120, compared with Wall, "A Study of Alcoholism in Women," 952.

77. Elizabeth Lapovsky Kennedy and Madeline Davis, "The Reproduction of Butch-Fem Roles: A Social Constructionist Approach," in Peiss and Simmons, eds., *Passion and Power*, 241–256. See also Lillian Faderman, *Odd Girls and Twilight Lovers: A History of Lesbian Life in Twentieth-Century America* (New York: Columbia University Press, 1991).

78. Curran, "Personality Studies in Alcoholic Women," 665. William C. Garvin, "Post Prohibition Alcoholic Psychoses in New York State," *American Journal of Psychiatry* 9 (January 1930): 747.

79. Curran, "Personality Studies in Alcoholic Women," 647, 649, for "conscious knowledge"; L. L. Orestein and W. Goldfarb, "A Note on the Incidence of Syphilis in Alcoholics," *Quarterly Journal of Studies on Alcohol* 1 (1940–1941): 442–443.

80. Banay, "Cultural Influences in Alcoholism," 267. A similar case was reported by Hart, "Personality Factors in Alcoholism," 127. See also Curran, "Personality Studies in Alcoholic Women," 649–650; Levine, "The Sexual Adjustment of Alcoholics," 676–677;

Wall, "A Study of Alcoholism in Women," 944–945; Van Amberg, "A Study of 50 Women Patients," 250; Wortis and Sillman, "Case Histories of Compulsive Drinkers," 322; and K. J. Tillotson and R. Fleming, "Personality and Sociologic Factors in the Prognosis and Treatment of Chronic Alcoholism," *New England Journal of Medicine* 217 (14 October 1937): 613.

Sober Husbands and Supportive Wives

Marital Dramas of Alcoholism in
Post–World War II America

LORI E. ROTSKOFF

IN 1953, THE *Quarterly Journal of Studies on Alcohol* published an article by a Texas social worker titled "Wives of Alcoholics: Four Types Observed in a Family Service Agency."[1] As a family caseworker, Thelma Whalen counseled dozens of women married to alcoholic men—and discovered "striking similarities" among them. Refuting claims that the alcoholic's wife was a helpless victim of circumstance, she contended that women contributed to their husbands' inebriety. "The wife of an alcoholic is not simply the object of mistreatment in a situation which she had no part in creating," Whalen wrote. "Her personality was just as responsible for the making of this marriage as her husband's was; and in the sordid sequence of marital misery which follows, she is not an innocent bystander. She is an active participant in the creation of the problems which ensue."[2] According to Whalen, the typical alcoholic's wife had an alleged need either to punish herself or to control another person; as a result, she selected a passive, irresponsible marriage partner—a man whose personality presumably predisposed him to alcohol abuse. For Whalen, then, alcoholism was a problem entwined in the psychological dynamics between husbands and wives.

Whalen was one of many professionals and lay experts to view alcohol abuse in terms of marital relationships during the post–World War II period. Many psychiatrists, sociologists, social workers, and public health advocates located the problem of alcoholism in the domestic sphere, in the private homes of women and men. Between 1940 and the early 1960s, Whalen's article was one of numerous studies focusing on the wives and marriages of alcoholics. At the same time, Alcoholics Anonymous—a not-for-profit "fellowship" dedicated to the treatment and recovery of compulsive drinkers—created an institutional context for such concerns. From its beginning in 1935, AA encouraged members' spouses to participate informally in the AA program of ritual disclosure, spiritual rebirth, and mutual support. AA's founders believed that family members could play a major role in perpetu-ating—or arresting—an alcoholic's drinking. In 1951, Lois Wilson, the wife of AA co-founder Bill Wilson, officially established the Al-Anon Family Groups, which encouraged wives to follow a twelve-step program similar to the one used by alcoholics themselves.[3] AA and Al-Anon leaders believed that women could help their husbands by creating an emotional and spiritual climate conducive to a life of sobriety.

The ideas of experts and AA leaders were communicated to the wider public through a series of effective public relations campaigns. Alcoholics Anonymous, the Yale Center for Alcohol Studies, and the National Council on Alcoholism (an agency for research and public education) had overlapping memberships and interlocking purposes—forming what some historians have called an "Alcoholism Movement." To heighten awareness about al-coholism and, moreover, to advance the idea that alcoholism was a *disease* rather than a moral failing, the alcoholism movement promoted a new med-icalized vision through the mass media as well as through therapeutic prac-tice.[4] Publishers of scholarly books sold thousands of volumes on the topic, while magazines and newspapers printed scores of articles on the use and abuse of alcohol.[5] While AA spokespersons kept to a relentless schedule of speaking engagements and radio interviews, the fellowship began to enjoy a national reputation as an effective treatment program. Attitudes toward al-coholism were also influenced by popular Hollywood films—including *The Lost Weekend*, which jolted audiences in 1945 with its grim depiction of a would-be novelist's besotted life; and *Come Back, Little Sheba* (1952), which explored the fraying marriage of a hard-drinking, downwardly mobile chi-ropractor and his disillusioned, disheveled wife. Through these various chan-nels, alcoholism gained recognition as a medical, psychological, and social problem.

In this essay I explore scientific and popular discourses of alcoholism in the 1940s and 1950s, focusing on the gendered thinking that informed Amer-icans' understanding and treatment of the disease.[6] Since the eighteenth-century physician Benjamin Rush first described alcohol as an addictive agent, chronic drunkenness has been perceived as a problem primarily af-fecting *men*. The decades surrounding World War II were no exception; in most medical literature during this time, the term "alcoholic" implicitly meant "male alcoholic." One study asserted that "it is fair to specify 'men'" when discussing alcoholism, citing the findings of a Harvard physician that "alcoholic addiction is seven times more prevalent among men than . . . among women."[7] Another sociologist agreed that "excessive drinking is largely a masculine affair."[8] When experts did focus on women, they noted it specifically, highlighting the more unusual status of female alcoholics. This assumption also held sway in AA during its early decades, when a predom-inately male—and largely white middle-class—membership prevailed.[9]

Because postwar discourses on alcoholism were informed by strong as-sumptions of sexual difference, they provide an excellent vantage point from which to explore the construction of gender roles and identities for men and women alike. Discourses on alcoholism both reflected and reshaped ideol-ogies of gender, constituting sites where norms of proper or "healthy" mas-culinity and femininity were produced and redefined. The historian Eliza-beth Lunbeck's analysis of psychiatrists in the 1910s and 1920s applies to later decades as well: "Gender conflict, real and rhetorical, shaped day-to-day practice and colored psychiatrists' and social workers' reflections upon it. It was encoded in the categories that ordered their observations, sometimes overtly . . . and sometimes silently." Lunbeck's study focuses on how mental health experts in the early twentieth century formulated concepts of "normal" manhood and womanhood. In their efforts "to aid the common man and woman to deeper, practical insights into everyday life," psychiatrists created a set of "normalizing judgments" about gender. Later authorities on alco-holism, concerned as they were with pathological deviations from the "nor-mal," nonetheless drew upon, and sometimes redefined, normative gender ideologies.[10]

The topic of the "alcoholic marriage" invites us to consider *gender for-mation* as a dynamic historical process in which both genders are formed and reformed, contested and negotiated in relation to each other.[11] Following Mariana Valverde's suggestion that historians pay more attention to the re-lationships between male and female gender norms, I focus on how profes-sional and lay alcoholism experts reinscribed assumptions about the rights and obligations accorded to husbands and wives by virtue of their sex and marital status. The historian Nancy F. Cott argues that "marriage has been a cardinal—arguably the cardinal—agent of gender formation and has in-stitutionalized gender roles" over the course of American history.[12] As cre-dentialed experts and twelve-step fellowships endeavored to make sober men out of alcoholics, they enlisted women, too, as supporting players in that effort—giving shape to the pathological drinker's complement, the modern figure of the "alcoholic's wife."

Given the gendered assumptions that infused ideas about excessive drink-ing, it is not surprising that alcoholism was linked to wider social concerns about the vitality of family life. If experts viewed overindulgence as a symp-tom of individual illness, such disease, in turn, signaled family pathology. In the aftermath of World War II, millions of Americans—at the behest of educators, advertisers, government officials and producers of popular cul-ture—subscribed to an ascendant domestic ideology which revised traditional familial values for the Cold War era. The dominant ideal of the white middle-class nuclear family was based on strictly divided gender roles: a husband was supposed to provide for his wife and children through his status as breadwinner, while wives worked as homemakers, consumers, and family caretakers. Government and industry harnessed this family ideology to a national effort designed to achieve economic growth and global political supremacy. Indeed, the legendary family of the 1940s and 1950s promised "to fulfill virtually all its members' personal needs through an energized and expressive personal life."[13] But while historians have painted a broad picture of postwar gender ideology, they have only just begun to uncover those conflicts and tensions which belied the family's mythic promise as a site of psychic fulfillment and material well-being. One such example was a husband's alcoholism, viewed as evidence of a "diseased" or "dysfunctional" family in which both spouses deviated from prevailing sex-role prescriptions.

Finally, the gendered dimensions of postwar alcoholism discourses should be related to the cultural history of temperance reform prior to national Prohibition (and Repeal) in the 1920s and 1930s. Mid-century social workers and spiritual mentors were hardly the first Americans to stress the harmful effects of alcohol upon family and nation. From the prayerful petitioners of the Woman's Christian Temperance Union to the loquacious lobbyists of the Anti-Saloon League, nineteenth- and early-twentieth-century temperance crusaders told heartbreaking stories of drunken husbands and forlorn wives. Reformers had long used sentimental narratives of marital misery and the symbol of the "drunkard's wife" in their quest to outlaw intoxicating beverages. By attacking "Demon Rum" as the root cause of domestic disintegration, temperance advocates imagined drink-induced family problems as social problems that required social and legal solutions. In the moralistic imagination of dry reformers, the drunkard was scorned, while the drunkard's wife was pitied, often seen as "ruined" beyond help.[14] After Repeal, however, the "normalization" of social drinking in the dominant culture led to a shift in how Americans viewed the effects of habitual drunkenness upon marriage.[15] In the post-Repeal therapeutic imagination, both husband and wife were players in a complex emotional drama—with each spouse exhorted to follow a different gendered script leading to "recovery" from domestic trauma.

Diagnosing the Alcoholic Marriage

Social workers were among the first professionals to regard the wives of alcoholics as a subject of research and treatment in their own right. In the 1930s, American psychiatrists published clinical studies of alcoholism, but they focused primarily on the "neuroses" of alcoholics themselves. In the mid-1940s, however, family caseworkers began to stress importance of treating the "alcoholic marriage," not just the alcoholic individual. In large part, this stemmed from a division of labor within the mental health professions that emerged in the 1910s and 1920s—as social workers, psychiatrists, and nurses engendered a "team approach" to therapeutic care. In contrast to the male-dominated realm of psychiatry, social work was generally a female profession.[16] When married couples sought treatment at clinics and hospitals, alcoholics were usually assigned to psychiatrists for evaluation and therapy, while spouses were "almost always assigned to a social worker."[17] Because female caseworkers spent the most time observing alcoholics' wives, they produced a large share of scholarship on the subject. Indirectly, however, psychiatrists wielded influence over psychiatric social workers, who had been utilizing psychoanalytic theory and methods for several decades.

One early study, published in the *Quarterly Journal of Studies on Alcohol* in 1945, painted a composite picture of twenty women married to alcoholic men. In the course of her work at an alcoholic treatment hospital in Boston, caseworker Gladys Price discovered a pattern in which a "basically insecure" woman had expected her husband to be a "strong, dependable, responsible person." But as her husband failed to manage the family's responsibilities, she felt increasingly unloved, resentful, and aggressive. In her disappointment, the wife "strove to prove that [her husband] was inadequate in order to justify his seeming lack of love for her." Eventually, she began to use his drinking as a way to "prove him and keep him inadequate," thus impeding his recovery.[18] Another writer offered a similar description of the alcoholic's wife: "She knocks the props from under him at all turns, seemingly needing to keep him ineffectual so that she feels relatively strong and has external justification for her hostile impulses. Thus she keeps the lid on her own inadequacies and conflicts."[19] Some psychiatrists agreed that wives had a vested interest in maintaining their husbands' incompetence; as one asserted, the typical wife "unconsciously, because of her own needs, seems to encourage her husband's alcoholism."[20]

Thelma Whalen offered a more nuanced account of the alcoholic spouse's psyche. Assuming that all wives chose husbands who would meet their underlying psychological needs, Whalen classified alcoholics' wives into four personality types with alliterative names: "Suffering Susan," "Controlling Catherine," "Wavering Winnifred," and "Punitive Polly." Suffering Susan, whose dominant characteristic was her need to punish herself, selected a mate "who was obviously so troublesome that her need to be miserable would always be gratified." Wavering Winnifred was motivated by insecurity and self-doubt; Winnifred "always chooses a husband who, to her, is weak, who she thinks 'needs her' and would therefore be unlikely to leave her." Such a woman cannot form "relationships with adequate, self-sufficient individuals because . . . she doubts her ability to hold their interest." "Controlling Catherine" and "Punitive Polly" played a less passive role in perpetuating their husbands' alcoholism. Catherine selected a spouse whom she could dominate and control; marriage to "a more adequate man" would be too threatening for her. To overcome economic insecurity, the controlling wife usually took a job herself—and gripped the family purse strings with an iron hand. Even more destructive was "Polly the Punisher," whose "relationship to her husband resembles that of a boa constrictor to a rabbit." Rather than allow her husband gradually to relinquish his marital duties, as Suffering Susan had done, Polly instinctively performed them herself—and emasculated him in the process. As Whalen explained, "Polly's husband always seems to her to be limited in some way in his essential masculinity. If he did not, she would have never married him." Polly spurned housework and child care—allowing her alcoholic spouse to indulge his "submissive and passive impulses" while she earned the family income. Polly treated her husband like a helpless child; their relationship was "similar to that of . . . a scolding but indulgent mother—and her very small boy."[21]

Psychiatric social workers perceived the wife's behavior as a sign of neurosis that existed prior to the onset of the partner's alcohol abuse.[22] All of Whalen's characterizations, for example, described the woman's decision to marry an ineffectual, alcoholic man as a sign of psychopathology in the woman *herself*. Implicit in Whalen's study is the assumption that "normal" women would seek strong, independent, self-sufficient husbands. In her view, "proper" husbands were responsible, dominant, and able to provide financially for their families; "normal" wives, in turn, had the good sense and psychological health to select them in the first place. But rather than emphasize the alcoholic's deviant behavior or his failure to conform to masculine norms, Whalen faulted wives for their misguided, destructive marital choices. Presumably, alcoholic men were not only sick themselves, they also suffered from the neuroses of their insecure or aggressive wives.

Whalen's depiction of Polly the Punisher is especially significant as a manifestation of postwar gender anxiety. During the 1940s and 1950s, social scientists, psychiatrists, and educators focused a great deal of attention on sex-role identification. Most experts believed that gender-appropriate behavior was not biologically determined; rather, it needed to be learned—just like a role in a high school play. Guided by the assumptions of functionalist sociology and psychoanalysis, experts aimed to discover the kind of child care that would produce children with "correct" sex-role characteristics. One parenting manual summarized sex-role theory with the simple question and answer, "What kind of parents are best for children? Manly men and womanly women." Two parental role models, one masculine and one feminine, were required to instill "healthy" sex-role identification in children.[23] But things did not always progress so smoothly. Boys, for example, could develop an identity crisis resulting from an overidentification with the female/mother figure. Indeed, some writers lamented a full-blown crisis of masculinity, whereby boys failed to develop the maturity and independence of "true manhood." The most damned offenders in this affair were American mothers and wives, who received their most scornful indictment in Philip Wylie's best-selling book *Generation of Vipers*. Wylie was infamous for his scathing attack on "Momism," which accused women of dominating their husbands and sons through their narcissistic, parasitic natures. According to Wylie, women sapped men of their masculinity in order to usurp power for themselves.[24] Behind this hatred and fear of women was a growing sense that men had somehow lost dominance and power in American society. At the heart of Wylie's vituperation, one scholar has noted, lay "the unappealing image of a new feminized man who had lost his traditional manhood, a demasculinized husband and father unable to hold his own in the face of restless and demanding women."[25]

A decade after *Generation of Vipers* first shocked American readers, "Momism" resurfaced in the psychological literature on alcoholism. Whalen's depiction of "Punitive Polly" matched Wylie's caricature in substance, if not in prose style. Polly was a power-hungry, domineering woman who preyed on her husband's weakness. She treated her spouse the way Wylie's "Mom" treated her son, smothering him with a crippling combination of indulgence and aggression. In the throes of such a dysfunctional marriage, the alcoholic man found that "drinking was often the only way he [could] find to assert himself." But such behavior only served to keep him submissive and passive in the face of his wife, "who is willing for him to have almost anything he wants—except his manhood."[26] In the context of postwar gender prescriptions for "manly men" and "womanly women," many experts viewed alcoholic husbands as failed men, their wives as deficient women. For social workers like Thelma Whalen, marital dramas of alcoholism played out when women—as well as men—failed to follow the proper psychological script.

While some experts regarded the wife's behavior as a result of her own preexisting neurosis, other researchers relied on a different conceptual framework. The sociologist Joan K. Jackson, who became a leading authority by the late 1950s, eschewed psychoanalytic determinism and viewed "the behavior of the wife . . . as a reaction to a cumulative crisis in which the wife experiences progressively more stress." Whereas Whalen viewed women in terms of fixed personality traits, Jackson argued that they passed through a series of chronological stages *in response to* their husbands' recurrent drinking. Previous writers had portrayed wives' behavior as "dysfunctional" because they viewed family dynamics in terms of what was best for the husband. But "when viewed in the context of the rest of the family," Jackson maintained, wives' behavior "might appear to be functional" instead. She believed that wives aimed not to punish their spouses, but to restore stability to their troubled families.[27] Describing seven stages of adjustment to alcoholism, she credited wives for "reorganizing" their households in the face of adversity. If Whalen's account sounded a shrill, anxious note in the postwar discourse on gender-role confusion, Jackson offered a more moderate, measured depiction of marital malaise.

Yet despite Jackson's sympathetic stance toward wives, the language of sex-role identification permeated her work as well. Though her analytical approach was more subtle than Whalen's, Jackson too provided a highly gendered account of women's behavior that reinforced the ideology of sexual difference inherent in psychiatric thought. Throughout her study, Jackson interpreted the family's response to alcoholism in terms of how the wife perceived her own "performance" *as a woman* in a domestic setting.[28] As Jackson described the first stage of family adjustment, "both husband and wife . . . try to play their conceptions of the ideal husband and wife roles . . . and create the illusion of a 'perfect' marriage." At this point, the wife desperately wants her family to be "normal." When her husband is sober, she defers to him "in his role as head of the household," and expects the children to obey their father. As her husband continues to drink, however, she resents him for not living up to her expectations. Yet rather than dwell on his behavior, the typical wife blames herself: "On her part, the wife begins to feel that she is a failure, that she has been unable to fulfill the major cultural obligations of a wife to meet her husband's needs. With her increasing isolation, her sense of worth derives almost entirely from her roles as wife and mother. Each failure to help her husband gnaws away at her sense of adequacy as a person." According to Jackson, the husband's deviance from prescribed norms causes the wife to question her own gender-role performance. With alcoholism comes frustration, hostility, and sometimes violence on the wife's part. Unable to maintain the calm, submissive demeanor of the ideal wife, she feels "intense shame at having deviated so far from what she conceives to be 'the behavior of a normal woman.'"[29] During these early stages, Jackson points out, the wife most resembles Whalen's "Wavering Winnifred" stereotype.

Over time, however, necessity requires that she act more like "Controlling Catherine." Realizing that she cannot rely on her husband, the typical spouse "begins to ease [him] out of his family roles . . . and assumes the husband and father roles" herself. In addition to her homemaking duties, she must also perform the manly roles of breadwinner, decision-maker, and discipliner of the children. As she "takes over control of the family with some degree of success," the alcoholic husband becomes "less and less necessary to the ongoing activity" of the household. Unlike Whalen, Jackson did not criticize women for taking over their husbands' duties, but rather complimented them for bringing "some semblance of order and stability" to their homes. In her view, such behavior allowed women to regain self-worth and to distance themselves emotionally from their husbands' destructive behavior.[30] But while Jackson rejected Whalen's rigid classification of women into four personality types—favoring instead a model of familial change over time—she borrowed Whalen's terminology and thus reinforced the same gendered assumptions.

Despite her empathy, Jackson viewed the family's sex-role inversion as a temporary compromise in trying circumstances. Her support of conventional gender norms is most evident in her discussion of family rehabilitation. While admitting that divorce was unavoidable at times, she applauded marital reconciliation when the husband achieved sobriety. In the last stage of domestic adjustment—the "recovery and reorganization of the whole family"—the wife needed to readjust to life with a sober partner. And on this matter, Jackson and Whalen generally agreed. "Counseling with Polly," Whalen wrote, "is always directed toward helping her reduce her controls and achieve satisfaction from more womanly and motherly roles." Whalen thus steered patients toward conformity to feminine ideals. Jackson, too, accepted the idea that sober men would reclaim their familial authority: at first, the wife "feels an unwillingness to let control slip from her hands." But at the same time "she realizes that reinstatement of her husband in his family roles is necessary to his sobriety."[31] Here Jackson supported the view that an alcoholic's recovery depended upon his wife's behavior. Both authors also assumed that men—if sober—were entitled to resume their dominant status. Another social worker was even more emphatic on this point: "The overly managing wife may be encouraged . . . to relax control as her husband starts to take over responsibilities which are clearly his own, and she may learn . . . to enjoy the new family situation which results."[32] Whether they saw wives' assertiveness as a response to crisis or as a sign of neurosis, the experts agreed on one thing: a "healthy" family required allegiance to traditional sex-role prescriptions.[33]

For the alcoholic's wife, then, the battle did not end with the husband's sobriety. Showing sensitivity to the wives' situation, Jackson explained that it was difficult for them to adjust to a new status quo and trust their husbands again. If performing her partner's duties had come to seem natural—or at least necessary—to a wife, how could she relearn her "proper" role? Significantly, experts conceptualized the wife's "readjustment" within the same therapeutic paradigm used for alcoholics themselves. If alcoholism was a "family illness," then the whole family would need to convalesce. If wives suffered from their husband's alcoholism, then they, too, would need to recover. But how could wives "recover" from their predicament? And what, exactly, did they need to recover from? In their scholarly articles, professional experts offered few answers to these questions. At least in their published writings, social workers and sociologists spent more time describing and diagnosing the alcoholic marriage than offering concrete suggestions for therapy.

When they did discuss therapeutic recommendations, social workers focused on helping women to express their feelings in more "constructive" ways. Typically, Gladys Price stressed that wives "stop mothering" their alcoholic husbands so the men had more incentive to take responsibility for themselves. Another goal was to dampen the wife's anger and hostility toward her spouse—so she could understand the emotional dynamics underlying the disease rather than harbor resentment.[34] And as discussed above, social workers also exhorted women to relinquish control of their husbands' "rightful" duties.

By the 1950s, however, several writers advocated treatment methods and programs that went beyond general description. Some psychiatrists and social workers published studies of professional group therapy with alcoholics' wives—a practice that became increasingly popular after World War II.[35] Moreover, Joan Jackson had a telling suggestion for wives: Alcoholics Anonymous. Toward the end of her article, Jackson opined that AA had much to offer both alcoholics and their spouses. "If the husband becomes sober through Alcoholics Anonymous and the wife participates actively in the groups open to her," she wrote, "the thoughts of what is happening to her, to her husband and to her family will be verbalized and interpreted within the framework of the [AA] philosophy and the situation will probably be more tolerable and more easily worked out." Jackson was familiar with AA— for in addition to interviewing wives of hospitalized alcoholics, she based her study on women members of the AA Auxiliary in Seattle.[36] And while she praised AA and Al-Anon as a means to successful family "reorganization," AA leaders, in turn, promoted Jackson's ideas in their national newsletter, *The Grapevine*.[37]

To understand how women learned to play out the final acts in their marital dramas of alcoholism, we need to move from the pages of scholarly journals to those of *The Grapevine* and other texts written by AA and Al-

Anon members. As important as professional experts were in regulating clinical practice, AA and Al-Anon were arguably more influential in shaping public opinion and experience.[38] During the 1950s, these fellowships enjoyed remarkable growth: AA's membership doubled from 100,000 in 1951 to over 200,000 in 1957, while the number of spouses' groups nationwide increased from eighty-seven in 1951 to 1,500 by 1963. The history of AA and Al-Anon reveals much about the gender ideologies embedded in alcoholism treatment. Moreover, it offers a virtually unexplored window into the norms and experiences that have defined marriage and family life for alcoholic and non-alcoholic families alike.

Rehabilitating the Alcoholic Marriage: Al-Anon and the Culture of Sobriety

In 1955, Alcoholics Anonymous commemorated its twenty-year anniversary at a national convention in St. Louis, where co-founder Bill Wilson declared that AA had officially "come of age." The convention was a defining moment for the fellowship, attracting over five thousand members from all fifty states, Canada, and several foreign countries. Most convention participants were men—but many came to St. Louis with their wives, who participated in panel discussions of their own. These meetings were officially sponsored by the Al-Anon Family Groups, an auxiliary or "sister" organization of local chapters throughout the country. According to Bill Wilson, the Al-Anon sessions were "among the biggest eye-openers" of the convention. During his keynote speech, Bill praised his wife Lois for coordinating Al-Anon at the national level. Proudly, he proclaimed that "AA is for the whole family," promising that adherence to AA philosophy could "do wonders for domestic relations." Soon after the conference, he even boasted that AA's divorce rate was "among the lowest in the whole world."[39]

Though Al-Anon was not officially organized until the early 1950s, the founders and members of AA had emphasized marriage and family since the fellowship's founding in 1935. In lectures and in print, Bill spoke warmly about the roles played by both Lois and Anne Smith, the wife of AA's other co-founder Robert Smith (known as "Dr. Bob"). When Bill and Dr. Bob first met at the Smiths' house in Akron, Ohio—the meeting that would later be defined as AA's formative moment—Anne provided good cheer and gracious hospitality while the fellow alcoholics talked about their problems. Though Lois herself was not present at this initial meeting (she was back at the Wilsons' home in New York), from the beginning both co-founders viewed their lives, their alcoholism, and their AA experience in a familial context. As AA expanded beyond the founders' home states of Ohio and

New York, the spouses of new members were encouraged to attend meetings and to socialize with other AA families. As early as 1940, AA wives began to meet on their own, helping each other with the common problems they faced. Though spouses were not officially AA members, women formed quasi-independent groups in their own communities throughout the 1940s. With names like "Non-AA," "AA Auxiliary," and "The Triple-A's," these groups affirmed their own identity within the larger social organization of AA itself.[40]

AA's first major publication, *Alcoholics Anonymous* (commonly known as the "Big Book") made explicit reference to alcoholics' family life. First printed in 1939, the book outlined the group's principles and demonstrated what alcoholics could hope to achieve by following them. Although the Big Book was published anonymously, the first half was actually written by Bill himself. The first chapter, titled "Bill's Story," established the use of autobiography as a means to narrate the history and ideology of AA, and invited members to tell their own stories as the cornerstone of the therapeutic process. The second half, edited by Bill, included twenty-nine brief autobiographical sketches. With one exception, all the personal stories were told from a man's perspective—revealing Bill's assumption that men would comprise the primary readership. Two chapters, though, addressed family members; one, titled "To Wives," was ostensibly narrated by several "wives of Alcoholics Anonymous." At the start of the chapter, the male narrator "introduces" the female narrators and offers a rationale for the discussion that follows: "With few exceptions, our book thus far has spoken of men. But what we have said applies quite as much to women. . . . But for every man who drinks others are involved. . . . Among us are wives, relatives, and friends whose problem has been solved, as well as some who have not yet found a happy solution. We want the wives of Alcoholics Anonymous to address the wives of men who drink too much. What they say will apply to nearly everyone bound by ties of blood or affection to an alcoholic."[41]

But although the "To Wives" chapter claims to be narrated by women, Lois Wilson's memoirs reveal that Bill actually wrote the chapter. Originally, Lois wanted to write it, as well as the following one, titled "The Family Afterward." But Bill believed that the first part of book should all be written in the same style. After Bill died, Lois admitted to feeling hurt by this, yet she deferred to her husband's editorial control.[42] Thus, to a great extent, the Big Book reflected *male* AA members' (and especially Bill Wilson's) ideas about wives' roles. But wives were quick to voice their own ideas and opinions—in letters to the *Grapevine*; in talks given at meetings; and eventually, in the pages of their own national newsletter, *The Family Forum*. In many cases, the wives' writings sound remarkably similar to Bill's chapters in the

Big Book. Indeed, given the overlapping beliefs and rituals of the two fellowships, it is not always easy to discern where the voices of male alcoholics end and those of female spouses begin. Sometimes, Al-Anon members expressed resistance to the ideas of male AA members (including their own husbands)—but in general, they recorded their views within an organizational context that originated within, and received continuing support from, AA itself.

The Big Book offered female readers a systematic plan for coping with their husbands' alcoholism. The purpose was twofold: first, to enlist wives' support of their husbands' involvement in the AA program; and second, to persuade women that their *own* emotional, psychological, and spiritual well-being required adherence to AA principles. Indeed, the first goal (support of a husband's sobriety) was figured as dependent upon the second (the wife's personal immersion in the AA way of life). AA's founders disseminated these ideas not only through the Big Book, but also through other publications, at local meetings, and at public speaking engagements.

Underlying AA's familial ideology was the assumption, shared by other experts, that the alcoholic's wife was "sick" herself. In 1948, the *Grapevine* published a letter from a Phoenix housewife titled "Your Wife May Be Sick, Too." The anonymous writer, who proudly identified herself as "an AA wife," wrote that "it seldom occurs to a new [sober] man that his wife is just as sick mentally, physically and emotionally as he is. His disease has a definite name and treatment. . . . The wife's maladjustment is a little more difficult to name and treat." Testing her own skills of diagnosis, the writer stated that the alcoholic's wife is "a bundle of screaming nerves" and "definitely is a neurotic as a result of what she has been through over the years." Earlier that year, the *Grapevine* published a similar letter arguing that the wife "is probably a pretty sick person, too, and helping her get rid of some of her complexes and neuroses will help her husband put his best foot forward faster." Other wives, viewing alcoholism in a metaphorical sense, argued that the disease afflicted all members of a family—not just the drinker himself. One female writer claimed that "alcoholic thinking" affects everyone in a household: "The family is just as intoxicated as the victim," she wrote. "It takes longer to get the family sober—but sober we all must be."[43]

What did this writer mean when she suggested that wives, too, had been intoxicated? If other family members had not literally been drunk, what would it mean for them to "get sober"? Bill Wilson offered an intriguing challenge to the AA spouse: "You can have more than alcoholic sobriety in your own family; you can have *emotional sobriety*, too. Even if the rest of the family . . . hasn't yet found stability, you can still have yours. And your own emotional sobriety often can hasten the happy day of change for them."[44] If literal sobriety is the goal for people who have overconsumed alcohol to dangerous extremes, the phrase "emotional sobriety" suggests a person who has "overindulged" in unsound, excessive emotions. If the literal alcoholic's illness stems from unhealthy, uncontrolled drinking, the metaphorical alcoholic's neurosis presumably stems from unhealthy, uncontrolled feeling. In large part, the twelve-step program centered on controlling and changing one's emotional responses to the environment and to other people. In essence, what AA and Al-Anon offered wives was a program of emotion management—one that identified certain patterns of thought and feeling as "unhealthy," while extolling other emotions as salubrious to the self and family alike.[45]

In published writings and personal correspondence, AA wives described their emotional reactions to alcoholic men. In the narrative persona of an AA spouse, Bill Wilson wrote that "we wives found that . . . we were afflicted with pride, self-pity, vanity, and all the things which go to make up the self-centered person."[46] In the *Grapevine*, one San Francisco wife confessed that she had "fairly swarmed with faults and deficiencies, prejudices, notions, neuroses, crooked thinking, cockeyed emotions, rampaging interior conflicts . . . and doubt and suspicion."[47] Another woman believed that her "emotionalism" mixed with her husband's liquor to create "an explosive cocktail" that threw the entire family "into absolute chaos."[48] Perhaps the most profound description of feeling-as-affliction was offered by Lois Wilson. Speaking for all alcoholics' wives, Lois described her reaction to Bill's drinking as a dangerous exercise in emotional intemperance: "Either we tried running things with too high a hand, weighted ourselves down with . . . guilt for another's drinking, tried too hard to stop it, or we soothed deeply hurt feelings with luxurious baths of self-pity—none of it good. In our own way, though not as obviously, we were just as excessive as our compulsive drinkers were. . . . Indulgence in hot anger, violent reproach, neurotic frustration, our attempt to retreat as completely as possible to avoid embarrassment or shame, was exactly as uncontrolled as our partners' drinking. Whether we acknowledged it or not, ours was a disease too—*a mental disorder we'd let ourselves fall into*" (emphasis added).[49] After their husbands stopped drinking—and as a result of their own involvement in AA—these women viewed their previous emotions as impulsive and destructive in their own right. Though Lois acknowledged her years of heartache and fear due to Bill's drinking, in retrospect she characterized her anger and resentment as excessive and self-indulgent.

These quotations provide telling clues about how women conceptualized their roles as wives, and how they viewed the social and emotional contract of marriage. AA leaders depicted the typical alcoholic home as a "battleground" in which the wife faced financial insecurity, emotional neglect, lone-liness, and sometimes violence. "How could men who loved their wives and children be so unthinking, so callous, so cruel?" asked the Big Book. Lois, for her part, devoted many pages in her autobiography to her years of self-sacrifice and despair—professing her undying love for a man whose alco-holism prevented him from fulfilling the promises entailed by their marital bond. Like social workers and psychiatrists at the time, Lois and other AA wives recognized alcoholic men's failure as husbands. And on the one hand, they acknowledged that wives would feel disappointed and resentful. But by characterizing wives' reactions as a "mental disorder" that they "let them-selves fall into," Lois suggested that they had wittingly engaged in destructive behavior just as their husbands had continued to "take chances" with alcohol. Though she viewed her feelings as a response to her husband's drinking, Lois nonetheless blamed herself for "falling into" an "unhealthy" reaction. Evidently, these women measured their reactions against an implicit standard of behavior and found themselves deficient. Though their husbands had reneged on their own marital responsibilities, many AA wives faulted them-selves for defying the emotional prescriptions that marital convention seemed to require of them.

What, then, were the emotional prescriptions, the "feeling rules" that AA endorsed for wives?[50] According to AA literature, the wife's first task lay in suppressing negative emotions. Though alcoholism had rendered her home a "battle-ground," the AA wife would need to act more like a peace keeper. As the Big Book counseled, "The first principle of success is that you should never be angry. Even though your husband becomes unbearable, and you have to leave him temporarily, you should, if you can, go without rancor. Patience and good temper are most necessary."[51] In an article about the AA auxiliary in Long Beach, California, a journalist described AA wives as "gal-lant women" who endured years of marital misery—but who no longer per-mitted "their natural fear and worry to show through their shining shields of hope." With AA's help, he explained, wives learned to project an image of "courage and confidence."[52] Thus, while a woman might "naturally" be worried or angry because of her spouse's drinking, it was her wifely duty to restrain those emotions, shielding them from view.

Not just marital harmony, but a husband's very sobriety depended on a woman's emotional restraint. For a man in the early stages of recovery, a wife's pessimism or "negative attitude" could spell disaster. According to the Big Book, a wife must never nag or condemn her husband for his behavior.[53] If a wife wanted to see herself as a warrior of sorts, the proper enemy was not her husband, but her husband's alcoholism. In 1945, a wife from Mont-pelier, Vermont, submitted a "Credo for an AA Wife" to the *Grapevine*, which encouraged wives to make the following pledge: "I believe that my husband is still the very human man I married and I will not expect him to do a complete about-face of character and personality, giving up all the little . . . faults that sometimes annoy me. . . . He will continue to gain . . . positive qualities that make a pleasing personality, . . . and I must never let my acceptance of this fact become humdrum . . . but offer frequent encouragement, stimulation and appreciation to arm him for his daily battle." Furthermore, she exhorted the AA wife to "maintain constant vigil" over her habits so as to "keep pace with the growth" of her recovering husband.[54] Depicting the alcoholic as an emotionally fragile person who could "go off the wagon" at the slightest provocation, this writer urged fellow wives to orient their thoughts and actions around the psychological needs of their husbands.

Not surprisingly, perhaps, the Big Book also encouraged this attitude, explaining that if a man "gets the idea that [his wife is] a nag or a killjoy," he might even "use that as an excuse to drink some more." The AA wife needed to be constantly "on guard not to embarrass or harm [her] husband." The impulse to criticize or express resentment could develop into a "great thundercloud of dispute," erupting into a "family dissension" of "deadly hazard to an alcoholic." It was the wife's task to "carry the burden of . . . keeping [conflict] under control." While the Big Book conceded that spouses could have "an honest difference of opinion," it nonetheless cautioned wives to "be careful not to disagree in a resentful or critical spirit." The AA spouse thus learned to differentiate between what she actually felt and what she "should" feel; between her inner, "natural" emotions and those she should reveal to others.[55]

According to AA ideology, a man's sobriety required a reformulated emotional contract between husband and wife. An alcoholic could face the arduous task of staying sober if his wife visibly affirmed and supported his efforts. A sober alcoholic would no longer "be so unthinking, so callous, so cruel" if his wife suppressed her resentment for past injustices. But while husband and wife each struggled to establish this new equilibrium, the work of emotion management was not evenly divided by gender. Indeed, the conditional nature of the above scenarios suggests that women bore the brunt of responsibility for ensuring marital success. The exhortations for wives to "maintain constant vigil" and "carry the burden" of diffusing conflict suggest that it was primarily the *wife's* job to ensure an auspicious emotional climate at home. One 1948 contributor to the *Grapevine* blatantly inscribed such gender distinctions: "An AA wife makes her home as pleasant as possible. She gives her family the stability and security it has lacked perhaps for years. The financial security is the husband's responsibility—but the emotional security is the wife's."[56] The task of maintaining sobriety required great psychological effort—and many men found a "payoff" for their efforts in a more harmonious marriage. But the emotional labor of marital cooperation fell disproportionately to wives.

And from the language women used to describe their efforts, it was a demanding, laborious job indeed. Several scholars have noted that the emotional obligations of family life are tied to the gendered division of labor in the household; historically women have performed the work of "feeling management" more than men. Arlie Hochschild describes the private realm as a kind of emotional gift exchange in which women—lacking power, authority, and material resources—"make a resource out of feeling and offer it to men as a gift in return for the more material resources they lack." Especially among middle-class couples, she argues, women "tend to manage feeling more because in general they depend on men for money, and one of the various ways of repaying their debt is to do extra emotion work—*especially emotion work that affirms, enhances, and celebrates the well-being and status of others* (original emphasis)."[57] This theoretical framework sheds light on the workings of AA and Al-Anon: as the recovering husband regained authority and his privileged role as breadwinner, the wife expanded her efforts to affirm, enhance, and celebrate his new, sober status. In exchange for her partner's "gift" of sobriety (and the material and psychic benefits it afforded), the wife increasingly oriented herself around her husband's needs.

The wife's emotion management also extended to her feelings about AA itself. AA publications admitted that wives often viewed AA in a negative light, especially at the beginning. Some women resented the amount of time their husbands spent attending AA meetings, talking with fellow members, and visiting alcoholics at hospitals. In the ostensible collective voice of AA spouses, the Big Book addressed wives on this matter directly:

> You may become jealous of the attention he bestows on other people, especially alcoholics. You have been starving for his companionship, yet he spends long hours helping other men and their families. You feel he should now be yours. The fact is that he should work with other people to maintain his own sobriety. Sometimes he will be so interested that he becomes really neglectful. Your house is filled with strangers. You may not like some of them. He gets stirred up about their problems, but not all about yours. It will do little good if you point that out and urge more attention for yourself. We find it a real mistake to dampen his enthusiasm for alcoholic work. You should join in his efforts as much as you possibly can.[58]

Ironically, while drink had once severed men's connection to hearth and home, now the recovery process threatened to distance men from their wives.

The above passage speaks volumes about AA's exhortations to members to devote time and effort to its therapeutic program. AA's strategy was to welcome wives into the fold as well, to make the fellowship itself into a family affair.

The ideal "AA wife" supported the social activities of the fellowship. Both before and after Al-Anon was officially founded, spouses' groups performed tangible services for AA members—serving homemade cookies at meetings; making and pouring coffee; planning pot-luck suppers and barbecues; decorating bulletin boards; and cleaning up after meetings. Recalling the earliest years of the fellowship in Dr. Bob's home city of Akron, one AA publication described the wives' group as a "non-alcoholic kitchen brigade" that "was allowed to wash dishes, make coffee, organize picnics, and things like that."[59] In a 1951 *Grapevine* article, Bill Wilson even honored the women for their "wifely dispensations of good cheer" which "smoothed the way and so lightened [the alcoholics'] burden of doubt."[60] Certainly, many wives took such tasks for granted—and found them an enjoyable way to socialize with other members. In any case, the gendered dimensions of these activities, which naturalized the wife's role as a supportive helpmate, dovetailed with the advice of professional experts for wives to resume, and even relish, their "proper" domestic orientation.

Some wives, however, resisted the AA program—and occasionally AA publications gave voice to their (often temporary) resentment. One anonymous wife urged fellow *Grapevine* readers to "guard against complacency" in their attitudes. Too many wives, she observed, complained that AA meetings were boring, the seats too hard, the people too dull. She countered that "the non-alcoholic wife's job . . . was to adjust [herself] happily and safely" to the changes that AA brought. In her view, the best way to prevent apathy was to embrace other wives with "warmth, hope and comfort."[61] Lois Wilson, for her part, went through a time when she resented Bill's work with other alcoholics. Her memoirs reveal that because she had not been able to cure Bill of his alcoholism, she resented the fact that others had done so. She was also "jealous of his new-found friends."[62] Another *Grapevine* contributor had even stronger negative feelings about AA. "When my husband first joined AA," she wrote, "it seemed as if he were being taken further away from me than ever. And by perfect strangers, too. . . . He was getting something out of his new associations—I was left out in the cold." Envious of the "sympathetic understanding" her husband was giving to fellow inebriates, she asked bitterly, "Why shouldn't I, who had borne the brunt in the past, rate a little of that commodity?" Defining "sympathetic understanding" as a "commodity," this writer referred to the faltering emotional economy of her alcoholic marriage; in her view, compassion was a scarce resource better spent within marriage than squandered on a group of AA "strangers."[63]

But like Lois, this wife eventually came to see AA in a positive light: not only would it ensure her husband's sobriety, it would provide a better life for herself as well. As she began to focus on her own character flaws rather than her husband's, she viewed AA as a means of personal and spiritual growth. "The sympathetic understanding, which I thought lacking . . . had been there all the time," she realized. Instead of seeking support from her husband alone, this woman turned to AA itself as a source of psychological well-being. As her *Grapevine* letter suggests, many wives turned to the AA and Al-Anon "family" to fulfill their emotional needs when the nuclear family fell short. As another contributor wrote, "friendship within her own sex is as important to a woman as are the bonds between men."[64] Just as former drinkers turned to one another for mutual support and camaraderie, so too could their wives benefit from fellowship. Alcoholism had made life lonely for men *and* women; AA and Al-Anon aimed to help both spouses overcome isolation, filling the emotional "holes" that remained in an alcoholic marriage.

Thousands of women accepted the fellowships' prescriptions for familial sobriety. Although the wives of AA and Al-Anon subscribed to a mutual-help program different from the psychoanalytic therapies pursued in hospitals and clinics, they embraced the notion that their own actions had affected (and would continue to affect) the drinking (or nondrinking) behavior of their partners. I am not arguing that Al-Anon members uncritically accepted either the ideas of the experts or the fellowship's rituals. In the 1950s, Al-Anon was a diverse constellation of local auxiliaries; it was not monolithic, and the extent to which individual groups or members embraced, ignored, or resisted the fellowship's program of emotion management certainly varied. Although the prescriptive content and laudatory tone of Al-Anon's textual evidence sheds little light on such resistance, we can assume that despite allegiance to a common set of principles, some members expressed ideas that were alternative or even subversive by the standards of the time. In general, however, AA and Al-Anon encouraged women to circumscribe their lives within a therapeutic and spiritual worldview, to contain their threatening emotions within the confines of a conventional family system.[65] Given how the fellowships imagined the emotional and material economy of marriage, they further depoliticized alcohol consumption—shifting the locus of responsibility for domestic trouble from the broader society inward to the nuclear family itself.

But while most AA and Al-Anon wives in the postwar era conformed to a family structure in which men were the heads of households and women were the subordinate helpmates, they believed they were transforming their lives in a powerful and empowering way. On the one hand, evidence suggests that Al-Anon accommodated married women to an inegalitarian social order: in a society which discouraged divorce and maintained formidable barriers to women's economic independence, Al-Anon could function to placate women who remained in less-than-desirable marriages (even after their husbands were sober.)[66] But we must also recognize the cultural constraints within which wives attempted to solve problems as *they* perceived them. For many, Al-Anon provided an outlet for gender-based identification (through support from other women) and in the process helped make their marriages seem more satisfactory. While hardly radical in its approach to domestic unhappiness—especially when compared to the feminist movement that had yet to emerge—Al-Anon should not simply be dismissed for failing to re-politicize alcohol-related problems or for recasting women's social, political, and economic subordination as a matter of psychological and spiritual suffering. In retrospect, we can evaluate the social consequences of the alcoholism movement while assessing mid-century participants on their own terms.

Conclusion: Alcoholism and the Cultural History of Marriage

How can we situate the history of alcoholism within a broader social and cultural context? What can we learn by exploring the role of gender in the creation of the alcoholic identities? In conclusion, I offer some speculative—and necessarily brief—arguments about the historical significance of the "alcoholic marriage" in mid-twentieth-century America.[67]

For one thing, therapeutic discourses on the alcoholic family help us better to understand the implications of a larger shift in attitudes toward habitual drunkenness. In the period before the enactment and repeal of Prohibition—that is, before the popular image of the depraved "drunkard" metamorphosed into the diseased "alcoholic"—temperance reformers blamed drinkers, drink manufacturers, and sellers for harming families and society at large. But as the historical sociologist Ron Roizen argues in his essay in this volume, the dissemination of the disease concept of alcoholism after Repeal absolved the drinker of much of the social harm he inflicted on others and encouraged society to avail the drinker of its ever-expanding therapeutic resources. In addition to engendering a more tolerant attitude toward drinking in American society, Roizen points out, the decriminalization of the liquor traffic bore social and economic implications for the alcohol industry and the addiction treatment professions. Yet as we have seen, new ideas about alcoholism also affected attitudes toward nonalcoholic spouses and influenced the treatment they received. As alcoholic men were viewed as the deserving recipients of benevolent treatment rather than social opprobrium, their wives, too, became objects of therapeutic scrutiny and practice. But so too did experts enlist wives in efforts to enhance their spouses' recoveries. No longer simply pitied, or used as a symbol to initiate social and legal reform, the postwar alcoholic's wife was pressured to orient herself around her husband's needs.

By the immediate postwar era, the culture of sobriety had begun to acquire the status of "common sense." More families accepted the idea that sobriety demanded a profound psychological adjustment between husband and wife. Perhaps the alcoholism movement enjoyed success because it meshed so well with other developments in American social and cultural life. Indeed, the very notion of personal "adjustment" calls for further consideration. Experts and AA members discussed the nonalcoholic wife's task in terms of "adjustment": first, adjustment to a husband's progressive disease; and later, re-adjustment to the new status quo of sobriety. But it was not just families of alcoholics who perceived life as a matter of environmental "adjustment"; indeed, this concept applied to all Americans facing the challenges of re-construction after World War II. In her history of psychology and public policy, Ellen Herman notes that the legislation known as the G.I. Bill was formally titled the Servicemen's Readjustment Act of 1944—as if to ac-knowledge that the social strains of "unemployment, housing shortages, ra-cial conflict, and the dawn of the nuclear age all tested the mental and emotional stamina of soldiers and citizens fatigued by years of war." National and world events led to increased affluence and geopolitical supremacy dur-ing the 1950s, but these trends were accompanied by anxieties suggesting "irrationality and madness lurking just beneath the thin veneer of a civilized social order." As people struggled to cope with the stresses of everyday life, psychological authorities gained newfound prominence. After 1945, Herman points out, "work associated with helping people adjust and cope constituted *the* popular reputation of psychological expertise during an era when the psychotherapeutic enterprise became, literally, a growth industry."[68]

Moreover, the quest for psychological health was inextricably tied to fam-ily relationships. As Elaine Tyler May writes, "the therapeutic approach that gained momentum during these years was geared toward helping people feel better about their place in the world, rather than changing it. It offered private and personal solutions to social problems. The family was the arena in which that adaptation was expected to occur; the home was the environ-ment in which people could feel good about themselves."[69] The emotional adjustment of men and women became an urgent issue throughout the na-tion, as sixteen million war veterans returned to the United States after a period of great social fragmentation. Experts fretted about the "problem" of the returning veteran and how best to reintegrate him into society after years of sacrifice and disruption. Susan Hartmann argues that experts viewed the home, and veterans' relationships with women, as the linchpin of men's satisfactory adjustment. They enlisted women to ensure men's morale, urging families to "do more adjusting to the veteran than the veteran to the family." Articles filled women's magazines, exhorting women to privilege men's feelings and prerogatives before their own. In assigning women the task of smoothing men's reintegration (even if it entailed self-abnegation), such writings exemplified a "larger trend in popular psychology and sociology . . . which saw women as the cause and/or potential redeemers of a deteriorating society."[70]

In this context, it is clear that a gender-based analysis allows for a more complete understanding of alcoholism in the postwar era. Alcoholism experts participated in a larger effort to establish the terms of social and emotional exchange within marriage. If the "typical" American family during the war years was bereft of masculine influence, the "typical" alcoholic family of the postwar years was similarly disadvantaged—not by the exigencies of war, but by the effects of disease. The gendered thinking that infused notions of marital duty and entitlement for "normal" couples also informed Americans' views of "problem" families. Given the threats the wartime social order posed to conventional family values, authorities developed allegedly therapeutic sanctions against deviance from sex-role prescriptions. Armed with a renewed conception of alcoholism as a disease, scientific and lay experts viewed deviation from cultural norms as a cause of bodily and mental illness.

Finally, an exploration of alcoholism's gendered history contributes to recent efforts by scholars to probe beneath the saccharine image of the postwar "Leave It to Beaver" family. Of course, the stereotype of the white middle-class consumer family was a prescription—not a description of how most Americans actually lived. But historians have often misunderstood this dominant family ideology; by adopting wholesale Betty Friedan's account of postwar values in her *Feminine Mystique* (1963), many studies ignore the ambiguities and internal contradictions inherent in postwar domesticity.[71] Countering Friedan's depiction of the "happy housewife" in popular culture, historians have shown that marriage counselors voiced a "discourse of discontent" which betrayed women's unhappiness even as it proclaimed the virtue of traditional female roles. In magazine articles read by millions, marriage experts urged women to scrutinize their domestic relations and strive for self-fulfillment at home. But at the same time, they admitted that many women were frustrated, lonely, or even miserable—a consequence, to be sure, of the inherent tension between the self-fulfillment and self-effacement their prescriptions required.[72] Paradoxically, while experts molded Americans into "well-adjusted" families, they conceded that family life remained fraught with problems. Despite the image of the happy family, an undercurrent of anxiety ran through postwar domestic culture.

And what situation embodied familial discontent more than alcoholism? As we have seen, experts documented the domestic "failure" of both spouses in an alcoholic marriage. AA invited members to look unflinchingly into the familial abyss, admitting that life with an alcoholic was no glib episode on a television sit-com. Yet underlying AA's philosophy, and perhaps its appeal, lay the possibility that the "pathology" of alcoholic marriage was not so unusual after all. As one *Grapevine* contributor, advising sober readers not to expect "domestic bliss" immediately, suggested: "Sometimes [sobriety] requires that husband and wife get to know each other all over again. . . . Fewer cases of post-drinking domestic upsets would occur if husbands and wives could realize that the need for continuing readjustment is very natural. As a matter of fact, domestic bliss is rarely something that comes automatically, with or without a drinking problem. More often it [must] be compromised for and guarded vigilantly at all times, in so-called 'normal' families. So why doesn't the same hold true for us? We're almost as screwy as normal people!"[73] With humor and irony, this writer reassured readers that so-called normal families were just as prone to domestic discord as alcoholic ones. In so doing, he spoke to the psychic toll that marital conventions exacted of all Americans who conformed to them.

We still have much to learn about the cultural history of marriage in the twentieth century. In her recent work on the connections between marriage as a private and public institution, Nancy F. Cott notes that marriage always reinforces or reshapes the gendered public order; it "operates as a systematic public sanction, enforcing privileges along with obligations."[74] While Cott stresses the role of marriage in the creation of public policy and citizenship, we must also pay attention to the emotional economy of marriage as a site of gender formation and cultural regulation. Because alcoholism so thoroughly destabilized the delicate balance of rights and responsibilities within postwar couples, it allows us to reconstruct gendered norms in illuminating detail. Although alcoholic beverages became a widely accepted feature of the American recreational landscape in the post-Repeal, post–World War II era, the addictive potential of alcohol meant that for some individuals, drinking was not merely part of a placid suburban lifestyle—but rather a destructive force that could shatter the very foundations of familial stability. Given the nation's deep psychological investment in marriage as a bedrock of tranquility and social order, it is apt that alcoholism's deleterious effects would increasingly be measured in familial, and especially marital, terms. In large part, the cultural construction of the "recovering" alcoholic marriage—comprised of sober husbands and supportive wives—gained public acceptance because it reflected and reshaped familiar values in American society at large.

Notes

1. Thelma Whalen, "Wives of Alcoholics: Four Types Observed in a Family Service Agency," *Quarterly Journal of Studies on Alcohol* 14, no. 4 (1953): 632–640; subsequently referred to as *QJSA*.

2. Ibid., 634.

3. The twelve steps begin with an admission that one is powerless over alcohol and that one's life has become unmanageable. (In Al-Anon, one admits to being powerless over an *alcoholic*.) The next two steps express belief in a Higher Power greater than oneself, and confirm one's decision to turn one's will over to the care of God as one personally understands Him. Steps three though ten entail admitting one's shortcomings and character defects, asking one's Higher Power to remove those shortcomings, making amends to other people one has harmed, and continuing to take a personal moral inventory. The eleventh step focuses on the need for prayer and meditation, and the twelfth step exhorts members to carry the AA or Al-Anon message to others. For the verbatim text of the Twelve Steps see *Alcoholics Anonymous*, 3rd ed. (New York: Alcoholics Anonymous World Services, Inc., 1976).

4. While the notion that alcohol addiction is a disease did not originate in the twentieth century, until the 1930s most social observers cast habitual drunkenness primarily in moral terms. Between the 1940 and 1960s, however, experts began to break down some of the moral stigma attached to drinking, favoring instead a "scientific" or medical view that defined the chronic drunkard as the victim of a physiological or psychological aberration. See Bruce Holley Johnson, "The Alcoholism Movement in America: A Study in Cultural Innovation," Ph.D. diss. University of Illinois, 1973, 233–234. For an overview of the popularization of the disease concept, see Jack S. Blocker, *American Temperance Movements: Cycles of Reform* (Boston, Twayne, 1989), 139–161. Since the 1960s, other scholars have challenged the disease concept of addiction; see, for example, Stanton Peele, *The Diseasing of America: Addiction Treatment Out of Control* (Lexington, Mass.: Lexington Books, 1989). My aim as a historian is not to assess the "truth" or social effects of the disease concept, but to explore how it gained hegemony and how it influenced and reflected other developments in American cultural life.

5. See, for example, Francis Sill Wickware, "Liquor," *Life*, 27 May 1946), 66–77; "What Makes an Alcoholic," *Newsweek*, 19 April, 1948, 98–99; and "Problem Drinking," *Time* 31 January, 1949, 54.

6. This essay explores writings by social workers and sociologists as well as material published by Alcoholics Anonymous and Al-Anon in the 1940s and 1950s. My book, titled *Love on the Rocks: Men, Women, and Alcohol in Post–World War II America* (Chapel Hill: University of North Carolina Press, 2002), investigates a wider range of documents and films from the 1910s through the early 1960s.

7. These quotes by psychiatrist Abraham Myerson were cited in *Science News Letter: A Weekly Summary of Current Science*, 13 January 1945, 22.

8. Selden D. Bacon, "Excessive Drinking and the Family," *Alcohol, Science and Society: Twenty-Nine Lectures with Discussions as Given at the Yale Summer School of Alcohol Studies* (New Haven: Quarterly Journal of Studies on Alcohol, 1945), 227.

9. For at least twenty to thirty years, the vast majority of AA members were men. On the fellowship's "masculinist" origins see Blocker, *American Temperance Movements*, 142–43; Elayne Rapping: *The Culture of Recovery: Making Sense of the Self-Help Movement in Women's Lives* (Boston: Beacon Press, 1996), 70–74; and Rotskoff, *Love on the Rocks*, chap. 3. For an excellent study of women and alcoholism see Michelle Lee McClellan, "Lady Lushes: Women Alcoholics and American Society, 1880–1960," Ph.D. diss., Stanford University, 2000.

10. Elizabeth Lunbeck, *The Psychiatric Persuasion: Knowledge, Gender, and Power in Modern America* (Princeton: Princeton University Press, 1994), 1–6; 46–48. On gender as a category of historical interpretation, see Joan W. Scott, "Gender, a Useful Category of Analysis," in her *Gender and the Politics of History* (New York: Columbia University Press, 1988), and Scott, "Deconstructing Equality-versus-Difference: Of, the Uses of Post-structuralist Theory for Feminism," *Feminist Studies* 14 (Spring 1988); Teresa de Lauretis, "The Technology of Gender," in her *Alice Doesn't: Feminism, Semiotics, Cinema* (Bloomington: Indiana University Press, 1984); and Gail Bederman, *Manliness and Civilization: A Cultural History of Gender and Race in the United States, 1880–1917* (Chicago: University of Chicago Press, 1995), 7–10.

11. Mariana Valverde's "Comment" in "Dialogue: Gender History/Women's History: Is Feminist Scholarship Losing Its Critical Edge?," *Journal of Women's History* 5 (Spring 1993): 123.

12. Nancy F. Cott, "Giving Character to Our Whole Civil Polity: Marriage and the Public Order in the Late Nineteenth Century," in Linda K. Kerber et al., *U.S. History as Women's History: New Feminist Essays* (Chapel Hill: University of North Carolina Press, 1995), 111.

13. Elaine Tyler May, *Homeward Bound: American Families in the Cold War Era* (New York: Basic Books, 1988), xxii. On postwar familial ideology, see also Wendy Kozol, *Life's America: Family and Nation in Postwar Photo-journalism* (Philadelphia: Temple University Press, 1994); and Stephanie Coontz, *The Way We Never Were: American Families and the Nostalgia Trap* (New York: Basic Books, 1992).

14. On the discursive history of the "drunkard's wife," see Robert C. Binkley, *Responsible Drinking: A Discreet Inquiry and a Modest Proposal* (New York: Vanguard Press, 1930), 134; and Elizabeth Pleck, *Domestic Tyranny: The Making of Social Policy against Family Violence from Colonial Times to the Present* (New York: Oxford University Press, 1987), 49–66. On the gendered politics of temperance reform, see Barbara Epstein, *The Politics of Domesticity: Women, Evangelism, and Temperance in Nineteenth-Century America* (Middletown, Conn.: Wesleyan University Press, 1981); Ruth Bordin, *Women and Temperance: The Quest for Power and Liberty, 1873–1900* (Philadelphia: Temple University Press, 1981); and Catherine Gilbert Murdock, *Domesticating Drink: Women, Men, and Alcohol in America, 1870–1940* (Baltimore: Johns Hopkins University Press, 1998).

15. Repeal symbolized a major shift in cultural values and behavior—eclipsing the dry worldview equating moral respectability and civic responsibility with abstinence from drink. On the "normalization" of social drinking, see John Burnham, *Bad Habits: Drinking, Smoking, Taking Drugs, Gambling, Sexual Misbehavior, and Swearing in American History* (New York: New York University Press, 1993), 10–22; 64–76.

16. Nancy J. Tomes, "The Rise of the Mental Health Professions in the United States, 1900–1970," unpublished manuscript, in author's possession.

17. Gladys M. Price, "Why I Want a Professional Social Worker on My Clinic Staff," *Selected Papers from the Sixth Annual Meeting of the National States' Conference on Alcoholism* (Portland, Ore., 1956), 27–31.

18. Gladys M. Price, "A Study of the Wives of Twenty Alcoholics," *QJSA* 5, no. 4 (March 1945): 623.

19. M. H. Boggs, "The Rise of Social Work in the Treatment of Inebriates," *QJSA* 4, no. 4 (March 1944): 557–567.

20. Samuel Futterman, "Personality Trends in Wives of Alcoholics," *Journal of Psychiatric Social Work* 23 (1953): 37–41.

21. Whalen, "Wives of Alcoholics," 632–640.

22. Margaret B. Bailey, "Alcoholism and Marriage: A Review of Research and Professional Literature," *QJSA*, 22, no. 1 (March 1961): 81–94.

23. The child-rearing book cited is Dr. David Goodman, *A Parent's Guide to the Emotional Needs of Children* (New York: Hawthorne Books, 1959), 246. See also Barbara Ehrenreich and Deirdre English, *For Her Own Good: 150 Years of the Experts' Advice to Women* (London: Pluto Press, 1979), 235–250; Wini Breines, *Young, White, and Miserable: Growing Up Female in the Fifties* (Boston: Beacon Press, 1992); and Robert Griswold, *Fatherhood in America: A History* (New York: Basic Books, 1993).

24. Philip Wylie, *Generation of Vipers* (New York: Holt, Rinehart and Winston, 1942), 184–204. There is no evidence that alcoholism experts read Wylie's book, but the cultural phenomenon of "Momism" was pervasive in the postwar period, striking a nerve among producers of popular culture. Most experts were exposed to anxious representations of female dominance and masculine weakness even if they did not read Wylie himself.

25. Breines, *Young, White, and Miserable*, 28, 44.

26. Whalen, "Wives of Alcoholics," 640.

27. Joan K. Jackson, "The Adjustment of the Family to the Crisis of Alcoholism," *QJSA*, 15, no. 4 (December 1954): 562–586.

28. No doubt, Jackson came to this interpretation in part because the women she observed described their situation in strikingly gendered terms *themselves*. Jackson's aim was to record the thoughts and behavior of actual women—not to offer her own abstract theory. But as with any social scientific study, the researcher's own assumptions influence the resulting interpretation. Sociological studies reveal much about the beliefs and actions of people in the past—but only as they were filtered through the interpretive lens of the observer.

29. Ibid., 567–575. All quotations are taken from Jackson's article in the *Quarterly Journal of Studies on Alcohol*, but it is worth pointing out that she published similar studies in various books and journals, including a special issue on alcoholism in the *Annals of the American Academy of Political and Social Sciences* 315 (January 1958): 90–98; *Marriage and Family Living* 18 (1956): 361–369; and D. J. Pittman and C. R. Snyder, eds., *Society, Culture, and Drinking Patterns* (New York: Wiley, 1962).

30. Jackson, "Adjustment of the Family," 575–582.

31. Ibid., 569–577, and Whalen, "Wives of Alcoholics," 641.

32. Jean V. Sapir, "Social Work and Alcoholism," *Annals of the American Academy of Political and Social Sciences* 315 (January 1958): 125–132.

33. For a useful overview of postwar family sociology, see Breines, *Young, White, and Miserable*, 25–46.

34. Price, "Why I Want a Professional Social Worker," 27–31.

35. In 1956, for example, a group of psychiatrists published an article titled "Group Therapy of Alcoholics with Concurrent Group Meetings of Their Wives," *QJSA* 17 (1956): 655–670. As historian Hillel Schwartz points out, group therapy actually began as a form of marriage counseling in the 1930s; it mushroomed during World War II due to a shortage of trained therapists for distressed soldiers. After the war, it was applied to a broader range of psychological problems, including alcoholism and other addictive behaviors. See Hillel Schwartz, *Never Satisfied: A Cultural History of Diets, Fantasies, and Fat* (New York: Free Press, 1986), 202–206.

36. Although the spouses' groups acquired the name "Al-Anon Family Groups" in 1951, many local groups continued to use their earlier names, including Seattle's "Auxiliary."

37. *Grapevine*, 12, nor 5 (October 1955).

38. I do not mean to inscribe a rigid separation between professional/medical authorities and the lay experts of AA and Al-Anon. There was much cross-fertilization of ideas among physicians, social workers, AA founders, and public health advocates. Many individuals were involved in several institutions, including research centers, hospitals, the National Council on Alcoholism, and AA. It is not my purpose to uncover the various linkages and divisions among these organizations, or to compare the relative cultural authority wielded by AA vs. other agencies. In any case, most Americans were probably unaware of these connections.

39. *Alcoholics Anonymous Comes of Age* (New York: Harper and Brothers, 1957), 32–34; 42–47; 97–98. From here on I often refer to Bill and Lois Wilson by their first names only, in part because it is simpler, but also because it reflects the way they presented themselves to the public—anonymously, as "Lois" and "Bill W."

40. For a general history of Al-Anon written from the perspective of organization itself, see *First Steps: Al-Anon . . . Thirty-Five Years of Beginnings* (New York: Al-Anon Family Group Headquarters, 1986).

41. *Alcoholics Anonymous: The Story of How Many Thousands of Men and Women Have Recovered from Alcoholism* (New York: Works Publishing, 1946), 117.

42. *Lois Remembers: Memoirs of the Co-Founder of Al-Anon and the Wife of the Co-Founder of Alcoholics Anonymous* (New York: Al-Anon, 1979), 114.

43. *Grapevine*, 5, no.7 (December 1948); *Grapevine*, 4, no. 11 (April 1948); and *Grapevine*, 5, no. 9 (February 1949). Each of these letters was written by a female spouse. Before Al-Anon launched a newsletter of its own, the *Grapevine* provided a limited outlet for wives to voice their opinions. That the editors of AA's newsletter printed their letters suggests their support of the wives' views (although it is impossible to know what letters they elected *not* to publish).

44. *Alcoholics Anonymous Comes of Age*, 34.

45. I borrow the term "emotion management" from the sociologist Arlie Hochschild, who offers a compelling theory about the ways in which people create an observable display of feeling through bodily display and verbal communication. In her definition, emotion management (or "emotion work") "requires one to induce or suppress feeling in order to sustain the outward countenance that produces the proper state of mind in others." In a given cultural context, the private realm of marriage and family life is governed by "feeling rules" which prescribe the terms of emotional exchange. Feeling rules establish a system of entitlements and obligations that defines what people expect to give and receive in their personal relationships. In this light, the family is seen quietly

to impose *emotional obligations* upon its members. Social roles, including those of husband and wife, not only entail prescriptions for activities like housework or money-making; they also establish rules for what emotional responses people think they owe others, or deserve to receive themselves. *See The Managed Heart: Commercialization of Human Feeling* (Berkeley: University of California Press, 1983), 1–75.

46. *Alcoholics Anonymous*, 129–30.

47. *Grapevine*, 4, no. 7 (December 1947).

48. Anonymous letter, "Al-Anon" file, Alcoholics Anonymous archives, New York City.

49. Undated Al-Anon memorandum by Lois Wilson, reprinted in *First Steps*, 13.

50. As Hochschild points out, the goals of psychologists and many institutions (including hospitals, schools, and churches) often entail influencing how people feel: "In times of uncertainty, the expert rises to prominence. Authorities on how a situation ought to be viewed are also authorities on how we should feel. . . . In the matter of what to feel, the social bottom usually looks for guidance to the social top. Authority carries with it a certain mandate over feeling rules" (*Managed Heart*, 75). As a fellowship of lay experts whose authority derived from personal experience, AA strove to promote sobriety in part by schooling participants in specific techniques of emotion management.

51. *Alcoholics Anonymous*, 124.

52. *Long Beach, California Press-Telegram*, 8 January 1950, Press Clippings Scrapbook, Alcoholics Anonymous Archives, New York City.

53. *Alcoholics Anonymous*, 132.

54. *Grapevine*, 1, no. 12 (May 1945).

55. *Alcoholics Anonymous*, 131. It is worth underscoring the prescriptive nature of these writings, especially the Big Book. As he acted as an anonymous advocate for other (usually male) alcoholics, Bill's exhortations here were obviously self-serving. Yet while Lois did not actually write these words, she greatly influenced Bill's ideas about wives' emotions. His prescription of the ideal wife—a model of "patience, tolerance, understanding, and love"—was an accurate description of Lois herself. Lois, through her own actions and character, helped shape her husband's prescriptions (which eventually influenced millions of subsequent readers.)

56. *Grapevine*, 5, no. 7 (December 1948).

57. Hochschild, *Managed Heart* 162–65. On other aspects of women's emotion work, see Micaela di Leonardo, "The Female World of Cards and Holidays: Women, Families, and the Work of Kinship," *Signs: Journal of Women, Culture and Society* 12 (Spring 1987): 440–453.

58. *Alcoholics Anonymous*, 133.

59. Undated memorandum, File 9.4, Al-Anon Archives, Virginia Beach, Va. Other documents in the Al-Anon archives discuss women's activities along these lines. One pamphlet printed by the Denver auxiliary in 1951 explained that members "scrubbed the floors when needed, washed the windows, washed the cups and spoons, cleaned the ash trays, furnished the cream and sugar, and did any other chore that came within the scope of need." Pamphlet titled "The Family Group of Alcoholics Anonymous," File D 1.6.

60. *Grapevine* 8, no. 6 (November 1951).

61. *Grapevine* 3, no. 6 (November 1946).

62. *Lois Remembers*, 98–99.

63. *Grapevine* 4, no. 11 (April 1948). There is more evidence of wives' criticism and even rejection of AA in the postwar period, but it helps to mine sources *not* produced by

the fellowships. In *The Cured Alcoholic: New Concepts in Alcoholism Treatment and Research* (New York: John Day, 1964), for example, AA critic Arthur Cain wrote that while most wives accepted their husbands' participation in AA, some confessed "that eating, sleeping, and talking AA twenty-four hours a day is almost worse than having an alcoholic husband." One Ohio wife explained that her husband had become a "religious fanatic"; she viewed his AA membership as a "terrible mistake" and found it difficult to support his efforts. (67; 95–96).

64. *Grapevine*, 3, no. 7 (December 1946).

65. For a perceptive discussion of these themes, see also the feminist psychologist Janice Haaken's brief historical analysis of Al-Anon in the 1950s, "From Al-Anon to ACOA: Codependence and the Reconstruction of Caregiving," *Signs: Journal of Women in Culture and Society* 18:2 (1993): 321–345.

66. Ibid. Al-Anon did not have an "official" position regarding divorce. In fact, when wives wrote to the national headquarters of Al-Anon in the 1950s, volunteers mailed out a form letter stating that the decision to separate or divorce was a "personal decision" that each woman must make herself. However, Al-Anon's general tendency in its early decades was to encourage marital reconciliation. Indeed, Lois Wilson exemplified the loyal wife who "stayed by her husband's side."

67. For a fuller discussion see Rotskoff, *Love on the Rocks*, 228–242.

68. Ellen Herman, *The Romance of American Psychology: Political Culture in the Age of Experts* (Berkeley: University of California Press, 1995), 1–15; 238–241.

69. May, *Homeward Bound*, 14.

70. Susan M. Hartmann, "Prescriptions for Penelope: Literature on Women's Obligations to Returning World War II Veterans," *Women's Studies* 5 (1978): 223–239.

71. Joanne Meyerowitz, ed., *Not June Cleaver: Women and Gender in Postwar America, 1945–1960* (Philadelphia: Temple University Press, 1994), especially the editor's introduction and her essay titled "Beyond the Feminine Mystique: A Reassessment of Postwar Mass Culture," 229–262.

72. Eva Moskowitz, "'It's Good to Blow Your Top': Women's Magazines and a Discourse of Discontent, 1945–1965," *Journal of Women's History* 8, no. 3 (Fall 1996): 66–98.

73. *Grapevine*, 3, no. 5 (October 1946).

74. Cott, "Giving Character to Our Whole Civil Polity," 107–110, 121.

III

Psychotropics, Psychedelics, and Cigarettes

No One Listened to Imipramine

NICHOLAS WEISS, M.D.

IN JULY 1997, Eli Lilly released its first "direct to consumer" advertisements for Prozac. Run in twenty-three popular magazines, including *Newsweek, Marie Claire, U.S. News and World Report,* and *Entertainment Weekly,* these were the first advertisements for prescription psychotropic medications shown directly to the public. Taking their place among new ads for other prescription medications, the two-page spreads announced beneath a gray rain cloud that "Depression hurts," and then beneath a vibrantly painted sun that "Prozac can help." This new degree of popular acceptance represents the most recent chapter in the forty-year history of the antidepressant medications, a history whose richness illustrates how varied are the factors which influence the social acceptance of licit, prescription psychotropic substances. Perceptions of illness, social forces, cultural biases, individual personalities, theoretical developments, and technological capacity all play a role in the development and dispersion of such legitimized drugs, just as all these elements enter into the history of alcohol, cigarettes, and narcotics.

The following account of the introduction of the first MAO-inhibitor and tricyclic into American medicine in the 1950s illustrates this interaction. More specifically, it shows how—despite the technological, even techno-utopian, rhetoric of their most flamboyant champion—the first-generation antidepressants were accepted not as consumer products appropriate for wide usage or general lifestyle enhancement, but as disease therapies to be kept strictly in the medical domain. I argue that the legitimacy and relative invisibility purchased via their promotion as specific remedies for a serious disease, clinical depression, insulated this class of drugs from any association with the recreational "drug culture," even as other prescription drugs, like the minor tranquilizers and the amphetamines, did come to acquire such associations. When the selective serotonin reuptake inhibitors (e.g., Prozac, then Zoloft and Paxil) emerged in the late eighties, they could simultaneously enjoy the medico-legal legitimacy of the "antidepressant" classification and profit from the huge market opened up by the broad popularization of the depression label, a sociocultural phenomenon that seems to have accelerated dramatically beginning in the early seventies. I end the essay with some tentative remarks on the relationship between these drugs and those substances, many illicit or controlled, which have taken on a far more negative legal, social, and cultural overlay.

Depression and Its Treatment at Mid-century

Discussions of the nature of depression reflected the theoretical congeries that reigned in psychiatry after World War II, which itself reflected the diversity of practical activities and professional commitments coexisting somewhat haphazardly under the discipline's mantle. "Neuropsychiatry," buoyed in prestige by apparent successes during the war, remained divided in its commitments between a huge network of state asylums, private mental hospitals, and an expanding industry of private practice psychotherapy. While Freud may have functioned more as icon and inspiration than as direct, unmediated influence on the theoretical formulations and practices of psychiatry and general medicine, psychodynamic formulations were undoubtedly rising in prestige. Even in the psychiatric hospitals the new popularity of group therapies meant that a rapidly increasing number of physicians, residents, and, of course, patients, were being exposed to psychodynamic ideas, which were, in any case, unavoidable in the popular press.[1]

Quite typical for the period was an informal synthesis of psychoanalytic theory and Adolf Meyer's "psychobiology." While both Meyer and Freud had acknowledged constitutional or hereditary predisposition, increasingly common was the assumption that the mechanisms responsible for depression, as for all mental dysfunction, were to be found in all normal individuals as well, thus focusing attention on the life experiences that might trigger this universal potential. Represented by early editions of the analyst Charles Brenner's popular *Elementary Textbook of Psychoanalysis*, a common approach was to view psychopathology through the lens of a metaphor culled from the physical sciences, to "view the phenomena of human mental functioning and behavior as ranging from the normal to the pathological in much the same way as the spectrum of an incandescent solid ranges from red to violet, with no sharp line separating one color from the next."[2] According to formulations like Brenner's, depression as such did not exist as a distinct disease category, as a condition, that is, with a unique etiology or well-defined boundaries, but was instead a vague emotional extreme that resulted from the ego's attempt to avoid anxiety. The mental conflict, not the emotional state, was the appropriate target of medical intervention, and so, for many partisans of this view, it made little sense to attack it with chemical agents.

During this period, when psychiatry was attempting in various ways to develop a larger presence outside of the asylum system, as well as a broader, less severely ill clientele, a spectrum theory of affective problems provided a useful theoretical base. It meant that psychiatry would be the appropriate destination for relatively healthy patients in search of professional assistance in managing their emotional lives.

The wider cultural consciousness tended not to recognize depression as a distinct disease category, and when it did it often identified the concept not with a common, everyday sort of condition, but with rare and extreme states like "involutional melancholia," an illness thought especially to mark the lives of menopausal women pained by the emptying nest and the loss of their sexual allure.[3] The professional literature suggested that those with what had come to be classed by some psychiatrists as mild or neurotic depression still generally avoided the term, and instead expressed their problems using somatic terminology. Out-patients, as one textbook put it, often will complain of "anything but depression," focusing instead on "vague or emphatic complaints of headache, often of an ill-defined and ill-localized type, and very persistent, of dyspepsia of various kinds, including lack of appetite, feelings of weight in the abdomen, a bad taste in the mouth, constipation, blurring of vision, irritability, especially to noises, lassitude, general weakness and . . . fatigue or actual exhaustion."[4] Those in more sophisticated circles might move away from somatic complaints toward the neurosis concept, but at mid-century few would describe themselves or others as having "depression," possibly because the term carried with it such haunting associations. One life insurance advertisement, for example, captured the common view of depression, or melancholia, as a bizarre condition far outside the range of normal experience. It employed a grotesque drawing of an emaciated involutional woman undergoing electroshock treatment, half the skull cut away and the brain exposed by the artist's imagination.

But drug prescriptions for depressive-type conditions and affects were, in fact, used in both psychiatry and general medicine. Though their use was only weakly supported by the official literature, advertising for amphetamines and related stimulants inevitably employed images of depressed-looking patients, sometimes portrayed as standard, or even caricatured, 1950s businessmen who seemed to be performing poorly at work, and promised both direct relief of symptoms and greater accessibility to psychotherapy for depression.[5] Often couched in the language of psychoneuroticism, these ads often played on the popular conception of the period as the "age of anxiety." As one plug for Burroughs Wellcome's Methedrine put it, "The mentally depressed patient who will neither 'fit in' with his surroundings nor cooperate in treatment presents an increasingly wide-spread problem in these anxiety-ridden times. Methedrine, given orally, has a remarkable stimulant effect which elevates the patient's mood and produces a sense of well-being." Schenley Laboratories billed its Euphased, a combination of desoxyephedrine and acetylbromdiethylacetylcarbamid, for "the patient feeling mighty LOW" (their emphasis), and placed its ads next to a similar one for a pure form of the carbamide that "quickly relieves the nervous tension and anxiety so often generated by modern life." Doctors may have had their suspicions about the drugs, but they were still used in great numbers. As one Philadelphia physician wrote in an article supporting the use of Dexamyl, Smith, Kline & French's combination of amphetamine and barbiturate, "Of course, the ideal treatment would be to discover the causes of the patient's emotional turmoil—the nagging wife or husband; the tyrannical parent; the unsuitable job; the financial burden—and remove it. Unfortunately, this is impracticable. Although dragging a secret worry out in the open—'getting it off one's chest'—is often in itself of benefit, it is not always enough."[6] Apart from expressing a common view of drug therapy, the physician captured in his statement the increasingly common view within medicine, and especially within psychiatry: that it was desirable to intervene medically in cases of "emotional turmoil" even in individuals whose distress fell quite close to that of the normal individual on the hypothetical affective spectrum.

The Introduction of Iproniazid and Imipramine

Perhaps no other postwar psychiatrist championed the professional management of the emotions as colorfully as the individual most associated with the introduction of the first MAO-inhibitor, Nathan S. Kline. After academic training in psychodynamic and biological psychology, Kline ran group therapy programs at the Veterans Administration Hospital in Lyons, New Jersey, and then served a period of time as director of research at Worcester State Hospital, where he participated in attempts to correlate endocrinological abnormalities with schizophrenia and depression. Kline only came into his own, however, after he was made director of the Rockland Research Institute in Westchester County, New York, in 1952. Well stocked with "closets full" of untried experimental drugs, supplied along with funds and equipment by several pharmaceutical firms, and surrounded by thousands of patients available for experimental treatments at the complete discretion of the attending physicians, Kline spearheaded an array of simultaneous mass drug trials.[7] His first major success, an experimental run with the tranquilizer reserpine, bolstered his confidence in the future of psychopharmacology and gained him rapid public recognition. Citing their "farsighted pioneering in the use of tranquilizing drugs in mental illness," the

Newspaper Guild of New York voted him and the Montreal researcher Heinz Lehmann the Page One Award for Science in March 1956—it would be followed soon after by the Adolf Meyer and Albert Lasker Awards—and Kline's position as chemopsychiatry's self-designated media spokesperson was set for life.[8]

Just after his initial work with reserpine, Kline became interested in the potential of a new medication. Developed originally by Hoffman-LaRoche in 1951 as a TB treatment to replace its parent compound, isoniazid, the drug iproniazid had been given to entire wards of convalescents before it was discontinued owing to its predecessor's lesser toxicity. The very first publications on the drug recognized "central nervous system stimulation" among patients taking it for TB, but with depression so far from the consciousness of the early researchers, this was considered little more than an undesirable side effect, one, in fact, that discouraged its use in favor of isoniazid.[9] Kline and others more interested in psychiatric issues, however, had seen the now famous photograph of ebullient patients dancing in the halls of the Sea View Sanatorium on Staten Island in the spring of 1953, but the only published study of the drug in mental patients—a Texas physician named Jackson Smith had tried it on a variegated group including individuals with catatonic schizophrenia and involutional depression—found little positive improvement and considerable side effects, and there was only cautious interest in trying the drug further.[10] Among the problems associated with the drug in TB trials were constipation, perverted sensations, neuralgia, dizziness, hypotension, dry-mouth, abnormal sweating, and, most serious, inflammation of the liver. Kline almost certainly kept the drug in the back of his mind while a few other researchers made claims for its efficacy in domains as varied as pain and lupus.

Then in 1956, just after receiving the Page One Award, in a joint effort deemed somewhat unusual at the time Kline worked with the Freudian analyst Mortimer Ostow on a theory of tranquilizer action that combined psychoanalytic and neurophysiological concepts, proposing a psychodynamic mechanism whereby chlorpromazine and reserpine diminished "psychic energy" by attenuating id drives that were localized, they speculated, in the globus pallidus. The theory suggested to him that the inverse process might also be chemically facilitated, and led to a statement to the American Psychoanalytic Association predicting that a "psychic energizer" would be found to complement the tranquilizers. Kline, that is, was not on the lookout for a specific remedy for a specific condition, depression, but for something like a long-term stimulant with action exclusively in the central nervous system.[11]

It is almost certain that Kline already had iproniazid in mind as an energizer. By his own recollection, he had seen the effects of the drug on lab animals at Warner Laboratories a year earlier, when he noticed its stimulating effect on experimentally reserpinized mice—it produced, as he called them, super-mice. "It occurred to me," he explained to the American Philosophical Society a few years later, "that it would be wonderful if we could get some of our apathetic and depressed patients even to remotely resemble these hyper-alert, hyper-attentive animals."[12] Kline and his colleague John Saunders also learned of the drug's likely action as an inhibitor of the enzyme monoamineoxidase, and wondered if iproniazid might achieve its euphoriant effect by making more catecholamine chemical messengers available to the receptors on brain cells. Believing that the only published psychiatric trials of the drug had unsuccessfully tested it as a tranquilizer, Kline began providing the medication to patients showing depressive symptomatology, announcing soon after that he had found his predicted energizer.[13]

With a combined research/publicity meeting held in New York City on November 29 and 30, 1957, Hoffman-LaRoche officially announced the drug's availability for general, nonexperimental use. The drug was moved quickly into larger-scale production—the FDA did not yet require demonstrations of efficacy—and by the end of the next year it was claimed that at least 400,000 patients had already been given iproniazid, now known generally by its commercial name, Marsilid. Its diagnostic target still quite fuzzy, the drug was likely to be referred to as an energizer, stimulant, euphoriant, eudaemonic, or mood brightener rather than as an antidepressant, though the term certainly existed and was promoted by researchers who preferred to conceptualize it as a specific remedy for a specific medical condition.

Despite the notable list of side effects, which at that point included sleeplessness, constipation, impotence, and hyperactivity, as well as the considerable variability in patient response and the lack of long-term data, Kline was thrilled with Marsilid. Describing the case of a suicidal baby nurse, he claimed that not only had her suicidality and unbearable somatic complaints been virtually eliminated, but "[e]ven her physical appearance changed. The scowling brow and the drawn mouth were replaced by a relaxed and smiling appearance, which incidentally made her look twenty years younger." In another patient, a housewife whose daily routine had been dominated by sleep, Kline proudly remarked that the drug had succeeded where seven years of analysis had failed: this patient was now so gratefully free of emotional and mental anguish that she felt continued treatment was worth the severe neuralgia of the throat and ears that seemed to be a side effect. He reported testimonials by enthusiastic colleagues, whose comments typically compared the drug's virtues to the deficiencies of the older stimulants with an air of excited progress. As one colleague reported to Kline, "Psychomotor stimulants speed up the pumps—Marsilid fills them." Kline himself could not help but extend his pronouncements far beyond the realm of the merely medical and link Marsilid with a utopian technological future. "It is characteristic of man," he wrote after describing the drug's effects to the press, "that he wanted to fly through the air and now into outer space, to travel under water, to communicate through thousands of miles instantaneously, and to do all matter of things. It is the most 'natural' of characteristics that man should attempt what is unnatural, unbelievable, or impossible and succeed."[14]

Kline became a tireless advocate for his self-described psychic energizer. After trying the drug on himself for three months in 1957 he announced to the press the happy results: not only was it safe and free of adverse side effects, but it had reduced his sleep need to three hours nightly, thereby doubling his professional productivity. "I felt absolutely fine during the whole time," Kline announced, "usually I slept sometime between 4 and 7 A.M., and woke up feeling fine. No alarm clock was needed." As *Newsweek* described this chemical feat, Kline had "used a pill for a pillow—a drug called iproniazid, a member of a chemical family that yields both rocket fuel and grass spray." Openly expressing his hope that the drug would serve not only to cure illness or alleviate suffering, but to enhance the performance of the ordinary individual, Kline responded to queries about the body's need for eight hours' rest with a potent engineering metaphor. "I just can't believe," he quipped, "that God made the human machine so inefficient that it has to shut down or be recharged one-third of its life span. One might ask, for that matter, why sleep is necessary at all since no one has conclusively demonstrated a biochemical or physiological explanation for it." In a preemptive strike, perhaps, against those who might accuse the drug of sapping the creativity that comes from inner struggle, Kline added proudly that iproniazid treatment had recently broken the painter's block of a "fairly well-known young artist," freeing him for a summer of brilliant, unparalleled artistic productivity.[15]

Just as Kline began his promotion of iproniazid, the introduction of imipramine, the first of the tricyclics, was being prepared in Germany by the psychiatrist Roland Kuhn. Apart from their faith in psychopharmacology, the two men could not have been more different. Kline saw himself as the very model of the optimistic American pragmatist. He looked to the promise of psychopharmaceuticals half through the eyes of a physician, and half through those of the self-confident, media-loving, technological visionary. Kuhn, on the other hand, was a reserved, contemplative European physician-humanist who attributed both his discovery and his understanding of his drug, imipramine, to an abstract, introspective philosophical tradition.

While also keen on promoting his medication, he limited his comments to the professional literature, where he argued that the drug reinforced, rather than undermined, the boundary between the sick and the healthy.

Kuhn had been trained in psychiatry under Jakob Klaesi, the Swiss psychiatrist who had introduced barbiturate sleep therapies into his university clinic in Zurich. In 1939 Kuhn became medical director of the public mental hospital in Muensterlingen, Switzerland, a 700-bed institution where Rorschach had perfected his testing technique. Strongly sympathetic to the existentialist psychiatry movement, but also eager to innovate with pharmaceuticals, Kuhn had accepted a free trial batch of chlorpromazine in the early fifties from its French producer, Rhone-Poulenc. He was enthusiastic about the results—especially the drug's ability to build a more cohesive hospital community—but the hospital's financial capacity made purchases of the drug impossible, and so, in the hopes of finding a substitute for chlorpromazine and simultaneously maintaining the flow of medications, he arranged with Ciba-Geigy's laboratory in Basel to try out some of their neuroleptic analogues. The results with one such compound tried in 1956, a synthetic molecule very similar to chlorpromazine that they had labeled G 22355, were striking. In a trial with three hundred patients, schizophrenic symptoms were unresponsive to the drug, but the mood of two apparently depressed patients seemed noticeably elevated. Further studies showed exciting results, and, like Kline, Kuhn proudly touted his testimonials. In a manner more typical of his central European milieu, however, he focused not on the restoration of professional productivity, but on the drug's apparent role in rebuilding family and community ties. One banner quotation, for example, came from a grateful mother: "I've rediscovered my relationship with my children, and can once again think of them."[16]

Since that time, Kuhn's discovery has been dogged by accounts he clearly finds unflattering—described by some as the serendipitous good fortune of a provincial asylum administrator, and by others as the illegitimate appropriation of an observation made not by Kuhn, but by a hospital employee, the recognition of G 22355's antidepressive effect, Kuhn himself insists, was dependent upon both the exemplary training of his staff and, even more important, his own philosophical background. As a follower of the existential psychiatrist Ludwig Binswanger, Kuhn argues, he was familiar with the former's conceptual division between functional and historical aspects of mental and emotional life, and therefore able to develop the conception of a biologically driven state of depression that was independent of external life events. In fact, the very conception of depression as a distinct disease state noncontinuous with normal emotional swings, and which might be the target of direct pharmacological treatment, was typical of that philosophical tradition in a manner different from the dominant perspective of contemporary American psychiatric theory. Like many of his Central European colleagues, Kuhn recognized a firm conceptual division between endogenous and reactive depressions.

Kuhn's existentialist psychiatry, with its self-proclaimed debt to European philosophers including Martin Heidegger and Edmund Husserl, suggested to him that those with mental disorders existed in conceptual and perceptual worlds that were quite different from that of the normal individual, especially with regard to the perception of time and space, and that each sort of illness itself gave rise to a different such world. For him, the division between endogenous and reactive depressions was a division not only based on causation, but one that implied a more global distinction between two types of basic experience. Imipramine, according to this perspective, was not just a mood elevator, but somehow had the capacity to modify, if only temporarily, the patients' distorted sense of space and time. Not surprisingly, one discerns in his original publications on imipramine some disappointment with the observation that the drug produced similar effects not only in those patients who had an ostensibly "endogenous" depression that logically ought to respond to pharmaceutical intervention, but also in those with a "reactive" condition. This fact was a challenge to the firm nosological division between these two pathways that Kuhn mentioned, but only in passing. His recognition of the gap between theoretical expectation and clinical experience, however, extended further. It was almost impossible, he explained after a year of experience with the drug, to predict the effect it would have on any given individual, since patients who seemed to suffer the same syndrome could show the expected elevation of mood when on the drug, a paradoxical deterioration of mood, or no effect at all.

Unlike Kline, Kuhn was not interested in recommending the drug for general personality enhancement, nor did he want it to become a well-known commercial product. Not only was it against his philosophical principles, but—probably to Kuhn's satisfaction—colleagues had found that imipramine sat poorly with "healthy" subjects, leading typically to a truncated emotional life, personality distancing, a lack of ability to concentrate, and diminished ability to do intellectual work. He insisted that depressed individuals, on the other hand, experienced essentially the opposite effect, making imipramine a fairly specific remedy for a pathological condition qualitatively distinct from the normal. In fact, Kline's conceptualization of iproniazid as an "energizer" that could move emotional life across a linear spectrum represented a type of thinking Kuhn found frankly repugnant, since it suggested a mechanistic view of biological function that failed to recognize the individual as a philosophical "whole." Well steeped in the German romantic, "holistic" tradition, which had considerably influenced central European medical and neurobiological thinking, Kuhn was clearly offended by theories of drug action that viewed the brain as, in his words, but "a machine that just runs faster or slower."[17] Instead, he pointed admiringly to Kurt Goldstein's neurological treatise *Construction of the Organism*, a work of holistic neurology, and insisted that psychopharmacology would progress by promoting natural processes of recovery, rather than by fighting hypothetical disease entities. Even so, he looked excitedly to the advent of newer, more specific drugs that would target just one of the various subtypes of depression proposed by his theoretical background, and thus validate his philosophical system.

An Ambivalent American Reception

Throughout the late fifties, Kline continued his proselytizing for the MAO-inhibitors, but above his enthusiasm hung a darkening cloud of concern. According to muckraking journalist Morton Mintz's *Therapeutic Nightmare* (1965), Roche began hearing reports of "deaths and injuries" connected with Marsilid in the fall of 1957. When, on April 10, 1958, a San Francisco coroner's jury ruled that fifty-five-year-old Frances Simpson had died from taking a prescribed dosage of Marsilid, one within the bounds of the manufacturer's guidelines, Department of Health officials in New York City embargoed high-potency packages of the drug and began investigating a possible link with other recent deaths. In response, Dr. David Bosworth criticized the over-hasty introduction of the drug into the realm of psychiatry, reaffirming the need for medical supervision in a statement to the Medical Society of New York, intoning that the drug was "not a 'pep pill' to be sold like a refreshing caffeinated drink," but a "potent, toxic drug, safely handled by prescription only, with the patient under close observation." In 1960, FDA officials negotiated a minor label change, and then forced a voluntary withdrawal of Marsilid. Meanwhile, other MAO inhibitors like phenelzine (Nardil), and then the first tricyclics, absorbed and then quickly surpassed Marsilid's market share.[18]

Fear of the drug's safety surely mingled with a more diffuse public worry over the propriety of modifying mood through chemistry: just as chlorpromazine and meprobamate had sparked worried commentary on the possibility of drugging the anxious, but attentive, public into apathy, the advent of iproniazid led to occasional critiques of a dangerously superficial culture and prompted lamentations over the pathogenicity of modern life. *Time*, for instance, had quoted one doctor's concern that meprobamate might "make millions of people significantly indifferent to politics," while others conjured up images of Huxleyian dystopias. In a society obsessed with the concept of anxiety, and particularly with its supposed humanizing function, those drugs associated in the public mind with its relief became richly symbolic, prompting fears even of mind control and chemically enforced conformity. Speaking to an audience of researchers in the fall of 1958, for instance, Pope Pius XII sanctioned the proper use of psychiatric drugs, but emphasized the danger of using them "for the sole purpose of systematically avoiding emotional difficulties, fears and tensions that are inseparable from an active life devoted to current human tasks." The sentiment was often echoed within the psychiatric profession, where many practitioners insisted that alleviating suffering without confronting the root psychodynamic causes would sap patients' motivation for insight therapies by masking psychic conflict.[19]

Kline responded to this public ambivalence with a speaking campaign waged in general support of psychopharmacology. Encouraged by the prestige of his honors, he spoke frequently in subsequent years to a wide array of concerned societies and organizations, often focusing on the potential public health benefits of the tranquilizers, but rarely failing to sing the praises of the energizers as well. By engendering acceptance of mental disorders as "real" illnesses, Kline insisted, the drugs had "begun to change centuries-old public attitudes towards mental disease," leading to "greater acceptance of patients back into the community." "The fact that a condition is treated with medication somehow guarantees in the public mind," he added, "that it is a genuine illness." He encouraged the average "family physician" to prescribe psychiatric drugs in office practice—especially iproniazid—thereby preventing the emergence of more serious mental illness and freeing psychiatrists for work on the most difficult and refractory cases. With the development of the psychopharmaceutical arsenal, Kline predicted, GP's would soon do as much psychiatry as dermatology, minor surgery, and gastroenterology. At other times, such as when speaking to the American Pharmaceutical Manufacturers' Association in February 1958, Kline suggested that drugs would soon be developed to prevent Alzheimer's, improve memory functions, treat drug addiction, and perhaps even facilitate extrasensory perception. "The development and successful application of the psycho-pharmaceuticals," he announced to that audience, "was a thermonuclear-like explosion which marked the end of one era and the beginning of another, and which may, in point of fact, be of markedly greater import in the history of mankind than the atom bomb." His most dramatic statement of this sort came in 1960 with the proposal that psychotropic drugs be employed to construct integrated "man-machine" units to be used for space travel—thus was born the concept of the "cyborg." (A decade later, when lithium was approved by the FDA, Kline suggested that it be placed in the water supply, like fluoride, as a preventative against general depression.)[20]

The public remained, however, remarkably unresponsive to the antidepressant issue, unwilling, it seemed, to see these drugs as technological wonders, or as harbingers of wonders to come. Despite Kline's efforts, the first generation of antidepressants never assumed the status of a well-known cultural icon. Unlike the MAO-inhibitors, which almost disappeared for a time because of their potential lethality, imipramine had moved fairly steadily into large-scale use. Dwarfed in sales and publicity by the major and minor tranquilizers, however—during the late fifties over thirty million prescriptions for tranquilizers were written each year—both sets of antidepressants led to comparatively little public discussion. Even the pharmaceutical manufacturers that sold them, while likely recognizing that there existed a potentially enormous market of individuals who might use the drugs, were somewhat hesitant in their early promotion—providing, for example, only discreet coverage to the antidepressants in their otherwise effusive annual reports. Rather than endorsing it, it seems as if the industry may have preferred to shield the antidepressants from association with Kline's techno-utopian rhetoric.[21]

When they were publicized, the industry fastened on a sales strategy that ran exactly counter to Kline's enthusiastic suggestion that these agents could be employed casually or used to enhance the normal individual and begin the construction of a "cyborg." They were, said the promotional literature, treatments for one type of serious illness, in this case a mental illness, but comparable to the antibiotics. At first Pfizer sold its MAO-inhibitor Niamid as a "mood brightener" particularly appropriate for cancer patients and "chronic fatigue" sufferers, and accompanied its advertisements with smiling, attractive faces of the sort found more commonly in the stimulant ads put out by less established drug companies. It then switched over to what became a standard marketing strategy for antidepressants, to emphasize not the appealing result of the therapy, but the gravity of the condition to be treated and the specificity of the medication. Forlorn faces only half exposed to the light typically looked out of the pages of the medical journals, their eyes glazed and vacant. Without access to archival materials from the drug firms one can only speculate, but this decision very likely reflected the historical position of the pharmaceutical industry circa 1960: having billed themselves as the bearers of modern technology's greatest gifts, the "ethical" drug companies were under strong pressure from the Kefauver hearings to justify their high prices, and they did so by emphasizing the serious, humanitarian nature of their enterprise. Though representing the most profitable industry in the

United States, industry spokespeople even claimed that their promotional efforts were not advertising, but physician education.

The number of prescriptions for the antidepressants grew rapidly, and the income added significantly to the expanding sales of firms like Pfizer and Hoffman-LaRoche, but the drugs remained relative unknowns, vastly overshadowed by the ubiquitous Miltown, and then the benzodiazepines Librium and Valium. It was those drugs, not the antidepressants, that came to absorb the country's concern about psychopharmacology's ostensible new power to tamper with basic aspects of humanity, however construed. And yet, with just about every new antidepressant that was introduced, distribution increased dramatically, so much so that by the hearings in 1964 congressional investigators argued that sales were so high that the drug firms must have been employing false or misleading advertising claims. This certainly reflected the lack of recognition of "depression" in the culture at large: it was inconceivable to those investigators that the condition was so widespread as to justify the fact that in 1964 enough of just one antidepressant, Parnate, had been sold for two million patients. That November, when Kline was given the prestigious Lasker Award for his introduction of iproniazid, the *New York Times* reported that over four million Americans used the antidepressants each year.[22]

Over the next decade, as usage of the antidepressants spread, a complicated situation developed within the psychiatric profession. On the one hand, even surveys of self-designated psychoanalysts suggested that clinical practice was fairly eclectic. The results of at least one sounding, in the southern California psychoanalytic community, showed that a high percentage of respondents used psychiatric drugs at least "sometimes" by 1967, with the strongest tendency to prescribe among older practitioners.[23] With nearly 200 million prescriptions for psychotropic drugs made that year (costing patients nearly $700 million), it seemed inevitable that all drugs would be combined with almost all types of psychotherapy, even if the topic received little explicit attention. Yet at the same time, it seemed that ideological camps were hardening within psychiatry, with entire schools of thought lining up for or against the use of the drugs. As early as 1961, Elvin Semrad, residency director at the Harvard-affiliated Massachussetts Mental Health Center, warned each new crop of residents that they dare not present patients to him who had been given such "poisons," while at just about the same time, the superintendent of St. Elizabeth's Hospital in Washington, D.C., did not hesitate to say that the agents were used quite casually on his wards for "depressions of all kinds, including mild psychoneurotics through severe psychotic depressive reactions." In short, this was a therapy that produced the most contrary opinions.[24]

To a degree, this situation emerged because little or no unambiguous information about the drugs was available. Through the sixties there was essentially no consensus on issues as basic as safety and efficacy, nor were there well-recognized methods for their evaluation. When a 1964 Senate subcommittee tried to investigate the association of one MAO-inhibitor, Parnate, with mortalities due to liver damage and hypertension, the investigators discovered that extreme differences of opinion and considerable uncertainties existed concerning the safety of the drug. The foreign medical press had reported numerous hypertensive crises, some lethal, in patients taking MAO-inhibitors, and the association between those crises and amine-containing foods had been suggested by British clinicians, but at least some American physicians continued to defend the drugs as harmless. One editorial in the *British Drug and Therapeutics Bulletin* contended that "both the frequency and severity of the [hypertensive] reaction have been seriously underestimated," and claimed that up to 20 percent of patients on Parnate had suffered severe reactions, while the chief medical director of the Veterans Administration reported "no fatal or alarming side-effects" in almost 6,000 patients.[25]

In terms of efficacy, the gaps between individual clinical experience and statistical evaluations were striking. Many physicians reported impressive successes with the antidepressants, but the statistical trials were anything but definitive, and there were essentially no hard data on long-term outcomes. In a letter written in 1964, the chief of the National Institute of Mental Health's Psychopharmacology Service Center, Dr. Jonathan Cole, placed the entire concept of antidepressant drugs in scare quotes, reporting that controlled clinical trials had often failed to show their superiority over placebo, and that "many clinicians [felt] that no drug was effective in depression, where the spontaneous improvement rate [was] high."[26] At the same time, however, he strongly supported the continued availability even of the MAO-inhibitor most associated with fatalities and least statistically proven, Parnate, asserting that "a substantial group of sound and responsible clinicians . . . [felt] this drug to be a valuable treatment." It was widely assumed that the drugs were helpful in managing suicidal patients, but the Senate subcommittee found that no statistical evidence had yet been published. Given the lack of conclusive efficacy data and the safety concerns, the FDA made an initial effort to remove the drug from general use, but the outcry from the medical profession—prompted at least partly by the manufacturer's letter campaign—was so strong that all those in Washington interested in the issue backed off.

To support the drugs in the face of this uncertainty, some physicians knowledgeable about research issues pointed to the developing "catecholamine hypothesis of affective disorders" as evidence that the drugs truly targeted what they claimed to be the biological roots of depression. The theory was born of the observation that the drug reserpine, a major tranquilizer introduced into American mental hospitals in the fifties, made many patients lethargic and unresponsive, a finding that was at first explained by at least some psychiatrists in elaborate psychoanalytic terms: the drug acted as a "disinhibitor," allowing "unacceptable angry feelings" to emerge from a previously suppressed state. The ensuing depression, serving as a psychological defense against these feelings, was then best understood as a secondary effect.[27] The subsequent discovery that reserpine depleted the stores of certain key chemical messengers in rat brains, however, shifted the focus to the brain itself. In its crudest form, the catecholamine theory proposed that human depression represented a deficiency of these chemical messengers, especially norepinephrine, at receptor sites on certain brain cells, and that the MAO-inhibitors and the tricyclics both corrected this deficiency, though by different means. While sophisticated advocates recognized that the theory was "at best, a reductionistic oversimplification of a very complex biological state," some partisans of the drugs, like Kline, tended to assume that illustration of a biological mechanism for drug activity supported the contention that depression's causation was also best understood through biological models, and that it was possible to identify, with a relatively large degree of certainty, "endogenous" depressions that were not triggered by life events, but by chemical malfunctions or imbalances.[28]

The research was, indeed, technically impressive. The ability of iproniazid to inhibit the breakdown of norepinephrine and another compound, serotonin, had been known since early in the fifties, and by 1964 NIMH neurobiologists Jacques Glowinski and Julius Axelrod had proposed a mechanism for imipramine's (and the other tricyclics') ability to inhibit the reabsorption of those messengers back into nerve endings (this would mean that more was available to stimulate the receiving brain cell). This work provided the theoretical impetus for research into more specific inhibitors that eventually produced the selective serotonin reuptake inhibitors (SSRIs). But other commentators argued that there was in fact no clear means of making correlations between the laboratory data and the clinical experience of patients or physicians, and that identification of a biological mechanism was in no way equivalent to identification of a biological cause for the condition. While clinical trials and basic research had become the official standards by which therapeutics were supposed to be evaluated, personal familiarity, advertising, word of mouth, and starting assumptions probably played a far greater role in determining practice.

In fact, the catecholamine hypothesis, though remaining the most important inspiration for a rapidly expanding body of biological investigation, was always controversial. As even its strongest supporters acknowledged, "apparent discrepancies" abounded, and though it was repeatedly claimed that "practical clinical applications" of the theory were on the horizon, the promise remained, it seems, unrealized. By the mid-seventies the theory competed for prominence with the indolamine hypothesis (apparently favored by European researchers) and its focus on serotonin over norepinephrine as the key player in depression, and then with the "neurotransmitter balance model," which proposed that the normal regulation of mood required an appropriate balance between those, and maybe many other systems of chemical messengers. Clinical lore held that certain subtypes of depression responded well to drugs, while others did not, and that among the former some types responded best to certain medications. This led, in turn, to the proliferation of competing classification schemes for depression that might help predict drug response, all of which faced confounding evidence and none of which gained universal support.[29] Some wondered whether depression was a scientifically meaningful concept, since the diversity of conditions falling under its rubric was so great.

The Age of Depression

If the fifties were the Age of Anxiety, we've now been living for almost three decades in something like the Age of Depression. While the popular press of the 1950s and 1960s typically emphasized anxiety in discussions of emotional health, depression gradually become far more prominent. It is admittedly difficult to periodize such a vague process, but it does seem that alongside the highly vocal fears of a new economic depression that accompanied the slump of the early seventies—by 1971 the press was full of grim comparisons with the late thirties on issues such as birth rate, job loss, and industrial decline—came the start of the rapid mainstreaming of "depression" as an illness label. Some popular books and articles on the topic had come earlier—Leonard Cammer's self-help guide *Up from Depression* in 1969 and Sylvia Plath's autobiographical novel *The Bell Jar* in 1971—but when, in July 1972, Democratic vice-presidential nominee Thomas Eagleton revealed to the public his history of hospitalizations and shock treatments for the condition, the media followed his disclosure and subsequent removal from the ticket with an unprecedented stream of depression journalism.[30]

Depression became the "disease of the '70s," the epidemic of the me generation. Articles in women's magazines explained to readers the difference between grief or "the drearies" and the "actual illness," sometimes encouraging self-diagnostic assessments based on questionnaires provided by the National Association for Mental Health. "You can't sleep, you can't eat, you don't feel like getting up in the morning. . . . These are the symptoms of depression," Ginger Ochsner of the Cornell School of Social Psychiatry explained in the December 1972 issue of *Harper's Bazaar*, "and we want people to be as acutely aware of them as they are aware of the symptoms of a cold."[31] A *New York Times Magazine* article from November 1973 opened with a profile of Barbara L., an "attractive and vivacious young Wall Street secretary" whose cheerful demeanor hid the despair within. The device, typical for the new depression journalism, was meant to demonstrate that the condition could attack even the most socially endowed, and to illustrate depression's preference for young women. *Depression: A Layman's Guide to the Symptoms and Cures* asked its readers "Are You Depressed?" and included a "Self-Scoring Depression Inventory" to help them decide.[32] With the 1974 publication of the paperback *From Sad to Glad: Kline on Depression*, Kline himself contributed energetically to the popularizing trend, providing to readers his easily self-administered SAD-GLAD Scale, useful for the "systematic assessment of depression" and the "graduated linear assessment of delight."[33] The psychologist Martin Seligman followed with the highly influential *Helplessness: On Depression, Development, and Death*.[34] That same year psychiatrist Ronald Fieve explained the value of lithium in *Moodswing*, while his colleague Harvey Ross recommended vitamin therapy in *Fighting Depression*.[35] A decade of depression research was now reaching a far broader audience, an audience that was receptive, psychiatric epidemiologists suggested, because the phenomena themselves were increasingly common, perhaps dramatically so, and especially among women.

The very diversity of the expert advice regarding the causes and treatment of depression suggests that the diagnosis served an important function for the mental health professions as a whole. Commentary ran the spectrum from firmly biological to firmly psychosocial in perspective, and those seeking help might fall in with any number of competing support services, psychodynamic therapists, cognitive therapists, behavior modifiers, psychopharmacologists, encounter groups, or pastoral counselors. Although most recognized the enormous diversity of conditions caught in the label's net, each school tended to suggest, especially when speaking to a lay audience, that its research program addressed the primary cause. For behaviorists it might be the lack of "response contingent positive reinforcement" or "learned helplessness," for Aaron Beck it was negative cognitive sets, for some neo-Freudians, hostility turned against the self. Social theorists saw the epidemic's roots in economic deprivation, sexism, or racism, biopsychiatrists in amine deficiencies. What most professionals shared, however, was a commitment to the diagnosis itself, even as much of the scientific research called

345

into question the coherence and distinctiveness of the category—a suspicion reflected in the gradual move toward the broader concept of "affective disorders" in the medical literature. With a common, but specific illness label that social workers, psychologists, psychiatrists of various theoretical persuasions, and the drug firms could all rally behind, it was probably that much easier to present something of a unified front in policy debates over the reality and seriousness of mental illness even among relatively healthy people in the general population. Given the decreased support mental health services were receiving from both government and insurance companies in the seventies, this alliance amidst contention and competition likely grew in importance.[36]

Based on numbers of prescriptions and sales figures, it seems that usage of the antidepressants grew throughout the 1970s, and then began a more rapid rise around 1980. In 1984 about 35 million prescriptions were written for antidepressants (including antidepressant tranquilizers), the result of a 12 percent increase over four years.[37] While psychotherapy remained extremely common, it was clear that both doctors and patients were increasingly willing to see their problem in terms of biological predisposition, rather than psychodynamics and life history.

The success of Prozac, whose annual sales reached $1 billion just a short time after its introduction in 1987, surely reflected as much this changed sociocultural situation as a new technological capacity, especially given the widespread professional consensus that the drug's "efficacy" as defined by symptom alleviation in clinical trials is no greater than that of the tricyclics. Reading through the medical press from just prior to its general release, one finds that few, if any, researchers felt that they had come across something dramatically novel. In fact, the drug's widely touted specificity for the serotonergic neurotransmitter system made it less, rather than more likely, to be a wonderdrug for depression, since serotonin had not been implicated more strongly than some other brain substances in much of the American depression research. With Prozac's introduction, and the subsequent advent of Zoloft and Paxil, antidepressants became one of the most discussed medical issues of our time, but the country's behavior and attitude regarding antidepressant drugs had probably been shifting for at least a decade, even if the technology itself may have changed very little.[38]

The new selective serotonin reuptake inhibitor antidepressants have now entered fairly solidly into mainstream shopping culture, complete with strong brand-name identification and nearly direct public advertising. As one internetter announced humorously, but tellingly, to the "Prozac Pez Page," "I used to have a Wonderwoman Pez, now I am taking Prozac and I feel as though I am Wonderwoman! My shrink tried to put me on Luvox, said it was Prozac's cousin, but I said I don't want the cousin or the brother, I want the real thing. Just like I prefer Levis to Lee jeans—maybe it's just all in my head, but I feel really great." The bright photos of smiling, attractive people that adorn the current ads for Prozac and Zoloft (and even, incidentally, for the antipsychotic Risperdol) now look more similar to the pictures found in clothing catalogs or on cigarette billboards than to those used to promote Elavil or Tofranil, and anecdotal reports suggest strongly that doctors are often simply rubber-stamping prescription requests that originate with the patients themselves. The use of these drugs has clearly become accepted, almost de rigueur in some quarters, a situation surely influenced by the lighter side-effect profile of the SSRIs and by the pharmaceutical industry's advertising blitz, but also indicative of the growing tendency for even quite functional individuals to define themselves as "depressed" or "dysthymic" and seek out pharmaceutical treatment for their condition. ("The fact is," explained a psychiatrist to New York Magazine in 1989, "we're all depressed. The whole world is depressed. I don't know a human being who isn't.")[39] Perhaps even more, however, it suggests that, having moved largely out of the conceptual realm of the "medical" and into that of everyday consumer product, these drugs and the industry that produces them no longer really need the authorization of a weighty illness category for their sale, only for their legally approved salability and insurance coverage. While Eli Lilly's official public stance continues to emphasize that Prozac is a medical treatment specifically developed to treat the disease clinical depression, the formal and informal indications for this and similar drugs have become so broad and the demand so wide, that it is likely available on request to those who can afford it.

Conclusion: Drugs and Diagnoses in the Twenty-first Century

The early history of antidepressants includes, but is not exhausted by, the history of technological innovation and scientific advance in psychiatric medicine, the history, that is, of drug development as often understood. It also demonstrates how the use and understanding of psychopharmaceuticals is deeply influenced by the local social and cultural context, and how an era's or individual's particular definition of psychiatric and emotional disorder strongly determines the conceptualization of pharmaceutical treatments. Both Kline and Kuhn were almost uncannily representative of their sociocultural milieus, and their particular takes on "their" medications illustrate this framing process. When first exposed to the drug, Kline understood iproniazid in the mechanistic terms of 1950s American technological enthusiasm, and saw a particular triumph for it in restored or enhanced professional production. Kline hoped he had discovered an "energizer," not a specific remedy. Kuhn on the other hand viewed "his" antidepressant through the lens of German holism and its vitalistic commitments, and felt the drug proved its value most vividly when it restored family and community relations. In fact, it is striking that Kline, working with a drug probably far more dangerous than Kuhn's, looked forward to widespread, almost casual use outside the boundaries of recognized medical conditions, while Kuhn probably never considered such a thing.

I've tried to use this comparison of personalities to raise several questions for which I have only speculative answers. If the inherent technological capacities of the SSRIs are genuinely so similar to the those of the MAO-inhibitors and tricyclics, why have the new drugs become such an enormous sociocultural sensation while the first generation remained so obscure? Why, despite vigorous efforts in the late 1950s, was Kline unable to engage the public's sense of technological awe toward these drugs, while Peter Kramer could do so quite easily with *Listening to Prozac* in 1993? Why were the drugs generally seen in a more "Kuhnian" way, that is, as antidepressants, rather than in a more "Klinian" manner, as energizers? Kline was clearly ahead of his time. In an era in which the pharmaceutical industry and the public preferred to think of medical advances as something qualitatively different from other technological lifestyle products, Kline's "cyborg" visions never caught on. Legitimacy for the drugs was gained instead by linking them firmly with clinical depression, a disease then considered to be fairly rare. Since the 1950s both the image of medicine and the image of depression have changed considerably. With the rise of birth control, cosmetic surgery, and other technologies that have stretched the medical role, the public is far more accustomed to seeing medicine as selling personal enhancement. Medical technologies no longer seem quite so different from other consumer technologies. In turn, the popularization of depression meant that the drugs could keep, to a certain degree at least, the legitimacy of being a disease remedy while reaching a vastly larger group of takers, and they could do so even amidst a general crackdown on the use of so many other psychotropic drugs.

Without entering into debates over the strictly pharmacological differences between those drugs designated antidepressants and those considered recreational drugs, debates that have gained some degree of popular recognition through articles alleging a strong similarity between, for example, Prozac and the street drug ecstasy, we can certainly speculate on crucial sociological differences. In this essay I have focused on one, the hardly inevitable and highly constructed linkage of this class of drugs with a diagnostic entity, depression, itself an intellectual abstraction whose boundaries have changed with the times. (One might, of course, instead emphasize related issues, such as the medical, as opposed to "informal," distribution network of the drug, or the nonstigmatized pool of users, an ever growing group of largely productive, middle-class persons.)

This focus suggests a comparison with alcohol and alcoholism. It has been argued that the promotion of "alcoholism" as a discrete disease affecting only a minority of drinkers helped to remove blame for alcohol-related social problems from the substance itself, shifting it instead to a subgroup of individuals who abused it, or to some pathological entity—whether biological or psychological—acting on those individuals. This enabled the alcohol beverages industry to sell its product despite widespread concerns about the dangers and evils of alcohol, as long as drinking was officially proscribed for that susceptible subpopulation. This role for the alcoholism concept would help explain the financial support given by the alcohol beverages industry to academic research organized around it.[40] The depression diagnosis may have functioned in an analogous, though inverse manner. By identifying a group of individuals who should become users, those with a current or potential medical depression, the pharmaceutical industry gained legitimacy for its product, antidepressants, again despite certain, though muted, public concerns about the propriety of selling and using mind-altering substances. The increasing body of research, especially genetic, linking depression with vulnerability to substance abuse makes this comparison still more relevant, since it raises the possibility that there is considerable overlap in the pools of potential alcoholics and depressives, or even of substance abusers and depressives more generally. With per capita alcohol, marijuana, minor tranquilizer, and cigarette use probably declining through the eighties—at least partly because of increasing social disapproval and governmental intervention—perhaps a market hungry for substitutes was being fashioned, thus making the antidepressants something like the informal, but well-legitimated maintenance drug for the nineties.[41] As such, the relationship between depression and the antidepressants illustrates, in an almost caricatured form, something typical of medicine more generally: that diagnostic categories serve both to recognize forms of distress and simultaneously to package that distress so as to make it available for socially sanctioned commercialization.

Notes

1. Gerald Grob, *From Asylum to Community: Mental Health Policy in Modern America* (Princeton: Princeton University Press, 1992); Nathan G. Hale, *The Rise and Crisis of Psychoanalysis in the United States* (Cambridge: Harvard University Press, 1995).

2. Charles Brenner, *An Elementary Textbook of Psychoanalysis* (New York: International Universities Press, 1955), 197.

3. For a fictional portrayal of this stock psychiatric character, see Mary Astor as Helen the involutional melancholic in "Journey to the Day," aired as part of the CBS series *Playhouse 90* on 4 April, 1960.

4. Quoted in Stanley W. Jackson, *Melancholia and Depression: From Hippocratic Times to Modern Times* (New Haven: Yale University Press, 1986), 204.

5. Other stereotypes: nervous housewife, debt-ridden worker, pressured executive, harried small businessman, oppressed civil servant, deprived slum dweller, victim of the age of anxiety.

6. Henry V. Grahn, "The Depressed Patient: Management with the Aid of a New Medicine," *American Practitioner* 18 (1950): 795.

7. Joseph Barsa, interview, tape recording, undated, Nathan Kline Institute, Rockland, N.Y.

8. "News Guild Names Lehmann for Award," *New York Times*, 2 March 1956.

9. Irving J. Selikoff, Edward H. Robitzek, and George G. Ornstein, "Toxicity of Hydrazine Derivatives of Isonicotinic Acid in the Chemotherapy of Human Tuberculosis," *Quarterly Bulletin of Seaview Hospital* 13 (1952): 17–26; quotation on 25.

10. J. A. Smith, "The Use of the Isopropyl Derivative of Isonicotinylhydrazine (Marsilid) in the Treatment of Mental Disease," *American Practitioner and Digest of Treatment* 4 (1953): 519–520.

11. E. Harrison, "Psychic Energy Reduced by Drug," *New York Times*, 8 December 1956; Mortimer Ostow and Nathan S. Kline, "The Psychic Action of Reserpine and Chlorpromazine," in Kline, ed., *Psychopharmacology Frontiers* (New York: Little, Brown, 1959); Mortimer Ostow and Nathan S. Kline, "The Effects of the Newer Neuroleptic and Stimulating Drugs on Psychic Function," in Gerald Sarwer-Foner, ed., *The Dynamics of Psychiatric Drug Therapy* (Springfield, Ill.: Charles C. Thomas, 1960).

12. Nathan S. Kline, "The Challenge of the Psychopharmaceuticals," *Proceedings of the American Philosophical Society* 103 (1959): 456.

13. E. Harrison, "TB Drug Is Tried in Mental Cases," *New York Times*, 7 April 1957; "Paper by Dr. Loomer," *New York Times*, 8 April 1957; M. Shumach "1964 Medical Prize Challenged in Suit by Associate of Winner," *New York Times*, 24 April 1965.

14. Nathan S. Kline, "Clinical Experience with Iproniazid (Marsilid)," *Journal of Clinical and Experimental Psychopathology* 19, Supplement 1 (1958): 76–77.

15. "Three Hours a Night," *Newsweek*, 27 June 1960; W. E. Laurence "Drug Called a 'Psychic Energizer' Found Useful in Treating Mental Illnesses," *New York Times*, 22 December 1957.

16. R. Kuhn, "Probleme der klinischen und poliklinischen Anwendung psychopharmakologisch wirksamer Substanzen," *Schweizerische Archiv für Neurologie und Psychiatrie* 84 (1959): 319–329; quotation on 324. For my general comments, see these articles by R. Kuhn: "Über die Behandlung depressiver Zustände mit einem Iminodibenzylderivat (G22355)," *Schweizerischer Medizinische Wochenschrift* 87 (1957): 1135–1140; "Probleme der praktischen Durchführung der Tofranil-Behandlung," *Wiener Medizinische Wochenschrift* 110 (1960): 245–250; "The Imipramine Story." in Frank Ayd and Barry Blackwell, eds., *Discoveries in Biological Psychiatry* (Philadelphia: J. B. Lippincott, 1970), 205–217; "Geschichte der medikametentösen Depressionsbehandlung—vom Opium zum Imipramin und seinen Derivaten," in O. K. Linde, ed., *Pharmakopsychiatrie im Wandel der Zeit* (Klingenmünster, Germany: Tilia-Verlag, 1988), 10–27; and "The Discovery of Modern Antidepressants," *Psychiatric Journal of the University of Ottawa* 14 (1989): 249–252.

17. Roland Kuhn, "Probleme der klinischen und poliklinischen Anwendung psycho-

pharmakologisch wirksamer Substanzen," *Schweizer Archiv für Neurologie und Psychiatrie* 84 (1959): 325.

18. Morton Mintz, *The Therapeutic Nightmare* (Boston: Houghton Mifflin, 1965); M. Illson, "Experts Defend Iproniazid's Use," *New York Times*, 17 May, 1958; U.S. Senate, Committee on Government Operations, Subcommittee on Reorganization and International Organizations, *Review of Cooperation on Drug Policies among Food and Drug Administration, National Institutes of Health, Veterans' Administration, and Other Agencies*, 88th Congress, 1st sess., 19 June 1963, 4; hereafter cited as U.S. Senate.

19. "Happiness by Prescription," *Time*, 11 March 1957; "Pope Upholds the Use of Tranquillizers but Warns of Peril in Improper Dosage," *New York Times*, 13 September 1958.

20. "What Tranquillizers Have Done," *Time*, 24 April 1964; "Drugged Future?" *Time*, 24 February 1958; Smith, Kline & French, *Annual Report, 1958* (Philadelphia: Smith, Kline & French, 1959); "Space-man Is Seen as Man-machine," *New York Times*, 22 May 1960; "A Simple Salt Promises Relief from Mania," *New York Times*, 12 April 1970.

21. See, for instance, Eli Lilly and Company, *Report to Shareholders, 1957* (Indianapolis: Eli Lilly and Company, 1958).

22. Two million figure from U.S. Senate, 2655; H. A. Rusk, "Gains Made in Mental Health," *New York Times*, 22 November 1964.

23. M. Hayman, "Drugs—and the Psychoanalyst," *American Journal of Psychotherapy* 21 (1967): 644–654.

24. U.S. Senate, 2648.

25. Ibid., 2652–2653.

26. Ibid., 2644. See also Isham Kimbell Jr., John E. Overall, and Leo Hollister, "Antidepressant Drugs: Myth or Reality," *Journal of New Drugs* 5 (January–February 1965): 9–12: "Although antidepressant drugs are widely used and the literature abounds in favorable reports, their true value remains in doubt because of the happy circumstance that many depressions improve spontaneously, making distinctions between treatments quite difficult. A series of controlled evaluations of antidepressant drugs have provided little evidence to support their efficacy or specificity."

27. Quoted in T. H. Harris, "Depression Induced by Rauwolfia Compounds," *American Journal of Psychiatry* 113 (1957): 950.

28. Joseph J. Schildkraut, "The Catecholamine Hypothesis of Affective Disorders: A Review of Supporting Evidence," *American Journal of Psychiatry* 122 (November 1965): 509–522; quotation on 517.

29. Joseph J. Schildkraut, "Current Status of the Catecholamine Hypothesis of Affective Disorders," in Morris A. Lipton, Albert DiMascio, and Keith Killam eds., *Psychopharmacology: A Generation of Progress* (New York: Raven Press, 1978), 1231. My comments in this paragraph are based on the entire section on affective disorders.

30. Leonard Cammer, *Up from Depression* (New York: Pocket Books, 1969); Sylvia Plath, *The Bell Jar* (New York: Harper and Row, 1971).

31. The common cold of psychiatry idea can also be found in Rona Cherry and Laurence Cherry, *New York Times Magazine*, 25 November, 1973, 38–135; Martin E. P. Seligman, "Fall into Helplessness," *Psychology Today* 7, no. 1 (June 1973): 43; and M. Rosen, "Christmas Depression and How to Deal with It," *Harper's Bazaar*, December 1972. See also David M. Alpern, "All About Depression," *Cosmopolitan*, August 1974, 133–136.

32. Paul J. Gillette, *Depression: A Layman's Guide to the Symptoms and Cure* (New York: Bookthrift, 1973), 136–141.

33. Nathan S. Kline, *From Sad to Glad: Kline on Depression* (New York: Ballantine, 1974).

34. Martin E. P. Seligman, *Helplessness: On Depression, Development, and Death* (New York: W. H. Freeman, 1975). Seligman also called depression the "common cold of psychopathology"; see 76 and 77.

35. Ronald R. Fieve, M.D., *Moodswing* (New York: Bantam, 1975); Harvey M. Ross, M.D., *Fighting Depression* (New York: Larchmont Books, 1975). Fieve explained that "Twenty million Americans a year—10 percent of the population of the United States—experience a clinically depressed mood and never know just what it is they are experiencing": 22. See also Peter M. Lowinsohn, *Control Your Depression* (Englewood Cliffs, N.J.: Prentice-Hall, 1978).

36. See Mitchell Wilson, "DSM-III and the Transformation of American Psychiatry: A History," *American Journal of Psychiatry* 150 (1993): 399–410.

37. C. Baum et al., "Prescription Drug Use in 1984 and Changes over Time," *Medical Care* 26 (1988): 105–114; U.S. Department of Commerce, Bureau of the Census, *Current Industrial Reports*, 1975–1995. Cherry and Cherry wrote in their 1973 *New York Times Magazine* article that 20 million antidepressant prescriptions were written in 1972, a doubling of the number written in 1965 (134).

38. For an early comparison of efficacy, see W. F. Boyer and J. P. Feighner, "An Overview of Fluoxetine, a New Serotonin-specific Antidepressant," *Mount Sinai Journal of Medicine* 56 (1989): 136–140. Greg Critser, "Dealing a New Antidepressant," *Harper's Magazine*, May 1993. The popularity and commercial success of the SSRIs provided support for a view of depression as caused by insufficient serotonin at the synapse, but the identification of an apparently effective antidepressant that stimulated serotonin uptake has thrown yet another wrench into the catecholamine hypothesis. See Marc Ansseau, "The Paradox of Neurochemical and Clinical Properties of Serotonergic Antidepressants," in S. Z. Langer, N. Brunello, G. Racagni, and J. Medlewicz eds., *Critical Issues in the Treatment of Affective Disorders*, International Academy for Biomedical Drug Research (Basel: Karger, 1994), 9: 127–135.

39. Fran Schumer, "Bye-bye Blues: A New Wonder Drug for Depression," *New York Magazine*, 8 December 1989.

40. As suggested by Ron Roizen in his essay in this volume.

41. Gerald D. Williams and Samar F. Debakey, "Changes in Levels of Alcohol Consumption: United States, 1983–1988," *British Journal of Addiction* 87 (1992): 643–648. U.S. Department of Health and Human Services, *Drug Abuse and Drug Abuse Research*, The Third Triennial Report to Congress, DHHS Pub. No. (ADM)91–1704. (Rockville, Md.: DHHS, 1991), 16. Marijuana use in the United States apparently peaked in 1979, cocaine use in 1985.

LSD before Leary

Sidney Cohen's Critique of 1950s
Psychedelic Drug Research

STEVEN J. NOVAK

IN CONGRESSIONAL HEARINGS on LSD held in 1966, Timothy Leary asserted that the drug was "remarkably safe," citing a key 1960 article by Dr. Sidney Cohen. When Cohen himself testified, however, he contradicted Leary. He told Congress that LSD was safe only if administered under strict medical supervision and that in the wrong hands it was "a dangerous drug."[1]

The conflict between Cohen, a physician, and Leary, a layman, prefigured subsequent divergent historical interpretations. There are no historiographical schools on the drug movement, but both critics and partisans of LSD have embraced Cohen's 1960 article. The medical establishment criticized overzealous 1960s enthusiasts like Leary for meddling in medical affairs: "In 1960, ten years after [LSD] was introduced into psychiatry, its therapeutic prospects were still considered fair and the dangers slight. Then the debate received an infusion of irrational passion from the psychedelic crusaders and their enemies. . . . Twenty years after its introduction it was a pariah drug, scorned by the medical establishment and banned by the law."[2] On the other hand, proponents of LSD have attributed the medical profession's opposition to the wire-pulling of the CIA or to doctors' fear of social change. Thus one account blasted an anti-LSD editorial by saying, "[Roy S.] Grinker cited no data to back up these rather serious charges. He cited no data for the simple reason that there were none—Sidney Cohen's 1960 study on adverse reactions was still unchallenged in the literature. What Grinker was doing was projecting his own professional biases."[3]

To illuminate this debate, this essay, based on new archival material and oral history interviews, analyzes Cohen's pioneering studies of the safety of LSD. Through this lens one can obtain a behind-the-scenes look at the tensions between physicians and intellectuals in defining LSD's meaning, plot the shift of LSD research from a scientific investigation into a cultural crusade, map the spread of LSD in the 1950s, and elucidate the medical profession's alarm over LSD, which led to government passage of tighter regulations of psychedelic drugs. Before Timothy Leary, who first took LSD in 1961, catapulted onto the national scene by being fired from Harvard in 1963, Sidney Cohen had sounded the alarm that LSD was being abused and hurting people.[4]

The Making of a Psychopharmacologist

Cohen came to LSD research with a strong background in pharmacology. Born in 1910 in New York City, he was one of seven children of a Lithuanian-Jewish shoe shop owner. He majored in pharmacology at City College of New York and Columbia University, then earned an M.D. in 1938 from the University of Bonn. During World War II he served in the Army Medical Corps in the South Pacific. After his discharge he took a residency at the Wadsworth Veterans Administration Hospital in Los Angeles, adjacent to the University of California, Los Angeles, and then accepted a position as an internist across the street at the Brentwood VA Hospital for mentally ill servicemen.[5] When Wadsworth and Brentwood affiliated with the new UCLA School of Medicine, Cohen became an assistant clinical professor, supervising interns and graduate students. Handsome and prematurely gray, he gained a reputation as a popular teacher with an infectious enthusiasm for research.

Cohen's interest in mental illness stemmed from his responsibilities at Brentwood. He puzzled over how to diagnose the physical ailments of his mute, catatonic, irrational patients. As he sought to explore the patients' physical symptoms, his first publications dealt with diagnostic physical probes. Next he shifted toward biochemistry, publishing a case study on Cushing's syndrome in which he warned that the overproduction of adrenal cortical steroids that caused the disease was often undetectable and that patients should be given frequent "urinalysis, blood chemistry studies, renal function and glucose tolerance tests."[6]

Cohen grew intrigued by the mental and behavioral side effects of diseases and drugs. In 1951, after an accidental overdose left a patient "acutely psychotic" and paranoid, he undertook a study of the effects of Banthine. Cohen also wrote a survey of toxic psychoses, temporary breaks with reality due to disruption of the body's biochemical homeostasis. He observed that toxic psychoses were "unexpected and almost unpredictable" and could result in "catatonic stupor, manic excitement, paranoid agitation, or a vivid hallucinosis." His toxic psychosis research led to his interest in LSD. In his 1953 survey he first mentioned other investigators' research on LSD, a drug that at this time he said caused "a transient psychosis in all subjects."[7]

LSD as a Model Psychosis

LSD-25, lysergic acid diethylamide, was a new investigational drug available only to physicians for research purposes. It had been synthesized in 1938 at the Basel, Switzerland, laboratories of Sandoz Pharmaceuticals, by the chemist Albert Hofmann. Hofmann discovered its mind-altering properties in 1943 when he accidentally ingested a minute quantity and thought he was going mad. For years psychiatrists had searched for a chemical cause of insanity but had failed to find measurable abnormalities in the blood or urine of psychotics. What made Hofmann's discovery so exciting was that LSD worked in almost infinitesimal doses. Other drugs were measured in milligrams, thousandths of a gram, but LSD was measured in micrograms, millionths of a gram. Hoping that LSD might have clinical applications, Sandoz brought it to the attention of scientists, and samples reached the United States in the fall of 1949.[8]

Though the idea that LSD per se caused insanity was soon abandoned, researchers began to experiment with LSD to induce a model psychosis in subjects. They sought to use it as a means of temporarily replicating the effects of mental illness, as a so-called psychotomimetic, like hashish and mescaline, which psychiatrists had previously employed. By the mid-1950s, LSD research was being conducted in major American medical centers as well as in Canada, England, and Europe. In the background of this research was the alleged "brainwashing" of American prisoners during the Korean War. Popular accounts of brainwashing claimed that "some drug or 'lie serum' may possibly be used to speed up collapse."[9] To determine whether LSD might be a truth serum or a form of chemical warfare, the Central Intelligence Agency secretly began to fund LSD research in 1953 and the Army Chemical Corps started its own tests in 1955.[10] Because LSD was originally perceived as hazardous, the subjects of the early experiments were often soldiers, mental patients, prisoners, conscientious objectors, animals, medical school staff members, and physicians themselves.[11] A few early investigators refused to take LSD, while others who tried it said they experienced only unpleasant or inconsequential effects.[12] To guard against untoward reactions, doctors conducted experiments in clinics and laboratories. Subjects were monitored by EEG machines and polygraphs, had their words tape-recorded, and were given lengthy psychological and intelligence tests.

Though reactions varied, the usual LSD session included visual illusions, luminous, intense colors, undulating lines and multiple images in geometric patterns; dissociation, loss of ego boundaries, distorted body image; an elongated sense of time; synesthesia—"seeing" sound or "hearing" sights; emotional lability, giggling and weeping, anxiety and detachment; and a tantalizing sense of portentousness or incompleteness. The question was what—if anything—these symptoms signified.

The early LSD researchers concluded that their subjects went through a temporary psychosis, most commonly categorized as schizophrenia or paranoia. Subjects performed poorly on tests, made perceptual errors, and exhibited loss of concentration and regressive behavior.[13] Even the euphoria sometimes present was defined as manic and hebephrenic.[14] Researchers had anticipated deleterious effects. The widely used questionnaire devised by the Harold A. Abramson lab in New York presented all of its questions in negative terms. Forty-eight percent of Abramson's subjects said they felt unsteady, 41 percent weak, 40 percent peculiar, 27 percent anxious, and 26 percent nauseous. By the mid-1950s, when this first wave of LSD research reached the public in popular magazines, undergoing the effects of LSD was portrayed as a harrowing experience.[15]

LSD as a Psychedelic Experience

That LSD produced a model psychosis was taken for granted when Cohen first took the drug on October 12, 1955. He expected to feel catatonic or paranoid, but instead, he wrote, "I was taken by surprise. This was no confused, disoriented delirium, but something quite different." His subsequent report described feeling an elevated peacefulness, as if "the problems and strivings, the worries and frustrations of everyday life vanished; in their place was a majestic, sunlit, heavenly inner quietude. . . . I seemed to have finally arrived at the contemplation of eternal truth."[16]

Cohen immediately launched his own LSD experiments. He sponsored three doctoral dissertations by UCLA graduate students in psychology that measured the effects of LSD on eighty-one members of the academic community.[17] The dissertations followed the standard model psychosis methodology of conducting extensive tests, and the results replicated prior studies: subjects showed impaired intellectual ability, lowered IQ, inability to concentrate, and breakdown of ego functioning. Afterward, they reported that under LSD they felt emptiness, loneliness, and isolation. Cohen was disappointed by these reactions, which differed from his own. At the 1959 Princeton LSD conference, he said, "Though we have been using the available measuring instruments, the check lists, the performance tests, the psychological batteries, and so forth, the core of the LSD situation remains in the dark, quite untouched by our activities."[18]

Rather than accept the dissertation findings as an accurate picture of the effects of LSD, Cohen took the crucial step of altering his approach. He shifted the focus of his LSD research to men of letters. The idea of filtering LSD reports through refined psyches was suggested by the Canadian psychiatrist Humphry Osmond, who first gave mescaline to Aldous Huxley. At a 1956 conference, Osmond said that one of the problems with LSD research was that there was a "dearth of subjects skilled in self-observation."[19]

Hoping for more articulate reports, Cohen tried LSD on psychoanalysts, supposed experts on the unconscious, but they either blocked the drug effects or had bad reactions. Next he turned to his friend Gerald Heard, an English expatriate freelance writer whose special interests were mysticism and popular science. In 1957 Heard wrote a friend that he was one of the "human guinea pigs in the lysergic acid research." He described the effect as "a shift of consciousness" that was "so clearly similar to the accounts given by the mystics that none of us feel able to deny that this is in fact the experience which we undergo."[20]

Cohen also collaborated with Heard's friend Aldous Huxley, whom he met in late 1955. The famous author of *Brave New World* was the literary lion of Los Angeles, where he had settled in 1937 to write for Hollywood.[21] Owing to his near blindness, which dated from his youth, Huxley was unable to engage in active scientific research himself, but he compensated by cultivating his talents as a conversationalist and stylist. Rather than explore the broad paths of thought, he searched the odd byways—hypnotism, ESP, flying saucers, and reincarnation. Long before Cohen met him, on May 4, 1953, Huxley had persuaded Osmond to give him a dose of mescaline, an experience that inspired him to write *The Doors of Perception* (1954) and *Heaven and Hell* (1956). In both books Huxley mentioned LSD, though he did not actually try it till December 1955, after the books were written.[22] Huxley redefined taking mescaline and LSD as a mystical religious experience. He claimed that these drugs allowed one to transcend the mundane world and enter the elevated state of consciousness usually reserved to poets, artists, and saints.

A few medical researchers questioned the validity of Huxley's account. Louis Lasagna considered *Doors of Perception* the result of "unusual . . . romantic proclivities." Ronald Fisher remarked that the book contained "99 percent Aldous Huxley and only one half gram mescaline." Joost A. M. Meerloo found Huxley's reactions "not necessarily the same as . . . other people experience."[23] Yet Huxley's critics were ignored, and his books became counterculture classics.

In redefining the meaning of the LSD experience, Huxley declared war on academic psychiatry. Despite accepting honors at psychiatric conferences, he privately scorned what he called "the Electric Shock Boys, the Chlorpromaziners and the 57 Varieties of Psychotherapists." Huxley converted Osmond and Albert Hofmann to the idea that taking LSD provided a transcendental experience, and possibly Cohen's own first reaction was shaped by a prior reading of Huxley.[24]

To make the public receptive to mescaline and LSD, Huxley sought to provide a new label for the drugs: "It will give that elixir a bad name if it continues to be associated, in the public mind, with schizophrenia symptoms. People will think they are going mad, when in fact they are beginning, when they take it, to go sane." With Huxley's help, Osmond discarded his former term for describing these experiences—hallucinogenic, which connoted mental illness—and in 1956 coined the word psychedelic, which signified "mind-manifesting." Osmond introduced the new term at a 1956 conference at which he declared that LSD's effects were not a model psychosis but, rather, a psychedelic experience. "For myself," he said, "my experiences with these substances have been the most strange, most awesome, and among the most beautiful things. . . . These are not escapes from but enlargements, burgeonings of reality."[25]

That physicians like Osmond and Cohen would turn to nonmedical thinkers like Huxley and Heard was partly due to psychiatry's lack of an adequate model of mental illness, such as the germ theory provided for infectious disease. At first Cohen deferred to these prominent intellectuals. He treated them more as collaborators than as subjects and trusted them with samples of LSD for self-experiments and to administer to others. He wrote in a posthumous tribute to Heard, "We learned from Gerald that, just as in some psychological experiments animals are inappropriate test subjects, *so in certain experiments with the psychedelics ordinary men are inadequate subjects.* . . . He was a skilled, articulate observer in entering into an indescribable, surging state, which could fragment some with its intensity and divert others with its entertaining visual displays."[26]

LSD and Psychotherapy

Besides turning to intellectuals, Cohen revised the reasons for giving LSD. He explored whether LSD might have a helpful effect in facilitating psychotherapy, curing alcoholism, and enhancing creativity. To test LSD in psychotherapy, he collaborated with Betty Eisner, a recent UCLA doctorate in psychology. The rationale underlying their study was the Freudian belief that the roots of maladjustment lay in trauma buried in the unconscious. Where Freud had used talk therapy to explore the unconscious, other psychiatrists tried to enter the subconscious by injecting their patients with drugs such as sodium amytal or causing them to inhale carbon dioxide.[27] This so-called narcoanalysis was much discussed in the 1950s. An English psychiatrist described LSD as "assisting the unconscious to reveal its secrets," though other psychiatrists were skeptical of its therapeutic potential.[28]

Cohen and Eisner sought to maximize LSD's potential by taming its terror. Cohen wrote Osmond, "We are going to study how and whether the LSD experience can be more 'healing.' . . . We are putting Betty Eisner to work on the development of an optimal technique and will see whether anything comes of it." They consulted with Al Hubbard, who first gave Huxley LSD and was using the drug in therapy in Canada. Hubbard was a mysterious figure, a charismatic, flamboyant entrepreneur with an extravagant lifestyle.[29] Huxley and the Canadian researchers hoped that Hubbard would finance LSD research, not realizing that he planned to make his fortune with the drug. Though not even a college graduate, Hubbard purchased a diploma-mill Ph.D., wore an Aesculapian tiepin, and, on his own, administered LSD, even though he was not a physician. To soften LSD's harsh effects, Eisner and Hubbard devised techniques such as starting with low doses, providing a domestic setting for "treatment," and establishing close rapport with patients before giving them the drug. Cohen was impressed by Hubbard's techniques but suspected that much of the effect was due to suggestion, which might not produce lasting improvement. He also worried that if subjects were merely reacting to the setting, the drug itself was not exposing their unconscious.[30]

In April 1957 Cohen and Eisner began giving LSD to psychotherapy patients. Over the next year and a half they treated twenty-two patients suffering from minor personality disorders. Unlike the model psychosis subjects, these patients expected that the drug would be therapeutic. Aware that evaluating therapy was subjective, Cohen and Eisner waited six months and then measured progress in the patients by behavioral criteria such as holding a job, sustaining a relationship, or giving up drinking. Working with these criteria, they reported a remarkable 73 percent improvement rate.

Their paper attributed these gains to giving patients what they called an "integrative experience, . . . a state wherein the patient accepts himself as he is. . . . There is a feeling of harmony with his environment." This mystical thrust was largely Eisner's doing. Like Huxley and Heard, she studied Eastern religions. She visited Heard's Vedanta monastery, Trabuco College, and had her personality analyzed by Krishnamurti. Even before their LSD experiment began, she confided, "I feel, and think that Sid does too, that the best possible therapeutic LSD experience is one in which a subject glimpses the unity of the cosmos."[31]

The second new thrust of Cohen's work with LSD was treating alcoholism, one of the most intractable forms of neurosis. The model for this approach came from Alcoholics Anonymous, founded in 1935 by Bill Wilson after he had "hit bottom" in Towns Hospital in 1934 and then had undergone a religious experience. There were two ideas about how LSD might cure alcoholism. In 1954, at Saskatchewan Hospital, Osmond and his partner, the psychiatrist Abram Hoffer, began giving alcoholics LSD on the theory that the traumatic drug experience resembled the delirium tremens (DTs) of hitting bottom.[32] On the other hand, their associate Al Hubbard believed that LSD brought alcoholics to awareness of the higher power to which AA said one must surrender one's will. The latter view gained support from Bill Wilson himself. Wilson was a friend of Heard's and through him met Osmond and Huxley and was drawn into trying LSD. Wilson's first LSD session took place in Los Angeles on August 29, 1956, with Cohen in attendance. Wilson took LSD again in February 1957 at Betty Eisner's house, along with her husband, Cohen, and an AA associate. Wilson dabbled in LSD for two years, comparing its effects on occasion to his mystical experience at Towns Hospital.[33] He started a private LSD group in New York, with LSD samples supplied by Cohen and Dr. Keith Ditman.

Ditman, one of Cohen's former Brentwood residents, was director of the UCLA Neuropsychiatric Institute's Alcoholism Research Clinic, where he tested LSD on alcoholics. A number of prominent figures passed through the clinic. Besides Wilson, Ditman gave LSD to Chuck Dederich, founder of the anti-drug commune Synanon, and Alan Watts, the popularizer of Zen. News of Wilson's involvement in LSD caused a scandal in AA, and Wilson accused Ditman of leaking his name. Ditman denied the charge but admitted that "when the word about LSD and our . . . studies got to one or two of the A.A. meetings, things became pretty lively."[34]

In his research Ditman gave LSD to seventy subjects. They received a single dose, without therapy, in a nonthreatening setting. Later, subjects rated three hundred card-sort statements. Ditman's first published finding was that LSD did not resemble the DTs. Whereas the DTs were marked by "anxiety, horror, depression, irritation, and paranoid thoughts," the LSD experience had been "typified by euphoria, humor, relaxation, and a nebulous sense of wonderment."[35]

Next Ditman published a full breakdown of the card-sort responses. When subjects were asked, "Looking back on your LSD experience, how does it look to you now?" 72 percent replied "a very pleasant experience," 66 percent "something I want to try again," and 66 percent "an experience of great beauty."[36] One would hardly think that this was the same drug used in the model psychosis research of the early 1950s. LSD was like a barometer measuring cultural change and preconceptions, and its subjective "meaning" was a social construct. Obviously, Ditman's subjects were having what Huxley had called a "psychedelic" experience.

By the end of the 1950s LSD was known as a miracle cure for alcoholism. In 1960, Huxley lectured at Harvard and met Leary, whom he regaled with LSD anecdotes: "Humphry Osmond curing alcoholics in Saskatchewan. Keith Ditman's plans to clean out Skid Row in Los Angeles." Likewise, the psychologist Abraham Maslow pointed to LSD research on alcoholics as proof of the therapeutic value of "peak experiences."[37]

The third new area of LSD research was testing its effect on the creative process. Model psychosis researchers had occasionally given mescaline or LSD to artists in order to track their mental deterioration, but psychedelic researchers like Huxley expected the drugs to enhance creativity.[38] The prevailing aesthetic of the day traced the origins of creativity to the unconscious. The reason people failed to be creative was that their conscious minds were encrusted by dull conventionality. Artists romanticized people who supposedly lived close to the unconscious—children, natives, outcasts, and the mentally ill.[39] The popular equation of art and neurosis was so strong that in the 1950s therapists complained that patients resisted getting well because of the "culturally noxious assumption . . . that one must be sick to be creative." A University of Chicago physiologist wrote that "from the young, the naive, the dreaming, the drug users, come a great spate of fresh imaginings."[40]

Cohen never published his findings regarding creativity, but he accepted for a time that LSD stimulated originality. The major figure testing LSD on artists was the psychiatrist Oscar Janiger, who often shared office space with Cohen. Janiger tested LSD on more than a hundred painters, writers, and composers between 1958 and 1962 and on a thousand subjects overall. Though his plan had been to test a cross-section of the population, "the artists began to come in a flood. Then I realized my demographic structure was going to be shot out the window," forcing him to turn artists away.[41]

To some psychiatrists, the fantastic claims being made for LSD seemed incredible. Investigators in the rest of the nation wondered why their subjects had not had transcendental experiences. They charged that West Coast investigators were biased in favor of LSD. Louis Jolyon West asserted that "either LSD is the most phenomenal drug ever introduced into treatment in psychiatry, or else the results were evaluated by criteria imposed by enthusiastic, if not positively prejudiced, people." Since it seemed "unlikely that subjects on the West Coast are organically different from those on the East

Coast," Jonathan O. Cole hypothesized that the differences must have re-sulted from "a therapist-induced mystical experience similar to religious con-version."[42]

Popularizing LSD

In 1959, as LSD was at its peak of medical acceptance, Cohen's antennae began to pick up danger signs. One disturbing trend was that researchers were growing lax in controlling the drug. They began to share LSD in their homes with friends. A 1958 article on experiments at the nearby Long Beach VA Hospital let slip that researchers were having "LSD-25 social parties." Sessions were held at Huxley's house in the Hollywood Hills and that of the Hollywood producer Ivan Tors. Ditman recalled that "LSD be-came for us an intellectual fun drug." By the late 1950s such socializing spread to the East Coast. On Long Island, Abramson began holding Friday-night LSD soirees in his home and was "besieged by people who wanted to take the drug." Cohen tried to avoid such gatherings; by 1968 he had taken LSD only seven times.[43]

Cohen was also concerned that LSD research was being mixed with pseu-doscience. Almost from the start, he and Eisner clashed about interpreting their therapy results. "I think that the material we have been getting makes him uncomfortable," she wrote. "In fact, he has said as much." By "material" Eisner meant the vivid sense subjects sometimes had that they were revisiting ancient Egypt, India, or Greece. Huxley, Heard, Hubbard, Eisner, and other researchers considered these impressions to be actual memories of past lives—proof of reincarnation.[44] What brought reincarnation to mind was the best-selling book *The Search for Bridey Murphy* (1956), in which an amateur hypnotist claimed to have uncovered the prior identities of his subject. Heard served as a consultant on the book and advised the author that the memories were authentic.[45]

In addition to reincarnation, pseudoscientists claimed that LSD facili-tated extrasensory perception. Huxley and Heard popularized paranormal psychology and published their accounts of LSD experiences in journals of psychical research. Eileen Garrett, founder of the Parapsychology Founda-tion, experimented with LSD in the 1950s and funded LSD research.[46] Her foundation sponsored conferences on psychedelics and ESP in New York City in 1958 and in France in 1959. Insofar as ESP, like reincarnation, lacked academic respectability, Cohen realized that being coupled with ESP would lessen LSD's credibility. He hoped to find a "middle ground" between sci-entific positivism, on the one hand, and "the Huxleys and Heards, . . . the Hubbards and witch doctors and the medicine men," on the other. LSD, he wrote, had "opened a door from which we must not retreat merely because we feel uncomfortably unscientific at the threshold."[47]

Yet Cohen did feel "uncomfortably unscientific." In 1960 he wrote his sponsor, "I deplore some of the fringy goings on with this group of drugs." By then he had distanced himself from some of his associates. He first rejected Hubbard. To gain credibility, Hubbard had created a mock institute called the Commission for the Study of Creative Intelligence. Huxley and Heard were board members, and Hubbard asked Cohen to join. In 1956 Cohen said yes, telling Hubbard, "I feel it an honor to be associated with them." But in 1957 he abruptly resigned.[48] His public reason was that the commission served no function and was merely "a letter-head for Al to use to impress his correspondents." He may also have been influenced by a shouting and shoving match between Ditman and Hubbard in the late spring of 1957, when Ditman vainly tried to stop Hubbard from acquiring a supply of LSD on the grounds that he was not a physician. Eisner admonished Hubbard, "I don't know what the Canadian laws are, but I do know that in the U.S. . . . no drug may be prescribed or administered except under the supervision of an M.D. And you and I, no matter what our training, experience, and background, are not M.D.'s. . . . If you give it to someone for philosophic or religious reasons, you are still prescribing a drug."[49] Only physicians were by law authorized to experiment with drugs, especially investigational drugs.

Next Cohen broke off from Eisner. At the end of their psychotherapy experiment she wanted to start another round of patients, but he begged off. Actually, he planned to launch a more strictly controlled study, but he confided that "it does not seem to me that Betty is the ideal therapist for an investigation of this sort. Her personal investment in the success of LSD therapy tends to reduce the validity of her results."[50]

Cohen even began to keep Heard at arm's length. They had written drafts of a book on LSD together, titled "Journey into Consciousness," and submitted it for publication. When the manuscript was rejected, Heard hoped to revise it, planning to stress the beneficial effects of LSD, but Cohen ended the collaboration. According to Heard, Cohen "felt it would be wiser for him not to be identified with so positive an approach. . . . He feels any reference that would go beyond recording the psychotomimetic side of the medicament's action is 'unscientific.'" Cohen not only retreated from their joint projects but even refused to write an introduction for Heard's proposed volume, explaining that Heard's manuscript was "intemperate in its hope for LSD." When Cohen's book *The Beyond Within: The LSD Story* appeared, Heard chided him for playing "public prosecutor."[51]

While Cohen grew nervous about the excesses of LSD zealots, a second wave of publicity presented LSD effects not as a model psychosis but as a panacea. Cohen himself took part in the publicity. He served as technical consultant on a 1957 television special entitled *The Lonely World*. He wrote a friend, "It is about LSD. . . . I'm not too proud about the story, but it is not completely incredible. It's the old compromise between fact and drama." The media's tendency to exaggerate plagued LSD researchers. Later that year Cohen served as an adviser on the eight-part *Focus on Sanity*, which again brought LSD to television. As the audience watched one of Cohen's attractive female subjects undergoing an LSD experience, Heard told viewers, "For most . . . it's an outstanding event in their lives." On March 12, 1958, Cohen gave LSD to Paul Saltman, a young University of Southern California biochemist, whose reaction was filmed for local television. Saltman hammed it up for the journalists, exclaiming, "It's wild, man, wild!"[52]

Newspaper coverage was similarly overdramatic. In June 1958, when Cohen and Eisner presented their LSD therapy findings at the American Medical Association convention in San Francisco, their talk caused such a stir that it led to a TV appearance and a front-page story. The *San Francisco Chronicle* reported that five LSD treatments, at a dollar per session, were more effective than "the standard sessions of psychoanalysis, which often require hundreds or thousands of hours, and many thousands of dollars." Traditional therapists were appalled by the account. Eisner wrote that while being on TV had been "fun," the newspaper's "garbled" article had made her "ambivalent about publicity." That fall, Ditman gave reporters a glowing account of the UCLA Alcoholism Research Clinic. "Many subjects who have undergone LSD experiences think highly of the beneficial effects of the drug," he declared. Janiger lectured frequently on LSD to art institutes. A newspaper declared, "Most exciting finding: apparently all of us have a creative faculty, and LSD shows there may be ways to unlock it at will."[53]

The biggest splash came in 1959, when Cary Grant told Hollywood gossip columnist Joe Hyams that he had taken LSD over sixty times in therapy since 1958. Grant bragged that because he took LSD "young women have never before been so attracted to me."[54] As might be expected, people clamored for the drug. Hyams recalled, "After my series came out, the phone began to ring wildly. Friends wanted to know where they could get the drug. Psychiatrists called, complaining their patients were now begging them for LSD. . . . In all, I got close to eight hundred letters." Historical accounts of media coverage of LSD have missed this pre-1960s publicity.[55] Obviously, by the end of the 1950s the public was well aware of LSD.

In addition to his concern about overzealous LSD apostles and widespread publicity, Cohen shared the medical profession's worries about the problems created for medical ethics by exploding pharmaceutical research.

Physicians feared that drug companies were introducing too many new drugs, too fast, turning doctors into drug company advance men and their patients into guinea pigs.[56] Participants in a 1956 conference concluded that, although physicians enjoyed legal immunity and insurance coverage for mishaps that occurred in the course of treating patients, "in giving drugs to volunteers the physician has no such legal protection. The death of a volunteer caused by taking an experimental drug would legally be homicide." Fearing lawsuits, at the 1959 Princeton conference Paul Hoch advised LSD researchers "to be very much aware of the legal implications of many of these things we are doing." In fact, psychiatric experiments entailed unknown risks. That same year psychiatrists conducting experiments on sleep deprivation and sensory isolation, which produced LSD-like hallucinations, discovered that these experiences could cause mental breakdowns.[57]

Unfortunately, just as the safety of LSD was becoming an issue, the drug was spreading into the undergraduate population. On March 20, 1959, Los Angeles newspapers carried a front-page story about the drug death of a freshman at the University of Redlands, eighty miles east of Los Angeles. The police investigation showed that he and five classmates had been experimenting with drugs, among them mescaline and LSD, in his dorm room. Closer to home, that same spring the UCLA biochemist Clara Szego kept two of her students from taking part in a campus LSD experiment. She had tested LSD on rats and recalls, "It was perfectly clear to me that this was no innocuous little substance that you could recover from."[58] She forced the investigators to stop their experiments.

Investigating the Safety of LSD

Almost a decade after LSD research began in the United States, Cohen took the unusual step of launching an investigation into the drug's safety. In February 1959 he sent a questionnaire to sixty-two LSD researchers, explaining his motivation in a cover letter: "A survey of this sort seems desirable at this time because reports of undesirable and unexpected reactions to lysergic acid diethylamide are not finding their way into the literature. Since it is coming into more widespread use, it may be possible, through an analysis of the collected data, to avoid some of the untoward events that might otherwise occur." He asked whether any of their subjects had died, committed suicide, or suffered mental breakdowns or other serious side effects. Forty-four of the sixty-two replied. Their responses provided demographic data about authorized LSD and mescaline use to that date. Researchers reported having administered the drugs over twenty-five thousand times to almost five thousand individuals. Though there had been occasional panic attacks, ten prolonged psychotic reactions, and a few flashbacks, no one had died by being poisoned by the drug.[59]

A key statistic was suicides. Frank Fremont-Smith said in 1959, "We are all worried that someone might commit suicide after taking the drug." Cohen had learned of five possible LSD suicides but concluded that only two of these had been "directly due to LSD."[60] In his published report, he calculated that the suicide rate of LSD subjects was 0.4/1,000—two suicides among five thousand cases. On the basis of this figure, he concluded that complications were "surprisingly infrequent" and that, in the hands of experimental clinicians, LSD and mescaline were "safe." Nevertheless, Cohen's article offered much advice on how to screen people who should not take the drug and on how doctors could terminate an LSD session gone awry.

LSD activists read Cohen's study as if it were a ringing endorsement. His statistic of 0.4 suicides per one thousand subjects was widely cited in subsequent years. A 1964 study quoted Cohen's figure as proof that LSD was "exceptionally safe." A model legal release form for LSD experiments offered Cohen's 1960 calculations as the only data about risks—vital information for informed consent. In 1966, as mentioned above, Leary cited the study in his congressional testimony.[61]

The trouble was that Cohen's study was tentative. The data were vague because he asked investigators only for approximate numbers and then rounded them off. The data were guesswork because not a single lab had carried out a follow-up of its subjects. Cohen acknowledged that his study was "doubtless incomplete" and that he suspected "serious complications" might have gone unreported because of investigators' "guilt feelings."[62] Eighteen researchers failed to reply to the questionnaire, and some key labs had withheld vital information. Cohen was not informed that in 1952 a patient at the Massachusetts Mental Health Center had committed suicide within hours of being injected with LSD.[63] He did not know of the Hoch patient who died in 1953 after being injected with a mescaline derivative. The CIA had successfully covered up the 1953 suicide of one of its subjects. An expert later speculated that if Cohen had been aware of the CIA suicide he might have reached different conclusions.[64]

But Cohen did not close his investigation in 1960. No sooner was the ink dry on his article than he began to obtain new data, especially on abuses by unqualified therapists that had caused adverse patient reactions. Therapists were drawn to LSD partly because it broke down patient defenses but also because it was lucrative. Although Sandoz Pharmaceuticals gave the drug away, therapists charged up to $500 for a session. As an investigational drug, LSD was supposed to be used exclusively for research, but to get around this rule therapists simply tabulated and wrote up their results—or said they planned to. Cary Grant's Beverly Hills psychiatrists, Arthur L. Chandler and Mortimer A. Hartman, published a paper in which they reported giving LSD 690 times to 110 patients, who showed a 69 percent improvement rate. A second group offering LSD therapy and research was the Menlo Park Foundation for Advanced Study, which operated both in the Bay Area and in southern California.[65] It charged $600 per treatment, and its founders dreamed of opening a string of LSD clinics across the nation. By the early 1960s at least a dozen Los Angeles psychologists were using LSD in therapy, including Huxley's wife Laura. Several incidents occurred, though a veil of silence hides many of the worst excesses. An LSD therapy handbook written by Canadian psychologists recommended that therapists take LSD along with patients to improve rapport, and some southern California psychologists who took the advice became involved in sexual activity with their patients and were charged with sexual abuse. In 1962 a middle-aged Long Beach man filed a $500,000 damage suit against his clergyman, the president of the Menlo Park Foundation, and several others on the grounds that they had enticed him to take LSD, a "dangerous" drug, which they were "unqualified" to administer. After taking LSD he had suffered depression, attempted suicide, and ended up in a mental institution.[66] By 1963 a number of local LSD investigators who were heavy users themselves had fallen afoul of legal and medical authorities; some had even been hospitalized. Cohen was bitter about the excesses of LSD psychotherapists. He charged that LSD therapists "have included an excessively large proportion of psychopathic individuals."[67]

Cohen's only connection to these for-profit LSD therapists was in treating their failures. One case in particular crystallized his concern. A forty-year-old woman who had undergone eight LSD treatments in Honolulu administered by Dr. William E. Stevens attempted to commit suicide in 1961 and ended up at the UCLA Hospital. In taking her history, Cohen discovered a painfully unstable life, including child abuse, murdered parents, prostitution, illegitimate children, divorces, suicide attempts, and electroshock treatments. He thought LSD was contraindicated in her case and upbraided Stevens: "I wondered why uncovering therapy was given this recently psychotic unstable woman. . . . Oddly enough, she wants LSD. I told her that she wanted magic and that this would be very risky. . . . I think she should be considered an LSD failure."[68]

In his defense, Stevens explained that this woman had suffered one of only two known disastrous experiences in the four hundred LSD sessions he had administered so far, though he told Cohen of other abuses in Hawaii. In reply, Cohen acknowledged that Los Angeles also had problems: "We, too, have our share of hair-raising LSD operations. Only today Keith [Ditman] and I saw a woman who had a panicky dissociated state following extensive LSD therapy. A second possibility is that her hallucinatory episode represented a folie à deux with her therapist. In general, this sort of eccentric LSD practice is diminished here due to Harry [Althouse]'s tighter control of the drug."[69]

Unfortunately, Cohen's faith that Althouse, the Sandoz detail man, could keep the lid on abuses was shattered in early 1962 when he and Ditman met a man at a Hollywood party who told them that he was making bootleg LSD. His sugar cubes contained 1,000 micrograms of LSD, ten times the normal dosage. Although the identity of the street acid maker is unknown, it may have been either Bernard Roseman or Bernard Copley. Roseman and Copley were the first men arrested, in 1963, for selling homemade LSD. They had been introduced to LSD in southern California experiments. Charged with smuggling the drug into the United States from Israel, they claimed that they had manufactured the LSD in Los Angeles in 1960.[70]

Alarmed that physicians were losing control over LSD, Cohen and Ditman quickly wrote a second article on the drug's side effects, warning the medical profession about the dangerous new complications they were seeing. They presented nine case studies. A child had accidentally swallowed an LSD sugar cube and suffered dissociation for months. A therapist had given a female patient LSD over three hundred times and left her an emotional wreck, surviving on sedatives. Avant-garde groups were mixing LSD with peyote, marijuana, barbiturates, amphetamines, and the like. Owing to the spread of LSD and the existence of a black market supply, Cohen and Ditman concluded that "the dangers of suicide, prolonged psychotic reactions, and antisocial acting out behavior exist."[71]

Federal Regulation of LSD Research

The impact of Cohen and Ditman's warning was magnified by the fact that it appeared just before the thalidomide tragedy hit the press. Women who had taken thalidomide, a sedative, gave birth to over ten thousand babies, two-thirds of whom lived, who suffered severe birth defects; most of these children were born in Germany and England, but there were six in the United States.[72] Like LSD, thalidomide was an investigational drug in the United States. Even before the thalidomide crisis broke, LSD researchers had been warned that they should stop giving the drug to pregnant women. In the medical community, LSD and thalidomide were linked. In Canada a new regulatory category of drugs was created, Schedule H, which could be neither sold nor distributed, and thalidomide and LSD were the first drugs placed on the list.[73]

The thalidomide crisis forced Congress to pass tougher regulatory controls over investigational drugs. Since December 1959, Senator Estes Kefauver had been conducting hearings on drug company price fixing. Suddenly, after the thalidomide scare, his committee was in the spotlight. In hearings held in August 1962, Senator Jacob Javits was amazed to learn that physicians could try out unproven drugs on patients without warning them that they were being tested. The head of the Food and Drug Administration, George P. Larrick, had to admit that, as the law then stood, "that is up to the physician." On October 10, 1962, Congress passed the Kefauver-Harris Drug Amendments, which went into effect in January 1963. Henceforth the FDA had to give prior approval for all testing of new investigational drugs, and such drugs would be authorized for sale only if they had been proven both safe and efficacious in curing some human ailment.[74]

The FDA and the Federal Bureau of Narcotics had been caught napping by this new outbreak of drug use. The FDA's first investigations of LSD abuse began in 1961, in southern California, where early "reports of misuse" focused on "physicians and psychologists who were not authorized to use the drug."[75] No one knows who tipped off the FDA, but in 1962 agents raided several Los Angeles therapists and seized their LSD supplies. Sandoz Pharmaceuticals took the opportunity provided by the new FDA regulations to cut off the supply of LSD to marginal investigators.[76] In 1963 Sandoz restricted LSD to researchers connected to the National Institute of Mental Health, state commissioners of mental health, or the VA, which cut the number from a couple of hundred to only seventy. But it was too late to stop the spread of LSD. In early 1963 Leary was fired from Harvard and launched his crusade to have the nation's youth "turn on, tune in, and drop out." Leary gained so much notoriety that we forget that the crackdown on LSD began before his escapades.[77]

As the popularization and use of psychedelic drugs increased, Congress further tightened regulations. In 1965 Congress passed the Drug Control Amendments, which prohibited the manufacture or sale of psychedelic drugs. In 1966 California and New York passed the first state laws on LSD. California Governor Edmund G. Brown Sr. invited Cohen and Ditman to the ceremonial signing. That same year, Sandoz withdrew its sponsorship and Congress cut off nearly all LSD research. To halt the spread of LSD, Cohen served as the first director of the NIMH Division of Narcotics Addiction and Drug Abuse from 1968 to 1970. His LSD subject Clare Boothe Luce teased him, "There is a certain irony in Dr. Sid's predicament. (LSD has been your Frankenstein monster!)"[78] Cohen thought it was time to tame the monster.

THE INTRODUCTION TO this essay showed that the historiography of the psychedelic drug movement starts with the assumption that Cohen proved the safety of LSD in 1960 and then tries to explain why, nevertheless, the medical profession and the government turned against the drug. I argue, on the contrary, that Cohen's study arose out of his concerns about its safety, that the 1960 study was admittedly incomplete and inconclusive, and that Cohen reversed himself only two years later. This interpretation sees medical opposition to LSD in the 1960s as due not to secret CIA conspiracies or to fear of the counterculture but to valid health concerns. The medical profession's rejection of LSD was not the result of its subservience to the government; rather, government restrictions on LSD followed pressure from physicians. The intrusion of "strangers at the bedside," as David Rothman has called increased governmental regulation of American medicine, was justified in the case of LSD research.[79]

This review of Cohen's LSD research also allows us to mark the time and place where the psychedelic drug movement began. The transformation of LSD research from a medical affair to a cultural crusade occurred not at Harvard in the early 1960s or in San Francisco in the 1967 summer of love but in Los Angeles in the late 1950s. It was here that Huxley and Heard redefined LSD's effects as a mystical experience. Southern California investigators extended the purview of LSD research from mental illness to neurosis, alcoholism, and creativity, causing word of LSD to spread among alcoholics, artists, writers, and actors. Premature media announcements stirred public expectations and excitement. Despite the drug's investigational status, therapists abandoned caution and adopted it in their clinical practice. Yet none of the hasty claims made for LSD withstood the test of time.

Cohen's collaboration with Heard and Huxley attempted to bridge the gap between what C. P. Snow called "the two cultures," the scientific and the literary. Cohen sought to find a middle way between scientism and mysticism, but he underestimated the extent to which his collaborators brought along their own agendas and values. LSD researchers in the 1950s understood the subjective nature of drug responses and how often the results merely mirrored subjects' personalities. To be valid, LSD experiments required a random sample of subjects with no preconceptions about the drug. Once Huxley and Heard had popularized their psychedelic interpretation, self-selected volunteers arrived primed to have a "Doors of Perception" experience. Bill Wilson read *Heaven and Hell* before his first LSD session. Ditman noted that several subjects came to his experiments "after reading Huxley's

Heaven and Hell or *Doors of Perception.*" Janiger's study participants often read Huxley before taking LSD. A subject in New York explained that he had volunteered in order to be "in good company—people like Aldous Huxley."[80] Experimental data from subjects like these were worthless because the subjects had been preconditioned.

By the mid-1960s Cohen had grown skeptical of Huxley's inflated claims for LSD. Cohen and the RAND Corporation psychologist William H. McGlothlin tried but failed to find statistically significant proof of the lasting effects of LSD. Though the effects produced by a dose of LSD felt tremendously significant, Cohen suspected that this was mainly self-deception. LSD revealed not a higher reality but antirationality.[81] By that time Cohen was describing the LSD state as a "completely uncritical one" with "the great possibility that the insights are not valid at all and overwhelm certain credulous personalities." His alternative to LSD came in advice he gave an audience near the end of his life: "I would like to commend the sober mind to you."[82]

Notes

1. U.S. Senate Subcommittee on Executive Reorganization, 24, 25, 26 May 1966, *Organization and Coordination of Federal Drug Research and Regulatory Programs: LSD* (Washington, D.C.: Government Printing Office, 1966) (hereafter cited as *Federal LSD Research*), 139, 145, 155.

2. Lester Grinspoon and James B. Bakalar, *Psychedelic Drugs Reconsidered* (New York: Basic, 1979), 232 (see 229 for Cohen's study). See also Roy F. Baumeister and Kathleen S. Placidi, "A Social History and Analysis of the LSD Controversy," *Journal of Humanistic Psychology* 23 (1983) 30–32; and Robert F. Ulrich and Bernard M. Patten, "The Rise, Decline, and Fall of LSD," *Perspectives in Biology and Medicine* 34 (1991): 572–575.

3. Jay Stevens, *Storming Heaven: LSD and the American Dream* (New York: Atlantic Monthly Press, 1987), 181 (quotation), 173. On the role of the CIA see Martin A. Lee and Bruce Shlain, *Acid Dreams: The CIA, LSD, and the Sixties Rebellion* (New York: Grove, 1985), 89–95; and John Marks, *The Search for the "Manchurian Candidate": The CIA and Mind Control* (New York: Times Books, 1979), 118–121.

4. The first notice of Leary in the *Reader's Guide to Periodical Literature* is "LSD and All That," *Time*, 29 March 1963, 72–73.

5. Dorothy Cohen interview, 27 February 1993. Unless otherwise noted, all interviews were conducted by the author and all interview tapes and notes are in his possession. I am grateful to Cohen's daughter for providing me with information about her father, photographs, and access to his personal papers (hereafter cited as Cohen Papers).

6. Sidney Cohen, "Cushing's Syndrome: Report of a Case," *Annals of Western Medicine and Surgery* 4 (1950): 288–293, on 289. For Cohen's earliest publications see Leonard M. Asher and Cohen, "Gastroscopic Perforation of the Esophagus and Stomach," *Gastroenterology* 12 (1949): 966–969; and Cohen, "The Management of Massive Esophageal Hemorrhage with Tamponade," ibid., 13 (1949): 141–151.

7. Sidney Cohen, "The Toxic Psychoses and Allied States," *American Journal of Med-*

icine 15 (1953): 813–828, on pp. 813, 817. Cohen attributed his interest in LSD to his research on toxic psychosis; he is quoted in Harold A. Abramson, ed., *The Use of LSD in Psychotherapy* (New York: Macy Foundation, 1960), 11. The Banthine overdose is described in Leonard Asher interview, 23 February 1993; for the resulting publication see Leonard M. Asher and Cohen, "The Effect of Banthine on the Central Nervous System," *Gastroenterology* 17 (1951) 178–183.

8. Albert Hofmann, *LSD, My Problem Child: Reflections on Sacred Drugs, Mysticism, and Science* (Los Angeles: Tarcher, 1983). The significance of LSD's microscopic dosage is emphasized in Humphry Osmond, "Chemical Concepts of Psychosis," in Max Rinkel, ed., *Chemical Concepts of Psychosis* (New York: McDowell, Obolensky, 1958), 3–26, on 10–11. A survey of the medical research with psychedelic drugs is Abram Hoffer and Humphry Osmond, *The Hallucinogens* (New York: Academic, 1967).

9. "Washed Brains of POW's: Can They Be Rewashed?" *Newsweek*, 4 May 1953, 37. See also Edward Hunter, *Brain-washing in Red China: The Calculated Destruction of Men's Minds*, 2d ed. (New York: Vanguard, 1953), foreword; and Jean Rolin, *Police Drugs* (New York: Philosophical Library, 1956).

10. Marks, *Search for the "Manchurian Candidate"* (cit. n. 3); and U.S. Army Medical Department, *LSD Follow-up Study Report* (Washington, D.C.: U.S. Army Medical Department, 1980). The army gave LSD to 4,826 soldier volunteers between 1955 and 1975. This research was supposed to be covert and was not fully revealed until the 1970s, but a few records were published by the end of the 1950s. See U.S. House Committee on Science and Astronautics, *Chemical, Biological, and Radiological Warfare Agents: Hearings before the Committee on Science and Astronautics*, 86th Cong., 1st sess., 16 and 22 June 1959 (Washington, D.C.: Government Printing Office, 1959); and Subcommittee on Disarmament of the United States, U.S. Senate Committee on Foreign Relations, *Chemical-Biological-Radiological (CBR) Warfare and Its Disarmament Aspects*, 29 August 1960 (Washington, D.C.: Government Printing Office, 1960).

11. Studies on LSD and schizophrenics include Gordon R. Forrer and Richard D. Goldner, "Experimental Physiological Studies with Lysergic Acid Diethylamide," *American Medical Association Archives of Neurology and Psychiatry* 65 (1951): 581–588; W. Mayer-Gross et al., "Further Observations on the Effects of Lysergic Acid Diethylamide," *Journal of Mental Science* 99 (1953):804–808; Bruce Sloane and John W. Lovett Doust, "Psychophysiological Investigations in Experimental Psychoses: Results of the Exhibition of D-Lysergic Acid Diethylamide to Psychiatric Patients," ibid., 100 (1954):129–144; Louis S. Cholden et al., "Clinical Reactions and Tolerance to LSD in Chronic Schizophrenia," *Journal of Nervous and Mental Disease* 122 (1955):211–221; and Herbert S. Cline and Harry Freeman, "Resistance to Lysergic Acid in Schizophrenic Patients," *Psychiatric Quarterly* 30 (1956):676–683. For LSD research on drug addict prisoners at the National Institute of Mental Health Addiction Research Center in Lexington, Kentucky, see Harris Isbell et al., "Studies on Lysergic Acid Diethylamide, I: Effects in Former Morphine Addicts and Development of Tolerance during Chronic Intoxication," *Amer. Med. Ass. Arch. Neurol. Psychiat.* 76 (1956): 468–478; Isbell et al., "Studies on the Diethylamide of Lysergic Acid, II: Effects of Chlorpromazine, Azacyclonol, and Resperine on the Intensity of the LSD-Reaction," ibid., 77 (1957):350–358; and Isbell, "Comparison of the Reactions Induced by Psilocybin and LSD-25 in Man," *Psychopharmacologia* 1 (1959): 29–38. For LSD research on prisoners in the federal penitentiary in Atlanta, Georgia, see Edmund W. J. DeMaar et al., "Effects in Man of Single and Combined Oral Doses of Resperine, Iproniazid, and D-Lysergic Acid Diethylamide," *Clinical Pharmacology and Therapeutics*

1 (1960): 23–30. Charles Savage administered LSD to Mennonite conscientious objectors at the NIMH; see Abramson, ed., *Use of LSD in Psychotherapy* (cit. n. 7), 193–194.

12. For Paul Hoch's refusal to try LSD, see Sanford Unger, "The Psychedelic Use of LSD: Reflections and Observations," in Richard E. Hicks and Paul Jay Fink, eds., *Psychedelic Drugs* (New York: Grune & Stratton, 1969), 199–209, on 200; for Milton Greenblatt's refusal see Milton Greenblatt interview, 5 November 1991. Unpleasant reactions are noted in Murray F. Jarvik interview, 24 March 1992; Nicholas A. Bercel interviews, 29 June and 24 August 1991; Max Rinkel, "Experimentally Induced Psychosis in Man," in Harold A. Abramson, ed. *Neuropharmacology: Transactions of the Second Conference*, 25, 26, and 27 May 1955, Princeton, N.J. (New York: Macy Foundation, 1956), 236; H. Jackson DeShon et al., "Mental Changes Experimentally Produced by L.S.D.," *Psychiat. Q.* 26 (1952): 33–53, on 41; Abramson, ed., *Use of LSD in Psychotherapy*, p. 236; and John M. Macdonald and James A. V. Galvin, "Experimental Psychotic States," *American Journal of Psychiatry* 112 (1956): 970–976, on p. 975.

13. Nicholas A. Bercel et al., "Model Psychoses Induced by LSD-25 in Normals, I: Psychophysiological Investigations, with Special Reference to the Mechanism of the Paranoid Reaction," *Amer. Med. Ass. Arch. Neurol.Psychiat.* 75 (1956): 588–618; DeShon et al. "Mental Changes," 41–48; Max Rinkel et al., "Experimental Psychiatry, III: A Chemical Concept of Psychosis," *Diseases of the Nervous System* 15 (1954): 259–264, on 260; Harold A. Abramson et al., "Lysergic Acid Diethylamide (LSD-25), I: Physiological and Perceptual Responses," *Journal of Psychology* 39 (1955): 3–60, on 34; Murray E. Jarvik et al., "Lysergic Acid Diethylamide (LSD-25), VIII: Effect on Arithmetic Test Performance," ibid., 465–473; A. Levine et al., "Lysergic Acid Diethylamide (LSD-25), XVI: The Effect on Intellectual Functioning as Measured by the Wechsler-Bellevue Intelligence Scale," ibid., 40 (1955): 385–396; W. M. Hirsch et al., "Lysergic Acid Diethylamide (LSD-25), XVIII: Effect of LSD 25 and Related Drugs upon Handwriting," ibid., 41 (1956): 11–21; and Rinkel, "Experimentally Induced Psychosis," 236.

14. DeShon et al., "Mental Changes," 37–42; J. Elkes et al., "The Effect of Some Drugs on the Electrical Activity of the Brain and on Behaviour," *J. Mental Sci.* 100 (1954): 125–128, on 125; Bercel et al., "Model Psychoses Induced by LSD-25," 588–618; and Rinkel, "Experimentally Induced Psychosis," 236.

15. The percentages are from Abramson et al., "Lysergic Acid Diethylamide (LSD-25)" (cit. n. 13), p. 34. On the questionnaire see Harold A. Abramson, ed., *Neuropharmacology: Transactions of the First Conference*, 26, 27, and 28 May 1954 (Princeton, N.J.: Macy Foundation, 1955), 263–264; Isbell, "Comparison of the Reactions" (cit. n. 11), 30 n. 2; and Abramson, "Lysergic Acid Diethylamide (LSD-25), XXX: The Questionnaire Technique with Notes on Its Use," *J. Psychol.* 49 (1960): 57–65, on 57. For reports in popular magazines see Sidney Katz, "My Twelve Hours as a Madman," *Maclean's*, 1 October 1953, 9–11, 46–55; Robert M. Goldenson, "Step into the World of the Insane," *Look*, 21 September 1954, 30–35; and Robert M. Yoder, "Help for the Living Dead," *Saturday Evening Post*, 22 October 1955, 41–43, 64, 66, 71.

16. Sidney Cohen, quoted in Abramson, ed., *Use of LSD in Psychotherapy* (cit. n. 7), 11; and Cohen, *The Beyond Within: The LSD Story* (New York: Atheneum, 1964), 107. Cohen's reactions were initially recorded in *Sidney Cohen LSD Report*, 13 October 1955; Leonard Asher provided me with a copy of this document. The bulk of the report was reprinted anonymously, and undated, in Cohen, *Beyond Within*, 106–111. One of Cohen's friends wrote, "The Gunz family were all fascinated by your Lysergic Acid experiment": Martin K. Gunz to Sidney Cohen, 29 October 1955, Cohen Papers. See also Oscar Janiger

interview of Sidney Cohen, 6 June 1978, Albert Hofmann Foundation, Santa Monica (hereafter cited as Hofmann Foundation).

17. Lionel Lazarus Fichman, "Psychological Effects of Lysergic Acid Diethylamide as Reflected in Psychological Test Changes," Ph.D. diss., UCLA, 1957; Leonard Korot, "The Application of the Semantic Differential to a Drug-Induced 'Dissociative State,'" Ph.D. diss., UCLA, 1959; and Eugene Morley, "Some Differences between the Lysergic Acid Diethylamide State and Three Naturally Occurring Psychoses on Rating Scales of Ego-Functioning," Ph.D. diss., UCLA, 1960. Cohen wrote, "There is considerable interest among the younger people training in psychology in lysergic acid": Cohen to Ewing W. Reilley, 7 March 1958, Cohen Papers.

18. Sidney Cohen, quoted in Abramson, ed., *Use of LSD in Psychotherapy* (cit. n. 7), 11. Ronald Sandison concurred: "I agree that psychological tests are singularly ineffective in helping us to define this response" (ibid., 15). The psychologist William McGlothlin, who worked on LSD experiments with Cohen in the early 1960s, later said, "We make absolutely no demands on the subjects. . . . They can do anything they wish. . . . They have no tests to take": William McGlothlin, quoted in Harold A. Abramson, ed., *The Use of LSD in Psychotherapy and Alcoholism* (Indianapolis: Bobbs-Merrill, 1967), 42. For the model psychosis test results see Fichman, "Psychological Effects" 85, 98–99, 105–106; for subjects' reported reactions see Sidney Cohen, Lionel Fichman, and Betty Grover Eisner, "Subjective Reports of Lysergic Acid Experiences in a Context of Psychological Test Performance," *Amer. J. Psychiat.* 115 (1958): 30–35.

19. Humphry Osmond, "A Review of the Clinical Effects of Psychotomimetic Agents," *Annals of the New York Academy of Sciences* 66 (14 March 1957): 418–434, on 422.

20. Gerald Heard to Ernest Hocking, 1 July 1957, Heard Papers, Collection 1054, Box 29-1, Department of Special Collections, University Research Library, UCLA, Los Angeles (hereafter cited as Heard Papers). On psychoanalysts' experience of LSD see Cohen to Alfred M. Hubbard, 13 September 1956, Cohen Papers; and Janiger interview of Cohen, 6 June 1978, Hofmann Foundation. Aldous Huxley wrote in 1957, "The only people who don't get anything from LSD or mescaline are psycho-analysts. There are 2 experimenters here who have given it to several Freudians. None of them got anything positive": Aldous Huxley, *Letters of Aldous Huxley*, ed. Grover Smith (New York: Harper & Row, 1969), 813.

21. "Your visit with Aldous Huxley sounds like a most interesting experience": Gunz to Cohen, 16 January 1956, Cohen Papers. On the influence of Huxley and Heard in general see David Robb, "Brahmins from Abroad: English Expatriates and Spiritual Consciousness in Modern America," *American Studies* 26 (Fall 1985): 45–60. Ironically, when *Life* magazine wanted to celebrate Los Angeles's intellectual coming of age, three of the four figures they selected—Huxley, Heard, and Christopher Isherwood—were English expatriates deeply involved in LSD; see "A Warm Climate for Cultural Life," *Life*, 20 June 1960, 89.

22. Huxley to Humphry Osmond, 23 December 1955, in Huxley, *Letters* (cit. n. 20), 778–779; Huxley, *The Doors of Perception* (London: Chatto & Windus, 1954); and Huxley, *Heaven and Hell* (London: Chatto & Windus, 1956).

23. Louis Lasagna and John M. von Felsinger, "The Volunteer Subject in Research," *Science* 120 (1954): 359–361, on 360–361; Ronald Fisher, quoted in Louis Cholden, ed., *Lysergic Acid Diethylamide and Mescalinein Experimental Psychiatry* (New York: Grune & Stratton, 1956), 67; and Joost A. M. Meerloo, "Medication into Submission: The Danger of Therapeutic Coercion," *J. Nervous Mental Dis.* 122 (1955): 353–360, on 358–359.

24. Huxley to Osmond, 11 May 1955, in Huxley, *Letters*, (cit. n. 20), 742–743. Huxley's address, "Mescaline and the 'Other World,'" was published in Cholden, ed., *Lysergic Acid Diethylamide*, 46–50. Humphry Osmond wrote me that his attitude toward the use of mescaline changed after observing Huxley's drug taking, reading *The Doors of Perception*, and talking with Huxley and his (first) wife Maria, which helped him understand that the "door in the wall" might give access to various kinds of experience: Osmond to Steven Novak, 1 March 1993. Hofmann explained his change of mind by writing, "In *The Doors of Perception* and *Heaven and Hell*, Huxley's newly-published works, I found a meaningful exposition of the experience induced by hallucinogenic drugs, and I thereby gained a deepened insight into my own LSD experiments": Hofmann, *LSD, My Problem Child* (cit. n. 8), 172.

25. Huxley to Osmond, 3 February 1955, in Huxley, *Letters*, 729 ("going sane"); and Osmond, "Review of Clinical Effects" (cit. n. 19), 428. For psychedelic see Huxley, *Letters*, 795n.

26. Sidney Cohen, unpublished, undated, untitled draft of an essay for a commemorative volume planned after Heard's death, Cohen Papers (emphasis added). On 29 November 1959 Huxley asked Osmond, "And talking of LSD—would it be possible for you to send me half a dozen doses of it? . . . I don't want to bother Sid Cohen too often": Huxley, *Letters*, 882.

27. Erich Lindemann, "Psychological Changes in Normal and Abnormal Individuals under the Influence of Sodium Amytal," *Amer. J. Psychiat.* 88 (1932): 1083–1091; S. J. Horsley, *Narco-analysis* (London: Oxford University Press, 1943); Roy R. Grinker and John P. Spiegel, *Men under Stress* (Philadelphia: Blakiston, 1945), 170–171, 394–395; Paul H. Hoch, "The Present Status of Narco-diagnosis and Therapy," *J. Nervous Mental Dis.* 103 (1946): 248–259; and L. J. Meduna, *Carbon Dioxide Therapy: A Neurophysiological Treatment of Nervous Disorders* (Springfield, Ill.: Thomas, 1950).

28. R. A. Sandison, "Psychological Aspects of the LSD Treatment of the Neuroses," *J. Mental Sci.* 100 (1954): 508–515, on 514; Sandison et al., "The Therapeutic Value of Lysergic Acid Diethylamide in Mental Illness," ibid., 491–507, esp. 497; Walter Frederking, "Intoxicant Drugs (Mescaline and Lysergic Acid Diethylamide) in Psychotherapy," *J. Nervous Mental Dis.* 121 (1955): 262–266, esp. 263; and Ian Stevenson, "Comments on the Psychological Effects of Mescaline and Allied Drugs," ibid., 125 (1957): 438–442. For some more skeptical views see Charles Savage, "Lysergic Acid Diethylamide (LSD-25): A Clinical-Psychological Study," *Amer. J. Psychiat.* 108 (1952): 896–900, esp. 899; James P. Cattell, "The Influence of Mescaline on Psychodynamic Material," *J. Nervous Mental Dis.* 119 (1954): 233–244, esp. 240, 243; and Paul H. Hoch, "Remarks on LSD and Mescaline," ibid., 125 (1957): 443–444.

29. Cohen to Osmond, 11 January 1957, Cohen Papers. On the first contacts with Hubbard see Cohen to Gunz, 8 December 1956, Cohen Papers: "This week I spent a lot of time with an Al Hubbard, a wealthy engineer from Vancouver. This chap has been using LSD and mescaline for the last couple of years up there as therapy for bottom-scraping alcoholics, muddled people, etc., with 'astounding' success. He sets up a sort of semi-religious situation, gives his 'friends' massive support and suggestion, and is able to turn problem alcoholics into social drinkers." Hubbard spun so many tall tales about himself that it is difficult to know what to believe about his life. I rely on the Oscar Janiger interview of Al Hubbard, 13 October 1978, Hofmann Foundation; extensive Hubbard correspondence in the Hoffer Papers, Saskatchewan Archives Board, University of Saskatchewan, Saskatoon (hereafter cited as Hoffer Papers), and in the Myron Stolaroff

Papers, privately held; and Todd Brendan Pahey, "The Original Captain Trips," *High Times*, November 1991, 38–40, 54–65.

30. Huxley described Hubbard as "a millionaire business man–physicist, scientific director of the Uranium Corporation"; Huxley to Eileen J. Garrett, 31 January 1955, in Huxley, *Letters*, (cit. n. 20), 729; see also 722–723. For a later perspective see Osmond to Abram Hoffer, 26 August 1963, Hoffer Papers; for Cohen's reservations see Cohen to Gunz, 8 December 1956, Cohen Papers.

31. Betty Grover Eisner and Sidney Cohen, "Psychotherapy with Lysergic Acid Diethylamide," *J. Nervous Mental Dis.* 127 (1958): 528–539; and Betty Eisner to Reilley, 13 February 1957, Eisner Papers. Information on Eisner's interests comes from Betty Eisner interviews, 9 August 1991 and 20 January 1993. Eisner allowed me to read her unpublished memoirs and to review her correspondence (hereafter cited as Eisner Papers).

32. "It is believed by Alcoholics Anonymous and by many alcoholics that alcoholics begin to recover after they have reached a state of existence called 'hitting bottom'": Hoffer and Osmond, *Hallucinogens* (cit. n. 8), 154. On the founding of AA see Bill Pittman, *AA: The Way It Began* (Seattle: Glen Abbey, 1988), 163–172. Wilson told of his experience in Bill W., *Alcoholics Anonymous: The Story of How Many Thousands of Men and Women Have Recovered from Alcoholism* (New York: Works, 1939); and Bill W., *Twelve Steps and Twelve Traditions* (New York: Harper, 1953). Added detail is found in Ernest Kurtz, *Not-God: A History of Alcoholics Anonymous* (Center City, Minn.: Hazelden, 1979); [Alcoholics Anonymous], *"Pass It On": The Story of Bill Wilson and How the A.A. Message Reached the World* (New York: Alcoholics Anonymous World Services, 1984); and Nan Robertson, *Getting Better: Inside Alcoholics Anonymous* (New York: Morrow, 1988).

33. The fullest account of Wilson's LSD experiences is in [Alcoholics Anonymous], *"Pass It On,"* 368–377. See also Bill Wilson to Cohen, 26 September 1956, Cohen Papers; Janiger interview of Cohen, 16 June 1978, Hofmann Foundation; Thomas E. Powers to Eisner, 16 February 1957, Eisner Papers; and Thomas E. Powers interview, 13 February 1995. For Wilson's comparison of the effects of LSD and his earlier mystical experience see Wilson to Cohen, 26 September 1956.

34. Keith Ditman to Wilson, 16 December 1957 (quotation), 4 February 1958, Ditman Papers. Wilson's distress that his taking LSD had become public knowledge is from Wilson to Cohen, 16 December 1957, Cohen Papers. See also Elizabeth Dixon interview of Chuck Dederich, 1962, in *Seven Voices from Synanon* (UCLA Oral History Program, 1964), Department of Special Collections, University Research Library, UCLA, 24–25; and Alan Watts, *In My Own Way: An Autobiography, 1915–1965* (New York: Pantheon, 1972), 342–344. Dederich looked at his drug trip in terms of Huxley, noting that Huxley had been taking LSD for a long time, though he said he did not have the enhanced color sense or the distorted perspective described in Huxley's *Heaven and Hell*.

35. Keith S. Ditman and John R. B. Whittlesey, "Comparison of LSD-25 Experience and Delirium Tremens," *Amer. Med. Ass. Arch. Gen. Psychia.* 1 (1959): 47–57, on 48; see also Ditman interviews, 8 and 29 April 1991.

36. Keith Ditman, Max Hayman, and John R. B. Whittlesey, "Nature and Frequency of Claims Following LSD," *J. Nervous Mental Dis.* 134 (1962) 346–352, on 347.

37. Timothy Leary, *High Priest* (New York: College Notes & Texts, 1968), 66 (quotation), 111–112; and Abraham Maslow, *Religions, Values, and Peak-Experiences* (Columbus: Ohio State University Press, 1964), 27 (quotation), 76. See also Richard J. Lowry, ed., *The Journals of A. H. Maslow* (Monterey, Calif.: Brooks/Cole, 1979), 205, 269; and Colin

Wilson, *New Pathways in Psychology: Maslow and the Post-Freudian Revolution* (New York: Taplinger, 1972), 189–195.

38. Huxley, *Doors of Perception* (cit. n. 22), 25 and passim. Compare model psychosis research: W. S. Maclay and E. Guttmann, "Mescaline Hallucinations in Artists," *Amer. Med. Ass. Arch. Neurol. Psychiat.* 45 (1941) 130–137; Rinkel, "Experimentally Induced Psychosis" (cit. n. 12), 252–253; and Rinkel, ed., *Chemical Concepts of Psychosis* (cit. n. 8), 78.

39. John D. Graham, one of the apostles of modernism, wrote that "the unconscious mind is the creative factor and the source and the storehouse of power and of all knowledge, past and future. The conscious mind is but a critical factor and clearing house. Most people lose access to their unconscious at about the age of seven. By this age all repressions, ancestral and individual, have been established and free access to the source of all power has been closed. This closure is sometimes temporarily relaxed by such expedients as danger or nervous strain, alcohol, insanity, and inspiration. Among primitive people, children, and geniuses this free access to the power of the unconscious exists in a greater or lesser degree": Graham, "Primitive Art and Picasso," *Magazine of Art* 30 (1937) 236–239, 260, on 237. This discussion owes much to John M. MacGregor, *The Discovery of the Art of the Insane* (Princeton, Princeton University Press, 1989); and W. Jackson Rushing, *Native American Art and the New York Avant-Garde* (Austin: University of Texas Press, 1995). See also Wolfgang Born, "The Art of the Insane," *Ciba Symposia* 7 (1946): 202–236; Margaret Naumburg, *Schizophrenic Art: Its Meaning in Psychotherapy* (New York: Grune & Stratton, 1950), 1–37; Francis Reitman, *Psychotic Art* (London: Routledge & Kegan Paul, 1951); Ernst Kris, *Psychoanalytic Explorations in Art* (New York: International Universities Press, 1952); and William Phillips, ed., *Art and Psychoanalysis: Studies in the Application of Psychoanalytic Theory to the Creative Process* (New York: Criterion, 1957).

40. Lawrence S. Kubie, *Neurotic Distortion of the Creative Process* (Lawrence: University of Kansas Press, 1958), 4 (quotation), 38, 46–47, 53, 142; R. W. Gerard, "The Biological Basis of Imagination," *Scientific Monthly* 62 (1946): 477–499, on 498; and Karen Horney, *Neurosis and Human Growth: The Struggle toward Self-Realization* (New York: Norton, 1950), 331, 13.

41. Oscar Janiger interviews, 26 August 1991 (quotation), 15 December 1992. See also Oscar Janiger, "The Use of Hallucinogenic Agents in Psychiatry," *California Clinician* 56 (1960): 222–224, 251–259; and Janiger and M. de Rios, "LSD and Creativity," *Journal of Psychoactive Drugs* 21 (1989): 129–134. Janiger's files on over a thousand LSD study participants form the core of the Hofmann Foundation collection. See also "The Uncanny Art of Twenty-seven Drugged Painters," *Maclean's*, 16 December 1961, 22–23. Cohen presented examples of paintings made under the influence of LSD in Time, Inc., *The Drug Takers* (New York: Time-Life, 1965), 104–105; see also Cohen, *Beyond Within* (cit. n. 16), 80–81. Among Cohen's subjects were the theologian John Courtney Murray and the playwright and diplomat Clare Boothe Luce.

42. Louis Jolyon West, quoted in Abramson, ed., *Use of LSD in Psychotherapy* (cit. n. 7), 185 (see also 51, 76, 90, 132, 186, 215–216, 227, 236–238); and Jonathan O. Cole, quoted in Seymour M. Farber and Roger H. L. Wilson, eds., *Man and Civilization: Control of the Mind* (New York: McGraw-Hill, 1961), 117 (see also 116–118).

43. Myron Feld, Joseph R. Goodman, and John A. Guido, "Clinical and Laboratory Observations on LSD-25," *J. Nervous Mental Dis.* 126 (1958): 176–183; Ditman interviews, 8 and 29 April 1991; and Abramson, ed., *Use of LSD in Psychotherapy*, 33. In 1965 Abramson said, "It was all I could do to prevent all of Brookhaven, people in the school system,

friends, and so on, to come to dinner with us on Friday evenings to take LSD": Abramson, ed., *Use of LSD in Psychotherapy and Alcoholism* (cit. n. 18), 475. See also Jarvik interview, 24 March 1991. On Cohen's limited self-experimentation see Cohen to Lisa Biberman, 22 May 1968, Cohen Papers.

44. Eisner to Osmond, 1 January 1958, Eisner Papers. On LSD experiences as evidence for reincarnation see Thelma Moss interview, 29 November 1992; Maurice Rapkin interview, 24 March 1993; Herman C. B. Denber to Eisner, 3 January 1958; and Osmond to Eisner, 2 October 1956, Eisner Papers. See also Ian Stevenson, *Twenty Cases Suggestive of Reincarnation* (New York: American Society for Psychical Research, 1966); Stevenson, *Cases of the Reincarnation Type*, 4 vols. (Charlottesville: University Press of Virginia, 1975–1983); and Stevenson, *Children Who Remember Previous Lives: A Question of Reincarnation* (Charlottesville: University Press of Virginia, 1987).

45. Morey Bernstein, *The Search for Bridey Murphy* (Garden City, N.Y.: Doubleday, 1956); "Hypnotic Adventure," *Time*, 9 January 1956, 48; Sigfried Mandel, "The Story behind 'The Search for Bridey Murphy,'" *Saturday Review*, 10 March 1956, 18–19; Ralph Daigh, "The Mysteries of Hypnosis," *Look*, 10 July 1956, 21–26; Milton V. Kline, ed., *A Scientific Report on "The Search for Bridey Murphy"* (New York: Julian, 1956); and Gerald Heard, "The Great 'Bridey Murphy' Furor," *Fortnight*, March 1958, 25–26.

46. R. Laurence Moore, *In Search of White Crows: Spiritualism, Parapsychology, and American Culture* (New York: Oxford University Press, 1977), 206. Garrett's LSD experiments in the 1960s, conducted in Palm Beach, Florida, are documented in the Hoffer Papers. Aldous Huxley, "The Case for ESP, PK, and PSI," *Life*, 11 January 1954, 97–98. Huxley published the first version of *Heaven and Hell* in *Tomorrow, the Quarterly Review of Psychical Research* 3 (Summer 1956): 7–35. See also Humphry Osmond, "Aldous Huxley's 'Doors of Perception,'" ibid., 2 (Spring 1954): 227–35; J. R. Smythies, "Our Transcendental World," ibid., 36–39; Ian Stevenson, "The Uncomfortable Facts about Extrasensory Perception," *Harper's*, July 1959, 19–25; Cedric W. M. Wilson, "The Physiological Basis of Paranormal Phenomena," *International Journal of Parapsychology* 4 (Spring 1962): 57–96, esp. p. 74–75; and Duncan Blewett, "Psychedelic Drugs in Parapsychological Research," ibid., 5 (Winter 1963): 43–74.

47. Cohen to Robert Lynch, 4 September 1959, Cohen Papers. On the conferences in New York and in France see *Proceedings of Two Conferences on Parapsychology and Pharmacology* (New York: Parapsychology Foundation, 1961). See also Ellen Huxley, "The Search for Ecstasy," *Tomorrow* 7 (Autumn 1959): 28–36; Ellen Huxley, "Parapsychology and Psychedelics," ibid., 7 (Winter 1959): 65–70; and Roberto Cavanna and Emilio Servadio, *ESP Experiments with LSD 25 and Psilocybin: A Methodological Approach* (New York: Parapsychology Foundation, 1964).

48. Cohen to Reilley, 20 December 1960; and Cohen to Hubbard, 13 September 1956, October 1957, Cohen Papers.

49. Cohen to Lynch, 4 September 1959, Cohen Papers; and Eisner to Hubbard, 30 April 1957, Eisner Papers. See also Eisner to Hubbard, 16 November 1957, Eisner Papers; and Osmond to Hoffer, 23 November 1957, Hoffer Papers.

50. Cohen to Reilley, 7 March 1958, Cohen Papers.

51. Heard to Lucille Kahn, 17 August 1959, Heard Papers, Box 36; Cohen to Reilley, 3 February 1961, Cohen Papers; and Heard to Cohen, 13 October 1963, Heard Papers, Box 38.

52. Cohen to Ganz, 8 December 1956, Cohen Papers. Scripts of the *Focus on Sanity* series are in the Heard Papers, Box 19-4A. Saltman's reactions are reported in Harry

Nelson, "Fantastic Sensations Gained with New Drug," *Los Angeles Times*, 13 March 1958, sec. 3, pp. 1, 8; and Omar Garrison, "New Explorations of the Human Mind," *Los Angeles Evening Mirror News*, 13 March 1958, sec. 2, pp. 1, 3. See also Paul Saltman interview, 2 February 1992; and Harry Nelson interview, 16 November 1991. Three weeks before Saltman's filmed LSD experience a UCLA professor of pharmacy had announced that LSD "does make everything seem beautiful": "Hallucinatory Drugs Defended by Doctor," *Los Angeles Times*, 21 February 1958, sec. 1, p. 14.

53. *San Francisco Chronicle*, 26 June 1958, sec. 1, pp. 1, 4; Eisner to Osmond, 17 July 1958, Eisner Papers; Harry Nelson, "UCLA Experts Searching for Way to Free Alcoholics," *Los Angeles Times*, 7 September 1958, sec. 2, pp. 1, 2 (quoting Ditman); and "More on LSD," *This Week* (Sunday supplement), *Los Angeles Times*, 3 January 1960, 12. See also Palmer Chase, "Psychiatrist Lauds Savage Tribe Drugs," *San Diego Evening Tribune*, 12 May 1959, A-1.

54. Laura Berquist, "The Curious Story behind the New Cary Grant," *Look*, 1 September 1959, 57–59, on 58; Joe Hyams, "What Psychiatry Has Done for Cary Grant," *New York Herald Tribune*, 20 April 1959, 16; Hyams, "Grant Tells Why Marriage Failed," ibid., 21 April 1959, 22; Richard Gehman, "The Ageless Cary Grant," *Good Housekeeping*, September 1960, 66–67, 144–160; and Hyams, "How a New Shock Drug Unlocks Troubled Minds," *This Week* (Sunday supplement), *Los Angeles Times*, 8 November 1959, 6–7, 9–10. See also Geoffrey Wansell, *Haunted Idol: The Story of the Real Cary Grant* (New York: Morrow, 1984), 232–234.

55. Joe Hyams, quoted in Bob Gaines, "LSD: Hollywood's Status Symbol Drug," *Cosmopolitan*, November 1963, p. 79. William Brazen asserted that press coverage of LSD began in 1963; see William Brazen, "LSD and the Press," in *Psychedelics: The Uses and Implications of Hallucinogenic Drugs*, ed. Bernard S. Aaronson and Humphry Osmond (Garden City, N.Y.: Anchor, 1970), 400–418. See also Charles C. Dahlberg et al., "LSD Research: The Impact of Lay Publicity," *Amer. J. Psychiat.* 125 (1968):137–141. In the early 1950s Nicholas Bercel complained that negative publicity about LSD was making it difficult for him to find volunteers; see Bercel et al., "Model Psychoses Induced by LSD-25" (cit. n. 13), 589.

56. Nathan S. Kline, "Relation of Psychiatry to the Pharmaceutical Industry," *Amer. Med. Ass. Arch. Neurol. Psychiat.* 77 (1957): 611–615; "Too Many Drugs?" *Time*, 25 April 1960, 78; Edgar F. Mauer, "A Physicians' Revolt: Objective: To Free the AMA of Drugmakers," *Saturday Review* 6 August 1960, 45–46; Walter Modell, "The Drug Explosion," *Clin. Pharmacol. Therap.* 2 (1961):1–7; Charles D. May, "Selling Drugs by 'Educating' Physicians," *Journal of Medical Education* 36 (1961): 1–23; and "Too Many Drugs," *Time*, 26 May 1961, 73.

57. For the 1956 conference conclusions see Jonathan O. Cole and Ralph W. Gerard, eds., *Psychopharmacology: Problems in Evaluation* (Washington, D.C.: National Academy of Sciences, 1959), 330; Hoch is quoted in Abramson, ed., *Use of LSD in Psychotherapy* (cit. n. 7), 60–61. See also Irving Ladimer, "Human Experimentation: Medicolegal Aspects," *New England Journal of Medicine* 257 (7 July 1957): 19–20; and William Furst and William Furst, "The Medico-Legal Aspects of Psychiatric Research," *Dis. Nervous System*, February 1960, 132–134. For experiments on sleep deprivation and sensory isolation see John T. Brauchi and Louis J. West, "Sleep Deprivation," *Journal of the American Medical Association* 171 (5 September 1959):97–100; Eugene L. Bliss et al., "Studies of Sleep Deprivation—Relationship to Schizophrenia," *Amer. Med. Ass. Arch. Neurol. Psychiat.* 81 (1959): 348–359; and Bernard Bressler et al., "Research in Human Subjects and the Ar-

tificial Traumatic Neurosis: Where Does Our Responsibility Lie?" *Amer. J. Psychiat.* 116 (1959): 522–526.

58. *Los Angeles Times*, 20 March 1959, sec. 1, pp. 1, 16; *Los Angeles Evening Mirror News*, 20 March 1959, sec. 1, p. 4; *Los Angeles Examiner*, 22 March 1959, sec. 1, p. 28; Michael S. Balter interview of Clara M. Szego, *Insight and Progress: Development of a Cell Biologist* (UCLA Oral History Program, 1989), Department of Special Collections, University Research Library, UCLA, 637–638; and Robert Sherins interview, 27 April 1993.

59. Oscar Janiger received the cover letter and questionnaire Cohen to Janiger, 6 February 1959, Hofmann Foundation. For Cohen's report of his findings see Sidney Cohen, "Lysergic Acid Diethylamide: Side Effects and Complications," *J. Nervous Mental Dis.* 130 (1960): 30–39.

60. Abramson, ed., *Use of LSD in Psychotherapy* (cit. n. 7), 63 (Fremont-Smith), 227 (Cohen).

61. Jerome Levine and Arnold M. Ludwig, "The LSD Controversy," *Comprehensive Psychiatry* 5 (1964): 314–321, on 318; "Authorization and Release of Responsibility for the Investigational Use of LSD-25 and Psilocybin (1964)," quoted in Jay Katz, comp., *Experimentation with Human Beings* (New York: Russell Sage, 1972), 389–390; and *Federal LSD Research*, 139.

62. Cohen, "Lysergic Acid Diethylamide: Side Effects and Complications" (cit. n. 59), 38–39. The only extant copy of the questionnaire I have found is that of Humphry Osmond in the Hoffer Papers.

63. Alison Bass, "Mentally Ill Patient in LSD Study Is Said to Have Killed Self," *Boston Globe*, 5 January 1994, 14. Two Boston psychiatrists who were present divulged this death to the press over forty years after it occurred. See also Robert Reid interviews, 1 February, 14 April 1994; and Paul Watson interview, 18 April 1994.

64. Marks, *Search for the "Manchurian Candidate"* (cit. n. 3), 67n, 73–86, 87–88, 93, 97, 100n, 205; and testimony of General R. R. Taylor, quoted in U.S. Senate, *Biomedical and Behavioral Research: Joint Hearings before the Subcommittee on Health of the Committee on Labor and Public Welfare and the Subcommittee on Administrative Practice and Procedure of the Committee on the Judiciary*, 94th Cong., 1st sess., 10, 12 September and 7 November 1975 (Washington, D.C.: Government Printing Office, 1976), 182–183.

65. Arthur L. Chandler and Mortimer A. Hartman, "Lysergic Acid Diethylamide (LSD-25) as a Facilitating Agent in Psychotherapy," *Amer. Med. Ass. Arch. Gen. Psychiat.* 2 (1960): 286–299. On the Menlo Park Foundation see Myron J. Stolaroff interview, 17 August 1993; and J. N. Sherwood, M. J. Stolaroff, and W. W. Harman, "The Psychedelic Experience—A New Concept in Psychotherapy," *Journal of Neuropsychiatry* 4 (November–December 1962): 69–80. See also Stolaroff, *Thanatos to Eros: Thirty-five Years of Psychedelic Exploration* (Berlin: Verlag für Wissenschaft und Bildung, 1994).

66. D. B. Blewett and N. Chewlos, "Handbook for the Therapeutic Use of LSD-25: Individual and Group Procedures" (mimeographed, 1959); and Murray Korngold interview, 21 May 1993. The lawsuit is reported in *Long Beach Express-Telegram*, 14 June 1962, sec. A, pp. 1, 4, and 21 June 1962, sec. B, p. 1.

67. Cohen to William Harlan Hale, 18 January 1963, Cohen Papers. On the problems of the LSD therapists see Board of Medical Examiners of the State of California, D-350, 6 August 1956, D-606, 31 August 1961, California State Archives, Sacramento; "Marijuana Charge Jails Psychiatrist," *Los Angeles Times*, 21 August 1963, sec. 1, p. 24; James

Goddard, in *Federal LSD Research*, 64; and Janiger interview, 26 August 1991. Cohen mentioned therapist breakdowns in *Beyond Within* (cit. n. 16), 217.

68. Cohen to William H. Stevens, 22 June 1961, Cohen Papers. Details of this woman's condition are in Sidney Cohen and Keith S. Ditman, "Prolonged Adverse Reactions to Lysergic Acid Diethylamide," *Amer. Med. Ass. Arch. Gen. Psychiat.* 8 (1963): 475–480, on 477.

69. Stevens to Cohen, 14 December 1961; and Cohen to Stevens, 21 December 1961, Cohen Papers.

70. Janiger interview of Ditman, 29 March 1978, Hofmann Foundation; and Ditman interview, 8 April 1991. On the arrest of the pair see *San Francisco Chronicle*, 4 April 1963, 4, 5 April 1963, 3. Photographs of the arrest are in the *Food and Drug Review*, May 1963, 3. FDA Commissioner James Goddard asserted that this was the first LSD arrest: *Federal LSD Research*, 65. On the trial see *San Francisco Chronicle*, 3 June 1964, 15; facts of the case are also found in the appeal: *Bernard Roseman and Bernard Copley v. United States of America*, 20 July 1966, in 364 F.2d 18 (1966). Roseman and Copley were sentenced to seventeen years in prison: *U.S. Food and Drug Administration, Annual Reports, 1950–1974* (Washington, D.C.: Government Printing Office, 1976), 294. Roseman wrote a fascinating account of his involvement with LSD and its effects on his life; see Bernard Roseman, *LSD and the Age of Mind* (Hollywood, Calif.: Wilshire, 1963), 2d ed. (1966), 22–40.

71. Sidney Cohen and Keith S. Ditman, "Complications Associated with Lysergic Acid Diethylamide (LSD-25)," *J. Amer. Med. Ass.* 181 (14 July 1962): 161–162. See also Harry Nelson, "Doctors Reveal Traffic in Hallucinations Drug," *Los Angeles Times*, 14 July 1962, sec. 3, p. 1. Cohen and Ditman published a more detailed summary of the complications in "Prolonged Adverse Reactions to Lysergic Acid Diethylamide" (cit. n. 68). In the same issue of the *American Medical Association Archives of General Psychiatry*, editor Roy R. Grinker Sr. denounced LSD investigators who "administered the drug to themselves, . . . became enamored of the mystical hallucinatory state," and ended up "disqualified as competent investigators." He charged that LSD had lost its usefulness as a research tool "due to unjustified claims, indiscriminate and premature publicity, and lack of proper professional controls": Roy R. Grinker Sr., "Lysergic Acid Diethylamide," *Amer. Med. Ass. Arch. Gen. Psychiat.* 8 (1963): 425. Apparently a number of physicians sent Cohen word of many adverse reactions to LSD after his article appeared. See Hoffer to Osmond, 11 July 1963, Hoffer Papers.

72. "Thalidomide Disaster," *Time*, 10 August 1962, 80; and "Tragedy from a Pill Bottle," *Newsweek*, 13 August 1962, 52–54. See also Phillip Knightly, Harold Evans, Elaine Potter, and Marjorie Walker, *Suffer the Children: The Story of Thalidomide* (New York: Viking, 1979).

73. On the warning against giving LSD in pregnancy see Frank Fremont-Smith's statement in Abramson, ed., *Use of LSD in Psychotherapy* (cit. n. 7), 88–90. At a 1961 London conference Linford Rees warned, "Here we have a drug which is of extreme potency . . . and which one might expect to have severe effects on the growing foetus": Linford Rees, quoted in Richard Crocket et al., *Hallucinogenic Drugs and Their Psychotherapeutic Use* (London: Lewis, 1963), 49. On Schedule H see Hoffer to Osmond, 22 October 1962, Hoffer Papers.

74. George P. Larrick, quoted in *U.S. News and World Report*, 13 August 1962, 57. On the consequences of the new legislation see Louis Lasagna, "Congress, the FDA, and New Drug Development: Before and After 1962," *Perspect. Biol. Med.* 32 (1989) :322–343.

75. James Goddard, quoted in *Narcotic Rehabilitation Act of 1966*, 321; and *Federal LSD Research*, 64. Richard H. Blum and Associates, *Utopiates: The Use and Users of LSD* 25 (New York: Atherton, 1964), first established that the early spread of LSD was due to professionals who shared the drug with their friends and families. On the 1961 FDA investigations, see the testimony of FDA Commissioner James Goddard in *Federal LSD Research*, 64; for a survey of LSD legislation see Grinspoon and Bakalar, *Psychedelic Drugs Reconsidered* (cit. n. 2), 309–312. See also David F. Musto, *The American Disease: Origins of Narcotic Control*, expanded ed. (New York: Oxford University Press, 1987), 252–253.

76. The belief that Sandoz feared litigation over LSD abuses appears in Hoffer to Osmond, 26 September 1962, Hoffer Papers. On the raids in Los Angeles in 1962 see Goddard, in *Federal LSD Research*, 64; and Janiger interview, 26 August 1991. Other therapists tried to distance themselves from their southern California brethren. Charles Savage wrote the chairman of the California State Assembly Committee on Criminal Procedure, 5 November 1963, "LSD therapy should not be seen from the narrow vantage point of Southern California where it has been vastly misused": California State Assembly Committee on Criminal Procedure, 13, 14, 15 November 1963, *Narcotics and Dangerous Drugs* (Sacramento, 1964), App. IV-c.

77. On the reduction of LSD researchers, see *Federal LSD Research*, 61–62.

78. Clare Boothe Luce to Cohen, 2 December 1965, Cohen Papers.

79. John R. Neill, "'More than Medical Significance': LSD and American Psychiatry, 1953 to 1966," *J. Psychoactive Drugs* 19 (1987): 39–45, esp. 44; and David J. Rothman, *Strangers at the Bedside: A History of How Law and Bioethics Transformed Medical Decision Making* (New York: Basic, 1991).

80. Wilson to Heard, 1 May 1956, Heard Papers, Box 29-2; Ditman et al., "Nature and Frequency of Claims" (cit. n. 36), 348–349, 352; and Harold Esecover et al., "Clinical Profiles of Paid Normal Subjects Volunteering for Hallucinogen Drug Studies," *Amer. J. Psychiat.* 117 (1961): 910–915, on 912. On volunteer bias in psychedelic drug tests see Lasagna and von Felsinger, "Volunteer Subject in Research" (cit. n. 23), 359–361; and Margaret R. Riggs and Walter Kaess, "Personality Differences between Volunteers and Nonvolunteers," *J. Psychol.* 40 (1955): 229–245.

81. On the failure to find proof of the lasting effects of LSD, see William H. McGlothlin, Sidney Cohen, and Marcella S. McGlothlin, "Short-Term Effects of LSD on Anxiety, Attitudes, and Performance," *J. Nervous Mental Dis.* 139 (1964): 266–273; and McGlothlin, Cohen, and McGlothlin, "Long Lasting Effects of LSD on Normals," *Amer. Med. Ass. Arch. Gen. Psychiat.* 17 (1967): 521–532. For Cohen's conclusion that LSD revealed only irrationality see Cohen, "The Return to the Primary Process," *Psychosomatics* 14 (1973): 9–11.

82. Cohen, in *Federal LSD Research*, 157; and Sidney Cohen, "The Antipodes of the Mind," *Journal of Substance Abuse Treatment* 1 (1984): 151–155, on 155. Cohen explained that "the discriminating, critical capacity is lost. The ability to observe oneself, to evaluate the validity of one's ideas and swift flowering fantasies, is lost": Richard Alpert and Cohen, *LSD* (New York: New American Library, 1966), 17.

From Nicotine to Nicotrol

Addiction, Cigarettes, and American Culture

ALLAN M. BRANDT

BEGINNING IN OCTOBER 1999, Philip Morris led the tobacco industry on a campaign to project a new image. Characterizing their tobacco business as "quality tobacco products, responsibly marketed," the company admitted that cigarette smoking, according to "overwhelming medical and scientific consensus" caused "cancer, heart disease, emphysema and other serious illnesses." Not stopping there, the company went on to admit that cigarette smoking was addictive "as that term is most commonly used today."[1] This new strategy—which Philip Morris as well as the other major U.S. tobacco companies continues to employ—reflects a transformative shift in the status and image of the cigarette.[2] The cigarette underwent a radical reconfiguration during the twentieth century, from a popular and prominent cultural icon to a central and stigmatized product of our drug culture. The status of cigarette use as nicotine addiction marks a remarkable historical transformation of one of the most successful commodities of twentieth-century American life.

In this essay I briefly review the complex history of nicotine addiction during the course of the past century. I suggest that any assessment of the history of a particular substance must simultaneously attend to the shifting criteria of addiction as a general concept; the particular meaning and nature of the substance; and the perceived status of those who use it. Although some have posited universal, transhistorical approaches to the mechanisms of addiction, as the editors of this volume have discussed, I argue that only in specific historical contexts can we see the social processes by which addictions are created and experienced, categorized and treated. The cigarette offers rich and complex possibilities for this examination.

Given that the Surgeon General's *Report* of 1988 was the first to confirm the addictive properties of nicotine, some might conclude that the realization of the addictive properties of tobacco and nicotine is only of recently vintage. Nineteenth-century observers, however, were confident that nicotine was both addictive and dangerous. Isolated in pure form as early as 1828 as the principal tobacco alkaloid, nicotine was widely recognized as one of the most toxic botanical substances in nature. Soon it was demonstrated that in its pure form even small doses were lethal.[3] There was also an understanding that at least for some users, tobacco was habit-forming. As an 1860 historical article about tobacco described, "The weed once inhaled, the habit once acquired, its seductions would not allow it to be easily laid aside . . ."[4]

Cigarettes proved an ingenious mechanism for the delivery of nicotine. Compared with pipe and cigar tobacco, the flue-cured bright burley tobaccos typically employed in the production of cigarettes were slightly acidic and easier to inhale. In fact, for nicotine to be absorbed, acidic tobacco must be inhaled into the lungs, where it is converted from acid to alkaline. Inhalation brings nicotine to the large surface of the lungs, where it is disbursed to the blood stream, the heart, and then the brain without any dilution.[5] The cigarette delivers nicotine to the brain much more efficiently than other forms of tobacco use. While nineteenth-century researchers did not explain the mechanisms of nicotine delivery to the brain, many observers drew a strong analogue to smoking opiates. As the tobacco reformer Charles B. Towns explained in 1915, "The smoker of cigarettes gets his narcotic by precisely the same mechanical process through which the opium-smoker gets his. The opium smoker would find it far too long and expensive a process to obtain the desired effect from opium by taking it into his stomach; but by burning a very much smaller quantity of the drug and bringing it into contact with the sensitive absorbent tissues of the throat and nose, he obtains the narcotic effect that his system craves."[6]

As cigarettes became increasingly popular in the last years of the nineteenth century and first decades of the twentieth, alarm about their addictive properties rose. Not only were they seen as having many baleful health consequences, they were typically identified as both "habit-forming" and poisonous. In the last decades of the nineteenth century, cigarettes were typically associated with delinquency and physical decline among boys. They predisposed some of their users, especially boys, it was thought, to the additional risks of alcohol use and other highly stigmatized behaviors. "Smoking when indulged in by boys is as pernicious a habit as if they commenced to tipple," noted the *New York Times* in 1882. "It stunts their growth, destroys digestion, obscures vision, and rendering them nervous, induces them to seek such stimulant as can be found in alcoholic fluids." Commentators were quick to distinguish the risks of cigarettes from those of other forms of tobacco use: "Cigarette smoking is more dangerous because it is usually done more frequently than cigar smoking, and also because cigarette smokers inhale the smoke, taking in 'air charged with nicotine.'"[7]

The difficulty of quitting, as well as ideas of both tolerance and withdrawal, led many to the conclusion (a century before the U.S. Surgeon General so declared) "that the smoking habit is addictive." By the early twentieth century, reports detailed the deviant behaviors of "cigarette fiends," typically identified as delinquent boys, often caught sneaking off from school. Commentators employed the language of addiction and habit interchangeably, or in tandem. "They were almost hopelessly addicted to the inhaling habit," noted the *Independent* in 1904. Those who tried to quit, it was often noted, failed. "The tobacco was stopped, and then followed a season of derangement and visions, less intense and terrorizing than those belonging to the alcoholic frenzy, but annoying and remarkable to the patient."[8] As one reformed smoker reported in the *Ladies Home Journal*: "I would wake in the morning with the double determination not to smoke and to do a full day's work, but I seldom was able to keep more than one of those determinations. My life became an alternation between idle days when I held to the determination not to smoke and days when, in desperation, I went to smoking again in order to concentrate my mind upon my work. I would go for several days, for a week, sometimes for nearly a month, without smoking. Then for several months I would give up the struggle."[9]

Attitudes and values concerning tobacco in the first decade of the twentieth century were closely tied to prevailing views of alcohol. Indeed, the Woman's Christian Temperance Union and other anti-alcohol reformers were eager to include the addicting dangers of tobacco (in its many forms) in their broadsides. Anti-tobacco leagues sought alliance with temperance organizations. According to late Victorian logic, both drinking and smoking emanated from the same center of depravity where idleness, waste, and a propensity to seek pleasure lurked. The nation's problem with addictive substances indicated a general lack of will and a failure of agency within a culture built on a historic premise of individualism and deferred gratification. Americans expressed powerful anxieties about the loss of control engendered by addiction. Whether the society could rely on individuals' control over themselves or resort to social prohibitions marked a critical social contest of the time.[10]

Dangerous substances were typically deemed deceptive and seductive, especially to the previously uninitiated. Addictions could catch the unaware by surprise and never let them go. Characteristic in the case of tobacco were descriptions of the power of Lady Nicotine; seductive and alluring, she captured men and held them in her smoke. This gendered vision symbolized the allure (and the anxiety) of a historically specific dependence on tobacco. J. M. Barrie, forced to quit smoking by his fiancée, waxed eloquent about both the aesthetic and enslaving characteristics of the habit. As women smokers joined the ranks in the early twentieth century, observers equated flappers with Lady Nicotine. "Obedient rings of perfumed smoke herald the haughty lady, . . . this 1927 version of my Lady Nicotine—the flapper herself," observed Ivor Griffith. . . . [A]s she cuts across the Boston Common— knee deep in silken stockings, high-heeled in artful slippers, her raven locks close trimmed—her face lifted and held secure in place with putty paste and pigments. Out of a crimson crevice crosswise on her face, protrudes a dainty sweet—Caporal."[11] Many were enjoined to take the risk by the femme fatale Lady Nicotine. One might contrast her image with that of Demon Rum, a morally unambiguous figure. The social costs of addiction seemed far more obvious with liquor than tobacco. Indeed, much of the concern over tobacco was its presumed link to alcohol. In this respect, tobacco was the first "gateway drug." "The laboring man and his family have no worse enemy than tobacco," explained Dr. Chalmers, "It often leads to drink, and drink leads to the devil."[12]

The coming of World War I and the triumph of the Eighteenth Amendment, however, severed the connection between alcohol and tobacco, heightening the perceived differences between the two substances. Nowhere was this cultural shift so clearly seen as during the Great War, when the YMCA, after much soul searching, decided to distribute cigarettes to soldiers overseas. In the context of the overwhelming dangers of war, the sustaining and reassuring associations of the cigarette trumped all previous concerns about its addicting characteristics. Given the "alternative vices" apparently available to the troops, cigarettes seemed an appropriate reward, a comfort without any major harmful consequences. The subsequent prohibition of alcohol after the war had the effect of further legitimating the use of cigarettes. Cigarettes now assumed many of the positive cultural and social attributes previously associated with drinking—leisure, pleasure, and sociability— without the risks of intoxication with its consequent social and familial pathologies. Cigarettes seemed, in this respect, the ideal substance for an industrial age of consumption. They were widely promoted as offering a range of significant benefits: by reducing stress and tension ("they won't jangle the nerves"); as an aid in digestion; or for a "quick pick me up." They could be smoked both at work and play, consumed through the day at the office and home.[13]

By the second decade of the twentieth century, as smoking became increasingly popular, a number of observers began to dissociate tobacco from other substances deemed more dangerous and addictive. It was often pointed out that anything could be dangerous if used excessively and that antismoking propaganda was typically based upon instances of abuse rather than reasonable use: "The folly lies not in smoking per se but in the overdoing it by an individual peculiarly susceptible. . . . The irrationally excessive use of tobacco, as of anything else, is usually practiced by those primarily neurasthenic, neurotic, or neuropathologically disposed; the tobacco abuse is a secondary phenomenon," noted *Current Opinion* in 1919. By the late 1920s, journals such as *Hygeia* reassured concerned smokers: "The general conclusion is that excessive smoking of tobacco is harmful, but tobacco taken in moderation by a healthy person does not produce any symptoms or any changes of importance."[14] Unlike earlier images of deviant boys, now smoking could be a moderate, pleasurable pastime, for men and women, young and old.

In much of the literature during the 1920s and 1930s, observers considered the nature of withdrawal as one means of assessing the addictiveness of cigarettes, often concluding that the habit could be broken without much trouble. "A substance to produce the condition known as addiction must affect the brain in such a way as to allow free play of the emotions . . . The factor which in the main is responsible for the evils of addiction has been the extraction and exploitation of active constituents [from plants as they occur in Nature]—morphine from opium and cocaine from coca. . . . Fortunately we have not reached a stage when it is desired to substitute nicotine for tobacco." As W. E. Dixon explained in 1926, "Tobacco smoking, then, does not lead to addiction. An addict to morphine or cocaine is held in bondage by the fear of withdrawal and the terrible craving which ensues. With tobacco this hardly exists; forgetfulness of one's smokes is an annoyance, but not a tragedy, and few, if any, cannot, when the necessity arises, entirely dispense with tobacco."[15] Another author suggested that the craving produced by cigarettes paled compared to other addictions, "That smoking produces a craving for more when an attempt is made to give it up . . . is undoubted, but it can seldom be accurately described as overpowering, and the effects of withdrawal, though there may be definite restlessness and instability, cannot be compared with the physical distress caused by withdrawal in morphine addicts. To regard tobacco as a drug of addiction may be all very well in a humorous sense, but it is hardly accurate."[16] Increasingly cigarettes were categorized as a social "habit" with strong psychological rather than physiological pulls. Defining smoking as but a "habit" rather than an addiction marked a critical aspect in the legitimization and popularization of the cigarette in the first half of the twentieth century.

As this categorization shifted, willpower became the focus in discussions of quitting. Throughout the first half of the century, smokers received advice about quitting from many quarters, including public health officials and reformed smokers. In a popular book called *How to Stop Smoking*, published in 1951, the journalist Herbert Brean asked, "Why do people smoke? Medically speaking tobacco is not habit forming; it does not worm its way into your physique or psyche, as opium or cocaine does. But it *is* habit-forming in the same way that three meals a day, or eight hours' sleep, or wearing clothes, are habit-forming. If you go without any one of them for awhile you become uncomfortable."[17] Public media offered much advice to those who wished to cut down and stop. A writer in *Reader's Digest* explained, "Of course you may say, 'I can't stop—the habit has got me,' or 'My system craves nicotine—it's the only thing that soothes my nerves.' Don't Believe any of this defeatist pish-posh. Your system does not crave nicotine. Smoking is not an irresistible hunger (as for dope) or a consuming thirst (as for alcohol). Your system is not a slave to a drug; you are a slave to a habit—a major habit made up of a connected series of minor habits."[18] Unlike the way earlier critics had conflated habit and addict, now they were sharply distinguished.

During and after Prohibition, the most likely analogue for addiction to cigarettes was addiction to alcohol. In both instances there was a tendency to assert that only certain individuals would develop problems with substance abuse. This model soon became explicit: certain substances could be quite dangerous if excessively used by those with particular vulnerabilities. Typically, these individuals, who were likely to become addicted if exposed to drugs, had an underlying mental disorder. For "normal" individuals, these substances posed little or no risk. This was a fundamental logic behind the repeal of Prohibition, which came to be widely perceived as punishing the many to protect the few.[19]

In each of these respects, cigarettes had come to fall beyond the contemporary boundaries of addiction. One can easily see how, in this context, trading other substances of dependence—such as alcohol or illicit drugs— for cigarettes was viewed as helping an individual traverse the boundary of deviance into the normative, and legitimate. Often cigarettes were seen as a vehicle for assisting in breaking addictions to more dangerous substances like alcohol or opiates. Even as concerns about the possible health consequences of smoking increased in the 1940s and '50s, Americans viewed cigarettes as a central aspect of their social life, an indicator of social and cultural power, autonomy, and attractiveness. All during this period, it is important to recognize that smoking was seen as having decided personal and social advantages that outweighed ongoing concerns about its alternative status as a "bad habit."[20] And, in fact, one of these utilities was that smoking was perceived especially among adolescents as being oppositional, rebellious, and even (moderately) dangerous. As the poet John Hollander recalled, "Abstention from nicotine couldn't help smacking of the self-righteous somehow. Also, even then, it was unquestionably better for one's health not to smoke, but only in the mildly problematic way that made the risk a moral virtue."[21]

It was in the context of widespread accepted cigarette use in the early 1960s that Surgeon General Luther Terry's blue ribbon investigation of the health consequences of cigarette smoking came to the considered conclusion that smoking was not addictive. In direct contrast with its pathbreaking assessment of the causal relationship between smoking and lung cancer, his committee's *Report* sought to dispel concerns that nicotine led to addiction. The *Report* did confirm that the cigarette could be habit-forming, explaining, "Smokers and users of tobacco in other forms usually develop some degree of dependence upon the practice, some to the point where significant emotional disturbances occur if they are deprived of its use." Still, the advisory committee reached the comforting conclusion that "[t]he evidence indicates this dependence to be psychogenic in origin." The committee, therefore, drew a sharp distinction between "habituation" and "addiction," assuring that "the biological effects of tobacco, like coffee . . . are not comparable to those produced by morphine, alcohol, barbiturates, and many other potent addicting drugs." Following definitions promulgated by the World Health Organization, the 1964 *Report* insisted that addiction was a much more severe condition than "habituation," indicating an underlying psychiatric disease. Addictions led to states of "periodic or chronic intoxication," "overpowering desire" to continue taking the drug and "to obtain it by any means." Further, addictive substances had a "detrimental effect on the individual and society." In contrast, habituation merely led to a "desire (but not a compulsion)" to continue using the drug, an absence of physical dependence. Most important, the detrimental impacts "if any" fell primarily on the individual.[22]

Further, the *Report* eagerly dissociated the use of cigarettes from the psychiatric disorders and social deviance usually associated with addiction. "It is generally accepted among psychiatrists that addiction to potent drugs is based upon serious personality defects from underlying psychological or psychiatric disorders which may become manifest in other ways if the drugs are removed." Terry and his colleagues effectively sought to avoid the pathologization of as much as half the adult American population. The *Report* made clear that in its judgment, "even the most energetic campaigner against smoking and nicotine could find little support for the view that all those who use tobacco, coffee, tea, and cocoa are in need of mental care. . . ."[23] Although many recognized the difficulty of quitting, nonetheless it seemed absurd to associate tobacco—a popular and legal product—with a range of drugs whose abuse created physical decline as well as familial and social decay.

Smoking simply did not conform to either medical or popular views of addiction. A recent Supreme Court opinion had concluded: "To be a confirmed drug addict is to be one of the walking dead. . . . The teeth have rotted out, the appetite is lost, and the stomach and intestines don't function properly. . . . Such is the torment of being a drug addict; such is the plague of being one of the walking dead."[24] Given the impressive popularity of cigarette smoking at mid-century and the legitimacy—even cogency—of smoking in American culture, identifying smokers as having a psychiatric disorder must have seemed extreme to the members of Terry's committee.

IN SUBSEQUENT DECADES, however, nicotine would come to be fundamentally incorporated into the medical and psychiatric nomenclature of addiction. A range of factors explain this critical transformation that led, ultimately, to Surgeon General Everett Koop's *Report on Nicotine Addiction* issued in 1988.[25] These included changes in values and attitudes about cigarettes and smokers, as well as shifts in theoretical and clinical approaches to addiction. If the goal of the 1964 *Report* was to demonstrate categorically that smoking caused pathology, in the two decades that followed smoking itself came to be seen as a pathology, an addiction to a powerful and dangerous drug. Increasingly, smoking was embedded in a new and emerging discourse of "substance abuse." Luther Terry's sharp differentiation between habit and addiction could not survive the vigorous medical and scientific assault on the cigarette, or the powerful process of medicalizing and biologizing addictions that became characteristic of the biomedical culture over the last quarter-century.

In the years following Terry's *Report*, medical and scientific data, both epidemiologic and clinical, confirmed, consolidated, and amplified the known harms of the cigarette. Never regarded as "safe," the cigarette quickly became synonymous with death and disease. By the early 1990s, the American Cancer Society would estimate that smoking caused more than 400,000 deaths per year—more than accidents, homicides, alcohol, and AIDS combined. Over the decades, incentives for quitting rose sharply, and many responded. Smoking rates among Americans declined steadily in the decades following Terry's *Report*; from a high of over 40 percent in 1964, to approximately 23 percent in 2000. Although 46.5 million Americans continue to smoke, nearly that many had successfully quit over the previous twenty-five years.[26] The very fact, however, that so many Americans gave up their cigarettes suggested to some that nicotine's addictive "valence" paled in comparison to other drugs.

During this period the very experience of smoking changed markedly. From a behavior associated with sociability, leisure, and pleasure, smoking increasingly came to be associated with compulsiveness, dirt, and personal disregard for one's health. Add to these developments a new recognition that cigarettes were dangerous not only to those who smoked, but also, at least to some degree, to so-called innocent bystanders as well.[27] Growing epidemiological evidence of the risks of passive smoking prompted a grassroots movement to limit smoking in public places. Anti-tobacco organizations lobbied successfully for sharp restrictions of workplace smoking, further isolating and ostracizing smokers and making them often the subject of public scorn, huddled masses on the doorstep.[28]

No doubt, these changes in both the venue and the meaning of smoking made its categorization as addiction far less problematic than would have been the case a generation earlier. Further, the demographics of tobacco use changed dramatically in these decades. A behavior that had been evenly distributed over the social terrain came to be associated with certain social groups—generally those less educated and of lower socioeconomic status. By the late 1980s, high school graduates were twice as likely to be smokers as were college graduates, and smoking prevalence among blacks had fallen far more slowly than among whites. In a culture prone to stigmatize its poor and disfavored, changing perceptions about the "average smoker" eased the growing attribution of addiction.[29]

During the 1970s and 1980s, many who attempted to quit failed. Most research showed that even among motivated individuals, generally only about one in five succeeded. A growing population of potential ex-smokers inspired a range of approaches to quitting. Hypnosis clinics, acupuncture, and cognitive therapies were all employed, with only infrequent successes. In the extreme case, aversion treatments boasted impressive results in the 1970s. In one clinic, individuals were reportedly wired to electrodes that periodically provided a jolt of electricity; "This is followed by 'inhalation therapy' requiring clients to 'smoke three cigarettes . . . at the almost impossible rate of ten deep puffs a minute. 'Inhale,' yells a therapist. 'You lady in blue, keep inhaling. Force yourself.' By the third cigarette, most patients are close to vomiting."[30] Many advocated "cold turkey" as the best way to quit, noting the need to maintain a supportive environment in the face of withdrawal. Despite the claims of new entrepreneurial outfits like SmokEnders and Smoke Watchers, nicotine proved "hard to kick."[31]

The impressive difficulties associated with stopping, as well as growing data that demonstrated that those who sought low-tar, low-nicotine cigarettes increased their consumption, suggested that nicotine more closely fit models of other addictive substances than previously suspected. During the 1970s, several studies demonstrated that smokers would adjust their smoking to maintain a given level of nicotine. Subjects given high-nicotine cigarettes smoked fewer, or puffed them more casually. Conversely, low-nicotine cigarettes led to more "nicotine-seeking"—smoking more, puffing more frequently, and inhaling more deeply. Other research now suggested that smoking was primarily done for the relief of withdrawal. The first cigarette of the day was typically more thoroughly smoked than those that followed. A pack—containing twenty cigarettes—had proven to be in perfect sync with the typical dose response. Depriving smokers of nicotine led to irritability, discomfort, and other symptoms—relieved by nicotine.[32]

Growing recognition of the harms of smoking and the difficulty of quitting spurred research into the pharmacodynamics of nicotine. Addiction to nicotine was incorporated into broader perspectives on the precise mechanisms of drug dependence. Researchers now were quick to point out that nicotine was a close analogue to other frequently abused drugs like heroin, alcohol, and cocaine. After a long history of cigarettes being dissociated from other addictive substances, nicotine now was reintegrated into the panoply of drugs. As the pharmacologist Neal Benowitz concluded in 1988, "nicotine readily crosses the blood-brain barrier and is distributed throughout the brain. Its uptake into the brain appears to involve both passive diffusion and active transport by the choroid plexus. Within the brain, the specific binding of tritiated S-nicotine is greatest in the hypothalamus, hippocampus, thalamus, midbrain, and brain stem, as well as in areas of the cerebral cortex. . . . Most of the effects of nicotine on the central nervous system are due to direct actions on brain receptors . . ."[33]

In addition to investigations of the effects of nicotine in the brain, researchers could also use the new findings in the neurosciences to describe the nature of the "neuroadaptation" characteristic of addictive drugs, such as tolerance and abstinence syndrome. Following out the logic of this analogy, the use of nicotine "substitution therapy" was soon proposed to assist in "detoxification, maintenance and tapering schemes," similar to programs using methadone to treat heroine addiction.[34]

The introduction of Nicorette chewing gum in 1984 further tightened the analogy to other addictive substances often treated with "substitutes." The FDA's approval of Nicorette underscored the pharmacologic properties of nicotine itself and enhanced its identity as an addictive drug. In addition to chewing gum, additional pharmacotherapies for nicotine addiction soon became available. Transdermal patches, inhalers, and nasal sprays, all laced with nicotine, offered smokers new opportunities for replacement therapy. "Ultimately," one nicotine expert explained, "the appropriate assignment of smoker to treatment will be as critical a choosing the proper antibiotic for infection."[35]

Parallel shifts occurred in psychiatry's construction of nicotine addiction. Before 1980, the American Psychiatric Association's *Diagnostic and Statistical Manual* contained no entry for nicotine addiction. However, as psychiatry came to increasingly distinguish addictions as diseases in and of themselves (and as medical perceptions of nicotine changed), by 1980 nicotine addiction rated an entry. By 1987 the *Manual* included "Nicotine-induced organic mental disorder," a syndrome typically associated with the withdrawal symptoms linked to quitting. No doubt, as more Americans attempted to quit they found themselves passing through this newly devised "disorder." The manual also included "305.10 Nicotine Dependence," noting somewhat tautologically, "people with this disorder are often distressed because of their inability to stop nicotine use. . . ." Here then were new syndromes created by the changing medical and social meanings of the cigarette. New medical incentives to quit helped to force the recognition of the difficulty of quitting. The difficulties associated with quitting, in turn, created a broad recognition of nicotine addiction.[36]

Soon after the APA's incorporation of nicotine into their rubric of addiction, the federal government came forward and substantiated these findings. In 1988, Surgeon General Everett Koop issued his *Report on Nicotine Addiction*. Never one to mince words, Koop declared that: (1) cigarettes and other forms of tobacco are addicting, (2) nicotine is the drug in tobacco that causes addiction, and (3) the pharmacologic and behavioral processes that determine tobacco addiction are similar to those that determine addiction to drugs such as heroin or cocaine. He suggested that a new label on cigarettes would now be appropriate; were he deciding the wording, he declared, "such a label would say tobacco 'is just as addictive as heroin or cocaine.'"[37]

Not surprisingly the tobacco industry sharply contested the categorization of nicotine as addictive. Brennan Moran, an industry public relations expert, argued, "Smoking is truly a personal choice that can be stopped if and when a person decides to do so." Another representative of the industry argued that Koop's findings, "contradict common sense and trivialize society's problems with illegal drugs." Others cited the large number of Americans who had quit over the previous decades as evidence that tobacco could not be addictive. Walker Merryman, the well-known spokesperson for the Tobacco Institute, responded to the Koop *Report* by noting, "I've not heard of anyone holding up a liquor store or mugging an old lady to get the money to buy cigarettes."[38] These arguments, while self-serving, appealed to an important ethic in American culture of personal responsibility and control.

The incorporation of cigarette smoking into the discourse of addiction nonetheless signaled the growth of a therapeutic ethos which would increasingly surround smoking. Nicotine addiction had been "medicalized" with the addition of diagnostic categories, the use of a sophisticated neuroscience and pharmacology to explain addiction, and the introduction of pharmacologic treatment. The implications of such medicalization in this instance were neither clear nor direct. On the one hand, nicotine addiction subverted traditional industry claims that smokers acted with rational free will. Further, with greater understanding of the addictive properties of the cigarette, it was suggested, perhaps smokers should no longer be treated as pariahs. "Health professionals and nonsmokers are being urged to see smokers in a more sympathetic light in the wake of the Surgeon General's recent report declaring nicotine to be an addictive drug that quickly turns most users into abusers," wrote Jane Brody in her *New York Times* health column.[39] Edwin B. Fisher Jr., a psychologist urged physicians to be "smoker friendly" instead of critical. "Smokers are not sickos, weak-willed or perverse if they can't drop their habit like a hot-potato."[40] Although declaring nicotine addictive might spare smokers such contempt, on the other hand it served to further pathologize a once popular behavior, with the consequence of potentially enhancing stigma. Smokers now joined the ranks of addicts; they had a diagnosable, if not easily treated disorder. Nonetheless, the attribution of addiction also served to further stigmatize and pathologize a population that persisted in the face of overwhelming health evidence to abuse their health in an increasingly health-conscious culture. Further, the medicalization of nicotine addiction often directed attention away from the social and cultural contexts in which smoking was embedded.

By the early twenty-first century, smoking had joined the ranks of "chronic disease." In *Treating Tobacco Use and Dependence*, the Clinical Practice Guidelines put out by the U.S. Department of Health and Human Services in June 2000, the authors warn that clinicians need to take into account that quitting is not something a majority of smokers will succeed at easily. Rather, they posit, "A more productive approach is to recognize the chronicity of tobacco dependence," defining it as a "long-term . . . disorder" with "periods of relapse and remission."[41] Dr. Nancy Rigotti, an expert on tobacco treatment and cessation, embraced this description in her 2002 discussion of tobacco dependence in the *New England Journal of Medicine*, explaining, "Smoking is a chronic problem, like hypertension or hyperlipidemia, that requires long-term management."[42] Correspondingly, twenty-first century guidelines have expanded to include Bupropion, a serotonin reuptake inhibitor (SSRIs) commonly prescribed as an antidepressant among the "first-line" treatments. Pharmaceuticals that do not simply substitute nicotine in another form but instead reduce that craving felt by the smoker have become a significant element of new treatment regimes.

At the same time that cigarettes were pathologized and incorporated into broader theoretical models of addiction, insistence upon individual responsibility for quitting sharply increased. In the last decades of the twentieth century, American culture came to be dominated by an ethic of control and personal mastery.[43] Many smokers apparently internalized this new ethic.[44]

Quitting became a powerful trope for control in the last two decades. Eth-nographers of the quitting experience found the triumph over the cigarette (as well as the agony of defeat) to be symbolic of more fundamental psy-chological and cultural anxieties about control and the assertion of agency over external forces (both chemical and corporate). As subjects from one anthropological study explained:

> Cigarettes run me ... I don't have control on this ... I can't walk away from it ... There is something down in me saying "smoke, smoke, smoke," and I'm saying "I don't want to, let me quit. ... ."

> It's either I have control over the nicotine, or the nicotine has control over me ... I'd like to see that I have myself, that I can control the situation.

> [Y]ou gain control over yourself once you give up ... and say, "heh, look, I did it. I do have control. ... ."[45]

Perhaps, in many ways, these anxieties reflected growing cultural concerns that control was so difficult to attain in the face of powerful political and economic forces, as well as biological and environmental threats, far beyond the ken of rational intervention. At such historical moments, it is perhaps not surprising to see rising anxieties about health and strong arguments that individuals must take responsibility for their health. In the United States, as well as other Western nations, such views were spurred by a new epidemi-ology of risk factors that often promised redemption through prescribed behavioral change. Now, it was argued, we have the data to take "control of our health."[46] Such arguments were deemed especially convincing in the United States, where cultural traditions of individual responsibility had a strong cultural valence. Nowhere was this phenomenon so clearly seen as in the dramatic decline in cigarette smoking and the elucidation of nicotine addiction.

In the mid-1980s, it appeared that smoking might remain a symbol of the assertion of individual agency and a powerful rhetorical vehicle for victim-blaming. The tobacco industry tried to foster this focus with a campaign highlighting "smokers' rights." However, conflicting sentiments ultimately placed blame in the lap of the industry rather than the consumer. By the late 1980s, social antipathy toward the tobacco industry began to emerge, opening up new possibilities for more intensive public regulation.[47] In the traditional tension between criminalizing the pusher or the user, new atten-tion has been directed at the activities of the powerful industry hawking a now addictive product.

The FDA regulations of nicotine have their immediate origins in an act of political theater staged in 1994 before Congressman Henry Waxman's

Subcommittee on Health and the Environment. Waxman's public elicitation of denials of the addictiveness of cigarettes from the seven major tobacco company CEOs destroyed the vestiges of credibility and legitimacy of a long-standing industry position. At the hearings, Food and Drug Commissioner David Kessler began a process of constructing a justification for FDA regulation of cigarettes. Kessler explained that his department was gathering evidence that "cigarette manufacturers may intend that their products contain nicotine to satisfy an addiction on the part of some of their customers." Although this conclusion, in and of itself, might not have stirred attention, he went on to add that it was the FDA's understanding that the companies "commonly add nicotine to cigarettes to deliver specific amounts of nicotine." Kessler concluded that the manufacturers "may be controlling smokers' choice by controlling the levels of nicotine in their products in a manner that creates and sustains an addiction in the vast majority of smokers." He further suggested that this was a deceptive practice since "most people assume that the nicotine in cigarettes is present solely because it is a natural and unavoidable component of tobacco." The recognition that nicotine could be taken out of tobacco and put back in—that the companies could control nicotine content in fine calibrations—opened the industry to charges of "spiking, manipulations, and juicing-up." Also, the former associate director of the Council for Tobacco Research, John Kreisher, explained at the hearings that additives, like ammonia compounds, reportedly enhanced the potency of nicotine. "Ammonia helped the industry lower the tar and allowed smokers to get more bang with less nicotine. It solved a couple of problems at the same time."[48]

The emergence of internal tobacco company documents served to strengthen the positions taken by Kessler and others at the hearings. Documents recovered in 1994 from the Brown and Williamson Company and BAT revealed that as early as 1963 tobacco industry scientists and executives had acknowledged that nicotine was addictive. A 1978 memo equated smokers' "satisfaction" with maintaining an adequate nicotine level. The production of ultra low-tar cigarettes (also low in nicotine), according to company documents, would have "severe implications for long-term market growth."[49] Additional documents indicated that Brown and Williamson had attempted to genetically engineer a tobacco plant with low-tar and high-nicotine content.[50] Further, Philip Morris researchers testified that industry executives had summarily suppressed studies on rats and nicotine addiction.[51] According to Kessler, as early as 1969, Philip Morris researchers had reported that "the ultimate explanation for the perpetuated cigarette habit resides in the pharmacological effect of smoke upon the body of the smoker."[52]

Following on these early revelations, there was growing evidence that the companies purposefully controlled nicotine content to enhance the addictiveness of their products in the 1980s and 1990s. Kessler stated, "In the spring of 1994, the FDA observed a trend that strongly suggested that the tobacco industry manipulated and controlled the level of nicotine in conventional cigarettes." Analyzing the FTC reports on tar and nicotine content, FDA investigators discovered that since 1982, nicotine content in cigarettes had been rising, with the largest increases occurring in low-tar cigarettes. Kessler concluded, "it seemed unlikely that the delivery of nicotine could increase independently unless the manufacturers had made deliberate design decisions."[53] Since 1982, nicotine levels in U.S.-produced cigarettes have risen by approximately 10 percent. As a result of testimony at the Waxman hearings and the evidence of suppressed documentation of the addictiveness of nicotine on the part of cigarette manufacturers, federal prosecutors and the Justice Department began probes into possible allegations of perjury.[54]

In the court of public opinion, Waxman, Kessler, and the anti-tobacco movement had scored a clear victory in this particular battle in the ongoing tobacco wars. A *New York Times*/CBS poll conducted following the public hearings and the powerful media reports they generated showed that 91 percent of Americans believed that smoking was addictive. Such findings no doubt encouraged President Clinton (a careful observer of public opinion) to take tobacco on as a political issue and to encourage Kessler's emerging initiative to regulate nicotine. Bob Dole's disclaimers about the addictiveness of tobacco proved to be a critical misstep in the 1996 presidential campaign, demonstrating how far out of touch he was with current views, as well as subjecting him to charges of being in the pocket of tobacco lobbyists.[55]

Kessler shrewdly tied the data on nicotine and addiction to growing concerns that the industry aggressively marketed cigarettes to children and adolescents. Echoing concerns of the late nineteenth and early twentieth century, Kessler labeled this a "pediatric disease." Epidemiological data confirmed that nicotine addiction usually begins among teenagers; more than half of all adult smokers had become regular "users" by age eighteen. Pointing to the very aggressive marketing that reaches children and adolescents, Kessler called for restrictions of vending machines, advertising, and other promotions pitched to youth, as well as stronger educational efforts to prevent smoking among teenagers. Central to his argument for jurisdiction over tobacco was the premise that young people could not adequately weigh the risks associated with tobacco in the face of such aggressive solicitation to use a product "intended to affect the structure or the function of the body." Underlying the FDA regulations was the attempt to undercut traditional justifications that tobacco use was a "choice" made by "consenting adults."[56]

By 1992, a textbook on substance abuse listed cigarette smoking as "the most common substance use disorder in the US."[57] More recently, even though the U.S. Supreme Court ruled in March 2000 that the FDA does not currently have jurisdiction over tobacco as a "drug delivery system" (as affirmed by the Federal District Court in 1997), they nonetheless recognized its addictive capacity.[58] Nicotine has become an increasingly "controlled" substance, embedded in a larger discourse of addiction, drug abuse, and treatment.

The cigarette and the risks inherent in smoking have come to represent a series of critical contests in late twentieth-century consumer culture. The cigarette, for much of the twentieth century an icon of consumption, a symbol of autonomy, attractiveness, and choice, has now become a symbol of the corruption of consumption. Tobacco companies are typically viewed as corrupt, greedy, deceptive, and manipulative. From what we know of the history of addictions and addicts, one might have anticipated a new round of victim-blaming as cigarettes came to be incorporated into the discourse of drug abuse. And of course there are powerful currents in our culture that define smokers as weak-willed and ignorant, who abuse their own health and others', while polluting the common environment. But in recent years increased attention has also been directed at the activities of the powerful multinational companies that produce cigarettes, a product seen increasingly as both dangerous and addicting. In this respect, in the modern history of the addictions, the tobacco companies may prove to be unrivaled villains, aggressively marketing—often to minors—a deadly and addictive, if legal, product.[59] Nowhere else in the drug wars has such traffic occurred so openly and explicitly. Drug pushing, in this context, is the activity of a legal industry, greedily seeking profits by soliciting youth to get hooked on their deadly product. In the current drug culture, the boundary between licit and illicit has therefore been erased.

During this same period, tobacco executives have continued to insist (very publicly, in testimony before Congress and in the numerous liability suits) that tobacco is not truly addictive. Hedging its bets, the industry has made a clear distinction between addiction to cigarettes and addiction to illegal drugs like cocaine and heroine. R. J. Reynolds, for example, asserted on its website in April 2000 that it "defies common sense and is contrary to much research" to claim that "everyday activities like smoking and drinking coffee" are addictive in the same sense as "use of hard drugs like heroin." By early 2003, however, R.J.R. toned down this argument, still stating, "we disagree with characterizing smoking as being addictive in the same sense as heroin, cocaine, or other substances," but no longer questioning the common sense of those who found it addictive. Admitting that "many smokers find it difficult to quit and some find it extremely difficult," the company website stated that smoking was addictive according to how "that term is commonly used today."[60]

THIS WAR IS far from over. At its center are deeply contested views of the meaning and nature of agency, responsibility, and addiction. Cigarettes hold a special place in this debate. A legal product, powerfully identified with the rise of our consumer culture, they are also a product of remarkable dangers. When such harms are incurred, how do we adjudicate responsibility? Where is the locus of control within individuals and society? Addiction has historically served a complex and even contradictory function of relieving some individuals of responsibility for their actions and at the same time generating moral outrage for individual irresponsibility. While many Americans have become convinced of the addictiveness of cigarettes— and increasingly understand the complicity if not the determinative role of the companies in creating these addictions—there remains a strong disposition to continue to hold smokers accountable for their actions. This tension remains at the heart of addiction discourse; while we insist medically and scientifically that addictions are diseases meriting support and treatment, we also insist that individuals must take responsibility for their plight if they are to be treated.

At stake in such debates are deep cultural norms and values about the nature of agency and the dynamics of social and personal control. On the one hand, we seem increasingly aware of the powerful corporate forces in modern societies that subtly and not so subtly shape opinion, behavior, and action, often in ways that do not conform with individual interests and health. Nonetheless, the need to believe that we can and must assert individual will over these forces is a characteristic element of our society. Embedded in this tension lies both our hostility to the cigarette and those who produce it, as well our ongoing skepticism and antagonism toward those who smoke. We continue, at least for the current historical moment, to live on this cusp.

Notes

1. "The Truth about Tobacco," Editorial, *New York Times*, 14 October 1999, A30; and Myron Levin, "Philip Morris' New Campaign Echoes Medical Experts," *Los Angeles Times*, 13 October 1999, C1.

2. See, for example, websites, (as of 4/13/00): http://www.philipmorris.com/tobacco _bus/tobacco_issues/health_issues.html; http://www.rjrt.com/TI/Pages/TIquiting.asp; and http://www.brownandwilliamson.com/1_hottopics/smoking_frame.html.

3. U.S. Department of Health and Human Services, *The Health Consequences of Smoking: Nicotine Addiction: A Report of the Surgeon General* (Washington, D.C.: GPO, 1988);

Wilhelm Heinrich Posselt and C. L. Reimann, "Chemische Untersuchungen des Tabaks und Darstellung des eigentümlichen Princeps dieser Planze," *Magazin für Pharmazie und die dahin einschlagenden Wissenschaften* 24–25 (1828–1829); A. Trousseau, "Tobacco-Poisoning, or Tobacconism," *Clinical Medicine Lectures*. 3d ed. (Philadelphia: P. Blakiston, 1882), 2: 964.

4. David William Cheever, "Tobacco," *Atlantic Monthly*, August 1860, 187–202. (http://www.theatlantic.com/unbound/flashbks/smoking/tobaccf.htm)

5. Robert K. Heimann, *Tobacco and Americans* (New York: McGraw-Hill, 1960); U.S. Department of Health and Human Services, *The Health Consequences of Smoking: Nicotine Addiction: A Report of the Surgeon General* (Washington, D.C.: GPO, 1988), 29–30.

6. Charles Barnes Towns, *Habits That Handicap: The Menace of Opium, Alcohol, and Tobacco, and the Remedy* (New York: Century, 1915), 165–166.

7. "M. Buley Is at the Head . . ." Editorial, *New York Times*, 17 October 1882, 4; "Cigarettes," *New York Times*, 14 August 1887, 4.

8. Charles Bulkley Hubbell, "The Cigaret Habit—A New Peril," *Independent*, 18 February 1904, 375–378; "Astounding Effects of Tobacco," *New York Times*, 8 April 1882, 2.

9. George H. Cleveland, "What's the Matter with My Pulse?" *Ladies Home Journal*, November 1914, 12.

10. Harry Gene Levine, "The Discovery of Addiction: Changing Conceptions of Habitual Drunkenness in America," *Journal of Studies on Alcohol* 39 (1978): 143–174; Joseph R. Gusfield, *Symbolic Crusade: Status Politics and the American Temperance Movement* (Urbana: University of Illinois Press, 1966).

11. J. M. Barrie, *My Lady Nicotine* (London: Hodder and Stoughton, 1890); Ivor Griffith, "My Lady Nicotine," *American Journal of Pharmacy* 99 (February 1927): 63.

12. Matthew Woods, "Some of the Minor Immoralities of the Tobacco Habit," *JAMA* 32, no. 13 (1 April, 1899): 683–687.

13. See Cassandra Tate, *Cigarette Wars: The Triumph of "The Little White Slaver"* (New York: Oxford University Press, 1999).

14. "A Physician's Vindication of Tobacco," *Current Opinion*, October 1919, 243; "Tobacco and Physical Efficiency," *Hygeia*, January 1928, 46.

15. W. E. Dixon, "Tobacco," *The Nineteenth Century*, April 1926, 565–566.

16. Sir Humphry Rolleston, "Medical Aspects of Tobacco," *The Living Age* (10 July 1926, 90.

17. Herbert Brean, *How to Stop Smoking* (New York: Vanguard Press, 1951); reprint (condensed) *Reader's Digest*, April 1954, 31.

18. J. P. McEvoy, "Are You a Man or a Smokestack?" *Reader's Digest*, August 1944, 103.

19. See for example Thomas R. Pegram, *Battling Demon Rum: The Struggle for a Dry America, 1800–1933* (Chicago: Ivan R. Dee, 1998).

20. John C. Burnham, *Bad Habits: Drinking, Smoking, Taking Drugs, Gambling, Sexual Misbehavior, and Swearing in American History* (New York : New York University Press, 1993).

21. John Hollander, "From Beyond the Cigarette: Notes of a Redeemed Smoker," *Harper's Magazine*, April, 1969, 87.

22. U.S. Public Health Service, *Smoking and Health: Report of the Advisory Committee to the Surgeon General of the Public Health Service* (Washington, D.C.: GPO, 1964), 350, 351.

23. Ibid., 351–352.

24. *Robinson v. California*, 370 U.S. 660, 1962, as quoted in Edward M. Brecher and the Editors of *Consumer Reports, Licit and Illicit Drugs* (Boston: Little, Brown, 1972), 21.

25. U.S. Department of Health and Human Services, *The Health Consequences of Smoking: Nicotine Addiction: A Report of the Surgeon General* (Washington, D.C.: GPO, 1988).

26. "Cigarette Smoking among Adults—United States, 2000," *Morality and Morbidity Weekly Report* (26 July 2002): 642.

27. U.S. Department of Health and Human Services, *The Health Consequences of Involuntary Smoking: A Report of the Surgeon General* (Washington, D.C.: GPO, 1986).

28. National Research Council, Committee on Passive Smoking, *Environmental Tobacco Smoke: Measuring Exposures and Assessing Health Effects* (Washington, D.C.: National Academy Press, 1986).

29. Allan M. Brandt, "The Cigarette, Risk, and American Culture." *Daedalus* 119, no. 4 (1990): 155–176.

30. *Newsweek,* 28 August 1972, 71

31. Sandra Blakeslee, "Nicotine: Harder to Kick . . . than Heroin, *New York Times Magazine,* (29 March 1987), 22.

32. Neal L. Benowitz et al., "Smokers of Low-Yield Cigarettes Do Not Consume Less Nicotine," *New England Journal of Medicine* 309 (21 July 1983): 139–142.

33. Neal L. Benowitz, "Pharmacologic Aspects of Cigarette Smoking and Nicotine Addiction," *New England Journal of Medicine* 319 (17 November 1988): 1318–1330.

34. Ibid., 1325.

35. M. Jarvik and N. Schneider, "Nicotine," in Joyce H. Lowinson, Pedro Ruiz, and Robert B. Millman, eds., *Substance Abuse: A Comprehensive Textbook,* 2d ed. (Baltimore: Williams & Wilkins, 1992), 350.

36. American Psychiatric Association, *Diagnostic and Statistical Manual of Mental Disorders: DSM-III-R.* (Washington, D.C.: American Psychiatric Press, 1987), 181.

37. Department of Health and Human Services, *The Health Consequences of Smoking* Martin Tolchin, "Surgeon General Asserts Smoking Is an Addiction," *New York Times,* 17 May 1988, A1.

38. Ed Bean, "Surgeon General's Stature Is Likely to Add Force to Report on Smoking as Addiction," *Wall Street Journal,* 13 March 1988, 21.

39. Jane E. Brody, "Health; Personal Health," *New York Times,* 7 July 1988, B6.

40. Quoted in ibid.

41. *Treating Tobacco Use and Dependence,* 9.

42. Nancy A. Rigotti, "Treatment of Tobacco Use and Dependence," *New England Journal of Medicine* 346, no. 7 (14 February 2002): 512.

43. Allan M. Brandt, "Behavior, Disease, and Health in the Twentieth-Century United States: The Moral Valence of Individual Risk," and Charles Rosenberg, "Banishing Risk: Continuity and Change in the Moral Management of Disease," both in Brandt and Paul Rozin, eds., *Morality and Health* (New York: Routledge, 1997), 53–78 and 35–52.

44. Paul Rozin, "Moralization," in ibid., 379–402.

45. Dennis G. Willms, "Experiences of Smoking and Smoking Cessation: An Anthropological Perspective" (Unpublished paper, Harvard Medical Anthropology Seminar Series, 15 May 1986), 31–32.

46. John Knowles, "The Responsibility of the Individual," *Dædalus* 106, no. 1 (Winter

1977): 57–80; U.S. Office of the Assistant Secretary for Health, *Healthy People: The Surgeon General's Report on Health Promotion and Disease Prevention* (Washington, D.C.: U.S. Dept. of Health, Education, and Welfare, Public Health Service, GPO, 1979); Robert A. Aronowitz, *Making Sense of Illness: Science, Society, and Disease* (New York: Cambridge University Press, 1998).

47. Robert L. Rabin and Stephen D. Sugarman, *Smoking Policy: Law, Politics, and Culture* (New York : Oxford University Press, 1993).

48. Richard Kluger, *Ashes to Ashes: America's Hundred-Year Cigarette War, the Public Health, and the Unabashed Triumph of Philip Morris* (New York: Alfred A. Knopf, 1996), 745, 744–745.

49. John Slade, Lisa A. Bero, Peter Hanauer, Deborah E. Barnes, and Stanton A. Glantz, "Nicotine and Addiction: The Brown and Williamson Documents," *JAMA* 274 (1995): 225–233.

50. Heather Bruce, "FDA Chief Says Nicotine Is Bolstered: Genetic, Chemical 'Manipulation' of Tobacco by Companies Charged," *Boston Globe*, 24 June 1994, 1.

51. Philip J. Hilts, "Scientists Say Cigarette Company Suppressed Findings on Nicotine,"*New York Times,* 29 April 1994, A1; Hilts, "Philip Morris Blocked '83 Paper Showing Tobacco Is Addictive, Panel Finds," *New York Times* 1 April 1994, A21.

52. David A. Kessler et al., "The Food and Drug Administration's Regulation of Tobacco Products," *New England Journal of Medicine* 335 (26 September 1996): 990. See also Kessler, *A Question of Intent: A Great American Battle with a Deadly Industry* (New York: Public Affairs, 2001).

53. Kessler, "The Food and Drug Administration's Regulation of Tobacco Products," 989.

54. John M. Goshko, "Federal Grand Juries to Investigate Testimony by Tobacco Firm Officials," *Washington Post* 26 July 1995, A5.

55. "Mr. Dole's Smoke Rings," Editorial, *New York Times*, 4 July 1996, A18.

56. Philip J. Hilts, "FDA Head Calls Smoking a Pediatric Disease," *New York Times*, 9 March 1995, A22; and Dolores Kong, "FDA Head Wants to Prevent Smoking Habit at an Early Age," *Boston Globe*, 16 May 1995, 24.

57. Jarvik and Schneider, "Nicotine," 350.

58. Marlene Cimons, "US Judge OK's FDA's Power to Regulate Tobacco," *Los Angeles Times*, 26 April 1997, A1; and U.S. Supreme Court, "Opinion of the Court," *Food and Drug Administration, et al., Petitioners v. Brown & Williamson Tobacco Corporation et al.,* Number 98–1152 (21 March 2000).

59. Philip J. Hilts, *Smoke Screen: The Truth behind the Tobacco Industry Cover-Up* (Reading, Mass.: Addison-Wesley, 1996).

60. R. J. Reynolds Tobacco Company, "Tobacco Issues: Quitting and Addiction," http://www.rjrt.com/TI/TIquitting.asp (accessed 20 February 2003).

Further Reading

Selected Historical Works on Alcohol

Early Histories of Temperance and the Liquor Problem

Blair, Henry William. *The Temperance Movement: or The Conflict between Man and Alcohol.* Boston: William Smythe, 1888.

Cherrington, Ernest. *Standard Encyclopedia of the Liquor Problem.* 6 vols. Westerville, Ohio: American Issue Publishing Company, 1925–1930.

Dorchester, Daniel. *The Liquor Problem in All Ages.* New York: Phillips and Hunt, 1884.

Gordon, Anna. *The Beautiful Life of Frances E. Willard.* Chicago: Woman's Christian Temperance Publishing Association, 1898.

Krout, Jack. *The Origins of Prohibition.* Chicago: University of Chicago Press, 1979.

Rush, Benjamin. *An Inquiry into the Effects of Ardent Spirits upon the Human Body and Mind, with an Account of the Means of Preventing, and of the Remedies for Curing Them.* Brookfield, Mass.: E. Merriam, 1814 (1784).

Temperance Movement

Blocker, Jack. *American Temperance Movements: Cycles of Reform.* Boston: Twayne, 1989.

Dannenbaum, Jed. *Drink and Disorder: Temperance Reform in Cincinnati from the Washingtonians to the WCTU.* Urbana: University of Illinois Press, 1984.

Gusfield, Joseph. *Symbolic Crusade: Status Politics and the American Temperance Movement.* Urbana: University of Illinois Press, 1963.

Lender, Mark. *Dictionary of American Temperance Biography: From Temperance Reform to Alcohol Research, the 1600s to the 1980s.* Westport, Conn.: Greenwood Press, 1984.

Tyrell, Ian. *Sobering Up: From Temperance to Prohibition in Antebellum America.* Westport, Conn.: Greenwood Press, 1979.

Pegram, Thomas. *Battling Demon Rum: The Struggle for a Dry America, 1800–1933.* Chicago: Ivan R. Dee, 1998.

Wagner, David. *The New Temperance: The American Obsession with Sin and Vice.* Boulder, Colo.: Westview Press, 1997.

Woman's Temperance Movement

Blocker, Jack. Jr. *Give to the Winds Thy Fears: The Women's Temperance Crusade.* Westport, Conn.: Greenwood Press, 1985.

———. "Separate Paths: Suffragists and the Women's Temperance Crusade." *Signs: Journal of Women in Culture and Society* 10 (1985): 460–476.

Bordin, Ruth. *Women and Temperance: The Quest for Power and Liberty.* New Brunswick: Rutgers University Press, 1990.

Epstein, Barbara. *The Politics of Domesticity: Women, Evangelism, and Temperance in Nineteenth-Century America.* Middletown, Conn.: Wesleyan University Press, 1981.

Giele, Janet Z. *Two Paths to Women's Equality: Temperance, Suffrage and the Origins of Modern Feminism.* New York: Twayne, 1995.

Levine, Harry Gene. "Temperance and Women in the 19th-Century United States." In Oriana Kalant, ed., *Research Advances in Alcohol and Drug Problems*, vol. 5, *Alcohol and Drug Problems in Women.* New York: Plenum Press, 1986, 25–67.

Reinarman, G. Craig. "The Social Construction of an Alcohol Problem: The Case of Mothers Against Drunk Drivers and Social Control in the 1980s," *Theory and Society* 17 (1988): 91–120.

Tyrell, Ian. "Women and Temperance in Ante-bellum America, 1830–1860." *Civil War History* 28 (June 1982): 128–152.

———. *Women's World/Women's Empire: The Woman's Christian Temperance Union in International Perspective, 1800–1930.* Chapel Hill: University of North Carolina Press, 1991.

Zimmerman, Jonathan. *Distilling Democracy: Alcohol Education in America's Public Schools, 1880–1925.* Lawrence,: University of Kansas Press, 1999.

Medicine

Appleton, Lynn M. "Rethinking Medicalization: Alcoholism and Anomalies." In Joel Best, ed., *Images of Issues: Typifying Contemporary Social Problems*, 2d ed. New York: Aldine De Gruyter, 1995, 59–80.

Babor, Thomas F. and Barbara Rosenkrantz. "Public Health, Public Morals, and Public Order: Social Science and Liquor Control in Massachusetts, 1880–1916." In Susanna Barrows and Robin Room, *Drinking: Behavior and Belief in Modern History.* Berkeley: University of California Press, 1991, 265–286.

Baumohl, Jim. "Inebriate Institutions in North America, 1840–1920." In Cheryl Krasnick Warsh, eds., *Drink in Canada: Historical Essays.* Montreal: McGill-Queen's University Press, 1993, 92–114.

Baumohl, Jim, and Sarah Tracy. "Building Systems for Inebriates: The Divergent Paths of California and Massachusetts, 1891–1920." *Contemporary Drug Problems* 21 (Winter 1994): 557–595.

Conrad, Peter, and Joseph Schneider. "Alcoholism: Drunkenness, Inebriety, and the Disease Concept." In Conrad and Schneider, *Deviance and Medicalization: From Badness to Sickness*, expanded ed. Philadelphia,: Temple University Press, 1992, 73–109.

Golden, Janet. "'An Argument That Goes Back to the Womb': The Demedicalization of Fetal Alcohol Syndrome, 1973–1992." *Journal of Social History* 33 (Winter 1999): 269–299.

Kurtz, Ernest. *Not-God: A History of Alcoholics Anonymous.* Center City, Minn.: Hazelden Educational Services, 1979.

Levine, Harry Gene. "The Discovery of Addiction: Changing Conceptions of Habitual Drunkenness in America." *Journal of Studies on Alcohol*, 39 (January 1978): 143–174.

Pauly, Philip. "The Struggle for Ignorance about Alcohol: American Physiologists, Wilbur Olin Atwater, and the Woman's Christian Temperance Union." *Bulletin of the History of Medicine* 64 (1990): 366–392.

———. "How Did the Effects of Alcohol on Reproduction Become Scientifically Uninteresting?" *Journal of the History of Biology* 29 (1996): 1–28.

Zimmerman, Jonathan. "'When the Doctors Disagree': Scientific Temperance and Scientific Authority, 1891–1906." *Journal of the History of Medicine and Allied Sciences* 48 (1993): 171–197.

Gender

Crowley, John W. *The White Logic: Alcoholism and Gender in American Modernist Fiction.* Amherst: University of Massachusetts Press, 1994.

Lender, Mark. "A Special Stigma: The Origins of Attitudes toward Women Alcoholics." In David Strug et al., eds., *Alcohol Interventions: Historical and Sociocultural Approaches.* New York: Hawthorne, 1986, 41–57.

Murdock, Catherine Gilbert. *Domesticating Drink: Women, Men, and Alcohol in America, 1870–1940.* Baltimore Johns Hopkins University Press, 1998.

Peiss, Kathy. *Cheap Amusements: Working Women and Leisure in New York City, 1880–1920.* Philadelphia: Temple University Press, 1985.

Powers, Madelon. *Faces along the Bar: Lore and Order in the Workingman's Saloon, 1870–1920.* Chicago: University of Chicago Press, 1998.

Rotskoff, Lori. *Love on the Rocks: Men, Women, and Alcohol in Post–World War II America.* Chapel Hill: University of North Carolina Press, 2002.

Ethnicity

Fahey, David. *Temperance and Racism: John Bull, Johnny Reb, and the Good Templars.* Lexington: University of Kentucky Press, 1996.

Herd, Denise. "The Paradox of Temperance: Blacks and the Alcohol Question in Nineteenth-Century America." In Susanna Barrows and Robin Room, *Drinking: Behavior and Belief in Modern History.* Berkeley: University of California Press, 1991, 354–375.

Kunitz, Stephen, and Jerrold Levy. "Changes in Alcohol Use among Navajos and other Indians of the American Southwest." In Roy Porter and Mikulas Teich, eds., *Drugs and Narcotics in History.* Cambridge: Cambridge University Press, 1995, 133–55.

Lender, Mark, and James Kirby Martin. *Drinking in America: A History*, 2d ed. New York: Free Press, 1987.

Lurie, Nancy. "The World's Oldest On-Going Protest Demonstration: North American Indian Drinking Patterns." *Pacific Historical Review* (1972): 311–332.

Mancall, Peter. *Deadly Medicine: Indians and Alcohol in Early America.* Ithaca: Cornell University Press, 1995.

Stivers, Richard. *Hair of the Dog: Irish Drinking and Its American Stereotype*, rev. ed., New York: Continuum, 2000.

Unrau, William. *White Man's Wicked Water: The Alcohol Trade and Prohibition in Indian Country, 1802–1892.* Lawrence: University of Kansas Press, 1999.

Pubs and Saloons

Conroy, David. *In Public Houses: Drink and the Revolution of Authority in Colonial Massachusetts.* Chapel Hill: University of North Carolina Press, 1995.

Duis, Perry. *The Saloon: Public Drinking in Chicago and Boston, 1880–1920.* Urbana: University of Illinois Press, 1983.

Peiss, Kathy. *Cheap Amusements: Working Women and Leisure in New York City, 1880–1920.* Philadelphia: Temple University Press, 1985.

Powers, Madelon. *Faces along the Bar: Lore and Order in the Workingman's Saloon, 1870–1920.* Chicago: University of Chicago Press, 1998.

Rosenzweig, Roy. *Eight Hours for What We Will: Workers and Leisure in an Industrial City, 1870–1920.* New York: Cambridge University Press, 1983.

General Alcohol

Barr, Andrew. *Drink: A Social History of America*. New York: Carroll and Graf, 1999.

Edwards, Griffith. *Alcohol: The World's Favorite Drug*. New York: St. Martin's Press, 2002.

Lender, Mark, and James Kirby Martin, *Drinking in America: A History*, 2d ed. New York: Free Press, 1987.

Levine, Harry Gene. "The Good Creature of God and the Demon Rum: Colonial Ideas about Alcohol, Crime, and Accidents." In Robin Room and Gary Collins, eds., *Alcohol and Disinhibition: Nature and Meaning of the Link*, NIAAA Research Monograph no. 12. Washington, D.C.: U.S. Government Printing Office, DHHS Publication no. [ADM] 83–1246, 1983, 405–2.

Room, Robin. "Alcohol Consumption and Social Harm: Conceptual Issues and Historical Perspectives." *Contemporary Drug Problems*, 23 (Fall 1996): 373–389.

———. "Alcohol, Science, and Social Control." In Edith Gomberg, Helene Raskin White, and John Carpenter, eds., *Alcohol, Science, and Society Revisited*. Ann Arbor: University of Michigan Press, 1982.

———. "Cultural Contingencies of Alcoholism: Variations between and within Nineteenth-Century Urban Ethnic Groups in Alcohol-Related Death Rates." *Journal of Health and Social Behavior* 9, (1968): 99–113.

———. "A 'Reverence for Strong Drink': The Lost Generation and the Elevation of Alcohol in American Culture." *Journal of Studies on Alcohol*, 45 (1985): 540–546.

———. "Sociological Aspects of the Disease Concept of Alcoholism." In *Research Advances in Alcohol and Drug Problems* 7. New York: Plenum Press, 1983, 47–91.

Room, Robin, and Susanna Barrows. *Drinking: Behavior and Belief in Modern History*. Berkeley: University of California Press, 1991.

Rorabaugh, William J. *The Alcoholic Republic: An American Tradition*. New York: Oxford University Press, 1979.

Walton, Stuart. *Out of It: A Cultural History of Intoxication*. London: Hamish Hamilton, 2001.

Prohibition

Behr, Edward. *Prohibition: Thirteen Years That Changed America*. New York: Arcade, 1997.

Burnham, John. "New Perspectives on the Prohibition 'Experiment' of the 1920's." *Journal of Social History* 2 (1968): 51–68.

Clark, Norman. *Deliver Us from Evil: An Interpretation of American Prohibition*. New York: W. W. Norton, 1976.

Hamm, Richard F. *Shaping the Eighteenth Amendment: Temperance Reform, Legal Culture, and the Polity, 1880–1920*. Chapel Hill: University of North Carolina Press, 1995.

Kerr, K. Austin. *Organized for Prohibition: A New History of the Anti-Saloon League*. New Haven: Yale University Press, 1985.

Krout, John. *The Origins of Prohibition*. New York: Knopf, 1925.

Kyvig, David. *Repealing National Prohibition*. Chicago: University of Chicago Press, 1979.

Levine, Harry Gene. "The Birth of American Alcohol Control: Prohibition, the Power Elite, and the Problem of Lawlessness." *Contemporary Drug Problems* (Spring 1985): 63–115.

Rumbarger, John J. *Profits, Power, and Prohibition: Alcohol Reform and the Industrializing of America, 1800–1930*. Albany: State University of New York Press, 1989.

Timberlake, James. *Prohibition and the Progressive Movement, 1900–1920*. Cambridge: Harvard University Press, 1963.

Selected Works on Drugs Other Than Alcohol

Works Published before 1900

Beard, George. *American Nervousness: Its Causes and Consequences*. New York: Putnam, 1881.
——. *Stimulants and Narcotics*. New York: G. P. Putnam and Sons, 1871.
Grob, Gerald, ed. *Origins of Medical Attitudes toward Drug Addiction in America: Eight Studies, 1791–1858*. New York: Arno Press, 1981.
Kane, Harry Hubell. *The Narcotic Habit*. Philadelphia: P. Blakiston, 1881.
Ludlow, Fitzhugh. *The Hashish Eater*. 1857.

Works on One or More Illicit Drugs

Acker, Caroline Jean. *Creating the American Junkie: Addiction Research in the Classic Era of Narcotic Control*. Baltimore: Johns Hopkins University Press, 2001.
Ball, John C., and Carl D. Chambers, eds. *Epidemiology of Opiate Addiction in the U.S.* Springfield, Ill.: Charles C. Thomas, 1970.
Chein, Isidor, Donald L. Gerard, Robert S. Lee, and Eva Rosenfeld. *The Road to H: Narcotics, Delinquency, and Social Policy*. New York: Basic Books, 1964.
Courtwright, David T. *Dark Paradise: Opiate Addiction in America before 1940*, enl. ed. Cambridge: Harvard University Press, 2001 (1982).
Grinspoon, Lester. *Marihuana Reconsidered*, Cambridge: Harvard University Press, 1971.
Helbrant, Maurice. *Narcotic Agent*. New York: Vanguard Press, 1941.
Jonnes, Jill. *Hep-Cats, Narcs, and Pipe Dreams: A History of America's Romance with Illegal Drugs*. New York: Scribner, 1996; Johns Hopkins University Press, 1999.
Light, Arthur B., Edward G. Torrance, Walter G. Karr, Edith G. Fry, and William A. Wolff. *Opium Addiction*. Chicago: The American Medical Association, 1929–1930.
Morgan, H. Wayne. *Drugs in America: A Social History, 1800–1980*. Syracuse: Syracuse University Press, 1981.
Musto, David F. *The American Disease: Origins of Narcotic Control*, 3d ed. New York: Oxford University Press, 1999 (1973).
Smith, Mickey C. *A Social History of the Minor Tranquilizers: The Quest for Small Comfort in the Age of Anxiety*. New York: Pharmaceutical Press, 1985, 1991.
Spillane, Joseph. *Cocaine: From Medical Marvel to Modern Menace in the United States, 1884–1920*, Baltimore: Johns Hopkins University Press, 2000.
Tate, Cassandra. *Cigarette Wars: The Triumph of "The Little White Slaver."* New York: Oxford University Press, 1999.
Terry, Charles, and Mildred Pellens. *The Opium Problem*. Chicago: The American Medical Association, 1928.
Wilner, Daniel M., and Gene G. Kassebaum, eds. *Narcotics*. New York: McGraw-Hill, 1965.

Understanding Users and Their Experiences

Agar, Michael. *Ripping and Running: A Formal Ethnography of Urban Heroin Addicts*. New York: Seminar Press, 1973.

Becker, Howard S. *Outsiders: Studies in the Sociology of Deviance*. New York: Free Press, 1963.

Biernacki, Patrick. *Pathways from Heroin Addiction: Recovery without Treatment*. Philadelphia: Temple University Press, 1986.

Bourgois, Philippe. *In Search of Respect: Selling Crack in El Barrio*. Cambridge: Cambridge University Press, 1995.

Courtwright, David, Don Des Jarlais, and Herman Joseph. *Addicts Who Survived: An Oral History of Narcotic Use in America, 1923–1965*. Knoxville: University of Tennessee Press, 1989.

Dai, Bingham. *Opium Addiction in Chicago*. Shanghai: Commercial Press, 1937.

Faupel, Charles E. *Shooting Dope: Career Patterns of Hard-Core Heroin Users*. Gainesville: University of Florida Press, 1991.

Feldman, Harvey W., Michael H. Agar, and George M. Beschner, eds. *Angel Dust: An Ethnographic Study of PCP Users*. Lexington, Mass.: Lexington Books, 1979.

Finestone, Harold. "Cats, Kicks, and Color." In Howard S. Becker, ed., *The Other Side: Perspectives on Deviance*. Glencoe, Ill.: Free Press, 1964, 281–297.

Keire, Mara L. "Dope Fiends and Degenerates: The Gendering of Addiction in the Early Twentieth Century." *Journal of Social History* 31, (1998): 809–822.

Lewin, Louis. *Phantastica*. Rochester, Vt.: Park Street Press, 1998 (1924).

Lindesmith, Alfred R. *Opiate Addiction*. Bloomington, Ind.: Principia Press, 1947.

———. "A Sociological Theory of Drug Addiction." *American Journal of Sociology* (1938): 593–613.

Preble, Edward, and John J. Casey. "Taking Care of Business—The Heroin Addict's Life on the Street." *International Journal of the Addictions* 4, 1969: 1–24.

Robins, Lee N. *The Vietnam Drug User Returns*. SAODAP Monograph, Washington, D.C.: GPO, 1974.

Rosenbaum, Marsha, *Women on Heroin*. New Brunswick: Rutgers University Press, 1981.

Waldorf, Dan. *Careers in Dope*. Englewood Cliffs, N.J.: Prentice-Hall, 1973.

Waldorf, Dan, Craig Reinarman, and Sheigla Murphy. *Cocaine Changes: The Experience of Using and Quitting*. Philadelphia: Temple University Press, 1991.

Weil, Andrew. *The Natural Mind: A New Way of Looking at Drugs and the Higher Consciousness*. Boston: Houghton Mifflin, 1972.

Zinberg, Norman E. *Drug, Set, and Setting: The Basis for Controlled Intoxicant Use*. New Haven: Yale University Press, 1984.

Treatment and Medical Constructions of the Addict

ABA and AMA Joint Committee on Narcotic Drugs. *Drug Addiction: Crime or Disease?* Bloomington: Indiana University Press, 1961.

Acker, Caroline Jean. "Stigma or Legitimation? A Historical Examination of the Social Potentials of Addiction Disease Models." *Journal of Psychoactive Drugs* 25 (1993): 193–205.

Gerstein, Dean R., and Henrick J. Harwood. *Treating Drug Problems*, 2 vols. Washington, D.C.: National Academy Press, 1990.

Kandall, Stephen R. *Substance and Shadow: Women and Addiction in the United States*. Cambridge: Harvard University Press, 1996.

Kolb, Lawrence. *Drug Addiction, a Medical Problem*. Springfield, Ill.: Thomas, 1962.

———. "Pleasure and Deterioration from Narcotic Addiction," *Mental Hygiene* 9 (1925): 699–724.

———. "Types and Characteristics of Drug Addicts." *Mental Hygiene* 9 (1925): 300–313.

Merton, Robert K. "Social Structure and Anomie." In Robert K. Merton, *Social Theory and Social Structure*. Glencoe, Ill.: Free Press, 1957.

Nyswander, Marie. *The Drug Addict as a Patient*. New York: Grune & Stratton, 1956.

Shavelson, Lonny. *Hooked*. New York: New Press, 2001.

Towns, Charles B. *Habits That Handicap: The Menace of Opium, Alcohol, and Tobacco, and the Remedy*. New York: Century, 1916.

Waldorf, D., M. Orlick, and C. Reinarman. *Morphine Maintenance: The Shreveport Clinic, 1919–1923*. Washington, D.C.: The Drug Abuse Council, 1974.

White, William L. *Slaying the Dragon: The History of Addiction Treatment and Recovery in America*. Bloomington, Ill.: Chestnut Hill Systems, 1998.

Williams, E. H. *Opiate Addiction: Its Handling and Treatment*. New York: Macmillan, 1922.

Winick, Charles. "Physician Narcotic Addicts." In Howard S. Becker, ed., *The Other Side: Perspectives on Deviance*. Glencoe, Ill.: Free Press, 1964, 261–279.

Understandings of Drug Effects and Drug Dependence

Acker, Caroline Jean. "Addiction and the Laboratory: The Work of the National Research Council's Committee on Drug Addiction, 1928–1939." *Isis* 86 (1995):167–193.

———. "Planning and Serendipity in the Search for a Nonaddicting Opiate Analgesic." In Gregory J. Higby and Elaine C. Stroud, eds., *The Inside Story of Medicines*. Madison: American Institute for the History of Pharmacy, 1997, 139–157.

Bishop, Ernest S. *The Narcotic Drug Problem*. New York: Macmillan, 1920.

Eddy, Nathan B. *The National Research Council Involvement in the Opiate Problem, 1928–1971*. Washington, D.C.: National Academy Press, 1973.

Eddy, Nathan, and Everette May. "The Search for a Better Analgesic." *Science* 181 (1973): 407–414.

Elster, Jon, ed. *Addiction: Entries and Exits*. New York: Russell Sage, 1999.

Pert, C. B., G. Pasternak, and S. H. Snyder. "Opiate Agonists and Antagonists Discriminated by Receptor Binding in Brain." *Science* 182 (1973):1359–1361.

Pettey, George E. *The Narcotic Drug Diseases and Allied Ailments: Pathology, Pathogenesis, and Treatment*. Philadelphia: F. A. Davis, 1913.

Ray, Marsh B. "The Cycle of Abstinence and Relapse among Heroin Addicts." In Howard S. Becker, ed., *The Other Side: Perspectives on Deviance*. Glencoe, Ill.: Free Press, 1964, 163–177.

Sonnedecker, Glenn. *Emergence of the Concept of Opiate Addiction*. Madison: American Institute for the History of Pharmacy, n.d.

Snyder, Solomon H. *Brainstorming: The Science and Politics of Opiate Research*. Cambridge: Harvard University Press, 1989.

Wikler, Abraham. *Opiate Addiction*. Springfield, Ill.: Thomas, 1953.

International Trafficking and Its Control

McAllister, William B. *Drug Diplomacy in the Twentieth Century: An International History*. New York: Routledge, 2000.

McCoy, Alfred W. *The Politics of Heroin in Southeast Asia*. New York: Harper & Row, 1972.

Walker William O., III. *Drug Control in the Americas*, rev. ed. Albuquerque: University of New Mexico Press, 1989.

———. *Opium and Foreign Policy: The Anglo-American Search for Order, 1912–1954.* Chapel Hill: University of North Carolina Press, 1991.

Policy Analysis and Policy Advocacy

Anderson, Warwick. "The New York Needle Trial: The Politics of Public Health in the Age of AIDS." *American Journal of Public Health* 81 (1991) 1506–1517.

Anslinger, Harry J., and Courtney Ryley Cooper. "Marijuana: Assassin of Youth." *American Magazine*, July 1937.

Bayer, Ronald, and Gerald M. Oppenheimer, eds. *Confronting Drug Policy: Illicit Drugs in a Free Society.* Cambridge: Cambridge University Press, 1993.

Bonnie, Richard J., and Charles H. Whitebread II. *The Marijuana Conviction: A History of Marijuana Prohibition in the United States.* New York: The Lindesmith Center, 1999 (1974).

Brecher, Edward M., and the Editors of *Consumer Reports. Licit and Illicit Drugs.* Boston: Little, Brown, 1972.

Campbell, Nancy D. *Using Women: Gender, Drug Policy, and Social Justice.* New York: Routledge, 2000.

The Drug Abuse Council. *The Facts about "Drug Abuse."* New York: Free Press, 1980.

Grinspoon, Lester, and James B. Bakalar. *Marihuana: The Forbidden Medicine.* New Haven: Yale University Press, 1993.

Heather, Nick, Alex Wodak, Ethan A. Nadelmann, and Pat O'Hare, eds. *Psychoactive Drugs and Harm Reduction: From Faith to Science.* London: Whurr, 1993.

Humphries, Drew. *Crack Mothers: Pregnancy, Drugs, and the Media.* Columbus: Ohio State University Press, 1999.

Inciardi, James A. *The War on Drugs II: The Continuing Epic of Heroin, Cocaine, Crack, Crime, AIDS, and Public Policy.* Mountain View, Calif.: Mayfield, 1992.

———. ed. *Handbook of Drug Control in the United States.* New York: Greenwood Press, 1990.

Jaffe, Arnold. *Addiction Reform in the Progressive Age: Scientific and Social Responses to Drug Dependence in the U.S., 1870–1930.* New York: Arno Press, 1981.

Kleiman, Mark. *Marijuana: Costs of Abuse, Costs of Control.* New York: Greenwood Press, 1989.

Lindesmith, Alfred R. *The Addict and the Law.* Bloomington: Indiana University Press, 1968.

MacCoun, Robert J., and Peter Reuter. *Drug War Heresies.* Cambridge: Cambridge University Press, 2001.

McWilliams, John C. *The Protectors: Harry J. Anslinger and the Federal Bureau of Narcotics, 1930–1962.* Newark: University of Delaware Press, 1990.

Nadelmann, Ethan A. "Drug Prohibition in the United States: Costs, Consequences, and Alternatives." *Science* 245 (1989): 939–947.

National Commission on Marihuana and Drug Abuse. *Marihuana: A Signal of Misunderstanding: The Official Report of the National Commission on Marihuana and Drug Abuse.* New York: New American Library, 1972.

O'Hare, P. A., R. Newcombe, A. Matthews, E. C. Buring, and E. Drucker. *The Reduction of Drug-Related Harm.* New York: Routledge, 1992.

Payne, E. George. *The Menace of Narcotic Drugs: A Discussion of Narcotics and Education,* New York: Prentice-Hall, 1931.

Reinarman, Craig, and Harry G. Levine, eds. *Crack in America: Demon Drugs and Social Justice*. Berkeley: University of California Press, 1997.

Room, Robin. "Drug Policy Reform in Historical Perspective: Movements and Mechanisms." *Drug and Alcohol Review 10* (1991): 37–43.

Szasz, Thomas. *Ceremonial Chemistry: The Ritual Persecution of Drugs, Addicts, and Pushers*. Garden City, N.Y.: Anchor Press, 1974.

Trebach, Arnold S. *The Heroin Solution*. New Haven: Yale University Press, 1982.

Walker, William O., III, ed. *Drug Control Policy: Essays in Historical and Comparative Perspective*. State College: Pennsylvania State University Press, 1992.

Wilson, James Q. "Against the Legalization of Drugs." *Commentary*, February 1990.

Zimring, Franklin E., and Gordon Hawkins. *The Search for Rational Drug Control*. Cambridge: Cambridge University Press, 1992.

Comparative Perspectives on Alcohol and Drugs (Historical and Contemporary)

Burnham, John. *Bad Habits: Drinking, Smoking, Taking Drugs, Gambling, Sexual Misbehavior, and Swearing in American History*. New York: New York University Press, 1993.

Courtwright, David. *Forces of Habit: Drugs and the Making of the Modern World*. Cambridge: Harvard University Press, 2001.

Gamella, Juan F. *Drugs and Alcohol in the Pacific: New Consumption Trends and Their Consequences*. Brookfield, Vt.: Ashgate, 2002.

Goldstein, Avram. *Addiction: From Biology to Drug Policy*, 2d ed. Oxford: Oxford University Press, 2001.

Goodman, Jordan, Paul Lovejoy, and Andrew Sheratt. *Consuming Habits: Drugs in History and Anthropology*. London: Routledge, 1995.

Jaffe, Jerome H., ed. in chief. *Encyclopedia of Drugs and Alcohol*. New York: Macmillan, 1995.

Levine, Harry Gene, and Craig Reinarman. "From Prohibition to Regulation: Lessons from Alcohol Policy for Drug Policy." *Milbank Quarterly, 69,* (1991): 461–94.

Matthee, Rudi. "Exotic Substances: The Introduction and Global Spread of Tobacco, Coffee, Cocoa, Tea, and Distilled Liquor, Sixteenth to Eighteenth Centuries." In Roy Porter and Mikulas Teich, eds., *Drugs and Narcotics in History*, Cambridge: Cambridge University Press, 1995, 24–51.

Nash, J. Madeleine, and Alice Park. "Addicted: Why Do People Get Hooked? Mounting Evidence Points to a Powerful Brain Chemical Called Dopamine," *Time*, 5 May 1997, 68–75.

Porter, Roy, and Mikulas Teich, eds. *Drugs and Narcotics in History*. Cambridge: Cambridge University Press, 1995.

Regan, Ciaren. *Intoxicating Minds: How Drugs Work*. New York: Columbia University Press, 2001.

Weil, Andrew. *From Chocolate to Morphine: Everything You Need to Know about Mind-Altering Drugs*, rev. and updated ed. Boston: Houghton Mifflin, 1998.

Notes on Contributors

CAROLINE JEAN ACKER received her doctorate in the history of the health sciences from the University of California, San Francisco, in 1993. She was the DeWitt Stetten, Jr., Fellow in the History of Biomedical Sciences and/or Technology at the National Institutes of Health from 1993 to 1994. Since then she has been a member of the Department of History at Carnegie Mellon University. Her book *Creating the American Junkie: Addiction Research in the Classic Era of Narcotic Control* was published in 2001.

JIM BAUMOHL is professor of social work and social research at Bryn Mawr College in Bryn Mawr, Pennsylvania. He has published widely on the history of alcohol and other drug treatments but is best known for his work on contemporary homelessness. Among other contributions to that literature, he is the editor of *Homelessness in America* (1996), a benefit book for the National Coalition for the Homeless.

ALLAN M. BRANDT is the Kass Professor of the History of Medicine at Harvard Medical School, where he directs the Program in the History of Medicine and the Division of Medical Ethics. He holds a joint appointment in the Department of the History of Science at Harvard University, where he is currently chair. His work focuses on social and ethical aspects of health, disease, and medical practices in the twentieth-century United States. He is the author of *No Magic Bullet: A Social History of Venereal Disease in the United States since 1880* (1985) and the editor of *Morality and Health* (1997). He is currently completing a book on the social and cultural history of cigarette smoking in the United States.

KATHERINE A. CHAVIGNY is assistant professor of history at Sweet Briar College. She writes on nineteenth-century American popular culture and social practices. Her dissertation is being revised under the title "Manly Confessions: Reformed Drunkards and the Origins of Therapeutic Culture."

TIMOTHY A. HICKMAN is a member of the history department at Lancaster University in England. He is currently working on a book manuscript entitled "The Secret Leprosy of Modern Days: Narcotic Addiction and Modernity in the United States, 1870–1920."

PETER C. MANCALL, professor of history at the University of Southern California, is author of *Deadly Medicine: Indians and Alcohol in Early America* (1995) and articles on alcohol use that have appeared in *Journal of the Early Republic, American Indian Culture and Research Journal,* and *Australian and New Zealand Journal of Psychiatry.* In 1998 he received the inaugural Alcohol Advisory Council of New Zealand ALAC Research Fellowship.

MICHELLE MCCLELLAN received her Ph.D. in American history from Stanford University. Her book entitled "Lady Lushes: Women Alcoholics and American Society, 1880–1960" is being prepared for publication. She teaches in the Honors College at the University of Georgia.

STEVEN J. NOVAK, formerly adjunct professor of American history at the University of California, Los Angeles, and senior editor of the UCLA Oral History Program, is currently director of professional education at City of Hope National Medical Center and associate dean for administration of the City of Hope Graduate School of Biological Sciences in Duarte, California. He studies the ethical issues involved in human subjects research.

RON ROIZEN is a research sociologist with over thirty years' experience in the various aspects of empirical social and epidemiological research. He has also pursued a variety of historical and theoretical studies. His writings have been published in a wide range of scholarly and scientific journals, including the *British Medical Journal, Contemporary Sociology, Social History of Alcohol Review, Journal for the Scientific Study of Religion,* and *Science.*

LORI E. ROTSKOFF has taught history and American studies at Yale University and Sarah Lawrence College. She is the author of *Love on the Rocks: Men, Women, and Alcohol in Post–World War II America* (2002).

SUSAN L. SPEAKER received her doctorate in the history of medicine from the University of Pennsylvania in 1992. She has taught courses in the history of science, medicine, drugs, and technology, and U.S. history at several institutions, including the University of Pennsylvania, Philadelphia College of Pharmacy, and Bucknell University. In 1998 she received a two-year publication grant from the National Library of Medicine to work on a history of American anti-drug rhetoric (in process). Since 2000, she has worked as a historian in the History of Medicine Division at the National Library of Medicine.

SARAH W. TRACY took her Ph.D. in the history and sociology of science at the University of Pennsylvania. She is an assistant professor at the Honors College of the University of Oklahoma, where she also directs the Medical Humanities Program. She is completing a book entitled "From Vice to Disease: Alcoholism in America, 1870–1920."

NICHOLAS WEISS, M.D., is a graduate of Harvard Medical School and is currently a resident in psychiatry at the University of California at San Francisco. He holds a master's degree in the history of science from Harvard University.

WILLIAM L. WHITE has worked in the field of addiction treatment for more than thirty years and is currently senior research consultant at Chestnut Health Systems, Bloomington, Illinois. He is author of *Slaying the Dragon: The History of Addiction Treatment and Recovery in America* (1998) and coauthor, with John W. Crowley, of *Drunkard's Refuge: The Lessons of the New York Inebriate Asylum* (2004).